palgrave macmillan law masters *focus*

# economic and social law of the european union

palgrave macmillan law masters *focus*

*Series editor*: **Marise Cremona**

palgrave macmillan law masters *focus*

# economic and social law of the european union

## jo shaw D.Phil, M.A.

Salvesen Chair of European Institutions
at the University of Edinburgh, UK

## jo hunt Jur.D. LLM

Lecturer at Cardiff Law School,
Cardiff University, UK

and

## chloë wallace M.A. B.C.L.

Lecturer at the School of Law,
University of Leeds, UK

**Series editor**: Marise Cremona
*Professor of European Law
European University Institute
Florence, Italy*

palgrave
macmillan

First published 2007 by
PALGRAVE MACMILLAN
Houndmills, Basingstoke, Hampshire RG21 6XS and
175 Fifth Avenue, New York, N.Y. 10010
Companies and representatives throughout the world

PALGRAVE MACMILLAN is the global academic imprint of the Palgrave
Macmillan division of St. Martin's Press, LLC and of Palgrave Macmillan Ltd.
Macmillan® is a registered trademark in the United States, United Kingdom
and other countries. Palgrave is a registered trademark in the European
Union and other countries.

ISBN-13: 978–0–333–63758–6
ISBN-10: 0–333–63758–5

This book is printed on paper suitable for recycling and made from fully
managed and sustained forest sources. Logging, pulping and manufacturing
processes are expected to conform to the environmental regulations of the
country of origin.

A catalogue record for this book is available from the British Library.

| 10 | 9 | 8 | 7 | 6 | 5 | 4 | 3 | 2 | 1 |
|----|----|----|----|----|----|----|----|----|----|
| 16 | 15 | 14 | 13 | 12 | 11 | 10 | 09 | 08 | 07 |

Printed and bound in Great Britain by
Cromwell Press, Trowbridge, Wiltshire

# Contents

# Preface and Acknowledgements

The broad objective of this book is to provide a coherent and contextualised introduction to the economic and social law of the European Union. While the book is aimed primarily at a student readership, each of the chapters has been informed by the latest research in the field. This objective has also shaped the structure of the book, in particular Chapters 1 and 2 which explore in some detail the context in which the EU operates as a project fostering integration in the economic and, increasingly, the social policy sphere between the Member States. Hence, departing from the core domain of the single market and closely associated policies such as external trade and competition policy, we proceed through the book to look at a number of flanking policies including those concerned with citizens (and indeed non-citizens) of the Union and those concerned with employment and the environment. Throughout, we have sought to bring into the mainstream not only the traditional 'Community' or 'Monnet' method for developing legal instruments and policies, but also the increasingly important sphere of so-called 'new governance'. Thus Chapter 2 in particular establishes a number of key themes which are picked up throughout the book, including the variety of instruments and institutions involved in the governance of the economy and the social sphere in the EU context, the interplay between the EU institutions and the Member States, the structuring function of constitutional principles, and the challenges of flexibility in an ever larger and more complex union.

Although the original idea for such a book on EU economic and social law came from Jo Shaw, and was based on the second half of her 1993 book *European Community Law* (the first half of which subsequently morphed into *Law of the European Union* on institutional and constitutional law, with a fourth edition in preparation), in practice the preparation of the book has been very much a collective endeavour, involving multiple drafts and rewrites. While Chloë Wallace took responsibility for the initial drafts of Chapters 6, 12, 13, 15, 17 and 19, final versions of these have been prepared by Jo Shaw (12, 13, 15 and 19) and Jo Hunt (6 and 17). Jo Shaw took responsibility for preparing Chapters 1, 2, 3, 7, 8, 10 and 11, Jo Hunt prepared Chapters 4, 5, 9, 14, 16 and 18. We sought wherever possible to ensure that authorship of a chapter was primarily the responsibility of a member of the team with a broad research interest in the specific field.

We would like to thank a number of people for their assistance and advice in preparing the book. Helen Bugler has been with us throughout, and has nurtured a child from birth to teenager-hood during the time that it has taken us to complete the project. Palgrave's forbearance has been remarkable. Marise Cremona, as series editor, has been consistently encouraging, and also made helpful comments on a number of chapters at an earlier stage. Bill Perry's copyediting efforts under the pressure of a very tight production timetable have been much appreciated. A number of students and assistants have helped us at various times with tasks such as preparing case lists and proof reading, including Chloe Vaughan, Michael Puzio, Laura Rochefort and Maksimilian del Mar, and we are very grateful to them all. Michael Cardwell, Gareth Davies, Tammy Hervey, Jeff Kenner, Urfan

Khaliq and Bob Lee provided helpful comments on individual chapters, and numerous other colleagues have given more generalised advice and encouragement to press on with what, at time, seemed like a project of monstrous proportions. Thanks too to friends and family for keeping us going.

Jo Shaw
Jo Hunt
Chloë Wallace

# Alphabetical List of Cases before the European Court of Justice

# Alphabetical List of Cases before the European Court of First Instance

# Cases before English Courts

# Numerical List of Cases before the European Court of Justice

# Opinions of the Court of Justice adopted on the basis of Article 300 EC

# Numerical List of Cases before the European Court of First Instance

# Part I

# Introduction

# Chapter 1

# Law and Economic Integration in the European Union

## 1.1 Introducing this Book

This is a book aimed at those who have already studied, or have at least a basic knowledge of, the law of the constitution and institutions of the European Union (EU). This includes understanding the effects of EU law, especially in relation to national law, and also the great variety of conditions and structures under which EU law is made. It assumes also a basic degree of familiarity on the part of the reader with the underlying history of the EU up to the present day. This is an increasingly complex narrative, but familiarity with the history is in any event a considerable aid to the study of the law of the EU, including the substantive social and economic law presented in this book. Important phases of the history of the EC/EU include:

- the launch of early economic 'Communities' of the 1950s, and the establishment of the European Economic Community (EEC) under the Treaty of Rome signed in 1957;
- the stagnation of the 1960s and 1970s, as the European integration project made little headway against a backdrop of an economic downturn in the Member States;
- the relaunch of the Community through the initiative from the mid-1980s onwards to complete the single market by the end of 1992, after the adoption of the Single European Act in 1986;
- the formal establishment of the European Union through the Treaty of Maastricht with its additional political concerns of foreign, security and defence policy and justice and home affairs policy;
- the creation of the single currency (the euro) in 1999, and its usage as a common currency in 'Euroland' from 2002;
- the solidification of political integration under the Treaty of Amsterdam in the late 1990s, and the additional progress contained in the Treaty of Nice which entered into force in 2003, both of which Treaties were intended to set the conditions for enlargement in the first decade of the twenty-first century;
- the important phases of Cold War enlargement, in particular with the accession of eight central and eastern European states among ten to join the Union in 2004, along with two more in 2007;
- the 'post-Nice' phase of discussions about how the European Union should develop in the future.

These latter discussions were still ongoing at the time of writing, as the Constitutional Treaty (OJ 2004 C310) which was signed in October 2004 has not thus far been ratified by the Member States (see 1.3)

This book describes and analyses the key features of what we shall generally term 'the economic and social law of the European Union'. The focus is on the internal and external dimensions of the law governing the operation of the single market, the creation and regulation of the single currency as an essential complement to the single market, the law governing the status of citizens and non-citizens in the EU in the context of the creation of an Area of Freedom, Security and Justice, and the law governing the EU's social dimension and other flanking policies such as environmental policy and policy on regional development. It is, therefore, a broad conception of economic and social law, and includes also citizenship-related matters under the heading of the Area of Freedom, Security and Justice, which fall within the scope of EU justice and home affairs law.

Studying the economic and social law of the EU involves examining the real business of the European Union: that is to say, to the extent that there do exist powers at the EU level in any particular area to make laws or regulations, we shall be looking at the choices made by the relevant policy-makers about the conditions under which citizens and other residents of the EU live their lives (learning, caring, working, doing business, travelling, pursuing leisure activities, using services and purchasing goods, etc.) and the circumstances in which those choices can be and are made. Underlying these policy-making activities are the EU Treaties themselves – the sources of legal competence in a limited powers system – which set the basic legal and constitutional principles, establish the institutions and the conditions under which they operate, and determine the rules on what the EU and its institutions can and cannot do. In addition, the most important principles of economic and social law such as the foundations of the internal market, economic and monetary union, the Area of Freedom, Security and Justice and the social dimension of the EU themselves appear in the Treaties. In many cases, these Treaty provisions, along with secondary legislation, have been interpreted and applied by the Court of Justice and national courts. The study of the economic and social law of the EU in this book will combine the following elements:

▶ the study and interpretation of treaty texts, and of the role of the Court of Justice and national courts in interpreting the treaties;
▶ the study of the acts of the institutions adopted to implement the Treaties, including the application and interpretation of these measures by the Court of Justice and other actors; and
▶ (to a more limited extent) the study of the ways in which these policies have been applied, including at the national level.

An important stepping-off point is the classic argument about what the EU is 'for' or intended to 'achieve'. The original European Communities of the 1950s had, according to Weiler (1999a: 239–44), a vocation to secure three goals by building on the wreckage of post-war Europe: peace, prosperity and supranationalism. By the last is meant a departure from the limiting confines of a destructive nationalism which caused so much damage in the first half of the twentieth century in Europe. The first can be seen in the placing of some of the principal tools of war, such as the coal and steel industries, in common hands under the European Coal and Steel Community (ECSC) established by the Treaty of Paris in 1951, and in the common sense adage that countries which are intimately linked through economic and social relations are unlikely to go to war against each other.

However, in some ways, it is the middle goal, that of prosperity, which has been the key instrument for achieving the other goals. It is the enhancement of prosperity which could be striven for directly from the very beginning through the establishment of the legal structures of three 'Communities' aimed at the creation of a common market and a customs union, and at the creation of a number of key common policies, for example the stabilisation of agricultural markets. In that sense, the business of what is now the European Union has come to be intimately linked to the implementation of this (socio-economic) goal of achieving greater prosperity, which in turn leads to the achievement of other (political and strategic) goals. This has come through successively in the project to complete the single market, the programme to create a single currency (the euro) and, more recently, the so-called 'Lisbon' agenda to make the European Union 'the most competitive and dynamic knowledge-based economy in the world capable of sustainable economic growth with more and better jobs and greater social cohesion'. However, what defines prosperity has changed in a variety of ways in the more than fifty years since the first Community was established, and policy-making at the EU and national levels has changed to reflect this. In common with other advanced economies, Western European societies have become simultaneously both more 'consumerist' and also more 'environmentalist' in orientation. Economic and social globalisation has accelerated in recent years, posing new challenges to the Member States. Furthermore, the original Community was conceived for a Western Europe caught in the middle of a Cold War between superpowers to the East and the West; since 1989, however, it has faced very different demands in relation to problems of economic and political transition and modernisation, and indeed maintaining peace on the European continent. We are now looking at a European Union stretching not only from the Arctic Circle to the Mediterranean and from the Atlantic Ocean to the Carpathian Mountains (achieved as of May 2004 with the fifth Enlargement of the Union), but even as far as the Black Sea in South Eastern Europe with the accession of Romania and Bulgaria on 1 January 2007. In this context, it becomes even more important to recognise that economic integration is not an end in itself, but part of a continuing process in which political goals are paramount, even though the political goals themselves have changed.

Accordingly, the original Treaties have evolved dramatically since they were first put in place to include ever more explicit political goals, especially since the adoption of the Treaty of Maastricht. We have seen the creation of a Common Foreign and Security Policy (CFSP) and the first steps towards a European Security and Defence Policy (ESDP), as well as the establishment of a framework for cooperation in the field of Justice and Home Affairs (JHA), covering internal security, police and criminal justice cooperation, immigration, asylum and the free movement of persons, and judicial cooperation in the civil justice field. These latter policies are now gathered together under the heading of the 'Area of Freedom, Security and Justice' (AFSJ), inaugurated by the Treaty of Amsterdam. Political integration is the primary business of the two non-Community pillars of the European Union, although it is also an inescapable dimension of the Community's first pillar itself. In the area of political integration, the current Treaty framework bears no resemblance to the original treaties.

If we focus upon the Community pillar, we will see in the paragraphs and chapters which follow that the basic Treaty framework concerned with the integration of markets and the creation of a common trading area with a single external economic identity has largely survived the passage of time. The most significant additions have been the provisions on Economic and Monetary Union (EMU) inserted by the Treaty of Maastricht and the further elaboration of policy goals and activities in relation to the free movement of persons. A number of key socio-economic goals have been added which are not wholly market-oriented, such as those in the arenas of environmental policy and labour market policy. 'Sustainable growth' was introduced as an objective of the European Community by the Treaty of Maastricht, and is complemented by an insistence on 'a high level of protection and improvement of the quality of the environment' (Article 2 EC). There has been a gradual, but inexorable, development of a stronger social dimension to the European Union and of the flanking policies both of a regulatory nature (e.g. environmental policy) and of a redistributive nature (e.g. regional policy, policy on economic and social cohesion). The social goals of the EU have been anchored increasingly firmly within the Treaty framework over the years, with statements on equality, social protection and the combating of social exclusion proliferating in the 'Principles' of Part One of the EC Treaty, and in the greatly strengthened Title XI on 'Social Policy, Education, Vocational Training and Youth'. In addition, Title VIII deals specifically with employment policy. It has long been a point of contention in studies of the EU whether it is the liberal market goals or the social goals concerned with quality of life which take priority. As we shall see, when we begin to study EU economic and social law by considering first the prism of a system of regional economic integration, it is hard to escape the conclusion that the economic still somehow precedes the social, in the sense that processes of market integration represent the dominant paradigm. At the same time, the Community pillar itself has become more political, especially in the wake of the Treaty of Amsterdam, as Title IV on 'Visas, Asylum, Immigration and Other Policies Related to Free Movement of Persons' was added which has both economic and political dimensions. This complements rather than detracts from the economic goals of the original Treaties.

## 1.2  The Approach Taken in this Book

The fields of EU economic and social law and policy covered in this book have been mentioned in outline in the previous section. The approach which we take is to sketch the general framework for each field of law, focusing on key principles and broad lines of legal and policy development. Attention is given to the basic EC Treaty framework, key secondary legislation and policy documentation, sketching lines of policy-making for the past, present and future, and relevant case law. Both the 'hard' and 'soft' dimensions of law are reviewed, with account taken where necessary of measures which are not strictly or fully binding on the Member States.

No claim is made that the book is offering comprehensive coverage of EU socio-economic law and policy in this text. Obvious omissions include transport policy, industrial policy, education policy other than as a by-product of citizens' rights to free movement, energy policy, fisheries policy, data protection and the regulation of intellectual property. There are other areas of recent intensive legislative action in the EU which are not covered in the book, even though they are of profound significance for the work of companies and enterprises in the EU, such as the regulation of chemical substances (European Parliament and Council Regulation 1907/2006 concerning the Registration, Evaluation, Authorisation and Restriction of Chemicals (REACH) and establishing a European Chemicals Agency, OJ 2006 L396/1). However, many of these fields are mentioned in passing in the chapters, highlighting how they link to the material which has been covered. Furthermore, within a single volume on the substantive law of the EU, it is possible to provide only a basic understanding of even the limited fields chosen for review, and to suggest case law, legislative and policy documents, secondary literature and other commentaries which can offer more detailed insights. Many of the subjects covered in the chapters of this book are analysed in larger volumes written by other scholars, and many of these are referred to in the 'Further Reading' sections at the end of each chapter. Specific references in the chapters are detailed in the Bibliography and References at the end of the book.

We work self-consciously in this book with the multiple objectives of the EU, and its complex legal and political status as a novel type of 'non-state polity', with semi-autonomous institutions, while acknowledging throughout the important underlying foundation of the EU in international treaties signed by sovereign states. These treaties confer only limited powers on the EU and its institutions. Our approach is informed also by our attempt to place EU economic and social law in its wider economic and political context, as well as to illuminate the complicated legal framework within its proper historical context in order to remind readers never to assume that the development of EU law has merely 'just happened'. A sense of EU law as a dynamic, evolving and contested framework is a core dimension of the approach taken here. For those who wish to understand more, the evolutionary approach is fully amplified in an edited volume on *The Evolution of EU Law* (Craig and de Búrca, 1999). Of course, the process of evolution of EC economic and social law has not been smooth. It is much like the process of integration itself which 'has always been characterized by fits and starts, by bursts of activity which have often been followed by crisis and relative inaction' (Tsoukalis, 1997: 1–2). We view it as important, therefore, to provide an insight within each chapter as to how the law and policy in the relevant field has evolved.

Developing this sense of EU law as a narrative and a process is not only the task for this first part of the book, comprising this introductory chapter, followed by a chapter on what we term 'socio-economic governance' amplified in its specific EU context; but it is also an approach which suffuses each individual chapter sketching the different fields of law. Reference is made where appropriate to non-legal literatures on the topics covered, in an effort to help bring a broader perspective. The first part of the book aims to set out also the core constitutional and legal principles derived from the treaties and the case law of the Court of Justice which govern law and policy-making in the EU and to show the great variety of techniques of socio-economic governance which apply across the different fields of law and policy-making with which the EU is currently engaged.

Overall, it is hoped that the reader will gain a sense of the operation of the legal order within a framework informed by the historical development of European Union integration processes and by the ever-changing preoccupations of the broader issues and the most important factors which have brought about such changes. Where once the discussion centred on the creation of the single market, and then on the launching of the single currency, the focus is now above all on the challenge of making a Union of twenty-seven Member States work. In matters of policy, the focus has turned to the challenges inherent in building the Area of Freedom, Security and Justice, and the issue of competitiveness within labour markets. These reflect the EU's twin themes of internal and external security in an ever more challenging world, and of economic reform to promote prosperity and sustainable development. In terms of external affairs, both the longstanding attempts to create a global free trade system within the General Agreement on Tariffs and Trade (GATT 1948) and the World Trade Organisation (WTO 1994), as well as the more recent US-led 'war on terrorism' which has significantly changed the state of affairs surrounding internal and external security matters, continue to shape the development of internal EU law and policy. Against these swiftly changing backgrounds, some aspects of the legal core of the EU can offer a haven of stability! As we shall see, the fact that the spotlight may shift away from a field of policy-making does not mean that the development of the law will actually stop. On the contrary, away from the full glare of attention, it may actually accelerate. In many fields of policy-making, it is apparent that a process of legislative renewal has been occurring under the management of recent Commissions headed by President Romano Prodi and President José-Manuel Barroso, reflecting often a principle of regulatory reform that encourages the EU to do more, but with fewer legislative instruments.

## 1.3 Terminology, Treaty Articles and Reform Processes

Wherever possible, reference is made throughout this book to the work, activities and institutions of the EU or the Union, although in strictly legal terms it is often correct in fact to refer to the European Community (EC) or simply the Community. Indeed, the Court of Justice commonly refers to 'Community law', and the term 'Union law' or 'EU law' is only just coming into usage in some legal documents of the EU and in the context of the emerging case law concerned with 'third pillar law'. Examples of documents which refer to Union law include the Charter of Fundamental Rights of the European Union of December 2000 (OJ 2004 C364/1) and the 2004 Constitutional Treaty (OJ 2004 C310/1), but the former is a declaratory instrument at present, while the latter has yet to be ratified and to enter into force, and seems unlikely to do so. In this book, we use the terms 'EU law' and the 'legal order of the EU' as general descriptors covering all legal aspects relating to the European Community and the European Union. Only when specifically delineating precise questions on the scope of Community competence under the EC Treaty will the terms 'EC' and 'Community' be used, in order to highlight the continuing legal distinction between the 'Community' and 'Union' pillars of the EU. In the latter context, reference will be made to the 'powers of the Union', in order to differentiate these from 'Community competence'.

In 1999, a significant renumbering exercise of Treaty provisions was brought into effect by the Treaty of Amsterdam. Throughout this work, provisions of the EC Treaty (e.g. Article 1 EC) and the Treaty on European Union (e.g. Article 1 EU) are referred to by their new post-Amsterdam numbers. Occasionally, for the avoidance of confusion, reference will be made to the earlier pre-Amsterdam numbering scheme. Thus, in quotations from cases or literatures where the old numbers are used, these are sometimes preserved if the sense requires this. Particular attention to the whole question of renumbering is paid wherever the periodic revisions which the treaties have undergone have resulted in the amendment, substitution or deletion of the original provisions. Tables of equivalences with the old and the new numbers are provided in all collections of primary materials on the EU, and readers are advised to consult them to resolve any confusion on the matter.

Since the early 2000s, the European Union has been going through a very significant reform process (Shaw, 2005). At the European Council meeting in Nice in December 2000, which finalised the text of the Treaty of Nice after an exceptionally difficult negotiation process, the leaders of the then fifteen Member States appended a Declaration on the Future of the Union to the Treaty. The Declaration committed the Member States to reflection upon some of the key issues which were felt to undermine the legitimacy of the EU. They raised issues such as the status of the Charter of Fundamental Rights of the EU, which had recently been drafted by a Convention established for that purpose during 2000, the division of powers between the EU and the Member States, and the role of national parliaments. However, even earlier in May 2000, German Foreign Minister Joschka Fischer had given a visionary speech in Berlin on the so-called 'finality' of European integration. Where might the EU finally end up? He suggested that the model of a federation of nation states might be useful.

There were therefore some very big ideas already on the table when the Member States came to consider these questions during the course of 2001, to which they had committed themselves. There were also still some 'nuts and bolts' institutional questions which had not been properly addressed in the Treaty of Nice or earlier Treaty amendments, relating to making the EU work better after enlargement. These included the size and composition of the European Commission, and the legislative process and system of qualified majority voting in the Council of Ministers. The idea would be to make the Commission smaller and more effective, and to change the system of qualified majority voting to make it easier to reach majority decisions after enlargement, at the same time as extending the list of areas where majority decision-making rather than unanimous voting would apply. Both the big ideas and the nitty-gritty challenges lay behind the adoption by the Member States of the Laeken Declaration in December 2001. This text provided an analysis of the challenges facing the EU, both in terms of its own internal workings and the environment in which it operates, and envisaged a set of responses to these challenges.

The first response was the establishment in February 2002 of the Convention on the Future of the Union, with ex-French President Valéry Giscard d'Estaing as its President. This was a body comprising representatives from a variety of constituencies, such as the national governments, the national parliaments, the European Parliament and the European Commission, and observers from a number of bodies such as the Committee of the Regions and the Economic and Social Committee. It included also representatives from the then thirteen candidate states, namely the ten which acceded in May 2004, plus Bulgaria, Romania and Turkey. The Convention worked steadily until mid-2003, through phases of listening, reflection and drafting, and eventually produced a report in the form of a draft Treaty establishing a Constitution for Europe. This draft Treaty was in turn sent to an Intergovernmental Conference (IGC) which was convened in October 2003 by the Italian Presidency.

An IGC is the conventional mechanism for Treaty amendment in the European Union under Article 48 EU, and involves just the representatives of the governments of the Member States as the decision-makers, with limited input from the Commission which must give an Opinion, and the European Parliament which only has observers present. Here the ten accession states were involved as full participants, although the IGC began before they actually acceded (1 May 2004), and the three other states were granted only observer status. Italy failed to achieve agreement among all the Member States on a single text by the end of December 2003. Particular difficulties arose among France, Germany, Poland and Spain over the definition of qualified majority voting. The Irish Presidency in the first half of 2004 worked steadily on resolving differences between the Member States, however, and agreement was reached in June 2004. The result was the Treaty establishing a Constitution for Europe ('Constitutional Treaty'), which is based in substantial measure upon the text elaborated by the Convention, with some additional changes introduced particularly to take into account the sensitivities of Member States. A good example of this concerns qualified majority voting in the area of harmonisation of national criminal laws and criminal procedure, where the Member States can apply an 'emergency brake' if they believe that proposed harmonisation measures in the EU compromise the integrity of their national legal systems. This means that if a Member State is unhappy about a proposal which could, in principle, be adopted by a qualified majority vote against their wishes, it can ask that the matter be referred to the European Council. This effectively means the dropping of the proposal.

Even though the Constitutional Treaty is not in force in the EU, some of its major proposals regarding changes to the EU's substantive laws and policies are referred to in the chapters which follow. In any event, it is worth noting that the text of the Constitutional Treaty contains important ideas for improving the effectiveness and coherence of the underlying legal structure of the EU which will influence any future reforms. However, it is important to emphasise that for the most part the Constitutional Treaty covers institutional and constitutional questions, and not issues of substantive policy-making. It does not affect, for example, the way in which the EU's single market continues to operate (see Chapter 3). On the other hand, it does suggest changes to some aspects of how the single currency is governed, and proposes substantial changes to the structure of policy-making in the area of justice and home affairs, in a way which would strengthen the input of the EU institutions into law-making, especially the European Parliament. Also, some of the institutional issues, such as the proposed simplification of the system of legal instruments which the EU institutions may adopt, are important for all fields of law and policy-making and are given brief coverage in this book as necessary. The basic institutional structure of the EU, with the European Parliament, the European Commission, the Council of Ministers and the Court of Justice, remains untouched.

The Constitutional Treaty is divided into four parts which are designated by Roman numerals:

▶ Part I is the general part of the Constitution, establishing Union objectives, values and competences. It includes provisions on institutions and instruments.
▶ Part II incorporates 'The Charter of Fundamental Rights of the Union' as a legally binding set of guarantees.
▶ Part III sets out 'The Policies and Functioning of the Union', and includes details on how the institutions as well as the policies actually work.
▶ Part IV contains 'General and Final Provisions'.

Overall, the Constitutional Treaty comprises 448 articles. Each article is designated with an Arabic and a Roman numeral. Thus, Article I-60 is the last provision in Part I, Article II-61 is the first provision of the next part, Article III-115 is the first provision of Part III, and Article IV-437 is the first provision of the final part. This notation is used in the chapters which follow whenever the text involves a discussion of the provisions of the Constitutional Treaty. Where there is no discussion of the Constitutional Treaty, it is because the Constitutional Treaty will not make any significant difference to the provisions which are being discussed. In such instances, the Constitutional Treaty is merely a renumbering exercise. A good example of this is the definition of the internal market contained in Article 14 EC and discussed in the next section. The definition is adopted in identical terms in Article III-130 of the Constitutional Treaty.

If it comes into force, the Constitutional Treaty will supersede the EC Treaty (as amended through to the Treaty of Nice) and the Treaty on European Union (likewise, as amended). However, at the time of writing, it could not be assumed that the Constitutional Treaty *will* in fact ever come into force, at least not in the form in which it was originally agreed in June 2004, and signed by the Member States in October 2004. Although by May 2005, the Constitutional Treaty had been ratified by nine of the 25 Member States, representing nearly a majority of the population, it failed its first test on 29 May 2005, when it was decisively rejected in a referendum in France by a majority of 55 to 45 per cent. This was followed by a negative referendum in the Netherlands on 1 June 2005, where nearly 62 per cent of those voting (on the basis of a 63 per cent turnout) voted 'no'. Despite this setback, ratification still continued in some Member States although the majority terminated their endeavours to achieve ratification, and by the beginning of 2007 eighteen Member States had approved the Treaty (including the incomers Bulgaria and Romania), representing more than a majority of the population of the Union. Given that ratification is required by all Member States before the Constitutional Treaty can come into force, the EU remained in a curious limbo throughout the rest of 2005 and through 2006, a time officially termed a 'reflection period' during which the Commission tried hard both to engender increased debate about the need for democracy and communication, and to focus the attention of both citizens and policy-makers on the delivery of policy initiatives in preference to the institutional changes which are the primary focus of the Constitutional Treaty.

Serious efforts to reignite the process of institutional reform, with something like a 'mini' Treaty reforming the existing EU and EC Treaties, were relaunched by the German Presidency in the first six months of 2007, and the Berlin Declaration, agreed by the Member States and the EU institutions on the occasion of the fiftieth anniversary of the signature of the Treaty of Rome in March 2007, referred rather vaguely to a hope for an institutional renewal of the Union before the date of the next European Parliament elections in 2009. This will be a much more modest affair than the Constitutional Treaty. It certainly seems very doubtful that the Member States will try to press ahead on the basis of the existing Constitutional Treaty, and attempt to reverse the negative referendum votes and persuade some rather eurosceptic Member States, such as the UK, Sweden, Denmark, Poland and the Czech Republic, to seek a positive ratification outcome. Indeed, it may be that even a modest reforming treaty will encounter ratification difficulties in some Member States. Meanwhile, the legal framework of the EU will continue unchanged as before, on the basis of the EC Treaty and the Treaty on European Union, as amended.

### 1.4    Regional Systems of Economic Integration and Different Levels of Economic Integration

The European Union is based upon a framework for regional economic integration, embodied primarily in the three Community treaties (EEC – now EC, ECSC and Euratom), as subsequently amended, and as supplemented by the Treaty on European Union, also as amended. This has to be the starting point for presenting the narrative and themes of EU social and economic law. To a certain extent the system of integration which the treaties provide for follows, in a recognisable way, theories of regional economic integration outlined by economists, although tailored to the specific requirements of the original Communities and now the EU.

The EU today is based on what the treaties call an 'internal market', that is, an area without internal frontiers where goods, services, persons and capital can move without hindrance (Article 14 EC), but with a common external frontier. In other words, it is also a 'customs union', with a single external tariff for imports, and it has, to a large extent, a common trading identity *vis-à-vis* the outside world. Since 1993 and the Treaty of Maastricht, it has been evolving towards an 'economic and monetary union', that is, an area with a common economic and monetary policy including a single currency, a single bank and controls over national economic policies. In broad terms, the form of integration chosen is that of market integration: a larger trading unit in which market forces operate freely and is created out of smaller diverse units. The EU is also a regulatory system, as the removal of trading borders between the Member States and the creation of a common trading area have often necessitated the replacement of diverse national regulations to protect interests such as the consumer, the worker and the environment, with common or harmonised EU-level regulations.

As a result of such processes of integration, economies are expected to specialise as they become increasingly interconnected, and to purchase imports from within the regional trading bloc rather than from outside. Thus, systems of regional economic integration are discriminatory *vis-à-vis* the rest of the world, and not automatically compatible with a system which aims at global free trade such as that based around the World Trade Organisation (WTO) which is now the principal international forum for trade negotiations and dispute settlement and comprises the old General Agreement on Tariffs and Trade from 1949 as amended (GATT), as well as newer agreements on trade in services (GATS) and intellectual property (TRIPS). The world trading environment of the post-Uruguay Round WTO and the increasing interconnectedness of the global economy have raised important challenges to the EU as a trading partner and as a regulatory system.

Economic integration can take different forms, depending essentially upon the degree of openness established towards the partner economies. The terms used here are not precise or static economic definitions, but rather descriptions of the types of features typically found in an evolutionary process of integration. A *free trade area* involves the removal of customs duties between the participating states, but does not involve the erection of a common external barrier. Participating states remain free to fix their own tariff levels in international trade. A free trade area will not lead to the removal of internal borders, as frontier controls will need to remain for the purposes of checking the origin of goods. The additional element of uniform external protection is added in a *customs union*, where the participating states agree upon the establishment of a common external tariff, and embark upon the task of creating a common external trade policy, for example, setting quotas and duty-free preferences. The EU is based on a customs union, but extends further in the sense that it is a *common market* in which there are to be no restrictions at all on the movement of commodities such as goods and services, or on the free flow of the factors of production such as labour, enterprise and capital.

The final stage of economic integration, in the sense that hitherto it was thought likely to be achieved only by groups of states which have become for all practical purposes a single political entity, is *economic and monetary union*. It was this stage of integration, involving the convergence of national economic policies and a gradual assumption of centralised responsibility for economic and monetary policy, leading to the creation of a single currency area within single monetary institutions and policies, which was envisaged by the Treaty of Maastricht. Many concrete steps towards its attainment have been taken, with the introduction of single banking institutions managing monetary policy, the locking of national exchange rates and the introduction of the euro as a single currency for 12 Member States from 1999, the phasing out of national currencies for 'Euroland' from 2002, and the introduction of greater centralised controls over national economic policies of the participating states from the mid-1990s onwards. The 'political identity' of the EU remains, however, a very uncertain issue (see 1.8). Another way of putting this matter is that these economic terms tell us nothing about how political entities such as nation states, international organisations such as the WTO, or intermediate bodies such as the EU, are supposed to achieve the changes necessary to move from one stage to another in the evolutionary process of economic integration.

## 1.5  Key Terms in European Economic Integration

When economic integration is discussed in the EU context, confusion often arises as to how some terms are used in the EU Treaties and literature on the EU, with terms used sometimes interchangeably. The best example is provided by the terms: *common, internal* and *single market*. In one sense, this is not a problem, given the somewhat fluid nature of all the different levels of economic integration, which are subject to influence from external factors such as current political ideologies or the state of the world economy. Not too much should be read into the shift from the term 'common market' used in the original EEC Treaty, to the term 'internal market', used in the EC Treaty from the Single European Act onwards, and 'single market', used in much political discourse throughout the 1980s. There was no stepping back in ambition between the original EEC Treaty and the Single European Act. The new terminology represented a break with the somewhat jaded concept of a common market, which had lost some of its political credibility as a realistic objective since it should have been established by 1970, but in fact never was established because of political stagnation and economic difficulties. Armstrong calls the single market merely 'a new spin on the idea of a common market' (Armstrong, 1999: 747).

The apparently confusing terminology can best be summed up in these terms:

- 'common market' is the term associated in the economic literature with a particular level of economic integration;
- the 'single market' has been a political project associated with the relaunch of European economic integration in the 1980s (the '1992 programme'); and
- 'internal market' is the term found most often in legal literatures, including the EC Treaty, documentation emanating from the European Commission including its White Paper which underpinned the '1992 programme', and much secondary legislation. According to Article 14 EC, the internal market is an area 'without internal frontiers', and much endeavour has been directed since the end of the period set aside for the completion of the programme, i.e. 31 December 1992, towards removing these frontiers, particularly for persons.

In sum, the differences are not based on the scope of what is meant (e.g. does the particular term include EMU and/or the flanking policies such as the environment, as well as commodity and factor of production mobility?) but rather the context in which the term is used, and the economic and political rather than the legal meanings of what is conveyed. As it is the term most closely associated with legal literatures, 'internal market' will be used throughout this book, except from time to time when specifically referring to the 1992 or single market programme where it is appropriate to use that term. However, and perhaps a little confusingly for our purposes, the Court of Justice generally refers to the 'common market' since this remains the term used in the EC Treaty in its original 1957 version, from which the Court derives most of its terminology.

A distinction is commonly drawn between *negative* and *positive* integration. Negative integration refers to the removal of existing impediments to trade and exchange, and less complex forms of economic integration consist almost entirely of negative dispositions. Typically, these obstacles to trade between states stem from measures adopted by states, such as product standards or provisions discriminating against non-national goods or services. Positive integration relates to:

'the modification of existing instruments and institutions and, more importantly, to the creation of new ones so as to enable the market of the integrated area to function properly and effectively and also to promote other broader policy aims of the [integration] scheme' (El-Agraa, 2004: 2).

Increased commitment to positive integration is necessitated by the move towards more complex levels of integration. There are numerous examples of the phenomenon identified by El-Agraa to be found in the EU. For example, it is arguable that there is a need, within the single market, to create EU-wide basic product standards to which all products put on the market should conform in the interests of consumer and environmental protection. This can be achieved by means of the harmonisation of national laws. Particular obstacles to the free movement of persons *within* the single market are evident which can only be removed by positive measures especially at the external borders, to create common standards on the admission of third country nationals. This allows the removal of internal frontier controls, as has occurred among the 'Schengen' states. A further example is the creation of new centralised policy instruments (Articles 81–86 EC) which enable the EU to restrain or punish undertakings or groups of undertakings which seek to recreate, through private behaviour, the same market segmentation which Member States are prohibited from retaining by the EU's guarantees of free movement (competition policy).

Two key difficulties exist with positive integration at the level of policy and decision-making, and at the level of implementation. Throughout this book we will revisit, through practical examples, the details of the rigidities and complexities of the EU's decision-making process. It was only after the adoption of the Single European Act in 1986 that there was a marked acceleration in the legislative activity of the EU. In practice, as we shall see, many of the achievements of the EU in the field of economic and social law, and especially in the domain of rights for individual economic actors or market participants, are a result of creative interpretations of the outer limits of negative integration by the Court of Justice. Often these have led to altered conceptions about the types of positive harmonising measures which are both expedient and necessary for the completion of the single market. In other words, the work of the Court has changed the conventional understanding of the difference between positive and negative integration.

The second difficulty is even more impervious to proactive changes brought about by the EU institutions. One often overlooked truth about the EU is that while the EU institutions may make decisions and thereby seek to exert control over the marketplace, they have little capacity to put their decisions into effect. In relation to most aspects of *implementation*, the EU institutions are in the hands of the national political, legal and administrative structures and actors. The EU institutions are limited to powers of *enforcement* which are often ineffective to deal with infringements, or are dependent upon the complaints or claims brought by aggrieved individual companies, traders or consumers.

Reference should finally be made to *sectoral integration*. Closer integration in particular sectors of the economy may be achievable only by interventionist policy-making which creates uniform regulatory mechanisms. The principal example in the EU, aside from the specific sectoral treaties, is the agricultural sector, where the various national mechanisms existing to subsidise agricultural activities and the earnings of farmers have, since the early 1960s, been replaced by a unified system of price support and intervention, buying whenever the market price falls below a specified guide price. This is not an example of the free market in operation. Recent steps towards reforming the agricultural policy have involved more structural action, for example encouraging changes in rural land use, supporting farmers to take care of the environment, or indeed leading to the re-nationalisation of certain policy choices in relation to agriculture. In none of these cases, however, is a free and unregulated market for agricultural activities and products proposed.

## 1.6   The Economic Benefits of Integration

Economists are greatly divided on the nature and degree of the economic advantages to be derived from integration. Models of customs unions developed within the classical theories of international trade would appear to show that there should be gains in terms of trade creation, but losses in terms of trade diversion. Trade creation occurs where the source of a particular good is switched to the most efficient source of production within the single trading bloc when customs duties which artificially increase prices are removed; trade diversion arises because the most efficient world producer may be excluded from that trading bloc, and its products may be rendered more expensive than those of the most efficient internal producer because of the effects of the customs duties at the external frontier. However, this theory relies upon a model of a static customs union which ignores factors such as the monopoly power of multinational undertakings, economies of scale, costs of transport and non-tariff barriers to trade erected by nation states. Consequently, the theory is based upon an unrealistic set of assumptions as to why systems of integration are formed. For example, the illustration of trade creation and trade diversion used here is an argument for global free trade, and against regional systems of integration. Global free trade would be the best way of maximising economic welfare, but in practice it remains unattainable. It follows, therefore, and is indeed undoubtedly true, that states have other reasons for embarking upon integration processes.

Regional integration offers other, dynamic benefits. These include the economies of scale and increased levels of competition which benefit both undertakings and consumers in a larger market, all of which may lead to accelerated restructuring and specialisation of economies. The integrated economic entity may also enjoy increased bargaining power in international trade, enabling better terms of trade to be negotiated with third countries. Integration involves openness of an economy towards the outside, and thus enhances transparency of the underlying regulatory framework. Overall, membership in a larger economic entity may make a state a more attractive location for inward investment from strong economies. Enhanced economic integration also leads onto other benefits, including increased political interdependence and increased influence upon global political events.

These dynamic benefits were emphasised particularly strongly in relation to the so-called 1992, or single market programme. For example, the Commission in its official papers pointed to the possible emergence of a 'virtuous circle of innovation and competition – competition stimulating innovation which in turn would increase competition' as a result of the lowering of the barriers. Certainly, one of the political successes of the programme was the harnessing of business commitment to the project with companies being successfully convinced that they needed to respond – in some way – to the changes being brought about.

However, although it may be possible to identify the economic factors which should, in theory, lead to growth resulting from customs unions and other forms of more intense economic integration, in practice these gains are very difficult to quantify. It is almost impossible to separate any additional economic growth which may have occurred in the Member States as a consequence of the existence of the EU from the growth in GNP which would in any case have occurred. This is especially true because of radical changes in the global economy since the inception of the European Community, the altered arrangements for the regulation of international trade especially since the creation of the WTO, and factors such as the internationalisation of capital movements and financial markets which have led to much greater global economic interdependency.

Undoubtedly it can be demonstrated that trade within the EU has increased greatly at the expense of trade between the EU and the outside world. This is often given as a reason why the UK, which has a particular tradition of trading outside Europe resulting from its history as a colonial power, may not have benefited as much from membership in the EU as other countries, since it has lost both the sources of many of its cheap raw materials and the destinations of many of its exports. Furthermore, trade within the EU is dominated by Germany which accounts for over 35 per cent of all exports of manufactured goods within the EU. Germany also runs a large trade surplus with the rest of the EU, since it accounts for only 25 per cent of all imports.

There is certainly a case for treating the original figures associated with anticipated growth from the completion of the single market with a certain scepticism, especially in the light of emerging evidence some years after the 1992 deadline. The possibility of increasing GDP by up to 5 per cent as a result of eliminating the 'costs of non-Europe' (i.e. the costs resulting from the failure to complete the single market) was naturally beguiling for both politicians and industrialists, not to mention ordinary consumers who would expect to see their spending power increase. This optimistic prognosis was propounded most famously in the Commission's own sponsored study in 'The Economics of 1992' (*Cecchini Report*) (Cecchini, 1988) and has been termed 'Christmas Tree' economics. In practice, however, many of the calculations put forward did not take into account the costs associated with industrial restructuring, shifts in patterns of employment and other regional effects of the creation of a larger market.

Jovanovic (1997: 199) cautioned that the single market programme is part of the long-range process in which it is difficult to disaggregate the precise effects of the changes introduced, and suggested in 1997 that it was still too early to conclude on the long-term benefits. Tsoukalis has warned against the temptation of producing numerical estimates of the macro-economic effects of the single market programme, while accepting that these are highly attractive to politicians. In 1997, he summarised the available evidence in cautious terms:

'Whichever way it is calculated, the macroeconomic impact of the internal market seems to have been rather small; and certainly smaller than expected. According to estimates released by the Commission, the impact of the internal market on GDP has been between 1.1 and 1.5 per cent, with the impact on investment being close to 3 per cent. Between 300,000 and 900,000 jobs have been directly attributed to the internal market, and approximately 1 per cent reduction in prices' (Tsoukalis, 1997: 77).

He attributed the difference between the *ex ante* estimates and *ex post* calculations of the macro-economic impact to the fact that expectations were deliberately inflated, and that the implementation of the single market programme has occurred in quite a hostile economic environment. The tenth anniversary of the completion of the single market, i.e. of the passing of the 1992 deadline, led to further attempts to estimate the effects of the single market programme, and the Commission concluded that EU GDP in 2002 is 1.8 percentage points or €164.5 billion higher thanks to the single market, and that about 2.5 million jobs have been created in the EU since 1992 that would not have been created without the opening up of frontiers.

Whatever the doubts about the figures, it cannot be denied that membership in the EU continues to be viewed as an attractive proposition. Evidence can be found not just in the 2004 enlargement, but also beyond, with Bulgaria and Romania having signed accession treaties in 2005, subsequently acceeding on 1 January 2007. In addition, in what is termed the EU's 'new neighbourhood' comprising countries such as Ukraine which continue the transition to full market economy status as well as to democracy, as well as those countries of South Eastern Europe which continue to cope with the fall-out from the break-up of Yugoslavia which undermines economic as well as political stability, membership in the EU is regarded as an important goal. It must be assumed therefore that all these countries, including the ten new Member States, envisage deriving economic gains from membership or, perhaps, avoiding losses which might result from non-membership. In addition, as many economists themselves note (e.g. El-Agraa, 2004), European integration involves many political choices as well as economic calculations.

## 1.7   Economic Integration and the Social Dimension

As Part IV of the book will show in detail, the EU has become gradually, but increasingly, involved in law and policy-making in many fields of social policy in the widest sense. In this book, for example, the discussion covers not only conventional redistributive social policies, but also environmental policy. Only belatedly are the Member States taking up the ringing declaration which they made in October 1972, at the Summit Meeting in Paris, just as the Community engaged with its first enlargement from six to nine members. The government leaders declared that 'they attribute the same importance to energetic proceedings in the field of social policy as to the realisation of the economic and financial union'. This suggests a grand principled rationale for the development of EU social policy. In practice, the reasons are more pragmatic.

According to Leibfried and Pierson, 'the economic and institutional dynamics of creating a single market have made it increasingly difficult to exclude social issues from the EU's agenda' (Leibfried and Pierson, 2000: 268). In developmental terms, EU social policy is widely understood to be the result of what are termed, in the language of integration theory, 'spill-overs' from one sector into another. The steps towards economic integration inherent in the concepts of the internal market and indeed economic and monetary union are not hermetically sealed with economic effects only. No one sector of the economy or society is isolated from all of the others.

The integration of markets, for example, can have a dramatic effect upon national welfare states. This is partly a result of labour migration which may change patterns of demand, but it is also a consequence of the increased marketisation and commoditisation of public services such as health care and social care. The level of resources put into national welfare systems through fiscal policy may remain essentially a matter for the Member States, but in many respects outputs are now constrained by the impact of principles such as non-discrimination, under which national welfare regimes must treat all EU citizens equally. This has led to the adaptation of national welfare state institutions as a consequence of the indirect pressures of integration as well as changes in the rules governing benefit allocation as a consequence of direct pressures to make them compatible with the rules of 'negative' market integration. Similarly, Economic and Monetary Union – in common with other dimensions of economic integration – has an effect on labour markets, demanding, for example, substantial restructuring efforts which will be more effective if coordinated across the Member States and the Commission itself. But most obviously, there have been growing pressures for positive integration, i.e. some measure of harmonisation in some fields of social policy, especially in relation to the social standards imposed on employers such as health and safety provisions, protection against employment risks such as redundancy, and the prohibition of discriminatory practices.

## 1.8 The Links between Socio-economic Integration and Political Integration in a Globalising Economy

Observing the EU at the outset of the twenty-first century, Laffan *et al* (2000: 101) commented that the central problem confronting the EU was the question, 'how is deep economic integration achieved and governed in the absence of centralised political authority?'

Systems of economic integration are rather unstable, and the theory of functionalism has been used to describe the 'spill-over effect' whereby the attainment of one level of economic integration tends to lead onto the next. For example, for many years there was considerable pressure from within business communities in the EU for the establishment of a single currency, which would both eradicate many of the uncertainties of floating, or even partially fixed, exchange rates, and reduce the transaction costs associated with dealing in more than one currency. Thus, the prospect of a larger accessible market sharpened awareness of the potential benefits of EMU and helped structure the processes which led to the Treaty of Maastricht and its implementation through the 1990s and into the 2000s. Moreover, in the types of mixed economy to be found in the Member States of the EU, the activities of the state are not restricted to erecting border controls, charging customs duties, imposing taxes and the management of macro-economic policy, but include numerous interventions in the economy through both regulatory activity and, in some areas such as the utility industries where these remain in public hands, commercial activity (Tsoukalis, 1997: 61–2). Tsoukalis concludes:

'In the context of such economies, a complete customs union or a common market can be nothing short of total economic integration; and this has become increasingly apparent in the case of the EU.'

It was an awareness of this which constituted the driving force behind the political movement in the EU, from the mid-1980s onwards, to complete the internal market in accordance with the timetable established in the Single European Act and the 'shopping list' of national obstacles to free trade identified in the Commission's White Paper of 1985. The primary barrier to full achievement of these objectives was the economic downturn experienced in the economies of the Member States in the early 1990s which significantly undermined, but did not eventually prevent progress towards EMU. All of this suggests both that the autonomy of the nation states within the legal framework provided by the EU Treaties has generally remained strong and that economic theory can sometimes underestimate the degree of political integration needed for the successful completion of a common market (Laffan *et al*, 2000: 103). In fact, it is generally accepted that the greater fetters upon the autonomy of the Member States have come from international market forces and that in fact states have ceded more power to the new economic orthodoxy of the free market and the global trading system than they have so far to the European institutions. Tsoukalis and Rhodes (1997: 19) suggested that:

> 'The main constraint in terms of national economy autonomy was for long the result of increased international capital mobility, and for many years regional integration had very little effect on it.'

Only as political realities have adjusted gradually to 'the growing Europeanisation (and internationalisation) of economic forces' (Tsoukalis and Rhodes, 1997: 29) have the European (Union) institutions slowly acquired more power at the expense of the national political institutions. This has occurred under the single market programme and, most recently, in relation to the development of EMU which involved the granting of significant powers to the European Central Bank (ECB). The initial reluctance of the Member States to concede the need for a parallel Intergovernmental Conference on Political Union to accompany the one on EMU which led to the Treaty of Maastricht and hence to the single currency and the establishment of the ECB is an important reminder of the obstacles to the balanced development of functional economic and political authority in the EU.

Political authority and hence political integration in the twenty-first century EU stands at a crossroads. On the one hand, as we shall see in the following section, political and socio-economic goals and policy-making instruments are now rather closely integrated together in the complex framework of Treaties which constitutes the present-day EU. In principle, the framework for a system of multi-level governance of the economies and societies involved in the EU is in place. As states and societies become more interdependent as a result of globalisation, as well as the process of European integration in fields as diverse as crime, immigration and the environment, policies have started to develop at the EU level, in close partnership with national policies. On the other hand, the nature of that governance system remains highly contested, as the EU appears to lose more and more popular support among the populations of the Member States and, moreover, it rarely appears to function particularly effectively or efficiently in response to growing technological and ethical challenges such as genetics or the need for sustainable energies. Public ignorance about and dissatisfaction with the EU are very high right across the EU, including in the new Member States of Central and Eastern Europe as public opinion surveys show. The campaign in France for a 'no vote' in the referendum on the ratification of the Constitutional Treaty reflected strongly felt and widespread public fears about globalisation and the preservation of national social systems and social models. Traditionally, the EU has offered protection against the harsh winds of globalisation. Some now fear that the EU itself is increasingly fostering the promotion of neo-liberal economic policies which push down labour market standards and force the privatisation of public services. The EU and its Member States have become increasingly obsessed with how to achieve growth and competitiveness at levels matching the United States (Sapir *et al*, 2004).

This book will not attempt to show how this legitimacy challenge could or should be faced, or to engage in details with the EU's current debate on governance or the 'Future of the Union', except insofar as these impinge directly upon the topics under discussion, such as the division of competences and the techniques of governance which the EU has at its disposal. It stands, however, for the more modest proposition that a better understanding of the legal framework of policy-making is a necessary prerequisite to making judgments about the desirability of the past, the present and the future of the European integration project.

## 1.9 The Objectives of the European Union and the Legal Framework for Policy-Making in the Socio-economic Domain

The legal framework underpinning the fields of policy-making analysed in this book cuts right across the three pillar structure of the EU, as established by the Treaty of Maastricht in 1993. This is shown schematically on p. 21. In this section, we sketch out that framework by reference to the foundational principles to be found in the Treaties. The Preambles to the EU and the EC Treaties set the stage, linking the vocation of the EU in terms of economic and social objectives to wider political goals related to liberty, democracy and respect for fundamental rights. The Preambles to both Treaties make general references strengthening economic and social progress, and to the unity and the convergence of the economies of the states. More specifically, Article 2 EU provides in its first paragraph that it is an objective of the EU:

> 'to promote economic and social progress and a high level of employment and to achieve balanced and sustainable development, in particular through the creation of an area without internal frontiers, through the strengthening of economic and social cohesion and through the establishment of economic and monetary union, ultimately including a single currency . . .'

This is the core socio-economic objective of the EU, strongly echoed in the EC Treaty, and indeed in key non-Treaty statements about the objectives of the EU, such as the Lisbon competitiveness agenda (see 1.1). Turning to the combined political and social objectives of the Union which are relevant to the development of policies covered in this book, we find also that the Treaty aims:

> 'to strengthen the protection of the rights and interests of the nationals of its Member States through the introduction of a citizenship of the Union;'

and

> 'to maintain and develop the Union as an area of freedom, security and justice, in which the free movement of persons is assured in conjunction with appropriate measures with respect to external border controls, asylum, immigration and the prevention and combating of crime.'

Part One of the EC Treaty which sets out 'Principles' appears to be simpler and indeed narrower, with Article 2 EC proclaiming the sole objective of the 'European Community' to be the following:

> 'The Community shall have as its task, by establishing a common market and an economic and monetary union and by implementing the common policies or activities referred to in Articles 3 and 4, to promote throughout the Community a harmonious, balanced and sustainable development of economic activities, a high level of employment and of social protection, equality

**PREAMBLE AND COMMON PROVISIONS OF THE EU TREATY [ARTS. 1–7 EU]**
- objectives and tasks of EU;
- common principles, e.g. subsidiarity;
- common values, e.g. fundamental rights, liberty, rule of law, democracy;
- single institutional structure;
- respect for national identities.

### THE THREE-PILLAR STRUCTURE OF THE UNION

*Pillar Two*                    *Pillar One*                    *Pillar Three*

Area of shared activity or cross-pillar structures, e.g. Schengen Acquis incorporated after Amsterdam; Title IV Part II EC Treaty as linked to PJC – **Area of freedom, security and justice**

**COMMON FOREIGN AND SECURITY POLICY (CFSP)** TITLE V EU ARTICLES 11–28 TEU 'Intergovernmental'

TWO (formerly three) COMMUNITIES HELD TOGETHER BY BOND OF 'SUPRANATIONALISM'

**EUROPEAN COMMUNITY** (EC) (subsumes since 23 July 2002 also the activities of the former Coal and Steel Community (ECSC)) **Covers** single market, customs union, EMU, social policy, etc.

**EURATOM or EUROPEAN ATOMIC ENERGY COMMUNITY**

**POLICE AND JUDICIAL COOPERATION IN CRIMINAL MATTERS (PJC)** TITLE VI EU ARTICLES 29–42 EU 'Intergovernmental' – but linked to first pillar . . . .

**TITLE VII EU (ARTICLES 43–45 EU)**
GENERAL CONDITIONS OF CLOSER COOPERATION
- special rules for pillar one (Art. 11–11a EC), pillar two (Art. 27a–e EU), pillar three (Art. 40–40b TEU).

**TITLE VI EU (ARTICLES 46–53 EU)** FINAL PROVISIONS
- jurisdiction of Court of Justice;
- arrangements for accession of new Member States;
- amendments to treaties;
- entry into force.

**PROTOCOLS APPENDED TO EU AND/OR EC TREATIES**, e.g.
- jurisdiction of Court of Justice;
- incorporation of Schengen Acquis;
- opt-outs for UK, Denmark, Ireland;
- subsidiarity and proportionality;
- European enlargement;
- Declaration on the Future of the Union.

**DECLARATIONS APPENDED TO TEU AND EC TREATY**
(not formally part of Treaty)

**CHARTER OF FUNDAMENTAL RIGHTS OF THE EUROPEAN UNION**

*The Architecture of the European Union*

between men and women, sustainable and non-inflationary growth, a high degree of competitiveness and convergence of economic performance, a high level of protection and improvement of the quality of the environment, the raising of the standard of living and quality of life, and economic and social cohesion and solidarity among Member States.'

However, as Article 2 EC indicates, a fuller guide to the legal framework for economic and social law in the EU is to be found in Articles 3 and 4 EC. Article 3 EC, which has been amended and broadened on the occasion of each new Treaty, sets out the activities of the European Community and includes:

'(a)  the prohibition, as between Member States, of customs duties and quantitative restrictions on the import and export of goods, and of all other measures having equivalent effect;

(b)  a common commercial policy;

(c)  an internal market characterised by the abolition, as between Member States, of obstacles to the free movement of goods, persons, services and capital;

(d)  measures concerning the entry and movement of persons as provided for in Title IV;

(e)  a common policy in the sphere of agriculture and fisheries;

(f)  a common policy in the sphere of transport;

(g)  a system ensuring that competition in the internal market is not distorted;

(h)  the approximation of the laws of Member States to the extent required for the functioning of the common market;

(i)  the promotion of coordination between employment policies of the Member States with a view of enhancing their effectiveness by developing a coordinated strategy for employment; [. . .]

(k)  the strengthening of economic and social cohesion;

(l)  a policy in the sphere of the environment; [and

(m)  to (u) which provide contributions to policies on competitiveness, research and technological development, the development of trans-European networks, health protection, education, training and culture, development cooperation, association of third countries, consumer protection, energy, civil protection and tourism.]'

Even then, the scope of the Community's activities as articulated seems a little narrow. Other than the reference to the free movement of persons in paragraph (c) of Article 3 EC, there is no reference in either Articles 2 or 3 EC to the citizenship objective articulated in the EU Treaty. This is a little anomalous, as the EC Treaty does indeed go on to create and regulate a 'citizenship of the Union' (Part Two of the EC Treaty, Articles 17–22 EC). These types of anomalies arise because the provisions of the EC Treaty on aims, objectives and activities have been constructed piecemeal since the original Treaty of Rome, via numerous amendments. Often, the final products do not make complete sense.

Article 4 EC, introduced by the Treaty of Maastricht, concentrates upon EMU. If doubt should remain after Article 3 EC, it firmly commits the EU to be a free market system, such that the activities of the EU now include:

'the adoption of an economic policy which is based on the close coordination of Member States' economic policies, on the internal market and on the definition of common objectives, and conducted in accordance with the principle of an open market economy with free competition.'

Article 4(2) EC introduces the objectives of:

'the irrevocable fixing of exchange rates leading to the introduction of a single currency . . . and the definition and conduct of a single monetary policy and exchange rate policy the primary objective of both of which shall be to maintain price stability and, without prejudice to this objective, to support the general economic policies in the Community, in accordance with the principle of an open market economy with free competition.'

All of these provisions which set out objectives need to be read in the context of the overall EC Treaty structure and contents and other principles articulated in Part One of the EC Treaty, as well as Article 6(1) of the Treaty on European Union which reminds us that:

> 'The Union is founded on the principles of liberty, democracy, respect for human rights and fundamental freedoms, and the rule of law, principles which are common to the Member States.'

The EU Treaty also commits the Union to respect fundamental rights (Articles 6(2) and 7 EU).

Turning to more specific principles contained in the EC Treaty, Article 3(2) EC 'mainstreams' gender equality, by requiring the Community to aim to eliminate inequalities and promote equality between men and women in all its activities. Environmental protection requirements are integrated into the definition and implementation of all policies by Article 6 EC, with a particular view to promoting sustainable development. Article 12 EC states the important principle of non-discrimination on grounds of nationality within the sphere of Community competence. Article 13 EC introduces not a principle of non-discrimination on a number of enumerated grounds, but a competence on the part of the Community to enact measures 'to combat discrimination based on sex, racial or ethnic origin, religion or belief, disability, age or sexual orientation'. Article 14 EC, already noted in 1.5, defines the internal market, adding an additional element which does not appear in Article 3(c), namely the elimination of internal frontiers. Although it ostensibly introduced an obligation to complete the internal market by the end of 1992 – an obligation with which the EU institutions and the Member States self-evidently failed to comply given all the areas of economic integration where the internal market project remains incomplete – nonetheless Article 14 EC does not entail many specific legal consequences. The Member States were aware of the risk that it might, and added a Declaration on Article 14 EC to the Final Act of the Single European Act expressing its political will to complete the internal market, but indicating that the date of 31 December 1992 does not 'create an automatic legal effect'. In Case C-378/97 *Wijsenbeek* ([1999] ECR I-6207), the Court held that Article 14 EC:

> 'cannot be interpreted as meaning that, in the absence of measures adopted by the Council before 31 December 1992 . . . the Member States [are required] to abolish controls of persons at the internal frontiers of the Community . . . [S]uch an obligation presupposes harmonisation of the laws of the Member States governing the crossing of the external borders of the Community, immigration, the grant of visas, asylum and the exchange of information on those questions' (para. 40).

Questions of competence are addressed in Article 5 EC, which elaborates the basic principle of the European Community as a body with limited powers, with the exercise of shared competences to be subject to the principles of subsidiarity and proportionality. There is further discussion of the general and constitutional principles structuring policy-making in the socio-economic sphere in Chapter 2, including principles which are not found explicitly stated in the treaties, but are in other instruments such as the Charter of Fundamental Rights of the Union adopted in 2000, or which are implicit in the case law of the Court of Justice. Part One of the EC Treaty also establishes the basic institutional framework.

The Constitutional Treaty in large measure replicates this system of aims, objectives and principles, as set out in the EC and EU Treaties. However, there is, of course, one single set of provisions, as the Constitutional Treaty sweeps away the 'pillar system' inaugurated by the Treaty of Maastricht, which separates out areas such as core economic and social policy-making activities, the common foreign and security policy, and cooperation in the areas of crime and policing. In comparison to the existing Treaties, the provisions of the Constitutional Treaty emphasise a little more clearly the EU's adherence to values such as fundamental rights, the diversity of its Member States and their cultures, and indeed the social rights and principles which underpin the so-called 'European social model'. In addition, Article I-7 of the Constitutional Treaty would give a single 'legal personality' to the EU, allowing it to make international treaties on its own behalf. Hitherto, only the separate European Communities have had international legal personality, allowing them each to conclude treaties. The EU as such, as established in 1993, had no formal legal personality, although in practice it has had the power to conclude some international agreements since the Treaty of Nice, by virtue of Article 24 EU. This has stunted in some ways the growth of the external dimension of the EU, although more in the political realm of common foreign and security policy, which lies beyond the scope of this book, rather than in the area of trade relations with third countries and with international organisations which is covered under the EC Treaty.

The Constitutional Treaty also deals with questions of competence in a manner different than before. It creates three explicit categories of competence: those which are *exclusive* to the EU, those which are *shared* between the EU and the Member States, and a category covering areas where the EU only has competence to support, coordinate or supplement the actions of the Member States. This is sometimes called *complementary* competence (Article I-12). Chapter 2 elaborates further on these categories, both by reference to the Constitutional Treaty, and also by reference to the existing Treaties, where they can already provide a useful way of categorising the different types of approaches to policy-making which the EU takes. The Constitutional Treaty also adopts unchanged the principles of subsidiarity and proportionality which are important in governing the exercise of competences, as well as the principle of limited powers, whereby the EU can only exercise powers which have been conferred upon it (Article I-11).

Part Three of the EC Treaty elaborates in greater detail many of the principal 'Community' activities identified in Article 3 EC, dealing separately with the mechanisms for establishing and maintaining the customs union, the removal of non-tariff barriers to trade in goods, and the elimination of restrictions on the free movement of services, the free movement of workers, enterprise and capital. Since the Treaty of Amsterdam, the EC Treaty has also included special provisions relating to 'Visas, Asylum, Immigration and other policies related to the Free Movement of Persons' (Title IV). These address directly the politically sensitive project of completing the internal market in relation to the free movement of people, creating a common external frontier and removing internal borders, while ensuring the necessary security measures are in place. In many cases, these policies are complemented by those on Police and Judicial Cooperation in Criminal Matters (the 'Third Pillar') governed by Title VI of the Treaty on European Union. Part Three also contains the basic framework for the harmonisation of national laws in pursuit of the single market objective, including the principal general law-making powers of Articles 94 and 95 EC. Separate Titles and Chapters within Part Three detail policies in other fields such as agriculture, transport and trans-European networks, competition, taxation, economic and monetary affairs, employment, external trade and customs cooperation, social policy, education, training and youth, culture, health, consumer protection, industry, economic and social cohesion (regional policy), research and technological development, environmental protection and development cooperation. Separate chapters are devoted in this book to the majority of these policy areas, and where appropriate they also detail those sections of Part III of the Constitutional Treaty which introduce important changes to EU policy-making.

Law is the principal mechanism available for turning the political and economic aspirations articulated in the Treaties into reality. The legal instruments of economic integration within the framework of the European Union are based on Treaties, that is, it is *prima facie* international law, and on the secondary legislation passed by institutions set up by the Treaties – where a variety of different regulatory techniques including both hard and soft law are used to require and to persuade the Member States to participate fully in the pursuit of the integration objectives. The case law of the Court of Justice is also a distinctive and important source of law in relation to economic integration and socio-economic regulation. The system of law set up under the Treaties displays special characteristics which enhance its effectiveness *vis-à-vis* the national legal systems, in particular where the focus is placed upon the 'Community' pillar where supranational decision-making methods involving the different institutions are the norm and where the Court of Justice has an authoritative role in relation to the interpretation and enforcement of legal provisions, under the rule of law. Article 10 EC binds the Member States to:

> 'take all appropriate measures, whether general or particular, to ensure fulfilment of the obligations arising out of this Treaty or resulting from action taken by the institutions of the Community. They shall facilitate the achievement of the Community's tasks. They shall abstain from any measure which could jeopardise the attainment of the objectives of this Treaty.'

The legal order of the EU is therefore generally termed supranational rather than international, even though there are strong international elements – notably under the second and third pillars – in relation to both decision-making structures which are intergovernmental and the effects of measures adopted. In many fields, however, the key economic and social law provisions of the EU have an impact within the Member States akin to constitutional provisions. Membership in the EU involves a loss of sovereignty, and the substitution of common political institutions for national political institutions. Indeed, in Case 294/83 *Parti écologiste 'Les Verts'* v. *European Parliament* ([1986] ECR 1339 at p.1365), the Court of Justice stated that the EC Treaty has the nature of a 'constitutional charter'. It is widely accepted that it is appropriate to analyse the EU's legal and institutional order as it evolves in constitutional terms, although it is accepted that the EU is not and will not become a 'conventional' state. This trend of analysis would, of course, enjoy a substantial boost in the event that the Constitutional Treaty is ratified and enters into force. In substance, the Constitutional Treaty is best understood as an incremental development of the existing Treaties and thus continues the emphasis on the international law origins of European integration combined with the strongly federal and supranational elements which have entered the legal order of the EU, both through the case law of the Court of Justice, and because of the extraordinary success in some fields at least of the EU in constructing a system of economic integration based on law. The use of the word 'constitution' in relation to the EU and its legal basis has fostered inevitably, however, a great deal of controversy, both during the drafting process and, most particularly, the ratification process where it has scratched at some of the evident sensibilities of the Member States and their citizens regarding national sovereignty.

Key provisions of economic and social law, such as those guaranteeing free movement, are justiciable before national courts (direct effect) and take precedence over national laws (supremacy). This is a case law principle under the system of EU law at present, but is explicitly enshrined in Article I-6 of the Constitutional Treaty. Those national courts faced with issues of EU law can and in some cases must refer questions on the interpretation and application of EU law to the Court of Justice, under the Article 234 EC preliminary reference procedure. Where the Community has fully exercised an exclusive competence to regulate in the economic domain, in particular in the field of agriculture, the existence of Community legislation will be regarded as precluding national legislation (the pre-emptive effect of Community law). In addition, the Community as a legal order exercising powers in the economic domain claims the legitimacy of adherence to the rule of law. The regulatory activities of the Community are therefore subject to tests of constitutionality and legality under the control of the Court of Justice.

## 1.10 Overview of the Structure and Contents of this Book

This book is divided into an Introduction and three substantive parts. Following this initial chapter, a further introductory chapter will set out the key principles, themes and approaches visible in the economic and social law of the EU. Part II then examines the law of the internal market and Economic and Monetary Union, covering both the general rules governing free movement and the harmonisation of national measures to facilitate the achievement and management of the internal market, and a number of special sectors and policies, such as agriculture, intellectual property and competition law. Both the internal and the external aspects of the regulation of the market are covered.

Because of the special circumstances which surround the case of persons, a separate part of the book is devoted to examining the legal situation of citizens and non-citizens of the Union, bearing in mind the general objective of creating an Area of Freedom, Security and Justice within the EU (Part III). Some dimensions of policy in relation to the creation of the Area of FSJ which are less directly related to socio-economic concerns are not discussed in detail, such as police and civil justice cooperation, and policies on criminal justice cooperation and organised crime and terrorism.

Finally, Part IV examines the social dimension of the EU, in its widest sense. It includes the 'flanking policies' such as policy on the environment and regional policy, which are closely related to the completion of the internal market.

Many of the subjects and policies considered here are not subjects which students of the law would necessarily study in the domestic context (e.g. regional development, development aid or the regulation of customs duties and imports/exports of goods). Moreover if they are studied they would often be the subject of many separate courses – for example on agricultural law, competition law, law and regulation, employment or labour law, discrimination law, social welfare law, environmental law, taxation, or immigration law, rather than being part of public law or regulation courses. One of the biggest challenges in studying EU social and economic law – with a dash of justice and home affairs law thrown in as well – is that of assimilating so many different fields of policy-making, and accomplishing this in a manner which is sensitive to the particular tensions of law and policy-making in a multi-level governance system where power and authority are distributed across a number of authorities, including the EU itself and the Member States. The reader will be constantly reminded of the many instabilities of the EU, both in terms of its policy-making systems and structures, but also most pertinently in the early twenty-first century, in terms of the extension of its geographical and geopolitical frontiers through enlargement towards the East.

## Summary

1. This chapter introduces the study of the social and economic law of the European Union. The objective of the chapter is to present the essential background to understanding law and economic integration.

2. This book assumes that the reader has a basic background knowledge of the EU's legal and political framework, including its historical evolution from the 1950s onwards. Only the most recent developments, such as the elaboration of the Treaty establishing a Constitution for Europe, are covered in more detail.

3. The key material reviewed includes the economic and social objectives of the EC Treaty and the Treaty on European Union, and a sketch of the way in which the Treaties approach the construction of a framework within which the institutions can develop policies. Law plays a key role in the economic integration system created by the Treaties, and the outlines of the policies can be identified looking at the provisions of the Treaties concerned with objectives and activities.

4. This chapter introduces the reader to key terminology in the study of regional systems of economic integration such as the EU, and the different levels of economic integration which can be achieved. It emphasises that the EU is a system of regional economic integration based on a customs union and a common market, with a system of economic and monetary union which extends to some of its Member States, which is still in development. It provides a short evaluation of the economic benefits of integration, highlighting that this issue is highly controversial. However, membership remains a very attractive proposition for outsiders.

5. The question of the social dimension of economic integration is also introduced briefly.

6. This chapter presents the basic structure of the rest of the book to the reader.

## Exercises

1. Distinguish between a free trade area, a customs union, a common market and an economic and monetary union. Why has the EU gradually developed through the stages to become a more closely integrated trading system?

2. What are the principal economic benefits of integration? Why do commentators disagree about the issue of the benefits of integration?

3. How and why does globalisation present both economic and political challenges to the EU as a system of regional economic integration?

## Further Reading

El-Agraa, A. (2004) *The European Union: Economics and Politics* (7th edn), Cambridge: Cambridge University Press. See especially chapter 1.

Gillingham, J. (2003) *European Integration 1950–2003: Superstate or New Market Economy?*, Cambridge: Cambridge University Press.

Guibernau, M. (ed.) (2006) *Governing Europe: The Developing Agenda*, Milton Keynes: Open University Press.

McCormick, J. (2005) *Understanding the European Union* (3rd edn), Basingstoke: Palgrave Macmillan.

Molle, W. (2006) *The Economics of European Integration: Theory, Practice, Policy* (5th edn), Aldershot: Ashgate.

Sapir, A. *et al* (2004) *An Agenda for a Growing Europe: The Sapir Report*, Oxford: Oxford University Press.

Shaw, J. (2005) 'Europe's Constitutional Future', Spring, *Public Law* 132.

Thompson, G. (2001) 'Governing the European Economy: A Framework for Analysis', and Lintner, V. (2001) 'The Development of the EU and the European Economy', in Thompson, G. (ed.), *Governing the European Economy*, London: Sage.

Tsoukalis, L. (2005) *What Kind of Europe?*, Oxford: Oxford University Press.

## Key Websites

The Europa server, the essential starting point providing access to materials on the institutions, policies, and documents of the European Union, is available at:
**http://europa.eu/index_en.htm**

On the Treaty Establishing a Constitution for Europe, see:
**http://www.europa.eu/constitution/index_en.htm**
which includes up-to-date information about the ratification of the Constitutional Treaty.

The 'Future of the European Union – Debate' or Futurum site, is a reference site on the process of debate accompanying the Constitutional Convention and the Intergovernmental Conference, and is available at:
**http://europa.eu/constitution/futurum/index.htm**

Stay up to date with news about the EU and European politics and economics by visiting, and signing up for updates from, a number of websites including –

EUPolitix, a source for developments in EU politics:
**http://www.eupolitix.com/**

EUObserver, a source for EU-related news:
**http://www.euobserver.com/**

Euractiv, a source for EU news and policy positions:
**http://www.euractiv.com/en/**

Excellent blogs on European politics include:
**http://www.economist.com/blogs/certainideasofeurope/**
**http://fistfulofeuros.net/**
**http://centreforeuropeanreform.blogspot.com/index.html**
**http://blogs.ft.com/brusselsblog/**

Blogs on EU law and specifically on the Court of Justice include:
**http://courtofjustice.blogspot.com/index.html**
**http://eulaw.typepad.com/eulawblog/**

# Chapter 2

# Law, Policy and Socio-economic Governance

## 2.1 Introduction

This chapter explains some of the core ideas and principles which are essential for the detailed study of individual areas of substantive EU law examined in the subsequent chapters. Some of the ideas set out here may seem a little abstract at this stage, and you are advised to return to this chapter more than once, as you work your way through the book.

Central to understanding the nature of economic law and socio-economic governance is an examination of a number of principles by reference to which governmental power is exercised in relation to market economies. First, we examine the nature of governmental interventions in the workings of market economies (2.2), turning then to the concept of 'governance' (2.3), the institutions and instruments of socio-economic governance (2.4 and 2.5) and the constitutional principles which underlie economic and social law in the EU, including those which restrain the role of the EU (2.6). Emphasis is placed upon the challenge of creating and maintaining a constitutional framework guaranteeing democratic, accountable and open government, in conditions of respect for the rule of law and individual rights, but in the very special conditions which must apply to the governance of socio-economic life *outside a state* or *beyond the state*, as is the case with the EU. Some of the concepts which are discussed in this chapter will be reasonably familiar, but others which are rather peculiar to EU law are less so, such as the concepts of competence, subsidiarity and proportionality. These are central to the exercise of the EU's powers, including the respective powers of the various institutions, as well as to the division of powers between the EU and the Member States (2.6 and 2.7). The chapter concludes with a presentation of how the idea of flexibility impinges in practice upon socio-economic governance (2.8).

All of this material is necessary background for the main focus of this book on the functions and contents of the rules which govern socio-economic activities. This is why we need to keep returning to the objectives of the EU as a project of socio-economic integration, as well as a political project of 'ever closer union'. Understanding the different fields of EU social and economic law involves reflecting on the process of 'selecting legal forms which can best achieve the instrumental goals of collective choice' (Ogus, 1994: v). In each field, policy-makers have to decide the best legal framework for the purposes of implementing agreed public policies. As we study the role of policy-makers, however, we have to remember that there are close links between the exercise of governmental power through the making of political choices about the form and content of rules, on the one hand, and processes of exchange within relatively free markets, on the other. In other words, our focus is not only on just and equitable governance under the rule of law, but also on effective governance in open mixed economies within an increasingly globalised world economy.

In many respects, the nature of *state* intervention in economic activities has changed since the inception of the European Communities in the 1950s. There has been a dramatic decline in central planning and state ownership of the means of production, from nationalised industries and publicly-owned utilities, and a shift towards regulation of private activities to ensure competition, especially in previously monopolised markets for utilities such as telecommunications and power supply. Thus, states everywhere continue to be active players in the economic sphere, not only encouraging and protecting competition, but also acting to protect the interests of groups such as consumers and the weaker and more vulnerable members of society, as well as diffuse interests such as those of the environment. In the arena of the welfare state, traditional paternalistic ideas of social protection have come to be challenged, not only as a result of the spiraling costs associated with ageing populations and shrinking working age populations in many European states, but also because of an ideological shift evident in many Member States towards individual and community-based self-reliance rather than state protection. At the same time, however, states do continue to provide the facilitative mechanisms of private exchange, by establishing laws governing property, contract and non-contractual obligations, as well as the rules governing the legal forms of economic association, such as corporate and partnership law for example, and by providing the means whereby disputes can be settled through the courts or by other means such as arbitration.

In sum, the exercise of governmental power is greatly constrained by the operation of, and changes within, the national, supranational and international economic orders. It is important to remember that much of the economic integration which has brought the Member States of the EU closer together may result as much from such factors as it does from the Treaties and the activities of the institutions themselves. The following paragraphs set out to describe some ways of understanding how governments might operate within systems based on predominantly open mixed economies and declining, but still highly significant, structures of universal welfare and social protection. They also sketch out some of the specific effects of the EU as a form of 'governance without statehood' (W. Wallace, 2005: 491) or, perhaps better, governance beyond the state.

## 2.2 Market Economies, State Intervention and the Exercise of Governmental Power

Majone distinguishes three generally accepted forms of public intervention in socio-economic life – redistribution, macro-economic stabilisation and regulation:

> 'The *redistribution function* includes all transfers of resources from one social group to another, as well as the provision of 'merit goods', that is, goods such as elementary education or publicly financed medical care, that the government compels individuals to consume. The *stabilisation function* is concerned with the preservation of satisfactory levels of economic growth, employment, and price stability. It includes fiscal and monetary policy, labour market policy, and industrial policy. Finally, the *regulatory function* attempts to correct various forms of 'market failure': monopoly power, negative externalities, failures of information, or insufficient provision of public goods such as law and order or environmental protection' (Majone, 1996a: 263) (emphasis in the original).

Cutting across these distinctions are the techniques of government. Government – sometimes called the executive in democracies – in a nation state context is the constitutionally independent organ entrusted with the implementation of agreed public policies. In other words, a government is the political authority which has been given a mandate through representative elections within an open party system. The EU, of course, does not have a government in the traditional sense, but it does exercise governmental power through complex interactions of its institutional structure as determined by the Treaties and the inputs of different interests including national interests, corporate interests (employers, trades unions, non-governmental organisations, etc.) as well as the distinctive European interest best embodied in the Commission.

Like national governments, those bodies which govern the European Union also possess a number of techniques of government. Daintith has distinguished three: *imperium, dominium* and *suasion* (Daintith, 1994: 212–13). *Imperium* describes 'the government's use of the command of law in aid of its policy objectives'; *dominium* covers 'the employment of the wealth of government'; *suasion* is reserved for the capacity of government to achieve its objectives by informing and persuading. A characteristic of government is that it is largely restricted to producing general rules, rather than individual adjudications.

A review of the activities of the EU shows that it engages in some aspects of each of the three forms of public intervention in socio-economic life, as well as using all three of the typical techniques of government. Furthermore, its work is in large measure focused upon the production of general rules and standards. The regulatory function is evident in the harmonisation activities in relation to the internal market, including the enactment of general and mandatory product standards or health and safety requirements. It has extended also to the regulation of many professional activities, where minimum standards have been set to enable the development of cross-border markets in fields such as financial services. These are clear examples of *imperium*. Other important illustrations include the liberalisation of the public procurement policies of the Member States, the liberalisation of the utilities sectors to facilitate competition in industries, such as telecommunications and energy supply, and much of the EU's activity in the field of environmental protection which has taken the form of 'command and control' legislation setting mandatory standards for Member States and industries. However, in some fields of activity, for example education and public health, harmonisation is specifically excluded from the range of permissible Community activities.

Redistribution has always been a key policy activity in the limited field of agriculture where prices and markets have been manipulated for wider political objectives. Its ambit has widened, however, since the mid-1980s, with the development of a more extensive regional policy aimed at offsetting some of the damaging effects of restructuring consequent upon the creation of the internal market and at buying the consent and acquiescence of poorer Member States to economic liberalisation. Here we have an example of *dominium*, although as with all EU policies there must be a legal basis in the Treaty and a legal framework underpinning the lawfulness of such activities as falling within the competences of the EU and its institutions. Funds are directed through the structural funds, such as the European Regional Development Fund, European Social Fund and, more recently, the Cohesion Fund, and policies are instrumentalised on the basis of partnerships involving the Member States and interested actors at local and regional levels, such as local authorities, charities and NGOs. Redistribution on an individual scale is not to any great extent the concern of the EU, since the provision of public goods such as health care, education and welfare remains largely in the seemingly increasingly fettered hands of the Member States. However, the EU does have an impact upon policies through 'incentive measures', especially in fields such as education and public health. Hence it would be misleading to suggest that the EU has any form of 'social regime', although it does have some aspects of a 'social dimension'.

Achieving and safeguarding macro-economic stability has come to the fore since the launch of the EMU project around 1990, and the involvement of the EU intensified once the Member States agreed to include a new chapter on labour market policy in the EC Treaty at the Amsterdam IGC (Articles 125–130 EC). However, there remains some uncertainty regarding the extent to which any of these provisions are coercive rather than merely persuasive upon the Member States – indeed a new approach to policy called the 'Open Method of Coordination' has emerged as the EU and its Member States have implemented the provisions on labour market policy. These are good examples of *suasion*, at least of Member States if not of citizens. A more pertinent example of *suasion* of citizens must be the frank and open publicity campaigns run by the Commission to seek greater public knowledge about and support for new initiatives such as the Treaty of Amsterdam and to persuade citizens to become involved in debates about 'Governance' or the 'Future of the Union'. However, as the issue of public support for the EU has become ever more intensely politicised, and as the ratification of the Constitutional Treaty has proceeded, even the Commission's involvement in activities of *suasion* has dissipated, as it has become ever more fearful of being accused of meddling in national debates.

## 2.3 The Concept of 'Governance'

A brief word of explanation is needed about the term 'governance', which has already been used on several occasions in both this chapter and the previous one. At one level, governance helps us to understand that the act of governing is increasingly separate from the institutions of government, and can involve private actors who, for example, set product or service standards which industry follows, or who regulate professions, or who act in partnership with public bodies to disburse funds such as subsidies or grants. It has seemed quite an apt term to apply to acts of societal steering, that is, the adoption of binding and non-binding rules and policies to secure certain ends, which are adopted away from the domain of the state, since it is the latter political entity which is traditionally associated with having a government. The EU does not have a government in the conventional recognisable sense, but it does regulate socio-economic life. It does this through the acts of its institutions, and through its various agencies and committees, responsible for formulating or implementing policy. It does this also through the agency of the national, regional and local governments of the Member States which implement and apply EU law; hence the frequently used term 'multi-level' governance. The EU accomplishes much of its work through partnerships with other bodies such as agencies, international organisations or the Member States. However, the EU does not have a monopoly of using the term 'governance'. The term 'governance' is also frequently applied at the global level, for example in relation to the activities of institutions as diverse as the World Bank and the United Nations Development Programme.

One widely used working definition of governance is general in nature:

'Governance refers to the process whereby elements in society wield power and authority, and influence and enact policies and decisions concerning public life, and economic and social development.

Governance is a broader notion than government (whose principal elements include the constitution, legislature, executive and judiciary). Governance involves interaction between these formal institutions and their spokesmen, and civil society.

Governance has no automatic normative connotation. However, typical criteria for assessing governance in a particular context might include the degree of legitimacy, representativeness, popular accountability and efficiency with which public affairs are conducted' (attributed to the International Institute of Administrative Sciences: Working Group on Governance, 1996; cited in Weiss, 2000: 797).

The last paragraph refers to the fact that discussions about governance often have connotations of what is good and what is bad. The EU engaged in a debate about 'good governance', in its White Paper on Governance, issued by the Commission in July 2001 (COM(2001) 428). From the Commission's point of view, it is part of a more general attempt to reconnect the EU with its citizens, and to stop the Member States from blaming Brussels for unpopular policy decisions for which they themselves should accept responsibility. Throughout the rest of this book, the term 'governance' will be used generally as a descriptive tool, and will include the range of activities in which the EU institutions and the Member States engage with a view to managing the particular problems relating to the pursuit of the objectives of the Treaties and the wider objectives of European integration identified in Chapter 1, namely peace, prosperity and supranationalism.

## 2.4   Institutions of Socio-economic Governance

The study of the substantive fields of EU economic and social law presupposes knowledge of the EU institutions, both in terms of what they are and what they can do. In large measure, this book assumes that readers will develop, or will have developed, that knowledge from reading other materials directly concerned with EU constitutional and institutional law.

Seemingly dry questions about the number of Commissioners, the operation of the Commission as a collegiate body, the emergence of the budgetary and legislative powers of the European Parliament, the precise details of what constitutes a qualified majority in the Council and the great complexity caused by the EU's plethora of different legislative procedures are fundamental to understanding how specific areas of EU economic and social law actually work. It is possible to understand by studying the available legal bases or the ways in which particular provisions of the Treaties are framed, why there is either a great deal or alternatively very little EU legislation in any given field, or indeed why such legislation takes particular forms (e.g. the choice between regulations, directives). All of these choices may be related to the difficulties of securing unanimous agreement in areas where unanimity is still mandated, such as social policy, or to the fact that some legal bases may rule out specific harmonisation measures, such as in the field of education policy under Article 149 EC. Alternatively, the content of a measure may reveal a particularly startling compromise between different positions, perhaps attributable to the fact that the European Parliament chose to flex its institutional muscles within the Conciliation Committee provided for under the co-decision procedure of Article 249 EC. Finally, the rather abstract idea that the outputs of the EU legislative process involve inputs from a multitude of bodies operating in different configurations and with different degrees of formality and informality depending upon the content of the Treaties or the practices of a particular Directorate General can be clarified by reference to the specifics of the ever growing importance of the so-called social dialogue involving representatives of the two sides of industry in the field of social policy-making.

Because of institutional paralysis and rigidity affecting the legislative process, the study of economic and social law was confined for a long time primarily to the study of the work of the Court of Justice. It concentrated especially on how the Court had interpreted the free movement provisions and those rules on social policy contained in the original Treaty, plus the limited range of legislative measures which had been adopted over the years such as those implementing the free movement of persons (Council Regulation 1612/68 on the rights of workers and their families, [1968] OJ L257/2, [1968] OJ Spec. Ed. 475) or implementing and extending the equal pay principle into broader issues of equal treatment in employment (Council Directive 75/117 on equal pay, OJ 1975 L45/19; Council Directive 76/207 on equal treatment in employment, OJ 1976 L39/40). Such cases often arose in the national courts, with recourse to the interpretative powers of the Court of Justice coming through the Article 234 EC preliminary reference procedure. From time to time, the Commission also brought enforcement actions under Article 226 EC against Member States for non-compliance with obligations under the Treaty. Comments concerning the Court's application of its powers in relation to actions brought directly before the Court of Justice itself by the Member States, the institutions or, where permitted, individual litigants tended to focus upon the Court's role as a constitutional or administrative court exercising judicial review within a supranational legal order. There was little dialogue concerning the relationship of these cases with developing patterns in particular policy fields such as customs and agriculture where they tended to cluster.

Treaty amendments have given the institutions new or enhanced powers in an ever increasing range of fields which have demanded interpretation by the Court. Consequently, the Court has faced a regular flow of 'legal basis' litigation since the mid-1980s, much of which sets the European Parliament or Member States in opposition against the Council. In such a case, the party bringing the action will typically allege that a measure should have been adopted under a different legal basis within the Treaties, often one which gives it enhanced participation rights within the legislative process. Occasionally, it may be argued that a particular legislative measure is without any legal basis within the EU Treaties. In addition, the ever increasing flow of legislative measures from the institutions have themselves often required interpretation and application in the context of national actions and preliminary references and, occasionally, even annulment at the behest of aggrieved institutions or individuals for breach of primary principles of EC law. Sometimes the suggestion is made that, as a result of these innovations, the Court's role is shifting from being primarily that of a constitutional court, exercising key choices about the nature of the EU as a polity, to being that of a Court limited to reviewing and applying the decisions of increasingly dynamic political institutions and subject to the overall control of the Member States as 'Masters of the Treaties'. The Court's role is becoming, allegedly, more technical and less political. This probably understates the extent to which the Court continues to operate as a policy actor, which we shall see when we examine recent cases where the Court has looked at the range of Community powers, although more often than not its language is cloaked now in a veneer of caution about its role.

As the EC developed into the EU, the institutional framework of socio-economic integration became more complex. The original four institutions of the EEC Treaty are still in place, even though changed: the European Parliament, the Commission, the Council, and the Court of Justice. The Court of Justice is now part of a wider 'Community judicature', with the addition of the Court of First Instance (Article 220 EC), and with the Treaty of Nice now in place it will become possible to attach judicial panels to hear certain types of specialised cases, such as in the intellectual property field. The consultative Economic and Social Committee now shares its original role of representing wider interests within the policy-making process with the Committee of the Regions. The EC Treaty also has established a range of additional sectoral Committees over the years, such as the Employment Committee (Article 130 EC), which advise the other institutions. The Commission largely retains the vital power to initiate new legislative measures by making formal proposals, but its role within the legislative process has been attenuated while that of the European Parliament has grown. Within the Council, not only the Committee of Permanent Representatives (Article 207 EC), but manifold Committees and Working Groups, prepare the work of the Ministers, who now share the decision-making role within the legislative process increasingly with the European Parliament. Financial probity in relation to the EU budget is ensured by the Court of Auditors, itself an institution under Article 7 EC. Several 'Structural' Funds, such as the European Social Fund and the European Regional Development Fund, which are derived from the EU budget, support projects promoting goals such as regional development. Often these projects are funded in partnership with funds from the Member States.

Article 211 EC appears, at first sight, to make the Commission responsible for the execution of policy laid down in the context of the EU and its institutions. In practice, the executive function in the EU has long been shared by the Commission with the Council and the Member States (Article 202 EC). Of particular importance is the structure of comitology, that is, committees of national representatives chaired by a representative of the Commission, which deal with the execution of legislative measures and maintain a very substantial degree of Member State control over this vital aspect of policy implementation. Over the years, a number of quasi-independent agencies and bodies have been set up, some of them rather longstanding such as CEDEFOP (European Centre for the Development of Vocational Training, 1975), but with rather limited roles and powers, particularly in relation to research and data gathering. Other agencies are of a more recent vintage, with more far-reaching roles, including the power to conclude their own agreements with third countries. One such agency is the European Police Office (Europol), which has been established to ensure operational cooperation between the police forces of Member States. In the field of the internal market, the European Medicines Evaluation Agency, which effectively provides a 'one-stop-shop' for medical products' approval in the EU, is probably the most significant agency. Recently, widespread public concern over health issues such as bovine spongiform encephalopathy (BSE) has led the EU to establish a European Food Safety Authority (EFSA). By acting as a focus for public concerns, the EFSA is intended to increase the public's confidence in the EU's ability to properly address health issues. It is the clustering of expertise in one location and the ability to specialise which speaks most strongly in favour of the creation and empowerment of independent agencies. Clearly, problems can be raised in relation to judicial control, accountability and the transparency of decision-making. Nevertheless, examples from the US are often cited as justifying further European experimentation as a means of resolving problems that arise in cases where there is no legislative body with the responsibility for primary legislation which can make all the rules necessary within a socio-economic system. Some form of delegated legislation and administration is an inevitable factor in modern life.

The most striking example of an agency is the constitutionally independent European Central Bank (Article 8 EC), which is charged with monetary policy management now that EMU is in place. Although not formally an institution of the European Union, the European Central Bank is treated on the Europa website as a different entity entirely. A whole specialised sub-branch of EU law is emerging, termed the law of the European Central Bank, which is concerned with this supranational organisation which has very specific powers and functions (Zilioli and Selmayr, 2001). Here too issues have been raised, frequently concerning judicial control and parliamentary accountability.

Less formal 'institutions' include the social dialogue, which involves representatives of management and labour at the European level – the so-called 'social partners'. Such a dialogue can lead to agreements on employment law matters which the Council can then enact through legislation (Article 139 EC).

National institutions are a further vital component of the overall multi-level EU framework. They make the operation of economic and social law a practical reality. As Daintith puts it:

> 'The Community ... looks to the Member States for the *implementation* of its law, not just its enforcement' (Daintith, 1994: 135) (emphasis in the original).

The involvement of the national institutions, which has been termed 'indirect rule', is derived from the obligation of Community loyalty under Article 10 EC, and every part of the national, regional and local state can be brought into the system. National courts have played a clear and identifiable role, in their capacity as 'Community courts' by virtue of the relationship between EC law and national law elaborated by the Court of Justice, particularly through their role under the Article 234 EC preliminary reference procedure (Maher, 1994). National legislatures are entrusted frequently with the vital task of implementing EU law, since so many measures take the form of directives which specifically require implementation under the principles contained in Article 249 EC. National administrations, and even sub-national bodies such as local or regional councils or public authorities, are also commonly called upon to undertake the detailed implementation and practical administration of EU rules. To a very large extent, the EU relies upon the functioning of state bodies in order to overcome the absence of a federal civil service, other than the Commission which is charged largely with policy-making and higher-order executive functions, and given only limited enforcement powers.

The Member States assume also the primary role in relation to the intergovernmental fields of cooperation falling within the second and third pillars of the EU, namely Common Foreign and Security Policy (CFSP) (Title V of the EU Treaty, Pillar Two) and Police and Judicial Cooperation in Criminal Matters (PJCC) (Title VI of the EU Treaty, Pillar Three). Whereas the Council dominates the policy-making arena, the Commission and the European Parliament have much more limited roles in comparison to the Member States in the fields falling within the second and third pillars of the EU. The Court of Justice has no jurisdiction in relation to CFSP, and very restricted jurisdiction in relation to PJCC. However, it retains the important role of policing the dividing lines between those pillars and the traditional arena of the Community, namely the EC Treaty (Pillar One).

## 2.5 Instruments of Socio-economic Governance

As we saw in 1.9, the Treaties lay down numerous general objectives and tasks for socio-economic governance in the EU. In addition, the Treaties also contain law-making powers or competences which the institutions may exercise in order to attain these objectives and undertake these tasks. The EU institutions do not have a completely free hand in relation to the instruments of socio-economic governance which they may make use of, even though, as we saw in 2.2, EU activities range quite widely across the recognised forms of state intervention in market economies. EU measures are limited in principle to the lists contained in the EC and EU Treaties for each of the three pillars. Under the EC Treaty, Article 249 EC contains a non-exhaustive list of the types of measures which the institutions may take, along with their legal effects. In the chapters which follow on specific policy areas, there will be numerous examples of the institutions adopting the classic binding measures – regulations, directives and decisions – as well as recommendations and opinions, which are not binding. This does not mean that the latter non-binding measures have no legal effects; rather they may be used as guides to interpret other measures. With a few exceptions, the Treaty gives the institutions charged with law-making a free hand to choose the most appropriate legal act to achieve the objective which they seek to attain.

Regulations are directly applicable and are best compared to national acts of parliament or primary legislation. They are of general application. Most regulations are justiciable before national courts, and both Member States and individuals are bound by their provisions. Regulations comprise the general framework of rules which govern the common organisations of the market in the field of agricultural policy. Directives bind only as to the result to be achieved, and leave choice of form and methods to the implementing Member States. Directives are typically used to harmonise or approximate diverse national laws, and offer considerable flexibility to the legislator. Provisions of directives which have not been transposed at national level, or which have been incorrectly transposed, may be invoked in national courts by aggrieved individuals, provided they are sufficiently precise, clear and unconditional. That is, like regulations, they may have direct effect. Directives are commonly used to harmonise national regulations which affect the functioning of the internal market for goods or services, such as product standards or banking rules, as well as in other flanking policy areas such as environmental policy or social policy. Decisions – although apparently designated as individual measures in Article 249 EC and relied upon frequently in fields such as competition law where the Commission is charged with applying the Treaty rules to conduct by individual firms and companies – are used often for more general policy purposes in the EU context. Decisions may be used to establish new bodies to assist the institutions, to set in place general plans or frameworks for policy, such as in the field of the environment, or to lay down general policies for the future of the EU, for example the Decision on Own Resources or the Decision establishing the framework for Comitology. Such normative acts are clearly not 'decisions' in the narrow sense of Article 249 EC.

It is therefore clear that Article 249 EC is not an exhaustive statement of the legal instruments which the EU institutions can adopt. The *sui generis* decision described above is the most important non-enumerated legal measure. The EC Treaty also refers in different places to 'guidelines' and 'conclusions' of the European Council (Article 128 EC in relation to employment policy), 'framework programmes' (Article 166 EC in relation to research and technological development policy) and 'action programmes' (Article 175 EC in relation to environmental policy). These are typically more flexible techniques which can be used to achieve policy objectives through persuasion rather than coercion. On the other hand, whenever they are turned into legally binding measures, the *sui generis* decision is most likely to be used.

Under the second and third pillars, special types of measures can be taken in the areas of foreign policy cooperation and police and judicial cooperation in criminal matters. These include joint actions and common positions, which are measures taken to implement common strategies which define the general approach of the EU to a foreign policy matter. They include also framework decisions under Pillar Three, which are intended to harmonise national laws in relation to matters of police and judicial cooperation in a manner similar to directives, which are explicitly excluded from having direct effect. Also under Pillar Three, the Council may adopt Conventions, which are like classical agreements under international law, except that they are not negotiated by parties at arm's length, but in the Council as an institution of the EU. Conventions require ratification at national level, just like other international agreements. None of the second or third pillar measures can have direct applicability akin to regulations, nor can they take effect automatically in the domestic legal orders or displace national law through any type of pre-emptive effect. However, according to the Court of Justice in the *Pupino* case (Case C-105/03 [2005] ECR I-5285), Member States are under an obligation to interpret national law in the light of a relevant Framework Decision.

The proliferation of different instruments under the second and third pillars, along with the confusion associated with the *sui generis* decision meant that the area of instruments was a field of EU law ripe for reform and simplification in the context of the work of the Convention on the Future of Europe and the subsequent IGC. The Treaty establishing a Constitution for Europe (OJ 2004 C310) therefore proposed some significant amendments in this area to resolve these concerns, and also to create a single set of instruments right across the range of EU policy-making activities.

Article I-33 CT lists and defines the different types of legal instruments which the EU could adopt. The scheme established in the Constitutional Treaty builds directly upon the system of the EC Treaty, but extends also to acts adopted in the fields of Common Foreign and Security Policy, and all areas of Justice and Home Affairs. To stop the proliferation of *ad hoc* types of acts not specified in the Treaty, Article I-33(2) requires the European Parliament and the Council to 'refrain from adopting acts not provided for by the relevant legislative procedure in the area in question'. Under Article I-33(1) CT, a new category of 'European law' replaces the 'regulation'. A European law is a 'legislative act of general application. It shall be binding in its entirety and directly applicable in all Member States.' European framework laws replace directives and framework decisions. A European framework law is a 'legislative act binding, as to the result to be achieved, upon each Member State to which it is addressed'. However it leaves to the national authorities the choice of forms and methods most appropriate for its implementation. European decisions are non-legislative acts, but they are binding in their entirety. Article I-33(1) also provides for non-legislative acts, confusingly called 'regulations', but these are implementing acts, rather than primary EU legislation.

Measures at the EU level are not adopted in a vacuum. They are linked, through the different programmes and policies pursued by the EU and its institutions, to the various functions and techniques of government identified in 2.2. In the internal market field, EU measures harmonise disparate national laws where the very disparity represents an obstacle to trade between Member States. That is, different national laws make it more difficult for manufacturers to sell their goods in other Member States because they are forced to comply with a new set of product standards, which inevitably increase production costs. In other words, the EU regulates in order to liberalise trade in accordance with the principles guaranteed in the EC Treaty itself through Articles 28, 39, 43, 49 and 56 EC. Its regulatory measures, for example a set of standards at EU level, may represent a heavier touch *vis-à-vis* the existing rules of some Member States in the sense of requiring higher standards, but a lighter touch *vis-à-vis* others. In relation to the latter, they could be said to be 'deregulatory' measures. Where there are common rules in place at the EU level, the Member States can no longer invoke the public health or public policy derogations contained in Articles 30, 39(3), 46 or 58 EC. This is a classical example of the EU operating as a 'quasi-state', employing the 'command of law' to achieve a specific result through the use of binding rules.

This approach to regulation is often termed in the EU context the 'classic' Community method, or even the 'Monnet' method, because of its association with Jean Monnet, one of the founding fathers of the EC Treaty, and the supranational approach to governance through quasi-autonomous institutions. In institutional terms, the foundations of the Community method are the Commission's exclusive right of legislative initiative, and the legislative and budgetary powers of the Council and the European Parliament. The effectiveness of these supranational powers was massively increased through successive Treaty amendments in 1987 (Single European Act), 1993 (Treaty of Maastricht) and 1999 (Treaty of Amsterdam), which widened the possibilities for qualified majority voting in the Council and enhanced the legislative role of the European Parliament through the cooperation procedure and the co-decision procedure (Articles 250 and 251 EC). Ironically, these changes also unleashed forces which have called into question not the effectiveness of the Community method, but its legitimacy, especially given the weakness of national parliamentary scrutiny of what national governments do in the guise of the Council. At the same time, national governments frequently blame Brussels for politically unpopular initiatives at the EU level, rather than taking full political responsibility for what is enacted, by a qualified majority vote, in the Council.

One response to this legitimacy crisis has been a move away from the classic Community method in some policy fields. This is especially the case in sensitive areas or areas at the margins of the current scope of Community competence, such as macro-economic policy, labour market policy or education policy. In recent years, there has been a marked trend towards what are often called 'new approaches' or 'new modes' of governance in the EU, the most distinctive example of which is generally termed the 'open method of coordination' (or OMC). The coordination of national policies in a non-coercive fashion has long been a recognised mode of governance under the EC Treaty. Under the original EEC Treaty, the Member States undertook to coordinate their economic policies, although in practice they rarely did (Article 103 EEC). Throughout the 1990s, and especially as a result of discussions at the European Council level between heads of state and government, a series of 'processes' have crystallised into a policy style which involves, according to Hodson and Maher (2001: 724), four key elements:

▶ setting short-, medium- and long-term guidelines for the EU with specific timetables for their achievements;

- establishing performance indicators and benchmarks tailored to each Member State and different sectors which allow comparison of best practices;
- translating targets from the European to the national and regional levels; and
- periodic monitoring, peer review and evaluation with the emphasis placed on the process of mutual learning.

Unlike the classic Community method, the task of driving forward policy initiatives is shared between the Commission and the Member States. The emphasis is more on what might be called 'policy transfer' between the Member States which is achieved through coordination and partnership arrangements in which the institutions are the handmaidens rather than the initiators of policy, rather than on the role of autonomous supranational institutions handing down EU policies in the form of directives or regulations. The Commission, therefore, has been wary of the introduction of the open method of coordination. Thus far, however, it has been restricted to the special cases of economic policy and labour market policy, where it is effectively mandated by the Treaty, and to other areas of shared responsibility between the Member States and the EU such as the information society, research policy, entrepreneurial and enterprise policy, as well as sensitive areas such as education policy, pension reform, policies to combat against poverty and immigration policy. Thus, many examples of the OMC in use can be seen in the chapters which follow, notably Chapters 14, 16 and 18. It is more frequently an instrument of *social* policy (albeit often with economic ends, such as the promotion of the reform of labour markets or the improvement of human capital through education and training), than it is an instrument of economic governance. The European Parliament is effectively excluded from a role within the open method. This is one of a number of legitimacy challenges which methods of new governance face (Scott and Trubek, 2002; de Búrca, 2003).

### 2.6 Constitutional Principles underlying Economic and Social Law: Concepts of Competence

Law-making and policy-making are governed by a legal and constitutional framework which determines how and under what conditions the powers given to the EU institutions can be exercised to make laws and policies. This section summarises these general principles. Subsequent chapters of the book will provide many examples of how the principles operate in practice in relation to specific policy areas.

A political argument is often made that there is a kind of 'competence creep' going on within the EU, and that the reserved powers of the Member States are being gradually eroded. To put it another way, the EU is gradually taking over all areas of socio-economic governance and consequently many important decisions are being taken too far away from the citizens who are directly affected by them. This concern has been expressed particularly clearly in states which have federal systems. For example, in Germany the states (*Länder*) have called for a clearer division of powers between the EU and the Member States, precisely because they are concerned about the erosion of their own powers under the German federal constitution. This illustrates the fact that to discuss who does what in the EU context in this way is to talk about the EU as if it were in fact a federal system involving two or indeed three separate but intertwined levels of government – a point that has been strongly resisted by successive British governments which have tended to insist that the EU is above all a union of states.

The characterisation that the EU is involved in a process of inevitable 'competence creep' is misleading for a number of reasons. In the first place, the most important examples of competence transfer to the Union have been those agreed unanimously by the Member States at successive IGCs, especially where they have agreed that such competences can be exercised under a system of majority voting in the Council. Moreover, as it stands, the EU does not have a system for the division of powers which truly resembles most federal systems. Although a system based around exclusive, shared and so-called complementary competences of the Union has been recommended for adoption by the Convention on the Future of Europe and the subsequent IGC in the Treaty establishing a Constitution for Europe, the current Treaties contain only a very small number of principles determining the conferment and exercise of powers. To understand in full how the system of competences actually works in the EU it is also necessary to take into account the case law of the Court of Justice.

The most basic principle is that of limited or attributed powers according to which the EU (or, more accurately, the Community) must act within the limits of the powers conferred upon it, and of the objectives assigned to it in the Treaty (Article 5 EC). Furthermore, under Article 7 EC the institutions must act within the limits of the powers conferred upon them. This competence question is translated in the EU context into the requirement that every act taken by the institutions must have a legal basis, either in the Treaties, or in some other piece of legislation which itself is based validly on the Treaties. The Court will police the existence of a valid legal basis if a challenge is brought under Article 230 EC, or a reference on validity is made by a national court under Article 234 EC. The Treaties also state what the objectives, tasks and activities of the EU are to be, and regulate each of these in a piecemeal way.

There is no single provision of the EU or EC Treaties which states in an *a priori* way who does what, and which powers are reserved for which level or shared between the two levels. There is not even a provision which articulates the principles upon which the division is based. Consequently, the division tends to be very poorly understood, particularly among politicians and opinion-formers who often accuse the EU of engaging in questionable if not prohibited activities. Some of the competences of the EU are sectoral, for example agriculture, transport and the labour market. Some are organised according to societal concerns, such as the protection of the environment, protection against discrimination or social exclusion, and the promotion of competitive markets. The largest groups of powers are specifically concerned with the EU's own functions in terms of economic integration, namely the powers to adopt measures for the purposes of completing the internal market and to prevent distortions of competition, and to ensure the establishment and functioning of economic and monetary union. There is also a residual power, or flexibility clause as it is now sometimes termed (Article 308 EC), which allows the Council to adopt by unanimous vote, measures, not otherwise provided for, but which are necessary for the achievement of the objectives of the Community.

Most EU competences are in practice shared with the Member States, although this is a point inferred from the system of EU law, rather than articulated in the Treaty. The EU has very few exclusive powers. The most important concern the common commercial policy or trade with third countries, two areas of competence which have been considerably strengthened as a result of the Treaty of Amsterdam and the Treaty of Nice. Other areas include the establishment of the Common Customs Tariff, and monetary policy in areas where the euro has been adopted (the 'Eurozone'). In addition, the EU has exclusive competence for most aspects of the common fisheries policy, such as the conservation of marine biological resources (i.e. fish). Under the Treaty on European Union, exclusive competence is confined to the establishment of joint bodies, such as Europol, which by definition are tasked with responsibilities that the Member States cannot undertake individually. Where the Community has legislated extensively in an area in which it shares competence with the Member States, the competence may become *de facto* exclusive, because there is no room left for national laws. This is termed 'pre-emption', and it results from the supremacy of EU law. However, it happens rarely. The internal market is a functional competence, and when the EU legislates to this end it often does so in fields of sectoral competence shared with the Member States.

Concurrent or shared competences are the largest group. The most important under the EC Treaty include citizenship, agriculture and some aspects of fisheries, the four freedoms (goods, people, services and capital), visas, asylum and immigration, transport, competition, taxation, social policy, environment, consumer protection, economic and social cohesion, energy, civil protection, and tourism. Under the EU Treaty, shared competences cover common foreign and security policy although not defence policy, and police and judicial cooperation in criminal matters.

The concept of 'complementary' competence or areas of supporting action refers to those areas in which the competence of the Union or Community is limited to supplementing or supporting the action of the Member States, such as adopting measures of encouragement or coordinating the action of the Member States. The bulk of the power to adopt legislative rules in these areas remains in the hands of the Member States and intervention by the Community cannot have the effect of excluding intervention by them. This category includes economic policy, employment, customs cooperation, education, vocational training and youth, culture, public health, industry, research and development, development cooperation, and a common defence policy (Pillar Two).

In each of these cases, the competence conferred on the Community or the Union is *explicit* in the Treaties. The Court has also recognised that in certain circumstances an *implied power* to act flows implicitly from the Treaty texts or their general structure in order to extend the Commission's power of decision (see Joined Cases 281, 283–285, 287/85 *Germany* v. *Commission (Migration Policy)* [1987] ECR 3203). More importantly, the Court has used the theory of implied powers in order to extend the Community's external powers and to create an extensive, if not complete, parallel between internal and external competence. This is intended to assist the implementation of the EU's aims which are discussed in detail in Chapter 11.

The Constitutional Treaty, if adopted, would provide a clearer overall framework for the study of competences given to the EU, and shared between the EU and the Member States. Articles I-11 to I-17 of the Constitutional Treaty explicitly adopt the categories of exclusive competences, shared competences and areas of supporting action which already *de facto* shape the system of competences under the EC and EU Treaties. Where exclusive competence is conferred on the EU in a specific area 'only the Union may legislate and adopt legally binding acts, the Member States being able to do so themselves only if so empowered by the Union or for the implementation of Union acts' (Article I-12(1) CT). Areas of exclusive competence pertain to the 'customs union; the establishing of competition rules necessary for the functioning of the internal market; monetary policy for the Member States whose currency is the euro; the conservation of marine biological resources under the common fisheries policy; and common commercial policy' (Article

I-13(1) CT). Article I-13(2) CT also covers a common area in which exclusive competence may arise as a result of pre-emption in the external field. It provides that:

'The Union shall also have exclusive competence for the conclusion of an international agreement when its conclusion is provided for in a legislative act of the Union or is necessary to enable the Union to exercise its internal competence, or insofar as its conclusion may affect common rules or alter their scope.'

Shared competences constitute the residual category, and a long, albeit representative, list is given in Article I-14 CT, and includes the internal market, social policy, economic and social cohesion, environment and so on. Where competence is shared between the EU and the Member States, both may legislate and adopt legally binding acts in that area. However, it is clear that the EU, in some respects, holds the upper hand in delineating the sphere of activities for the Member States, as '[t]he Member States shall exercise their competence to the extent that the Union has not exercised, or has decided to cease exercising, its competence' (Article I-12(2) CT). Finally in areas of supporting and coordinating action, the EU may only carry out actions to 'support, coordinate or supplement the actions of the Member States, without thereby superseding their competence in these areas' (Article I-12(5) CT). The adoption of measures harmonising national legislation is explicitly excluded. Article I-17 CT lists the areas for supporting action and includes 'protection and improvement of human health; industry; culture; tourism; education, youth, sport and vocational training; civil protection; and administrative cooperation'.

Some areas escape categorisation under this neat scheme. These include the coordination of national employment and economic policies (Articles I-12(3) and I-15 CT) and common foreign and security policy (Articles I-12(4) and I-16 CT). This suggests that although the attempt in Part I of the Constitutional Treaty is to provide an all-encompassing scheme in order to express clearly (especially for an audience comprising EU citizens) what the EU can and cannot do, in practice it is hard to shoehorn the different fields of activity into a set of restricted categories. Just as it is essential to read the detail of the legal powers conferred in relation to each area of policy-making within the EC Treaty and the Treaty on European Union, so too will it remain essential to read the details of the Constitutional Treaty, especially Part III which sets out each area of EU policy-making.

## 2.7   Principles Governing the Exercise of Powers by the EU

The EC Treaty also articulates expressly many of the general principles which govern the way the various competences conferred upon the EU are exercised. The most important are contained in the second and third paragraphs of Article 5 EC:

'In areas which do not fall within its exclusive competence, the Community shall take action, in accordance with the principle of subsidiarity, only if and insofar as the objectives of the proposed action cannot be sufficiently achieved by the Member States and can therefore, by reason of the scale or effects of the proposed action, be better achieved by the Community.

Any action by the Community shall not go beyond what is necessary to achieve the objectives of this Treaty.'

Notwithstanding the political importance of subsidiarity, ever since it was introduced by the Treaty of Maastricht, the Court has in fact never explicitly used it as the basis for finding that a legislative measure in an area of shared or concurrent competence should not have been adopted. In practice, the legislative impact of subsidiarity is largely limited to its insertion into institutional practices. As part of the process of assessing the appropriateness of legislative action, the institutions take steps to ensure that they have reviewed the question of subsidiarity and applied a comparative efficiency test as mandated by the Treaties.

Other principles guide the shape of EU policy-making. Environmental protection requirements must be integrated into the definition and implementation of all Community policies and activities, with a view to promoting sustainable development (Article 6 EC). In relation to all of its activities referred to in Article 3 EC, the Community must aim to eliminate inequalities and promote equality, between men and women (Article 3(2) EC). These are examples of values which are not strictly economic, being 'mainstreamed' into EU policy-making. More generally, of course, the EU legislature is bound by fundamental rights, by virtue of the case law of the Court of Justice (Case 11/70 *Internationale Handelsgesellschaft* [1970] ECR 1125), and by virtue of Articles 6(1) and (2) EU. Article 6(1) provides that:

'The Union is founded on the principles of liberty, democracy, respect for human rights and fundamental freedoms, and the rule of law, principles which are common to the Member States.'

Fundamental rights are guaranteed within the EU legal order as general principles of law, inspired by sources such as the constitutional traditions common to the Member States and international human rights instruments, notably the European Convention on Human Rights and Fundamental Freedoms. No explicit reference is made in the Treaties to the EU's own Charter of Fundamental Rights, solemnly proclaimed by the Presidents of the three political institutions at the Nice European Council in December 2000 (OJ 2000 C364/1), and its legal status has been uncertain hitherto, although it has been recommended for inclusion as a legally binding instrument in the draft Treaty establishing a Constitution for Europe. However, the Commission, which actively promotes the role of the Charter within the EU legal order, regularly refers to its provisions when it draws up legislative proposals, as a way of demonstrating that it has considered the human rights implications of the measures which it is proposing. As general principles of law, fundamental rights are just one example among several which the Court has recognised, or which are enshrined in the Treaty. Others include the prohibition on discrimination on grounds of nationality contained in Article 12 EC, the general principle of equality.

Economic integration itself provides a general frame of reference and set of principles which guide EU policy-making. The dominant economic concept in the European Community, at least until the adoption of the Single European Act, was the notion of a 'common market'. In Case 15/81 *Schul* v. *Inspecteur der Invoerrechten* ([1982] ECR 1409) the Court stated that the concept of a common market:

'involves the elimination of all obstacles to intra-Community trade in order to merge the national markets into a Single Market bringing about conditions as close as possible to those of a genuine internal market' (para. 31).

Traditionally, the Treaty provided two mechanisms for achieving this: 'provisions ... relating to "the elimination of barriers" and "fair competition" both of which are necessary for bringing about a single market' (Case 32/65 *Italy* v. *Council and Commission* [1966] ECR 389 at p.405). In the early days, it was the 'negative' aspect of the elimination of barriers which predominated with the interpretation and application of the *fundamental freedoms*. The introduction of Article 14 EC defining the internal market, and the rapid emergence and implementation of the programme for the completion of the internal market by the end of 1992, broke away from that traditional framework by emphasising the importance of legislative measures aimed at securing fair competitive conditions.

Economic and social law does have an undoubted constitutional significance for the institutions, which are not permitted to act in ways which endanger the unity of the market (Barents, 1990). The fundamental character of the free movement provisions for the EU itself emerges clearly from Joined Cases 80 and 81/77 *Société Les Commissionnaires Réunis SARL* v. *Receveur des Douanes* ([1978] ECR 927), where the Court of Justice indicated that actions by the Community which infringed the free movement rules would be a form of:

> 'prejudice to what the Community has achieved in relation to the unity of the market [which] moreover risks opening the way to mechanisms which would lead to disintegration contrary to the objectives of progressive approximation of the economic policies of Member States set out in Article 2 of the Treaty' (para. 36).

A characteristic feature of the EU legal order is its treatment of the individual. This includes not only the recognition of the range of individual rights, especially fundamental rights, highlighted in this section, but also a more general injunction in relation to the rule of law. Like Member States, individuals are the subjects of EU law. The treatment of the individual thus also incorporates the principle of individual legal protection, which has emerged from the constitutionalisation of the EU Treaties principally by the Court of Justice. EU law has been ascribed the value of *supremacy* or primacy *vis-à-vis* all forms of national law and furthermore penetrates the national legal orders and becomes part of national law. It is because of this process that EC law is commonly termed a *supranational* form of law, rather than a species of *international* law. Much of this constitutional edifice is built upon Article 10 EC which states the core principle of 'Community loyalty' binding the Member States to the achievement of the objectives of the Treaties. A key way of instrumentalising the constitutional framework conferring formal federal-type authority upon EC law which has been developed by the Court, involves giving individuals rights which they derive from specific provisions of EC law which are sufficiently precise and unconditional to be capable of judicial enforcement (*direct effect*). Furthermore, where the EU has fully exercised a power to regulate a particular area, this will have a *pre-emptive* effect upon national law, displacing the national power to regulate. National procedural rules and remedies continue to govern proceedings in national courts in relation to EU law, subject to the principle that the national remedies must not be less favourable than those relating to similar domestic claims and 'must not be such as in practice to make it impossible or excessively difficult to obtain reparation' (Joined Cases C-46 and 48/93 *Brasserie du Pêcheur* v. *Germany*, and *ex parte Factortame (Factortame III)* [1996] ECR I-1029, at para. 67).

These fundamental principles remain essentially unchanged in the text of the Constitutional Treaty.

## 2.8 Flexibility, Enhanced Cooperation and Opt-outs

The last decade has seen a marked increase in the instances in which the EU Treaties either create an 'opt-out' in which one or more Member States do not participate in a given policy, or provide mechanisms for the adoption of legislative measures applying only to a limited group of Member States. This reflects the concept of flexibility, a concept through which the Member States and the institutions seek to manage the contradictory impulses of integration and the protection of diversity. Indeed, flexibility has been built into the very system of the internal market since the Single European Act. Under the provisions of Articles 95(4)–(8) EC, a Member State may derogate from a single market harmonisation measure on grounds of major needs such as public health or consumer protection.

Flexibility also operates at the level of primary law. Not all of the Member States participate in the several policy activities detailed in this book. The best example is Economic and Monetary Union. When the single currency was first launched in 1999, only eleven states participated. Subsequently, before the euro displaced the national currencies on 1 January 2002, Greece joined the eleven. 'Euroland', or the 'eurozone' as it is more frequently termed, now comprises all the pre-2004 enlargement Member States apart from the UK, Denmark and Sweden. Sweden's non-participation is somewhat different compared to that of the UK and Denmark, as it did not benefit, as did the other two states, from certain special arrangements written into the Treaty of Maastricht from the very beginning. It has a type of *de facto* exemption which it has effectively written for itself, which was in turn reinforced as a result of Sweden holding a referendum on the basis of the proposition that it should join the eurozone in September 2003, which was defeated. On that basis, the other eurozone participants could hardly insist that Sweden join the euro, against the expressed will of its people. Estonia, Lithuania and Slovenia joined members of the European Exchange Rate Mechanism, which serves as a precursor to adopting the euro, soon after joining the EU but so far only Slovenia has actually adopted the euro, from 1 January 2007.

However, it would be wrong to assume that any of the non-participating states are completely unaffected by the economic and monetary disciplines which are associated with the role of the European Central Bank in managing monetary policy within the eurozone, such as the avoidance of excessive public sector deficits. Some of the rules apply to all the Member States, albeit in differing ways. For example, where participating states are bound by 'stability programmes' in relation to budgetary disciplines, the non-participating states are bound only by 'convergence programmes'.

The Schengen Agreement is another area where a set of variable solutions applies. A group of Member States developed the Schengen system outside the framework of the EU Treaties, as a laboratory for integration in relation to the free movement of persons. It instituted, for the participating states, a single external border and the removal of internal frontiers, accompanied by measures relating to the sharing of information between the participants. By the time of the Treaty of Amsterdam, all the Member States except the UK and Ireland were participating in Schengen. Norway and Iceland, non-Member States linked with Denmark, Finland and Sweden in a passport union, are also involved in the system. The Treaty of Amsterdam initiated the incorporation of the Schengen system into the EU, so that autonomous EU laws should gradually displace their Schengen equivalents. The UK and Ireland were given an opt-out from Schengen at the time of its incorporation, as well as to the new Title in the EC Treaty on the free movement of persons, although they have the opportunity to opt back into various aspects of the programme of legislation in relation to the free movement of persons, asylum and immigration. Both states have taken advantage of the possibility of selective opt-ins in relation to some types of measures; the UK, for example, has opted in to the information exchange aspects of the Schengen system. Denmark also has authority under a protocol attached to the Treaties to treat Schengen-related matters as international law, within its domestic legal order, but not as EU law. This is the basis on which it also participates in subsequent developments of existing Schengen law or the 'Schengen *acquis*' as it is known. The post-2004 and post-2007 new Member States are obliged to adopt the Schengen *acquis* and they will become part of Schengen, but only when the existing members are confident about their systems of border control and information management.

Potentially the most widespread form of flexibility is enhanced, or closer, cooperation. The Treaty of Amsterdam witnessed the introduction into the Treaties for the first time of provisions empowering a limited group of Member States to adopt secondary legislation applying only to themselves. This is intended to operate only as a 'last resort' when measures cannot be adopted under provisions applicable to all Member States. The Amsterdam provisions were further amended by the Treaty of Nice to loosen some of the conditions applying to the adoption of such measures, while at the same time assuring those who do not participate, that enhanced cooperation is not a Trojan horse leading inexorably towards the break up of the Union. Enhanced cooperation is now governed by Articles 43–45 EU (general principles), plus Article 11a EC (first pillar), Articles 40–42 EU (second pillar) and Articles 27a–e EU (third pillar). In fact, these provisions have never been used, although their possible usage has been threatened from time to time. In other words, their potential has yet to be tapped, although there is some doubt that it will ever be explored (Shaw, 2004). Perhaps the most credible threat on the part of the majority of the Member States to use closer cooperation *vis-à-vis* a dissenting Member State was that made to Italy, when it sought to block the adoption of a European Arrest Warrant measure under the Police and Criminal Justice Cooperation provisions (13.14). The adoption of the warrant measure was part of a package of provisions designed to assist the fight against crime, particularly in the aftermath of the terrorist attacks in the US on 11 September 2001. In the end, Italy conceded the point and voted for the measure.

The Constitutional Treaty, if adopted, would preserve the arrangements for flexibility in relation to the euro and the Schengen Agreement, and further adapts the criteria for enhanced cooperation, in particular by creating a single set of criteria which apply to all areas of EU policy-making (Federal Trust, 2005).

The tensions of flexibility versus uniformity and of integration versus diversity will be consistent themes embedded throughout this book.

## Summary

1. This chapter provides essential background to the study of the substantive economic and social law of the EU, particularly by focusing on the role of public authorities in the regulation of economic activity and on concepts such as 'governance'.

2. A general definition of 'governance' is used in the chapter: 'governance refers to the process whereby elements in society wield power and authority, and influence and enact policies and decisions concerning public life, and economic and social development.'

3. One unique facet of the EU is that it is trying to fashion a system of 'governance beyond the state', or 'governance without statehood'. This poses particular challenges when it comes to all three generally accepted forms of public intervention in socio-economic life: the redistribution function; the stabilisation function; and the regulatory function.

## Summary cont'd

4. It is useful to combine the review of these three functions with three techniques of government distinguished by Daintith: *imperium* (command of law); *dominium* (wealth of government); and *suasion* (capacity of government to inform and persuade).

5. A review of EU law and policy highlights the important role of *imperium* and the regulatory function in much of EU law-making, especially as regards the harmonisation of national laws for the purposes of promoting the internal market. The EU has much more limited powers in relation to redistribution and *dominium*, especially at the individual level. The EU often resorts to *suasion*, insofar as it uses policy techniques which do not rely upon legal sanctions to try to change national policies in many areas.

6. Studying EU social and economic law begins the process of placing the EU institutions into context, since it becomes increasingly clear what governance functions the Commission, the Council of Ministers, the European Parliament and the Court of Justice actually fulfil. The same point can be made about the system of legal instruments under the EC and EU Treaties (regulations, directives, decisions, etc.).

7. This chapter briefly reviews the institutional structure and legal instruments of the EU, and provides summary coverage of some important amendments suggested by the Constitutional Treaty.

8. Law-making and policy-making in the area of socio-economic life in the EU are governed by constitutional principles. The Court of Justice polices the application of many of these principles.

9. The EU can only act where it has competence. Broadly speaking, EU competences fall into three categories: exclusive, shared and areas of supporting activity. The Constitutional Treaty articulates a more detailed scheme of competences according to these broad distinctions. However, the most important principles which affect the allocation of competences are the detailed legal bases to be found currently in the EC and EU Treaties, and under Part III of the Constitutional Treaty. The Court of Justice will annul measures which are not taken on the correct legal basis.

10. Subsidiarity and proportionality are the most important principles which govern the exercise of competences, especially of shared competences. EU law includes a set of fundamental rights, which are protected as general principles of law.

11. Flexibility has become a very important element of the system of integration under the EC and EU Treaties. Flexible integration can allow Member States to have opt-outs from certain policy activities. For example, only a minority of 12 out of 25 current Member States had the euro as their currency in 2005. The UK, Ireland and Denmark have opt-outs from the Schengen system which provides for border-free movement between Member States. However, the system of enhanced cooperation, which would allow groups of Member States to break away and adopt closer integration policies in specific areas, under conditions specified under the treaties, has never been used under the EC and EU Treaties.

# Exercises

1.  What is meant by the term 'governance' and how does it help us to understand what the EU does and how it acts?

2.  What are the typical functions of public authorities in market economies? Make a list at this stage of your studies, and include on the list all the functions which the EU undertakes of which you are currently aware. Keep this list and return to it, as you work through the subsequent chapters and topics in the book, in order to evaluate the impact which the EU has, through its substantive policy-making, upon the lives of its citizens and residents. You should also become increasingly aware of the extent to which the EU is better equipped to intervene in some areas, by using certain types of techniques and instruments, than it is in other areas.

3.  What difference would it make to the EU if it had the power to tax and thereby raise its own revenues?

4.  What is meant by 'competence' in the EU context, and why is it of constitutional significance for the scope and nature of EU law and policy-making?

5.  How do the principles of subsidiarity and proportionality constrain policy-makers?

6.  How flexible is the EU in relation to law and policy-making?

## Further Reading

de Búrca, G. (2003) 'The Constitutional Challenge of New Governance in the European Union', 28 *European Law Review* 814.

Federal Trust (2005) *Flexibility and the Future of the European Union*, A Federal Trust Report, October 2005, available at: **www.fedtrust.co.uk**

Gillingham, J. (2003) *European Integration 1950–2003: Superstate or New Market Economy?*, Cambridge: Cambridge University Press. See especially chapter 15.

Gormley, L. (2006) 'The Internal Market: History and Evolution', in Nic Shuibhne, N. (ed.), *Regulating the Internal Market*, Cheltenham: Edward Elgar.

Hodson, D. and Maher, I. (2001) 'The Open Method as a`New Mode of Governance: the Case of Soft Economic Policy Co-ordination', 39 *Journal of Common Market Studies* 719.

Majone, G. (2005) *Dilemmas of European Integration. The Ambiguities and Pitfalls of Integration by Stealth*, Oxford: Oxford University Press.

Rhodes, M. (2002) 'Globalization, EMU and Welfare State Futures', in Heywood, P., Jones, E. and Rhodes, M. (eds.), *Developments in West European Politics 2*, Basingstoke: Palgrave Macmillan.

Scott, J. and Trubek, D. (2002) 'Mind the Gap: Law and New Approaches to Governance in the EU', 8 *European Law Journal* 1.

Tsoukalis, L. (2005) *What Kind of Europe?*, Oxford: Oxford University Press. See especially chapter 5.

Wallace, H. (2005) 'An Institutional Autonomy and Five Policy Models', in Wallace, H., Wallace, W. and Pollack, M. (eds.), *Policy-Making in the European Union* (5th edn), Oxford: Oxford University Press.

Weatherill, S. (2006) 'Supply of, and Demand for Internal Market Regulation: Strategies, Preferences and Interpretation', in Nic Shuibhne, N. (ed.), *Regulating the Internal Market*, Cheltenham: Edward Elgar.

De Witte, B. (2004) 'Future Paths of Flexibility: Enhanced Cooperation, Partial Agreements and Pioneer Groups', in de Zwaan, J. *et al* (eds.), *The European Union: An Ongoing Process of Integration*, The Hague: TMC Asser Instituut.

## Key Websites

A Citizens' Guide providing a useful starting point to understanding the work of the EU and its institutions is available at:
**http://www.europa.eu/institutions/index_en.htm**

The European Commission's website on governance, including the Governance White Paper of 2001, is available at:
**http://europa.eu/comm/governance/index_en.htm**

A forum of short academic papers discussing the EU's governance agenda is available at:
**http://aei.pitt.edu/74/01/GovernanceForum.html**

The website of the European Central Bank is available at:
**http://www.ecb.eu**

# Part II

# The Internal Market

# Chapter 3

# Introduction to the Law of the Internal Market

## 3.1 Introduction

This chapter builds on the general introduction to the socio-economic project of the European Union, and on the nature of socio-economic governance addressed in Chapters 1 and 2. It presents an outline of the law of the internal market as it has been developed both by the Court of Justice through its case law and by the political institutions through legislative and other measures. By looking at both these sources of law, it takes further the distinction between positive and negative integration made in 1.5. It is inevitable that some of the questions which this chapter asks and the developments which it discusses will be easier to understand once a more detailed study of the free movement case law of the Court of Justice has been completed. Readers may therefore wish to return to this chapter at a later stage of their studies.

This chapter begins by presenting the basic outline of the Treaty rules governing the liberalisation of trade in commodities (goods and services) and of factor movements (labour, capital, enterprise) between the Member States (3.2). Brief reference is made in 3.3 to how the Court of Justice has interpreted these basic provisions, although detailed consideration of the Court's case law on the free movement of goods, services, capital and persons is reserved for Chapters 4–8 and 12. The specific objective here is to highlight both the strengths and weaknesses of the Court's approach and how this fed into the project to complete the single market by 1992 – a project launched in the mid-1980s, and linked to the amendments to the EC Treaty introduced by the Single European Act of 1986. Completing the single market was the EU's most important undertaking of the late 1980s and early 1990s. The internal market programme itself will be discussed in more detail in 3.6. Harmonisation measures, however, are not unique to the single market programme, and 3.4 and 3.5 will provide important background by discussing in more general terms policies and methods of harmonisation, and the heritage of harmonisation up to the Single European Act. Some of this material is therefore useful background for later chapters in this book, such as those on social policy and the environment – that is, flanking policies where harmonisation of national laws has been widely used as a policy tool.

The nature of the single market programme will be discussed in 3.7 which addresses the so-called 'new approach' to harmonisation which was one of the *leitmotivs* of that programme. However, harmonisation has never been the only, nor perhaps even the dominant method of market governance in the EU, and 3.8 presents some of the other steps taken towards the realisation of the single market objective aside from harmonisation. Turning to the crucial institutional framework for the adoption of single market measures such as harmonisation, the legal basis of which is contained in Article 95 EC, 3.9 discusses specific problems resulting from the complex derogation and flexibility rules contained in that provision. The scope of EU competence for the adoption of legislation in relation to the internal market is presented briefly in 3.10. Bringing the narrative concerned with the development of the internal market up to date, 3.11 widens the focus to examine the full range of legal and policy instruments which the Commission in partnership with the other institutions now uses to secure its continued development. Many of these 'new governance' techniques are themselves quite flexible and responsive to demands for differentiated integration. This chapter concludes by examining, in 3.12, the enforcement of internal market law, especially by the Commission.

Internal market law is not in any substantial way affected by any of the changes proposed in the Constitutional Treaty. The changes to the legislative procedure and to the system of legal instruments referred to in Chapter 1 will concern the adoption of legislation affecting the internal market, but not in any greater way than, say, social law or environmental law. The Constitutional Treaty preserves the underlying constitutional structure of the internal market referring to the basic liberal features of the market (free and undistorted competition) in the context of the Union's objectives in Article I-3 CT. Internal market measures fall within the shared competence of the Union and the Member States (Article I-14(2) CT). Chapter 1 of Title III of Part III of the Constitutional Treaty retains most of the detailed parts on internal market freedoms and the adoption of internal market legislation contained in the EC Treaty. Consistent with the Constitutional Treaty's vocation to simplify and clarify EU law, the terminology of the 'common market' is dropped, and the text refers throughout only to the 'internal market'.

## 3.2 A Sketch of the EC Treaty Rules on the Liberalisation of Trade and Factor Mobility

This section builds upon 1.9, which presented the basic objectives of the European Union in the socio-economic field, as well as the broad legal framework for policy-making in this domain. Fundamental to the establishment of the 'common market' upon which the European Union is based (Article 2 EC retains the original language of the Rome Treaty) is the definition of an internal market which is characterised by 'the abolition, as between Member States, of obstacles to the free movement of goods, persons, services and capital' (Article 3 EC), and is an area 'without internal frontiers' (Article 14 EC). These more general objectives and obligations are of less significance than the specific prohibitions which follow later in the Treaties. Even so, in Case 15/81 *Schul* v. *Inspecteur der Invoerrechten* ([1982] ECR 1409) the Court stated that the concept of a common market:

> 'involves the elimination of all obstacles to intra-Community trade in order to merge the national markets into a Single Market bringing about conditions as close as possible to those of a genuine internal market' (para. 33).

Traditionally, the EC Treaty provides two mechanisms for achieving this: 'provisions . . . relating to "the elimination of barriers" and . . . "fair competition", both of which are necessary for bringing about a single market' (Case 32/65 *Italy* v. *Council and Commission* [1966] ECR 389 at p.404). In the early days, the 'negative' aspect of the elimination of barriers predominated the interpretation and application of the *fundamental freedoms* especially by the Court of Justice and national courts. The introduction of Article 14 EC defining the internal market, and the implementation of the single market programme in the 1980s and 1990s, broke away from that traditional framework of judicially-led development by emphasising the importance of legislative measures aimed at securing fair competitive conditions.

One general provision of the EC Treaty is of considerable significance to the internal market and to free movement, and that is Article 12 EC. Prohibiting discrimination on grounds of nationality, this provision reinforces all the specific provisions on commodity and factor mobility:

'[w]ithin the scope of application of this Treaty, and without prejudice to any special provisions contained therein, any discrimination on grounds of nationality shall be prohibited.'

The Council, acting in accordance with the co-decision procedure of Article 251 EC, may adopt measures with the European Parliament prohibiting such discrimination (Article 12(2) EC). In one sense, non-discrimination reinforces each of the individual economic freedoms, namely the requirement not to discriminate against non-national traders, providers of services, capital, companies, entrepreneurs and workers. The following chapters will examine how and to what extent discrimination analysis truly underpins the conceptual framework which the Court of Justice has put in place to secure trade liberalisation.

Title I of Part Three of the EC Treaty regulates the free movement of goods. Article 23 EC provides that the Community is based upon a customs union covering all trade in goods, and involves the prohibition as between the Member States of customs duties on imports and exports and all charges having equivalent effect, and the adoption of a common customs tariff in Member States' relations with third countries. The detailed rules on the Customs Union (Chapter 1 of Title I: Articles 25–27 EC) and on the prohibition of quantitative restrictions and other types of non-tariff barriers to trade in goods (Chapter 2 of Title I: Articles 28–31 EC) apply to 'goods in free circulation'. These are either goods originating in the Member States, or goods originating in a third country in which all import formalities have been observed, including the payment of any customs duties or charges having equivalent effect (Article 24 EC). There are complicated rules, of course, on concepts of origin where goods may have mixed origins, or may have been processed in different countries. In the context of the development of the Customs Union, it has been extremely important that the EC Treaty prohibits not only charges formally termed 'customs duties' – long abolished between the Member States and superseded in trade with third countries by the Common Customs Tariff – but also 'charges having equivalent effect'. The latter comprise any other pecuniary impositions on the movement of goods across borders. There are no exceptions in the EC Treaty to these mandatory rules. The details of the Customs Union, including both the internal and external dimensions, are examined in Chapter 4. Closely linked to the provisions on pecuniary obstacles to the free movement of goods is Article 90 EC which prohibits the imposition of higher levels of internal taxation upon imported goods than upon domestic ones. Chapter 7 addresses this provision, and related matters concerning the elimination of taxation barriers to trade between Member States.

Chapter 2 of Title I of the EC Treaty prohibits other non-pecuniary barriers to the free movement of goods between the Member States, beginning with quantitative restrictions on trade between Member States (quotas) and so-called measures having equivalent effect to a quantitative restriction (MEEs or MEEQRs). Member States are prohibited from imposing these on both imports from (Article 28 EC) and exports to (Article 29 EC) other Member States (see Chapter 5). These provisions do not extend to external trade with third countries. In contrast to Articles 25–27 EC which address the Customs Union, the EC Treaty provides for exceptions to the prohibition on quotas and MEEs or MEEQRs. These are dealt with in secondary measures adopted under Article 133 EC, such as the common rules for imports (see Chapter 11). Article 30 EC provides:

> 'The provisions of Articles 28 and 29 shall not preclude prohibitions or restrictions on imports, exports or goods in transit justified on grounds of public morality, public policy or public security; the protection of health and life of humans, animals or plants; the protection of national treasures possessing artistic, historic or archaeological value; or the protection of industrial and commercial property. Such prohibitions or restrictions shall not, however, constitute a means of arbitrary discrimination or a disguised restriction on trade between Member States.'

Article 31 EC requires Member States to adjust state monopolies of a commercial character. These are increasingly rare in the days of privatisation and deregulation, but examples include the Swedish and Finnish state alcohol monopolies.

The provisions on the free movement of persons, services and capital, and the right of establishment, are gathered together in Title III of Part Three of the EC Treaty. In this book, services (a traded commodity) are dealt with in Chapter 6 alongside the right of establishment for the self-employed and legal persons (a form of human capital and a factor of production in classic economic analysis). The reason for this lies in the relationships drawn in EU law between the free movement of services and freedom of establishment in relation to the regulation of enterprise. Article 49 EC prohibits restrictions on freedom to provide services within the Community in respect of nationals of Member States who are established in a State of the Community other than that of the person for whom the services are intended. The Council is permitted to extend the benefit of the provisions on the free movement of services to nationals of a third country who provide services and who are established within the Community. Liberalisation directives aimed at particular services can be adopted by the Council under Article 52 EC, acting by a qualified majority. It is clear that the Member States envisaged, when drafting the Treaty, that there would be difficulties in achieving the free movement of services not because 'movement' itself is regulated, but rather many services themselves (such as those provided by lawyers, doctors, architects, engineers, etc.) are highly regulated internally for public policy reasons and in order to protect consumers. From the beginning, the Member States were committed to applying the non-discrimination principle, and to regulating services provided by non-nationals in the same way as those provided by nationals (Article 54 EC). Article 46 EC provides derogations for services similar to those available to goods contained in Article 30 EC:

> 'The provisions of this Chapter . . . shall not prejudice the applicability of provisions laid down by law, regulation or administrative action providing for special treatment for foreign nationals on grounds of public policy, public security or public health.'

This is a shorter list of derogations compared with those available for trade in goods. In addition, Article 45 EC disapplies the liberalisation provisions with respect to service activities within a Member State which are connected 'even occasionally, with the exercise of official authority'.

The provisions governing the right of establishment, which will be discussed in more detail in Chapter 6, follow a similar pattern. Article 43 EC provides that:

> 'Within the framework of the provisions set out below, restrictions on the freedom of establishment of nationals of a Member State in the territory of another Member State shall be prohibited. Such prohibition shall also apply to restrictions on the setting up of agencies, branches or subsidiaries by nationals of any Member State established in the territory of any Member State.

Freedom of establishment shall include the right to take up and pursue activities as self employed persons and to set up and manage undertakings, in particular companies or firms . . . under the conditions laid down for its own nationals by the law of the country where such establishment is effected . . .'

Once again the Member States foresaw obstacles to achieving freedom of establishment solely on the basis of negative prohibitions. Article 44 EC provides for the adoption of directives by the Council, with some specific instructions in relation to the types of priorities which the institutions should pursue in achieving liberalisation through harmonisation of the conditions attaching to particular activities. In addition, Article 47(1) EC provides specifically for the adoption of directives establishing the mutual recognition of diplomas, certificates and other evidence of formal qualifications, and Article 47(2) EC enables the harmonisation of national rules concerning the taking-up and pursuit of economic activities such as the liberal professions or the provision of financial services. The derogations contained in Articles 45 and 46 EC on the exercise of public authority and on public policy considerations apply to freedom of establishment.

Enterprise, that is, freedom of establishment, is only one of three factors of production covered by the EC Treaty. Capital and (employed) labour are also included in the Treaty's scope. The free movement of capital is governed by Chapter 4 of Title III, but it represents a special case in comparison to the other fundamental freedoms. The original EEC Treaty provisions on capital were drafted as softer provisions, committing the Member States to progressive abolition of obstacles to free movement, but precluding guarantees enforceable in the courts. The current versions of the provisions, which were introduced by the Treaty of Maastricht in 1993 (Articles 56–60 EC), match more closely the pattern of the other fundamental freedoms. Article 56(1) EC provides:

'. . . all restrictions on the movement of capital between Member States and between Member States and third countries shall be prohibited.'

Article 56(2) EC extends the same prohibition to restrictions on the movement of payments. There are a number of qualifications applicable with respect to movements between Member States and third countries in the provisions which follow. Article 58 EC allows Member State exemption with respect to certain provisions of taxation law and measures necessary for the prudential supervision of financial institutions, or measures which are justified on grounds of public policy or public security. Detailed coverage of the free movement of capital, along with that other major heading of monetary integration, the establishment of an economic and monetary union, is contained in Chapter 8.

Finally, the free movement of (employed) labour forms part of a wider network of provisions governing in general terms the free movement of persons. Article 18 EC guarantees 'the right to move and reside freely within the territory of the Member States' to all citizens of the Union, although this is 'subject to the limitations and conditions laid down in this Treaty and by the measures adopted to give it effect'. This general right of free movement and residence is in itself extremely important, as Member States may only impose proportionate restrictions upon it. However, a number of specific provisions, not only those governing the self-employed (see the previous discussion of services and establishment), but also those on the free movement of *workers* (Articles 39–42 EC), continue to be extremely important. Article 39(2) EC guarantees freedom of movement for workers:

'Such freedom of movement shall entail the abolition of any discrimination based on nationality between workers of the Member States as regards employment, remuneration and other conditions of work and employment.'

Freedom of movement for workers entails, 'subject to limitations justified on grounds of public policy, public security or public health' (Article 39(3) EC), the right to accept offers of employment, to move freely within the territory of the Member States for these purposes, and to stay in a Member State for the purpose of employment. Article 39(4) EC appears to exclude public service employment from the scope of the liberalisation provisions, but in fact this provision has been narrowly interpreted by the Court of Justice. Only migrant workers who are EU citizens are protected under Article 39 EC. Article 40 EC allows the adoption of implementing or supplementing measures under the co-decision procedure referred to in Article 251 EC. Article 42 EC organises the coordination of social security entitlements for migrant workers, allowing for the aggregation of contributions made in several countries. Three directives from 1990 laid down free movement rights for students, pensioners and those of independent needs, but these were repealed and consolidated in a single 2004 Directive on the right of citizens of the Union and their family members to move and reside freely within the territory of the Member States (European Parliament and Council Directive 2004/38 OJ 2004, L158/77). Third country nationals, who are members of the families of EU citizens, where the latter rely upon the free movement provisions in order to move to another Member State, also receive protection under EU secondary legislation. These are derived rights only, enacted to ensure that enjoyment of free movement rights on the part of EU citizens is not hindered because, for example, they are married to a third country national, or they have dependent relatives who are third country nationals. Such third country nationals have no direct or personal right to free movement under EU law, although Title IV of Part Three of the EC Treaty, introduced by the Treaty of Amsterdam, established a progressive programme for the adoption of measures to regulate through harmonisation, visas, asylum, and other issues related to the free movement of third country nationals, which is vital to the project of securing the abolition of internal frontiers. These aspects regarding the free movement of EU citizens and third country nationals are covered in Chapters 12 and 13. Significantly, none of these measures afford a direct personal right of entry to the EU and its Member States on the part of third country nationals. Member States continue to control immigration from outside the EU.

Treaty provisions prohibiting discrimination or requiring the removal of restrictions, however, were never expected to be sufficient on their own to achieve the level of integration envisaged by the original EEC Treaty, i.e. the creation of a common market. From the outset, the EEC Treaty enabled the institutions to adopt a variety of secondary legislative measures. These have been concerned largely with giving effect to principles of negative integration (Craig, 2002: 4–5). For example, they may provide guidance on the scope and interpretation of basic Treaty provisions such as Article 28 EC, or they may require Member States to notify the EU of any new technical product regulations they wish to adopt, or they may set out detailed procedures necessary to implement the free movement rights, or they may limit the discretion afforded Member States seeking to limit free movement, such as the derogations permissible under Article 39(3) EC. The most comprehensive body of secondary legislation of this type concerns the free movement of workers and their families, and addresses related questions such as the rights of retired workers, educational rights of migrants and their children, and the reduction of border formalities for those exercising their free movement rights.

Secondary legislation is concerned, of course, with the promotion of positive integration. In addition to the harmonisation measures foreseen in Article 47 EC relating to freedom of establishment and Article 52 EC relating to the freedom to provide services, a general provision on the harmonisation of national laws was included in the EEC Treaty in what was originally Article 100 EEC (now Article 94 EC). However, there were always considerable difficulties in making substantial progress in this dimension of positive integration. Unanimity among the Member States was required for the adoption of harmonisation measures under Article 100 EEC, and thus it proved an inadequate tool for the realisation of the internal market. Detailed discussion of the policies and methods of harmonisation in the EU and the key dimensions of the history of harmonisation before the Single European Act are contained in 3.4 and 3.5. The issue of harmonisation after the Single European Act continues in 3.6 and 3.7.

What was not necessarily envisaged by the founders of the Treaties, however, was the extent to which the Court of Justice would take a proactive role in interpreting and applying the basic prohibitions contained in the Treaties. In relation to goods, services, establishment, workers and the post-Maastricht provisions on capital, the Court has held that the basic free movement provisions are enforceable by individual economic actors such as traders, providers of services, companies or workers before national courts. In other words, such provisions have direct effect. Traders and other economic operators are thus able to resist the application of national measures found to be in breach of the basic prohibitions contained in Articles 23, 25, 28, 29, 39, 43, 49 and 56 EC. The Court's interpretation of the Treaty has had the effect of ensuring that the key actors in the process of economic integration include individual economic operators and the national courts. This 'indirect' enforcement process operates to support the Commission's efforts of ensuring Member States' compliance with the provisions of the Treaty through the medium of Article 226 EC enforcement proceedings before the Court of Justice.

## 3.3  Strengths and Weaknesses of the Court's Approach

Discussion of the details of the Court's interpretation of the individual free movement provisions is reserved for the following chapters which address each of the various freedoms. A snapshot which focuses on some of the strengths and weaknesses of the Court's approach suffices here.

It is worth recalling that it was in the context of a case on the free movement of goods (Case 26/62 *Van Gend en Loos* [1963] ECR 1) that the Court first formulated the concept of direct effect. An importer of chemicals from Germany into the Netherlands challenged the imposition of what it alleged was an increased customs duty on the goods before the national courts in the Netherlands. Increases in customs duties were prohibited under what was then Article 12 EEC (now Article 25 EC). Despite submissions from the Belgian, German and Netherlands governments arguing against the possibility that the foundational principles of the common market could be enforceable in national courts, the Court of Justice concluded otherwise. The Court relied upon the objectives of the Treaty, including its Preamble, and on the existence of 'institutions endowed with sovereign rights'. It found that the Community constitutes:

'a new legal order of international law for the benefit of which the states have limited their sovereign rights, albeit within limited fields, and the subjects of which comprise not only Member States but also their nationals.'

Applying the principle of direct effect to the provisions of an international treaty enacted for the purposes of promoting economic integration may have been quite a startling innovation on the part of the Court, although the notion of the self-execution of international treaty provisions was not completely unknown in international law. Once the principle was accepted, its further application by the Court to a wide range of provisions on the free movement of goods, including those on quotas and MEEs, all of which are drafted in a dispositive and unconditional style, was considerably less surprising. More surprising was the Court's willingness to extend the principle of direct effect to cover freedom of establishment, even though the provisions in question appeared at first sight to suggest that they needed to be fleshed out by legislation before they could be applied as complete obligations. Indeed, the Court in *Van Gend en Loos* cited the need for 'legislative intervention' as a reason why a provision might *not* have direct effect.

In Case 2/74 *Reyners* v. *Belgium* ([1974] ECR 631), the Court referred to the 'obligation to attain a precise result' imposed by what is now Article 43 EC, when it concluded that the principle of the free movement of services could be directly effective. The Court warned that 'the fulfilment of [this obligation] had to be made easier by, but not made dependent on, the implementation of a programme of progressive measures'. It was therefore no obstacle to direct effect. This constitutes the Court acting as a 'legislative catalyst' (Craig, 2002: 2), even though the legislative organs of the European Communities in the 1970s were not in fact quick enough to follow the Court's lead. On the contrary, throughout the 1970s and into the 1980s, the Court ploughed a largely lonely furrow, giving purposive interpretations to key Treaty provisions, such as Article 28 EC which prohibits quantitative restrictions and measures having equivalent effect on imports between Member States. In the long term, however, the approach adopted by the Court has served as a major catalyst for what has become the single market programme.

Moving away from legal effects to interpretations given to the scope of the free movement rights, the Court, in Case 8/74 *Procureur du Roi* v. *Dassonville* ([1974] ECR 837), gave a liberal interpretation to Article 28 EC which prohibits 'measures having equivalent effect' to 'quantitative restrictions' on interstate trade in goods. It held that:

> '[a]ll trading rules enacted by Member States which are capable of hindering, directly or indirectly, actually or potentially, intra-Community trade are to be considered as measures having an effect equivalent to quantitative restrictions' (para. 5).

The Court's most innovative contribution came in its formulation of the mutual recognition principle in the seminal *Cassis de Dijon* case (Case 120/78 *Rewe-Zentrale AG* v. *Bundesmonopolverwaltung für Branntwein* [1979] ECR 649). Under German law, certain liqueurs had to be of sufficient alcoholic strength to be marketed in Germany. German authorities refused to allow the importation of the French liqueur 'Cassis de Dijon' because the drink was not of sufficient alcoholic strength. Faced with the effects such disparate national regulatory schemes would have on trade between the Member States, the Court accepted that Member States were free to regulate the production and marketing of alcohol, since there were no common rules at the EU level. However, the Court concluded that such rules could in principle infringe Article 28 EC, even though they did not discriminate between national products and imported products. The Court introduced the concept of mutual recognition, noting that once a product has been lawfully produced and marketed in one Member State, there could be no valid reason why the sale of such products in any other Member State should be prohibited. In its reasoning, however, it did allow for the possibility that Member States might have reasons – what it called 'mandatory requirements', although they might be better termed 'justifications in public policy' – which would justify restrictions on the sale or marketing of a product, whether imported or domestically produced. However, a proportionality test would have to be applied. In *Cassis* an outright ban was excessive, since the objective of protecting the consumer from confusion about the amount of alcohol he or she was consuming could be achieved by the less restrictive means of labelling requirements.

In *Cassis*, the Court cited the effectiveness of fiscal supervision, the protection of public health, the fairness of commercial transactions and the defence of the consumer as reasons justifying restrictive national measures. Since *Cassis*, the Court has added the protection of the environment to the list. This approach has been termed the 'rule of reason', and it comprises a wider list of justifications for state action than Article 30 EC provides. However, the *Cassis* list of mandatory requirements can be applied only to the type of 'indistinctly applicable' measure at issue in that case, that is, the types of measures which do not differentiate on the face of it between domestic and imported products. The measures, of course, may well place a greater burden in fact on imported products which may have difficulties in complying with both the regulations in the home state of production as well as the regulations in the host state.

Although the precise reasoning in *Cassis* has not been applied explicitly to the other freedoms, it still represents the cornerstone of the EU's internal market policies, both in the Court of Justice and before the political institutions. The principle of mutual recognition has influenced many dimensions of EU internal market law. These include the general approach to harmonisation taken since the Single European Act in the context of the programme to complete the single market by 1992, and the extent to which national laws have had to be adjusted to satisfy the demands of the internal market so that they themselves have had to be amended to incorporate mutual recognition clauses in certain circumstances (3.10 below, the *Foie Gras* case). The driving force of the mutual recognition principle is a trend which commentators generally term 'deregulatory', in the sense that it has undermined some systems of national regulation, or at least required national regulators to consider again the reasons for regulating matters as diverse as the ingredients of beer or the conditions under which confectionary can be marketed.

Under each 'head' of free movement law (goods, persons, establishment, services, capital), it is accepted that the prohibitions in the Treaty can apply in principle to measures which apply equally to domestic and imported goods, services, etc. This point was made perhaps most dramatically when the Court applied the principle to the free movement of workers. In Case C-415/93 *Union Royale Belge des Sociétés de Football Association ASBL* v. *Jean-Marc Bosman* ([1995] ECR I-4921), the Court concluded that national football associations' rules on transfers restricting the freedom of contract of football players seeking to change clubs fell within the scope of the prohibition on restrictions on the free movement of workers under Article 39 EC, even though the rules did not discriminate on grounds of nationality. Although the original concern was the ability of players such as Bosman to play football for a club in another Member State (Bosman wanted to move from Belgium to France to play for another club, but was unable to secure the release of his registration from his original club in Liège), in practice the effect has been applied to the market for all out-of-contract footballers in the EU, regardless of whether they contemplate a move abroad.

In Case C-55/94 *Gebhard* v. *Consiglio dell'Ordine degli Avvocati e Procuratori di Milano* ([1995] ECR I-4165), the Court addressed the propriety of restrictions placed on a German national who was pursuing professional activities as a lawyer in Italy under the title *avvocato*, despite the fact that he was not admitted to the Milan Bar and his training, qualifications and experience had not been formally recognised in Italy. The Court reiterated its general approach that Member States may, in the absence of Community rules, justifiably subject the pursuit of self-employed activities to *bona fide* rules relating to the organisation of the profession, including its qualifications and ethical standards. However, the Court went on to develop a general principle regarding the exercise of the fundamental freedoms and the extent to which national measures can be applied:

> 'It follows, however, from the Court's case law that national measures liable to hinder or make less attractive the exercise of fundamental freedoms guaranteed by the Treaty must fulfil four conditions: they must be applied in a non-discriminatory manner; they must be justified by imperative requirements in the general interest; they must be suitable for securing the attainment of the objective which they pursue; and they must not go beyond what is necessary in order to attain it' (para. 37).

This tells national courts faced with such cases what to do once it is clear that they are dealing with a national measure which restricts one of the fundamental freedoms in a way which is caught by the Treaty. They must subject the rules to strict scrutiny in line with the principle of proportionality. The Court has tended to assume that consumers are reasonably cautious and informed, and that labelling requirements and the provision of information to consumers should generally be preferred to restrictions or bans on goods or services. What it does not provide is a decisive marker indicating in what circumstances national or local regulatory schemes conflict *in principle* with the basic concept of the integrated market which underpins the EC Treaty. The question here is not whether national schemes are *justified,* but whether they are irrelevant in any event to the task of completing the internal market, simply because their impact upon patterns of interstate trade in commodities or factor mobility is so remote. The quotation above mentions national measures 'liable to hinder or make less attractive the exercise of fundamental freedoms'. This is not, however, a clear enough jurisdictional criterion, especially when considered in relation to the free movement of goods where there has been a proliferation of cases brought at national level to challenge all manner of market regulations such as restrictions on Sunday trading or shop trading hours. In a somewhat controversial decision, the Court of Justice declared in Joined Cases C-267 and 268/91 *Criminal Proceedings against Keck and Mithouard* ([1993] ECR I-6097) that selling arrangements for goods did not come within the scope of Article 28 EC, and so did not require justification. The Court ruled, however, that the relevant selling arrangements must apply to all affected traders within the national territory and that the arrangements affect in the same manner, in law and in fact, the marketing of both domestic and imported products. The distinction between selling arrangements and other rules relating to the marketing of products is not always easy to identify with certainty, and is discussed in detail in Chapter 5. Although no decisive line can be discerned as yet from the Court's case law on goods, persons, services, establishment or capital, one influential argument, supported by academics and Advocates General in the Court of Justice, in particular Advocate General Francis Jacobs, argues that the case law is in fact 'converging around a principle of "market access" ' (Barnard and Deakin, 2002: 197):

'According to this principle, national legal measures which have the effect of either *preventing or seriously hindering* access to the home market (or a relevant part of it) from another Member State would either be *per se* illegal or would have to be justified by a version of the "rule of reason"' (emphasis in the original).

Indeed, in relation to the free movement of persons, it has been suggested recently that none of the theories generally applied in the context of goods and services, such as market access, or discrimination and double burden, satisfactorily explain the burgeoning case law. On the contrary, the Court has increasingly started to protect the European citizen 'as citizen', and not 'as mover' (Spaventa, 2004).

These ideas and the extent to which they are reflected in current Court case law will be fleshed out in the detailed chapters to come on the free movement rules which underpin the internal market concept. At this point, it is sufficient to note that the Court's case law has had a dramatic effect on the capacity of individual traders, employees, companies, etc. to challenge the conditions under which they trade, work, transact business, etc. in the national courts. As a consequence, the reach of the process of integrating markets into everyday market operations has become much more intense than could have been envisaged when the Treaties were drafted initially. The policies and methods applied to the approximation or harmonisation of national laws in the EU, although likewise envisaged as an important activity for the institutions from the inception of the integration project, have also been transformed in important ways as a result of the Court's free movement case law.

## 3.4  Policies and Methods of Harmonisation in the EU

The harmonisation of laws means the adjustment of diverse legal systems and the creation of a situation of sufficient commonality and unity between the systems to secure a given objective. Harmonisation is a means to an end, not an end in itself. When undertaken with the specific object of the completion of the internal market in view, successful harmonisation can be defined as that which removes the disparities between the national legal systems to the extent necessary to secure the unity of the market. The directive as a form of Community legislation provides a valuable mechanism for securing such a goal. Under Article 249 EC, Member States have a choice of 'form and methods' in relation to the implementation of directives, as long as the underlying goal of the directive is achieved. A directive requires Member States to achieve a particular objective, but does not impose substantive or procedural uniformity upon them. It does not rob the national systems of their sovereignty by requiring total uniformity. To do so would imply the 'unification of laws', a process which typically occurs within the sphere of international law. For example, a group of states may agree to unify an aspect of their law (e.g. the law of contract, commercial sales or carriage of goods) and agree consequently upon an international instrument (e.g. a convention or a treaty) embodying this uniform law which must then be ratified and adopted internally before taking effect.

Some aspects of the internal market programme have sought to create uniform, or even unique structures. The Commission has sought the adoption of supranational structures for doing business on an EU-wide front, sometimes referred to as 'creating a propitious environment for business cooperation'. In this context, a regulation may be a more appropriate policy instrument than a directive, since it provides a uniform and mandatory legal framework. An example of this approach is the Regulation on the European

Economic Interest Grouping (Council Regulation 2137/85, OJ 1985 L199/1) which provides a flexible form of structure for undertakings from the various Member States seeking to cooperate on a cross-national basis. This has been adopted recently in a much more moderate form after decades of controversy as the Regulation on the Statute for a European Company or *Societas Europeae* (SE) (Council Regulation 2157/2001, OJ 2001 L294/1). Interestingly enough, the provisions on worker participation which form part of the SE Statute take the form of a directive (European Parliament and Council Directive 2001/86, OJ 2001 L294/22), allowing the Member States to transpose one of a number of different options on worker participation which correspond to the different models of corporate governance in the EU. This represents a unique blend of uniformity and flexibility. It is not yet clear how or whether this will work, however, given the fact that lengthy implementation periods delayed the effect of the SE until 2004 onwards, and Member States delayed taking the necessary steps to ensure the application of the EU rules at the national level.

Harmonisation is positive integration in practice. It recognises that negative integration in the form of prohibitions upon barriers to trade in commodities or factor mobility cannot lead to total market integration. Moreover, negative integration cannot always deal with the reasons Member States might allege to resist the dismantling of certain types of rules which are restrictive of trade, namely the imperative need to protect important public interests such as health or the environment. These are precisely the derogations which the Court has allowed Member States to cite when attempting to resist the application of the prohibitions contained in the treaties. Harmonisation substitutes national rules with a uniform set of rules which incorporate interests requiring protection. Consequently, this precludes the operation of exceptions contained in Articles 30 and 46 EC, and the mandatory requirements which the Court has articulated in cases such as *Cassis*. Thus, the Court's approach is not simply deregulatory in nature, but rather it seeks to incorporate a re-regulatory approach, substituting EU-based notions of the public interest for nationally-based interests.

The EU has made use of different methods of harmonisation. In broad terms, there is a distinction between the simpler forms of harmonisation which are closest to unification and involve the substitution of diverse rules with a *uniform rule,* and various forms of *differentiated* or *flexible* harmonisation. This distinction between uniformity and flexibility reflects also deeper patterns within processes of integration in the EU, which go beyond the scope of the internal market (de Búrca and Scott, 2000).

Uniform rule harmonisation generally aims at *total* or *complete harmonisation*. The EU measure will state definitively the system for products or services throughout the EU, allowing no derogation except for safeguard measures. As a method it is inflexible, and severely restricts the powers of the Member States. One can draw a link between the manner in which such a harmonisation measure is framed and its effects under EC law. Typically, the effect of legislative harmonisation of this nature is to 'occupy the field' and to pre-empt the exercise of national competence. An example of this can be found in Case 60/86 *Commission* v. *United Kingdom (Dim-dip lighting devices)* ([1988] ECR 3921) where the Court found Council Directives 70/156 (OJ 1970 L042/1) and 76/756 (OJ 1976 L262/1), governing lighting and light-signalling devices for motor vehicles, to have exhaustively regulated the field, leaving no scope for the introduction of any different type of lighting device such as the dim-dip mechanism. The Court held that:

'Member States cannot unilaterally require manufacturers who have complied with the harmonized technical requirements set out in Directive 76/756 to comply with a requirement which is not imposed by that directive, since motor vehicles complying with the technical requirements laid down therein must be able to move freely within the common market' (para. 12).

Conversely, if the harmonisation measure operates in this way it precludes the application of general Treaty rules on free movement, thus excluding recourse to the exceptions or derogations contained in Article 30 or 46 EC.

From the early 1970s onward, Member States were disillusioned with the total harmonisation method, even though it had been seldom used. Instead, *partial* or *optional* harmonisation was chosen, both of which seek to allow two regimes to co-exist for domestic and interstate trade (Slot, 1996: 383–4). The advantage of optional harmonisation is that it leaves to the trader the choice of whether to comply with either harmonised or national standards. The advantage of complying with the harmonised standards is that this will open up access to the entire market subject to the harmonisation rules. The advantage of complying only with national standards is that this may be cheaper, and also sufficient in practice if the national standards in question are recognised in the destination market. In such a case, compliance with EU-level standards is unnecessary. Partial harmonisation only requires states to ensure protection for products traded across borders, and allows them to retain the possibility of separate standards for domestic trade.

Similarly, *minimum* harmonisation affords some degree of discretion to the national authorities. The harmonisation measure sets only minimum standards, which are mandatory, but leaves it to the national authorities to choose, if they so wish, to apply stricter standards. The distinction between total harmonisation and minimum harmonisation is neatly demonstrated by the contrast between two labelling cases: Case 148/78 *Pubblico Ministero* v. *Ratti* ([1979] ECR 1629) and Case C-11/92 *R* v. *Secretary of State for Health, ex parte Gallaher Ltd and others* ([1993] ECR I-3545).

*Ratti*, best known among EU law *cognoscenti* as the case which established the principle that the provisions of directives are capable of giving rise to rights enforceable by individuals only *after* the expiry of the deadline set for implementation, concerned the effects of Council Directive 73/173 (OJ 1973 189/7) on the labelling of solvents. This directive contained both a clause prohibiting Member States from allowing the marketing of products not complying with its labelling requirements, and a market access clause requiring access to be given to products which did comply. The directive was interpreted by the Court as setting all the parameters for the regulation of labelling, precluding Member States from imposing different or even stricter standards.

The labelling requirements at issue in *Gallaher* concerned the printing of the tar and nicotine content of cigarettes on packets in accordance with Council Directive 89/622 (OJ 1989 L359/1). The terms of the directive stated that all packets of cigarettes must carry such a notice covering *at least* 4 per cent of the package's outer surface area. Tobacco products complying with these requirements were allowed access to all national markets. The UK's implementing regulations required at least 6 per cent of the package's outer surface area to be covered with the tar and nicotine content notice, but also provided that free movement was guaranteed for those imported products which complied with the legislation of other Member States introduced to implement the directive. In other words, they imposed stricter standards for home-produced products. The Court interpreted the directive as allowing this differentiation on the part of the UK, concluding that contrary to the submissions of the applicant cigarette manufacturers, the directive did not establish a single common rule. The distinction is, significantly, a matter of *interpretation*.

A number of provisions in the EC Treaty now specifically recognise this trend. Regarding the adoption of consumer protection measures, Article 153(5) EC provides that:

'Measures adopted pursuant to [the co-decision procedure of Article 251 EC and after consulting the Economic and Social Committee] shall not prevent any Member State from maintaining or introducing more stringent protective measures. Such measures must be compatible with this Treaty.'

Similarly, Article 176 EC on environmental protection measures provides that:

'The protective measures adopted pursuant to Article 175 shall not prevent any Member State from maintaining or introducing more stringent protective measures. Such measures must be compatible with the Treaty.'

Thus, minimum harmonisation recognises explicitly the sharing of competence between the Member States and the EU. This is emblematic of current general trends against exclusivity for the EU which has been both praised and criticised (Weatherill, 1994: 23–6). For example, Weatherill and Beaumont (1999: 558) comment:

'In a sense, such provisions detract from the notion of uniformity in a common market. Yet more realistically, they reflect the notion that the Community cannot legislate in advance to cover all problems that may arise. They reflect initiatives taken at national level and suggest the development of different levels of regulatory competence in the Community.'

Alongside the greater recognition and use for minimum harmonisation are other forms of flexibility which include more use of options and derogations within directives. A good example is the Product Liability Directive (Council Directive 85/374, OJ 1985 L210/29) which introduced strict liability for defective products. This directive allowed Member States a number of choices especially in relation to the inclusion of the 'development risks' defence which allows a manufacturer to escape liability by reference to the state of scientific knowledge. Under Article 15(1)(b) of the directive, Member States have been able to exclude this defence and seek a more absolute form of strict liability (Weatherill and McGee, 1990: 582). Although the proliferation of derogations and options, not to mention the use of all manner of instruments of flexibility, does not change the fundamental character of the provisions of EU law, it does raise complex questions of interpretation for the Court of Justice, while affording greater implementation latitude to Member States. Conversely, the very flexibility may also create pitfalls for the Member States if the terms of the directive are ambiguous, or when it is unclear as to which obligations the Member States must establish and when they must be implemented. An example of this has been the Working Time Directive (Council Directive 93/104, OJ 1993 L307/18). It is often clear that variations in the regulatory pattern of directives are a product of the political trade-offs and deals which are essential both within the Council itself, especially under qualified majority voting, and among the Council, the Commission, as initiator of legislation, and the European Parliament, as co-legislator in many fields of harmonisation policy.

The principle of *subsidiarity* in Article 5 EC, despite the imprecision of the definition given in the Treaty, is a further important factor in this context. Its subsequent interpretation by the Court of Justice in cases such as the *Working Time Directive Case* (Case C-84/94 *United Kingdom* v. *Council* [1996] ECR I-5755; see de Búrca, 1998), permitting wide legislative discretion to the EU institutions, seems to suggest that, as a principle, it may add little to the terms of provisions such as Article 95 or 153 EC, which we shall examine below (3.9). All of these issues are linked to a wider debate about *differentiation* and *flexibility* within the EU (de Búrca, 2000). To what extent does the objective of the single market presuppose that there must be uniformity *throughout* the EU after harmonisation, and to what extent can a 'two-tier' or even 'multi-speed' Europe be tolerated without undermining the fundamental principles of the integration project? The Treaty of Amsterdam, as well as the amendments introduced by the Treaty of Nice, have put into place definite constitutional mechanisms for permitting institutionalised differentiation within the integration process. Since then, flexible integration even within some of the core activities of the EU is possible in principle. As the restrictions on the use of the enhanced cooperation technique will remain tight, even after they have been loosened by the Treaty of Nice, it remains unclear to what extent they will add to the existing flexibility of harmonisation policy in most fields.

Finally, distinctions may be drawn as to the degree of detail contained in harmonisation measures. The objective of harmonisation can be achieved by means of *reference to standards* established by standards' institutes rather than through the elaboration in the harmonisation measure of detailed standards by the legislature itself. This can work well in conjunction with a uniform rule which states only the basic minimal prerequisites for a given product (a 'framework directive'), leaving the detailed rules to be elaborated in the work of the standards' institutes. The result is a minimal, but nonetheless total harmonisation approach, in which there is a privatisation of the harmonisation process whereby detailed standard-setting is delegated to standards' institutes which are in fact private bodies composed of industry bodies, rather than public bodies such as regulators (see 3.7). A horizontal approach can also be applied to the harmonisation of standards appropriate to general classes of professions and products, rather than a vertical approach to specific professions or products. Such an approach is now favoured within the EU, and will be discussed in further detail in relation to the internal market programme in 3.6.

## 3.5 Harmonisation: From the Treaty of Rome to the Single European Act

Harmonisation, or as it is often termed, the approximation of laws, has been an objective of the European Community since its inception (Vignes, 1990). Article 3(1)(h) EC, which remains without amendment since 1957, calls for the activities of the Community to include:

> 'the approximation of the laws of Member States to the extent required for the functioning of the common market.'

Early harmonisation measures in the field of product standards date back to the early 1960s, when directives on food additives were introduced. Subsequently, the Member States in the Council agreed upon a systematic programme for the harmonisation of national laws in the General Programme of 28 May 1969, for the elimination of technical barriers to trade that result from disparities between the provisions laid down by law, regulation or administrative action in Member States (OJ 1969 C76/1). Up until 1984, the Council had adopted just over 150 measures, most of which were based on what was then

Article 100 EEC. This provision remains in force, since renumbered Article 94 EC, but it is no longer the most important legal basis available. It provides:

> 'The Council shall, acting unanimously on a proposal from the Commission and after consulting the European Parliament and the Economic and Social Committee, issue directives for the approximation of such laws, regulations or administrative provisions of the Member States as directly affect the establishment or functioning of the common market.'

There are two important procedural matters contained in Article 94 EC: unanimity is required in the Council, and Parliamentary input is limited to the right to be consulted. However, difficulties in achieving the adoption of proposals within the Council have run deeper than basic questions of process, and concern also the methods of harmonisation used. Typically, 'old style' harmonisation involved attempts to achieve total harmonisation, although that was only one of several methods of harmonisation envisaged in the General Programme which contemplated the use of, for example, the technique of optional harmonisation. Most of the directives adopted contain minutely detailed technical regulations dealing with every aspect of the product in question, organised around a picture of a mandatory product standard. Consequently a great deal of time was needed for the preparation, adoption and implementation of measures. Reaching a consensus with manufacturers, standards' institutes and Member States on the technical specifications to be included in a measure was often a lengthy process. Unfortunately, proposals rarely made use of whatever standards did already exist at European level (the reference-to-standards approach), and thus no attempt was made to lighten the work of the institutions by diverting some of the burden towards the European standards' institutes. Proposals often remained on the Council's agenda for a decade or more prior to adoption, or, in some cases, definitive abandonment. Even when adopted, such detailed directives could present serious implementation problems for the Member States, not to mention enforcement problems for the Commission.

Furthermore, it is often argued that measures of 'total' harmonisation risk destroying the benefits of national diversity within the EU, by creating excessive uniformity among products ('Euro-cheese'; 'Euro-sausage'). Such measures are also unreceptive to technological change, although some directives have provided for a rather cumbersome committee structure working in conjunction with the Commission under which technical standards may be changed in the light of new developments. With rapidly developing products and slow decision-making processes, however, some directives risk becoming outdated even before they are adopted. Even so, the Council has made insufficient use of the opportunity to delegate powers to the Commission to adapt directives to technical progress.

Progress towards a more flexible approach has stemmed from a number of causes. One has been the more open approach to trade liberalisation under the free movement rules. This was most clearly heralded in *Cassis de Dijon*, especially the mutual recognition principle, and in the development of the concept of mandatory requirements in *Gebhard* (3.3). The adoption of such an approach tells us that not all national rules need be harmonised to create a sufficient degree of uniformity. Only national provisions which survive scrutiny under the application of the free movement rules and the various exceptions and derogations to these rules require harmonisation. In 1983, the Council adopted Directive 83/189 (OJ 1983 L109/8) creating a 'mutual information' system which obliges Member States to notify the Commission of drafts of new technical regulations which they intend to adopt. This has enabled the Commission to maintain a better understanding of the state of technical barriers to trade within the EU, since it is premised on the principles of mutual recognition and transparency. In May 1985, the Council adopted a Resolution on a new approach to technical harmonisation and standards, which contained clear guidelines on a simpler approach based on mutual recognition and harmonisation through reference to standards in an Annex (OJ 1985 C136/1). The more flexible approach finally came to fruition with initiatives in the political sphere, and with the launch of the single market project by the Commission in 1985, under Jacques Delors' leadership which ensured that this new approach soon came to be well used.

## 3.6 The Project to Complete the Single Market

Good progress was made in the early days of the Community towards creating the Customs Union, and the Court pursued its task of interpreting and applying the free movement rules in a manner which tended to maximise the scope of EC law. However, it would have been an exaggeration to describe the European Community as a 'common market' during the period of stagnation from the mid-1960s until the mid-1980s. The tendency during that time, which saw a number of worldwide economic recessions, was towards national protectionism, and the fragmentation of the Community market through restrictive national public procurement policies in which national governments bought only national products, and commissioned only national companies for public works and services. In addition, the period witnessed the proliferation of all kinds of barriers to trade. The political relaunching of the Community came after the arrival of the first Commission headed by Jacques Delors in 1984, who sought a new meaning for the Community through a realisation of its economic underpinnings through the single market programme. The political programme was given a formal and institutional frame by the Single European Act, which introduced the aim of establishing the internal market over a period expiring on 31 December 1992, through Article 7A EEC (now Article 14 EC), and which gave the Council and the European Parliament the necessary legislative powers, in particular in the form of Article 100A EEC (now Article 95 EC), to achieve the establishment of the internal market. This provision allows measures to be adopted on the basis of a qualified majority in the Council, involving the European Parliament fully in the legislative process through the co-decision procedure of Article 251 EC. The whole programme galvanised the European integration project more generally, such that other important aspects of what is now EU policy-making, such as EMU and economic and social cohesion or regional policy, as well as the broader movement for political union, must be traced to this new beginning.

The project began with a Commission White Paper on Completing the Internal Market (COM(85) 310) which identified three types of barriers which had formed the main obstacles to the achievement of a single internal market:

- physical barriers (i.e. physical controls on persons and goods crossing borders);
- technical barriers (i.e. non-tariff barriers such as product standards, public procurement policies, etc.);
- fiscal barriers (i.e. VAT and excise duties).

This categorisation is somewhat arbitrary and was adopted mainly for convenience. It is not comprehensive. For example, it does not address directly the crucial question of the relationship between the more integrated internal market and the wider world market. The removal of physical barriers comprises four main elements: the elimination of controls on goods (e.g. checking of documentation etc.); the total harmonisation of plant and animal health controls; the abolition of controls on road transport (e.g. vehicle checks normally carried out at frontiers to be assimilated into national road safety policies and carried out in the interior of the state); and the abolition of frontier controls on persons. Physical barriers, in particular controls on persons, have been regarded as having a special symbolic significance in the context of need for the EU to be a 'People's Europe'. The removal of fiscal barriers implies shifting the place of taxation away from the frontier and achieving the degree of harmonisation of VAT and excise rates required to prevent distortions of competition when internal frontiers are removed. The category of technical barriers comprises a wide range of potential barriers to trade requiring a variety of flexible legislative responses. These include:

- technical and product standards;
- national rules on public procurement;
- restrictions on the free movement of persons, services and capital;
- liberalisation of transport policy;
- creating suitable conditions for cooperation between businesses;
- removal of barriers formed by the national basis of laws governing industrial and intellectual property.

The original White Paper identified some 300 measures which were listed in a detailed timetable annexed to the body of the report. In fact, since that time more than 1500 measures have been adopted which can be associated in some respect with the single market programme. By 1990, the Commission claimed to have presented all the necessary proposals, and the legislative onus fell principally on the Council and the Parliament. By autumn 1992, over 90 per cent of the proposals had been adopted, but residual difficulties lay (and indeed still lie) in pressure points such as the abolition of all frontier controls on persons, indirect taxation and company law. This has meant that not only could the 1992 programme not have been completed in its entirety by the end of that key year, but that even now, some 15 years later, gaps in the regulatory system are still evident in fields such as taxation. The continued application of unanimous voting in the Council has been the crucial obstacle, an obstacle that in the context of the work of the Convention on the Future of Europe and its preparation of a draft Treaty establishing a Constitution for Europe, the Member States showed no inclination to remove. Chapters 5–7 will offer more detailed coverage of the extent to which the internal market as a 'regulatory project' is complete, especially in some of the more troublesome areas, as well as provide a sketch of some of the success stories. The following section elaborates on the so-called new approach to harmonisation which has provided a framework for many of these successes.

### 3.7    Applying the New Approach to Harmonisation

What distinguished the work on the 1992 programme from other attempts to relaunch the integration process was not only the political will to succeed, but also the adoption of new techniques in the legislative domain to make that will a reality. In terms of legislative technique, the harmonisation programme embarked upon represents a break with the past, employing the full range of more flexible options which were outlined in 3.4. This is best evidenced in the approach taken to removing technical barriers, especially divergent national technical and product standards, where recourse was made to various aspects of a new approach to harmonisation, including reference to standards, minimum harmonisation measures, and increased acceptance of options and derogations within directives. Moreover, harmonisation has been undertaken only where necessary. If mutual recognition will suffice, then harmonisation will be unnecessary. Although termed the 'new' approach, its heritage can be traced to a much earlier directive, concerned with low voltage electrical equipment, which adopted very much the same approach to harmonisation (Council Directive 73/23, OJ 1973 L77/29).

The principles of harmonisation are stated in the Council's Resolution of 7 May 1985, on a new approach to technical harmonisation (OJ 1985 C136/1). This Resolution limits legislative harmonisation to the setting out of 'essential safety requirements (or other requirements in the general interest) with which products put on the market must conform'. Technical standards-setting will be delegated to organisations specialising in this work, and remain voluntary, although compliance with a technical standard set by such a body will provide conclusive evidence that a particular product complies also with the essential requirements contained in the directive, and is therefore to be guaranteed freedom of movement throughout the EU. For this system to work, the essential requirements need to be sufficiently detailed and sufficiently clear to allow them to be applied by the national authorities. Manufacturers may also prove compliance with the directive by demonstrating that their products satisfy the essential requirements by some means other than by satisfying the technical standards set by the standards' institutes. In practice, of course, there will be a great deal of pressure on manufacturers to comply with such standards which is often the most cost-effective way of achieving free movement.

An example of the new approach in operation is the Toy Safety Directive (Council Directive 88/378, OJ 1988 L187/1), implemented in the UK as the Toy (Safety) Regulations made under the Consumer Protection Act of 1989 (SI 1989, No. 1275). Evidence of the existence of EU-wide safety standards for toys can be seen in the form of the 'CE' mark which is affixed to toys which comply with these standards and which benefit automatically from the right of free movement. Pursuant to the principle that goods in free circulation should be treated the same as goods of EU-origin, third country products which have been lawfully marketed in one Member States should be able to circulate freely within other Member States provided they satisfy the essential requirements.

Clearly the new approach has had significant advantages. It is much faster and simpler than the traditional approach, enabling the Council and the European Parliament to adopt many more sectoral directives than previously, rather than directives confined to specific products or professions. In addition, it avoids excessive standardisation and uniformity, while encouraging diversity and competition within the traditional methods of manufacture, for example, the different ways of making cheese. New harmonisation directives are much easier for the Member States to implement, and thus the Commission's supervisory tasks are made easier. However, it should not be thought that the new approach is entirely without problems.

For example, there have been doubts as to whether there are at the EU-level already sufficiently coherent consumer and health protection policies to substitute for existing national policies, or whether it is not in fact the case that harmonisation on the basis of essential requirements is actually detrimental to the interests of the consumer in the sense that harmonisation undermines the high safety standards which have been achieved in some Member States. There are concerns that since harmonisation of essential safety standards is taking place within the confines of what is a market liberalisation programme, consumer safety may be sacrificed in the interests of short-term economic gains as a result of pressure from commercial interests. The structure of the new approach to harmonisation encourages manufacturers to find cheaper and more efficient ways of satisfying the essential requirements, but in practice this approach may undercut the standards already adopted as the result of consumer group pressure, particularly in the more safety-conscious Member States. In such circumstances there may be a conflict between the public interest and free trade.

There may also be problems resulting from the transfer of functions to the standardisation bodies. Under the new approach, the establishing of minimum requirements and the setting of standards have been separated, with the latter function passing to European standards' bodies which group together the national standards' bodies. The most significant of these are CEN (the *Comité Européen de Normalisation*), CENELEC (the *Comité Européen de Normalisation Electrotechnique*) and ETSI (European Telecommunications Standards Institute). Taking into account the current state of technical knowledge, the standards set by these organisations can be changed without amending the relevant directives.

Arguably the new approach consists of replacing national legal rules with privately determined EU standards. This raises problems of accountability. CEN and CENELEC are private associations incorporated under Belgian law, while ETSI is headquartered in France. Is it permissible, or even desirable, for the EU to delegate a power to make standards to such bodies, given that their decisions are not easily subject to judicial control? The mutual recognition approach results in a division of powers between the public and private spheres which may be problematic from the perspective of the protection of individual rights. Furthermore, who controls the standard-setters? The Commission claims that it can ensure that standards conform to the requirements of the individual directives, and that there is no major problem because the standards are voluntary. This is disingenuous on the part of the Commission. The standards are not easily characterised as justiciable, because they are privately determined, but they are quasi-mandatory because of the legal and factual benefits which they can confer.

While it may be faster and simpler for the Council and the European Parliament, assisted by the Commission, to adopt harmonisation measures under the new approach, the actual standards-setting process remains as time-consuming and labour-intensive as ever. It simply now takes place within a private arena, namely that of the European standardisation bodies. As a consequence, legislative stagnation within the EU legislature has been replaced, to a certain extent, by a bottleneck within CEN, CENELEC and similar standardisation organisations (Chalmers *et al*, 2006: 491–7).

Undoubtedly, the effectiveness of the standardisation element in the new approach to harmonisation can be enhanced by the development of a comprehensive EU policy on standardisation. Indeed, the Commission has worked steadily, if sometimes slowly, towards this goal. In more recent years, the role of oversight of standardisation efforts, as well as the task of managing and developing the *acquis* in relation to internal market measures more generally, has passed from the Internal Market Directorate-General

(MARKT) to the Directorate-General for Enterprise and Industry (ENTR). The Council's core statement of policy dates from 1999 (OJ 1999 C141/1), when it confirmed in a Resolution that: 'standardisation is a voluntary, consensus-driven activity, carried out by and for the interested parties themselves, based on openness and transparency, within independent and recognised standards organisations, leading to the adoption of standards compliance with which is voluntary.' In a 2004 Communication on the role of European standardisation in the framework of European policies and legislation (COM(2004) 674), the Commission positioned its standardisation policy within the broader framework of the EU's policies to engage in 'better regulation', which is more efficient and focused on its tasks. This has been an important broad motif of post-1992 internal market policies, which will be discussed in more detail in 3.11.

## 3.8   Beyond Harmonisation: Mutual Recognition and the Exchange of Information

Aside from harmonisation, the single market programme also comprises a range of complementary measures, many concerned with either procedural questions and the exchange of information, or with buttressing the mutual recognition principle which underpins the entire legal edifice. A 2002 Commission report on mutual recognition estimated the value of trade within the EU which is covered by the mutual recognition principle at approximately €430 billion annually (COM(2002) 419). The same report suggests that mutual recognition operates well for products which pose few safety problems, such as bicycles, storage tanks and containers. Less well-served by the principle of mutual recognition are technically complex products, such as buses, lorries, construction materials and products produced from precious metals, as well as products which can pose safety or health problems, such as food supplements and nutritionally fortified products. Often this is because national administrations are unfamiliar with the principle as a result of a lack of information, the absence or refusal of dialogue, or the lack of administrative cooperation. The Commission's 2001 Report on the functioning of Community product and capital markets (COM(2001) 736) concluded that non-application of the mutual recognition principle decreased trade within the EU by up to €150 billion in 2000.

This does not mean that there is an absence of general mechanisms concerned with mutual recognition and the exchange of information which should assist national administrations. On the contrary, under the General Product Safety Directive (European Parliament and Council Directive 2001/95, OJ 2002 L11/4, replacing Council Directive 92/59, OJ 1992 L 228/24) products are presumed to be safe, in the absence of EU rules governing their safety, so long as they are manufactured in accordance with national standards and rules. European standards are also important in demonstrating the question of safety. Safety in these terms means that a product can circulate freely in the internal market, although Member States can take steps to prevent access to the market in circumstances where the product is dangerous. If a Member State does this, it must inform the Commission of its actions. If the risk is not confined to the territory of the Member State, it must also use the Community Rapid Information System (RAPEX) introduced by Council Decision 84/133 (OJ 1984 L 70/16) to inform the Commission and the other Member States about the risk arising from the use of consumer products and the reasons for taking action. *Ex post* notification of national measures which may undermine the free movement of goods is also required under European Parliament and Council Decision 3052/95 (OJ 1995 L321/1) establishing a procedure for the exchange of information on national measures derogating from the principle of the free movement of goods within the Community, and Council Regulation 2679/98 (OJ 1998 L 337/8) on the functioning of the internal market in relation to the free movement of goods among the Member States, which even requires Member States to notify the Commission about *private* measures, for example motorway blockades, which might interfere with the functioning of the internal market. The origins of this regulation lay in an important Court of Justice case, the so-called *Strawberries* decision (Case C-265/95 *Commission* v. *France (French Farmers)* [1997] ECR I-6959) in which the Court held that the French Government was in breach of Article 28 EC when it failed to take sufficient measures to prevent *private* sabotage actions by French farmers which resulted in the regular destruction of agricultural produce from the UK and Spain. France had failed to take adequate measures to protect the free movement of goods insofar as they had failed sufficiently to police these matters, or to prosecute offenders.

The new approach to harmonisation, and indeed the whole standardisation approach, is complemented by use of the *prior* notification system under European Parliament and Council Directive 98/34 (OJ 1998 L204/37), replacing Council Directive 83/189 (see 3.5). In an important clarification, the Court of Justice held in Case C-194/94 *CIA Security International SA* v. *Signalson SA and Securitel SPRL* ([1996] ECR I-2201) that technical regulations which a Member State had failed to notify to the Commission in accordance with the directive's procedures cannot be enforced against a third party in a national court. In Case C-443/98 *Unilever Italia SpA* v. *Central Food* ([2000] ECR I-7535), the Court also found that a notified provision brought into force without regard to the standstill provision in Article 9 of the directive is likewise unenforceable against an individual.

Mutual recognition applies to services as much as it does to goods. It has been particularly significant in the area of financial services, where the basis of a single banking licence for operation throughout the EU was established by legislation. Similarly, the new approach to recognising professional qualifications marks a departure from old-style vertical regulation to a horizontal approach based on the presumed equivalence of national qualifications coupled with supplementary measures to protect consumers and the reputation of the professions.

## 3.9  The Institutional Environment for Developing the Internal Market: A Focus on Article 95 EC

This section concentrates upon the institutional environment for internal market measures offered by the application of Article 95 EC and its interaction with a number of other key provisions.

Article 95 EC provides, in part:

1. By way of derogation from Article 94 and save where otherwise provided in this Treaty, the following provisions shall apply for the achievement of the objectives set out in Article 14. The Council shall, acting in accordance with the procedure referred to in Article 251 and after consulting the Economic and Social Committee, adopt the measures for the approximation of the provisions laid down by law, regulation or

administrative action in Member States which have as their object the establishment and functioning of the internal market.

2. Paragraph 1 shall not apply to fiscal provisions, to those relating to the free movement of persons nor to those relating to the rights and interests of employed persons.

3. The Commission, in its proposals envisaged in paragraph 1 concerning health, safety, environmental protection and consumer protection, will take as a base a high level of protection, taking account in particular of any new development based on scientific facts. Within their respective powers, the European Parliament and the Council will also seek to achieve this objective.

This provision was introduced originally in the Single European Act and amended subsequently by the Treaty of Maastricht, which introduced co-decision in lieu of the cooperation procedure, and the Treaty of Amsterdam. The latter amendments concern particularly the derogation arrangements for Member States discussed below.

A number of important factors distinguish Article 95 EC from Article 94 EC. First, there is no reference to a direct effect upon the establishment of the internal market. Second, Article 95 EC envisages the adoption of measures in pursuit of the objectives set out in that provision, whereas Article 94 EC restricts the Council to adopting directives. Finally, and in this respect Article 94 EC is the broader power, Article 95(2) EC excludes certain key areas in which harmonisation may be necessary for the attainment of the internal market from the application of the provisions of Article 95(1) EC. This exclusion has been particularly important in respect of fiscal measures, especially since the Treaty of Amsterdam both established a specific chapter of the EC Treaty relating to the free movement of persons and significantly strengthened the social policy provisions of the Treaty. For fiscal measures the alternative legal basis is Article 93 EC, which likewise requires the achievement of unanimity within the Council, but which has not been amended by any of the subsequent Treaties.

The nature of Article 95 EC as a legal basis has given rise to considerable debate, both in terms of its relationship with other overlapping law-making powers, and in terms of where the overall limits of Community competence are set in relation to the completion of the internal market. The latter question will be dealt with in 3.10.

In Case C-300/89 *Commission* v. *Council (Titanium Dioxide)* ([1991] ECR I-2867) the Commission, with the support of the Parliament, successfully challenged the Council's decision to rely upon what was then Article 130S EEC (now Article 175 EC) as the legal basis for Council Directive 89/428 (OJ 1989 L19/16) approximating national programmes for the reduction and eventual elimination of pollution caused by waste in the production of titanium dioxide. At the time of its adoption, Article 130S EEC involved a unanimous decision of the Council after mere *consultation* with the Parliament. The motive of the Court's judgment may have been to protect the integrity and effectiveness of the legislative procedure, since Article 100A required at the time the application of the cooperation procedure. However, the effect of the Court's decision appeared to be also to emphasise the Community's internal market objective over its other objectives, and, arguably, to destroy the effect of the saving words in Article 95(1) EC – 'save where otherwise provided in this Treaty' (Crosby, 1991). In a later case on the Waste Directive, the Court concluded in favour of the use of Article 130S EEC, since the chief purpose of the directive was to safeguard the environment through the efficient management of waste, rather than to facilitate free movement and the creation of the internal market (Case

C-155/91 *Commission* v. *Council (Waste Directive)* [1993] ECR I-939). According to Craig (2002: 17), the 'general test propounded by the ECJ for the resolution of such boundary disputes was that regard should be had to the nature, aim, and content of the act in question'.

The permissible intensity of measures adopted on the basis of what is now Article 95 EC has likewise been the subject of litigation before the Court. For example, Article 9 of Directive 92/50 on general product safety (since replaced by Directive 2001/95, see 3.8), established a procedure whereby the Commission could take temporary measures to ensure the free movement of a product whenever one or more Member States had taken restrictive measures. The temporary measures could take the form of decisions addressed to the Member States. The Court rejected an argument put forward by Germany that Article 95 EC could not be used as the valid legal basis for a provision allowing for such individual measures (Case C-359/92 *Germany* v. *Council (General Product Safety)* [1994] ECR I-3681). It also rejected Germany's argument that the possibility of introducing such measures violated the general principle of proportionality established under Article 5 EC.

When Article 100A EEC was first introduced, it was expected that its most controversial part would have been paragraph 4 since it attracted a great deal of critical attention from commentators (see especially Pescatore, 1987). Article 100A(4) EEC allowed Member States to retain national measures on grounds of major needs referred to in what was then Article 36 EEC (now Article 30 EC) such as public health. In addition, Article 100A(4) EEC included national provisions 'relating to the protection of the environment or the working environment', although it allowed the Commission to manage such derogations by bringing alleged infringements before the Court of Justice via a truncated infringement procedure. This provision was introduced as part of the trade-off for the introduction of qualified majority voting into Article 95 EC in order to facilitate the internal market programme (Ehlermann, 1987: 389). Yet, the concept of a real trade-off largely ended when the politicians left the negotiating table. Article 95 EC as a whole has been a significant launching pad for the entire integration process, not just the internal market programme. On the other hand, paragraph 4 has been relied upon only sparingly, with very few authorisations being sought or given. In 1994, the Court confirmed that it would place a narrow interpretation on the scope of these provisions (Case C-41/93 *France* v. *Commission (PCP)* [1994] ECR I-1829). The Court annulled a decision which would have allowed Germany to continue to apply certain national provisions, on the grounds that the decision was inadequately reasoned. In addition to confirming the narrow scope of the exceptions permissible under Article 95(4) EC, the Court emphasised the need for the Commission to exercise proper supervision over the Member States and reinforced its own right to control the Commission's supervisory powers.

One of the problems with the pre-Amsterdam procedure was the fact that if the Commission did not respond to the request, the Member State was precluded from applying its legislation. This point was made very clearly in Case C-319/97 *Kortas* ([1999] ECR I-3143), where the Court rejected an argument made by Sweden regarding what it considered to be the Commission's failure to reply within a reasonable time to its notification of certain measures derogating from a directive on additives in confectionery. To conclude otherwise, said the Court, could undermine the effectiveness of the harmonisation process. The effects of *Kortas* are limited, however, since it was decided after the conclusion of the Treaty of Amsterdam, but before its May 1999 entry into force. The amendments to Article 95 EC are therefore quite important in this respect. The derogation provisions are now set out in more detail in paragraphs 4 through 9 of Article 95 EC, distinguishing between two situations in which a Member State retains in force *existing* provisions (Article 95(4) EC) or purports to introduce certain types of *new* measures based on new scientific evidence (Article 95(5) EC):

4. If, after the adoption by the Council or by the Commission of a harmonisation measure, a Member State deems it necessary to maintain national provisions on grounds of major needs referred to in Article 30, or relating to the protection of the environment or the working environment, it shall notify the Commission of these provisions as well as the grounds for maintaining them.

5. Moreover, without prejudice to paragraph 4, if, after the adoption by the Council or by the Commission of a harmonisation measure, a Member State deems it necessary to introduce national provisions based on new scientific evidence relating to the protection of the environment or the working environment on grounds of a problem specific to that Member State arising after the adoption of the harmonisation measure, it shall notify the Commission of the envisaged provisions as well as the grounds for introducing them.

6. The Commission shall, within six months of the notifications as referred to in paragraphs 4 and 5, approve or reject the national provisions involved after having verified whether or not they are a means of arbitrary discrimination or a disguised restriction on trade between Member States and whether or not they shall constitute an obstacle to the functioning of the internal market.

   In the absence of a decision by the Commission within this period the national provisions referred to in paragraphs 4 and 5 shall be deemed to have been approved.

   When justified by the complexity of the matter and in the absence of danger for human health, the Commission may notify the Member State concerned that the period referred to in this paragraph may be extended for a further period of up to six months.

7. When, pursuant to paragraph 6, a Member State is authorised to maintain or introduce national provisions derogating from a harmonisation measure, the Commission shall immediately examine whether to propose an adaptation to that measure.

8. When a Member State raises a specific problem on public health in a field which has been the subject of prior harmonisation measures, it shall bring it to the attention of the Commission which shall immediately examine whether to propose appropriate measures to the Council.

9. By way of derogation from the procedure laid down in Articles 226 and 227, the Commission and any Member State may bring the matter directly before the Court of Justice if it considers that another Member State is making improper use of the powers provided for in this Article.

The post-Amsterdam procedure, although a little more cumbersome, allows a better balancing of the national and EU interests and has been successfully invoked by the Member States on a number of occasions (for detailed analysis see de Sadeleer, 2003).

### 3.10    The Court of Justice and EU Competence in Relation to the Internal Market

In 3.3, the focus of the discussion was upon the strengths and weaknesses of the Court's contributions to the EU's internal market programme. The significance of the Court's decision in *Keck* was not so much that it represented a hindrance to the momentum of market construction, but rather that it sought to focus attention upon the main objective of the mutual recognition principle, namely the bulk of national technical regulations related to products as well as services. Craig (2002: 35) asserts that it seems relatively unimportant that certain types of selling arrangements might escape the prohibition of quantitative restrictions under Article 28 EC and instead fall outside the scope of EU law. On the contrary, perhaps the Court's most important contribution in recent years to the effectiveness of the mutual recognition principle has been its relatively overlooked decision in the *Foie Gras* case (Case C-184/96 *Commission* v. *France* [1998] ECR I-6197). The Court upheld the Commission's argument that French law imposing requirements for the composition of *foie gras* ought to contain a mutual recognition clause *explicitly* permitting *foie gras* lawfully marketed in another Member State to be marketed in France.

Regarding the scope of EU competence in relation to the internal market, the Court's most significant contribution has come from its decision in the *Tobacco Advertising* case (Case C-376/98 *Germany* v. *Parliament and Council* [2000] ECR I-8419). Germany challenged the adoption of a directive banning tobacco advertising on the basis of Article 95 EC, arguing that it was a public health measure masquerading as an internal market measure. It was clear that public health concerns were uppermost in the minds of those who adopted the measure, and that this impacted upon the assessment of the market impacts of the measure. In brief, the Court held that the effects of the measure in harmonising conditions of competition or facilitating trade between Member States were too minor and uncertain to justify its adoption under Article 95 EC. The real problem lay in the fact that the ban on tobacco advertising was too broad. It extended not only to mobile media and sponsorship, but also to static advertising such as billboards where the cross-border impact on trade of having diverse national regulations was negligible and there was no significant risk of distorting competition. In other words, the Court took seriously the requirement that measures adopted under Article 95 EC must 'have as their object the establishment and functioning of the internal market'. Consequently, the Court severely restricted the possibility that other policies could be constructed on the back of Article 95 EC. Of course, it remains the case that so long as a measure genuinely aims at promoting the establishment and functioning of the internal market, its validity will not be undermined by the fact that it might *also* aim at promoting public health. To conclude otherwise would be to render the mandate contained in Article 95(3) EC requiring the Commission to have regard to a high level of health protection in its proposals nugatory.

### 3.11    The Internal Market after 1992

Few believed that the completion of the internal market would have been accomplished by the target date of 31 December 1992. Since then, however, the focus has shifted in a number of different ways. First, there is a stronger emphasis on monitoring and evaluation (3.12). Secondly, the internal market is seen ever-increasingly as an evolving and dynamic project, rather than a definable end. Thirdly, there has been a reconceptualisation of the internal market which is viewed now in the light of a diverse number of broadly related agendas. The internal market is not in itself an agenda for deregulation, and for the releasing of market forces. It is closely allied to other 'flanking' objectives and policies relating to consumer protection, the protection of the environment, and social and employment affairs. Progress in the internal market needs to be viewed, for example, in the light of the Commission's strategies on consumer policy, which is managed by a different Directorate-General (see COM(2002) 208, Consumer Policy Strategy 2002–2006). There is also now a distinct strand within internal market policy focusing on economic reform, and hence the reform of markets themselves, which are reviewed regularly under what is known as the Cardiff review process (see COM(2001) 736). The European Council's spring meeting focuses on economic reform and competitiveness, issues which have become increasingly urgent in light of evidence which suggests that a worldwide recession may severely affect some Member States more than others. This focus on markets, however, has to be seen in light of the Lisbon agenda, which is to make the European Union the world's most competitive economy *because of*, and not *despite*, the protection and maintenance of the European social and welfare model.

Fourthly, internal market policy-making now encompasses quite explicitly a broader range of policy instruments, including both soft and hard law. Since 1993, there has been a proliferation of action programmes, strategy papers and policy documents, of both a general and sectoral nature. The general tenor of such documents is to laud the progress that has been made, especially in terms of its contribution to prosperity and to individual liberty, but to refer in terms of ever greater urgency to the areas where progress has been slow. In addition, the Commission has begun to focus more closely upon adjustments needed to maintain the dynamism of the internal market in an enlarged EU. Finally, in a linked move, the internal market has been one area subjected to review in terms of the simplification of instruments and better law-making, in order to facilitate transparency and the legitimacy of governance arrangements.

The 1999 Internal Market Strategy (COM(1999) 624) identified four strategic aims, namely modernising markets, improving the conditions for doing business, meeting citizens' needs in relation to the internal market, and anticipating the effects of enlargement. It is now well accepted that high levels of consumer confidence, as well as a commitment to focusing on the needs of business, are essential to the success of the internal market.

Among the sectors where current regulatory measures are receiving particular attention is the area of financial services, where 32 out of 42 measures contained in an action plan (COM(1999) 232) have been adopted. To a certain extent, this success story offsets the bleak assessment of the Commission's recent internal market strategy document for 2003–2006 (COM(2003) 238):

'Considerable differences in regulation from one Member State to the next – and the lack of confidence in each others' regulatory systems – are the main reason why free movement of services has so far been more a legal concept than a practical reality. Because of the complex and intangible nature of many services and the importance of the know-how and qualifications of the service provider – they are generally subject to more wide-ranging and complex legal rules than goods.'

In addition, in an effort to improve the conditions for conducting business within the EU, the 2003 strategy document focuses on the removal of tax obstacles, ensuring high-quality network industries, and improving the opportunities for cross-border public procurement, which will benefit both governments and consumers. The Commission argues that the role of such a strategy, with its review and monitoring procedures, 'is to provide decision-makers with a road map' for the short to medium-term, and 'to show how the different actions fit together' (COM(2002) 171). It also frequently talks of having fewer, but more realistic and realisable targets for its activities, although admittedly the achievement of these targets rests with the Council, the European Parliament and the Member States. In practice, although the emphasis of the action plans and strategy documents has changed somewhat over the years since the expiry of the 1992 deadline, especially in response to renewed emphasis at the strategic European Council level on economic reform, many of the same obstacles remain, such as the impossibility of achieving a better taxation environment because of the persistence of the requirement of unanimity in the Council.

## 3.12　Application and Enforcement of Internal Market Law

The application and enforcement of EU law is one of the principal tasks of the Commission in the exercise of its role as 'Guardian of the Treaties' under Article 211 EC. Each year it issues a general report on monitoring the application of Community law. The Commission's most recent report is its XXIIIrd Annual Report on monitoring the application of Community law for 2005, published on 24 July 2006 (COM(2006) 416). In a number of fields, however, including the internal market, there are specific targets and monitoring exercises concerned with the application of EU law. The European Council's spring meeting now sets transposition targets for internal market directives, and the Commission issues 'scoreboards' every six months which assess progress against these targets. For example, the general target in 2003 was to have 1.5 per cent or fewer unimplemented directives by the Member States at the time the deadline passes for implementation. In circumstances where the deadline for implementation of directives has expired more than two years previously, the target is 100 per cent implementation. After a number of years of steady progress, the biannual scoreboard witnessed its first increase in the 'implementation deficit' in May 2003 although a gradual improvement could be discerned again by 2005. By the end of 2005, the Commission was reporting that the implementation deficit in single market legislation had reached an average of 1.6 per cent across the Member States, slightly above the 1.5 per cent target, but the lowest recorded percentage nonetheless.

Non-implementation of directives is not the only difficulty which the Commission encounters with the enforcement process. It also finds that it has a steady increase in infringement proceedings under Article 226 EC, whenever Member States fail to fulfil an obligation under the Treaty, even after a judgment has been handed down by the Court of Justice. Often such cases can take up to four years to come before the Court. Consequently, the Commission has identified alternative mechanisms for resolving disputes concerning internal market issues, in its 2002 Communication on Better Monitoring of the Application of Community Law (COM(2002) 725). It decides on a case-by-case basis whether to use formal infringement proceedings, or more informal mechanisms such as the SOLVIT network. SOLVIT is an on-line problem-solving network in which EU Member States work together to resolve problems caused by the misapplication of internal market law by public authorities. There is also a SOLVIT centre in every Member State where citizens and business can receive help with handling complaints. Initial results, published in May 2003, showed that SOLVIT resolved more than 70 per cent of its cases, many within the 10 week target deadline.

# Summary

1.  This chapter summarises the main outlines of the law of the internal market. It provides background to the detailed discussion of the individual economic freedoms discussed in subsequent chapters.

2.  The EC Treaty regulates the free movement of goods, services, persons and capital, requiring the Member States to liberalise cross-border trade in each of these areas. In each case, free movement is subject to a number of derogations relating to public policy matters. This constitutes negative integration.

3.  The Court of Justice has played an important role in the development of EU free movement law. It has long held that the key provisions of the EC Treaty can be enforced directly by individual economic actors in national courts – i.e. they have direct effect. It has taken a teleological approach to the interpretation of the scope of the free movement provisions, which has tended to restrict the capacity of Member States to regulate many aspects of the marketplace, such as product composition or the circumstances in which services may be marketed.

4.  Although there are no strictly common principles applicable across the different heads of free movement law (goods, services, persons, capital), in practice the law has tended to converge around principles such as market access and non-discrimination, protecting traders from outside the domestic market.

5.  Harmonisation of national laws is an important tool of positive integration. Harmonisation can take a number of different forms, and can allow greater or lesser degrees of divergence among the national laws which are harmonised or approximated. Recently, the trend has been towards more flexible instruments of harmonisation, especially under the aegis of the programme to complete the EU's single market by the end of 1992.

6.  The project to complete the internal market by 1992 was an important step towards the relaunching of the EU's integration project, which had been stalling since the 1970s. The political and economic project was combined with institutional reforms through the Single European Act, making it easier for the Council of Ministers to adopt harmonisation legislation by means of a qualified majority vote.

7.  The single market programme was associated with a 'new approach' to harmonisation under which the EU institutions were able to adopt broader, more sectorally-based directives, relying also upon the elaboration of EU-level standards by standards-setting bodies such as CEN and CENELEC. The EU's approach has often been characterised as re-regulatory, rather than purely deregulatory, as it often replaces national rules with EU-level rules which deal with public policy concerns about safety, consumer protection or the environment.

8.  Other mechanisms to promote the functioning of the internal market include the principle of mutual recognition and the development of regulatory techniques, requiring the Member States to exchange information with the European Commission.

9.  Article 95 EC was introduced by the Single European Act and is the most important legal basis for the adoption of internal market measures. It includes important derogation mechanisms upon which the Member States can rely in limited circumstances to protect national legislation. Article 95 EC is limited to legislation related directly to the achievement of the internal market and cannot be used to construct EU-level policies on, for example, the protection of public health.

## Summary cont'd

**10.** Since 1992, the European Commission has continued the ongoing challenge of developing the internal market, less through new legislation adopted by the Council of Ministers and the European Parliament, and more often through monitoring and seeking the application and enforcement of existing legislation.

## Exercises

1. Why did the Court of Justice conclude that the basic free movement principles contained in the EC Treaty have direct effect? What could have been the consequence of it deciding that these principles did not have direct effect?

2. What are the main strengths and weaknesses of the Court's approach?

3. What is meant by 'harmonisation of laws'? Why does the EU have a policy of the harmonisation of national legislation in the internal market field?

4. From the perspective of approaches to harmonisation, what was significant about the programme to complete the single market by the end of 1992?

5. What pitfalls have arisen in relation to the completion of this project, and where have the main obstacles arisen?

6. Why has Article 95 EC proved to be such an important institutional innovation for the EU?

## Further Reading

Barnard, C. (2004) *The Substantive Law of the EU: The Four Freedoms*, Oxford: Oxford University Press. See especially chapter 1.

Chalmers, D. *et al* (2006) *European Union Law*, Cambridge: Cambridge University Press. See especially chapter 11.

Craig, P. (2002) 'The Evolution of the Single Market', in Barnard, C. and Scott, J. (eds.), *The Law of the Single European Market: Unpacking the Premises*, Oxford: Hart Publishing.

Craig, P. and de Búrca, G. (2003) *EU Law: Text, Cases and Materials*, (3rd edn), Oxford: Oxford University Press. See especially chapter 28.

Dougan, M. (2000) 'Minimum Harmonization and the Internal Market', 37 *Common Market Law Review* 853.

Mortelmans, K. (1998) 'The Common Market, the Internal Market and the Single Market, What's in a Market?', 35 *Common Market Law Review* 101.

Mortelmans, K. (2002) 'The Relationship between the Treaty Rules and Community Measures for the Establishment and Functioning of the Internal Market – Towards a Concordance Rule', 39 *Common Market Law Review* 1303.

Oliver, P. and Roth, W.H. (2004) 'The Internal Market and the Four Freedoms', 41 *Common Market Law Review* 407.

De Sadeleer, N. (2003) 'Procedures for Derogations from the Principle of Approximation of Laws under Article 95 EC', 40 *Common Market Law Review* 889.

Spaventa, E. (2004) 'From *Gebhard* to *Carpenter*: Towards a (Non)-Economic European Constitution', 41 *Common Market Law Review* 743.

Weatherill, S. (2006) *Cases and Materials on EU Law* (7th edn), Oxford: Oxford University Press. See especially chapter 19.

<u>**Further Reading cont'd**</u>

Young, A. (2005) 'The Single Market', in Wallace, H., Wallace, W. and Pollack, M. (eds.), *Policy-Making in the European Union* (5th edn), Oxford: Oxford University Press.

# Key Websites

A comprehensive website focusing on virtually all aspects of the internal market is available at:
**http://www.europa.eu/comm/internal_market/index_en.htm**

The European Committee for Standardisation (*Comité Européen de Normalisation – CEN*) is the organisation which contributes to the objectives of the European Union by promoting voluntary technical standards in support of internal market policies. Their website is available at:
**http://www.cen.ee**

A similar organisation, operating in the field of electrotechnical standards, is the European Committee for Electrotechnical Standardization (*Comité Européen de Normalisation Electrotechnique – CENELEC*). Their website is available at:
**http://www.cenelec.org**

A third organisation producing telecommunications standards is the European Telecommunications Standards Institute (ETSI). Their website is available at:
**http://www.etsi.org**

The website for SOLVIT, the European Union's problem-solving network is available at:
**http://europa.eu/solvit/site/index_en.htm**

The website for the European Union's Scoreboard approach to completing the internal market is available at:
**http://ec.europa.eu/internal_market/score/index_en.htm**

The website for the European Commission's Directorate-General on Enterprise and Industry is available at:
**http://www.europa.eu/comm/enterprise/index_en.htm**

Providing information on the New Approach to technical harmonisation and the Global Approach to conformity assessment, legislation and standardisation is the New Approach website available at:
**http://www.europa.eu/comm/enterprise/newapproach/index_en.htm**

The New Approach Standardisation in the Internal Market website is available at:
**http://www.newapproach.org**

The European Commission's website on the Application of Community Law is available at:
**http://ec.europa.eu/community_law/eulaw/index_en.htm**

# Chapter 4

# The Customs Union

Introduction

Our discussion of the substantive fields of EU economic law begins with one narrow segment: the rules governing the external and internal operation of the customs union. The customs union is described and explained in Article 23(1) EC:

'The Community shall be based upon a customs union which shall cover all trade in goods and which shall involve the prohibition between Member States of customs duties on imports and exports and of all charges having equivalent effect, and the adoption of a common customs tariff in their relations with third countries.'

This chapter covers two topics:

▶ a description of the workings of the common customs tariff (CCT) imposed on imports of goods *into* the EU (the *external* dimension of the customs union), and
▶ an analysis of the principles under which tariff barriers and so-called 'charges having equivalent effect to a customs duty' (CHEEs) have been eliminated *between* the Member States, and continue to be policed under EU law (Articles 23–25 EC) (the *internal* dimension of the customs union).

The removal of tariff barriers on its own will not result in the completion of market integration for products. All manner of other barriers to free movement within the EU must also be removed. These include national rules regulating product standards or product markets, discrimination in public procurement practices by national governments, rules on intellectual property, and the way in which national taxation systems operate. These barriers will be examined in Chapter 5, in which the centre point of much discussion will be Article 28 EC, which prohibits non-tariff barriers to interstate trade in goods, and Chapter 7 on taxation.

The current chapter will begin with a consideration of the law relating to the external dimension of the customs union. The establishment and successful operation of this outer shell is a functional prerequisite to the completion of the internal market. Goods passing the external frontier of the Union and upon which all relevant duties and charges have been levied and customs formalities completed are thereafter deemed to be 'goods in free circulation' (Article 24 EC). Once within the Union, these goods are able to benefit from free movement within the Union by virtue of the uniformity of external protection offered by the CCT.

This chapter needs to be set against a general analysis of the EU's external trade policy, the common commercial policy (CCP), which will be discussed in Chapter 11. The CCT is just one of the several limbs of an external trade policy which is based on the basic principles of the creation of a single EU-based trading area and uniformity of treatment *vis-à-vis* third countries.

While undoubtedly privileging its own Member States through the creation of a customs union and an internal market, the EU is not opposed to the furtherance of *global* free trade. Article 131 EC links together the customs union, the CCP and the pursuit of free trade:

'By establishing a customs union between themselves the Member States aim to contribute, in the common interest, to the harmonious development of world trade, the progressive abolition of restrictions on international trade and the lowering of customs barriers.

The common commercial policy shall take into account the favourable effect which the abolition of customs duties between Member States may have on the increase in the competitive strength of undertakings in those states.'

It should be noted that these articles are phrased in terms of encouragement to action, rather than obligation. They do not create justiciable duties on the part of the Member States acting jointly as the European Community to lower their customs barriers towards third countries, but at most, articulate a duty to negotiate in good faith for the achievement of free trade within organisations such as the World Trade Organisation (WTO). The WTO, created in 1995, at the end of the General Agreement on Tariffs and Trade's (GATT) eighth round of negotiations (the Uruguay Round), seeks to create, through legal agreements and dispute resolution processes, open, fair and undistorted competition on a global scale. The WTO replaces GATT as an international organisation; however, GATT continues to exist as the relevant WTO Treaty on trade in goods. The WTO currently has some 150 members, including each of the EU Member States individually, as well as the European Community in its own right (the EU as such has no separate legal personality, though the Treaty establishing a Constitution for Europe would amend this). Within the WTO/GATT system, it is largely the EC which negotiates and concludes agreements, rather than the individual Member States. The international obligations of the EC under the WTO are incorporated into Community customs legislation, the basic Regulation being the Community Customs Code (Council Regulation 2913/92, OJ 1992 L302/1). However, testing the compatibility of EC customs measures with the requirements of the WTO before European courts has proved a particularly knotty problem for applicants and the courts (see 4.7).

One of the consequences of a series of negotiations under the aegis of the GATT has been a generalised global reduction in tariffs. Following the implementation of the Uruguay Round of negotiations, average tariffs on industrial goods traded between the developed market economies of the EU, Japan, the US and Canada are less than 4 per cent. The current round of negotiations, the Doha Development Round, was opened in 2001 with a particular focus on trade issues concerning developing countries. The negotiations, as yet unresolved after six years, aim to further reduce, or eliminate, tariffs and subsidies on industrial and agricultural goods.

One consequence of the worldwide reduction on customs duties has been the steady decrease in the percentage of that part of the EU's 'own resources', its budget, which is generated from customs duties paid on goods passing the Union's external frontier. Currently, the revenue collected amounts to around 15 per cent of the EU's annual budget. In 2004, some €12 billion were collected in charges. Revenue collection is undertaken by national customs authorities, with a proportion collected being kept by the Member States. Providing the EU and Member States with budgetary resources is one of three strategic objectives of the customs union, along with the provision of a framework for international trade, and the protection of society against unfair, illegal or dangerous international trade (Commission Communication concerning a strategy for the Customs Union (COM(2001) 51). This latter objective is of ever greater significance. In 2004, some 100 million counterfeit items were seized by customs officials, along with dangerous products including weapons and illegal medicines.

The 2001 Communication also highlights limitations in the operational aspects of the customs union. For practical purposes, the customs union is run by national customs officers, whose task is to apply the legislative rules adopted by the EU. The Community Customs Code Regulation is supplemented by an extensive body of implementing measures, commonly adopted by the Commission exercising delegated powers, under the comitology framework. The Commission has indicated its concerns about divergences in the operational capacity of the different national administrations, and is seeking to foster a more coherent and cohesive approach among the Member States, with better coordination between them. This is being stimulated through a series of action programmes, the most recent being 'Customs 2007' (European Parliament and Council Decision 253/2003, OJ 2003 L36/1). This programme focuses on exchanges of experience, the sharing of best practice and benchmarking of performance, with the aim of improving efficiency and effectiveness. A package of Commission Communications from 2003 (COM(2003) 452) outlines a programme which seeks to simplify and rationalise existing customs legislation. Support for this programme is contained in a Commission Proposal for a Regulation modernising the Customs Code (COM(2005) 608) which will replace the existing Regulation, and a Commission Proposal for a Decision promoting Electronic Customs (COM(2005) 609), which advocates increased reliance upon information technology. These moves are designed to reduce the opportunities for divergences between the different Member State administrations. A further area of concentration over recent years has been on increasing the security aspects of the customs union (European Parliament and Council Regulation 648/2005, OJ 2005 L117/13, amending Council Regulation 2913/92 establishing the Community Customs Code).

## 4.2    Goods

The provisions contained in Articles 23–30 EC on the customs union and on quantitative restrictions apply to all trade in 'goods'. At no point, however, does the Treaty provide a definition of this concept. In Case 7/68 *Commission* v. *Italy* ([1968] ECR 423), the Court of Justice addressed a disputed tax levied on the export of articles of an artistic, historic, archaeological or ethnographic nature. The Italian government argued that such articles were not 'goods' for the purposes of the customs union, which should include only 'ordinary merchandise', that is 'consumer goods or articles of general use'. The Court disagreed, ruling that 'by goods, within the meaning of [Article 9 (now Article 23) EC], there must be understood products which can be valued in money and which are capable as such, of forming the subject of commercial transactions' (at p.428). Further, it has been established that goods may have a negative value, such as shipments of non-recyclable waste in Case C-2/90 *Commission* v. *Belgium (Walloon Waste)* ([1992] ECR I-4431). In addition, 'goods' need not necessarily be physical objects, for example electricity, a disputed import tax upon which was addressed in Case C-213/96 *Outokumpu Oy* ([1998] ECR I-1777).

## 4.3    The Common Customs Tariff

According to Lyons, 'a study of Community customs law, is in large measure, a study of achievement' (2001: 1). Legislatively, the customs union was completed some eighteen months ahead of schedule. The transitional period had been fixed for 1 January 1970, however the common customs tariff (CCT) was established and fully operational on 1 July 1968, by the adoption of Council Regulation 950/68 (OJ 1968 L172/1).

The CCT comprises three main elements:

▶ a *nomenclature* for the classification of goods;
▶ rules on the *valuation* of goods;
▶ rules on the *origin* of goods.

Once it has been determined what the goods are for customs purposes, how much they are worth and where they came from, it is then possible to determine on an *ad valorem* percentage basis what duty is payable. A definition of the customs territory is also necessary for the operation of the CCT. This is based broadly on the countries which are from time to time included among the Member States of the EU, and those which are excluded, for example Gibraltar. In addition, international agreements are concluded by the Community with third countries establishing a customs union. Such countries include Turkey, the Republic of San Marino and the Principality of Andorra. Although extremely close economic relations are established within the European Economic Area (EEA) between the EC and Iceland, Liechtenstein and Norway, it does not include the establishment of a customs union. However, the EEA does establish a free trade area with no *internal* customs duties and it also allows for considerable simplification of the customs arrangements between the EEA and the EU, inspired by the arrangements in place between Switzerland and the EU.

The rules on nomenclature, valuation and origin discussed in this chapter are indispensable to the operation of the CCT. Without them, the CCT would not provide uniform external protection, and 'tariff-shopping' would be a common practice. Surprisingly then, there was no explicit provision in the Treaty for the adoption of such rules. Initially, the necessary rules on nomenclature and valuation were provided by the international customs instruments to which all Member States were party. There was, however, no international agreement in place concerning rules on the origin of goods when the CCT was established in 1968, and autonomous legislation in the form of Council Regulation 802/68 (OJ 1968 L148/1) needed to be adopted. Necessarily, the residual law-making power in Article 308 (former 235) EC was used as the legal basis for the origin Regulation. This basis was used subsequently for the adoption of Regulations on nomenclature and valuation, following the decision in Case 8/73 *Hauptzollamt Bremerhaven* v. *Massey-Ferguson* ([1973] ECR 897), which established clearly the case for harmonised customs legislation, as opposed to simply relying on the international customs instruments to which all the Member States were party. The harmonising Regulations give effect to the various international obligations to which the EC is party, and these measures have been significantly amended, updated and added to over the years.

In 1992, much of the existing legislation on the CCT was brought together in Council Regulation 2913/92, the Community Customs Code, to which there is an accompanying Implementing Regulation (Commission Regulation 2454/93, OJ 1993 L343/1). The Customs Code was introduced under former Articles 113 (the CCP), 100a and 28 (now Articles 133, 95 and 26) EC. This was in line with the case law of the Court, which had shifted towards reducing the scope for application of the general law-making power in Article 235 (308) EC, in favour of stressing the availability of more specific law-making powers (Case 45/86 *Commission* v. *Council (Generalised Tariff Preferences)* [1987] ECR 1493). The new regime came into force on 1 January 1994. The Customs Code and its Implementing Regulation repeal a large number of earlier measures and seek to provide a global, rather than a sector-by-sector, approach to the customs treatment of goods. The pressure for such a consolidation came from external and internal sources (Gormley, 1996: 125–7). The external pressures came from both the EC's own legal commitments to improve and simplify customs arrangements with neighbouring states, as well as from the large number of international developments to produce common standards and procedures in the customs field in which the EC was involved. The internal pressures originated in the programme to simplify and consolidate EU legislation, with a view to ensure greater transparency (Maher, 1995). The Code changed little of the applicable substantive law, except in relation to individual appeal procedures. An amendment proposed by the European Parliament to allow the Commission to exercise its implementing powers delegated from the Council under the less interventionist of the comitology committees, the Advisory Committee, was rejected. Instead, when the Commission exercises its delegated powers in respect of nomenclature, it does so subject to the oversight of a Management Committee, while the Valuation and Origin Committees are regulatory committees; the latter two must give favourable opinions before the Commission can adopt implementing measures. The Nomenclature Committee exercises less restrictive blocking powers. A committee structure also exists to assist the Commission in making decisions as to whether a product is entitled to a duty-free exemption or reduction (see 4.9).

Operationally, the 'Integrated Tariff', known as TARIC, draws together all relevant customs provisions, including nomenclature, preferences, quotas and rates of duty, which are set, according to Article 26 EC, by the Council, on a proposal by the Commission, and by a qualified majority. The TARIC allows traders to determine the rules applicable to particular goods. It is maintained by the Commission, is constantly updated, and is now freely accessible via the Europa website.

### 4.4  Nomenclature for the Classification of Goods

Until 1988, the CCT nomenclature was based on the 1950 Customs Cooperation Council Nomenclature Convention. This was the nomenclature used by the Member States before the establishment of the Communities, and the EC succeeded to the rights and duties of the Member States (Case 38/75 *Nederlandse Spoorwegen* v. *Inspecteur der Invoerrechten* [1975] ECR 1439). This has been replaced by the International Convention on the Harmonised Commodity and Description and Coding System (OJ 1987 L198/3), established under the auspices of the World Customs Organisation (WCO) (formerly the Customs Cooperation Council), and which the EC was involved in negotiating. The intergovernmental WCO, with 171 Members, works closely with the WTO, and its role is to contribute to the harmonisation of international customs procedures. A new nomenclature was needed in order to achieve a common worldwide approach to problems of classification, to develop a more sophisticated system which could be used for statistical as well as customs purposes and under which transactions could be computerised, and to adapt the earlier classification to technological progress. This Convention was given effect within the EU legal order by Council Regulation 2658/87 (OJ 1987 L256/1), which establishes the Combined Nomenclature. The separate headings by which the nomenclature classifies products are set out in an annex to this regulation, and an updated version of this is adopted annually by means of a Commission regulation.

All products crossing the EU's external frontier are recorded under the relevant classification code. Uniformity in the interpretation of the nomenclature across all Member States' customs authorities is essential if the CCT is to operate effectively. There is however scope for uncertainty and divergences in the application of the nomenclature. Indeed, it is not always immediately apparent under which heading a particular product will fall, and thus the applicable rate of duty that is payable upon a particular import. Guidance is available in the form of explanatory notes issued by the WCO, although it is important to note that while these may be 'an important aid to the interpretation of the scope of the various tariff headings . . . [they] do not have legally binding force' (Case C-405/97 *Mövenpick* v. *Hauptzollamt Bremen* [1999] ECR I-2397 at para. 18). However, where 'an interpretation reflects the general practice followed by the contracting parties, it can be set aside only if it appears incompatible with the wording of the heading concerned or goes manifestly beyond the discretion of the [WCO]' (Case 38/75 *Nederlandse Spoorwegen*, at para. 25).

Legally binding guidance is available from the Commission, operating with the assistance of the Customs Code Committee. Article 9 of Council Regulation 2658/87 provides that the Commission, operating under delegated powers, may issue by regulation, interpretations on product classification. Commission Regulation 1578/2006 (OJ 2006 L291/3), for example, informs us of the correct classification code – neither that for a toy, nor a lifesaving device – of 'a pair of inflatable plastic rings, each with two air chambers . . . designed to be worn by children around the arms in order to keep them afloat in shallow water'. Guidance is also available from national authorities, in the form of 'Binding Tariff Information' (BTI). According to Article 12 of the Community Customs Code Regulation, BTI is available from the customs authorities of any of the Member States. The authorities will identify the relevant heading under the customs nomenclature for the particular product in question and, once issued, the BTI remains binding in respect of all Member States, not simply the Member State issuing the BTI. Generally, the BTI is binding for a period of six years. However, the BTI will cease to be valid upon the adoption of a contrary Commission classification regulation. It is crucial to the integrity and coherence of the CCT that issued BTI is reported immediately to the Commission. Article 12 of Implementing Regulation 2454/93 imposes such an obligation upon Member State authorities.

Given the possible financial implications of customs classifications decisions, it is not surprising that traders are prepared to pursue legal action in an effort to seek redress for their grievances relating to interpretations of the customs nomenclature made by the Commission and national customs authorities. Article 243(1) of the Customs Code establishes common criteria which governs standing in order to challenge the decisions of the national customs authorities before national courts. The adoption of common rules has been seen as highly important given that there are significant variations in national procedural laws. However, while agreement was forthcoming on standing, a proposal by the Commission to create uniform grounds for review was rejected (Gormley, 1996: 113). Procedural rules operating at national level have also been subject to considerable scrutiny by the European Court. In Case C-453/00 *Kühne and Heitz NV* ([2004] ECR I-837), a Dutch poultry exporter brought an action seeking refunds of export payments which were withheld on the basis of a contested interpretation of the customs nomenclature. In accordance with the principle of cooperation arising from Article 10 EC, the Court ruled that unless a reasoned rejection of the application is given, an administrative body is under an obligation to review a decision it has taken in order to consider the interpretation of a relevant provision of EU law given in the meantime by the Court. This obligation is subject to four conditions. First, under national law, the administrative body must have the power to reopen that decision; second, the administrative decision in question must become final as a result of a judgment of a national court ruling at final instance; third, that judgment must, in the light of a later interpretation by the Court of Justice, be based on a misinterpretation of EC law and no reference to the Court must have been made under Article 234 EC in the action; and fourth, the person concerned must have complained to the administrative body immediately after becoming aware of the relevant decision by the Court.

Given that classification decisions are generally adopted as regulations, aggrieved traders challenging EU measures often find that they have difficulties in establishing the requisite standing to mount a challenge to the decision's legality before European courts. Article 230 EC restricts standing to individuals who can show 'direct and individual concern' in the contested measure. While the Court was initially opposed to individuals' bringing actions under Article 230 EC for annulment of tariff classification regulations on the basis of the regulations' general and abstract nature (Case 40/84 *Casteels* v. *Commission* [1985] ECR 667), it has more recently shown itself prepared to examine whether a trader may have the requisite direct and individual concern, regardless of the general and abstract qualities of the regulation. In this respect, Case T-243/01 *Sony* v. *Commission* ([2003] ECR II-4189) is of particular significance. The trader was granted standing since he was already in receipt of Binding Tariff Information in relation to the product, which was subsequently overruled by the Commission Regulation. For those denied standing before the Court of Justice, an alternative channel may exist through challenges to the national implementing decisions brought before national courts. Such challenges may serve as a means of attacking the disputed EU measure through a reference to the European Court on validity.

Finally, while the Court's role may be considered crucial given that the uniform interpretation of the customs nomenclature is fundamental to its effectiveness, there has been perhaps too ready a recourse to the Court of Justice, where many of the CCT questions asked have appeared to be essentially questions of fact rather than law. As Lyons observes (2001: 132):

> 'The founding fathers of the Community surely did not imagine that the Court of Justice, established to oversee the legal order of the new Community, would need to rule that, for the purposes of Community law, "nightdresses" includes "undergarments which, by reason of their objective characteristic, are intended to be worn exclusively or essentially in bed"' (citing C-338/95 *Wiener* v. *Hauptzollamt Emmerich* [1997] ECR I-6495).

## 4.5    Valuation of Goods

Customs duties are imposed on an *ad valorem* basis, that is, they are set as a percentage of the value of the goods being declared. The task of valuing the goods coming across the external frontier falls to the national authorities. A uniform system of valuation is needed, as is one that is not easily susceptible to abuse through the artificial lowering of the 'true' price. The original valuation system of 1968 was based on the 1950 Customs Cooperation Council Valuation Convention, to which all the Member States were parties. This was superseded by an agreement reached under Article VII of the GATT in the context of the 1979 Tokyo Round of multinational negotiations. This led to the adoption of Council Regulation 1224/80 (OJ 1980 L124/1), which was subsequently replaced during the process of the consolidation of customs legislation, with provisions in the Customs Code Regulation (Articles 28–36) and the Implementing Regulation (Articles 141–181).

The common rules on valuation are based on the GATT Customs Valuation Code. The basic principle is that the value for customs purposes of imported merchandise should be based on the actual value on which duty is assessed, rather than on some notional value. The valuation system provides for five valuation methods which are applied successively to any given imported product until the appropriate method has been ascertained. Where none is found to be applicable, recourse to any reasonable method of valuation may be taken (Articles 29–31 Customs Code Regulation). The five basic valuation methods take into account the following:

- transaction value of the goods;
- transaction value of identical goods;
- transaction value of similar goods;
- deductive value of the goods; and
- computed value of the goods.

Transaction value is based on the sale price at the time of entry. In contrast, deductive value is based on sale price after entry, less certain expenses, and computed value is based on the costs of production and transport, etc., with an added element for profit. The transaction value can be applied only when certain conditions are satisfied. There must be no restrictions on the disposal or use of goods by the buyer, other than those imposed by public authorities; the transaction must not be subject to some further consideration for which a value cannot be determined; the buyer and seller must not be related, or, if they are related, the transaction value must be acceptable for customs purposes; and no part of the proceeds of any subsequent sale must accrue directly or indirectly to the seller unless an appropriate adjustment has been made.

A considerable body of case law exists in which the Court has been asked to judge which expenses are to be included in the customs valuation, and which are to be excluded. Article 33 of the Customs Code Regulation provides an indication of expenses which may be excluded. These include charges for the transport of goods after their arrival at the place of introduction into the customs territory of the EU (Case C-17/89 *Hauptzollamt Frankfurt am Main-Ost* v. *Olivetti* [1990] ECR I-2031), and charges for the construction or assembly of the imported goods. Additional exclusions include interest payments on the purchase price, and buying commissions paid by an importer to an agent who obtains goods to be imported from a producer or supplier in a third country, on behalf of the importer. In all cases, however, the Customs Code Regulation requires that the excluded costs should be 'distinguished from the price actually paid or payable' on the customs declaration. In Case C-299/90 *Hauptzollamt Kahlsruhe* v. *Hepp* ([1991] ECR I-4301), the Court ruled that this requirement was deemed to have been fulfilled, despite the fact that no explicit reference was made to the buying commission in the customs declaration. Only the net price, that is, the value less the commission was recorded on the invoice. This judgment has been followed in respect of non-declared interest payments in Case C-152/01 *Kyocera Electronics* v. *Hauptzollamt Krefeld* ([2003] ECR I-13821). In contrast, in C-379/00 *Overland Footwear* v. *Commissioners of Customs and Excise* ([2002] ECR I-11133), the invoice recorded the net price plus the commission, but it did not distinguish between them. The importing company was unsuccessful in challenging the requirement to pay duty on the full amount, since the Court held that the Regulation's requirement to distinguish the potentially excluded amount from the actual price had not been fulfilled. However, in a second reference to the Court in this same matter, it ruled that where the national customs administration finds that the declared customs value erroneously included a buying commission, the customs administration is required to regularise the situation by reimbursing the import duties applied to that commission (Case C-468/03 *Overland Footwear Ltd* v. *Commissioners of Customs and Excise* [2005] ECR I-8937).

The normal task of the valuation system is to prevent the undervaluation of goods for customs purposes. Case 65/79 *Procureur de la République* v. *Chatain* ([1980] ECR 1345) raises the more unusual problem of how the rules should be applied to goods overvalued for customs purposes. Chatain, the French subsidiary of Sandoz, appeared to have used excessive invoice prices on goods acquired from the parent company, in order to transfer profits to Switzerland and to avoid paying French tax. It was prosecuted for making false declarations and unlawfully transferring capital abroad. The question arose whether the customs authorities were permitted under EU law to reduce the price. The Court ruled that the essential purpose of Council Regulation 803/68 (OJ Special Edition 1968 I, p.170), which then governed customs valuation, was to prevent goods from being undervalued, and that EU law could not therefore be used to reduce the value.

## 4.6 Origin of Goods

In addition to the classification and valuation of a product, it is essential to know the origin of a product for the correct application of the CCT. Certain countries will benefit from preferential trade agreements with the EC under the Common Commercial Policy, and may be subject to reduced or suspended duties. In principle, of course, such preferential treatment must be in line with the EC's international commitments – though the long running banana saga, where African, Caribbean and Pacific (ACP) producers were ruled by the WTO Dispute Settlement Body and Appellate Body to have received preferential treatment, is an example of the EC's repeated failure to comply with its WTO obligations (McMahon, 1998a and 2005; Smith, 2000).

The Customs Code contains rules to determine the 'economic nationality' of a product. While this may be clear in respect of goods wholly obtained or produced in one country (see Article 23 Customs Code), it will be less clear where a product has been subject to manufacturing processes in more than one country, including, of course, a country of the EU. In the case of products with a mixed heritage, Article 24 of the Customs Code provides that goods produced in one or more country are considered as originating in the country in which they underwent their 'last, substantial economically justified processing or working in an undertaking equipped for that purpose and resulting in the manufacture of a new product or representing an important stage of manufacture'. This was defined in Case 49/76 *Überseehandel* v. *Handelskammer Hamburg* ([1977] ECR 41) which gave the product resulting from the manufacturing process 'its own properties and a composition of its own, which it did not possess before that process or operation'. Change in tariff classification is a guide, but is not decisive. The test may be judged also in accordance with the extent to which the processing brings added value to the product. This is illustrated by Case 34/78 *Yoshida Nederland BV* v. *Kamer van Koophandel* ([1979] ECR 115) and Case 114/78 *Yoshida GmbH* v. *Industrie- und Handelskammer Kassel* ([1979] ECR 151) which concerned the incorporation of Japanese-made sliders into slide fasteners in the Netherlands. It was held that the sliders were only an element in the completed product, and that the price of the sliders was not decisive in determining the final price of the slide fasteners. Consequently, the finished products were held to be of EU origin. In Case 26/88 *Brother International* v. *Hauptzollamt Giessen* ([1989] ECR 4253), the Court held that the assembly of products may be sufficient to confer EU origin, but only if it constitutes a decisive stage of production. For example, production must require a skilled workforce, or specially equipped premises. If it does not the added value to the finished product brought about by the assembly process would be considered. In this case, an added value of less than 10 per cent was deemed insufficient to confer EU origin.

The operation of origin rules is clearly of considerable importance to multinational enterprises. In addition to shifting profits to areas where the tax burdens are less, such enterprises seek to shift the various stages of production of finished products around the world in order to take advantage of cheap labour markets, favourable origin rules and preferential tariff treatment (see Case 65/79 *Chatain* [1980] ECR 1345). Article 25 of the Customs Code provides that whenever processing is moved to another country solely to circumvent the EU rules, and benefit from the origin rules, the sought after country of origin will not be conferred. In *Brother International*, the Court held that the fact that the assembly of a product is transferred to another country does not automatically raise the presumption that it has been transferred solely for the purpose of avoiding unfavourable origin rules, unless the transfer coincides with the entry into force of those rules, in which case the manufacturer must show other valid reasons for the transfer. The burden of proving origin lies on the importer, although a Member State may not require from importers more information about the origin of goods than they may be reasonably expected to know.

With respect to goods which originate from countries with preferential trade agreements with the EU, additional and specific rules may apply as to the determination of origin. In accordance with the provisions in the Customs Code Implementing Regulation (Articles 68 *et seq.*), it is generally necessary to show that the product in question is composed of at least 90 per cent of materials originating in that country. In circumstances where a greater proportion of materials in the product originate elsewhere, it must be shown that these materials have been subject to 'sufficient working or processing'.

### 4.7   The Exclusive Nature of the Common Customs Tariff

The CCT provides for uniform tariffs in all Member States. Consequently, it would be contrary to the system established by the CCT for Member States to be permitted unilaterally to impose additional tariffs, or charges having equivalent effect to customs duties (CHEEs) on imported products. In Joined Cases 37 and 38/73 *Sociaal Fonds voor de Diamantarbeiders* v. *NV Indiamex* ([1973] ECR 1609), the Court considered the validity of contributions to the Belgian Social Fund for diamond workers, payable by importers of rough diamonds and calculated on the basis of the diamonds imported. According to the Court, the fact that no specific mention is made of CHEEs in the provisions dealing with the CCT, does not mean that they are not prohibited. On the contrary, it is because CHEEs are at variance with the objective of the CCT, which is to create uniformity of protection, that they are therefore prohibited. The Court held that the CCT:

'is intended to achieve an equalisation of customs charges levied at the frontiers of the Community on products imported from third countries, in order to avoid any deflection of trade in relation with those countries and any distortion of free internal circulation or of competitive conditions' (para. 9).

The Court established that no *new* charges could be applied after 1 July 1968. The option conferred on Member States to retain existing charges is narrowly construed, and in Case C-126/94 *Cadi* v. *Ministre des Finances and Directeur Général des Douanes* ([1996] ECR I-5647) the Court ruled that raising the level of charges, or extending their application to other categories of products, meant that a charge was 'new' even if still levied under the same name as a charge existing in 1968. Thus, in *Cadi,* the *octroi de mer* levied on goods imported into French overseas departments and territories, and which is also levied on goods coming from elsewhere within metropolitan France and elsewhere within the EU, is a CHEE under the *Diamantarbeiders* principle.

There have been many difficulties arising from the application of these principles to health inspections carried out at the EU's external frontiers, and to charges levied for such inspections. Recent years have seen the development of a significant programme of harmonised veterinary checks and health inspections of imported products from third countries (see Council Directive 97/78, OJ 1997 L24/9). These checks are further buttressed by the work of the Commission's Food and Veterinary Office, which, *inter alia,* conducts inspections of the inspectors in the Member States, as well as missions to third countries. Full harmonisation has not been achieved yet, however, and, in the interim, Member States have been able to carry out, and charge for, inspections which would be compulsory in intra-EU trade and would be carried out on the basis of harmonised rules (Case 70/77 *Simmenthal* v. *Italian Finance Administration* [1978] ECR 1453). The fees charged can even exceed those carried out for similar inspections on EU goods, in order to avoid more favourable treatment of imported goods (Case 30/79 *Land Berlin* v. *Wigei* [1980] ECR 151). Even where the inspection undertaken is not one uniformly conducted by all the Member States, charges may be imposed, at least insofar as the charge corresponds to the cost of the inspection (Case 1/83 *Intercontinentale Fleischhandelsgesellschaft* v. *Freistaat Bayern* [1984] ECR 349). With GATT also moving towards uniform international rules, as seen with the adoption of an Agreement on the Application of Sanitary and Phytosanitary Measures, annexed to the agreement establishing the WTO, the *Wigei* case seems to be in conflict with the EU's international obligations. Annex C 1(f) requires that any fees imposed for the procedures on imported products should be equitable in relation to any fees charged on like domestic products and should be no higher than the actual cost of the service.

The Court has also been called upon to address the possible application of Article 90 EC in the external trade context. Article 90 EC prohibits discriminatory internal taxation (see generally Chapter 7). The question arose in Case 193/85 *Cooperativa Co-frutta Srl* v. *Amministrazione delle finanze dello Stato* ([1987] ECR 2085), whether Article 90 EC applied to measures which discriminate against products from non-EU countries. It appeared from Case 148/77 *Hansen* v. *Hauptzollamt Flensburg* ([1978] ECR 1787) that Article 90 EC was to be interpreted strictly as not applying to third country products, since they are not explicitly mentioned. However, in *Co-frutta,* which concerned an Italian tax on the consumption of fresh bananas which was imposed on bananas originating in Colombia and imported into Italy from the Benelux, the Court held that Article 90 EC precludes the charging of a consumer tax on certain imported fruit where it may protect domestic fruit production. Such a tax may not be imposed on goods which are in free circulation, that is, goods which have been imported into another Member State from a third country, and which must be assimilated in all respects to goods originating in the EU. In sharp contrast, the position is different in respect of goods imported directly from third countries into the Member State where the tax is imposed. In Joined Cases C-228–234, 339 and 353/90 *Simba SpA and others* v. *Ministero delle finanze* ([1992] ECR I-3713), which concerned the same Italian tax on bananas, the Court held that Article 90 EC does not apply to goods imported directly into the Member State where the tax is imposed, and that the application of such a tax is not incompatible with the general principles governing the Common Commercial Policy. However, as Usher suggests, this is 'an open invitation to distortions of trade' (Usher, 1996: 116). It may conflict, moreover, with the EC's international obligations, since Article III: I of GATT 1994, requires imported products to be given treatment no less favourable than that accorded to national products as regards the imposition of taxes and regulations. It may also conflict with specific bilateral international commitments undertaken by the EC.

Although there may be cases where the rules formulated by the EU infringe the GATT, any attempts to rely upon these international rules may founder upon the Court's continuing reluctance to allow the invocation of the GATT in proceedings involving EU legislation in order to protect the rights of individuals (Peers, 2001; Lavranos, 2005). The trend established in Joined Cases 21–24/72 *International Fruit Company NV* v. *Produktschap voor Groenten en Fruit* ([1972] ECR 1219) was confirmed by the Court of Justice in Case C-280/93 *Germany* v. *Council (Bananas)* ([1994] ECR I-4973) on the validity of the EU's banana regime where the Court held:

'it is only if the Community intended to implement a particular obligation entered into within the framework of GATT, or if the Community act expressly refers to specific provisions of GATT, that the Court can review the lawfulness of the Community act in question from the point of view of the GATT rules' (para. 9).

Further, the Court has taken a restrictive reading of when the Community can be regarded as intending to implement particular obligations. The applicants in Case T-383/00 *Beamglow* v. *Parliament, Council and Commission* ([2005] ECR II-5459) were one of a number of EU-based exporters who claimed to be affected by trade reprisals from the US, which had increased by 100 per cent customs duties on various products from the EU. This was in apparent retaliation for the continued non-compliance of the EU's banana regime with WTO rules (both Council Regulation 404/93, OJ 1993 L47/1 on the Common Organisation of the Market in Bananas, and its replacement, Council Regulation 1637/98, OJ 1998 L 210/28, being found by the WTO Dispute Settlement Body (DSB) to be in breach of WTO commitments). The applicants brought an action seeking damages against the Council and Commission, on the basis that their failure to perform their obligations under the WTO agreements thwarted the applicants' legitimate expectations in respect of its sales and investments in the US. The Court ruled that in undertaking to comply with the WTO rules through the adoption of Council Regulation 1637/98, and after the DSB decision of 25 September 1997, the Community did not intend to assume a specific obligation in the context of the WTO capable of justifying an exception to the principle that WTO rules cannot be relied upon before the Community courts. On the contrary, the Court confirmed its stance that Community courts could not review the legality of the conduct of Community institutions by referring to WTO rules.

### 4.8    Customs Procedures

All goods entering the EU customs territory must be conveyed without delay to the customs authorities and placed under their supervision in order to complete the necessary formalities (Articles 37 *et seq.* Customs Code). The arrival of the goods should be notified to the authorities, and a customs declaration made. Attempts to simplify and streamline the administration of the customs union have resulted in tools such as the Single Administrative Document which is the standard form for declarations. The declaration will indicate, *inter alia*, under which of the different customs procedures the importer is seeking to place the imported goods. These procedures include, first and foremost, the release of the goods into free circulation within the EU. Article 79 of the Customs Code provides that this confers on non-EU goods the customs status of EU goods. As the Court explained in Case 41/76 *Donckerwolcke* ([1976] ECR 1921), this results in the imported goods becoming 'definitely and wholly assimilated to products originating in Member States'. Where a customs debt arises in respect of the goods, they will not be released until the debt is paid or secured (Article 74 Customs Code).

As an alternative to completing full customs procedures at the point of entry into the EU, the external transit procedure may be applied. Under the Community Transit System, customs duties are suspended along with the completion of full customs formalities until the final destination point in the EU. The transit system also operates in the event that goods travelling between two points in the customs union travel through a third country. As with all customs procedures, the goods must be available for inspection at the external border, at which point, checks on the goods will be conducted, and if counterfeit goods are discovered, they may be seized and subsequently destroyed. A New Computerised Transit System (NCTS) should enable the effective tracking of the transit of goods throughout the EU, to their ultimate destination. However, the significance of internal frontiers has not been obliterated completely by the process of integration and the completion of the internal market. Customs authorities in the countries in which the goods pass through will be advised in advance of the anticipated arrival of the goods, and an electronic declaration will be made. Upon arrival, a second declaration will be made and, if any irregularity is suspected which could result in abuse of the customs procedures, inspection of the goods may be made (Article 352 Implementing Regulation).

A further range of alternative customs procedures again allow duties to be suspended temporarily, and in some cases, waived completely. These include: customs warehousing, which allows for the temporary storage, free from customs duties, of non-EU goods, until their next destination is decided upon; inward processing, where materials are imported free from duties, for processing in the EU, subject to their subsequent export; and temporary importation, which allows for goods to be used in the EU without payment of duty, subject to their being exported afterwards in the same state as that in which they were imported originally. Recent amendments to the Customs Code Regulation have sought to modernise, simplify and streamline these procedures, and to counter the many procedural differences which have grown up between operations in the different Member States. In addition, a 2005 proposal calling for a modernised Customs Code (COM(2005)

608 and 609) proposes that, in line with the 2000 EU Charter of Fundamental Rights (OJ 2000 C3641/1), in addition to the right of appeal against any decision taken by the customs authorities, there should be a right for every person to be heard before any decision is taken which would adversely affect them. Many such challenges would properly lie before the national court, as decisions on authorisations for suspension or waiver of duty lie with national customs authorities, albeit following consultation with the Customs Code Committee. However, as the European Court ruled in Case C-11/05 *Friesland Coberco Dairy Foods BV* v. *Inspecteur van de Belastingdienst* ([2006] ECR I-4285), 'a duty to consult the Committee cannot be treated as a duty to adopt its conclusion' (para. 31). On this basis, the Court refused to review the Committee's conclusion that waiving of duties under the inward processing rules would not be granted to a Dutch fruit juice manufacturer.

## 4.9  Common Customs Tariff: Exemptions or Reductions

Preferential trade agreements with particular states may have the effect of reducing or even exempting duties otherwise due, and the various customs procedures set out above in 4.7 may have the effect of suspending duties altogether. Further reductions and exemptions are possible. For example, on the basis of what is now Article 26 EC, the Council adopted Regulation 1255/96 (OJ 1996 L 158/1), which permits the suspension of CCT duties on the importation of certain industrial and agricultural products on the grounds that EU production of these particular products was inadequate or non-existent, and producers could not meet the needs of user industries in the EU.

Council Regulation 918/83 (OJ 1983 L305/1) meanwhile sets out a more methodical system of relief from customs duties, and includes those educational, scientific and cultural materials listed in the Annex to the Regulation: certain goods destined for charitable or philanthropic organisations; tourist information materials; as well as the more popularly known example of 'duty-free' imports, that is, goods in travellers' personal luggage intended for their personal consumption, rather than commercial use. The distinction between goods intended for personal consumption and those intended for commercial use was addressed in Case C-99/00 *Lyckeskog* ([2002] ECR I-4839). Following Mr Lyckeskog's conviction for attempted smuggling, in which he brought 500 kilograms of rice into Sweden from Norway, the Court of Justice ruled that 'personal use' must be examined on the basis of an overall assessment of the circumstances of each case. Wherever appropriate, account must be taken of the traveller's lifestyle and habits, including his or her family environment. The Court rejected the national administrative practice of setting a ceiling for the amount of goods, above which import was deemed to be for commercial purposes. In *Lyckeskog*, the ceiling for rice had been set at 20 kilograms. The Court did not support this practice, however, finding that EU law precludes national administrative practices which impose binding quantitative limits before customs duties would apply, or which would have the effect of creating a rebuttable presumption that the importation concerned is commercial by reason of the quantity of goods imported.

Having initially exempted or granted a reduction in duty to goods imported, national customs authorities may subsequently seek to re-impose the duty, a procedure which is known as 'post-clearance recovery'. A common circumstance of post-clearance recovery occurs when authorities subsequently discover that the documentation presented by the importer has been falsified or forged. Good faith on the part of importers alone will not protect them from post-clearance recovery (Joined Cases C-153 and 204/94 *R* v.

*Commissioners of Customs and Excise, ex parte Faroe Seafood Co. Ltd* [1996] ECR I-2465). It may also occur when authorities discover at a later stage that they have been operating under incorrect rules. Because of the complexity of the field, this is not an infrequent occurrence. The general principle is governed by Article 220 of the Customs Code, which allows for a waiver of post-clearance recovery. Three cumulative conditions are applied:

▶ the duties must have been collected as a result of an error on the part of the competent authorities (error is assessed in the light of the complexity or sufficient simplicity of the rules concerned, and the period of time during which the authorities persisted in their error – see Case C-499/03P *Biegi and Commonfood Handelsgesellschaft* [2005] ECR I-1751);

▶ the person liable must have acted in good faith, that is, they could not reasonably have detected the error made by the competent authorities (taking into account the nature of the error, the professional experience of the person liable, and the degree of care they exercised: Case C-370/96 *Covita AVE* v. *Greece* [1998] ECR I-7711);

▶ he or she must have observed all the provisions laid down by the rules in force as far as customs declarations are concerned (Case C-292/91 *Weis* v. *Hauptzollamt Wurzburg* [1993] ECR I-2219).

In practice, the test for acting in good faith had proved a controversial one. Consequently, Article 220(b) of the Customs Code was amended in 2000 (Regulation 2700/2000, OJ 2000 L311/17) in an effort to bring clarity, and a better balance between the interests of the individual and the EU. The text now provides, for example, that good faith will be lacking in circumstances where the European Commission has published a notice in the *Official Journal of the European Communities*, stating that there are grounds for doubt concerning the proper application of the preferential arrangements by the beneficiary country. Amended Article 220(b) of the Customs Code has been held by the Court to be an interpretative provision, and as such, the new text may apply to actions involving situations existing before its entry into force (Case C-293/04 *Beemsterboer Coldstore Services* v. *Inspecteur der Belastingdienst – Douanedistrict Arnhem* [2006] ECR I-2263).

The 2003 amendments to the Customs Code brought increased decentralisation to the administration of the already highly decentralised customs regime. The amendments increased the threshold from €50,000 to €500,000, the amount at which Member States are obliged to request that the Commission determine whether recovery should be made. Below this amount, the matter must be settled by the Member State. Where the decision rests with the Commission, an appeal against that decision may be brought before the Court of First Instance, although the decision is addressed to the Member State, and not to the applicant (Case T-42/96 *Eyckeler and Malt* v. *Commission* [1998] ECR II-401).

## 4.10 The Internal Dimension of the Customs Union: The Nature and Scope of the Prohibition on Customs Duties and Charges Having Equivalent Effects (CHEE)

Having considered the external aspects of the customs union, our discussion turns now to the internal dimension, that is, the impact of the customs union as between Member States. The prohibition on customs duties and charges having equivalent effects to customs duties (CHEEs) between the Member States is 'a fundamental principle of the

Common Market' (Joined Cases 80 and 81/77 *Société Les Commissionnaires Réunis SARL* v. *Receveur des Douanes* [1978] ECR 927, at para. 24). The prohibition is clearly stated in Article 25 EC:

'Customs duties on imports and exports and charges having equivalent effect shall be prohibited between Member States. This prohibition shall also apply to customs duties of a fiscal nature'.

Customs duties and the related CHEEs are one of the two forms of fiscal barriers prohibited by the EC Treaty; the other prohibited fiscal barrier is a system of discriminatory taxation (Article 90 EC Treaty). The two prohibitions are mutually exclusive (Case 57/65 *Alfons Lütticke* v. *Hauptzollamt Saarlouis* [1966] ECR 205), but complementary in the sense that they are both concerned with fiscal obstacles to trade. A charge is either a customs duty or a CHEE, or it may be part of a system of internal taxation. The latter group of charges will be dealt with in Chapter 7.

The EC Treaty provides for the absolute prohibition on customs duties and CHEEs, and this prohibition binds the Member States unconditionally, though not private parties outside the control of the Member State. The prohibition also binds the EU institutions themselves. For example, in *Société Les Commissionnaires Réunis SARL*, a Council Regulation which authorised Member States to impose charges on intra-EU trade in wine was held invalid on the grounds that it was incompatible with the principles of the customs union, although it was adopted within the context of the Common Agricultural Policy (CAP) and the common organisation of the market in wine.

The Court has elaborated a comprehensive definition of customs duties and CHEEs which is qualified by few exceptions. According to the Court in Joined Cases 90 and 91/63 *Commission* v. *Luxembourg and Belgium (Dairy Products)* ([1964] ECR 625 at p.633), 'any possible exception, which in any event must be strictly construed, must be clearly laid down'. There are no general exceptions in the public interest such as those set out in Article 30 EC which, as will be seen in Chapter 5, permit derogations from the prohibition on non-tariff barriers to trade. The only possible exceptions are those concerned with charges for services to importers and exporters which the Member States may legitimately impose and charges for inspections prescribed by EU law. The remaining 'exception' applies to situations where the 'charge' is in fact levied as part of an internal system of taxation, in which case it will be considered under Article 90 EC, and, unless discriminatory, allowed to stand. The dividing line between Article 25 EC and Article 90 EC remains a contested one, and has given rise to a steady flow of preliminary references under Article 234 EC before the Court of Justice. This has been the case particularly in the context of taxes which are imposed on all goods, but which are reimbursed in full or in part for domestically produced goods (see 4.16). The EC Treaty does not prohibit systems of internal taxation. It requires them, however, to be neutral in their treatment of imported and domestic goods in order to avoid distortions of competition within the market. It is, therefore, the concept of 'discrimination' which is the key to the application of Article 90 EC (see Chapter 7).

Under the original EEC Treaty, provision was made for the progressive elimination of existing customs duties and CHEEs (completed by 1968), as well as for the prohibition on the imposition of new duties. This prohibition, which was set out in the 'standstill clause' of ex-Article 12 EC (now Article 25 EC), provided the Court of Justice with its first opportunity to espouse the principle of the justiciability of obligations under EC law in national courts. It was, of course, Article 12 EC which the Court was called upon to interpret in Case 26/62 *Van Gend en Loos* v. *Nederlandse Administratie der Belastingen* ([1963] ECR 1). The Court held that the aggrieved importers must be able to rely upon Article 12 EC before the Dutch courts in order to support their argument that an increase in customs duties after the entry into force of the EEC Treaty resulting from the reclassification of goods under a new tariff heading carrying a higher tariff rate was prohibited and could not be enforced.

### 4.11 ▮ What is a CHEE?

In Case 24/68 *Commission* v. *Italy (Statistical Levy)* ([1969] ECR 193), the Court elaborated a definition of a CHEE, which has since become standard. More recently, in Case 72/03 *Carbonati Apuani* v. *Comune di Carrara* ([2004] ECR I-8027) the Court stated:

> 'As the Court has held before on many occasions, any pecuniary charge, however small and whatever its designation and mode of application, which is imposed unilaterally on domestic or foreign goods by reason of the fact that they cross a frontier, and which is not a customs duty in the strict sense, constitutes a charge having equivalent effect within the meaning of Article 23 of the Treaty' (para. 20).

It is simply the fact that a charge has been imposed as a result of goods crossing a frontier which makes it a CHEE. However, the charge need not actually have to be imposed at the frontier. Thus, charges made in the context of customs clearance occurring in special warehouses in the interior of the country fall within the prohibition (Case 132/82 *Commission* v. *Belgium* [1983] ECR 1649). Further, it is not only charges payable upon the crossing of national frontiers which are prohibited, but also those levied at regional frontiers. Thus, charges payable on goods imported into the French overseas *département d'outre Mer* (DOM) of Réunion, which forms part of the territory of the European Union, could constitute CHEEs. It had been argued that they should escape this classification, on the grounds that they were not levied by reason of the fact that a *national* frontier had been crossed. The charges were payable on goods coming in from any of the Member States, including mainland France. According to the Court however:

> 'a charge levied at a regional frontier by reason of the introduction of products into a region of a Member State constitutes an obstacle to the free movement of goods which is at least as serious as a charge levied at the national frontier' (Case C-163/90 *Administration des Douanes et Droits Indirectes* v. *Legros* [1992] ECR I-4625, at para. 16).

This point arose also with respect to duties payable on goods entering the Greek Dodecanese Islands from any other region in Greece (Joined Cases C-485 and 486/93 *Simitzi* v. *Municipality of Kos* [1995] ECR I-2655), and with respect to a charge payable on marble taken out of the Italian municipality of Carrara, but remaining within Italy (Case 72/03 *Carbonati Apuani*).

The fact that the charge is not imposed for the benefit of the Member State, or that it has no discriminatory or protectionist effect, is irrelevant. There is no *de minimis* rule. Thus, even though the charge may be so small that it does not lead to an increase in prices, the prohibition applies nonetheless. Indeed, the Court has stated that even small charges constitute obstacles to free movement which are 'aggravated by the resulting administrative formalities' (Case 18/87 *Commission* v. *Germany (Live Animals)* [1988] ECR 5427). The absence of equivalent or competing domestic goods is likewise irrelevant to the existence of a CHEE. For example, in Joined Cases 2 and 3/69 *Sociaal Fonds voor de Diamantarbeiders* v. *Brachfeld and Chougol Diamond Co.* ([1969] ECR 211), a charged imposed by Belgium on all imports of diamonds was held to be a CHEE, even though the charge was intended to provide social benefits for diamond workers, and despite the absence of a Belgian diamond industry which might benefit from the imposition of the charge.

### 4.12  Prohibitions on CHEEs on Exports

In Case 7/68 *Commission* v. *Italy (Italian Art)* ([1968] ECR 423) the Court held that a tax imposed on the export of artistic, historical and archaeological treasures from Italy infringed Article 25 EC Treaty. The Court did not admit an exception on the grounds of the sensitivity of the articles in question (they were classed as 'ordinary' goods), or on the grounds of public policy. Later, in Joined Cases 36 and 71/80 *Irish Creamery Milk Suppliers Association* v. *Ireland* ([1981] ECR 735), the Court condemned internal charges on exports as CHEEs if they fall more heavily on exports than on domestic products. However, the imposition of a charge on domestic goods alone, and not on imported goods, is permissible under Articles 23–25 EC, provided the proceeds of the charge are not used to finance activities incompatible with EU law, such as a 'Buy National' campaign (see Case 249/81 *Commission* v. *Ireland* [1982] ECR 4005).

### 4.13  Exceptions to the Prohibition

According to the established case law of the Court of Justice, there are three situations in which a charge will fall outside the prohibition on CHEEs. These are set out in Case 18/87 *Commission* v. *Germany (Live Animals)* ([1988] ECR 5427):

> '[T]he Court has held that such a charge escapes that classification if it relates to a general system of internal dues applied systematically and in accordance with the same criteria to domestic products and imported products alike . . . , if it constitutes payment for a service in fact rendered to the economic operator of a sum in proportion to the service . . . , or again, subject to certain conditions, if it attaches to inspections carried out to fulfil obligations imposed by Community law' (para. 6).

The first of these situations, in which the charge is classified as part of a system of internal taxation, will be subject to scrutiny under Article 90 EC, and will be unlawful if it is found to be discriminatory, is considered in more detail in 4.16. Payment for services is treated in 4.14, and 4.15 covers compensation payable to the state for the conduct of inspections imposed by Community law. As will be seen, this category has recently been extended to cover compensation for state compliance with other Community obligations.

### 4.14  Fees for Services Performed

Services may only be charged if they provide a tangible benefit to the importer (such as a storage service) and not for services rendered in the general public interest. In Case 24/68 *Commission* v. *Italy (Statistical Levy)* ([1969] ECR 193), the Court held that a levy on all imports into, and exports from Italy, used to finance the collection of statistical material for use in discerning trade patterns for the benefit of importers and exporters, was in breach of Articles 9 and 12 (now Articles 23 and 25) EC. The Court determined that the advantage to importers was so general and uncertain, that the charge could not be considered a payment for services rendered.

Member States certainly may not charge for undertaking actual customs formalities. In Case 340/87 *Commission* v. *Italy* ([1989] ECR 1483), Italy sought to justify its charge for customs formalities on the grounds that the charge was needed to cover the cost of the performance of customs services outside the Italian civil servants' normal working day (six hours a day, while EU law required customs posts to be open for at least 10 hours a day). The Court rejected Italy's argument. However, where customs checks are taking place outside the stipulated 10 hour period, these may be regarded as a service to be performed for a commensurate fee (Case C-209/89 *Commission* v. *Italy* [1991] ECR I-1575).

Elsewhere, the Court has ruled that charges imposed for the temporary storage of imported goods are unlawful where the storage is required while customs clearance is being completed (Case 132/82 *Commission* v. *Belgium* [1983] ECR 1649). However, Member States may charge for carrying out customs formalities conducted on the importer's own premises, but fees must be calculated in relation to the cost of the service, not the value of the goods, and must not exceed the cost of the actual customs services (Case 170/88 *Ford España* v. *Spain* [1989] ECR 2305). The dividing line appears to be that whenever the service is imposed on the importer by the state, any charge will be classified as a customs duty or CHEE, while charges for services requested by the importer will be permissible.

### 4.15 Compensation to the State

In addition to payment for services, and the general system of taxation (which will be discussed at 4.16), there is the well-established exception for charges for the conduct of health inspections. Health and safety inspections may be legitimately undertaken under EU law. Although *prima facie* non-tariff barriers to trade, such inspections will normally fall under Article 30 EC, which permits derogations on public health grounds from the prohibition in Article 28 EC, unless they are carried out with a protectionist motive in mind. However, where the inspections are themselves in violation of EU law, any charges will of course be unlawful. Such was the circumstance in Case C-272/95 *Bundesanstalt für Landwirtschaft und Ernährung* v. *Deutsches Milch-Kontor GmbH* ([1997] ECR I-1905), in which Germany imposed systematic inspections on all consignments of powdered skimmed milk entering its territory, despite the fact that EU Regulations had been passed authorising spot checks.

While certain inspections may be legitimate under EU law, this does not automatically result in the legitimacy of the charges relating to them. Charges may be legitimately imposed only for inspections in any of the three following situations, and then subject to certain conditions. The first set of circumstances occurs when the same inspection is undertaken on domestic products as on imports, in which case the same fee must be charged on imports (Case 50/85 *Schloh* v. *Autocontrôle Technique Sprl* [1986] ECR 1855, in which a valid test ensuring the roadworthiness of imported vehicles was imposed on domestically produced vehicles as well).

The second set of circumstances concerns inspections which are mandatory under harmonised EU rules on the health and safety of products (Case 46/76 *Bauhuis* v. *Netherlands* [1977] ECR 5). In Case 18/87 *Commission* v. *Germany (Live Animals)*, the Court held that Germany was permitted to impose fees for inspections of imported live animals under EC legislation, which introduced harmonised arrangements for such inspections (though not the fees themselves) in the Member States. Unlike other services covered in 4.14, the fact that certain inspections are prescribed for the general interest of the EU does not mean that the trader cannot be charged. In *Commission* v. *Germany (Live Animals)*, the

Court rationalised the fee as 'the financially and economically justified compensation for an obligation imposed in equal measure on all the Member States by Community law'.

Thirdly, under the same principles, fees may be charged for inspections undertaken by Member States pursuant to international agreements to which the Community is bound, or to which all the Member States are parties, and which encourage the free movement of goods (Case 89/76 *Commission* v. *Netherlands* [1977] ECR 1355). For example, in Case C-111/89 *Netherlands* v. *Bakker Hillegom* ([1990] ECR I-1735), it was held that the Netherlands was justified in imposing charges for field inspections of plants carried out under an international convention intended to encourage the free importation of plants into the country of destination, by establishing a system of inspections in the exporting state, recognised and organised on a reciprocal basis. The reason for permitting such charges is that they tend to discourage recourse by importing Member States to unilateral inspection measures which would be permissible under Article 30 EC, and that therefore they promote the free movement of goods. However, charges may not be imposed simply because an inspection is expressly permitted, though not mandatory, under EU law (Case 314/82 *Commission* v. *Belgium* [1984] ECR 1543).

In circumstances where a charge may be imposed, it may not be higher than is necessary to cover the cost of the inspection (Case 46/76 *Bauhuis* v. *Netherlands*). To enable this to be assessed accurately, there needs to be a link between the amount of the fee and the costs related to the actual inspection. Thus, the Court held in *Bakker Hillegom* that the fee may not be calculated according to the weight of the products or the invoice value of the products, but rather according to factors such as the duration of the inspection, the number of persons required and the cost of materials used.

Particular difficulties arise in charging for inspections which are carried out on all products, but where the cost is imposed only on imported products. For example, in *Bakker Hillegom*, field inspections were carried out on all plants, but 75 per cent of the costs of the inspections was borne by exporters, which corresponds to the 75 per cent of plants grown which were then exported. The remaining 25 per cent of the cost was borne by the state and not charged to the products intended for the home market. The Court held that such a charging structure would amount to a CHEE on exports, if the products intended for the home market derived any benefit from the inspection for which they were not charged.

This logic of a valid 'compensation' charge being payable to the state where it acts in furtherance of legal obligations which promote the free movement of goods has recently been extended to cover compulsory contributions by exporters of waste to a 'solidarity fund' established to finance the return of illegally exported waste. EU environmental law required Member States to guarantee the return of such waste (Case C-389/00 *Commission* v. *Germany* [2003] ECR I-2001).

### 4.16  The Distinction between CHEEs and Systems of Taxation

Only a 'genuine' taxation system falls outside the prohibition under Articles 23 25 EC, and is subject instead to scrutiny under Article 90 EC. According to the Court in Case 90/79 *Commission* v. *France (Levy on Reprographic Machines)* ([1981] ECR 283), a genuine tax is one relating:

> 'to a general system of internal dues applied systematically to categories of products in accordance with objective criteria irrespective of the origin of the products' (para. 14).

For example, in Joined Cases 2 and 3/62 *Commission* v. *Belgium and Luxembourg (Gingerbread)* ([1962] ECR 425), the Court held that a 'compensatory' tax on imports of gingerbread, alleged to offset the high domestic cost of rye, an ingredient of gingerbread, caused by a national price support system for rye, was not a 'genuine' tax, but a CHEE governed by Article 12 (now Article 25) EC. This is an example of a general principle expounded later in Case 132/78 *Denkavit Loire* v. *France* ([1979] ECR 1923), whereby if a charge is to be treated as part of a system of internal taxation, it must be imposed according to the same criteria on domestic and imported products. For example, it must be imposed at the same stage of marketing, and by the same taxation authorities. In Case 29/72 *Marimex SpA* v. *Ministero delle Finanze* ([1972] ECR 1309), an Italian 'veterinary inspection tax' imposed on imported meat to ensure that it conformed to Italian health standards was held to be a CHEE. Although similar domestic products were subject to inspections and taxes, they were imposed by different bodies under different criteria. In Case C-109/98 *CRT France International SA* v. *Directeur Régional des Impôts de Bourgogne* ([1999] ECR I-2237), a tax on the supply of imported CB radios was held to be a CHEE, since this tax differed from the general system of taxing the user of radio receivers and transmitters.

In contrast, an import surcharge, charged until 1990 as a percentage of general goods duty payable on all goods loaded, unloaded or otherwise handled within Danish ports, was held to be part of a general system of internal dues subject to Article 90 EC (Case C-90/94 *Haahr Petroleum Ltd* v. *Åbenrå Havn et al* [1997] ECR I-4085). The Court based its reasoning initially on an assessment of the general goods duty which was imposed on all goods, domestic and imported, according to the same objective criteria. It then viewed the surcharge as a part of the system of dues, since it was charged as a percentage on those dues. Any discriminatory effect was consequently subject to assessment under Article 90 EC. A pragmatic approach to the operation of the tax/CHEE test is in evidence in Case C-234/99 *Nygård* v. *Svineafgiftsfonden* ([2002] ECR I-3657), where a measure was held to be a tax, despite apparent differences in the taxation regime for exported pigs and those remaining in the home market. The trigger event for the imposition of the tax was the presentation for slaughter of the pigs remaining on the domestic market, while for those intended for export it was on leaving the domestic market. The Court determined both to be the same marketing stage, with both operations being carried out with a view to releasing the pigs from national primary production. Moreover, the fact that the tax was payable by the producer in the case of pigs for the domestic market, and the exporter for those leaving the market, was not fatal to the measure's classification.

If a tax is part of a general system of internal dues, it will be irrelevant that there is little or no domestic production of a particular product. Good examples are taxes on cars in Portugal (Case C-343/90 *Lourenço Dias* v. *Director da Alfandga do Porto* [1992] ECR I-4673), or in Denmark (Case C-47/88 *Commission* v. *Denmark* [1990] ECR I-4509 and Case C-383/01 *De Danske Bilimportører* v. *Skatteministeriet* [2003] ECR I-6065). However, even though such a tax may not fall within Articles 23–25 EC, it will still be subject to scrutiny for discrimination under Article 90 EC (Chapter 7).

Finally, if the revenue from a tax which has been levied on domestic and imported products in accordance with identical criteria is intended to finance activities for the advantage of the taxed domestic products, it will be designated an unlawful CHEE, at least where it fully offsets the fiscal burden carried by the domestic product (Joined Cases

C-78–83/90 *Compagnie Commerciale de l'Ouest* v. *Receveur Principal des Douanes de La Pallice Port* [1992] ECR I-1847 and Case C-72/92 *Scharbatke GmbH* v. *Germany* [1993] ECR I-5509). Where the offset is only partial, the tax will continue to be regarded as potentially discriminatory (Case 73/79 *Commission* v. *Italy* [1980] ECR 1533 and Case C-347/95 *Fazenda Pública* v. *UCAL* [1997] ECR I-4911).

## 4.17   The Recovery of Unlawfully Levied Charges

As a general principle of EU law, where charges are levied unlawfully by national authorities they must be reimbursed to aggrieved importers and exporters. In Case 199/82 *Amministrazione delle Finanze dello Stato* v. *SpA San Giorgio* ([1983] ECR 3595), the Court reiterated the well-established point that national remedies for breach of EU law must be both the same as those available for breach of equivalent domestic prohibitions, and also not such as to render the enforcement of EU law impossible in practice.

The Court has also stated that national authorities are permitted to apply national principles of unjust enrichment in order to justify not reimbursing some or all of the tax, in the face of evidence that the burden of the tax has been passed downstream to its customers by the claimant. However, the authorities are not entitled to assume that this has happened (Case 104/86 *Commission* v. *Italy (Repayment of Illegal Taxes)* [1988] ECR 1799). In some circumstances, national law effectively requires the tax to be passed on, as in Joined Cases C-192–218/95 *Société Comateb and Others* v. *Directeur Général des Douanes et Droits Indirects* ([1997] ECR I-165), where the referring French court assumed that the unlawfully levied *octroi de mer*, or dock dues, must have been passed on by the traders upon whom it was imposed, because of the French prohibition upon resale at a loss. The Court held that the national court could not impose a presumption that the tax had been passed on, nor that it was for the trader who paid the tax to prove otherwise. The burden lay on the Member State to prove that the tax had been passed on in its entirety to another party before it could resist repayment of that part which had not been passed on. Most intriguingly, the Court then went on to cut away at the unjust enrichment defence which it had developed by pointing out that in some circumstances, a trader may claim that the very imposition of dock dues reduces general levels of profitability, even if it is passed on to a third party, by raising prices, reducing imports and leading to a decrease in sales. In those circumstances, if that general loss is recoverable under national law in the context of the main proceedings for recovery, the national court must give effect to the claim. Alternatively, the trader may bring a more general claim based on the EU legal principle of state liability developed in Joined Cases C-46 and 48/93 *Brasserie du Pêcheur* v. *Germany* and *ex parte Factortame (Factortame III)* ([1996] ECR I-1029) for reparation of the loss caused by the levying of the charges in breach of EU law. Finally, in Joined Cases C-441/98 and 442/98 *Kapniki Mikhaïlidis* v. *IKA* ([2000] ECR I-7145), the Court rejected an attempt to make the increase in the price of exported goods and a reduction in the volume of sales of those goods serve as the requirements for a successful action for repayment of unlawfully levied charges, instead of having them serve as the basis of a separate cause of action such as in *Comateb*.

## Summary

1. Article 23(1) EC Treaty establishes that the Community is based on a customs union. This customs union has both internal and external dimensions.

2. The external dimension applies to trade between EU states and the rest of the world. The EU operates a Common Customs Tariff (CCT), under which duties on goods entering the EU will be the same, wherever they enter the Union. There is an international commitment to lower, or remove, such tariffs.

3. The external customs union and the CCT have the objectives of: providing the EU with budgetary resources; providing a framework for international trade; and protecting against unlawful or dangerous trade.

4. The amount payable on goods crossing the CCT is calculated on the basis of their nomenclature, valuation and origin.

5. The customs union and the CCT are administered by national authorities, within a regulatory framework created by the EC institutions. It is important to identify the correct author of a legal act if challenges to the legality of customs decisions are to be made – this is not always straightforward.

6. Once goods are in free circulation in the EU, member states may not impose customs duties or charges having equivalent effect to customs duties (CHEE) on products moving around the EU. States must also avoid levying discriminatory or protectionist levels of taxation on them.

7. The prohibition against customs duties and CHEE in Article 25 EC Treaty is interpreted strictly. No Treaty-based exceptions to this rule are available.

8. The Court has recognised that charges may legitimately be levied on traders: when the charge is imposed in return for a service undertaken at the request of the trader, and which is commensurate to the service received; when the charge may be regarded as 'compensation' payable to the state for its actions in compliance with EU/international law where these have the objective of furthering the goal of free movement of goods, as with certain health inspections; and when the charge is properly to be regarded as an aspect of the state's taxation system.

## Exercises

1. What are the objectives of the external and internal dimensions of the customs union?

2. Why is it important to know where a product originates from?

3. What guidance is available on establishing the correct nomenclature of a product under the CCT?

4. What is the role of national administrations in the operation of the CCT?

5. Outline the key difficulties applicants may have challenging the validity of decisions taken in the context of the CCT.

6. What are the characteristics of a charge having equivalent effect to a customs duty?

7. Under what circumstances will a charge escape classification as an unlawful CHEE?

8. What distinguishes a customs duty/CHEE from an internal taxation measure?

## Further Reading

Barnard, C. (2004) *The Substantive Law of the EU: The Four Freedoms*, Oxford: Oxford University Press, chapter 3.

Gormley, L. (1996) 'Consolidation, Codification and Improving the Quality of Community Legislation – The Community Customs Code', in Emiliou, N. and O'Keeffe, D. (eds.), *The European Union and World Trade Law*, London: Wiley.

Lavranos, L. (2005) 'The Communitarisation of WTO Dispute Settlement Reports: an Exception to the Rule of Law', 10 *European Foreign Affairs Review* 313.

Lyons, T. (2001) *EC Customs Law*, Oxford: Oxford University Press.

Maher, I. (1995) 'Legislative Review by the EC Commission: Review without Radicalism', in Shaw, J. and More, G. (eds.), *New Legal Dynamics of European Union*, Oxford: Clarendon.

McMahon, J. (1998) 'The EC Banana Regime, the WTO Rulings and the ACP: Fighting for Economic Survival?', 32 *Journal of World Trade Law* 101.

McMahon, J. (2005) 'International Trade; Customs; European Union; Food; "The Longstanding Banana Saga" – Towards an Acceptable Solution: Part 1', 11 *International Trade Law and Regulation* 181.

Peers, S. (2001) 'W.T.O. Dispute Settlement and Community Law', 26 *European Law Review* 605.

Smith, F. (2000) 'Renegotiating Lomé: the Impact of the World Trade Organisation on the European Community's Development Policy after the Bananas Conflict', 25 *European Law Review* 247.

Usher, J. (1996) 'Consequences of the Customs Union', in Emiliou, N. and O'Keeffe, D. (eds.), *The European Union and World Trade Law*, London: Wiley.

## Key Websites

The European Commission's website for customs law and policy is at:
**http://ec.europa.eu/taxation_customs/index_en.htm**

The website for the World Trade Organisation (WTO), the global international organisation dealing with the rules of trade between nations, is available at:
**http://www.wto.org/**

The website for the World Customs Organisation (WCO), an independent intergovernmental body whose mission is to enhance the effectiveness and efficiency of Customs administrations, is available at:
**http://www.wcoomd.org/ie/index.html**

# Chapter 5

# Non-Tariff Barriers to Trade in Goods

**5.1**    Introduction

The removal of tariff barriers to trade is not enough by itself to create the conditions for a single market for trade in goods. Standing in the way of a single, internal market are a wide range of non-tariff barriers, which may need to be removed, or harmonised, in the interests of the EU market-making exercise. This chapter focuses on these non-tariff barriers to interstate trade, and in particular, on the contribution of the Court of Justice to their elimination. It also considers various harmonisation strategies employed by the EU in respect to certain non-tariff barriers. The concept of non-tariff barriers is potentially vast in scope. Obvious non-tariff barriers to trade include bans, quotas and other quantitative restrictions imposed on the entry of goods into their territory by Member States. There are however many other non-tariff measures which may equally result in the segmentation of the EU market along national lines, not least divergent product and technical standards, which may block entry to the domestic market of products manufactured elsewhere in the EU in accordance with alternative standards. Indeed, almost any regulatory divergence between two national markets represents a potential hindrance to trade. For example, divergent retail market rules (e.g. advertising rules, shop opening hours, product licensing, price regulation, even divergent labour market regulation measures) may restrict the marketing of goods coming from outside national markets, and hence the process of market integration.

This chapter commences with a presentation of basic provisions and concepts, before embarking on an examination and assessment of the Court's interpretation of the core provisions on non-tariff barriers. These are found in Articles 28 and 29 EC (former Articles 30 and 34 EC), which provide for the prohibition of measures having equivalent effect to quantitative restrictions (MEEQRs), subject to exemptions to be found in Article 30 EC (former Article 36 EC). The Court has struggled with its task of determining where the proper reach of these articles ought to lie, and has sometimes been inconsistent. Clearly of the view that the functional demands of creating the market required more than simply removing overtly discriminatory and protectionist national measures, the Court's expansive interpretation of the free movement provisions resulted in seemingly ever increasing situations where national regulatory choices would be opened up to scrutiny under Article 28 EC. Amidst criticisms that the Court had overextended the scope of Article 28 EC, it embarked on a no less controversial revision of its approach. Having considered the case law which sets where the limits of Articles 28 and 29 EC lie, this chapter turns to examine the grounds on which national measures which otherwise interfere with the free movement principle may be saved. In 5.16 the focus shifts from negative integration, and the removal of national laws and practices conflicting with the requirements of the internal market, to a consideration of examples of positive integration, and the creation of common regulatory frameworks to facilitate the free movement of goods, building upon the material covered in Chapter 3.

## 5.2  The Treaty Provisions

Article 28 EC provides:

> 'Quantitative restrictions on imports and all measures having equivalent effect shall be prohibited between Member States.'

This is supplemented by Article 29 EC which states:

> 'Quantitative restrictions on exports, and all measures having equivalent effect, shall be prohibited between Member States.'

Article 30 EC provides for derogations from these prohibitions:

> 'The provisions of Articles 28 and 29 shall not preclude prohibitions or restrictions on imports, exports or goods in transit justified on grounds of public morality, public policy or public security; the protection of health and life of humans, animals or plants; the protection of national treasures possessing artistic, historic or archaeological value; or the protection of industrial and commercial property. Such prohibitions or restrictions shall not, however, constitute a means of arbitrary discrimination or a disguised restriction on trade between Member States.'

Since the end of the transitional period, the direct effect of these provisions has not been in doubt, and was stated expressly by the Court in relation to Article 28 EC in Case 74/76 *Ianelli and Volpi SpA* v. *Meroni* ([1977] ECR 557) and in relation to Article 29 EC in Case 83/78 *Pigs Marketing Board* v. *Redmond* ([1978] ECR 2347). While vertically directly effective, these provisions are not recognised as being horizontally directly effective, and as such cannot be directly relied upon against private parties before national courts. This is because the provisions are not recognised as binding on private parties. In Case 311/85 *Vlaamse Reisbureau's* ([1987] ECR 3821) the Court stated explicitly that Articles 28 and 29 EC 'concern only public measures and not the conduct of undertakings' (para. 30). Consequently, the provisions do not apply to the obstacles which individuals place in the way of economic integration, such as refusing to buy or sell imported goods, or refusing to deal with undertakings from other Member States. A variety of less overt forms of potentially trade-inhibiting action, resulting from contractual relations between private parties, will also fall outside Articles 28–30 EC, such as the requirement to place a 'green dot' recycling logo on products for participation in a company's collection and recycling scheme (Case C-159/00 *Sapod Audic* v. *Eco-Emballages* [2002] ECR I-5031).

The non-application of the free movement of goods rules to private parties is now out of line with the Court's interpretation of the Treaty provisions on the free movement of persons. Arguably the text of Articles 28 and 29 EC does not explicitly exclude the provisions' application to the acts of private parties. Further, given the fundamental importance of securing the free movement of goods, it may be thought surprising that the Court has not brought private parties clearly within the scope of application of the provisions. However, by requiring the purchasing preferences of individuals to be monitored and open to legal challenge could rightly be regarded as a step too far for EU law. Also, the actions of private undertakings is already subject to the operation of the Treaty's competition law regime, which would be severely disrupted if Articles 28–30 EC were deemed to have horizontal direct effect (see Van den Bogaert, 2002: 139–40).

As well as binding the Member States, the provisions bind the institutions, and they are therefore precluded from authorising otherwise unlawful Member State actions, for example, in respect to the common agricultural policy (Case 9/73 *Schlüter* v. *Hauptzollamt Lorrach* [1973] ECR 1135). The only exception is where they are expressly or implicitly authorised to do so by other provisions of the Treaty.

## 5.3　State Measures

Articles 28–30 EC are concerned with *state measures*. 'Measures' have been held to include not only legally binding acts, but also practices 'capable of influencing the conduct of traders and consumers' (Case 249/81 *Commission* v. *Ireland (Buy Irish)* [1982] ECR 4005), and administrative practices, if they have 'a certain degree of consistency and generality' (Case 21/84 *Commission* v. *France (Franking Machines)* [1985] ECR 1355). This case concerned a French administrative requirement that prior approval be given to postal franking machines, where approval was not granted to UK machines.

Further, the situations in which actions are ascribed to the state have been widely drawn. They include, as with the *Buy Irish* example, the situation where a private company organises a buy national campaign, where it receives instructions and funding from the government. In Case 222/82 ([1982] ECR 4083), the Court ruled that the activities of the UK's *Apple and Pear Development Council* were capable of infringing Article 28, owing to the Council's statutory basis, and the fact that it operated on the basis of compulsory contributions from its members. On the same grounds, the actions of a private company, which awarded quality labels to German-produced goods, were also brought within Article 28 EC (Case C-325/00 *Commission* v. *Germany (Quality Mark)* [2002] ECR I-9977). Professional associations which operate with powers conferred by national legislation may also be brought within Article 28, as in Joined Cases 266 and 267/87 *R* v. *Royal Pharmaceutical Society of Great Britain, ex parte Association of Pharmaceutical Importers* ([1989] ECR 1295), in which the Society had been granted disciplinary powers extending to the removal from the register of persons authorised to exercise the profession in question.

The Court has also held that state measures for the purposes of Article 28 may include state *inaction* in the face of private individuals' actions which obstruct the free movement of goods. In Case C-265/95 *Commission* v. *France (French Farmers)* ([1997] ECR I-6959), at issue was the French state's response to ongoing demonstrations held by farmers in France, which involved blockades and the destruction of agricultural goods produced in other states. The Court, drawing on both the fundamental role of Article 28 and the Article 10 EC duty of loyal cooperation, which requires states to take 'all appropriate measures, whether general or particular, to ensure fulfilment of the obligations arising out of [the] Treaty', held that France had failed to take necessary and proportionate measures to deal with the problem, and was thus in breach of its obligations. In Case C-112/00 *Schmidberger* ([2003] ECR I-5659), meanwhile, the Austrian authorities' decision not to ban a one-day environmental demonstration which resulted in the temporary closure of the Brenner motorway (resulting in obstacles to entry, exit and transit of goods through Austria) was held to be caught by the free movement provisions. However, the Court eventually concluded Austria was not in breach of its obligations under the Treaty, on the grounds that the authorities' response to the demonstrators (and specifically, by respecting their fundamental rights of freedom of expression and assembly) rendered their inaction 'objectively justified' as being in the public interest.

## 5.4    Quantitative Restrictions and Measures Having Equivalent Effect

Quantitative restrictions are 'measures which amount to a total or partial restraint of, according to the circumstances, imports, exports or goods in transit' (Case 2/73 *Geddo* v. *Ente Nationale Risi* [1973] ECR 865). Thus, they are measures capable of limiting imports to a finite quantity, including zero, and clearly include both import bans (Case 34/79 *R* v. *Henn and Darby* [1979] ECR 3795, involving a ban on imports of pornographic material into the UK).

While quantitative restrictions are usually readily identifiable, the definition of the category of measures having equivalent effect to quantitative restrictions (MEEQR) has provided the Court with more challenging questions. An early view on the precise scope of Article 28 EC came from the Commission in Directive 70/50 (OJ Spec. Ed. 1970, p.17), which was issued at the conclusion of the transitional period, and which is now no longer in force. The directive divides national measures restrictive of trade into two categories:

▶ those which distinguish overtly between imported and domestic products, referred to as *distinctly applicable* measures; and
▶ those which are *indistinctly applicable* to all products – that is, which apply without any formal distinction based on national origin.

Article 2(2) of the directive lists as falling under the prohibition in Article 28 EC in particular the following distinctly applicable measures:

'measures which make imports or the disposal, at any marketing stage, of imported products subject to a condition – other than a formality – which is required in respect of imported products only, or a condition differing from that required for domestic products and more difficult to satisfy. Equally, it covers, in particular, measures which favour domestic products or grant them a preference, other than an aid, to which conditions may or may not be attached.'

Article 2(3) lists numerous examples of the types of measures covered including measures which control the prices or profit margins in respect of imported products alone, which require imported products to be marketed via a national agent, and which restrict the access of imported products to the national market.

Article 3 confirms that indistinctly applicable measures are subject to the prohibition in Article 28 EC, but only subject to certain qualifications:

'This Directive also covers measures governing the marketing of products which deal, in particular, with shape, size, weight, composition, presentation, identification or putting up and which are equally applicable to domestic and imported products, where the restrictive effect of such measures on the free movement of goods exceeds the effects intrinsic to trade rules. This is the case, in particular, where:
▶ the restrictive effects on the free movement of goods are out of proportion to their purpose;
▶ the same objective can be attained by other means which are less of a hindrance to trade.'

This definition, offered by the Commission, was reached without assistance from case law of the Court. The Court's own classic definition of a MEEQR was first presented in Case 8/74 *Procureur du Roi* v. *Dassonville* ([1974] ECR 837). The case concerned criminal proceedings in Belgium against a trader who acquired a consignment of Scotch whisky in free circulation in France, and imported it into Belgium without being in possession of a certificate of origin from the UK customs authorities. This was a violation of Belgian customs requirements, the UK at that time not being part of the customs union.

Dassonville prepared his own certificate of origin and was prosecuted for forgery. The Court of Justice, on a reference from the Belgian court, held:

> 'All trading rules enacted by Member States which are capable of hindering, directly or indirectly, actually or potentially, intra-Community trade are to be considered as measures having an effect equivalent to quantitative restrictions' (para. 5).

This is an extremely broad definition, which has acquired the status of a classic statement of the scope of Article 28, and has been cited repeatedly by the Court as justifying its decisions in subsequent cases. It is an effects-based test and, while intention to discriminate is sufficient for a measure to be caught, it is by no means necessary. These effects need only be 'potential', not realised, and, as further established in Joined Cases 177 and 178/82 *Criminal Proceedings against Van De Haar and Kaveka de Meern* ([1984] ECR 1797), it does not matter how slight the effect of the trading rule on interstate trade is, it will still be caught by Article 28, as there is no *de minimis* rule. Nonetheless, the Court has on occasion held measures to be outside the reach of the Treaty prohibitions where the effects of the national measure are considered too remote to impact on trade. Thus, national rules which apply without distinction to domestic and imported goods, and which are not designed to regulate trade in goods with other Member States, and whose restrictive effects on the free movement of goods are too uncertain and indirect, will avoid censure. Case C-69/88 *Krantz* v. *Otvanger der Directie Belastingen* ([1990] ECR I-583), concerning a national law permitting tax authorities to seize goods and hold them against the tax debts, is a good example. Case C-20/03 *Burmanjer et al* ([2005] ECR I-4133) contains a shift in language, excluding national measures which are 'too *insignificant* and uncertain to be regarded as being such as to hinder or otherwise interfere with trade between Member States'. Nonetheless, this may still be viewed as a question of causation and remoteness, and is not the same as the question of whether trade is, or would be only minimally, affected.

The *Dassonville* definition has been interpreted as covering both distinctly and indistinctly applicable measures, the latter having proved particularly problematic as the Court has struggled to fix the proper limits of the reach of Article 28. After all, by making 'all trading rules' which may hinder trade open to challenge under Article 28, the Court has made a significant incursion into Member States' autonomy in their public policy choices: for example, national rules placing bans or even less onerous restrictions on the sale of products regarded as harmful, such as drugs, alcohol or cigarettes, may *prima facie* fall within Article 28, albeit that such measures may ultimately be saved by a successful pleading of the public interest exemptions.

### 5.5 Article 28 EC and Distinctly Applicable MEEQR

Distinctly applicable measures are those measures that in some way hinder access to a state's market as a result of a difference in treatment of goods on the basis of their national origin. These measures may not necessarily block the entry of the imported product onto a state's market, but may, for example, increase the costs borne by the import, or in some other way divert consumer choice away from the imported good. The case law of the Court has provided a wealth of examples of the application of Article 28 to such measures, including:

▶ *Import licences* The requirement to obtain licences prior to importing a product, even when these licences are issued automatically and are a pure formality, is a

MEEQR: Case 124/81 *Commission* v. *United Kingdom (Imports of UHT Milk)* ([1983] ECR 203) and see Case C-434/04 *Criminal Proceedings against Ahokainen and Leppik* ([2006] ECR I-9171) concerning Finnish rules requiring licences for the import of high strength alcohol.

▶ *Origin marking*   In Case 113/80 *Commission* v. *Ireland (Souvenirs)* ([1981] ECR 1625) the Court condemned the Irish requirement that Irish-themed souvenirs manufactured outside Ireland be marked 'foreign'; in Case C-30/99 *Commission* v. *Ireland (Precious Metals)* ([2001] ECR I-4619), the Court condemned the requirement that imported precious metal articles bear different hallmarks from domestically manufactured precious metal articles.

▶ *'Buy national campaigns'*   Case 249/81 *Commission* v. *Ireland (Buy Irish)*; compare Case 222/82 *Apple and Pear Development Council*, in which the Court acknowledged that a carefully formulated promotion campaign which draws attention to the qualities of typically national varieties of goods and organises campaigns to promote the sale of such goods, will be compatible with Article 28 provided that it does not discourage the purchase of imported goods or disparage the qualities of such goods in the eyes of consumers. Germany attempted, but failed, to present their quality mark scheme as compatible with Article 28 under these terms in Case C-325/00 *Commission* v. *Germany (Quality Mark)*.

▶ *Inspections or checks*   In Case 4/75 *Rewe-Zentralfinanz* v. *Landwirtschaftskammer Bonn* ([1975] ECR 843), the Court held that Article 28 applied to an inspection of imported apples designed to control a pest called San Jose scale; in Case 42/82 *Commission* v. *France* ([1983] ECR 1013) Article 28 was held to cover excessive delays in customs clearance, resulting from systematic checks of wine to ensure that it complied with quality standards.

▶ *Discriminatory purchasing requirements*   Article 28 covered a requirement that all importers of oil into Ireland purchase 35 per cent of their requirements of petroleum products from the Irish National Petroleum Co. at a price to be fixed by the Minister (Case 72/83 *Campus Oil Ltd* v. *Minister for Industry and Energy* [1984] ECR 2727); it is also worth noting Case C-398/98 *Commission* v. *Greece* ([2003] ECR I-7915), which made marketing companies' use of storage facilities at refineries in Greece dependent on their purchase of minimum stocks of petroleum from these refineries.

▶ *Discriminatory public procurement measures*   Article 28 may restrict the use of regional policy legislation which is linked to the procurement of goods by public bodies; it was held to cover the requirement under Italian law that all public or semi-public bodies buy a fixed quota of their supplies from companies operating in the Mezzogiorno (Case C-21/88 *Du Pont de Nemours Italiana SpA* v. *Unita Sanitaria Locale No. 2 di Carrara* [1990] ECR I-889).

It should be noted that any of these measures may be justified potentially under the derogations from Article 28 contained in Article 30.

## 5.6   Article 28 EC and Indistinctly Applicable MEEQR

The distinctly applicable measures considered above may be equated with directly discriminatory measures. Discrimination may be direct, in the sense that an overt distinction is drawn between goods on the basis of nationality, relating to different treatment in law and in fact for domestic and imported goods. It may also be indirect, that is, it may be covert discrimination, involving the application of the same rule to both domestic and imported goods, but that rule has a more onerous impact on the imported good. It would appear from Directive 70/50, and the examples of distinctly and indistinctly applicable measures provided there, that Article 28 was expected to bite on both directly and indirectly discriminatory measures.

However, it must be noted that in developing its category of indistinctly applicable measures for the purposes of Article 28, the Court moved beyond a discrimination-based test. Rather than requiring a comparison between domestic and imported goods to be made, and proof of differential impact and damaging effect on the latter be adduced, the Court focused instead simply on the question of whether there were disparities between national regulatory systems which could give rise to restrictions to trade. This approach was already present in *Dassonville*, and was confirmed in respect to indistinctly applicable measures in the next case in the free movement canon: Case 120/78 *Rewe-Zentrale AG* v. *Bundesmonopolverwaltung für Branntwein (Cassis de Dijon)* ([1979] ECR 649).

*Cassis de Dijon* involved a German law which prohibited the marketing of liqueurs with an alcoholic strength of less than 25 per cent. This made it impossible for the plaintiff to import a consignment of Cassis de Dijon, a French blackcurrant liqueur, with a strength of between 15 and 20 per cent, into Germany. The liqueur could therefore not compete with the stronger, and more expensive, German equivalent. There were no restrictions on the production and marketing of the weaker liqueur in France. The German Government claimed that the fixing of minimum alcohol contents had two functions. First, it avoided the proliferation of alcoholic beverages on the national market, in particular alcoholic drinks with a low alcohol content; the Government argued that such products may more easily induce a tolerance towards alcohol than drinks with a high alcohol content; and secondly, it protected the consumer against unfair practices on the part of producers and distributors of alcoholic drinks consisting of lowering the alcohol content in order to obtain a competitive advantage in price.

The Court of Justice considered that the restriction on trade stemmed from the disparity between the French and German legislation on liqueurs. It concluded that in principle, there is no valid reason why, provided they have been lawfully produced in one of the Member States, alcoholic drinks should not be introduced into any other Member State. The only exception to this principle, termed 'mutual recognition', is where the disparities result from national provisions which are recognised as being necessary in order to satisfy certain 'mandatory requirements'. *Cassis de Dijon* contained a non-exhaustive list of these mandatory requirements, i.e. measures in the general interest, which comprised the protection of public health, the effectiveness of fiscal supervision, the fairness of commercial transactions and the defence of the consumer. This list of measures in the general interest has since been substantially added to by the Court (see 5.11).

Applying the principle of mandatory requirements, sometimes termed the 'rule of reason', to the measure in question in *Cassis*, the Court used a proportionality test. It looked to see, first, whether the justifications raised fell within the concept of mandatory requirements; second, whether there was a serious and coherent national policy actually being operated; and third, whether the measures adopted were reasonably necessary to pursue the policy operated, and whether they were proportionate to the aims. As regards the argument on health put forward by the German Government in *Cassis de Dijon*, the Court held that there was in fact no coherent public health policy being pursued through the ban on low alcohol liqueurs, since in practice a whole range of alcoholic beverages of varying alcohol contents was available in Germany. It also concluded that a ban was a disproportionate way of protecting the consumer against unfair practices. A system of labelling could have achieved the same effect in a less restrictive way.

*Cassis* then established clearly that indistinctly applicable measures could be caught by Article 28. Subsequently two lines of case law evolved covering two main types of indistinctly applicable measures. The first type are indistinctly applicable measures akin to those at issue in *Cassis*, which concern product requirements, that is, rules regulating the physical attributes of a product which is to be put on sale, its composition and labelling, for example. The second concerns indistinctly applicable rules regulating the circumstances under which products may be sold or marketed, for example, restricting sale to licensed premises, or restricting advertising. The Court's approach to these two types of measure differs, with indistinctly applicable product requirement rules being presumed to fall within Article 28 (as discussed in 5.7), while there is a (rebuttable) presumption that indistinctly applicable selling arrangements fall outside Article 28 (see 5.8). In relation to both types of measures, where Article 28 does apply, the possibility for justifying the national measure extends to encompass the broader mandatory requirements, as well as the Article 30 grounds.

## 5.7  Indistinctly Applicable Product Requirement Rules

In *Cassis*, the Court found that disparities existing between the relevant French and German rules on alcoholic strength of fruit liqueurs resulted in a restriction on trade. French-produced wine which complied with French standards was barred from accessing the German market owing to the different standards required there. Subjecting products to two sets of regulatory requirements, home and host state, has been described as subjecting them to a 'dual burden'. This can be compared with the single burden carried by domestic products placed on the domestic market. The clearest examples of such dual burden rules include cases concerning product requirements, that is, measures which specify how something is to be made, what it is to consist of and how it is to be presented for sale.

Such 'dual burdens' may result in goods being barred from national markets, or it may make their manufacture more time-consuming and expensive than it would have been absent the further regulatory requirements, as manufacturers seek to alter their products to make them acceptable for the host state market. Following *Cassis*, and in particular from the mutual recognition principle, it is clear that when the importing, host state imposes stricter – or simply different – contents requirements than the home state of manufacture, these will have to be justified under the mandatory requirements principle (or under Article 30) if they are to remain applicable.

Significant use has been made by traders of Article 28 and the mutual recognition principle to overcome obstacles to free movement arising from a wide range of indistinctly applicable regulations governing the requirements to be met by products intended for sale on the market. While some product regulations imposed by the state may have been artfully constructed so as to protect the market for national products, and amount to protectionism or overt discrimination, very many more are the unintended consequences of a state's regulation in the public interest (such as consumer protection, protection of health and of the environment), and others, simply, are the result of ingrained national practices, conforming with the way that things have always been done.

Thus, the rules on the presentation of products may be caught by Article 28. In Case 261/81 *Walter Rau* v. *de Smedt* ([1982] ECR 3961) the Court held that a Belgian law requiring margarine to be packed in cube-shaped boxes, allegedly introduced in the interests of consumers in order to enable them to distinguish margarine from butter, fell within Article 28. The reservation of certain types of container for particular products likewise falls *prima facie* within Article 28. Case 16/83 *Prantl* ([1984] ECR 1299) concerned bulbous-shaped bottles from Italy, which closely resembled the German 'Bocksbeutel' which is reserved under German law for a quality wine from a particular region of Germany; the Italian bottles themselves were also traditional to Italy. The Court held that the restriction fell within Article 28.

Also caught are rules on the composition of products. Examples include rules on the permitted contents of bread in the Netherlands (Case 130/80 *Keldermann* [1981] ECR 527), the permitted ingredients of pasta in Italy (Case 407/85 *Drei Glocken* v. *USL* [1988] ECR 4233) and of sausages in Germany (Case 274/87 *Commission* v. *Germany* [1989] ECR 229), as well as national restrictions on the addition of vitamins, nutrients, minerals and other supplements to foods (Case 174/82 *Officier van Justitie* v. *Sandoz* [1983] ECR 2445; Case C-192/01 *Commission* v. *Denmark* [2003] ECR I-9693; and Case C-24/00 *Commission* v. *France* [2004] ECR I-1277).

Closely related are attacks on denomination requirements, such as the German *Reinheitsgebot* which restricted the use of the term 'Bier' to drinks containing only certain barley, hops, yeast and water (Case 178/84 *Commission* v. *Germany (Reinheitsgebot)* [1987] ECR 1227) and the reservation of the name 'chocolate' to products made with cocoa butter alone, and no other form of fat (Case C-14/00 *Commission* v. *Italy* [2001] ECR I-513 and Case C-12/00 *Commission* v. *Spain* [2001] ECR I-459). Indeed, in the event that national legislation on product content and denomination fails to provide for mutual recognition equivalent to products marketed under the same terms in other states, then the state will have failed to fulfil EU law obligations (Case C-184/96 *Commission* v. *France (Foie Gras)* [1998] ECR I-6197).

Sometimes states may seek to protect the use of particular names and designations, allowing only goods made in a particular region, and in accordance with a particular process to use such names. Where such product names have become generic, and are no longer indicative of a product produced in a particular region, the *Cassis* approach will be applied. If the imported product was made in accordance with the requirements imposed in the state of production, then, unless mandatory requirements are successfully raised, the goods should be able to be marketed in the host state. For example, in Case C-448/98 *Guimont* ([2000] ECR I-10663), a successful challenge was brought against French rules which required cheese marketed as 'Emmenthal' to have a rind, although no such requirement was in place in the Member State of production. Conversely, in Joined Cases C-465 and 466/02 *Germany and Denmark* v. *Commission* ([2005] ECR I-9115) the Court ruled that Feta cheese was not generic. Where such 'indications of provenance' (which identify the geographical source of the product) and 'designations of origin' (which further identify that particular defined methods of production have been employed) have not fallen into generic use, they may be protected under the system of registration now found in Council Regulation 510/2006 (OJ 2006 L93/12) (replacing Regulation 2081/92 (OJ 1992 L208/1)), which allows restrictions on the marketing of such products bearing this title. This is discussed further in 5.17 where measures of positive integration are considered.

The restrictions arising in these cases result from disparities in national regulatory regimes – they arise where harmonising legislation, introducing common Europe-wide regulatory solutions in the interests of, for example, health and safety, and consumer protection does not exist, or only partially occupies the relevant field. For many commentators (Bernard,1996; Hilson, 1999; Nic Shuibhne, 2002), the effects of placing additional obstacles before imports, owing to different product standards being operated by host and home states, are such that host state product requirements should be classified as indirectly discriminatory measures. It should be reiterated however that the Court has not always used the discrimination concept or language as regards these cases. As Oliver and Jarvis make clear (2002: 124), with regard to product requirement rules, it is the fact that the national measures are restrictive of trade (albeit potentially) which is critical for the Court, not that they are discriminatory.

## 5.8  Indistinctly Applicable Selling Arrangement Rules

Product requirement rules are presumed to fall within Article 28, requiring justification under Article 30 or one of the mandatory requirements. The Court takes a rather different approach to measures which deal with the rules governing circumstances in which goods are sold or marketed. These selling arrangement rules are presumed to fall outside the scope of Article 28, and will not require justification, as their impact on trade is assumed not to put imports at a disadvantage. However, this is a rebuttable presumption, and indistinctly applicable selling arrangements which do not affect 'in the same manner, in law and in fact, the marketing of domestic products and of those from other Member States' will fall within Article 28 and require justification if they are to stand.

The distinction between selling arrangements and product requirements was introduced in Joined Cases C-267 and 268/91 *Criminal Proceedings against Keck and Mithouard* ([1993] ECR I-6097). *Keck* concerned a criminal action brought against two supermarket managers for offering products for sale at a price lower than the supermarkets' actual purchase price. This was in contravention of the French law which prohibited resale at a loss. Keck and Mithouard argued that the law under which they had been convicted itself breached Article 28, as it constituted a hindrance to the free movement of goods. The Court did not agree. While the French law closed down one means of sales promotion for products, and may as a consequence have reduced the overall volume of goods sold, the Court ruled that if the national measure affects 'in the same manner, in law and in fact, the marketing of domestic products and of those from other Member States', the measure should fall outside the reach of Article 28 as interpreted in *Dassonville*, as it 'is not by nature such as to prevent access to the market or impede access any more than it impedes the access of domestic products' (*Keck*, paras. 16 and 17).

Selling arrangements deal with where, when and by whom goods may be sold. Specific examples of such measures include:

▶ rules on the hours during which particular goods can be sold at locations such as petrol stations (Joined Cases C-401 and 402/92 *Criminal Proceedings against Tankstation 't Heustke vof and J.B.E. Boermans* [1994] ECR I-2199);
▶ rules restricting Sunday trading (Joined Cases C-69 and 258/93 *Punto Casa SpA* v. *Sindaco del Commune di Capena* [1994] ECR I-2355);

▶ a requirement that bakers, butchers and grocers have permanent establishments in those administrative districts (or neighbouring ones) in which they wish to have delivery rounds (Case C-254/98 *Schutzverband gegen unlauteren Wettbewerb* v. *TK Heimdienst Sass GmbH* [2000] ECR I-151);

▶ the prohibition of the sale of pharmaceutical products by mail order (Case C-322/01 *Deutscher Apothekerverband* v. *0800 DocMorris NV and Jacques Waterval* [2003] ECR I-4887); and

▶ the prohibition of the sale of jewellery in private houses (Case C-441/04 *A-Punkt Schmuckhandels* v. *Schmidt* [2006] ECR I-2093).

Also included in the definition of selling arrangements are rules concerning sales promotion and advertising, and a range of prohibitions and restrictions on advertising and marketing strategies have been identified as such by the Court, such as:

▶ restrictions on advertising of products by pharmacists (Case C-292/92 *Hünermund* [1993] ECR I-6787);

▶ restrictions on television advertising for the distribution sector (Case C-412/93 *Société d'Importation Edouard Leclerc-Siplec* v. *TFI and M6* [1995] ECR I-179);

▶ bans on advertising directed at children (Joined Cases C-34–36/95 *Konsument-ombudsmannen* v. *De Agostini* [1997] ECR I-3843);

▶ bans on the advertising of alcohol (Case C-405/98 *Konsumentombudsmannen* v. *Gourmet International* [2001] ECR I-1795).

Where the measure impacts on the intrinsic physical characteristics of the product itself, it will be considered a product requirement, and not a selling arrangement. For example, an Austrian prohibition on prize competitions in magazines required German magazines carrying them to be altered to enter the Austrian market (Case C-368/95 *Vereinigte Familiapress Zeitungsverlags- und vertriebs GmbH* v. *Heinrich Bauer Verlag* ([1997] ECR I-3689), and as such constituted a product requirement. Thus, to take a hypothetical example, national legislation prohibiting the sale of cigarettes exceeding maximum tar and nicotine levels would be considered to be a product requirement measure, while national rules restricting the sale of cigarettes to licensed premises, or prohibiting their advertising, would be selling arrangements.

Having identified a measure as a selling arrangement, the next step is to consider whether the measure fulfils the conditions set out in *Keck* and thus falls outside Article 28: does it apply to all relevant traders operating within the national territory and does it affect in the same manner, in law and in fact, the marketing of domestic products and of those from other Member States? Following *Keck*, if the national measure impacts in an even-handed manner on traders, it will fall outside Article 28, as the measures in *Tankstation 't Heuske* and *Punto Casa* were assessed to do. In *Heimdienst*, the Court suggested that the national measure, restricting the operation of grocery delivery services to those with a permanent establishment in the area to be served, did not treat traders equally, as grocers established elsewhere would have to set up another permanent establishment in the area in which they wished to deliver. 'Consequently, in order for goods from other Member States to enjoy the same access to the market of the Member State of importation as domestic goods, they have to bear additional costs' (para. 26). The measure did not treat traders equally in fact, impeding access to the market of imported products more than it impeded access for domestic products.

Unequal impact was also found in *DocMorris*, concerning a German ban on mail order sales from pharmacies:

'A prohibition such as that at issue in the main proceedings is more of an obstacle to pharmacies outside Germany than to those within it. Although there is little doubt that as a result of the prohibition, pharmacies in Germany cannot use the extra or alternative method of gaining access to the German market consisting of end consumers of medicinal products, they are still able to sell the products in their dispensaries. However, for pharmacies not established in Germany, the internet provides a more significant way to gain direct access to the German market. A prohibition which has a greater impact on pharmacies established outside German territory could impede access to the market for products from other Member States more than it impedes access for domestic products' (para. 74).

The national ban on jewellery parties in private homes at issue in *A-Punkt* was identified as closing off a marketing strategy which was particularly appropriate for traders specialising in low value jewellery. However, the Court ruled that the fact national rules close down an efficient and profitable marketing method is not in itself enough to bring a measure within Article 28. The effects of prohibiting a particular marketing strategy must affect products from other Member States more than it affects domestic products.

The emphasis in these judgments on the importance of marketing as a way of gaining a foothold in another market, bringing, in an effective manner, a broader choice of products and traders to consumers has parallels with the approach taken in the advertising cases. This matter was little addressed in the earlier selling arrangement cases such as *Hünermund*, though in *Leclerc-Siplec* Advocate General Jacobs called upon the Court to be 'extremely vigilant' when considering restrictions on advertising, given the importance of advertising for breaking into new markets, and for challenging the established preferences for 'familiar' domestic products. Measures prohibiting, or severely restricting, advertising, according to Advocate General Jacobs, 'tend inevitably to protect domestic manufacturers and to disadvantage manufacturers located in other Member States' (para. 21). In his opinion, the Advocate General, who proposed a new test for the application of Article 28 of whether a measure amounted to a substantial hindrance on market access, suggested that as the national measures restricted only one form of advertising, leaving other channels open, such an impact could not be found. In its judgment, the Court applied the 'equal in law and fact' *Keck* test, and not that of Advocate General Jacobs, finding restrictions on television advertising affected the marketing of imported and domestic products in the same manner, similarly pointing to the fact that only one form of advertising was prohibited. In subsequent cases, the Court may be seen to have undertaken a more detailed assessment of the impact of restrictions on advertising. In *De Agostini*, concerning a magazine publisher's challenge to the Swedish ban on directing advertising on television to children under the age of 12, the Court ruled that 'it cannot be excluded that an outright ban, applying in one Member State, of a type of promotion for a product which is lawfully sold there might have a greater impact on products from other Member States' (para. 44). Then, in *Gourmet International*, the ban on the advertising of alcoholic beverages, 'the consumption of which is linked to traditional social practices and to local habits and customs', was considered to fall within Article 28, as:

'a prohibition of all advertising directed at consumers in the form of advertisements in the press, on the radio and on television, the direct mailing of unsolicited material or the placing of posters on the public highway is liable to impede access to the market by products from other Member

States more than it impedes access by domestic products, with which consumers are instantly more familiar' (para. 21).

## 5.9 Assessments of the Bifurcated Approach to Indistinctly Applicable Measures under Article 28 EC

The *Keck* judgment which formalised a difference in treatment for measures categorised as either product requirements or selling arrangements was described by the Court as a necessary re-examination and clarification of case law. The necessity resulted, it said, from 'the increasing tendency of traders to invoke Article [28] of the Treaty as a means of challenging any rules whose effect is to limit their commercial freedom even where such rules are not aimed at products from other Member States' (*Keck*, para. 14). The most notorious example of such actions to reach the European Court is the Sunday Trading case (Case C-145/88 *Torfaen BC* v. *B & Q plc* [1989] ECR 3851). The case was part of a strategy of litigation by out-of-town DIY stores to challenge UK rules prohibiting Sunday trading. The argument advanced by B & Q was that restricting the volume of possible sales by making shops close on a Sunday resulted in a reduction in the volume of goods that could be sold and, in consequence, imported. The Court was prepared to regard such a measure as at least potentially caught by Article 28, though told the referring court that it needed to weigh up the public interest objectives of restriction against its effect on trade. This led to a variety of responses from national courts receiving actions. The *Torfaen* trading case marked a high water mark in a line of actions which were perceived as illegitimately overstretching the scope of Article 28, catching measures which were not protectionist or discriminatory (whether directly or indirectly), nor in any other way likely to increase the regulatory burden on importers more than they did on domestic traders.

With *Keck*, the Court sought to set limits on the scope of Article 28, and remove the inconsistencies which had emerged in the case law in respect to measures which imposed an equal burden on importers and domestic traders. Conflicting lines of jurisprudence had developed on equal burden type measures – while the wide *Torfaen* approach had been seen in the earlier *Cinéthèque* case concerning a French prohibition on the rental or sale of videos in the first year following their cinema release (Joined Cases 60 and 61/84 *Cinéthèque* v. *Fédération Nationale des Cinémas Français* [1985] ECR 2605), in other cases the Court ruled the equal burden measure to fall automatically outside Article 28. For example, in *Quietlynn*, the Court described a national restriction on the sale of sex toys to licensed establishments as 'merely a rule regarding . . . distribution, regulating the outlets through which the products may be marketed. In principle therefore marketing of products imported from other Member States is not rendered any more difficult than that of domestic products' (Case C-23/89 *Quietlynn* v. *Southend Borough Council* [1990] ECR I-3059, para. 9). A similar approach was taken in the subsequent Sunday trading case (Case C-169/91 *Stoke on Trent and Norwich City Councils* v. *B & Q* [1992] ECR I-6635).

*Keck* confirms the approach of the latter line of cases, taking the newly created category of 'selling arrangement' type measures which have an equal burden in fact and in law on importers and domestic traders, outside the scope of Article 28. While a tightening up of the scope of Article 28 was generally welcomed, the manner in which it had been done was severely criticised. Weatherill for example attacked the ruling on a number of grounds:

'The ruling was flawed by the absence of an adequate articulation of just why it was possible to conclude that no sufficient impact on trade between states was shown; it was diminished in its value as a turning point in the case law by the Court's failure to name (at least some) of the decisions overruled; and it was marred by the Court's peevish hint that over-ambitious traders were at fault in seeking to exploit peculiarities which had been introduced into the law by the Court itself. Most of all, the *Keck* test . . . has a disturbingly formalist tone' (1996: 887).

Weatherill's concerns about the 'formalist' tone of the *Keck* test were that the rule would be mechanically and rigidly applied, inappropriately excluding measures which in fact present obstacles to the internal market. As has been seen, however, the Court, through cases such as *Gourmet* and *DocMorris*, has afforded an increasingly sensitive reading to the discrimination test at the heart of *Keck*. For some, however, this reading may run the risk of being so broad as to render the distinction drawn between product requirements and selling arrangements meaningless, 'and the entire *Keck* approach will collapse' (Oliver and Jarvis, 2002: 133).

Concerns about the usefulness of a separate test have led some to propose a return to a single test for measures under Article 28. For Advocate General Jacobs in his opinion in *Leclerc-Siplec* for example, it is simply 'inappropriate to make rigid distinctions between different categories of rules, and to apply different tests depending on the category to which particular rules belong' (para. 38). Instead, he suggests a test based upon the 'guiding principle' he perceives to underpin the internal market: that all undertakings should have unfettered access to the whole of the EU market. On that basis, 'the appropriate test in my view is whether there is a substantial restriction on that access', a test subject necessarily to a *de minimis* rule. The *Keck* approach, Jacobs argues, is unwelcome also for its emphasis on discrimination. This he says is 'inappropriate':

'The central concern of the Treaty provisions on the free movement of goods is to prevent unjustified obstacles to trade between Member States. If an obstacle to inter-state trade exists, it cannot cease to exist simply because an identical obstacle affects domestic trade . . . Indeed the application of the discrimination test would lead to the fragmentation of the Community market, since traders would have to accept whatever restrictions on selling arrangements happened to exist in each Member State, and would have to adapt their own arrangements accordingly in each state' (para. 39).

Such an approach would apply to measures like that in *A-Punkt*. In that case, the jewellery trader was prohibited under Austrian law from using the sales technique of holding jewellery parties in people's homes, a technique she used successfully in other Member States. In the absence of discrimination between the trader and Austrian traders however, Article 28 would not be breached. Should Jacob's broader approach apply, the Austrian rule would fall for examination under Article 28, though Austria would still retain the opportunity to make out a justification for its national rules. In a similar vein, Weatherill (1996) has endorsed an approach which looks beyond discrimination, capturing measures which amount to a substantial restriction on market access. However, Oliver and Jarvis have argued that such approaches, requiring assessments of the degree of restriction caused, which requires the evaluation of complex economic data, and which may change from one month to the next, would be inclined to lead to less legal certainty than the *Keck* approach (2002: 129–31).

Following a rather different tack, Weiler (1999b) likewise advocates a common approach to measures under Article 28, but one that emphasises the importance of combating discrimination. He has proposed introducing a 'general rule of free movement', under which all measures discriminating in law or in fact would require justification. This general rule would then be supplemented by a special rule requiring all measures to be justified which, while not discriminatory, prevent access.

Arguably, in terms of its effects, the case law of the Court has arrived at the same point as Weiler's new tests would lead – if one takes the product requirement cases as examples of indirect discrimination (Nic Shuibhne, 2002, but compare Oliver and Jarvis, 2002: 124). Non-discriminatory selling arrangement rules which nevertheless prevent access are also caught by *Keck*, especially as in more recent cases the Court has laid particular emphasis on para. 17 of the *Keck* judgment, in effect turning this into the operative part of the test, rather than it simply being a statement of the consequences of para. 16 being fulfilled, by stating that:

> 'if national provisions restricting or prohibiting certain selling arrangements are to avoid being caught by Article 30 of the Treaty, they must not be of such a kind as to prevent access to the market by products from another Member State or to impede access any more than they impede the access of domestic products' (*Gourmet*, para. 18).

While the *Keck* case law has been in a state of constant refinement and revision, and while many of the major concerns highlighted in respect to its operation have been addressed by the Court through this process, it remains the case, as will be seen in the following chapters, that the case law on the free movement of goods is out of line with a broader 'market access' approach applied across the other free movement provisions.

## 5.10 Article 29 EC: The Prohibition on MEEQR on Exports

Article 29 prohibits quantitative restrictions and MEEQR on exports. For example, in Case 53/76 *Procureur de la République Besançon* v. *Bouhelier* ([1977] ECR 197) a requirement in France for watches destined for export to be given an export licence following a quality inspection was held to breach Article 29 as no inspection and licensing requirement existed for watches destined to be sold in France. Also breaching Article 29 was the requirement for exporters of potatoes from the island of Jersey to be registered with the Jersey Potato Marketing Board and have entered into agreements about the area of land to be cultivated for export crops. This case also demonstrates that as with the rules on tariff barriers, the prohibitions on non-tariff barriers apply to trade within the regions of a state – here Jersey and the UK, to which exports were destined, were treated as being one territory. The rationale for the application of Article 29 in this case was that there was nothing to rule out the possibility that such potatoes, once within the United Kingdom, might then be re-exported to other Member States (Case C-293/02 *Jersey Produce Marketing Organisation* v. *States of Jersey and Jersey Potato Export Marketing Board* [2005] ECR I-9543).

The Court does not apply the Article 29 prohibition with the same rigour as it does Article 28 to indistinctly applicable measures. For example, a Dutch ban on the possession of horse meat by manufacturers of meat products, intended to ensure that meat exports to countries which prohibit the sale of horse meat are not affected by the suspicion that horse meat might have been used in their manufacture, was held not to breach Article 29, even though it represented an obstacle to export (Case 15/79 *Groenveld* v. *Produktschap voor Vee en Vlees* [1979] ECR 3409). The Court held:

> '[Article 29 EC] concerns national measures which have as their specific object or effect the restriction of patterns of exports and thereby the establishment of a difference in treatment between the domestic trade of a Member State and its export trade in such a way as to provide a

particular advantage for national production or for the domestic market of the state in question at the expense of the production or of the trade of other Member States' (para. 7).

Similarly, the Court has found that Article 29 was not infringed by Belgian rules restricting night working and delivery hours in respect of bakery produce, even though it had the effect of preventing Belgian bakers selling their wares in other neighbouring Member States in time for breakfast (Case 155/80 *Oebel* [1981] ECR 1993).

Thus, unlike the situation with imports, Article 29 bites only on distinctly applicable, discriminatory measures. According to Weatherill and Beaumont (1999: 606), this more restricted reading in respect of exports can be justified on the grounds that 'there is no *Cassis*-style dual burden' felt by the export as a result of the imposition of rules by its own state. A dual burden will only arise if the state of importation imposes additional, or different, rules and these can, if necessary, be challenged under *Cassis* principles on imports. While this may be so, it should be recognised that the Court's approach in the field of goods is now out of line with that taken in the area of workers, services and establishment.

In line with the Court's approach to imports and, indeed, in common with its approach across the free movement provisions, the Court is prepared to find no breach of Article 29 where the effects on trade of the challenged national measure are 'too uncertain and indirect'. For example, Case C-412/97 *ED Srl* v. *Italo Fenocchio* ([1999] ECR I-3845) concerned a prohibition of 'summary payment orders' to debtors outside the national territory, and while this was recognised as subjecting traders to different procedural rules according to whether they supplied goods within the Member State concerned or exported them to other Member States, 'the fact that nationals might therefore hesitate to sell goods to purchasers established in other Member States is too uncertain and indirect for that provision to be regarded as liable to hinder trade between Member States' (para. 11).

Finally, as with imports, measures breaching the Treaty prohibitions may nonetheless be saved by the successful pleading of one of the Article 30 grounds. Thus, in Case C-469/00 *Ravil* v. *Bellon and Biraghi* ([2003] ECR I-5053) a MEEQR was found to exist with the reservation of the name 'Grana Padano' to cheese, where it otherwise fulfilled the conditions for this designation of origin only where it had been grated and packaged in the region of production, and not outside the region to where it may have been exported. The legislation was found to have the specific effect of restricting patterns of exports of cheese, establishing a difference in treatment between domestic trade and export trade. However, designations of origin may fall within the scope of industrial and commercial property rights, recognised and protected under Article 30 (and by specific protective legislation: see 5.17). Such was the case here, where it was found that the restriction was justified on the grounds that it was designed to preserve the reputation of the designation by guaranteeing the product's authenticity and the maintenance of its qualities and characteristics (see also Case C-388/95 *Belgium* v. *Spain* [2000] ECR I-3123 on bottling rules for the use of the denomination Rioja).

## 5.11 Exceptions: Article 30 EC and the Mandatory Requirements

The Court of Justice's readiness to recognise that measures fall within the scope of application of Articles 28 and 29 has resulted in states regularly being placed in the position of having to justify national regulatory choices, and under such a system 'the pressure on the derogation clause becomes enormous'(Weiler, 1999b: 363). This clause is set out in the Treaty at Article 30, and provides an exhaustive list of the grounds of derogation which the Court has held must be interpreted strictly, like any other exception from the basic principles of free movement. These grounds are:

▷ public morality, public policy, public security;
▷ protection of health and life of humans, animals or plants;
▷ protection of national treasures possessing artistic, historic or archaeological value; and
▷ protection of industrial and commercial property.

Of these permissible derogations, restrictions on the grounds of health and the protection of industrial and commercial property are by far the most commonly successfully invoked. Separate consideration of the Court's treatment of these grounds is given in 5.12 and 5.14. Limited use has been made of the other grounds. There has been no use of the national treasures ground, and the Court has limited, through a highly restrictive reading, the potentially wide ground of public policy. It has however accepted arguments based on public morality. For example, it was successfully pleaded in *Henn and Darby*, in respect to a UK ban on indecent or obscene pornographic materials, in which there was no lawful trade in the UK. The public morality ground failed however in Case 121/85 *Conegate Ltd v. Commissioners of Customs and Excise* ([1986] ECR 1007), in respect to the seizure of consignments of inflatable rubber dolls and other items of erotica imported into the UK from Germany, as there was no equivalent national ban. The public security ground was successfully invoked in *Campus Oil*, which concerned a requirement that all oil importers buy a certain amount of oil from the Irish National Petroleum Company. The public security interest protected was that of guaranteeing the continuity of oil supplies by ensuring the survival of a national oil refinery.

Concerning indistinctly applicable measures, further grounds for justification may be available in addition to those set out in Article 30. This is through the mandatory requirements principle, first recognised in *Cassis*. The list of grounds provided in *Cassis* (protection of public health, the effectiveness of fiscal supervision, the fairness of commercial transactions) has remained open, with the Court prepared to consider and recognise other 'overriding reasons in the general interest' put before it. Such reasons must be in accordance with the aims of the Treaty. To the *Cassis* list has since been added, *inter alia*:

▷ environmental protection (e.g. Case 240/83 *Procureur de la République* v. *Association de défense des brûleurs d'huiles usagées* [1985] ECR 531 (disposal of waste oil); Case 302/86 *Commission* v. *Denmark (Disposable Drinks Containers)* [1988] ECR 4607; Case C-389/96 *Aher-Waggon* [1998] ECR I-4473);
▷ worker protection (*Torfaen*);
▷ measures to maintain the financial balance of the social security system (Case C-120/95 *Decker* [1998] ECR I-1831);
▷ maintenance of the diversity of the press (Case C-368/95 *Vereinigte Familiapress*);
▷ the protection of fundamental rights (*Schmidberger*);
▷ consumer protection (*A-Punkt Schmuckhandels* v. *Schmidt*).

The Article 30 derogations and the mandatory requirements are only available where states have retained regulatory competence over the issue, that is, where they have not been precluded from action by harmonising EU legislation. Where the state does retain this competence (for example, because there is no relevant EU legislation, or there is only partial harmonisation, through for example minimum standards legislation), successful reliance on one of the derogations (either Treaty based or Court recognised) will require a number of hurdles to be passed. As Article 30 makes explicit, the derogations will not apply to measures which are a means of arbitrary discrimination or a disguised restriction on trade between Member States. To avoid such a categorisation, measures must be shown to be part of a coherent policy applying also to domestic products, where appropriate. Thus, in *Cassis*, the German Government failed to convince the Court of Justice that its ban on low alcohol liqueurs (which excluded the French Cassis de Dijon from the market) was part of a coherent public health policy. The Government's argument, that it was a health protection measure, on the grounds that low alcohol products more easily induce a tolerance towards alcohol than high alcohol products, was undermined by the wide range of drinks of varying alcohol contents available on the German market. Similarly, in Case 40/82 *Commission* v. *United Kingdom (Imports of Poultry)* ([1982] ECR 2793) an import licence requirement imposed on imports of turkeys and other poultry products into the UK was held not to be justified. Amounting to a total ban on imports from six Member States (over a period including Christmas) the requirement was not part of a seriously considered health policy, but operated as a disguised restriction on trade.

Crucially, as regards both the Article 30 grounds and the mandatory requirements, the measure must also be proportionate, and this requires a three-limb test to be satisfied. The measure must be:

▶ suitable to achieve the stated aim;
▶ necessary to achieve the stated aim; and
▶ no more restrictive than is absolutely necessary for the purposes of achieving the stated aim.

Of course, in direct actions brought before the Court of Justice by the Commission under Article 226 EC, the issue of proportionality must be settled by the Court of Justice. In the case of Article 234 EC preliminary references though, the issue of proportionality is one that is properly left to the national court. In *Gourmet International*, for example, the Court stated that the question of whether the ban on advertising of alcoholic products was proportionate:

> 'and in particular as to whether the objective sought might be achieved by less extensive prohibitions or restrictions or by prohibitions or restrictions having less effect on intra-Community trade, calls for an analysis of the circumstances of law and of fact which characterise the situation in the Member State concerned, which the national court is in a better position than the Court of Justice to carry out' (para. 33).

Nevertheless, this principle of shared jurisdiction is not always respected by the European Court. In *Cassis de Dijon*, for example, the Court of Justice dealt with the proportionality issue itself, in respect to the second of the German Government's attempted justifications, that the ban protected consumers against unfair practices on the part of producers and distributors of alcoholic drinks consisting of lowering the alcohol content in order to obtain a competitive advantage in price. The Court ruled that a ban on these grounds was disproportionate, and that the objective could have been achieved by a less restrictive labelling requirement. Indeed, as Oliver and Jarvis identify, a 'golden rule' has developed that 'the sale of a product should never be prohibited when the consumer will be sufficiently protected by adequate labelling requirements' (Oliver and Jarvis, 2002: 291). Anything more restrictive would be disproportionate.

The Court has conventionally proceeded on the basis that overtly discriminatory measures may only be justified under Article 30, while the broader mandatory requirements are reserved for indistinctly applicable rules. In Case 113/80 *Commission v. Ireland (Souvenirs)* for example, the Court held that consumer protection grounds could not be invoked to justify a discriminatory measure, as Article 30 contains no consumer protection clause. However, the Court has increasingly – though not consistently – shown itself to be somewhat less rigorous in the application of this division. This is particularly, though not exclusively, the case with regard to questions of environmental protection (see further 5.13). Further, in *Decker*, a challenge was brought against national rules which required prior authorisation to be obtained for reimbursement of the costs of medical products bought outside the home market. The measure should undoubtedly be considered a distinctly applicable one – a clear difference in law existed between the treatment of goods purchased at home and those purchased elsewhere in the EU. The Court, however, appeared prepared to consider (though ultimately reject in the context of the facts of this case) a justification for the measure which is not recognised under Article 30: that of the need to maintain the financial balance of the social security system which could otherwise arise. It should be noted that this ground seems to undermine somewhat the otherwise established point that there is no general derogation from Articles 28–30 on economic grounds to protect Member States against the possibly damaging effects of enhanced competition as a result of free trade, a point established in the first case on Article 30 to come before the Court of Justice (Case 7/61 *Commission v. Italy* [1961] ECR 317).

## 5.12　Protection of Health and Life of Humans

Article 30 EC provides a derogation on the grounds of 'the protection of health and life of humans, animals and plants'. However, a clear hierarchy exists among these elements, and indeed among all the recognised derogations, since '[i]t is settled case-law that the health and life of humans rank foremost among the assets or interests protected by Article 30 EC' (*DocMorris*, para. 103). Protecting the health of humans is of course also one of the mandatory requirements recognised in *Cassis*. However, when considering the protection of human life and health, the Court makes no distinction between indistinctly and distinctly applicable rules; the same approach, taken under Article 30, is used in respect to both (see, for example, Joined Cases C-1 and 176/90 *Aragonesa de Publicidad Exterior SA* [1991] ECR I-4151). The balancing act between the internal market imperative, on the one hand, and the protection of non-economic interests, on the other, is perhaps most acute and sensitive regarding this ground more than any other, and the Court maintains a precautionary, if robust approach to justifications advanced by Member States. The recent spate of public health scares surrounding the safety of certain foods has resulted in a steady stream of cases before the Court concerning issues such as dioxins in food, genetically modified food and additives. The legislative response to such risks, in terms of positive integration strategies in the area of free movement, will be considered below.

At this juncture the Court's general approach to these perceived health risks will be outlined.

The starting point, articulated in cases such as Case C-41/02 *Commission* v. *Netherlands (Additives)* ([2004] ECR I-11375), is that:

'it is for the Member States, in the absence of harmonisation and to the extent that uncertainties continue to exist in the current state of scientific research, to decide on their intended level of protection of human health and life and on whether to require prior authorisation for the marketing of foodstuffs, always taking into account the requirements of the free movement of goods within the Community' (para. 42).

For the Article 30 derogation to apply, the state must establish on the basis of the latest scientific data, that a real risk to health exists. However, the Court recognised in Case C-95/01 *Greenham and Abel* ([2004] ECR I-1333), that:

'[i]t is clear that such an assessment of the risk could reveal that scientific uncertainty persists as regards the existence or extent of real risks to human health. In such circumstances, it must be accepted that a Member State may, in accordance with the precautionary principle, take protective measures without having to wait until the existence and gravity of those risks are fully demonstrated' (para. 43).

The Court has ruled that risk assessment cannot be based on 'purely hypothetical' considerations (see Case C-236/01 *Monsanto Agricoltura Italia and Others* [2003] ECR I-18105). Instead, a proper application of the precautionary principle requires:

'in the first place, the identification of the potentially negative consequences for health of the proposed addition of nutrients, and, secondly, a comprehensive assessment of the risk for health based on the most reliable scientific data available and the most recent results of international research' (C-192/01 *Commission* v. *Denmark* [2003] ECR I-9693, para. 51).

The justifiable adoption of restrictive measures under the precautionary principle may take place:

'where it proves to be impossible to determine with certainty the existence or extent of the alleged risk because of the insufficiency, inconclusiveness or imprecision of the results of studies conducted, but the likelihood of real harm to public health persists should the risk materialise.'

Applying the precautionary principle, and the proportionality principle, the Court ruled that, while there may be concern about the possible harmful effects of an excessive consumption of vitamins and minerals, a Danish measure which only permitted the marketing of foods fortified with vitamins and minerals meeting a nutritional need in the Danish population was not justified. Nor, in the absence of an in-depth, case-by-case assessment of the possible effects on public health, was a Dutch blanket ban on the marketing of fortified foods (Case C-41/02 *Commission* v. *Netherlands (Additives)*).

Other justifications which are frequently argued before the Court by the Member States include national policies concerning medical and pharmaceutical products. For example, in Case C-369/88 *Delattre* ([1991] ECR I-1487), the Court held that the French monopoly which reserved the sale of medicinal products by pharmacists, including products defined as medicines in France but freely available in other Member States, could be justified on health (and consumer protection) grounds. Some tightening up of this approach, in the interests of the internal market, may now be underway, however. *DocMorris* involved an attempt at national level to enforce a German ban on the mail order sale of medicines, against a Dutch pharmacy offering prescription and non-prescription medicines to people based in a number of Member States, including Germany, over the internet. While the prohibition on the supply of prescription medicines was held to be justified under Article 30 (on the basis of the health risks posed by, *inter alia*, medicine labelling in other languages, and abusive, or inappropriate, use of prescriptions), the ban on the supply of non-prescription medicines was not.

## 5.13 Environmental Protection

Article 30 EC contains no reference to justifying measures on the basis of environmental protection, though it does of course mention the protection of the health and life of humans, animals and plants. While the Court could perhaps have chosen to take a broad interpretation of this ground and recast it, half a century after it was written, as suggesting an environmental protection ground, the Court has not proceeded in so explicit a manner, leaving the law in a rather unsatisfactory state. There is little problem in respect to indistinctly applicable measures. The *Cassis* mandatory requirements were extended to include environmental protection through the cases of Case 240/83 *Procureur de la République* v. *Association de défense des brûleurs d'huiles usagées* and Case 302/86 *Commission* v. *Denmark (Disposable Drinks Containers)*. The latter case involved a Danish measure making a deposit-and-return system compulsory in order to enforce the re-use of containers for beer and soft drinks. This was held to be covered by the mandatory requirement of protection of the environment. It also held that the recycling system itself was a proportionate measure for Denmark to adopt. On the other hand, the Court took a different approach to the practice of requiring drinks to be sold only in approved containers, in order to restrict the range of containers on the market and to encourage maximum re-use by allowing consumers to return empty bottles to any drinks retailer. The practice of allowing only approved containers has a strong effect of partitioning off the Danish market against the penetration of new imported drinks, and although drinks could be sold in non-approved containers, a maximum quantity *per annum* was imposed. The Court held that the restriction of the quantity of products to be sold in non-approved containers was disproportionate to the aim pursued, since a system of returning non-approved containers is still capable of protecting the environment. This decision was handed down in the period before EU environmental policy really came of age, with the enhanced constitutional position and the mainstreaming of environmental protection across all policy fields which took place through later Treaty revisions (see Chapter 17).

Despite the upgrading of environmental concerns in the Treaty, the Article 30 grounds have not been amended since their original drafting. Without the Member States' intervention in recasting the grounds for justification, the Court of Justice's reticence to explicitly re-read Article 30 as giving a general basis for the protection of the environment is understandable, though the Court has strained to ensure such interests are given sufficient regard. Unfortunately, this has involved inconsistency in the case law and some sleight of hand. An 'environmental protection' reading was given to Article 30 in Case C-67/97 *Criminal Proceedings against Ditlev Bluhme* ([1998] ECR I-8033), where, in principle, it recognised the possibility of justifying a ban on the importation of particular species of bees onto a Danish island as a means of protecting the indigenous bee population and, more broadly, 'the maintenance of biodiversity'. Somewhat more controversial, however, has been the Court's approach to apparently distinctly applicable/directly discriminatory measures under *Cassis*, thus opening up the broader grounds of the mandatory requirements. Evidence of the Court's approach may be found in Case C-2/90 *Commission*

v. *Belgium (Walloon Waste)* ([1992] ECR I-4431), which concerned a prohibition by the Belgian region of Wallonia on the storage or dumping of any waste there which did not originate in Wallonia, and *Aher-Waggon*, which imposed stricter noise standards on aeroplanes registered outside Germany. In other cases, the Court has clearly recognised the discriminatory nature of the measure, then proceeded to consider the possible application of justifications recognised as mandatory requirements, rather than Article 30 grounds. Such was the Court's approach in Case C-379/98 *PreussenElektra* v. *Schleswag* ([2001] ECR I-2099), in which a national law that placed an obligation on energy providers to source a proportion of their supplies from local renewable energy installations was justified under the environmental protection head. In the interests of legal certainty, as well as the constitutionalised principle of environmental protection, a reform of the Article 30 grounds is demanded, and is long overdue.

## 5.14  The Protection of Intellectual Property

The derogation regarding the protection of industrial and commercial property, more commonly referred to as intellectual property, which is contained in Article 30, cannot be properly understood without a brief discussion of how Article 28 has been interpreted as applying to national provisions which protect intellectual property. *National* protections of inventions, designs and logos and symbols which give the holder certain exclusive rights in respect to manufacture and marketing of protected products, can have the effect of segmenting the single market. According to the Court, while the existence of intellectual property rights is not challenged by EU law, the exercise of those rights may be contrary to EU law (Case 78/70 *Deutsche Grammophon* v. *Metro* [1971] ECR 487, para. 11). For example, patent holders may seek to exclude imports between states by relying on domestic legislation which protects their patents. While this protection will be available where the patent holder holds the patent in the state alone, it will not be available where the patent holder seeks to extend patent protection to parallel imports, that is, products under the same or a parallel patent held by them imported from another state. The Court has developed an 'exhaustion of rights' doctrine to prevent intellectual property rights, and the national legislation which upholds them, being used to obstruct the free movement of goods in this way. Under this doctrine, patent holders who have marketed their products, or who have consented to them being marketed (e.g. by an agent, licensee or otherwise economically linked undertaking) in another Member State will be precluded by Article 28 from excluding imports. As well as covering the more obvious case of blocking imports, this doctrine will also preclude patent holders from creating differential pricing systems in which the patented product is sold at higher prices in certain Member States, since intellectual property legislation cannot be used to screen off the national market against imports of cheaper patented products bought up by a parallel importer in another Member State (Case 15/74 *Centrafarm BV* v. *Sterling Drug Inc.* [1974] ECR 1147).

In Case 19/84 *Pharmon BV* v. *Hoechst AG* ([1985] ECR 2281), the Court limited the scope of what is meant by 'consent' for the purposes of the exhaustion of rights doctrine, concluding that where a compulsory licence has been granted to a third party for the exploitation of a patent in a Member State where the patent holder has never exploited it, does not amount to the patent holder giving his or her consent. It remains possible, therefore, to use national legislation which is saved by the Article 30 derogation, to restrict imports of the patented product from the Member State where the compulsory licence has been granted into another Member State where patent protection is also held. By according this protection, the Court claims to be protecting the 'specific subject matter' of the intellectual property rights, namely the reward which the patent holder (or holder of a trademark or a copyright) should derive from his or her invention, innovation or design. In relation to patents, this specific subject matter of the protection is the right to put a product on the market for the first time. In relation to copyright, the specific subject matter includes the exclusive right to reproduce the copyrighted work, or to perform it (Case 158/86 *Warner Brothers* [1988] ECR 2605), and the specific subject matter of design rights covers the prevention of third parties from manufacturing and selling or importing, without consent, products incorporating the design (Case 238/87 *Volvo* v. *Veng* [1988] ECR 6211), though not the prevention of their intra-Community transit (Case C-23/99 *Commission* v. *France* [2000] ECR I-7653).

As regards trade marks, the specific subject matter includes the right to market the trade-marked product for the first time, as well as a prohibition on the unauthorised use of the trade mark (Case C-16/74 *Centrafarm* v. *Winthrop* [1974] ECR 1183). Further, in Case 102/77 *Hoffmann-La Roche* v. *Centrafarm* ([1978] ECR 1139), concerning, as very many cases in this area do, the parallel importation of pharmaceuticals, the specific subject matter of the trade mark was held to include the right to prevent trade marks from being affixed to products repackaged for the target market. According to the Court, rather than protecting the trade mark holders' interests, the primary purpose of trade marks is consumer protection, guaranteeing the identity of the trade-marked product's origin by enabling him to distinguish it without any risk of confusion from products of different origin. With this in mind, the ability of trade mark holders to block imports of repackaged goods is not considered absolute. As was further clarified in Joined Cases C-427, 429 and 436/93 *Bristol-Myers Squibb* v. *Paranova* ([1996] ECR I-3457), the parallel importation of repackaged products will be permitted where:

▷ 'it is established that the use of the trade-mark right by the owner, having regard to the marketing system which he has adopted, will contribute to the artificial partitioning of the markets between Member States;

▷ it is shown that the repackaging cannot adversely affect the original condition of the product;

▷ the owner of the mark receives prior notice before the repackaged product is put on sale; and

▷ it is stated on the new packaging by whom the product has been repackaged' (para. 49).

In Joined Cases C-414–416/99 *Zino Davidoff* v. *A & G Imports Ltd* and *Levi Strauss & Co.* v. *Tesco Stores Ltd* ([2001] ECR I-8691), the Court considered the geographical limits of the exhaustion of rights doctrine, and the question of consent. The cases concerned the attempts by trade mark holders to block the marketing of trade-marked goods brought in from outside the European Economic Area (EEA). The Court confirmed that the placing of products on the market outside the EEA will not exhaust rights for the EEA market unless the trade mark holder consents to their being marketed in the EEA. The Court ruled that the concept of consent had to carry a uniform EU meaning, and such consent had to be 'unequivocally demonstrated'. This would most probably be done by express statement though, in certain situations, it could be inferred from 'facts and circumstances prior to, simultaneous with or subsequent to the placing of the goods on the market outside the European Economic Area' (para. 47). However, the Court continued, implied consent cannot be inferred from the mere silence of the trade mark holder, or from the fact that the goods do not carry any warning that it is prohibited to place them on the market within the EEA.

## 5.15   Fundamental Rights

In Case C-112/00 *Schmidberger*, the Austrian authorities' decision not to ban a one-day environmental demonstration which resulted in the temporary closure of a major trade route through Austria was found to be a justified restriction on the free movement of goods. The basis for this was the overriding interest in respecting citizens' fundamental rights of freedom of expression and assembly. As Advocate General Jacobs recognised in his opinion, the case is the first in which a Member State has invoked the necessity to protect fundamental rights to justify a restriction of one of the fundamental freedoms of the Treaty:

> 'Such cases have perhaps been rare because restrictions of the fundamental freedoms of the Treaty are normally imposed not to protect the fundamental rights of individuals but on the ground of broader general interest objectives such as public health or consumer protection. It is however conceivable that such cases may become more frequent in the future: many of the grounds of justification currently recognised by the Court could also be formulated as being based on fundamental rights considerations.'

The increasing significance of the EU's own Charter of Fundamental Rights could lead conceivably to an increase in such cases. The Charter contains an extensive body of civil, political, economic and social rights. Whenever such rights conflict, there will need to be a careful assessment on the grounds of proportionality. While *Schmidberger* establishes that respect for fundamental rights may be accepted as a mandatory requirement, it is not yet clear what the response would be should a fundamental rights argument be raised in respect to Article 30 attempts to justify distinctly applicable measures. To date, the Court has only indicated that national justifications must themselves be compatible with 'the fundamental rights the observance of which is ensured by the Court' (Case C-260/89 *Elliniki Radiophonia Tileorassi* [1991] ECR I-2925, para. 43). Proposed national justifications based on fundamental rights may conceivably go beyond current interpretations of the Article 30 grounds, and while, as Jacobs recognised, the existing Article 30 grounds may capture certain fundamental rights, a broader reading of the public policy ground in Article 30 may evolve.

## 5.16   Legislative Intervention in the Free Movement of Goods Regime

By and large, the measures challenged as hindrances to trade under Articles 28 and 29 all share the same underlying cause, namely a disparity between the regulatory responses taken by different states to the same issue. The discussion up to this point has focused on one response to addressing such disparities, that is, the removal of the national rules conflicting with basic Treaty requirements. This is a deregulatory process of *negative harmonisation*. An alternative to this would be to remove the disparities through a programme of harmonisation of state laws, of supranational re-regulation, otherwise known as *positive integration*. The final sections of this chapter examine examples of positive integration in the field of goods, with a focus on food law.

Articles 94 and 95 EC provide the legislative basis for the introduction of harmonising measures necessary for the establishment and functioning of the internal market. These bases have been used for the harmonisation of both product requirement type rules, as well as selling arrangements. Of the former, examples include Council Directive 76/768/EEC (OJ 1976 L262/169) on the approximation of the laws of the Member States relating to the composition, labelling and packaging of cosmetic products which contains, *inter alia*, a negative list of substances which cosmetics must not contain. An example of the latter is Council Directive 85/577/EEC (OJ 1985) L372/31) to protect the consumer in respect of contracts negotiated away from business premises, also known as the Doorstep Selling Directive. Both measures refer in their preambles to disparities in the laws of the Member States on these matters, and proceed on the basis that these need approximating to overcome the effects of such disparities on the functioning of the internal market. Whether this logic is necessarily convincing in every case (see specifically on selling arrangement measures Davies, 2005; and generally Weatherill, 2004) it has fostered nonetheless an extensive programme of harmonisation. As was discussed in Chapter 3, a more detailed whole-scale and comprehensive programme of harmonisation has been jettisoned in favour of more selective interventions, utilising a range of lighter touch governance tools. As Weatherill points out, this shift reflects the perception that 'in a geographically and functionally expanded European Union the establishment of common rules is not only increasingly difficult to achieve, it is also increasingly undesirable as a suppression of competitive and cultural diversity' (2004: 11). Furthermore, such legislative interventions as are currently undertaken are increasingly underpinned by a strong consumer protection thrust. These developments, and the role of harmonising legislation in respect to the free movement of goods more generally, will be briefly explored through a consideration of certain aspects of the legislative regime applying to the free movement of foodstuffs.

### 5.17 Compositional and Manufacturing Requirements

The German restriction on the use of the word 'Bier' for drinks containing only certain barley, hops, yeast and water (Case 178/84 *Commission* v. *Germany (Reinheitsgebot)*, see 5.7) is an example of a *national* recipe law, that is a law setting out the compositional requirements that need to be met if a product is to be marketed lawfully under that name in the relevant territory. As was seen, such recipe laws are *prima facie* indistinctly applicable hindrances to trade under Article 28. One means of overcoming such hindrances, and facilitating the free movement of foodstuffs throughout the internal market, would be through the adoption of harmonised EU-level recipe laws, setting common compositional requirements. In 1969, a programme 'for the elimination of technical barriers to trade in foodstuffs which result from disparities between the provisions laid down by Law, Regulation or Administrative Action in Member States' was adopted (OJ 1969 C76/1). This programme identified a range of foodstuffs for each of which it was intended to introduce a 'vertical' directive, setting out compositional and manufacturing requirements for products to comply with if they were to carry generic product names throughout the Union.

Such vertical directives have been adopted *inter alia* in respect of honey (originally Council Directive 74/409 (OJ 1974 L221/10), replaced by Council Directive 2001/110 (OJ

2001 L10/47)) and chocolate, with the relevant directive defining terms such as milk, white, plain and filled chocolate, and the compositional requirements of each if they are to be marketed under those names (originally contained in Council Directive 73/241 (OJ 1973 L356/71), replaced by European Parliament and Council Directive 2000/36 (OJ 2000 L197/17)). While harmonising certain aspects of the compositional requirements of products, these directives nonetheless may not be exhaustive in their coverage, leaving Member States scope for action which may still be contrary to the requirements of Articles 28–30.

The later replacement versions of the original recipe directives show a rather lighter touch than the originals, and certainly any expectation of there being comprehensive coverage of all foodstuffs through detailed legislation is no longer, and indeed may never have been, realistic. Instead, there has been a shift to placing more emphasis on assuring certain essential consumer protection and health and safety issues, along with a greater reliance on informing consumers through labelling (see 5.18). The shift also reflects broader concerns about harmonisation expressed by Weatherill, that:

> 'harmonisation as a technical process devoted to market making tends to disregard the rich and deep roots of the national laws that are subjected to its influence. And the ornate strands of cultural tradition that pattern national laws are thereby sacrificed to the cold calculations of economic gain' (2004: 13).

Indeed, one set of legislative interventions by the EU, far from sacrificing these 'ornate strands of cultural tradition', enables them to be maintained and protected. The preamble to Council Regulation 510/2006 (OJ 2006 L93/12), on the protection of geographical indications and designations of origin for agricultural products and foodstuffs, notes that 'a constantly increasing number of consumers attach greater importance to the quality of foodstuffs rather than to quantity. This quest for specific products generates a growing demand for agricultural products or foodstuffs with an identifiable geographical origin.' The regulation allows for the registration and restriction on the use of specific names for traditional, typically produced foodstuffs, as either protected geographical indications (PGIs), for example for Scottish beef and Worcestershire cider, or as protected designations of origin (PDOs) such as Manchego cheese, Beurre d'Isigny and Blue Stilton cheese, which as well as identifying the geographical source of the product further identify that particular defined methods of production have been employed. The 2006 Regulation replaces an earlier one from 1992 (2081/92, OJ 1992 L208/1) which was ruled by a Panel of the WTO Dispute Settlement Body to be contrary to WTO obligations in respect to aspects of the regime of registration of PDO and PGI in third states (see Handler, 2006).

Such restrictions on the use of product names would otherwise be caught under Article 28, and require justification as hindrances to trade. For the sorts of names protected under the regulation, which are those that have not fallen into generic use, the possibility of justification for restricting their use was initially recognised on the Article 30 grounds of the protection of industrial and commercial property (see Case C-3/91 *Exportur* [1992] ECR I-5529, concerning the Spanish confectionary Turron de Alicante and de Jijona). The regulation creates a framework of *a priori* registration and protection of specific names, though the scope of protection offered by registration under the regulation is often brought into question in the context of cases at national level alleging breaches of registered PDO or PGI. In both Case C-108/01 *Consorzio del Prosciutto di Parma and Salumificio S. Rita SpA* v. *Asda Stores Ltd and Hygrade Foods Ltd* ([2003] ECR I-5121) (concerning the slicing and packaging of Parma ham outside the region of production) and Case C-469/00 *Ravil SARL* v. *Bellon and Biraghi* (concerning the grating of Gran Padarno cheese outside the region of production), the Court ruled that while the relevant registered PDO prohibited such activities if the product was to be sold with that name, the principle of legal certainty meant that the use of a simplified registration procedure, which did not provide for the publication in EU legislation of the specifications, meant that the PDO could not be enforced against economic operators contravening the PDO specifications.

### 5.18 Food Labelling

In *Cassis de Dijon*, proper labelling, providing consumers with necessary information about the nature of the product, was seen as a suitable alternative to national rules which would otherwise halt the marketing of imported products. Attempts to justify national minimum alcohol content rules on the basis of the fairness of commercial transactions would fail, for example, as the Court declared it to be 'a simple matter to ensure that suitable information is conveyed to the purchaser . . . on the packaging of products'. Thus, labelling has a crucial role in facilitating the free movement of goods. Indeed, shortly before the *Cassis* decision was handed down, the Council had adopted a directive on the labelling, presentation and advertising of foodstuffs, the preamble acknowledging that 'differences between the laws, regulations and administrative provisions of the Member States on the labelling of foodstuffs may impede the free circulation of these products and can lead to unequal conditions of competition . . . therefore, approximation of these laws would contribute to the smooth functioning of the internal market' (Council Directive 79/112, OJ 1979 L33/1).

The Food Labelling Directive marked a shift from the vertical, recipe law directives, to a more general, horizontal approach. The directive sets out certain requirements which have to be met – labelling must not be misleading and must cover such matters as the product's name, ingredients, their quantity and the best before or use by dates. The directive states in the preamble that 'the prime consideration for any rules on the labelling of foodstuffs should be the need to inform and protect the consumer'. According to Slater (2003), the consumer protection focus of the measure was subsequently, through the *Cassis* decision, to have superimposed on it a free-trade-centred general principle. This has been seen most clearly in respect of the directive's provisions on the restrictions that states may impose on the names that imported products may bear. These rules, which at first appeared to suggest that the rules applying in the state of sale take precedence over those of manufacture, have been interpreted in line with the mutual recognition principle (which now explicitly features in the replacement Labelling Directive – European Parliament and Council Directive 2000/13, OJ 2000 L109/29), so that, as a general rule, the names under which products are lawfully marketed in the state of production must be accepted in the state of sale. Difficulties with this principle emerge, however, where the product name is regarded as generic – that is, names which are now generally used for a product, such as bread, or chocolate, or indeed, more specifically, names such as Emmenthal or Edam cheese. In such cases, the state of sale may have national recipe laws, though these may be defeated by the application of the mutual recognition principle. The directive and the Court's case law both recognise that a product may have to be renamed, however, if the two products bearing the same generic name are very different, as regards composition and manufacture, and the provision of additional information is insufficient to guarantee that consumers are not confused. In Case C-448/98 *Guimont*, for example, the court suggested that additional labelling was sufficient to overcome possible consumer confusion between a more 'traditional' Emmenthal with rind and that produced without – they were not so completely different as to require renaming. However, according to MacMaoláin (2001), the Court's approach in cases such as *Guimont* could lead ultimately to a lowering of product quality standards, with its insufficient promotion of consumer interests, its false reliance on the usefulness of labelling, its overemphasis on the interests of free movement and given consumers' generally low levels of attention.

The Court has developed a notion of the consumer who is 'reasonably well informed and reasonably observant and circumspect' (for example, Case C-220/98 *Estée Lauder Cosmetics* v. *Lancaster Group* [2000] ECR I-117, para. 30), who reads and understands the information presented on product labels. While such consumers may in fact be few and far between, reliance on labelling and information provision is central to both the EU's consumer protection policy (Howells, 2005) and to the free movement of goods. In addition to the general labelling rules, more specific legislation operates in respect to foodstuffs which have attracted, for some, a more 'high risk' profile, and for which consumers may seek more information to allow them to buy with confidence. Thus, European Parliament and Council Regulation 1760/2000 (OJ 2000 L204/1) on the labelling of beef requires the meat to be labelled with the details of where the animal was born, reared, fattened, slaughtered and cut, enabling foodstuffs to be traced through the chain of production and distribution, the principle of traceability being central to the EU's new food safety regime, built around the proposals in the 1999 White Paper on Food Safety (COM(1999) 719). Food supplements marketed as foodstuffs must, under European Parliament and Council Directive 2002/46 (OJ 2002 L183/51), carry additional information, including a statement that supplements should not be used as a substitute for a varied diet, and information about daily recommended doses. Since 1997, EU legislation has also made mandatory additional labelling of genetically modified (GM) food for products that consist of generically modified organisms (GMO) or contain GMO, and for products derived from GMO. This was done first under the Novel Foods Regulation (European Parliament and Council Regulation 258/97, OJ 1997 L43/1), and now under European Parliament and Council Directive 2001/18 (OJ 2001 L106/1) as supplemented by European Parliament and Council Regulation 1830/2003 (OJ 2003 L268/24). However, doubts have been expressed as to whether legislation on GM labelling goes far enough, in that food does not need to be labelled GM if it contains less than 0.9 per cent of genetically modified material (see further MacMaoláin, 2003).

## 5.19   Restrictions on Foodstuffs

In recent years, the issue of risk, its existence and the reasonable responses that Member States and EU institutions can adopt, has been brought regularly before the Court as a result of the public health scares surrounding, for example, bovine spongiform encephalopathy (BSE), GM foods, dioxins in animal feed and food additives. The EU has responded by reviewing its approach to food safety issues, seeking to bring greater coherence in its activities, and restore and maintain consumer confidence. Central to the new framework on food safety is the European Food Safety Authority (EFSA) (European Parliament and Council Regulation 178/2002, OJ 2002 L21/1). The recitals to this Regulation begin with the statement that 'free movement of safe and wholesome food is an essential aspect of the internal market and contributes significantly to the health and well being of citizens'. The EFSA may issue advisory opinions on the safety or otherwise of food products. If no opinion is in existence, then the standard mutual recognition approach will operate. If the EFSA has issued an opinion, certifying a product as safe, it will still be possible for a Member State to seek to justify restrictions on the marketing of such products seeking entry onto their national market, under Article 30. According to Chalmers, this possibility will be denied to the Member State if the EFSA's opinion is incorporated into EC legislation (2003: 554). This is on the basis that such harmonising legislation will have occupied the field, making individual Member State action unlawful. However, most harmonising legislation will provide for safeguard clauses, such as those found in the GM directive, and the food additives directive, which will allow a state 'as a result of new information or a reassessment of existing information' to temporarily halt the sale of products otherwise deemed 'safe'. This will then be considered by the Commission through the comitology system (making use of the Standing Committee on the Food Chain and Animal Health) and, if necessary, the relevant legislation will be amended to cover the new assessment of risk. As is shown by Italy's continued refusal to come into line with the Commission's view of its unnecessary invocation of the safeguard clause in respect to certain GM products, this process is by no means straightforward and may be very highly charged (Berends and Carreno, 2005).

As well as certifying foods as safe, legislation may also impose bans on the sale of certain foodstuffs throughout the EU. The Food Supplements Directive, for example, uses a positive list approach, whereby only listed minerals and vitamins are 'safe' (following verification by the EFSA) and may be used in food supplements. The Court, in an Article 234 EC preliminary reference questioning the validity of the directive, supported the use of a positive rather than negative list system (the latter prohibiting just those things listed), as reliance on such a system:

> 'might not suffice to achieve the objective of protecting human health . . . [for] . . . as long as a substance is not included on the list, it can freely be used . . . even though, by reason of its novelty for example, it has not been subject to any scientific assessment apt to guarantee that it entails no risk to human health' (Joined Cases C-154 and 155/04 *R* v. *Secretary of State for Health, ex parte Alliance for Natural Health and National Association of Health Stores* [2005] ECR I-6451).

Such positive lists must operate under a procedure allowing products to be added to the list which complies with 'general principles of Community law, in particular the principle of sound administration and legal certainty' (para. 72). Beyond the blocks on marketing of certain products taken under specific legislation, the general Food Safety Directive, which was also set up by the EFSA, now provides for an emergency procedure (Articles 53 *et seq.*) allowing the Commission, on its own initiative, or at the request of a Member State, to suspend the placing of particular products on the market, or take any other interim measure considered appropriate. This new power fills significant lacunae in the powers of the Commission, highlighted in previous food-related scares (Berends and Carreno, 2005).

# Summary

1. Articles 28–30 EC prohibit quantitative restrictions and measures having equivalent effect to quantitative restrictions (MEEQRs) on imports and exports, subject to derogations furthering the public interest.

2. The Article 28 and 29 prohibitions are directed against state measures, and the provisions are vertically directly effective. Actions of quasi-public and private actors may, in some circumstances, be attributed to the state.

3. The definition of MEEQRs under Article 28 has been very widely drawn by the Court. Its starting point is the test in *Dassonville*.

4. Both Articles 28 and 29 will catch national measures which are distinctly applicable – that is, measures which draw an explicit difference between domestic products and those which are imported/exported. Distinctly applicable measures need to be justified under Article 30 if they are going to stand.

5. Article 28 also catches 'indistinctly applicable' measures – measures which, in law, apply equally to domestic products and imports but which may hinder trade. A distinction is drawn between indistinctly applicable rules relating to product requirements and those governing marketing and other 'selling arrangements'.

6. Product requirement rules are presumed to fall within Article 28, and must be justified by the state if they are to stand. In addition to Article 30, a set of broader grounds, the mandatory requirements, are available. These are a non-exhaustive set of public good reasons first raised in the *Cassis* case.

7. Following *Keck*, selling arrangement rules are presumed to fall outside Article 28 unless they are shown to prevent access to a market or to make it more difficult for imported products to gain a foothold in the market. National rules on advertising restrictions have been found to be caught by Article 28. States may then seek to justify the measure under the Article 30 grounds, or, as it is indistinctly applicable, under the mandatory requirements.

8. The protection of health and life of humans and animals ranks foremost among the interests protected under Article 30 and the mandatory requirements. Under this ground, states may apply the precautionary principle and, as with all the possible grounds of justification, must demonstrate that the measure is proportionate.

9. The successful justification of national measures which hinder trade will often lead to legislative intervention by the EU institutions, and the adoption of a piece of EU-wide harmonising legislation, which both protects the interests successfully raised under Article 30/the mandatory requirements, and facilitates trade.

# Exercises

1. What are Measures having Equivalent Effect to a Quantitative Restriction?

2. Why did the Court draw a distinction between product requirement rules and selling arrangement rules? Was it right to do so?

3. Should Article 28 catch all measures which hinder market access, or only those which are discriminatory?

Exercises cont'd

4. What are the mandatory requirements? In what way do they differ from the Article 30 derogations?

5. To what extent does the jurisprudence of the ECJ on Articles 28–30 EC Treaty maintain an acceptable balance between the promotion of the free movement of goods and respect for national diversity?

# Workshop

Brian is a manufacturer of power saws, based in Cardiff, UK. Over recent months, he has experienced a number of difficulties in respect of his trade with other Member States. In the light of EC law on the free movement of goods, advise him of his legal position in the following situations:

(a) He is required to obtain an import licence to import his saws into Greece. This requirement was enacted by the Greek government to keep a record of imports of power saws following public pressure after a number of 'copycat' Texan chainsaw massacres.

(b) In Italy, he is prosecuted for putting the saws on the market in breach of an Italian law which requires, on safety grounds, that the handles of power saws, both imported and domestic, be made of special hardened plastic.

(c) In Germany, he finds that power saws may only be sold in registered specialised shops. The justification for this requirement is that it protects the existence of small tool shops, and protects the profession of retail tool sellers. He finds it hard to break into the German market as a result.

(d) His sales are very low in Denmark, where advertising, to the general public, of power tools is prohibited on public safety grounds.

(e) He finds his products subjected to an organised boycott by French retailers, who are anxious to protect the French saw industry.

## Further Reading

Barnard, C. (2004) *The Substantive Law of the EU: The Four Freedoms*, Oxford: Oxford University Press. See especially chapter 3.

Berends, G. and Carreno, I. (2005) 'Safeguards in Food Law – Ensuring Food Scares are Scarce', 30 *European Law Review* 386.

Bernard, N. (1996) 'Discrimination and Free Movement in EC Law', 45 *International Comparative Law Quarterly* 82.

Chalmers, D. (2003) '"Food for Thought": Reconciling European Risks and Traditional Ways of Life', 66 *Modern Law Review* 532.

Chalmers, D. *et al* (2006) *European Union Law: Text and Materials*, Cambridge: Cambridge University Press, chapter 15.

Davies, G. (2003) *Nationality Discrimination in the European Internal Market*, The Hague: Kluwer Academic Publishers.

Davies, G. (2005) 'Can Selling Arrangements be Harmonised?', 30 *European Law Review* 371.

Handler, M. (2006) 'The WTO Geographical Indications Dispute', 69 *Modern Law Review* 70.

Hilson, C. (1999) 'Discrimination in Community Free Movement Law', 24 *European Law Review* 445.

## Further Reading cont'd

Howells, G. (2005) 'The Potential Limits of Consumer Empowerment by Information', 32 *Journal of Law and Society* 349.

MacMaoláin, C. (2001) 'Free Movement of Foodstuffs Quality Requirements and Consumer Protection: Have the Court and the Commission Both Got It Wrong?', 26 *European Law Review* 413.

MacMaoláin, C. (2003) 'The New Genetically Modified Food Labelling Requirements: Finally a Lasting Solution?', 28 *European Law Review* 865.

Nic Shuibhne, N. (2002) 'The Free Movement of Goods and Article 28 EC: An Evolving Framework', 27 *European Law Review* 408.

Oliver, P. and Jarvis, M. (2002) *Free Movement of Goods in the European Community* (4th edn), London: Sweet & Maxwell.

Slater, D. (2003) 'Would Chocolate by Any Other Name Taste as Sweet?: A Brief History of the Naming of Generic Foodstuffs in the EC with Regard to the Recent Chocolate Cases (Case C-12/00 *Commission* v. *Spain* and Case C-14/00 *Commission* v. *Italy*)', 4(6) *German Law Journal*. Available at: **http://www.germanlawjournal.com**

Van den Bogaert, S. (2002) 'Horizontality', in Barnard, C. and Scott, J. (eds.), *The Law of the Single European Market: Unpacking the Premises*, Oxford: Hart Publishing.

Weatherill, S. (1996) 'After *Keck*: Some Thoughts on How to Clarify the Clarification', 33 *Common Market Law Review* 885.

Weatherill, S. (2004) 'Why Harmonise?', in Tridimas, P. and Nebbia, P. (eds.), *European Union Law for the Twenty-First Century: Rethinking the New Legal Order, Volume 2*, Oxford: Hart Publishing.

Weiler, J. (1999) 'The Constitution of the Common Market Place: The Free Movement of Goods', in Craig, P. and de Búrca, G. (eds.), *The Evolution of EU Law*, Oxford: Oxford University Press.

## Key Websites

The website for the Commission's Enterprise and Industry Directorate-General is available at:
**http://ec.europa.eu/enterprise/regulation/goods/index_en.htm**

The mutual recognition principle is examined in detail, and proposals made for a regulation at:
**http://ec.europa.eu/enterprise/regulation/goods/mutrec_en.htm**

The European Parliament has a factsheet on the free movement of goods:
**http://www.europarl.europa.eu/facts/3_2_1_en.htm**

# Chapter 6

# Freedom to Provide Services and Freedom of Establishment

## 6.1 Introduction

Free movement of services is one of the classic four freedoms protected by the original Treaty of Rome. Freedom of establishment can be presented as a facet of the broader notion of the free movement of persons, providing as it does rights for the self-employed (and companies) to set themselves up in another Member State. For reasons which will be discussed in 6.2 of this chapter, services and establishment are usually considered together, as they have many similarities. Both areas of law concern the rights of Union citizens and companies established in the EU to carry out their activities in other Member States, and the conditions of access which apply to them.

This is a fast-growing field of law, reflecting the growth of the service economy and in particular the growth of the kinds of services and activities which can be provided on a cross-border basis. It has also, more recently, become a highly politicised and controversial field of law. One important aspect of the so-called 'Lisbon' agenda to make the European Union 'the most competitive and dynamic knowledge-based economy in the world capable of sustainable economic growth with more and better jobs and greater social cohesion' was the request made by the European Council to the Commission to propose an internal market strategy to remove barriers to services, recognising both the growing importance of the service economy and the continued existence of significant barriers to free movement. While the service economy itself is a highly significant contributor to national GDP (accounting for an average of between 60 and 70 per cent of economic activity with Member States, and responsible for a similar level of the employment rate), interstate trade in services remains underdeveloped, certainly in comparison with trade in goods. Barriers to interstate service provision are largely constituted by Member State regulation of certain services and professions, often justified in the name of consumer protection or the maintenance of high standards and integrity in particular professions.

The strategy produced by the Commission (COM(2000) 888) proposed a large-scale harmonisation of regulations in order to remove barriers. In its report on the state of the internal market in services, the Commission further observed that the Lisbon goals would not be achieved unless 'sweeping changes' were made in the market for services (COM (2002) 441 at p.70). This in turn led to the proposal for a general directive on services in the internal market (COM(2004) 2). The depth of the debate and disagreement within the Council and the Parliament surrounding this proposal, and the extent to which public debate on the subject in some Member States (notably France) has connected the directive to the purportedly 'neo-liberal' character of the Constitutional Treaty, brought political significance to the draft directive far beyond its practical legal impact. For example, the rapporteur for the European Parliament's Internal Market Committee, Evelyne Gebhardt, stated during the Parliamentary debate on 15 February 2006 that the directive is 'the most important piece of EU legislation apart from the Constitution'. The directive was finally adopted towards the end of 2006 in a much watered-down form, mostly because of amendments introduced by the European Parliament during the co-decision procedure (European Parliament and Council Directive 2006/123 on services in the internal market, OJ 2006 L376/36). In large measure, the directive consolidates the case law of the Court of Justice on restrictions which Member States may place upon the cross-border establishment of self-employed persons or companies providing services, or upon the cross-border provision of services without establishment, although it attempts to simplify the administration of any authorisation requirements which Member States continue to impose upon cross-border establishment. The anticipated legal impact of the directive will be addressed in the relevant parts of this chapter.

Cross-border activities in the field of services frequently occur without any physical movement on the part either of the provider or the recipient of the service. For this reason, it is becoming increasingly possible and indeed desirable to distinguish the personal rights attached to those persons moving to provide or to receive services, and the regulatory conditions under which the services themselves are provided. In this book, therefore, the two issues are dealt with separately. The *personal* rights of individuals moving in order to exercise their freedom to provide or receive services or to become established in another Member State (including the exceptions and derogations which Member States may impose) will be dealt with in Chapter 12, which addresses the status and rights of EU citizens. This chapter will consider the conditions under which economic activities may be carried out on a cross-border basis. These conditions take as their starting point the general right to non-discrimination which means that the economic activity of the self-employed person, company or service provider should not be carried out under conditions which are less favourable than those applying to persons or companies operating within their Member State of origin.

Section 6.2 sets out the basic distinction between the concepts of 'establishment' and 'services'. Section 6.3 considers the provisions' application to private actors, and 6.4 then focuses in more detail on the establishment provisions and, in particular, their application to companies. The apparently residual nature of the services provisions and the nature of activities to which the provisions apply are considered in 6.4–6.6. The following five sections (6.7–6.11) focus on the kinds of barriers to free movement which have been addressed in the case law of the Court of Justice; these are barriers which, for the most part, are connected to the different mechanisms used to regulate the exercise of trades and professions in Member States. Possible grounds for justification are considered in 6.12 and 6.13. Certain of the most contentious aspects of the new Services Directive are then outlined in 6.14. The problems that have arisen with the diversity of regulatory frameworks around the EU have made positive integration measures for setting up EU-level regulatory frameworks all the more urgent, and these processes will be discussed in outline in the latter part of the chapter.

## 6.2 The Distinction between Establishment and Services

As freedom to provide services and freedom of establishment are dealt with by two separate sets of provisions in the EC Treaty (Articles 43–48 EC: establishment; Articles 49–55 EC: services), it continues to be important to distinguish the two. However, it should be clear from the outset that the distinction, while initially apparent in the legislation, is becoming more and more artificial. The Court of Justice increasingly interprets the two key provisions of Articles 43 and 49 EC in parallel, and differences between the ways they were approached have more or less been eroded. Much legislation also treats both provisions together. The Services Directive, for example, establishes general provisions intended to facilitate the exercise of freedom of establishment and freedom to provide services in respect of service activities and occupations albeit under different conditions, and thus is based upon both Articles 47(2) and 55 EC. This trend has led O'Leary to comment that there is a lack of clear blue water between the two concepts (O'Leary, 1999).

Nevertheless, the distinction maintains some relevance. While some legislation does apply to both establishment and services, other positive integration measures separate them; a good example is provided by the Lawyers' Services Directive (Council Directive 77/249, OJ 1977 L78/17) and the Lawyers' Home Title Directive (European Parliament and Council Directive 98/5, OJ 1998 L77/36) (discussed in 12.17). The distinction is also often emphasised in case law, in that the sets of provisions are considered to be mutually exclusive (see Case C-55/94 *Gebhard* v. *Consiglio dell'Ordine degli Avvocati e Procuratori di Milano* [1995] ECR I-4165). It will also be seen that the Court's approach, as with that of the legislation, is to accord a greater degree of control by the host state over the activities of those that establish themselves there, than those who simply provide services there. To confuse matters, however, there have been a number of recent judgments where the Court does not clearly distinguish between the provisions (see Case C-272/91 *Commission* v. *Italy (Lottomatica)* [1994] ECR I-1409), simply because there is no need to do so, and here the Court applies both sets of provisions (as well as the goods and workers' provisions) cumulatively (see Case C-348/96 *Calfa* [1999] ECR I-11). The relationship between the different free movement provisions must therefore be understood as flexible. However, it does remain important to distinguish them, as in the more straightforward cases only one set of provisions will apply.

According to Article 50 EC Treaty, the concept of services applies to activities provided for remuneration 'in so far as they are not governed by the provisions relating to freedom of movement for goods, capital and persons'. The services provisions have thus traditionally been approached as a residual category (though see 6.5), and this has extended to the relationship between services and establishment: the Court of Justice has tended to proceed by setting out a definition of freedom of establishment, and then treating economic activities which do not fit within this definition as instances of freedom to provide services, subject to the fulfilment of certain conditions (outlined in 6.5 and 6.6). The applicable test was given in *Gebhard*, where the Court stated that a person is established in a state when they 'participate, on a stable and continuous basis, in the economic life of a Member State other than his state of origin' (para. 25). For establishment to be shown, some sort of infrastructure should be maintained within the state of establishment: an office, perhaps some staff. It is not, however, necessary for the person or company to remain permanently within the Member State in order to be established there. In *Gebhard* the Court was at pains to point out that it is possible, and indeed to be encouraged, that people or businesses should establish themselves in more than one Member State at a time and therefore, particularly in the case of a sole trader or small company, might only spend a part of their time in any one state.

The critical distinction between establishment and services is the degree of stability of involvement in the host state. While the Court in *Gebhard* indicated that attention should be paid to the duration of the provision of economic activity in the host state, as well as its 'frequency, periodicity, or continuity', it has made clear that it is not as simple as looking at the duration and frequency of economic activity, with 'greater' being conclusive evidence of establishment and 'less' of services. In Case C-215/01 *Schnitzer* ([2003] ECR I-14847), which involved the provision of building services over a three year period, the Court ruled that 'services within the meaning of the Treaty may cover services varying widely in nature, including services which are provided over an extended period, even over several years'. Having some degree of infrastructure in the host state, as necessary to be able to provide the services in question, will not cause services to be reclassified as establishment (*Gebhard*). Services cases such as *Schnitzer* most often involve economic activity that is episodic – that is, as in this case, a contract to undertake plastering on a building project. Establishment meanwhile does not have this episodic quality, applying to those who pursue a professional activity on a stable and continuous basis in another Member State where economic actors hold themselves out 'from an established professional base to, amongst others, nationals of that Member State' (*Schnitzer*, para. 29). Hatzopoulos and Do (2006) have suggested that the Court now proceeds by adopting an 'economic' rather than legalistic approach to the concept of services, and no longer regards it as a residual category.

## 6.3 Horizontal Application of the Free Movement Provisions?

In the previous chapter, it was seen that the provisions on the free movement of goods apply to state measures – and while this concept has been quite broadly interpreted, the acts of private parties are only tangentially engaged (for example, Case C-265/95 *Commission* v. *France (French Farmers)* [1997] ECR I-6959). It will subsequently be seen in Chapter 12 that the European Court has fully extended the scope of the free movement of workers' provisions to cover the acts of private parties restricting that free movement (in Case C-281/98 *Angonese* v. *Cassa di Risparmio di Bolzano* [2000] ECR I-4139). The approach to the scope of application of the services and establishment provisions falls someway between these two positions. The Court has held that the acts of private associations may be caught, where these regulate, in a collective manner, the provision of services or the carrying out of business in another Member State. Thus, the International Cycling Union's rules which required pacemakers to be of the same nationality as the racing cyclist could be challenged under Article 49 EC (Case 36/74 *Walrave and Koch* v. *Union Cycliste Internationale* [1974] ECR 1423) and, in Case 90/76 *Srl Ufficio van Ameyde* v. *UCI* ([1977] ECR 1091), an agreement between national motor insurance bureaux which restricted the institutions that could handle insurance claims could be challenged, the Court ruling that it is irrelevant whether the discrimination results from actions of public authorities.

## 6.4 Establishment: Natural and Legal Persons, and Company Law Implications

Article 43 EC Treaty prohibits restrictions on the freedom of establishment of Member State nationals in another Member State. For natural persons, the right of establishment includes the right to operate in a self-employed capacity, as well as to set up and manage an undertaking. According to Article 43, also covered by the establishment provisions is secondary establishment – the setting-up of agencies, branches or subsidiaries by nationals already established elsewhere in the EU, where they retain their primary establishment.

Freedom of establishment is also extended to companies themselves, under Article 48 EC, which provides that:

'companies or firms formed in accordance with the law of a Member State and having their registered office, central administration or principal place of business within the Community shall . . . be treated as in the same way as natural persons who are nationals of Member States.'

These provisions do not however apply to non-profit-making undertakings (on the possible interpretations of this concept, see Stöger, 2006: 1547, who argues that the definition of profit-making undertakings taken from the field of tax law, that of trying to achieve profits for its members, is unsuitably narrow for application in the field of establishment).

In principle, therefore, companies based in a Member State have right to primary and secondary establishment in any other Member State. However, significant obstacles to their exercise of freedom of establishment are created by national company law systems. Beginning in 1968, the EU has undertaken a programme of company law harmonisation, with measures introduced under the legal basis provided in Article 44 EC. Among other things, these measures have harmonised rules on disclosure of company documents (First Company Directive, Council Directive 68/151, OJ 1968 English Special Edition Series I, 41), on annual accounts (Fourth Company Directive, Council Directive 78/660, OJ 1978 L222/11) and have made the private limited company available as a corporate vehicle to one single shareholder (Twelfth Company Directive, Council Directive 89/667, OJ 1989 L395/40). However, this programme of harmonisation has by no means been comprehensive, and many areas of significant difference remain (Wouters, 2000). These differences may lead to further complications in identifying the 'home' state of a company, as the Member States apply different theories to identifying the 'nationality' of a company. Under the 'incorporation' theory, practised by the UK for example, the determining factor is the place of company incorporation. Under the 'real seat' approach, operated, among many others, by Germany, the crucial factor is where the company's head office or principal place of business of the company is (Wymeersch, 2003).

As regards a company's right to primary establishment in another Member State, there is nothing stopping a company terminating its existence in one state and re-incorporating in another, though of course it must then comply with the new state's rules on incorporation and its company law regime. A more problematic scenario is where the company seeks to move its principal place of business, but retain a presence in its original state. In Case 81/87 *R* v. *H. M. Treasury and Commissioners of Inland Revenue, ex parte Daily Mail and General Trust plc* ([1988] ECR 5483), an attempt by a holding company to move its central management from the UK to the Netherlands, while remaining incorporated in the UK, was made subject to approval by the UK Treasury. This requirement was challenged as an obstacle to free movement. The Court of Justice, however, influenced perhaps by the company's clear intention to relocate so as to avoid the tax consequences of a share sale, ruled that such home state control over the free movement of companies was allowed. In Case C-208/00 *Überseering* v. *Nordic Construction Company* ([2002] ECR I-9919) meanwhile, Überseering moved its centre of administration from the Netherlands to Germany, while remaining registered in the Netherlands. Under Germany's real seat theory, the company should now be governed by German law. However, as it was not lawfully constituted as a German company, it was not recognised as having legal capacity, and as a consequence, was unable to bring legal action in the German courts. The Court of Justice found this action by Germany to be unlawful. Rather than simply placing restrictions on Überseering's right to take advantage of the establishment provisions, the German rule negated this right entirely and was not open to justification.

A legislative response to the moving of company seat was first mooted a decade ago, and calls for the adoption of the Fourteenth Company Directive on cross-border seat transfer were repeated in the Report to the Commission of the High Level Group of Company Law Experts in November 2002, which resulted in the Commission's Company Law Action Plan (COM(2003) 284). While this measure remains at an early stage of development, recent years have seen the adoption of a number of measures which had been stalled in the legislative quagmire, in some cases for decades. These measures have implications for cross-border company establishment. The eventual adoption of the European Company Statute now allows for public companies located in different Member States to merge and form a new corporate form, the European Company, or *Societas Europea* (Council Regulation 2157/2001, OJ 2001 L294/1) (Edwards, 2003). The breakthrough in enabling this measure to be adopted was the agreement on worker participation provisions (see further 16.15), and this also cleared the way for the adoption of the Tenth Company Directive on cross-border mergers (European Parliament and Council Directive 2005/56, OJ 2005 l310/1). Before the date of transposition had passed, the European Court handed down its judgment in Case C-411/03 *SEVIC Systems* ([2005] ECR I-10805). SEVIC, a German company, sought to merge with a Luxembourg company, SVC. On merger, SVC would cease to exist, its liabilities and assets being transferred to SEVIC. German law only permitted the registration of company mergers where both companies were resident in Germany. This German rule was successfully challenged as a restriction on freedom of establishment before the European Court, the Court having first confirmed, contrary to the submissions of both Germany and the Netherlands, that a merger constituted an act of 'establishment'. While the Court recognised that there was potential for the national measure to be objectively justified, it directed that it would not succeed in this case.

In *SEVIC*, the act of merger, through the acquisition of another company, was likened to the establishment of a secondary establishment in another state. The case law on secondary establishment has caused particular controversy, as it would seem to indicate that companies are permitted to forum shop for the most convenient legal framework for their principal establishment, which then enables them to establish secondary branches or subsidiaries elsewhere, despite the main focus of their business being in the state of secondary establishment. Such was the situation in Case C-212/97 *Centros* v. *Erhvervs- og Selskabsstyrelsen* ([1999] ECR I-1459). Centros was incorporated in the UK, by a Danish couple, but it did not trade there. Instead, it sought to establish a branch in Denmark, where its day-to-day trading would take place. By incorporating in the UK, it was able to avoid the high minimum capital investment rules applicable in Denmark. The Danish authorities refused to register the company branch in Denmark. This was found by the European Court to be a restriction on the freedom of establishment, and the Danish attempts to objectively justify their refusal on the grounds of creditor protection were unsuccessful. The Court subsequently repeated its approach in Case C-167/01 *Kamer van Koophandel en Fabrieken voor Amsterdam* v. *Inspire Art* ([2003] ECR I-10155). The combined effects of the case law on both secondary and principal establishment significantly erode the 'real seat' theory, and significantly generate a ' "mobility of company laws" as well as a cross-border "mobility of companies' headquarters" ' (Behrens, 2006: 1669).

## 6.5   Freedom to Provide Services: A Residual Provision?

Article 49 EC provides:

'. . . restrictions on the freedom to provide services within the Community shall be prohibited in respect of nationals of Member States who are established in a state of the Community other than that of the person for whom the services are intended.'

Article 50 EC outlines the nature of the activities that are covered. These include: activities of an industrial character; activities of a commercial character; activities of craftsmen; and activities of the professions. Such services will be covered by the Treaty provisions:

'where they are normally provided for remuneration, in so far as they are not covered by the provisions relating to the free movement of goods, capital and persons.'

The formulation of Article 50 EC would therefore appear to suggest that the services provisions should only apply where no other free movement provisions are applicable. This is not necessarily the case. Often, the provision of services will involve some cross-border movement of goods. The servicing of a car by a garage, for example, is a service which may involve, as part of that service, the supply of certain goods, such as spare parts (Case C-55/93 *Van Schaik* [1994] ECR I-4837). Where the provision of a service involves the ancillary provision of goods, the Court will apply the services provisions: as is also seen in cases involving the lease of goods to the service recipient, including slot machines (Case C-6/01 *Anomar* v. *Portugal* [2003] ECR I-8621) and the equipment to operate laser 'play to kill' games (Case C-36/02 *Omega* v. *Oberbürgermeisterin der Bundesstadt Bonn* [2004] ECR I-9609). On occasion, the Court has considered national restrictions in the light of both the services and goods provisions (as in the case concerning the Swedish ban on alcohol advertising, Case C-405/98 *Konsumentombudsmannen* v. *Gourmet International* [2001] ECR I-1795). According to Hatzopoulos and Do (2006: 956), the Court's particularly broad interpretation of the type of national measures which will fall for consideration under the services provisions has increasingly led to litigants proceeding under the services provisions, when the goods provisions would also be applicable.

The distinction between workers and services in terms of personal scope is fairly clear, as the provisions on services apply only to self-employed people. However, problems have arisen where the provision of a service is dependent on the activities of a number of employees of the service provider. Employees carrying out services in another Member State are not classified as workers exercising their free movement rights. Thus, rules concerning social security (Case C-272/94 *Guiot and Climatex* [1996] ECR I-1905) and work permits (Case C-43/93 *Vander Elst* [1994] ECR I-3803) may not be applied to the employees of the service provider by the state where the service is being carried out. These matters are now dealt with in more detail under the Posted Workers Directive (European Parliament and Council Directive 96/71, 1996 OJ L18/1). This measure is discussed in 16.12 in the context of EU employment law, though, in short, the directive provides that cross-border service providers using their own workforce from their home state must respect certain host state rules on basic workers' rights. Equally, the employees may not seek access to the labour market of the host state on the basis of their free movement rights as service providers. Should they do so, they will be covered by the provisions on job-seekers rather than services.

## 6.6 'Cross-Border' Provision of Services

The range of situations where freedom to provide services can be invoked is becoming increasingly wide and complex. The original set of rules was aimed at a situation where an individual, either as a self-employed person or as the representative of a company, travelled across the border in order to provide services in another Member State. This situation has never been uncommon and the issues it raises are particularly critical in those areas of EU territory which are close to borders between Member States. However, subsequent case law clarified that the provisions also apply to people who want to travel to receive services (Joined Cases 286/82 and 26/83 *Luisi and Carbone* v. *Ministero del Tesoro* [1984] ECR 377, see 8.2) and to people who, while travelling, receive services (Case 186/87 *Cowan* v. *Le Trésor Public* [1989] ECR 195, see 12.5). Further, with the increasing use of telecommunications and internet technology in the business community, more and more services can be provided across borders while neither the service provider nor the service recipient moves from their home state. Finally, in the case of transport services, both the service recipient (i.e. a person being transported) and/or the object of the service (e.g. goods) as well as the service itself are involved in moving across borders.

Where either the service provider or the service recipient physically crosses a border, it is straightforward to show the cross-border element traditionally required for application of free movement provisions. It is also unproblematic in cases where the service provider and the service recipient are in different Member States and the activity takes place over the telephone or on the internet (Case 15/78 *Société Générale Alsacienne de Banque SA* v. *Koestler* [1978] ECR 1971). More difficulties arose in Case 62/79 *Coditel* v. *SA Ciné Vog Films* ([1980] ECR 881) and Case 352/85 *Bond van Adverteerders* v. *Nederlands* ([1988] ECR 2085), where, while both the service providers (of cable television) and the service recipients (customers) were in one Member State, the service itself (the television broadcasts) originated from another Member State. The Court managed to avoid addressing the question, but Advocate General Mancini in *Bond van Adverteerders* argued that, because the service itself is inherently 'without frontiers', it should fall within the scope of EU law. Since that case, the Broadcasting Directive (Council Directive 89/552, OJ 1989 L298/23) has taken broadcasting outside the scope of the general provisions (although some issues continue to be raised before the Court of Justice, such as, for example, the annual municipal tax on the owners of satellite dishes discussed in Case C-17/00 *De Coster* v. *Collège des bourgmestre et échevins de Watermael-Boitsfort* [2001] ECR I-9445).

In some cases the Court has made it clear that it is less interested in the location of the service provider and/or the recipient, and more interested in the provision of services as such and mobility between Member States (see, for example, Case C-381/93 *Commission* v. *France (Marine Cabotage)* [1994] ECR I-5145 where the nationality of the individuals and companies concerned was irrelevant as long as freedom of movement was inhibited). Hatzopoulos sees this move, in conjunction with other cases (Case C-118/96 *Safir* [1998] ECR I-1919 and Case C-158/96 *Kohll* v. *Union des Caisses de Maladie* [1998] ECR I-1931), as a move away from an emphasis on the free provision of services (to individuals) towards a more abstract conception of the free movement of services (without a particular focus on the providers or recipients). Thus services are increasingly viewed as an objective economic reality, rather than an activity of persons (Hatzopoulos, 2000). The Court of Justice has stated (for example in Case C-398/95 *SETTG* v. *Ypourgos Ergasias* [1997] ECR I-3091) that the heart of the service provisions lies not in ensuring that there are no barriers to the physical crossing of borders but in scrutinising measures which could have some effect on interstate trade. This broad statement mirrors much of what has been said about the free movement of goods, and some of its consequences will be explored later.

### 6.7    Economic Value of the Activity

Article 49 EC defines a service as an activity normally provided for remuneration. The crucial aspect is that the service must have some economic value. As long as there is a profit motive, it is not necessary that the activity be paid for by its consumers; in *Bond van Adverteerders*, it was clarified that broadcasting services, free to the consumer but paid for by advertisers, can constitute services within the meaning of Article 49. However, activities conducted on a voluntary basis for charitable or other purposes do not constitute services (Case C-159/90 *Society for the Protection of the Unborn Child* v. *Grogan* [1991] ECR I-4685).

What though of welfare services, those which have traditionally been operated by the state, according to principles of territoriality and universality, and underpinned by ideas of solidarity? Does EU free movement law create rights for economic operators to provide 'welfare' services, such as health services, social housing provision and education in a host state, whether under the services or establishment provisions? As the discussion in 14.8 (on the social dimension and, specifically, health care policy) will show, the Court has recognised rights for citizens to access both private and, more controversially, public health services in another state – the latter being possible at the expense of the home Member State where treatment is not readily available in the home state (Case 157/99 *Geraets-Smits and Peerbooms* [2001] ECR I-5473). This result may be seen as surprising in the light of the Court's 1988 judgment in Case 263/86 *Belgium* v. *Humbel* ([1988] ECR 5365) which held that state provision of secondary education was not a service under the Treaty provisions as the essential characteristic of remuneration was absent. This was because, first, 'the state, in establishing and maintaining such a system, is not seeking to engage in gainful activity but is fulfilling its duties towards its own population in the social, cultural and educational fields. Secondly, the system in question is, as a general rule, funded from the public purse and not by pupils or their parents' (at para. 18). However, similar considerations have not been such as to remove health services from the scope of Article 49. Furthermore, with services becoming increasingly 'marketised', and shifts away from traditional forms of state provision taking place, the scope for involvement for economic actors from other states also increases, and with Davies submitting that 'pretty much all of the services provided by welfare states could, if organised the right way, fall within free movement . . . law' (Davies, 2006: 6), the potential, and highly controversial, significance of free movement law for national social welfare systems becomes apparent (see further 6.14).

As cases such as *Sodemare* (Case C-70/95 *Sodemare* v. *Regione Lombardia* [1997] ECR I-3395) demonstrate however, the Court has shown itself to be sensitive to the concerns held by states in this field. Attempts by a Luxembourg company to operate old people's homes in Italy were thwarted by Italian rules restricting their operation to non-profit-making companies (and thus, the establishment provisions could not be relied upon). The Court held that such a restriction could be legitimate, nothing precluded Italy's decision to exclude profit-making companies from the market, which enabled social aims to be pursued as a matter of priority.

## 6.8  Unlawful Activities

A particular problem arises when certain states prohibit on their territory activities which are permitted in other states. In cases of this kind, some states have tried to argue that unlawful services are not services within the meaning of the Treaty, and that attempts to provide unlawful services should not be covered by EU law. While accepting that states have the right, on their own territory, to prohibit such activities as they see fit, the Court of Justice nevertheless maintains the jurisdiction to consider the position under EU law of individuals established elsewhere providing unlawful services in a host Member State. This jurisdiction applies solely to Article 49, as freedom of establishment can always be restricted by rendering a particular activity unlawful, provided, of course, the law is applied without discrimination on grounds of nationality. The matter of services remains more complex, and the following cases have clarified the circumstances under which the illegality of an activity in one Member State can restrict its provision by a national or company of another Member State.

The prohibited activity at issue in *SPUC* v. *Grogan* was the provision of abortion services in the Republic of Ireland. The defendants had been distributing information about travelling to the UK to get an abortion, and the Society for the Protection of Unborn Children, a pressure group, brought an action against them. The defendants in turn argued that a restriction on providing information about abortions in the UK was a restriction on the freedom of Irish citizens to travel to receive services. The argument failed because the defendants were working on a voluntary basis and had no economic link with the provision of the services; there was no profit or financial motive. However, the Court did make it clear that, while Ireland had the sovereign right to prohibit abortion on its territory, its sovereignty extended only to its territory, and did not allow for a prohibition on Irish citizens from travelling to other Member States to receive abortion services lawfully provided there. States, therefore, can control by means of prohibition what happens on their territory, but cannot control the activities of their citizens when they are not in their territory.

Case C-275/92 *HM Customs and Excise* v. *Schindler* ([1994] ECR I-1039) meanwhile concerned the prohibition within the UK of lotteries other than those authorised by statute. The German defendants were charged by the UK authorities with offences relating to running a lottery then illegal in the UK, because they had advertised their lottery in the UK and made it possible for UK citizens to take part. The UK's first argument was that the case did not fall to be considered under the Treaty at all, because the fact that the service concerned was unlawful within the UK took it outside the scope of Article 49 EC. The Court responded that, as long as an activity was lawful in some Member States (as such lotteries are), it could be considered as a legitimate service under the Treaty, although individual states retain the right to prohibit it on their territory. The second question was whether the German lottery was taking place on the territory of the UK and thus covered by the prohibition, given that neither the operators of the lottery nor the UK-based participants crossed any borders. The Court held that the essential activity of the lottery was taking place in Germany, as that was where the information was collated and the draw made, and thus the lottery must be understood as taking place in Germany and falling outside the UK's prohibition. Consequently, the UK was not entitled to prohibit the distribution of information or the participation of its residents in an activity which took place outside its territory.

## 6.9   The Prohibition on Discrimination

Articles 43 and 49 prohibit discrimination against companies or individuals established or providing services in a Member State other than their state of origin. This prohibition was held to have direct effect in Case 2/74 *Reyners* ([1974] ECR 631) (Article 43) and Case 33/74 *Van Binsbergen* ([1974] ECR 1299) (Article 49). Looking first at the establishment case law, *Reyners* concerned a clear case of direct discrimination, as it involved a requirement imposed by Belgian authorities that lawyers in that country had to have Belgian nationality. Case 71/76 *Thieffry* v. *Conseil de l'Ordre des Avocats à la Cour de Paris* ([1977] ECR 765) meanwhile extended the reach of Article 43 to indirectly discriminatory measures, rules that do not draw an explicit distinction on the grounds of nationality, but which impose a requirement that is more likely that nationals fulfil, in this case a French measure restricting authorisation to practise to professionals holding qualifications obtained in France. While a person seeking to establish themselves in a regulated profession may be excluded if his or her qualification is not satisfactory (and the question of the equivalence of academic, vocational and professional qualifications will be addressed in Chapter 12), this cannot simply be because the qualification is from a different Member State. Discrimination, direct or indirect, is also prohibited in the case of secondary establishment. Thus, in Case 107/83 *Ordre des Avocats* v. *Klopp* ([1984] ECR 2971) the Court held that a rule stating that any advocate admitted to the Paris Bar could not be registered at any other Bar and must not have any establishment other than in Paris was, *prima facie*, contrary to Article 43. The consequence of the rule was to require advocates established elsewhere to cut all their ties with their home Bars in order to practise in Paris. Other indirectly discriminatory (or indistinctly applicable) rules include residence requirements for company shareholders and directors, as seen in Case C-221/89 *R* v. *Secretary of State for Transport, ex parte Factortame (Factortame II)* ([1991] ECR I-3905).

The measures considered so far all have the effect of affecting the right of economic operators to take up an economic activity in another state. They are of the nature of restricting access to the market. Also covered by Article 43 are national measures which while not barring access, nevertheless impose discriminatory conditions on their pursuit of an economic activity. Again, such measures will clearly be caught if they are distinctly applicable (or directly discriminatory), as with the French nationality requirement for artists wishing to rent studio space in a fishermen's shed (Case 197/84 *Steinhauser* v. *City of Biarritz* [1985] ECR 1819), or indistinctly applicable/indirectly discriminatory, as with Belgian rules exempting the self-employed from paying social security contributions if they were also employed in Belgium (Case C143/87 *Stanton* v. *INASTI* [1988] ECR 3877).

As regards services, Article 49 also prohibits straightforward non-discrimination on grounds of nationality (or, in the case of companies, the state of registration or incorporation). Thus, in Case C-375/92 *Commission* v. *Spain* ([1994] ECR I-923), a requirement that tour guides be Spanish nationals was a clear breach of the services provisions. The imposition of a residence requirement is also a breach of the provisions (*Van Binsbergen*). The necessity of this is particularly obvious in the field of freedom to provide services where the prohibition by a Member State of the provision of services by non-resident Member State nationals would frustrate the very purpose of Article 49. Many service cases deal with measures akin to indistinctly applicable dual burden rules, such as those in the *Cassis* case in respect to goods (Case 120/78 *Rewe-Zentrale AG* v. *Bundesmonopolverwaltung für Branntwein (Cassis de Dijon)* [1979] ECR 649, see 5.6). The

Court has responded to the particular nature of service provision, which is temporary and often irregular, by making it clear that (subjective to possible objective justification) for a Member State to require service providers from other Member States to comply with the same regulations as service providers established on their own territory would deprive Article 49 of its purpose. If a service provider is required to comply with a new set of regulations and/or qualifications in order to provide their service in another Member State they will be discouraged and the free movement of services will be hindered. This was highlighted in Case 279/80 *Criminal Proceedings Against Webb* ([1981] ECR 3305), where a Dutch requirement that recruitment agencies should have a licence to operate was considered by the Court and held to fall under Article 49 because of its imposition of an extra requirement on foreign recruitment agencies which would place an extra burden on them if they wished to operate within the Netherlands.

The existence of a non-discrimination rule is therefore clear. However, the case law on establishment and services has followed the same trajectory as that on free movement of goods, in that the Court of Justice soon proceeded to hold that the existence of discrimination was not the only factor which would make a restriction fall foul of the Treaty provisions. This conclusion is buttressed also by Articles 14 and 16 of the Services Directive.

## 6.10   Beyond Discrimination: Freedom of Establishment

As with the case law on goods (Chapter 5), the Court has extended the reach of the free movement provisions to cover measures which, while non-discriminatory in law or in fact, nonetheless hinder market access. Many of the rules in the company law cases considered in 6.4 were approached by the Court not in terms of any directly or indirectly discriminatory effects on the grounds of place of registration or incorporation (which, it has been seen, may be a complex criterion to operate in this field), but on the grounds that the measure in question was 'liable to hinder or make less attractive the exercise of fundamental freedoms' (*Centros*, at para. 30). This formulation was first introduced in the field of establishment in the *Gebhard* case, which concerned a requirement to be registered with the national bar. Gebhard, a German national and resident in Italy, was established in the latter but had not formally registered, and could thus not use the official title *avvocato*. While Daniele has argued that a professional who is established within a Member State should, in principle, be subject to the same rules as are applied to nationals of that state (Daniele, 1997), the position of the Court of Justice is that any application of national rules different from those of the state of origin is suspect and must be justified. This position can be understood in the context of the Court's preoccupation with preserving the right of secondary establishment. States may maintain their regulations only if they can be objectively justified. The approach in respect to measures which concern the pursuit of an economic activity rather than the initial right of establishment itself in another state is rather less expansive, discrimination remaining a feature of the Court's jurisprudence (Case C-442/02 *Caixa Bank France* v. *Ministere de l'Économie, des Finances et de l'Industrie* [2004] ECR I-8961, see Chalmers *et al*, 2006: 730–4).

It should be noted that the Services Directive lists the prohibited requirements which Member States may not place upon access to the services activities falling within the scope of the Directive through establishment in the host state (Article 14), and it also contains a list of requirements to be evaluated by the Member State (Article 15), to ensure that they satisfy the requirements of non-discrimination, necessity and proportionality (see 6.13). This represents a shift of emphasis away from the case-by-case scrutiny fostered by the happenstance of litigation arising in national courts or as a result of the Commission bringing an enforcement action under Article 226 EC, and towards the proactive assessment of the restrictive effects of national restrictions and requirements.

## 6.11  Beyond Discrimination: Free Movement of Services

In Case C-76/90 *Säger* v. *Dennemeyer & Co. Ltd* ([1991] ECR I-4221), a case concerning German regulations about the qualifications required to act as a patent agent, the Court introduced the hindrance to the market approach to its services case law, albeit that the case itself could be categorised as one of indirect discrimination, or a 'dual burden'. The Court stated that if a UK company which was able to carry out this activity in the UK were not also to be allowed to do it in Germany without obtaining a fresh set of qualifications, its freedom to provide services would be hindered. The case most often seen as clarifying the scope of Article 49 as going beyond discrimination is Case C-384/93 *Alpine Investments BV* v. *Minister van Financiën* ([1995] ECR I-1141). Alpine Investments was a Dutch introductions broker, acting as a contact between commodities brokers and their clients. Under Dutch law, however, they were prohibited from approaching potential clients without written permission to do so; a practice known as 'cold-calling'. Alpine Investments argued that this restricted their ability to find new clients and therefore to carry out their business effectively and that, in particular, it restricted their ability to offer their services outside the Netherlands. The Court refused to go as far as accepting that there was a restriction on services 'solely by virtue of the fact that other Member States apply less strict rules to providers of similar services established in their territory' (para. 27). Nonetheless, it did accept a *prima facie* breach of Article 49 on the grounds that the national rule deprived the company of a 'rapid and direct technique for marketing' (para. 28).

*Alpine Investments* thus extends the reach of Article 49 to cover non-discriminatory rules on the 'export' of services (which goes beyond the interpretation offered to national rules hindering the export of goods, 5.10). It also witnessed unsuccessful attempts to have a *Keck*-style restriction read into the case law on services (Joined Cases C-267 and 268/91 *Criminal Proceedings against Keck and Mithouard* [1993] ECR I-6097, see 5.8). The UK and Dutch governments submitted that as the measure was 'generally applicable and non-discriminatory' . . . and 'affects only the way in which the services are offered, it is analogous to the non-discriminatory measures governing selling arrangments' under *Keck.*

The Court rejected the anology. In the Court's defence, one could raise the very different nature of persons and products, or of citizenship rights and economic rights. The product requirement/selling arrangement distinction made within *Keck* is difficult to operate in the context of services. Services have no abstract nature like a product, but are always understood in the context in which they are provided or sold (Hatzopoulos, 2000). Free movement of goods can be said to involve a completely different set of factors from those involved in the free movement of persons, services and establishment. The latter three freedoms concern the movement of people, as well as or instead of products, and thus raise a different set of social and cultural circumstances for consideration. In particular, they often involve, not restrictions on access to a particular market, but rather restrictions on the right to carry out a trade or profession or on the way in which that trade or profession is carried out. The services market is far more heavily regulated than the market in goods, and the vast majority of barriers to cross-border services are regulatory barriers.

It can be suggested that the growing emphasis of the EU on citizenship of the Union means that the law relating to persons should be less restrictive than that relating to economic goods and products, because citizenship is intended to grant individual citizens the freedom of movement in the widest possible terms around the territory of the EU. This argument would suggest that, if a distinction is to be made, it should not be made between the market in goods and the other markets (services, labour and capital), but rather between the free movement of persons and the free movement of products or services. This, in fact, is the organisational principle adopted in this book. The Court itself has suggested, in its Opinion 1/94 on the WTO agreement ([1994] ECR I-5267) that, under certain circumstances, goods and services can be equated to each other, and differentiated from the law relating to persons. The adoption of this organisational principle as the basis for substantive distinctions in legal rules would require a distinction to be made between those applications of the freedom to provide or receive services which involve the cross-border movement of people, and those which involve the cross-border nature of the service. Such a distinction may, in practice, often be difficult to make.

However, concerns with the refusal to apply the *Keck* restriction in the field of services were raised early in the post-*Keck* period, when challenges were brought to measures under both Articles 28 and 49, and the scheme appeared different depending on the Article under which the national measure was considered. Thus, in Joined Cases C-34–36/95 *Konsumentombudsmannen* v. *De Agostini (Svenska) Forlag* ([1997] ECR I-3843), it was held that legislation on television advertising could be considered under both Articles 28 and 49 and that, while the legislation was considered a non-discriminatory selling arrangement and thus excluded from the ambit of Article 28, it also fell under Article 49 in so far as advertisers were restricted from providing their service effectively within particular markets and could, in principle, be held to be unlawful. Later cases from both fields have gone some way to answer these concerns. As has been seen in other advertising cases (e.g. the Swedish ban on the advertising of alcohol considered in Case C-405/98 *Gourmet International* [2001] ECR I-1795, see 5.8) the Court has become less formulistic in its application of the *Keck* exemption. Selling arrangement rules are not automatically outside Article 28, and will be prohibited (unless justifiable) if they prohibit access or otherwise impact more adversely on imported products. In *Gourmet*, the Court's finding on the possible breach of Article 28 was mirrored by its findings on the restriction of services. The language of market access, of prohibitions on measures which prevent access or which impede access more for non-national products or providers, is now commonly applied across the free movement of goods and services provisions. Case C-17/00 *De Coster* ([2001] ECR I-9445), for example, concerned an annual municipal tax on the *owners* of satellite dishes. This tax was held as being 'liable to impede more the activities of operators in the field of broadcasting or television transmission established in [other] Member States . . . while giving an advantage to the internal Belgian market and to radio and television distribution within that Member State' (at para. 35). This was because Belgian broadcasters had unlimited access to (untaxed) cable distribution for their programmes, while broadcasters in other states did not, and had to rely on satellite broadcasting.

However, as Hatzopoulos and Do identify, the Court has recently embarked on a 'retreat and an effort at rationalization' in its services case law (2006: 958). In Joined Cases C-544 and 545/03 *Mobistar SA* v. *Commune de Fléron,* and *Belgacom Mobile SA* v. *Commune de Schaerbeek* ([2005] ECR I-7723) the Court considered the lawfulness of a Belgian rule requiring providers of telecommunications services to pay a one-off tax on transmission equipment. The requirement led to higher costs to consumers, and was challenged by service providers. The Court ruled (at para. 31) 'measures, the only effect of which is to create additional costs in respect of the service in question and which affect in the same way the provision of services between Member States and that within one Member State, do not fall within the scope of Article [49] of the Treaty'. The implications of this judgment are yet to fully play out. Certainly it does not appear to mark the significant and controversial rupture in jurisprudence that *Keck,* and its early mechanistic application by the Court, introduced into the goods case law. *Mobistar* has as yet been referred to in only one judgment, Joined Cases C-94 and 202/04 *Cipolla* v. *Fazari,* and *Macrino* v. *Capodarte* ([2006] ECR I-11421), which concerned Italian rules setting minimum fee rates for the provision of legal services. These were held to be a restriction on the free movement to provide services, as they deprive 'lawyers established in a Member State other than the Italian Republic of the possibility, by requesting fees lower than those set by the scale, of competing more effectively with lawyers established on a stable basis in the Member State concerned and who therefore have greater opportunities for winning clients than lawyers established abroad' (at para. 59). Thus, the rules did not affect in the same way the provision of services between Member States and that within one Member State.

## 6.12 Justifications for Restrictions on the Freedom of Establishment and Free Movement of Services

The discussion so far has outlined the extensive reach of Articles 43 and 49 EC. Measures imposed by both the target and the originating state of the service provider or economic operator seeking to establish elsewhere may constitute restrictions on free movement, even if they are non-discriminatory. Such restrictions may nevertheless be able to be justified – either under the Treaty-based justifications available, or, for measures which are indistinctly applicable, a broader set of Court-condoned objective justifications. This mirrors the approach already seen in Chapter 5 in relation to goods, and will be seen again in Chapter 12, on free movement of people.

Article 45 EC provides that the:

'provisions of this chapter shall not apply, so far as any given Member State is concerned, to activities which in that state are connected, even occasionally, with the exercise of public authority.'

The public authority exemption is extended to cover the chapter on services by Article 55 EC. The Court affords this provision a limited reading, any restriction on the exercise of the fundamental freedoms needing to be narrowly construed. In the *Reyners* case, the Court rejected an attempt by the Belgian Bar to exclude the whole profession of *avocat* from the scope of the free movement provision by virtue of the fact that 'it is connected organically with the functioning of the public service of the administration of justice'. The Court ruled that the exercise of the *avocat*'s role 'leaves the discretion of judicial authority and the free exercise of judicial power intact', and could not be seen as having the necessary 'direct and specific connection with the exercise of official authority' (paras.

53–54). Even if this connection were present, it is only where the exercise of functions connected with the exercise of official authority cannot be separable from other elements of the profession that an entire profession could be excluded. Equally unsuccessful were Italy's attempts to restrict the pool of those tendering to provide computer services for the operation of the state lottery. While certain tasks were held by the public administration, such as the approval of winning tickets and paying out, these were not activities which the provider of computer services would be directly involved in (Case C-272/91 *Commission* v. *Italy (Lottomatica)* [1994] ECR I-1409).

Article 46 EC, also extended to cover services by Article 55 EC, provides:

'The provisions of this Chapter . . . shall not prejudice the applicability of provisions laid down by law, regulation or administrative action providing for special treatment for foreign nationals on grounds of public policy, public security or public health.'

The scope of the public policy derogation was considered in Case C-268/99 *Jany* v. *Staatssecretaris van Justitie* ([2001] ECR I-8615) which concerned the status of Czech and Polish prostitutes in the Netherlands. Having established that they fell to be considered under the provisions on establishment, rather than workers (see 12.4), the Court considered whether they could be excluded on the basis of public policy, and specifically, public morality. The Court stated:

'Although Community law does not impose on Member States a uniform scale of values as regards the assessment of conduct which may be considered to be contrary to public policy, conduct may not be considered to be of a sufficiently serious nature to justify restrictions on entry to, or residence within, the territory of a Member State of a national of another Member State where the former Member State does not adopt, with respect to the same conduct on the part of its own nationals, repressive measures or other genuine and effective measures intended to combat such conduct . . . Consequently, conduct which a Member State accepts on the part of its own nationals cannot be regarded as constituting a genuine threat to public order' (at paras. 60–61).

The absence of a 'uniform scale of values' reappeared in *Omega*, concerning Germany's banning of the laserdrome shoot-to-kill games, lawful elsewhere in the EU, and with implications for service providers located in other states. Accepting the lawfulness of the restriction, which was based on a constitutional principle of respect for human dignity, the Court stated that 'the specific circumstances which may justify recourse to the concept of public policy may vary from one country to another and from one era to another. The competent national authorities must therefore be allowed a margin of discretion within the limits imposed by the Treaty' (at para. 31). Nevertheless, 'the concept of "public policy" in the Community context, particularly as justification for a derogation from the fundamental principle of the freedom to provide services, must be interpreted strictly, so that its scope cannot be determined unilaterally by each Member State without any control by the Community institutions' (at para. 30).

The public health ground is regularly raised in justification, and the Court has shown itself ready to accept a range of measures under this heading. Thus, in Case C-158/96 *Kohll* v. *Union des Caisses de Maladie* ([1998] ECR I-1931), discussed further at 14.8, the Court ruled that 'Member States may restrict the freedom to provide medical and hospital services in so far as the maintenance of treatment capacity or medical competence on national territory is essential for the public health, even survival of the population' (at para. 51). Advertising restrictions, prohibiting the advertising of alcoholic drinks, are also potentially permissible under the public health heading (*Gourmet International*), while, from the field of regulated professions, a restriction on those permitted to conduct eye examinations, being ophthalmologists, rather than opticians generally, was regarded as being capable of falling under the Article 46 derogation, being seen as 'an appropriate means by which to ensure attainment of a high level of health protection' (Case 108/96 *Mac Quen et al, Criminal Proceedings against* [2001] ECR I-837, at para. 30).

Although the Court may accept that the policy goal put forward by the Member State falls under one of the Article 46 EC headings, it must still be shown that the measures in question are a necessary and proportionate response to achieving that goal. Under a 234 EC reference this is properly a role for the national courts. Proportionality will be considered further below. At this stage it is sufficient to acknowledge that the Court has held that 'the fact that one Member State imposes less strict rules than another Member State does not mean that the latter's rules are disproportionate and hence incompatible with Community law' (*Mac Quen*, at para. 33).

## 6.13 Objective Justification

The test of objective justification, which, when properly made out, allows Member States to maintain national restrictions in the general public interest, was set out clearly in *Gebhard* (at para. 37). Measures must:

- be applied in a non-discriminatory manner;
- be justified by imperative requirements in the general interest;
- be suitable for securing the attainment of the objective which they pursue; and
- must not go beyond what is necessary in order to attain it.

This approach is also employed across the services cases. However, a distinction is apparent in the way the test operated between establishment and services cases, with the Court affording more leeway to Member State regulation in the case of establishment. In relation to non-discriminatory restrictions, the Court's view is that the regulation of the conduct of trades, professions and other activities may be necessary. Thus, in *Gebhard*, it stated that 'where the taking-up of a specific activity is not subject to any rules in the host state, a national of any other Member State will be entitled to establish himself on the territory of the first state and pursue that activity there. On the other hand, where the taking-up or the pursuit of a specific activity is subject to certain conditions in the host Member State, a national of another Member State intending to pursue that activity must in principle comply with them.' The Court has recognised that a stricter regulatory regime needs to be applied to those businesses which are established in a Member State than that applied to services which are provided on a temporary basis in other Member States. Regulation is regarded as most appropriately carried out in the Member State of establishment. However, there is the possibility under this approach that service providers could, because of the temporary nature of their activity, avoid all regulation emanating from the Member State where they are operating. This is particularly problematic where their state of establishment has a less regulated market in the service they are offering. However, the existence of regulation can be a serious disincentive to service providers to provide their services across a border. This may be because the regulations in different Member States vary significantly, making it difficult to comply with all of them, or because different Member States require procedures to demonstrate essentially the same thing (e.g.

professional skill or financial probity) which necessitates lengthy bureaucratic procedures. This can thus have the effect of fragmenting the market quite considerably, as well as of chilling innovations in relation to service provision which result from a more competitive and cohesive market. The temporary nature of services means that service providers will be less inclined to comply with a second set of regulations and so will choose not to offer their services within a particular Member State. The Court's response has been to be more ready to find qualification, registration and authorisation requirements applying to service providers unlawful, especially where they duplicate home state controls, in accordance with the principle of mutual recognition. This is seen in respect of measures requiring a French-obtained law qualification (*Thieffrey*); the requirement for building service suppliers to be entered on the trade register (*Schnitzer*); and for companies providing security services to be authorised by the Dutch state and their workforce to wear Dutch authority-issued ID badges (Case C-189/03 *Commission v. Netherlands (Private Security Firms)* [2004] ECR I-9289). While Member States may find it difficult to justify the imposition of regulations on businesses established in other Member States and providing temporary services on their territory, they will find the Court more amenable to allowing them to regulate businesses established on their territory even if they originate from, and/or are also established in another Member State (see Case 271/82 *Auer v. Ministère Public* [1983] ECR 2727). However, where national rules prevent access to the market (as with Case 107/83 *Klopp*, and many of the company law cases), the Court's review of the attempt at objective justification will be particularly stringent. The terms of the new Services Directive place a number of requirements on states if their demand for authorisation for economic service providers seeking establishment is to be lawful: in addition to the *Gebhard* criteria, the national measure must also be transparent, clear and unambiguous, made in advance and in public. It must also not duplicate any equivalent controls to which the economic operator is already subject (Article 9).

*Gebhard* itself, it will be remembered, concerned a registration requirement for practice at the Italian bar. Following *Thieffry*, the Court acknowledged that 'the taking-up and pursuit of certain self-employed activities may be conditional on complying with certain provisions laid down by law, regulation or administrative action justified by the general good, such as rules relating to organization, qualifications, professional ethics, supervision and liability' (at para. 35). Other public interests which can be protected are the reputation of the national financial sector (*Alpine Investments*), road safety (*Van Schaik*), the protection of workers (*Guiot and Climatec*), the financial balance of the social security system (*Kohll*), the protection of creditors (*Centros*), the protection of insurance policy holders (Case 205/84 *Commission v. Germany* [1986] ECR 3755), consumer protection, conservation of the national artistic heritage, dissemination of knowledge of artistic and cultural heritage of a country (Case C-180/89 *Commission v. Italy* [1991] ECR I-709), protection of the urban environment (*De Coster*) and the prevention of both fraud and incitement to squander on gambling (Case C-124/97 *Läärä and Others* [1999] ECR I-6067, Case C-67/98 *Zenatti* [1999] ECR I-7289 and Case C-243/01 *Gambelli* [2003] ECR I-13031).

Having established that the measure in question can be classified as an imperative requirement in the general interest (and this is an open-ended list), the measure must also be accepted as suitable for securing the attainment of the objective which it pursues, and must not go beyond what is necessary in order to attain it. The application of this test of necessity and proportionality is, according to Hatzopoulos, the way in which the Court tends to use its power to hold regulations to be unlawful. Most goals of public policy put forward by the Member States are accepted without question and the Court focuses on assessing whether the measures concerned are necessary and proportionate to that aim (Hatzopoulos, 2000). Many examples can be found of the Court refusing to accept that the measure is appropriate to achieve the aim set (or, at least, suggesting strongly to the national court how they should exercise their powers of review here). Thus, the tax on satellite equipment in *De Coster* was strongly questioned as being an appropriate and proportionate means to achieve the aim of protecting the urban environment, the Court stating that 'there are methods other than the tax in question in the main proceedings, less restrictive of the freedom to provide services, which could achieve an objective such as the protection of the urban environment, for instance the adoption of requirements concerning the size of the dishes, their position and the way in which they are fixed to the building or its surroundings or the use of communal dishes' (at para. 38). From among the recent stream of gambling cases, the restriction on those able to run betting services and take bets in *Gambelli* was not amenable to objective justification on the public interest grounds put forward by the Italian state. They were debarred from doing so because of the state's support of the activity. While an activity (such as gambling) does not need to be totally prohibited for state restrictions regulating that activity to be potentially justifiable (*Läärä* and *Zenatti*), the Italian state could not rely on a justification based on public order concerns relating to the need to reduce opportunities for betting 'in so far as the authorities incite and encourage consumers to participate in lotteries and games of chance and betting to the benefit of the public purse' (at para. 69). Any national restriction would also need to go no further than was necessary to achieve its aim, and criminal sanctions for breach of such national rules are inappropriate. It should be recognised that the Court's treatment of national attempts at objective justification is not always as stringent. The level of scrutiny in some cases appears to depend on the nature of the measure. In *Alpine Investments*, for example, the prohibition on cold calling imposed by the Dutch government was intended to maintain the good reputation of the Dutch financial sector. The Court assumed that this was a valid goal, and did not scrutinise particularly hard the need for the prohibition in order to achieve this goal. It is perhaps significant that this was a measure which was not discriminatory in any way, and this perhaps prompted the Court to allow the Netherlands wide regulatory choice when it came to such a measure.

## 6.14  The Services Directive

The most controversial element of the original proposal for a Services Directive (referred to as the Bolkestein Directive, after the then Commissioner for the Internal Market) was the inclusion of a general 'country of origin' principle applicable to temporary service provision. This amounted to a broad statement of mutual recognition and home state control, which appeared to go beyond the strict text of the EC Treaty and also the case law of the Court of Justice. The principle stated that any service provider operating temporarily in a Member State other than their own should be subject only to the national provisions of their own Member State, and not to any regulation emanating from the host Member State (Article 16). This was, however, subject to a limited number of excluded fields of activity (Article 17) where the host Member State would be permitted to regulate. Such a proposal appeared to exclude the opportunity for the host Member State to objectively justify any regulation in the manner which the Court of Justice had thus far permitted.

This approach was vehemently rejected by the European Parliament in its discussion of the proposal, and the Parliament's position was supported by the Council of Ministers. The proposed directive had attained an extraordinary political significance, and was held up as an example of over-regulation and a source for downward pressure on national social systems, especially in France, where its fate and that of the Constitutional Treaty became inextricably linked. Thus the final version of the adopted directive, based on the revised 'McCreevy' proposal (the name change reflecting a change in Commission personnel) sees Article 16 restate the Treaty and the current law of the Court of Justice, in that the fundamental legal principle is 'freedom to provide services', subject to the right of host Member States to justify the existence and application of regulations which are non-discriminatory, necessary for reasons of public policy, or public security, or the protection of health and the environment, and proportionate. It is possible that the necessity requirement could in due course be interpreted as narrower than the very broad set of policy grounds which the Court currently accepts as justifying Member State regulations, although there is no authoritative guidance on this question at this stage. Elsewhere, Article 16 brings little change to the current legal situation, affording EU legislative authority to the pragmatic compromise which the Court has developed over many years.

A second controversy surrounding the Services Directive concerned the extent to which it would apply to Services of General Interest (SGIs). SGIs are what are often referred to within Member States as 'public services' or, at the very least, services where the providers are subject to public service obligations. In 6.7, consideration was paid to the extent to which the Court currently requires such services to be covered by the free movement provisions. The piecemeal extension of the case law on these matters has been extremely controversial, as indeed was the proposed application of the original Commission proposal for a Services Directive to SGIs. The final version limited this application considerably, in that its application to non-economic services of general interest (Article 2(2)(a)), healthcare services (Article 2(2)(f)) and social services relating to social housing, childcare and support of families (Article 2(2)(j)) is excluded. Also excluded after significant lobbying pressure are, among others, the gambling industries (Article 2(2)(h)) and private security services (Article 2(2)(k)). The operation of the free movement principles in these areas remains subject to the general Articles 43 and 49 EC scheme, rather than the 'special' scheme that would have been introduced by the directive. In addition to these generally excluded areas, the final form of the directive also maintains the list of services which fall under the Article 17 'additional derogations' – activities to which the principle of home state control in Article 16 were not to apply, such as services covered by other EU legislation, such as electricity supply, gas, postal services and those operating under the Posted Workers Directive.

Given the degree to which derogations and exceptions litter the directive, its real value as a tool of removing outstanding restrictions to the free movement of services and establishment is to be doubted. The revised form of the directive, it has been argued, reduces the impact of the directive on development of the internal market 'to practically zero, if not even to a negative effect' (Editorial, 2006: 307).

## 6.15 Positive Integration in Establishment and Services

The case law discussed above has involved the Court often seeking to balance two separate, and often opposing, interests. On the one hand, it is essential for the development of the internal market, particularly given the increasing size of the service-based economy, that freedom of movement of services and freedom of establishment should be achieved with as few barriers as possible. On the other hand, service providers, self-employed individuals and companies are often engaged in activities which, for the sake of consumer protection and economic stability, need to be regulated. It is these kinds of regulations which most often form barriers to trade in services or to cross-border establishment. Although in many cases such regulation is necessary, there is always a risk that they may be protectionist, either in intent or in effect. The Court has tried to do this by holding a wide range of regulations to be *prima facie* contrary to EU law, although it has allowed many of them to be saved if they are necessary in order to fulfil a legitimate public policy goal. This approach, however, has two weaknesses. First, it can lead to an undermining of the regulatory framework in certain areas, as national regulation requires constant justification. Second, and more importantly, it means that, provided that they can justify them, Member States are still entitled to maintain different regulations from those of their neighbours, leading to a fragmentation of the market.

As a consequence, and mirroring the development in other areas of the internal market, the legislative institutions have moved towards EU-level regulation of certain activities, and the liberalisation of certain trades and professions, with controls set at EU level. The Treaty offers legal bases to do this under Article 44 (freedom of establishment) and Article 52 (freedom to provide services). The differences between these two legal bases should perhaps be noted. Both provisions require the institutions to proceed by means of directives, in order to give Member States the choice as to how Community-level regulation can be incorporated into their systems. However, Article 44 requires the co-decision procedure to be used, while Article 52 simply requires consultation of the Parliament and Economic and Social Committee, and a qualified majority in Council. Article 44 gives a general competence to legislate in order to attain freedom of establishment, but it requires the Commission and the Council to give 'priority treatment to activities where freedom of establishment makes a particularly valuable contribution to the development of production and trade' (Article 44(2)(b)). This would emphasise the focus of legal regulation on the economic development of the internal market. Article 52 refers more specifically to the liberalisation of services, rather than to the attainment of free movement of services, and requires priority to be given to services which directly affect production costs or where liberalisation promotes trade in goods. Again, an emphasis on the economic development of the internal market can be found.

Positive integration has generally tended to take place on a sector-specific basis. One of the purposes of the original proposed Services Directive, as it was conceived by the Commission, was to move away from sector-specific harmonisation and towards a general horizontal approach to the removal of barriers, by means of the country of origin principle. However, the number of excluded sectors in the final version and the removal of the country of origin principle mean that sector-specific harmonisation remains an important area of activity. This chapter ends with a very brief overview of some of the main sectors of the service economy where harmonisation and liberalisation have taken place, covering transport and financial services.

## 6.16    Areas of EU Legislative Activity

Transport services are clearly of great importance when it comes to ensuring cross-border trade. Article 51 EC specifically states that transport services are not governed by the general provisions on the free movement of services but rather under the provision of the Title relating to transport (Title V of Part Three of the Treaty). Thus transport is governed by the specific of the Common Transport Policy, which aims at the harmonisation of the conditions under which goods are transported throughout the territory of the Union, while at the same time liberalising the market in transport services. In addition, measures are demanded to ensure that transport is sustainable, addressing the high pollution costs that are the result of the dominance of road transport for passenger trips, and its heavy use in haulage across the EU.

Among the measures adopted under the Common Transport Policy, using the legal base of Article 71 EC, are regulations on maritime transport. Maritime transport accounts for some 90 per cent of external trade movement, and 40 per cent of internal trade within the EU. Council Regulation 4055/86 (OJ 1986 L378/1) opened up the possibility of shipping companies gaining contracts to provide maritime services operating between Member States, and between Member States and third countries, regardless of their (member) state of establishment. Measures which restrict such operations, for example, through indirectly discriminatory taxation of vessels (Case C-430/99 *Sea-Land* [2002] ECR I-5235) will breach the regulation in the same way that they would be found to breach Article 49 EC, were the general principles to apply. Hatzopoulos and Do have identified significant 'cross-fertilization' between the sector-specific and general legislation (2006: 930). In the same way, there has been a programme of liberalisation in the air transport sector (e.g. Regulation 2408/92, on access for Community air carriers to intra-Community air routes, OJ 1992 L15/33), to which the same principles found in the Article 49 EC jurisprudence apply (Case C-70/99 *Commission* v. *Portugal (Airport Taxes)* [2001] ECR I-4845). The programme of liberalisation had, according to the Commission, by 2005 contributed to an increase in the number of intra-Community routes by more than 40 per cent, and an increase in the number of companies by 25 per cent. Within the road transport sector, a variety of measures have been introduced, including rules harmonising conditions for admission to the occupation of road haulage operator and road passenger transport operator in the European Union (Council Directive 96/26, OJ 1996 L24/1 as amended by Council Directive 98/76, OJ 1998 L/17). The operators must fulfill three qualitative criteria of good repute, financial standing and professional competence. This is justified for several reasons, including the facilitation of establishment. Additionally, for road transport operations taking place between Member States, operators must hold a Community licence, issued by the Member State of establishment, which gives free access to the whole single market. To obtain it, operators must meet the conditions of Council Regulation 881/92 (OJ 1992 L95/1). The right to provide temporary haulage services from any EU state is further provided by Council Regulation 3118/93 laying down the conditions under which non-resident carriers may operate national road haulage services within a Member State (OJ 1993 L279/1).

The *financial services* sector is one which has traditionally been subject to intensive national regulation. However, once more, liberalisation of the sector is seen as an essential component of the achievement of the internal market. Financial services have, over time, and in a piecemeal manner, been liberalised and regulated, firstly in conjunction with the liberalisation of capital, as required by Article 51(2) (see Chapter 8). The SEA, with its drive to the completion of the internal market, stimulated some activity across the financial services sector, for example with the adoption of the Second Banking Directive (Council Directive 89/646, OJ 1989 L386/1; this, and the 1977 First Directive and a raft of later measures have now been replaced by European Parliament and Council Directive 2006/48 relating to the taking-up and pursuit of the business of credit, OJ 2006 L177/1) and measures in the field of insurance (see below). The legislative programme was recently significantly advanced through the Commission's action plan to secure a single market in financial services by 2005 (COM(1998) 625). The thrust of the EU's approach to financial services is to undertake sufficient coordination and harmonisation which will enable the operation of a system of mutual recognition and a 'single passport' system, which allows financial services operators legally established in one Member State to establish/provide their services in the other Member States without further authorisation requirements. This Financial Services Action Plan (FSAP) sought to provide an overarching policy in financial services, which cover such sectors as banking, insurance, and securities and investment funds. The priorities of the FSAP were: to create an integrated securities and derivatives market and to remove barriers to raising capital on an EU-wide basis; an open market for financial services (e.g. mortgages, insurance, banking, pensions); to ensure the stability of financial markets; and to eliminate tax barriers to liberalisation and harmonisation. While the target date has passed, the Commission continues to monitor the transposition of the measures adopted under it, while at the same time working to achieve its objectives for financial services policy for the period to 2010. These are set out in the White Paper on Financial Services Policy 2005–2010. As in many sectors, the Commission views the current period as one where there is limited scope for new legislation, instead the priorities are on consolidating progress and ensuring sound implementation and enforcement of existing rules. Also prioritised under the White Paper is the creation of more competition between service providers, especially those active in retail markets. It also focuses more emphasis on retail integration than before, and will involve an examination of barriers associated with the use of bank accounts, with a view to enabling consumers to shop around all over Europe for the best savings plans, mortgages, insurance and pensions, with clear information so that products can be compared.

Within the broader category of financial services, specific attention has been paid to a number of important sectors, such as services provided in relation to pensions schemes. This is not least because of the close relationship between the free movement of persons and pension provision. The transferability of pensions across borders would offer a significant boost to labour mobility. EU action currently focuses on the liberalisation of the pensions market, and in particular on the broadening of investment possibilities to include cross-border investment. At the same time, safeguards need to be put into place to protect investors. The common policy on pension schemes is currently quite limited. State pensions are not touched by EU law, and policy decisions about pension provision remain in the hands of the Member States. In the absence of legislation, the general rules on services apply – as seen in Case C-422/01 *Skandia and Ramstedt* ([2003] ECR I-6817), in which the Court ruled that it was contrary to Article 49 EC for a state to treat an occupational pension insurance policy issued by an insurance company established in another Member State differently in terms of taxation from those provided by home state companies. In May 2003 the Council and the European Parliament approved a directive on the harmonisation of occupational pensions which are linked directly to employment (European Parliament and Council Directive 2003/41, OJ 2003 L235/10). This will allow for more liberal investment rules to take advantage of the internal market, and would also allow for the cross-border management of funds, which has not previously been permitted. A more harmonised taxation system would be of great benefit to the pensions market but, under current conditions, is not likely to be achieved in the near future.

Insurance services are one area where a significant Community-level regulation has taken place. The objective of EU involvement is to liberalise the insurance market, enabling insurance providers to operate across the EU, while ensuring protections for the consumers of their policies. As before, a level of harmonisation is required as a basis for mutual recognition to take place. The earliest measure was Council Directive 73/239 (OJ 1973 L228/3) on non-life assurance (excluding third party motor insurance), which set out freedom of establishment for insurance companies and also the authorisation procedures for them. Council Directive 79/267 (OJ 1979 L63/1) did the same for life assurance. These 'first generation' measures were subsequently joined by the 'second generation' measures, introduced on the back of the SEA and which regulate the location of supervision procedures for different types of insurance (Council Directive 88/357 on non-life assurance, OJ 1988 L172/1; Council Directive 90/619 on life assurance, OJ 1990 L330/50). Finally, the 'third generation' measures introduced a single authorisation procedure for insurance services (Council Directive 92/49 on non-life assurance, OJ 1992 L228/1; Council Directive 92/96 on life assurance, OJ 1992 L360/1). The three directives on life insurance were replaced by one single measure in 2002 (European Parliament and Council Directive 2002/83, OJ 2002 L345/1). Comparable consolidation and streamlining have yet to take place in respect to non-life assurance.

Significant activity has taken place in respect of motor insurance, which is seen as particularly important given the incidence of interstate travel by car. There are now five motor insurance directives. The First (72/166, OJ 1972 L103/1), on the approximation of the laws of Member States relating to insurance against civil liability in respect of the use of motor vehicles, and to the enforcement of the obligation to insure against such liability, imposed requirements on Member States to provide for a system of compulsory insurance of vehicles, and removed the right for states to conduct systematic checks on the insurance status of vehicles entering their territory. The system was based upon agreements between national insurance bureaux according to which each national bureau guaranteed the settlement of claims in respect of accidents occurring in its territory caused by vehicles normally based in the territory of another Member State, whether or not such vehicles are insured. Ongoing variations in Member State rules on compulsory insurance were addressed in the Second Directive (Council Directive 84/5, OJ 1984 L8/17), which set certain minimum levels of compensation and, in addition, required the states to set up compensation bodies, responsible for meeting the cost of claims for damage to property or personal injuries caused by an unidentified or uninsured vehicle. The Third Directive (Council Directive 90/232, OJ 1990 L192/33) introduced harmonising measures in particular in respect of the insurance protection of vehicle passengers. The Fourth Directive (European Parliament and Council Directive 2000/26, OJ 2000 L181/65) meanwhile introduced further bodies against whom claims could be brought by 'visiting victims', including insurance companies' claims representatives across the EU states, or, as a fall back, compensation bodies established or approved by the state. The Fifth and most recent Directive (European Parliament and Council Directive 2005/14, OJ 2005 L149/14) brings clarification to some of the existing provisions, including defining the 'territory in which the vehicle is normally based' as the state of which the vehicle bears the registration plates, as well as increasing the minimum insured sum levels.

## Summary

1. The establishment (Articles 43 and 48 EC) and services (Article 49 EC) provisions concern the rights of Union citizens and companies established in the EU to carry out their activities in other Member States, and the conditions of access which apply to them.

2. While the service economy itself is a highly significant contributor to national GDP (accounting for an average of between 60 and 70 per cent of economic activity with Member States, and responsible for a similar level of the employment rate), interstate trade in services remains underdeveloped.

3. The Services Directive was intended to stimulate wide ranging liberalisation in the services sector. However, it became highly politically controversial and was finally adopted in a much watered down form.

4. This chapter considers the conditions under which economic activities may be carried out on a cross-border basis The *personal* rights of individuals moving in order to exercise their freedom to provide or receive services or to become established in another Member State are dealt with in Chapter 12.

5. According to Article 50 EC Treaty, the concept of services applies to activities provided for remuneration 'in so far as they are not governed by the provisions relating to freedom of movement for goods, capital and persons'.

6. Establishment is defined in *Gebhard* as participation on a stable and continuous basis in the economic life of the state.

7. For EU law to be applicable to a situation there must be a cross-border element to the provision of services. It is not necessary that individuals physically cross borders. This reflects an increasing emphasis on the objective economic status of services, separate from the people who provide them.

8. The acts of private associations may be caught, where these regulate, in a collective manner, the provision of services or the carrying-out of business in another Member State.

9. Companies based in a Member State have a right to primary and secondary establishment in any other Member State. However, significant obstacles to their exercise of freedom of establishment are created by national company law systems. Both negative and positive harmonisation measures have been taken to address these obstacles.

10. To fall under the Treaty provisions, the service must have some economic value. As long as there is a profit motive, it is not necessary that the activity be paid for by its consumers. There is considerable controversy over the application of the provisions to social or welfare services.

11. While Member States retain the sovereignty to prohibit certain economic activities on their territory, they may not prohibit the distribution of information about such activities carried out lawfully in another Member State (*Grogan*), nor may they prevent their own citizens from participating in such an activity, provided that it is carried out on the territory of another Member State (*Schindler*).

12. Direct and indirect discrimination on the grounds of nationality and residence are prohibited between service providers and between those established in a Member State. All rules relating the right to take up an activity in a Member State on a permanent basis are subject to careful scrutiny in order to ensure that there is no restriction of freedom of establishment. Rules governing the conditions under which such activity may be carried out are subject to a lesser level of scrutiny, in order to allow Member States effectively to regulate the field.

## Summary cont'd

13. Rules governing the temporary provision of services are subject to significant scrutiny, to ensure that they do not operate so as to discourage the cross-border provision of services (*Alpine Investments*).

14. All restrictions – whether distinctly or indistinctly applicable, are open to justification under the recognised Treaty grounds of exercise of public authority (Article 45 EC), and on grounds of public policy, public security or public health (Article 46 EC).

15. Non-discriminatory measures can be objectively justified in the public interest. Objective justification is easier to show for rules relating to establishment than for rules relating to the temporary provision of services.

16. Rather than rely on the Court of Justice permitting national regulations, the legislative institutions have moved towards the European-level harmonisation of the regulation of economic activities and services.

# Exercises

1. What is the difference between being established in a Member State and providing services there?

2. What is the significance of the judgment in *Alpine Investments*?

3. How can a Member State justify regulatory barriers: (a) to establishment; and (b) to the cross-border provision of services?

4. What differences will the Services Directive bring to this area?

5. Why is the positive integration of regulatory structures important?

# Workshop

André is a computer engineer. He is a French national and lives and works in Montpellier. However, he has contacts in Barcelona and frequently travels over the border to Spain to carry out work there. Because he has a lot of sensitive technical equipment, he has rented an office in Barcelona to store things in, and he also keeps a flat in Barcelona, where he can stay overnight during long jobs. His wife and family continue to live in Montpellier, and he continues to do a lot of work in France. Which set of Community law provisions covers his situation?

In Spain, the (fictitious) Software and Data Protection Law is passed. This provides, *inter alia*, that all software engineers must be licensed by the regional authority to carry out their trade. The licensing procedure constitutes a police check and a short interview, to ensure that the engineer is legitimate and can be trusted with the often confidential information he or she may come across. No such requirement for a licence exists in France. André is not sure whether or not he needs to apply for a licence. Advise him.

André decides to apply for the licence. He goes to the relevant office in Barcelona, and is told by a civil servant that he will not be granted a licence. This is because it is a complex and expensive business for the Spanish authorities to run a police check in France, and therefore the rule is that licences are only granted to people who have been living in Spain for the past five years. What should André's response be?

On receipt of his licence, André goes back to Montpellier. However, he notices that he is getting no work from his contacts in Barcelona. When he approaches them to ask about this, he is told that a new regulation exists, whereby software engineering contracts must be coordinated by a central body, and cannot be contracted out privately. He telephones the relevant body, and is told that, on payment of a fee of 1000 euro per year (which is the fee that is charged to all contractors, whether Spanish or not), he may register with them and be allocated contracts whenever suitable ones arise. Is the Spanish regulation lawful?

Following the break-up of his marriage, André decides to settle in Barcelona. In the interests of making a new start, he decides to give up the software engineering business and become a bookmaker. However, under the (fictitious) Betting and Lottery Law, only state-owned betting shops and services may operate in Spain – anyone else trying to operate as a bookmaker will be convicted of a criminal offence. André therefore convinces his friend Gérard, back in Montpellier, to run a telephone betting service from France, which Spanish citizens can call to place bets. André's contribution is to publicise the service and to advise on the odds offered. Subsequently, the French government introduce the (fictitious) Telephone Sales Act, which prohibits companies in France from publicising their own telephone services in other countries. Does André have a defence under EU law to:

▶ a Spanish prosecution of him for breach of the Betting and Lottery Law;
▶ a French prosecution of him for breach of the Telephone Sales Act?

## Further Reading

Barnard, C. (2004) *The Substantive Law of the EU: The Four Freedoms*, Oxford: Oxford University Press, chapters 12, 13 and 14.

Chalmers, D. *et al* (2006) *European Union Law*, Cambridge: Cambridge University Press, chapters 16 and 17.

Daniele, L. (1997) 'Non-Discriminatory Restrictions on the Free Movement of Persons', 22 *European Law Review* 191.

Davies, G. (2006) 'The Process and Side Effects of Harmonisation of European Welfare States', Jean Monnet Working Paper 02/06, available at: **http://www.jeanmonnetprogram.org**

Editorial (2006) 'The Services Directive Proposal: Striking a balance between the promotion of the internal market and preserving the European Social Model', 43 *Common Market Law Review* 307.

Edwards, V. (2003) 'The European Company – Essential Tool of Eviscerated Dream?', 40 *Common Market Law Review* 443.

Hatzopoulos, V. (2000) 'Recent Developments of the Case Law of the ECJ in the Field of Services', 37 *Common Market Law Review* 43.

Hatzopoulos, V. (2002) 'Killing National Health and Insurance Systems but Healing Patients? The European Market for Healthcare Services after the Judgments of the ECJ in Vanbraekel and Peerbooms', 39 *Common Market Law Review* 683.

Hatzopoulos, V. and Do, T. (2006) 'The Case Law of the ECJ Concerning the Free Provision of Services: 2000–2005', 43 *Common Market Law Review* 923.

Littler, A. and Fijnaut, C. (eds.) (2007) *The Regulation of Gambling: European and National Perspectives*, Leiden/Boston: Martinus Nijhoff Publishers.

O'Leary, S. (1999) 'The Free Movement of Persons and Services', in Craig, P. and de Búrca, G. (eds.), *The Evolution of EU Law*, Oxford: Oxford University Press.

Roth, W.H. (2003) 'From *Centros* to *Ueberseering*: Free Movement of Companies, Private International Law, and Community Law', 52 *International and Comparative Law Quarterly* 177.

## Further Reading cont'd

Snell, J. and Andenas, M. (2000) 'How Far? The Internal Market and Restrictions on the Free Movement of Goods and Services', Part I, 2 *International and Comparative Corporate Law Journal* 239 and Part II, 2 *International and Comparative Corporate Law Journal* 361.

Weatherill, S. (2002) 'Pre-emption, Harmonisation and the Distribution of Competence to Regulate the Internal Market', in Barnard, C. and Scott, J. (eds.), *The Law of the Single European Market: Unpacking the Premises*, Oxford: Hart Publishing.

Wouters, J. (2000) 'European Company Law: Quo Vadis?', 37 *Common Market Law Review* 257.

Wymeersch, E. (2003) 'The Transfer of a Company's Seat in European Community Law', 40 *Common Market Law Review* 661.

## Key Websites

The Commission's informational website on services and establishment is at:

**http://ec.europa.eu/internal_market/top_layer/index_19_en.htm**

The Commission's transport website is at:

**http://ec.europa.eu/transport/index_en.html**

There is a separate website dedicated to financial services at:

**http://ec.europa.eu/internal_market/top_layer/ index_24_en.htm**

## Chapter 7

# Taxation and the Internal Market

**7.1** Introduction

The raising of revenues through direct taxation on individuals and companies is, within the EU, a matter for the Member States. The power to tax is a jealously guarded aspect of national sovereignty, although national taxation systems are subject to the disciplines of the internal market, in the sense that they must be non-discriminatory in nature. One form of indirect taxation – the turnover-based value-added tax – is a common form of taxation instituted in 1977, which operates on a common basis governed by EU directives, although rates of taxation may vary between the Member States. Other indirect taxes, such as taxes on goods or services, remain governed by national law, again subject to the non-discrimination principle.

This chapter looks at some of the principal implications of EU law for taxation imposed by the Member States, concentrating on the taxation of goods as governed by Article 90 EC, which prohibits discrimination. It is therefore closely linked to other aspects of the free movement of goods (see Chapters 4 and 5). The free movement implications of taxation which is imposed by the Member States on services, persons and corporations, and especially the application by the Court of Justice of the non-discrimination principle to various forms of direct taxation, are raised briefly also in Chapters 6 and 12. Long after the question of taxation barriers to interstate trade was raised as a central concern in the Commission's original plan to complete the internal market (*Completing the Internal Market*, COM(85) 10), concerns still continue about whether the Member States' tax systems impact equally upon domestic and imported products. These concerns as well as the wider cross-border implications of the national systems are echoed in the paragraphs which follow. Some more general questions about the evolution of EU taxation policy are addressed at the end of the chapter.

The Treaties have relatively little to say directly about the question of taxation, with a meagre four provisions in the EC Treaty (Articles 90–93). Article 90 EC prohibits the Member States from imposing discriminatory taxation on domestic and imported products. Article 91 EC prohibits refunds of taxation on exports which exceed the internal taxation imposed upon them, and Article 92 EC also deals with repayments in respect of taxation on exports. Article 93 EC offers an important legal basis for the adoption of measures harmonising national legislation relating to 'turnover taxes, excise duties and other forms of indirect taxation to the extent that such harmonisation is necessary to ensure the establishment and functioning of the internal market'. Article 93 EC operates as a *lex specialis* compared to other internal market legal bases, such as Articles 94 and 95 EC. It requires a unanimous vote in the Council and involves only consultation with the European Parliament. Fiscal provisions are explicitly excluded from the scope of Article 95 EC, which provides for qualified majority voting and Council–Parliament co-decision in relation to most measures which are to be adopted for the purposes of the completion of the internal market (Article 95(2) EC). Articles 94 and 308 EC, both of which also require a unanimous vote in Council, have also been used to adopt harmonisation measures dealing with aspects of taxation. Harmonisation is confined to cases where direct or, more frequently, indirect taxation impacts upon the free movement of goods, services, persons or capital and the right of establishment for companies and individuals. A good example of a recent proposal from the Commission concerns taxation on passenger cars, presented in July 2005 (COM(2005) 261). According to the Commission's press release (IP 05/839, 5 July 2005), the proposal for a directive:

'would require Member States to re-structure their passenger car taxation systems. The proposal aims to improve the functioning of the Internal Market by removing existing tax obstacles to the transfer of passenger cars from one Member State to another. It would also promote sustainability by restructuring the tax base of both registration taxes and annual circulation taxes so as to include elements directly related to carbon dioxide emissions of passenger cars. The proposal aims only to establish an EU structure for passenger car taxes. It would not harmonise tax rates or oblige Member States to introduce new taxes.'

As we shall see below, there have been a number of cases before the Court of Justice concerned with allegedly discriminatory national systems of taxation on motor vehicles, and many such systems have environmental concerns as their rationales. To the Commission, therefore, it obviously made sense to make a proposal for a directive on the structure of passenger car taxation systems to increase the possibility that the EU and its Member States might reach their ambitious emissions reduction targets, while allowing for tax competition to continue between the Member States on taxation rates. However, the proposal is based on Article 93 EC and requires unanimous agreement among the Member States for it to be adopted, and while the measure was approved under the consultation process with relatively minor amendments by the European Parliament in 2006, it is unclear whether it will receive the support of all twenty-seven Member States.

Article 269 EC requires the EU budget to be wholly financed from its own resources – which include a percentage of VAT revenue collected at the national level, as well as agricultural levies, customs duties and GNP-based resources. However, the EU has no power to create or levy taxes, and indeed nothing is stated in the Treaty about a taxation policy for the EU. Such a policy would be expected to include not only ways of responding to the challenges resulting from the inevitable cross-border implications of national taxation systems, especially those operating within an internal market and an economic and monetary union, but also some attempt to harness the possibilities that taxation offers as an instrument of economic regulation and as a means of promoting wealth creation and of redistributing income, especially in relation to concerns about protecting the environment (particularly climate change and energy supply issues) and promoting employment. This is ever more important in an increasingly global economy, as is clear from the fact that there are more than a dozen Commission proposals pending before the Council for adoption, not to mention numerous reports, communications and programmes which the Commission has sought to promote on the subject of taxation, which is indeed an important matter for the EU. Most, if not all, EU policies now have a 'tax dimension'. Three main challenges have been identified for EU tax policy:

- stabilising Member States' tax revenues;
- ensuring the smooth functioning of the internal market in the context of sustainable development; and
- promoting employment.

It is still worth reiterating the general proposition that the taxation systems in the internal market, with the exception of the VAT system which has effectively been a common system since 1977, are instituted by the Member States and not by the EU. The principle of the diversity of systems is therefore very important, and taxation is recognised as being extremely important to national sovereignty. Progress on taxation policy in the form of 'hard law' measures has, however, always been slow. The development of the VAT system and other aspects of EU tax policy which affect the workings of national taxation systems are addressed in a little more detail in 7.8 and 7.9. The main part of this chapter looks in detail at Article 90 EC, including its relationship to other provisions of the Treaty.

## 7.2 The Nature and Scope of the Basic Prohibition in Article 90 EC

Article 90 EC provides two bases for assessing the discriminatory element in systems of taxation. It states:

> 'No Member State shall impose, directly or indirectly, on the products of other Member States any internal taxation of any kind in excess of that imposed directly or indirectly on similar domestic products.
>
> Furthermore, no Member State shall impose on the products of other Member States any internal taxation of such a nature as to afford indirect protection to other products.'

Article 90 applies only to goods originating in other Member States, and to goods in free circulation in the Member States. It does not apply to goods imported directly from third countries (Case C-130/92 *OTO* v. *Ministero delle Finanze* [1994] ECR I-3281). The essential purpose of Article 90 is not to engender a principle of equivalence in national taxation regimes. This would be impossible given the diversity of national regimes which continue to exist, since the Member States retain fiscal autonomy as regards the raising of revenue and the use of taxation as an instrument of redistributive policy. Taxation must, however, be neutral and the Treaty restricts the prohibition to measures which are discriminatory in form or in effect, provided normally in the latter case that there is a protectionist effect in addition. According to the Court of Justice, in Case 127/75 *Bobie* v. *Hauptzollamt Aachen-Nord* ([1976] ECR 1079), Article 90:

> 'seeks to ensure, by means of the prohibition which it lays down, that an importing Member State does not, by means of internal taxation of imported products and similar domestic products give domestic traders preferential treatment as compared with their competitors from other Member States who sell similar products on the market of that state' (at p.1086).

The Court sets a high standard when evaluating systems of taxation. According to the Court:

> 'a system of taxation may be considered compatible with Article [90] of the Treaty only if it is such as to exclude any possibility of imported products being taxed more heavily than similar products' (Case C-228/98 *Dounias* v. *Ypourgio Oikonomikon* [2000] ECR I-577, para. 41).

To determine whether a system of taxation is discriminatory or not, the Court will consider not only the rate of tax, but also the basis of assessment and the detailed rules for levying the various duties. As the Court held in Case C-68/96 *Grundig Italiana SpA* v. *Ministero delle Finanze* ([1998] ECR I-3775):

> 'The decisive criterion for purposes of comparison with a view to the application of Article [90] is the actual effect of each tax on domestic production, on the one hand, and on imported products, on the other. Even where the rate is the same, the effect of the tax may vary according to the

detailed rules for the assessment and collection thereof applied to domestic production and imported products' (para. 13).

In this case, the Italian Government applied a different set of criteria to calculate the taxable amount in respect of a consumption tax imposed on certain audiovisual and photo-optical goods for domestic and imported products. The inclusion of costs and charges for delivery to the Italian border in the taxable amount had the effect of disadvantaging the imported products. The Court repeated its settled case law that:

> 'the prohibition on discrimination laid down in Article [90] is infringed where a tax is assessed on the value of a product if, in the case of the imported product alone, assessment criteria are taken into consideration which are likely to increase its value *vis-à-vis* the corresponding domestic product' (Case C-68/96 *Grundig*, para. 16; see also Case 74/76 *Iannelli and Volpi SpA* v. *Meroni* [1977] ECR 557).

Scrutiny of collection methods is also important. The Court held in *Grundig* that it is incompatible with Article 90 for the national authorities to reserve for the domestic production alone a facility such as deferred payment, while demanding payment at the border in respect of imported products. These are cases of direct discrimination on the part of the national authorities and cannot in any circumstances be justified.

The prohibitions in Articles 90(1) and (2) are unconditional and capable of judicial enforcement in national courts. Indeed both paragraphs have been held to be directly effective (Case 57/65 *Alfons Lütticke GmbH* v. *Hauptzollamt Saarlouis* [1966] ECR 205 (Article 90(1)); Case 27/77 *Firma Fink-Frucht GmbH* v. *Hauptzollamt München Landsbergerstrasse* [1968] ECR 223 (Article 90(2))). Accordingly, although there have been numerous cases of the Commission bringing enforcement proceedings under Article 226 EC against Member States in respect of their taxation systems, including, for example, some important cases on alcohol and vehicle taxation discussed in the following paragraphs, the majority of the cases on Article 90 have arisen before national courts with traders seeking to resist demands for a tax, or to seek recovery of taxes which they claim have been levied unlawfully. Two recent cases, for example, arose from challenges before Polish and Hungarian courts to national rules imposing excise duties on imported second hand cars, while no duty was payable on domestic second hand cars (Case C-313/05 *Brzeziński* v. *Director of the Warsaw Customs Office*, judgment of 18 January 2007, and Joined Cases C-290 and 333/05 *Nádasdi and Németh* v. *Directorate of the Customs and Finance Guard for the Region of Észak-Alföld* [2006] ECR I-10115). These cases are significant because they were the first two Article 234 references involving the post-2004 Member States in which economic operators have successfully managed to persuade national courts to make a reference to the Court of Justice which has resulted in a judgment which will have a substantial liberalising effect at national level (in the field of car taxation). In other words, they highlight the gradual normalisation of the post-2004 Member States into the legal and economic order of the EU and, at the same time, the role which economic law will play in allowing economic operators to attack national provisions in a single market.

An important role of the national court is to evaluate the national legislation, especially to decide whether the tax under scrutiny falls within the scope of Article 90, or Articles 23–25 EC, which prohibit customs duties and charges having equivalent effects, although in practice the Court usually gives detailed guidance on this question in its preliminary rulings (see 4.16 and 7.7). More challenging for the national court is to determine whether there has been discrimination in the amounts charged on domestic and imported products, by looking at financial equivalence over a reference period (Case C-234/99 *Nygård* v. *Svineafgiftsfonden* [2002] ECR I-3657). A finding that a tax is in breach of Article 90 does not lead necessarily to the abolition of the offending provisions by the national authorities. On the contrary, the national authority must adjust the tax to ensure that the tax burden is equivalent and eliminate any discrimination (Case 68/79 *Hans Just I/S* v. *Danish Ministry for Fiscal Affairs* [1980] ECR 501, para. 14) or, if there has been a finding that Article 90(2) has been infringed, remove the protective effect which favoured national products. Thus, any differences in the taxation of domestic and imported products must be abolished, since this is the only way of avoiding direct or indirect discrimination against imported products (Case 21/79 *Commission* v. *Italy* [1980] ECR 1, para. 16).

## 7.3 The Differences between the Two Paragraphs of Article 90 EC

Article 90(1) applies where there are 'similar' imported and domestic products. Similar products must be taxed equally, unless there are compelling economic policy reasons for differentiating between them, and the policy of differentiation is in any case applied indistinctly to national and imported products. Article 90(2) is broader, using a more general criterion of indirect protection afforded by the domestic taxation system. The goods in question, while not necessarily similar, must still be in competition with domestic products, even if this is partial, indirect or potential. Goods in competition may be taxed differently, so long as the taxation does not have a protective effect. The element of protection is assessed on the basis of a broader economic measurement of the impact of the taxes.

The definition of 'similarity' applied by the Court, ascertains whether goods 'have similar characteristics and meet the same needs from the point of view of consumers' (Case 106/84 *Commission* v. *Denmark* [1986] ECR 833, para. 12). For example, in relation to cars, the Court has held in Case C-421/97 *Tarantik* v. *Direction des Services Fiscaux de Seine-et-Marne* ([1999] ECR I-3633) that goods are 'similar' if:

> 'their characteristics and the needs which they serve place them in a competitive relationship and, second, that the degree of competition between two models depends upon the extent to which they meet various requirements regarding price, size, comfort, performance, fuel consumption, durability, reliability and other matters' (para. 28).

The Court has emphasised the need for flexibility in relation to the assessment of similarity (Case 168/78 *Commission* v. *France (Taxation of Spirits)* [1980] ECR 347). Goods may be deemed 'similar' if they are in the same classification category for tax, tariff or statistical purposes, although this point is not decisive. Rum and whisky have been held to be similar, although they are in separate categories (Case 169/78 *Commission* v. *Italy* [1980] ECR 385). A broad economic approach is required to the question of similarity. For example, in Case 243/84 *John Walker & Sons Ltd* v. *Ministeriet for Skatter og Afgifter* ([1986] ECR 875) the Court addressed the question whether fruit wines and whisky are similar, and in its response offered a range of objective criteria, such as origin, method of manufacture and alcohol content, as well as subjective criteria, such as whether the goods are capable of meeting the same need from the point of view of consumers. These criteria are used together in the assessment of 'similarity'. Here, whisky was held not to be similar to fruit wines, as it has twice the alcohol content.

Many different alcoholic drinks, although not similar, have been held to be in competition. For example, in Case 170/78 *Commission* v. *United Kingdom* ([1983] ECR 2265) the Court had to consider whether wine and beer are competing products. The Court held that in fact they are, at least as regards certain categories of light and cheap wine, in respect of which the degree of product substitution with beer is potentially highest. It can be difficult, however, to assess whether products are in competition on the basis of consumer habits, since these may themselves have been formed by discriminatory national taxation structures. In Case 356/85 *Commission* v. *Belgium* ([1987] ECR 3299), the Court confirmed that beer and wine are in competition, when it was called upon to examine the Belgian VAT regime under which wine (not produced in Belgium) was taxed at 25 per cent, while beer (which it does produce) was taxed at 19 per cent. In perhaps its broadest approach, in Case 168/78 *Commission* v. *France (Taxation of Spirits)* the Court found in relation to the question of the relationship between spirits produced from grain and spirits produced from fruits, that some spirits were similar and some were merely in competition. Thus, there was a case for the application of Article 90 as a whole, bearing in mind that all spirits have certain characteristics in common. This is called the globalised approach to Article 90 by Barnard (2004: 57).

## 7.4 The Basis for Fiscal Comparisons

Fiscal comparisons undertaken to identify the presence of discrimination are generally straightforward in circumstances where the products in question are the same. For example, in Case C-327/90 *Commission* v. *Greece* ([1992] ECR I-3033), the Court condemned a system of taxes on private vehicles under which imported vehicles were taxed using a calculation based on a notional value of the vehicles, while vehicles produced in Greece were taxed using a calculation made on the basis of the real price of the vehicles at the factory gate. The basis of the assessment of the tax must be the same for imported and domestic products. Nor may national products be advantaged through the operation of administrative instructions regarding the functioning of the taxation system, even if the relevant legal measures are themselves formally neutral. In addition, Article 90(1) is infringed where taxation on the imported product and that on the similar domestic product are calculated in a different manner on the basis of different criteria which lead, if only in certain cases, to higher taxation being imposed on the imported product. The point is well made by Case C-213/96 *Outokumpu Oy* ([1998] ECR I-1777). In respect of the Finnish system of taxation on electricity production, which was intended to serve environmental aims, the Court held that there will be discrimination:

> 'where, under a system of differential taxation . . ., imported electricity distributed via the national network is subject, whatever its method of production, to a flat-rate duty which is higher than the lowest duty charged on electricity of domestic origin distributed via the national network.
> The fact that electricity of domestic origin is in some cases taxed more heavily than imported electricity is immaterial in this connection since, in order to ascertain whether the system in question is compatible with Article [90] of the Treaty, the tax burden imposed on imported electricity must be compared with the lowest tax burden imposed on electricity of domestic origin' (paras. 35–36).

The Court is consistently unsympathetic to the claims of national authorities that it may be practically difficult to tax imported and domestic products on the same basis. Importers should be given the same basis as domestic producers to demonstrate, for example, the manner in which their products have been produced, in order to benefit from lower rates of domestic taxation.

Assessment of the taxation levels imposed on competing products is more complex. In Case 184/85 *Commission v. Italy* ([1987] ECR 2013), the Court was asked to assess whether a tax on the consumption of bananas was discriminatory. It held that bananas are not similar to table fruit produced in Italy (e.g. apples, peaches, apricots, mandarins, etc.) but are in at least partial competition with them. The Commission was able to demonstrate that the tax level on bananas was nearly half the price on importation, and the Court agreed that the tax was discriminatory.

In general, however, the Court does not make clear statements about the criteria which it prefers to use in fiscal comparisons. Problems are particularly acute in the case of alcoholic drinks where at least three possible bases for comparison exist. Conventionally, alcohol is taxed by reference to volume, value or alcoholic strength. A tax on volume may need to be adjusted in light of the differing levels of consumption of various alcoholic drinks, to ensure that beer drinkers, for example, do not make an excessive contribution to tax revenues. Taxes on alcoholic strength may be adjusted also in light of legitimate health concerns about the effects of stronger drinks. In Case 170/78 *Commission v. UK*, the Court refused to state a preference for the basis of fiscal comparisons, holding that regardless of which approach was used the conclusion must be reached that there were substantially different tax burdens on the two competing products – beer and light, cheap wines. No one method is capable of yielding reliable results on its own, but rather each will give 'significant information' allowing the assessment of the tax system. Ultimately, the Court's conclusions as to whether the system is legitimate will depend upon the weight given to each criterion and its assessment of the degree of national fiscal autonomy permitted in the pursuit of legitimate public policy goals such as combating alcoholism. However, the effect of the UK tax system was, the Court concluded, to stamp wine with the hallmark of a luxury beverage.

## 7.5 Eliminating Discrimination and Protection: The Problem of National Fiscal Autonomy

The Court has frequently reinforced the extent of national fiscal autonomy in relation to the design and application of taxation systems. In Case C-213/96 *Outokumpu Oy*, it reiterated that:

> 'in its present state of development Community law does not restrict the freedom of each Member State to establish a tax system which differentiates between certain products, even products which are similar within the meaning of the first paragraph of Article [90] of the Treaty, on the basis of objective criteria, such as the nature of the raw materials used or the production processes employed. Such differentiation is compatible with Community law, however, only if it pursues objectives which are themselves compatible with the requirements of the Treaty and its secondary legislation, and if the detailed rules are such as to avoid any form of discrimination, direct or indirect, against imports from other Member States or any form of protection of competing domestic products' (para. 30).

For example, the Member States are not precluded by the absence of similar domestic products from imposing taxation on imported products. In Case 27/77 *Firma Fink-Frucht GmbH v. Hauptzollamt München Landsbergerstrasse* ([1968] ECR 223), the Court was asked to consider a turnover equalisation tax imposed on sweet peppers imported from Italy, although no similar or comparable domestic products existed. It held that:

'Article [90] is intended to remove certain restrictions on the free movement of goods. But to conclude that it prohibits the imposition of any internal taxation on imported goods which do not compete with domestic products would appear to give it a scope exceeding its purpose. Internal taxes, and turnover tax in particular, are essentially fiscal [i.e. revenue-raising] in purpose. There is therefore no reason why certain imported products should be given privileged treatment, because they do not compete with any domestic products capable of being protected. Where such a tax is imposed at the import stage, even on products which do not compete with domestic products, its purpose is to put every kind of product, whatever its origin, in a comparable fiscal situation in the territory of the state imposing the tax. It must therefore be concluded that Article [90] does not prohibit Member States from imposing internal taxation on imported products when there is no similar domestic product, or any other domestic products capable of being protected' (at p.231).

*A fortiori* systems of domestic taxation which do protect domestic products are liable to strict scrutiny under Article 90. For example, in Case 112/84 *Humblot* v. *Directeur des Services Fiscaux* ([1985] ECR 1367), a French car tax which imposed much higher levels of taxation on cars over 16 CV (fiscal horsepower) was condemned by the Court. There were no French cars over 16 CV. The Court pointed out that the effect of the tax was to reduce the competition faced by French cars, and could not therefore be regarded as neutral, even though it was not imposed using a criterion overtly based on nationality. On the other hand, in Case C-132/88 *Commission* v. *Greece* ([1990] ECR I-1567) the Court upheld a taxation system which imposed much heavier tax burdens on cars with engines with a cylinder capacity above 1800 cc, even though no cars produced in Greece had engines with a cylinder capacity above 1600 cc, because it found that the tax did not have a protectionist effect.

Tax regimes which are, however, effectively protectionist have in some circumstances escaped condemnation under Article 90, provided they are operated in a non-discriminatory way. For example, in Case 21/79 *Commission* v. *Italy (Regenerated Oil)* ([1980] ECR 1), it was held that tax concessions must be extended to non-domestic products, even though this may make controls upon their operation more difficult. In Case C-213/96 *Outokumpu Oy*, the regime of electricity taxation introduced by Finland for environmental reasons, which differentiated by reference to how electricity was produced, was held to be, in principle, acceptable under EU law, except that it was operated in a discriminatory manner which did not extend the benefits of lower taxation to imported products. In Case 148/77 *Hansen* v. *Hauptzollamt Flensburg* ([1978] ECR 1787), which concerned a German regime of tax relief available in respect of spirits made from fruit by small businesses and collective farms, the Court addressed the reasons why certain types of tax regimes which implicitly benefit national products may be compatible with Article 90:

'At the present stage of its development and in the absence of any unification or harmonisation of the relevant provisions, Community law does not prohibit Member States from granting tax advantages, in the form of exemption from or reduction of duties, to certain types of spirits or to certain classes of producers.

Indeed, tax advantages of this kind may serve legitimate economic or social purposes, such as the use of certain raw materials by the distilling industry, the continued production of particular spirits of high quality, or the continuance of certain classes of industry such as agricultural distilleries' (at p.1806).

The only requirement is that the preferential system must be extended without discrimination to spirits of the same class coming from other Member States.

Regional policy objectives cannot be pursued through measures which differentiate explicitly between products according to whether they originate in a particular region. Such a measure may not be classed as part of a system of internal dues at all, but as a charge having an equivalent effect (CHEE) prohibited under Article 25 EC (Case C-163/90 *Administration des Douanes et Droits Indirectes* v. *Legros* [1992] ECR I-4625).

Case 46/80 *Vinal SpA* v. *Orbat SpA* ([1981] ECR 77) demonstrates the 'chicken and egg' problem of permitting taxation regimes which benefit national products in the interests of regional or social policies. Under the Italian tax regime, alcohol of agricultural origin was taxed less heavily than chemically-based alcohol, which is not produced in Italy (because of the heavy tax?). Although the system was clearly discriminatory in that it taxed similar products differently, and also protectionist in the sense that no domestic products fell into the higher tax band, it nonetheless escaped condemnation by the Court. It was not directly discriminatory on the basis of nationality, as non-domestic alcohol of agricultural origin benefited from the tax concession. The Court held that 'the system of taxation pursued an objective of legitimate industrial policy' compatible with Community principles, namely that of ensuring a reasonable level of employment in certain areas, and of ensuring the survival of agricultural distilleries.

## 7.6 The Relationship between Article 90 EC and Other Provisions of the Treaty

There is no overlap between the prohibition on discriminatory taxation in Article 90 and the prohibitions on customs duties and charges having equivalent effect (CHEEs) on imports and exports contained in Articles 23–25 EC. The two sets of provisions are mutually exclusive. As was discussed in Chapter 4, a CHEE is:

> 'any pecuniary charge, whatever its designation and mode of application, which is imposed unilaterally on goods by reason of the fact that they cross a frontier and which is not a customs duty in the strict sense' (Case C-234/99 *Nygård* v. *Svineafgiftsfonden*, para. 19).

In contrast, Article 90 applies to general systems of internal dues which apply systematically to categories of products according to objective criteria without regard to the origin of the products. This definition applies even where there is no or negligible national production, so that Member States are not precluded from subjecting such products to internal taxation (Case 193/85 *Cooperativa Co-frutta Srl* v. *Amministrazione delle Finanze dello Stato* [1987] ECR 2085). Problems have arisen in differentiating between CHEEs and charges levied under general systems of taxation in cases where a levy has been imposed at the frontier on imported products apparently to compensate for a comparable charge levied on national products. Such charges are often termed 'parafiscal charges'; these are tax-like charges which are collected outside the tax system. In such circumstances, the charge will be classed as a CHEE unless the charge to be applied at the frontier imposes the same duty as applied to domestic products, at the same marketing stage, based on an identical triggering chargeable event. According to the Court in Joined Cases C-441 and 442/98 *Kapniki Mikhaïlidis* v. *IKA* ([2000] ECR I-7145):

> 'to exempt a charge levied at the frontier from being classified as a charge having equivalent effect when it is not imposed on similar national products or is imposed on them at different marketing stages, because that charge aims to compensate for a domestic fiscal charge applying to the same products, would make the prohibition on charges having equivalent effect to customs duties empty and meaningless' (para. 23).

Cases where the Court has found such charges to be covered by Article 90 are relatively rare. Examples include Case 29/87 *Dansk Denkavit ApS* v. *Danish Ministry of Agriculture* ([1988] ECR 2965), concerning a Danish levy charged for the purposes of covering the costs of checking samples, and Case C-234/99 *Nygård* v. *Svineafgiftsfonden,* concerning a Danish levy imposed according to identical criteria on pigs intended for slaughter on the domestic market and those intended for live export to other Member States.

The Court also takes into account the purpose for which the revenue derived from the charge is applied. Thus, a charge levied in ostensibly non-discriminatory ways on both imported and domestic products may still fall foul of Article 90, if it is used to finance activities for the special advantage of the taxed national products, to the detriment of the imported products. Indeed, in such cases the assessment is complicated not only because it may be difficult to discern whether the charge is covered by Article 90 or Articles 23–25, but also because the provisions governing the incompatibility with the common market of certain forms of state aid given to undertakings (Articles 87–89 EC) will come into play if the revenue from the national exchequer is directed towards the support of certain groups of undertakings. There is no unconditional prohibition in Articles 87–89 EC on aid schemes, but the scrutiny of aid is within the exclusive competence of the Commission. In other words, Article 87 EC does not have direct effect and cannot be applied by national courts. However, the Court has confirmed that this division of powers does not preclude national courts from examining the compatibility of such a taxation scheme with either Article 90 or Articles 23–25, as the case may be, even in circumstances where the Commission has given an authorisation to the national aid scheme (Case C-234/99 *Nygård* v. *Svineafgiftsfonden,* para. 64).

The dividing line between Articles 90 and 23–25 remains a little uncertain. In Case 77/72 *Capolongo* v. *Azienda Agricolo Maya* ([1973] ECR 611), the Court held that a charge imposed by Italy on all egg boxes, intended to finance the production of paper and cardboard in Italy, was a CHEE, as it was intended exclusively to benefit the domestic product. However, in subsequent cases, the doctrine was refined, and in Case 105/76 *Interzuccheri SpA* v. *Ditta Rezzano e Cavassa* ([1977] ECR 1029), the Court set out three conditions which must be satisfied before a tax (in that case a levy on sales of sugar whether imported or domestic, to benefit the domestic sugar industry in the form of subsidies to beet producers and sugar processors) will be a CHEE, rather than part of a system of taxation subject to scrutiny under Article 90, or an aid to domestic producers subject to Article 87 scrutiny. The conditions are:

- the charge must be exclusively for the financing of activities which for the most part benefit national products subject to the charge;
- the imported product subject to the tax and that benefiting from it must be identical;
- the burden imposed on the national product must be completely compensated.

A charge which does not satisfy these criteria, but involves, for example, only a partial reimbursement of the burden of the tax on the domestic product will be discriminatory under Article 90, and/or subject to scrutiny by the Commission as a state aid under Article 87 (Joined Cases C-149 and 150/91 *Sanders Adour et Guyomarc'h Orthez Nutrition Animale* [1992] ECR I-3899). The Court continues to reiterate these principles in more recent cases, such as Case C-347/95 *Fazenda Pública* v. *UCAL* ([1997] ECR I-4911) which concerned a Portuguese charge on the marketing of dairy products which was applied to benefit the domestic agri-foodstuffs industry. In cases of doubt, as in *UCAL* itself, it is for the national court to determine what the legal characterisation of a particular charge will be. The tax does not as a consequence of such a finding have to be completely abolished, but it does have to be rendered neutral as regards the basis for imposition and reimbursement. For example, it can be altered to use facially non-discriminatory criteria (e.g. it is imposed by reference to certain production methods which are typically national) which in practice benefit domestic production. Such taxes are capable of justification despite their discriminatory effect on the grounds that they serve some overriding and legitimate national policy interest (e.g. the protection of vulnerable regions, or the promotion of specialist regional products). This line of case law demonstrates that the Court implicitly recognises the dual purpose of taxes both to raise revenue for the state and also to pursue wider economic, social, political, cultural or environmental goals through redistributive policies. Finally, as the Court stated in Case C-343/90 *Lourenço Dias* v. *Director da Alfandga do Porto* ([1992] ECR I-4673), the fact that part of a system of taxation is discriminatory does not make the whole system contrary to Community law. The Member State will only be required to change the system of taxation in respect of those products which are discriminated against.

## 7.7 The Recovery of Unlawfully Levied Charges and Taxes

In accordance with the general principles governing domestic remedies for breach of Community law, unlawfully levied charges and taxes must be reimbursed to aggrieved importers and exporters. In Case 199/82 *Amministrazione delle Finanze dello Stato* v. *SpA San Giorgio* ([1983] ECR 3595), the Court reiterated the well-established point that national remedies for breach of Community law must be both the same as those available for breach of equivalent domestic prohibitions, and also not such as to render the enforcement of Community law impossible in practice. The Court also stated that national authorities are permitted to apply national principles of unjust enrichment in order to justify not reimbursing some or all of the tax, in the face of evidence that the burden of the tax has been passed downstream to its customers by the claimant. However, the authorities are not entitled to assume that this has happened (Case 104/86 *Commission* v. *Italy (Repayment of Illegal Taxes)* [1988] ECR 1799), or to apply presumptions or rules of evidence intended to shift onto the trader the burden of proving that the charges unduly paid have *not* been passed on to customers or others and to prevent the trader from adducing evidence in order to refute any allegation that the charges have been passed on (Joined Cases C-441 and 442/98 *Kapniki Mikhaïlidis* v. *IKA*, para. 42).

## 7.8 The VAT System in Brief Outline

The (then six) Member States took the first steps towards replacing their various indirect taxation systems with a common system of value-added tax (VAT) in 1967. The Sixth VAT Directive of 1977 created a broadly identical 'VAT base' in 1977, with Member States levying VAT on more or less the same transactions. However, there are still numerous anomalies, which the EU has been trying and failing to iron out since that time. EU VAT law is not contained in a single code, like the Customs Code, but in numerous separate directives, with an important body of interpretative Court of Justice case law. The Commission's website (see 'Key Websites' at end of chapter) gives an excellent short summary of the major features of VAT, which is:

- A **general tax** that applies, in principle, to all commercial activities involving the production and distribution of goods and the provision of services.
- A **consumption tax** because it is borne ultimately by the final consumer. It is not a charge on businesses.
- Charged as a percentage of price, which means that the actual tax burden is visible at each stage in the production and distribution chain.
- Collected **fractionally**, via a system of partial payments whereby taxable persons (i.e. VAT-registered businesses) deduct from the VAT they have collected the amount of tax they have paid to other taxable persons on purchases for their business activities. This mechanism ensures that the tax is **neutral** regardless of how many transactions are involved.
- Paid **to** the revenue authorities by the seller of the goods, who is the 'taxable person', but it is actually paid **by** the buyer to the seller as part of the price. It is thus an indirect tax (emphases in the original).

In intra-Community trade, because differing rates of taxation still applied, the Member States continued to apply the destination principle which is common in international trade. Under this principle, the tax on goods intended for export is remitted or the goods are zero-rated, and the same rate of taxation as for domestic goods is applied in the destination state. This meant, however, that border controls were still needed to police exports and remit taxes. Under the programme to complete the internal market by the end of 1992 (Commission, 1985), this situation was obviously identified as an obstacle to the removal of border controls. The Commission's original 1987 proposal was to approximate VAT rates within two bands in an effort to remove distortions of trade. Even this mere 'approximation' was never agreed, not least because of the UK's reluctance to give up its practice of zero-rating certain items such as food and children's clothes. Consequently, all that happened was that the Finance Ministers made a *political* agreement – the UK refusing to be bound by a binding measure such as a directive – that the *normal* minimum rate of VAT would be 15 per cent and the reduced rate will be 5 per cent. The Commission also wanted the EU to move over to the origin system whereby goods are taxed at the place of origin, but this would have resulted in quite substantial transfers of tax revenues, for which a clearing system would have been necessary to ensure reallocation. Consequently, only a partial and transitional move to the origin system was achieved before the internal market deadline, in relation to sales to final consumers. This is essentially why the travellers' duty-free allowance disappeared after 1993, and also why so-called duty-free sales also disappeared.

The Commission has continued to push for the creation of a common system of VAT, with major initiatives in 1996, and again in 2000, with a Communication entitled *A Strategy to Improve the Operation of the VAT System within the Context of the Internal Market* (COM(2000) 348). However, it has abandoned some of its original objectives such as a 'big bang', one-off move to a new system in favour of the graduated introduction of changes. Once again, the majority of the measures it has proposed continue to languish in the Council, despite the passing of numerous self-imposed deadlines. When Treaty change has come into consideration, including in the context of the Constitutional Treaty, the Member States have always failed to agree upon the move to qualified majority voting which would ease the decision-making blockage. One of the major drawbacks of the current system is its complexity, making it susceptible to fraud. The Member States have yet to fully harness the possibilities which new technologies offer in relation to increasing transparency and efficiency in the VAT system which would thus make it easier to detect fraud. Nor have the Member States made the most of the opportunities of administrative cooperation between the national taxation authorities, despite initiatives such as the Community Action Programme 'Fiscalis 2003–2007' (European Parliament and Council Decision 2235/2002 adopting a Community programme to improve the operation of taxation systems in the internal market (Fiscalis programme 2003–2007)).

## 7.9    Other Aspects of EU Tax Policy

In recent years, the Commission has sought to emphasise that at the EU level, as in the Member States, taxation policy should be 'joined up' policy. It must integrate with policies on labour markets and employment, on enterprise and industry, on the environment and energy, and on health and consumer protection. The EU's goals in relation to tax policy must fit with other EU goals, such as the goal set by the European Council at Lisbon in March 2000 of making the EU economy the most competitive and dynamic knowledge-based economy in the world. The Commission has also given support to the goal of seeking durable reduction in the overall tax burden in the EU, while recognising the role that public finances can and do play in promoting growth and stability. The Council appears to share this concern in relation to the impact of national direct taxation policies, but does not appear inclined to take any decisive legislative action. A good example of the Council's approach comes from a recent set of Council Conclusions (ECOFIN Council, 27 March 2007):

> 'The Council underlined that the functioning of the internal market may be improved through cooperation on taxation among Member States and where appropriate at the European level, while respecting national competencies. While recognising the principle of preserving an effective allocation of the power to tax, the Council recognised the value of discussions on enhancing cooperation between Member States in specific areas of direct taxation to ensure that their domestic direct tax systems work together within the framework of Community law. The Council noted that appropriate solutions may take a variety of forms, in accordance with the subsidiarity principle.'

Unsurprisingly, this is a field where there is a superabundance of Commission proposals and initiatives – many of which are summarised in the Commission's 2001 Communication entitled *Tax Policy in the European Union – Priorities for the years ahead* (COM(2001) 260) – but a paucity of measures actually adopted by the Council. In relation to harmful tax competition between the Member States, a so-called 'taxation-package' has been formulated, supposedly to have been adopted by the end of 2002. This 'taxation-package' was to limit tax obstacles to competition between companies in different Member States and to prevent interest on savings in other countries avoiding taxation. Ambitiously, the Commission has suggested moves towards creating a common tax base for companies operating across more than one Member State (COM(2006) 157), and it has also sought to implement a common framework for energy taxation concurrently with the liberalisation of the energy markets, and the elimination of the tax obstacles to cross-border pensions. Most recently, it has proposed a directive on a common structure for taxation on passenger cars (see 7.1).

On the other hand, realising that the removal of the unanimous vote on 'mainstream' taxation harmonisation measures is not likely to occur within the short term, the

Commission has also mooted other options, such as the use of a wide range of policy instruments including soft law measures, and the application of the enhanced cooperation provisions contained in the EC Treaty (2.7) to allow a limited number of Member States to press forward to closer integration in the taxation field, for example in relation to energy taxation. More generally, taxation issues have moved increasingly to the top of the agenda in the context of environmental policy (see Chapter 17).

# Summary

1. Within the EU, it is the Member States which raise revenue through taxation. With the exception of the VAT system, Member States are free to decide upon the systems of direct and indirect taxation which they wish to adopt, and the rates of taxation which they wish to apply.

2. The development of EU tax policy is limited by the Member States' reluctance to relinquish national sovereignty in relation to their taxation systems, which is evident above all in the retention of the requirement of unanimity in relation to legal bases in the EC Treaty for the introduction of measures in relation to taxation under Article 93 EC.

3. The principle of non-discrimination on grounds of nationality is an important constraint upon the Member States in relation to the application of their taxation systems, both specifically in relation to taxation on goods (Article 90 EC) and more general in relation to other aspects of the single market.

4. Where a system of taxation is found to be discriminatory, it must be adjusted to ensure the tax burden is equivalent, or where appropriate the protectionist element must be eliminated. Taxpayers who have paid a tax levied in violation of Article 90 may recover the tax from the national authorities by bringing an action in the national court.

5. Article 90 EC prohibits direct and indirect discrimination in national measures applied to groups of products both where the imported and the national product are 'similar' (para. 1) and where they are 'in competition' (para. 2).

6. While directly discriminatory national measures imposing a greater tax burden upon imported products cannot in any circumstances be justified, in practice the much more common case of indirectly discriminatory measures may be justified by national authorities by reference to objective criteria which serve legitimate economic and social purposes, such as the protection of certain types of regional protection.

7. Article 90 EC complements the prohibition in Articles 23–25 EC on charges having equivalent effect to a customs duty, as well as the restrictions on state aid, which is incompatible with the common market contained in Articles 87–89 EC.

8. Thus far, the EU's VAT system is incomplete, in particular because the Member States refuse to harmonise their levels of taxation; in other fields of tax policy, the Commission has concentrated on encouraging the Member States to adopt measures which reduce harmful tax competition.

# Exercises

1.  In what ways does the prohibition on discriminatory internal taxation contained in Article 90 EC complement the provisions of Articles 23–25 EC?

2.  To what extent is national fiscal autonomy in relation to internal taxation on goods preserved, notwithstanding the prohibition in Article 90 EC?

3.  Why was Italy allowed to retain a system of internal taxation which imposed heavier dues on chemically produced alcohol than on alcohol produced from agricultural sources?

4.  What difficulties does the Court of Justice face when it is asked to assess the impact of systems of taxation which the Member States choose to operate in respect of alcoholic drinks?

## Further Reading

Barnard, C. (2004) *The Substantive Law of the EU: The Four Freedoms*, Oxford: Oxford University Press, chapter 4, Article 90: internal taxation.

Hedemann-Robinson, M. (1990) 'Indirect Discrimination: Article 95 EC Back to Front and Inside Out?', 1 *European Public Law* 439.

van der Hoek, M.P. (2003) 'Tax Harmonization and Competition in the European Union', 1 *eJournal of Tax Research* 19 (**http://www.austlii.edu.au/au/journals/eJTR/**)

## Key Websites

The website for the Commission's Taxation and Customs Union Directorate-General is available at:
**http://ec.europa.eu/taxation_customs/index_en.htm**

The website for the EU Tax Policy Strategy is available at:
**http://ec.europa.eu/taxation_customs/taxation/gen_info/tax_policy/index_en.htm**

A general overview of VAT in the EU is available at:
**http://ec.europa.eu/taxation_customs/taxation/vat/how_vat_works/index_en.htm**

# Chapter 8
## Monetary Integration

Introduction

There are several key elements to a system of monetary integration, including in particular freeing up capital transfers and the irrevocable fixing of exchange rates between participating currencies. Both aspects of monetary integration so defined are examined in this chapter. It looks at Economic and Monetary Union (EMU) as instituted by the EC Treaty, this being a set of arrangements which goes beyond a mere exchange rate union. EMU establishes a single currency which replaces the national currencies, and fosters and promotes the free movement of capital under the EC Treaty, with the result that the EU and the Member States are much closer to the desired state of capital market integration.

As of 1 January 1999, the European Union's single currency or euro, as it has come to be called, was brought into being as a result of the irrevocable tying of the exchange rates of the Member States of the European Union which are participating in the euro and which are therefore members of the 'Eurozone'. The 'Eurozone' is the term most commonly applied to designate the EU's geographically partial monetary union. The creation of the euro marked the beginning of the Third Stage of the plan for progressive achievement of monetary union detailed in the Treaty of Maastricht and now forming part of the EC Treaty. After 1 January 1999, the euro was formally the currency in the Eurozone, but most payments continued to be denominated in the separate national currencies. In 2000, Greece joined the original group of eleven countries in time for it to participate in the next step, the issuing of notes and coins. Indeed, for most of the public, the decisive date for monetary union was really 1 January 2002, when the euro notes and coins were first issued, followed by the rapid disappearance of the legacy currencies during the course of that year.

As yet, the United Kingdom, Denmark and Sweden of the 'old' Member States have not adopted the euro, and of the 'new' Member States, only Slovenia was permitted to join as of 1 January 2007. Lithuania's application to join at the same time was rejected by the Commission in May 2006, on the grounds that it failed to satisfy one of the convergence criteria under the Treaty – that of having an annual inflation rate of less than 2.4 per cent. Estonia withdrew its application to join in 2007, before the stage of review by the Commission was reached. The other new Member States have mainly set target dates for entry between 2008 and 2010, although Poland has yet to set a target date at all. In fact, Poland, as well as other post-2004 Member States, may join the long-term non-participants among the old Member States. Before Member States are allowed to join the euro, reports must be submitted by the European Central Bank and the Commission. Final decisions to allow Member States to join the euro are taken by the Council of Ministers. Indeed, the original decision to create the single currency on the basis of the eleven states then ready, able and willing to proceed, was taken by the Council sitting, unusually, in the composition of the Heads of State and Government (i.e. the European Council) (Article 121(2) EC).

Alongside the internal market, EMU is conceived by the Treaty as an instrument promoting the growth and development of the European economy. Thus, the achievement of EMU remains closely linked to the project to complete the internal market and to the four fundamental freedoms. In particular, the free movement of capital and payments within the internal market, which is also discussed in this chapter alongside EMU, is crucial. Movements of capital and payments, and efficient cross-border financial services, are essential to the free movement of goods, services and persons. Equally, both price stability and exchange rate stability (i.e. the elimination of risks related to these questions) are themselves central to the achievement of a single marketplace for capital and financial services in the EU.

The original Treaty of Rome (EEC) provisions in respect of the free movement of capital were much weaker than those applying to the other fundamental freedoms. One of the main reasons for this was that the Member States feared substantial capital flight as a consequence of liberalisation. The synergy between EMU and the free movement of capital is evidenced most categorically by the decision of the Member States to replace the Treaty provisions on capital with provisions resembling those governing the other fundamental freedoms at the same time as they introduced, through the Treaty of Maastricht, the provisions necessary to achieve EMU. In fact, such provisions were not strictly necessary because *secondary* legislation, introduced as part of the single market programme in 1988, had already effectively required the liberalisation of capital movements. By then, the Member States had also realised that with international capital movements becoming increasingly easy, they were forcing their domestic firms to pay a higher price for capital by enforcing capital movement restrictions in the context of a global marketplace, and also reducing their attractiveness as a location for foreign direct investment. In view of these links between EMU and the internal market, this chapter begins with a brief presentation of the EC Treaty provisions on the free movement of capital and payments (8.2) and of the now substantial body of Court of Justice case law on the interpretation of the capital provisions of the EC Treaty (8.3).

The second half of this chapter is devoted to EMU. EMU is seen more as a process, rather than simply a goal. It has long been a controversial project within the context of European economic integration, and the decision to move towards EMU and a single currency was as much a political decision as it was an economic one (Snyder, 1999). That it is not primarily a project delivering economic growth is borne out by the fact that growth rates within the Eurozone have remained stubbornly sluggish since the establishment of the single currency and by the fact that the fastest growing economies in the EU – those of the new Member States, especially the Baltic states and Slovakia, are currently not in the Eurozone and, in the case of Lithuania, have been specifically excluded despite seeking entry. There is certainly no doubting its huge historical significance for the wider project of European integration and its immense political and economic, as well as legal ramifications. As 8.4 shows, the history of EMU is a somewhat patchwork narrative, and ironically some of the earlier attempts to bring about exchange rate stability, such as the European Monetary System (EMS), were themselves undermined by the attempts to achieve capital market liberalisation for the purposes of pursuing the internal market objectives. These obstacles were eventually gradually overcome, and the late 1980s and 1990s were a decisive period for planning and finally action to bring into being the single currency under the Treaty of Maastricht framework. Monetary policy is now therefore managed by a single institutional framework (the European Central Bank), discussed in 8.5.

The steps taken to put the single currency in place, including the operation of the conditions elaborated in the Treaty, are detailed in 8.6. The ongoing and as yet incomplete elements of EMU will be discussed in 8.7, including the Stability and Growth Pact and other aspects of economic governance. The ongoing process of economic governance needs to be seen in the light of the continuing struggle to complete complementary aspects of the internal market, such as those relating to taxation and especially harmful tax competition. This chapter is linked therefore, not only to Chapters 3–6 on the internal market, the customs union, the free movement of goods and services, and freedom of establishment, but also to Chapter 7 on taxation.

## 8.2   Free Movement of Capital and Payments under the EC Treaty

The original Treaty of Rome provisions on the free movement of capital differed sharply from those governing the free movement of goods, services and persons. Although Article 67(1) EEC did provide that during the transitional period, Member States should progressively abolish between themselves all restrictions on the movement of capital belonging to persons resident in Member States, and any discrimination based on nationality or place of residence of the parties or on the place where such capital is invested, this applied only 'to the extent necessary to ensure the proper functioning of the common market'. Member States were to endeavour to be 'as liberal as possible' in granting exchange authorisations (Article 68(1) EEC) and under Article 71 EEC Member States had to endeavour to avoid introducing within the Community any new exchange restrictions on the movement of capital and current payments connected with such movements, and endeavour not to make existing rules more restrictive.

Unsurprisingly, the Court held in Case 203/80 *Casati* ([1981] ECR 2595) that these provisions did not give rise to any obligations which individuals could rely upon in national courts to combat national rules restricting capital movements, although it did conclude in Joined Cases 286/82 and 26/83 *Luisi and Carbone* v. *Ministero del Tesoro* ([1984] ECR 377) that the separate provisions on the free movement of payments related to the *other* fundamental freedoms under Article 106(1) EC were directly effective. Equally unsurprisingly, in the absence of a dispositive framework, Member States did not show any particular inclination to liberalise capital movements, although, for example, the UK did abolish exchange control restrictions from 1979. *A fortiori* the extensive Court of Justice case law on national restrictions on free movement and permissible exceptions was not reflected in the field of capital movements.

A number of measures were adopted by the Council especially during the 1960s, when there was increased interest in monetary integration, despite the weakness of the original EEC Treaty provisions. But by far the most important measure was not adopted until the late 1980s, as part of the overall internal market package. Council Directive 88/361 (OJ 1988 L178/5) effectively introduced legally binding obligations on the Member States to liberalise capital movements and to bring about a single market for capital. Ironically, the free movement of capital became the only one of the four freedoms to be realised through the means the original Treaty apparently intended – via secondary legislation. In Joined Cases C-358 and 416/93 *Bordessa and Mellado* ([1995] ECR I-361), the Court held that Article 1 of the 1988 Directive has direct effect.

Alongside the negotiation on the provisions on EMU, the Member States agreed upon the replacement of the provisions on the free movement of capital and payments, so that

Articles 67–73 EEC were replaced by what are now, post-Amsterdam, Articles 56–60 EC (former Articles 73b–73g). They came into force on 1 January 1994, some two weeks later than the rest of the Treaty of Maastricht amendments, to coincide with the transition to the second stage of EMU. Article 56 EC now provides:

'1. Within the framework of the provisions set out in this Chapter, all restrictions on the movement of capital between Member States and between Member States and third countries shall be prohibited.
2. Within the framework of the provisions set out in this Chapter, all restrictions on payments between Member States and between Member States and third countries shall be prohibited.'

The rules on capital and payments are unified now therefore in a single framework. Article 57 EC constitutes a 'grandfather' clause relating to the continuation of existing restrictions on third country capital movements. Article 58 EC lays down certain exceptions to the free movement principle. Member States retain the right 'to apply the relevant provisions of their tax law which distinguish between taxpayers who are not in the same situation with regard to their place of residence or with regard to the place where their capital is invested' (Article 58(1)(a) EC) and 'to take all requisite measures to prevent infringements of national law and regulations, in particular in the field of taxation and the prudential supervision of financial institutions, or to lay down procedures for the declaration of capital movements for purposes of administrative or statistical information, or to take measures which are justified on grounds of public policy or public security' (Article 58(1)(b) EC). Any national measures, however, 'shall not constitute a means of arbitrary discrimination or a disguised restriction on the free movement of capital and payments' (Article 58(3) EC). Articles 59 and 60 EC deal with certain types of exceptional measures, which can be taken with regard to third countries in an emergency. In Joined Cases C-163, 165 and 250/94 *Criminal Proceedings against Lucas Emilio Sanz de Lera* ([1995] ECR I-4821), the Court held that Articles 56(1) and (2) EC have direct effect. It has also since applied the exceptions. No cases have yet arisen on the third country dimension of the provisions, which are unique to this Chapter of the EC Treaty.

It might, of course, be wondered why there was a need for these Treaty provisions given the previous adoption of Directive 88/361. The introduction of the third country dimension is one good reason for requiring Treaty change. The most significant reason, however, is that by definition provisions introduced by secondary legislation are potentially more 'amendable' than provisions contained in the Treaty, and it seemed appropriate to give the same primary or constitutional status to the rules on capital movements as applied to the other fundamental freedoms.

The Court is now clear that the free movement of capital is a fundamental principle of the Treaty. Its statement in Case C-463/00 *Commission* v. *Spain* ([2003] ECR I-4581) illustrates this point:

'The free movement of capital, as a fundamental principle of the Treaty, may be restricted only by national rules which are justified by reasons referred to in Article 58(1) EC or by overriding requirements of the general interest. Furthermore, in order to be so justified, the national legislation must be suitable for securing the objective which it pursues and must not go beyond what is necessary in order to attain it, so as to accord with the principle of proportionality' (para. 68).

## Recent Case Law Testing the Boundaries of the Post-EU Treaty Provisions on the Free Movement of Capital

Since the early 1990s, there has been an increasingly substantial body of case law on the free movement of capital, much of which mirrors the types of concerns which have animated the Court's interpretations of the other free movement provisions. In 1997, the Commission made use of some of that case law in order to issue a Communication on legal questions related to intra-EU investment to try to give some guidance to Member States on avoiding infringements of the Treaty and to economic operators on what their rights might be (OJ 1997 C 220/15). Since then, developments, including a number of flagship infringement cases brought by the Commission against Member States under Article 226 EC in respect of the restrictions they have placed in relation to shares in privatised enterprises, have continued at a rapid pace.

Evaluations of the case law are mixed. Peers (2002) fears that the Court is not only repeating some of the mistakes made in relation to the other fundamental freedoms, but is also interpreting some of the provisions, especially Article 58(1)(a) EC on taxation, in a way which was not intended by the Member States. Flynn (2002), in contrast, suggests that although there are a number of important outstanding questions, such as on the exact relationship between the various freedoms, especially freedom of establishment, there is plenty of evidence of convergence between the free movement of capital and the other freedoms, and that there are grounds to congratulate the Court for developing a sophisticated case law remarkably rapidly.

As the concept of capital is not defined in Articles 56–60 EC, the Court of Justice has had recourse to a non-exhaustive list of possible types of capital movements contained in an annex to Directive 88/361. This has led it to conclude that capital movements covered by the provisions include, for example, mortgages used to secure loans linked to the sale or purchase of real estate (Case C-222/97 *Trummer and Mayer* [1999] ECR I-1661), investments in real estate by non-residents (Case C-302/97 *Konle* v. *Austria* [1999] ECR I-3099), investments in companies by non-residents (Case C-98/01 *Commission* v. *United Kingdom (BAA)* [2003] ECR I-4641) and transactions in securities (Case C-483/99 *Commission* v. *France (Elf-Aquitaine)* [2002] ECR I-4781). The key groups of capital movements are summarised as follows (Chalmers *et al*, 2006: 509):

> 'direct investments, such as investment in a company or finance provided to an entrepreneur; investments in real estate, such as a purchase of a house; operations in securities, be it trading in bonds, shares and any other money market instruments; financial loans and sureties; operations in current and deposit accounts with financial institutions; transfers relating to insurance contracts, and finally, personal capital movements, such as gifts, inheritances or personal loans.'

For the rules to apply, there must, of course, be a cross-border element, but in none of the cases which have so far come before the Court of Justice has this proved to be a stumbling block.

Article 56 EC refers to 'restrictions' on capital and payment movements. The Court has considered on many occasions the types of restrictions which might fall within the scope of Article 56. It has made it clear that the restrictions which fall within Article 56 are not just those which actually discriminate between national and non-national investors, for example, but also include those which, although they may not 'give rise to unequal treatment', nonetheless are 'liable to impede the acquisition of shares in the undertakings concerned and to dissuade investors in other Member States from investing in the capital of those undertakings' (*Elf-Aquitaine*, para. 41). The Court has used the 'liable to dissuade' terminology on a number of occasions, for example in relation to a national restriction preventing the denomination of a mortgage in another currency (*Trummer and Mayer*, para. 26) and in relation to a Luxembourg provision restricting the grant of State interest rate subsidies on home construction loans to borrowings made from banks established in Luxembourg (Case C-484/93 *Svensson and Gustavsson* [1995] ECR I-3955, para. 10). It has also addressed national legislation, such as an Austrian stamp duty imposed on loans which discriminated according to where the loan was contracted, being 'liable to deter' residents from contracting loans with non-national lenders.

At issue in *Commission* v. *United Kingdom (BAA)* were provisions contained in the Articles of Association of BAA plc, limiting the possibilities for investors to acquire voting shares, and maintaining a procedure requiring the consent of the national authorities in respect of certain actions in relation to the company's assets, including disposal and winding-up. These provisions related to measures put in place when the British Airports Authority was privatised under the Airports Act 1986, which gave the Secretary of State power to approve the Articles of Association and also instituted a One Pound Special Share ('golden share') held by the Secretary of State for Transport. Through the Special Share and the powers under the Airport Act, the Secretary of State exercised considerable control over BAA plc, and the Court firmly rejected the argument that these arrangements resulted solely from the application of private company law mechanisms. The UK asked the Court to consider applying its own *Keck and Mithouard* case law to the circumstances of the case (Joined Cases C-267 and 268/91 [1993] ECR I-6097), on the grounds that the measures in question did not restrict access to the market. The Court did not as such expressly reject the possibility of *Keck*-type reasoning applying in the context of the free movement of capital. However, it held in brief terms that the measures in question, although applicable without distinction to both residents and non-residents, would nonetheless:

'affect the position of a person acquiring a shareholding as such and are thus liable to deter investors from other Member States from making such investments and, consequently, affect access to the market' (para. 47).

The real question in the golden share cases, as with many of the cases which have come before the Court of Justice, is not so much the applicability of the capital provisions in principle. On the contrary, the Court has so far shown an inclination to cast the net quite widely to include a wide range of national provisions, even at the risk of 'overreach' as has been seen with other freedoms (Chalmers *et al*, 2006: 511). Rather it is the possibility that the offending national provisions may be justified either under the various provisions in Article 58 EC, or by reference to the unwritten 'mandatory requirements' which the Court has once again, as with goods, services and persons, written into the rules as possible justifications for non-discriminatory national provisions. Thus, in Joined Cases C-515 and 527–540/99 *Reisch* ([2002] ECR I-2157), the Court addressed the restrictions put in place by an Austrian system of prior authorisation/notification in respect of the acquisition of immovable property concerned with restrictions on second homes in certain parts of Austria. The Court held that the rules would be compatible with EU law if they:

'pursue, in a non-discriminatory way, an objective in the public interest and if they observe the principle of proportionality, that is if the same result could not be achieved by other less restrictive measures' (para. 33).

The Court went on to say that a restriction imposed by a Member State:

'in order to maintain, for regional planning purposes, a permanent population and an economic activity independent of the tourist sector, may be regarded as contributing to an objective in the public interest' (para. 34).

The Court also referred approvingly to other concerns which may underlie the same measures such as protection of the environment. As to proportionality, the Court found that a notification system was proportionate, but an authorisation system was not. Similarly, in another golden share case, Case C-463/00 *Commission* v. *Spain* ([2003] ECR I-4581), the Court found that a prior authorisation system relating to the disposal of public shareholdings was disproportionate, although the Court accepted in that case and in others on golden shares that Member States may be justified in retaining a degree of influence over privatised undertakings 'where those undertakings are active in fields involving the provision of services in the public interest or strategic services' (para. 66; see also, for example, Case C-367/98 *Commission* v. *Portugal* [2002] ECR I-4731). In a report published in 2005, the Commission identified special rights in privatised companies as an important obstacle to intra-EU investment which is necessary for the development of the internal market, but also pointed to a diminishing role for special rights in recent years (Commission reports satisfactory progress in eliminating unjustified special rights in EU privatised companies, IP/05/998, 22 July 2005).

The specific derogations from Article 56 EC, especially those in Article 58(1)(b) EC relating to fiscal cohesion and public policy or public security, either have not been widely discussed or particularly successfully invoked by Member States. In Case C-478/98 *Commission* v. *Belgium (Eurobond)* ([2000] ECR I-7587), the Court rejected the invocation of the 'fiscal coherence' limb of Article 58(1)(b) on the grounds that the Belgian rule in question which restricted the access of Belgian residents to the Eurobond market was not directly linked to any fiscal advantage or disadvantage that needed to be preserved to ensure coherence. Furthermore a rather generalised appeal to a presumption of tax evasion was found disproportionate and unable to justify the measure. In Case C-54/99 *Association Eglise de Scientologie* ([2000] ECR I-1355), a French rule requiring prior authorisation for capital investments which threatened public policy or public security could in principle fall within Article 58(1)(b), but did not do so in practice because it was too vague and imprecise about the specific threats. The Constitutional Treaty would have provided a new power for the EU institutions themselves to create common legislative derogations from the provisions on the free movement of capital with a view to facilitating the fight against terrorism. Article III-160 would allow the adoption of European laws to:

'define a framework for administrative measures with regard to capital movements and payments, such as the freezing of funds, financial assets or economic gains belonging to, or owned or held by, natural or legal persons, groups or non-State entities.'

This would replace the current approach which requires the adoption of such confiscation measures under the framework of policy on justice and home affairs, under Title VI of the Treaty on European Union, or under various residual competences under the EC Treaty, with a single focused provision instead.

## 8.4 Economic and Monetary Union in the Context of European Economic Integration

As Swann (2000: 191) notes, it is clear that while the original EEC Treaty called explicitly for the creation of a customs union and a common market, it did not – as such – provide for the creation of an economic union. That is not to say that the original treaty had nothing to say about economic policies of the Member States, but that all measures concentrated on the need for consultation between the Member States and the institutions, and on coordination measures, and contained few binding commitments on the part of the Member States in relation to economic policy. Article 3 EEC stated that the activities of the Community should include 'the application of procedures by which the economic policies of the Member States can be co-ordinated and disequilibria in their balance of payments remedied', and the original Article 104 EEC required each Member State to pursue the economic policy needed to ensure the equilibrium of its overall balance of payments and to maintain confidence in its currency. Finally, under the original Article 105(1) EEC, Member States were to coordinate their economic policies so as to facilitate the attainment of those obligations. Article 102a EEC was added by the Single European Act and provided for the convergence of economic and monetary policies 'necessary for the further development of the Community', and added a new chapter heading: 'Co-operation in Economic and Monetary Policy'. Article 102a EEC now appears as part of the provisions on EMU in Article 124 EC. Notably, in Opinion 1/91 on the *European Economic Area* (EEA) *Agreement* ([1991] ECR I-6079), when interpreting the meaning of the then EEC Treaty, the Court of Justice held that the European Community in fact *already had* the objective of achieving Economic and Monetary Union under the terms of the version of the Treaty then in force. This was even before the signing of the Treaty of Maastricht.

As a political objective, since the early 1970s, the Member States had been attempting to move towards Economic and Monetary Union. Until the Treaty of Maastricht, however, progress was very slow. The early political work included an agreement in 1969, by the Heads of State and Government at The Hague, to work together to create an EMU. This led to the Werner Committee Report proposing the achievement of an EMU by 1980, an unrealised objective which was endorsed by the Council of Ministers in 1971. One of the problems was that the Werner Report was premised on a wider international system of fixed exchange rates, but this economic reality was eroded from the early 1970s onwards, largely as a result of problems experienced by the US economy and the collapse of the Bretton Woods system. As the European currencies began increasingly to 'float', a so-called 'snake' was devised, which was intended to confine their movements within certain limits. In practice, again, it proved impossible to keep all of the currencies within that band of fluctuation and so, in 1978, the European Monetary System was established by a European Council resolution. This instituted the Exchange Rate Mechanism (ERM) and the European Currency Unit (ECU). The latter eventually became the euro. The overall value of the ECU was determined from a basket of national currencies, and the ERM then set each national currency a rate against the ECU. The values were set collectively and could only be altered collectively. The ERM worked by setting a normal margin of fluctuation for each currency of 2.25 per cent, with an exceptional band of 6 per cent. The ERM effectively fell apart during the currency crises in 1992–93, which placed market pressures on the bands which national central banks were unable to resist. The lira and the pound were suspended from the ERM and the bands were eventually widened to 15 per cent.

At the very same time, ironically, the Member States were moving towards the ratification of the Maastricht plan for EMU. The problems encountered by the ERM at that time hardly seemed to presage a successful transition to monetary union during the course of the 1990s. In the event, as the successful launch of the single currency in 1999 demonstrated, economic recession and monetary turbulence did not fatally weaken the political commitment to achieve the single currency.

The Maastricht plan was an initiative driven to a very significant extent by Jacques Delors, the President of the Commission in the 1980s and early 1990s, who was also responsible in large measure for the successful promotion and prosecution of the programme to complete the internal market. He pushed for EMU to come onto the political agenda as the essential complement – as he saw it – to the single internal market. It was taken up from 1988, when the European Council established a committee mainly comprised of central bank presidents from the Member States, which he chaired, to consider and propose a plan for monetary union. The Delors Committee recommended a three stage plan for monetary union. Stage One required the completion of the internal market, closer economic convergence and membership of all Member States in the ERM. It set, in effect, certain background conditions which did not require new Treaty powers. Stage Two was an important institutional stage with the establishing of an independent European System of Central Banks (ESCB) which would be tasked with coordinating monetary policies and formulating a common monetary policy. This required Treaty amendments. Finally, Stage Three would see the irrevocable locking of exchange rates and the emergence of a common currency, which would be managed by the ESCB, which would have price stability as its central goal. This required not only Treaty amendments, but also ongoing convergence in the area of economic management by the Member States to create the conditions necessary for a single currency. The decision to embark upon Stage Three of EMU would require, in any event, a separate political decision on the part of the Member States.

The effective inclusion of the Delors Report in the EC Treaty via the Treaty of Maastricht illustrates a remarkable synergy of economic interests and high politics. There was always considerable French enthusiasm for a single currency, and although the finance minister and the governor of the *Bundesbank* in Germany were less enthusiastic, Chancellor Kohl pressed strongly for the project. Already from July 1990, the European Council decided to proceed to the first stage of EMU, which coincided with the achievement of capital movement liberalisation in eight of the then twelve Member States. The decision to call an intergovernmental conference (IGC) on economic and monetary union was also taken in 1989. At the Rome European Council meeting in October 1990, it was decided that Stage Two of EMU would begin in January 1994, and this was enshrined in Article 116 EC. Even before the IGC started its official work in December 1990, a great deal of preparatory behind-the-scenes work had been undertaken to ensure that the eventual negotiations themselves were relatively straightforward. Political opposition in states such as the UK was overcome, as was the reluctance of some central bank governors. In large measure the move was political; economic arguments in favour of monetary union were effectively used to legitimate a previous political decision, and in fact many economists remained sceptical about the benefits of, or need for, a monetary union in the EU. In practical terms, the agreement of the UK to the introduction of the EMU project was secured through the inclusion of a Protocol explicitly reserving the decision to participate in EMU to the UK Government and Parliament (and – by virtue of a promise made by Labour Party leader Tony Blair even before his government was elected in 1996 – a referendum as an inducement to voters). Denmark also secured a similar Protocol, which it exercised to reserve for itself the decision on participation.

## 8.5 The Legal and Institutional Framework of Economic and Monetary Union

The Treaty of Maastricht resulted in the inclusion in the EC Treaty of a range of institutional and policy provisions calling for the achievement of monetary union no later than 1 January 1999 (Article 121(4) EC). In addition, Protocols on the Statute of the European System of Central Banks and the European Central Bank and on the excessive deficit procedure were agreed. The irrevocable fixing of exchange rates, foreseen by Article 4(2) EC as one of the activities of the Community, could have been achieved earlier, had political will allowed but, in the event, the Member States went ahead with the default Treaty date. Article 4(2) EC also provides that 'the irrevocable fixing of exchange rates' will lead 'to the introduction of a single currency, the ECU, and the definition and conduct of a single monetary policy and exchange rate policy', and that the primary objective of the latter policies will be to maintain price stability (i.e. low inflation).

The reference to the ECU in Article 4(2) EC illustrates the extent to which the provisions of the EC Treaty do not correctly reflect all aspects of the present arrangements for monetary management in the EU. The Member States in 1995 decided that the currency unit of the new monetary union should be called the 'euro' (€) and not the European Currency Unit, or ECU, as it still appears in the Treaty. However, the reform of the EMU provisions of the EC Treaty was not undertaken in the context of negotiating either the Treaty of Amsterdam or (for the most part) the Treaty of Nice, for fear that opening up debate on even a purely technical issue such as substituting 'euro' for 'ECU' might lead to the unravelling of some of the more sensitive aspects of the EMU arrangements. Consequently, since the Treaty of Amsterdam, the provisions of Title VII of Part III of the EC Treaty retain the only (four) remaining examples of the use of the cooperation procedure for the adoption of legislation. Incidentally, the Constitutional Treaty would correct this anomaly in relation to the use of the term 'euro'. Moreover, since some of the provisions currently covered by the cooperation procedure involve the taking of measures which are more *executive* than *legislative* in character, Article I-33 of the Constitutional Treaty would provide for the adoption of executive acts (European regulations and decisions) under the new scheme established in the Constitutional Treaty. For executive acts, the full participation of the European Parliament under the default legislative procedure (i.e. co-decision) is not appropriate, but rather the European Parliament and the European Central Bank are merely to be consulted.

Article 4(1) EC provides for the other limb of EMU – economic management:

> 'the activities of the Member States and the Community shall include ... the adoption of an economic policy which is based on the close coordination of the Member States' economic policies, on the internal market and on the definition of common objectives, and conducted in accordance with the principle of an open market economic with free competition.'

It should be noted that the Treaty amendments did not create any new instruments or powers in relation to the conduct of fiscal policies, but rather the result has been an inbuilt asymmetry in relation to EMU. Participants have ceded control over most of the governmental instruments which can be used to promote balanced economic growth and protect the national economy, such as exchange rate policy, money supply and interest rates (all now in the hands of the independent European Central Bank). However, the EU political institutions have not been given the means, such as fiscal powers, either to conduct appropriate policies at an EU level or to provide for interstate transfers, which might be necessary if one particular state suffered particular hardship as a result of a change in the world economy (e.g. the change in price of a particular commodity). National fiscal autonomy prevails, but within the constraints allowed by the convergence criteria controlling national economic policies and particularly the Stability and Growth Pact agreed in 1997, to beef up the levels of centralised control over, for example, Member States' national budgetary deficits. Consequently, it constrains heavily national fiscal autonomy. The unhappy history of the Stability and Growth Pact is discussed in more detail in 8.7.

The provisions of Title VII of the EC Treaty can be grouped as follows, to explain thematically the structure of legal and institutional arrangements governing EMU:

▷ Chapter 1 on Economic Policy;
▷ Chapter 2 on Monetary Policy;
▷ Chapter 3 on Institutional Provisions; and
▷ Chapter 4 on Transitional Provisions.

The Transitional Provisions are largely of historical interest although they deal with arrangements for enlarging the Eurozone by setting out the conditions for new entrants. The provisions on Economic Policy build on and extend the earlier EEC Treaty provisions which make national economic policies a matter of common concern, and which create a framework for convergence of economic policies, especially through the issuing of Broad Economic Policy Guidelines annually by the Council (Article 99 EC), and establish the principle that Member States must avoid excessive government deficits (Article 104 EC). Article 104 EC also lays down the procedures for monitoring such deficits, and this must be read in light of the Protocol on Excessive Deficits and, more recently, the Stability and Growth Pact. This will be discussed further in 8.7.

Chapters 2 and 3 are best discussed in combination, since the nature of the EU's monetary policy is inseparable from the institutional structures established to carry it out, in particular the establishment of the European System of Central Banks (ESCB) governed by the independent European Central Bank (ECB). The primary objective of the policy and of the institutions is to maintain price stability. This is reflected in the provisions of the Treaty (Article 105 EC), and in Article 2 of the Protocol on the Statute of the European System of Central Banks and of the European Central Bank. This principle guides the work of the ECB in running the monetary policy of the EU, especially in relation to its policy on interest rates and money supply.

The ESCB comprises the ECB and the national central banks. It represents a decentralised and two-tier system for monetary management, but the system is unequivocally governed by the ECB, rather than being a classical federal system with powers assigned to each level (Zilioli and Selmayr, 2001: chapter 2). Decentralised tasks are assigned to the national central banks which have not been abolished in the context of the effective centralisation of monetary power. However, the Member States were obliged to ensure, before the beginning of Stage Three of EMU, that the statutes of the national central banks must be compatible with the Treaty. That has involved giving independence to the national central banks – a lead followed also by the UK, in large measure, although the legislation governing the Bank of England would require some amendment before the adoption by the UK of the euro.

The ECB has legal personality, has guaranteed independence within the system of the EU (Article 108 EC) and has its own resources, budget and decision-making bodies, powers and modes of action (Article 110 EC). It is not exactly an 'institution' of the European Union, but rather an independent and autonomous entity within the system, which remains subject to the principles of EU law and the rule of law as upheld by the Court of Justice. This was unequivocally established in the first case on the status of the ECB within the EU legal order, a case in which the Commission challenged the validity of a decision by the ECB on fraud prevention (Case C-11/00 *Commission* v. *European Central Bank (OLAF)* [2003] ECR I-7147). The ECB had effectively sought to opt out of the general EU fraud prevention system based around OLAF, the European Anti-Fraud Office established by a 1999 Commission Decision. Council Regulation 1073/1999 (OJ 1999 L136/1) deals with investigations conducted by OLAF which it is permitted to conduct within *all* the EU's bodies and institutions, and officials of all the institutions and bodies are obliged to inform OLAF if they suspect fraud against the EU and its interests. In a 1999 decision adopted by its Governing Council (OJ 1999 L291/36), the ECB sought to opt out of the general system of fraud prevention and to establish its own independent control and audit mechanisms. The Court rejected all arguments by the ECB that the 1999 Council Regulation and the work of OLAF did not apply to the ECB, and that the regulation itself was invalid because, for example, there had been a failure properly to consult the ECB. On the contrary, the 1999 ECB decision was annulled on the grounds that it failed to apply the system established by the regulation, which constituted a superior and binding source of law within the EU legal order, and the ECB 'exceeded the margin of autonomy of organisation which it retains for the purpose of combating fraud' (Case C-11/00 *Commission* v. *European Central Bank (OLAF)*, para. 182).

The Court pointed out that the guarantee of independence was intended to:

> 'shield the ECB from all political pressure in order to enable it effectively to pursue the objectives attributed to its tasks, through the independent exercise of the specific powers conferred on it for that purpose by the EC Treaty and the ESCB Statute' (para. 134).

In other words, its independence is 'policy independence', not legal autonomy. It went on to say that:

> 'recognition that the ECB has such independence does not have the consequence of separating it entirely from the European Community and exempting it from every rule of Community law' (para. 135).

It was clear from the Treaty that the principle of attributed powers applies to the ECB, as do the principles of judicial review. That meant that, where appropriate, the EU institutions could freely adopt legislative measures – such as those on fraud prevention – which could validly apply to the ECB.

Under Article 105(2) EC, the ESCB has the key monetary tasks for EMU, including defining and implementing the monetary policy of the EU, conducting foreign exchange operations, subject to certain powers reserved to the Council in relation to the making of agreements on the exchange-rate system for the euro in relation to non-EU currencies

(Article 111 EC), holding and managing the official foreign reserves of the Member States, and promoting the smooth operation of payment systems. The ESCB also contributes to the smooth conduct of policies relating to prudential supervision of credit institutions. The ECB may be given specific extra tasks by unanimous decision of the Council (Article 105(6) EC). It has the exclusive right to authorise the issuance of banknotes, although Member States may issue coins subject to approval by the ECB on the volume (Article 106 EC). The ECB, which governs the ESCB via its decision-making bodies, also has the right to be consulted on proposed EU acts within its 'fields of competence' (Article 105(4) EC but, as the *OLAF* case has demonstrated, this is related to *its specific functions and competences*, i.e. in relation to EMU) and does not restrict the EU institutions in relation to *general legislative* measures which could affect its internal organisation. In that respect, it is to be treated no differently from any other EU institution or body (Case C-11/00 *Commission* v. *European Central Bank (OLAF)*, para. 111).

The decision-making bodies of the ECB are its Governing Council and the Executive Board (Article 107 EC). The Governing Council comprises the members of the Executive Board and the Governors of the national central banks (Article 112(1) EC). The Executive Board comprises the President, the Vice-President and four other members. The six persons are appointed:

> 'from among persons of recognised standing and professional experience in monetary or banking matters by common accord of the governments of the Member States at the level of Heads of State or Government, on a recommendation from the Council, after it has consulted the European Parliament and the Governing Council of the ECB' (Article 112(2)(b) EC).

Only nationals of the Member States can be members of the Executive Board. The term of office of Executive Board members is eight years, non-renewable. The first Governor of the ECB, after it was established in 1999, was Wim Duisenberg, of the Netherlands, although his appointment was surrounded in controversy as it was only accepted by the French Government on the basis that he informally agreed not to serve a full term, but to step aside at some point after the issue of the euro notes and coins at the beginning of 2002, to make way for the preferred French nominee Jean-Claude Trichet. In some ways, this could be said to compromise the independence of the office of Governor, and was a rather shabby story reflecting badly on Member States' jealousy with each other with regard to appointments of key positions. Trichet's appointment was confirmed in due course in the summer of 2003.

### 8.6  Progress towards a Single Currency . . . in Some Member States

Even though the Treaty of Maastricht appeared to set the EU on an irrevocable course towards a single currency by setting the default start date of 1 January 1999 for Stage Three of EMU, it was by no means clear in the early 1990s, as the ERM effectively collapsed and as the Treaty of Maastricht encountered considerable difficulties in relation to ratification, that this achievement would be realised. Considerable preparations were still needed. Commentators often note that there are marked variations within the degree of precision laid down in the Treaties transitional provisions relating to the different aspects of progress towards a single currency. In particular, the Treaty laid down certain 'convergence criteria' to be tested by the Commission, the Council and a transitional banking institution, the European Monetary Institute (EMI), which was superseded at the beginning of the third stage by the ECB. The convergence criteria (Article 121(1) EC) were intended to ensure a sufficient degree of readiness in the national economies for EMU before embarking upon the third stage. The criteria include:

▶ the achievement of a high degree of price stability through low inflation rates;
▶ the sustainability of governmental financial positions, evidenced by Member States not having excessive deficits;
▶ successful participation in the EMS for at least two years, within the normal fluctuation rates; and
▶ long-term interest rates close to the rest of the Member States indicating durable convergence.

Although relatively precisely defined, in practice the criteria were not always strictly applied. Once the political will among a sufficient number of Member States was evidently present, the requirement that each Member State participating be sufficiently convergent in relation to these criteria no longer appeared to be an insuperable obstacle. In December 1995, at the Madrid European Council, it was confirmed that the third stage of EMU would begin on 1 January 1999. An important question, however, was: 'which states would participate?'. Member State participation is also governed by Article 121 EC, although the decision is to be taken by a qualified majority. Transitional provisions precluded the creation of EMU unless a majority of Member States were able to participate, but this became a theoretical question only. In May 1998, it was agreed by the European Council that eleven of the Member States should be allowed to participate in the third stage of EMU, even though it was evident that a number of the Member States did not have appropriate public debt ratios. Furthermore, Greece, the only Member State in 1998 deemed willing but unable to join, was allowed to join from 2000 – sufficiently early enough for it to be ready for the issue of notes and coins from 1 January 2002, even though it had not participated for a sufficiently lengthy time in the EMS. Sweden did not pass the convergence criteria tests – but then it had no wish to do so, as politically it did not wish to participate in the single currency at the time, and a subsequent referendum has seen participation rejected for the time being. Denmark had already exercised its option to stay outside EMU for the time being, having in 2000 held a referendum in which the vote was 53 per cent to 47 per cent, on a high voter turnout of more than 87 per cent. The UK has also remained outside EMU, although the euro remained a vital question of internal politics at least until the mid-2000s, with Chancellor of the Exchequer Gordon Brown fixing five tests to be passed, which he found in June 2003 had not yet been passed. The Governments of Prime Minister Tony Blair have been committed, since the mid-1990s, not to commit the UK to joining the euro unless there has been a positive vote in a referendum, but the prospect of such a referendum has receded from view since 2003.

In 1997 and 1998, the Council adopted a number of crucial pieces of legislation necessary for the transition to a single currency, including Council Regulation 1103/97 on certain provisions relating to the introduction of the euro (OJ 1997 L162/1) and Council Regulation 974/98 (OJ 1998 L139/1). These provided that, as of 1 January 1999, the euro would be the currency of the participating Member States, but that it would be represented up to 1 January 2002 by the national currencies of the states. Council Regulation 2866/98 (OJ 1998 L359/1) irrevocably fixed the exchange rates of the participating currencies against the euro. Other important measures required for the changeover to euro notes and coins starting on 1 January 2002, included measures on forgery and counterfeiting, including Council Regulation 1338/2001 (OJ 2001 L181/6) laying down measures necessary for the protection of the euro against counterfeiting, extended by a linked Council Regulation 1339/2001 (OJ 2001 L181/11) also to those Member States which have not adopted the euro as their currency.

The legal framework for EMU is made more complex because it is premised on a scheme of variable geometry, that is, there will be 'ins' and 'outs'. So far, the distinction has largely been a political one, in the sense that all the Member States which are willing have adopted the euro, and those which have not done so, are largely deciding according to internal political contingencies rather than strict economic questions. In other words, if they were willing, doubtless the convergence criteria could be interpreted in such a way as to deem their ability to join EMU quite quickly. That is no longer the case after enlargement in May 2004. Too rapid assimilation of the new Member States into EMU after enlargement would be unwise for both those states and for the EU itself. The transitional economies of the new Member States could well be harmed by precipitate adoption of the euro. In turn, the stability of the euro as a currency, as well as the objective of price stability, could be endangered by enlargement of the Eurozone.

Strictly speaking, a Member State not participating in the euro is a 'Member State with a derogation'. There are some differences, especially between the UK and the rest, but the general principle is that certain obligations and rights do not apply to those states. The status of 'Member State with a derogation' is envisaged to be temporary, since under Article 122(4) EC, at least once every two years, or at the request of a Member State with a derogation, the Commission and the ECB must report to the Council in relation to convergence criteria under Article 121 EC. Under the Protocol on Certain Provisions relating to the UK, Article 4(2) EC does not apply to the UK once it had given notice that it would not participate in the third stage. However, it is worth noting that according to the Court of Justice (see Opinion 1/91, 8.4 above) there is an underlying Treaty objective of achieving monetary union.

The following provisions do not apply to Member States with a derogation: Articles 104(9) and (11) EC on sanctions relating to the excessive deficit procedure, various provisions of Article 105 EC on the functions of the ECB, Article 106 EC on the issue of banknotes, Article 110 EC on the issue of secondary legislation by the ECB, Article 111 EC on external monetary policy and Article 112(2)(b) EC on the appointment of the Executive Board of the ECB. As some of these provisions are decision-making provisions, the voting arrangements within the Council have been altered to allow for the suspension of the votes of those states with a derogation. Under Article 122(5) EC, a qualified majority is defined as two-thirds of the votes of the representatives of the Member States without a derogation, weighted in accordance with the (normal) rules on vote weighting in Article 205(2) EC. Economic policy coordination is in the hands of the Council of Economics and Finance Ministers of the European Union (Ecofin Council), which meets before its regular sessions in the configuration of the 'Eurogroup', that is, the twelve states participating in the euro (although the non-participating Member States are allowed to attend, but are excluded from discussions on matters central to the operation of the euro as a currency, such as its value in relation to the US dollar). Until 2005, this group was usually chaired by the Finance Minister of the Member State holding the Presidency, unless that was a Member State holding a derogation, in which case it was chaired by the Finance Minister of the Member State next due to hold the Presidency. Since 2005, the Eurogroup has adopted the practice of having stable two year presidencies, with the first Chair of the Eurogroup for two years from 1 January 2005 being the Prime Minister and Finance Minister of Luxembourg, Jean-Claude Juncker. One reason for this stability of leadership was to give the Eurogroup a more prominent voice complementing the centralised and stable leadership of the European Central Bank.

## 8.7 Economic and Monetary Management in the Eurozone

Under the arrangements for EMU, Member States retain not only a large measure of fiscal autonomy, but also responsibility for conducting their general economic policies. However, they are now subject to a number of important obligations set out not only in the Treaty and the Protocol on the Excessive Deficit Procedure, but also in the 1997 Stability and Growth Pact which was intended to give additional teeth to the tools for monitoring national budgetary policies and public finances. In practice, although economic policy coordination extends to all twenty-seven Member States, it is most intense in relation to the Member States participating in the euro, since they share a single monetary policy and a single exchange rate with other currencies, as well as in relation to those new Member States actively aspiring to achieve Eurozone membership, although for them it is the convergence criteria which have real teeth. There are in principle very substantial powers within the Council in relation to excessive public finance deficits in particular, including the imposition of fines and the issuing of an invitation to the European Investment Bank to reconsider its lending policy towards a delinquent Member State. The objective, according to Chalmers *et al* (2006: 533) is:

'to avoid situations where the unsustainability of the fiscal position of a national government would generate financial instability, threatening the normal operation of the monetary system of the whole eurozone.'

The 1997 Stability and Growth Pact comprises a number of more formal and informal elements. These are: a Resolution of the European Council meeting at Amsterdam in June 1997 (OJ 1997 C236/1), which signalled the political will of the Member States to achieve convergence and discipline in budgetary matters at the highest level; Council Regulation 1466/97 (OJ 1997 L209/1) on the strengthening of the surveillance of budgetary positions and the surveillance and coordination of economic policies; and Council Regulation 1467/97 (OJ 1997 L209/6) on speeding-up and clarifying the implementation of the excessive deficit procedure. Member States participating in the euro must annually, according to a timetable, submit a stability programme. Non-participating Member States must submit a convergence programme. These texts build upon Treaty language mandating that Member States should avoid excessive government deficits (Article 104 EC), and that there would be sanctions and penalties if a Member State failed to correct its deficit. Excessive budget deficits are effectively those in excess of 3 per cent of a Member State's gross domestic product (GDP), or public debt exceeding 60 per cent of the GDP. The Stability and Growth Pact is intended to ensure that the Excessive Deficit Procedure is applied strictly, so that sanctions should be applied if the rules are broken.

By 2004, France, Germany, Italy and Portugal had all been subject to adverse reports on the part of the Commission, entailing scrutiny of various aspects of their national budgetary policies. However, the Council – i.e. the Member States collectively – continued to tolerate non-compliance by the delinquent Member States, a failure which the Commission consistently objected to as it weakened the Stability and Growth Pact. Eventually, the Commission decided to take legal action in respect of Council conclusions adopted in relation to France and Germany in November 2003, merely noting that these states had made political commitments to bring their public finances within the limits of the Stability and Growth Pact, and stating that the Excessive Deficit Procedure for these states would be held in abeyance so long as they acted in accordance with these commitments. In any event, the litigation proved rather inconclusive (Case C-27/04 *Commission* v. *Council* [2004] ECR I-6649). While, on the one hand, the Court of Justice found that the Commission's action for annulment under Article 230 EC was admissible in principle, in the sense that the conclusions under review were found to be reviewable acts, intended to have legal effects, and indeed annulled the conclusions on the grounds that the Council had effectively deviated from the procedure laid down in Regulation 1467/97, nonetheless the Court's conclusion appeared to be that there was nothing that could be done to force the Council to enforce the Stability and Growth Pact and the Excessive Deficit Procedure.

Responding to this, the Commission proposed, and the European Council effectively accepted, 'strengthening' the procedures for economic governance which actually introduced more, not less, discretion in the management of national deficits. In a sense, this recognised not only the delinquency of the Member States up to 2004, but also the significant increase in the heterogeneity of the national economies after the 2004 enlargement. Thus more account is to be taken of the medium-term prospects in relation to public debt, rather than the year-on-year deficit. A number of measures formally amended the Stability and Growth Pact measures: Council Regulation 1055/2005 amending Regulation 1466/97 (OJ 2005 L174/1) and Council Regulation 1056/2005 amending Regulation 1467/97 (OJ 2005 L174/5). The political backup is provided by a Council Report to the European Council, effectively paying lip service to a rules-based system.

In addition to the monitoring of national budgetary policies and public finances, economic management in the EU has a number of other elements, such as economic surveillance of the state of the economy in the EU and the Eurozone, conducted by the Commission, and broader economic policy coordination which applies to all the Member States. Under the multilateral surveillance procedures of Article 99 EC, the Ecofin Council monitors economic developments in each of the Member States against so-called 'Broad Economic Policy Guidelines' (BEPG) which are laid down annually. Over the years, the procedures laid down in outline in Article 99 EC have been linked to a wider set of objectives in relation to growth and structural economic reform, notably the Lisbon objective of 2000 which seeks to make the economies of the EU's member States the most competitive in the world. Procedurally, this has been linked to the use of the so-called 'Open Method of Coordination' (2.5) to encourage competitive convergence of national policies in relation to employment and social welfare, as well as macro-economic matters.

# Summary

1. This chapter examines both Economic and Monetary Union (EMU) and the free movement of capital under the EC Treaty. These are two essential pillars of monetary and economic integration. The EU's single currency – the euro – was formally created on 1 January 1999, as a result of the irrevocable locking of the exchange rates between the participating countries, and euro notes and coins were first issued on 1 January 2002, rapidly replacing the legacy currencies.

2. Twelve Member States participate in the euro. Of the pre-2004 Member States, three do not participate: Denmark, Sweden and the United Kingdom. None of the post-2004 Member States participated until 2007, when Slovenia was the first new Member State to be allowed to join. Lithuania's application to join at the same time was turned down because of its inflation rate. Most of the other Member States are expected to join in the following five years, although Poland has yet to set a target date to join.

3. The free movement of capital was regulated under the original EEC Treaty in a very different manner from the other fundamental freedoms (goods, services and persons). The provisions were drafted such as to give discretion to the Member States, and consequently they were held – with the minor exception of certain rules related to the free movement of payments – not to have direct effect. Legislative changes were made in combination with the programme to complete the Single Market by the end of 1992, to give effect to the free movement of capital, and provisions of the relevant directives were held by the Court of Justice to have direct effect. In addition, significant amendments to the Treaty text were effected by the Treaty of Maastricht, confirming the direct link between the free movement of capital and EMU.

4. The provisions on the free movement of capital have in recent years been interpreted by the Court of Justice in a manner which is broadly in line with its approach to the other fundamental freedoms. Not only discriminatory restrictions on the movement of capital, but also non-discriminatory restrictions which are liable to dissuade nationals of other Member States from undertaking a transnational capital or payment movement, will fall within the scope of provisions.

5. The history of EMU in the EU is long and somewhat fraught. Although the antecedents of the project to institute a single currency for the EU date back to the 1960s, in practice it was the initiative to create the Single European Market, and the political pressure stemming from the work of Jacques Delors and supportive leaders particularly in France and Germany, which generated the concrete plan to achieve EMU which is enshrined in the EC Treaty.

6. The provisions on EMU in the EC Treaty are largely those introduced by the Treaty of Maastricht, and they have not been substantially amended by subsequent Treaty amendments. They contain a number of anomalies, most notably the reference to the EU's currency as the European Currency Unit (ECU).

7. The legal and institutional framework for EMU comprises a rather weak set of provisions on economic policy, provisions on monetary policy which enshrine the strong and independent role of the European Central Bank, and sets of transitional provisions which remain important because the majority of Member States remain at the present time outside the euro.

8. The convergence criteria which are designed to determine which Member States were ready and able to participate in a single currency are based around price stability, the sustainability of government financial positions, successful participation in the European Monetary System for two years and long-term interest rates close to the rest of the Member States, indicating durable convergence. Some doubted whether these were applied strictly in the first instance, for example when Greece was allowed to join the original group of eleven Member States which went ahead with the euro in 1999.

## Summary cont'd

9.  Economic management in the Eurozone is designed to be based around the Stability and Growth Pact, which is intended to introduce economic discipline in relation to government budgetary deficits on a year-on-year basis, and also around the long-term sustainability of the overall national debt. However, the Member States have been reluctant to discipline themselves, and have not applied any sanctions on the Member States, in relation to which the Commission has started procedures in relation to their excessive deficits. As a result the Commission took the Council before the Court of Justice and successfully sought the annulment of a set of Conclusions drawn up by the Council in November 2003, which effectively suspended the Excessive Deficit Procedures against France and Germany. However, the result of this legal procedure appears to be greater, not less, flexibility in economic governance in the Eurozone.

# Exercises

1.  Why did the EEC Treaty contain weak provisions on the free movement of capital, and in what ways have the original provisions affected the subsequent development of this fundamental freedom?

2.  What is a 'golden share' and why might it be problematic under EU law?

3.  Why did it take so long to achieve Economic and Monetary Union, and what were the conditions which eventually made it possible?

4.  What are the most important institutional specifics of the law governing economic and monetary union, when compared to the rest of the law governing economic integration within the internal market?

5.  Does the Stability and Growth Pact work?

## Further Reading

Barnard, C. (2004) *The Substantive Law of the EU: The Four Freedoms*, Oxford: Oxford University Press, chapter 17.

Chalmers, D. *et al* (2006) *European Union Law*, Cambridge: Cambridge University Press, chapter 12.

Doukas, D. (2005) 'The Frailty of the Stability and Growth Pact and the European Court of Justice: Much Ado about Nothing?', 32 *Legal Issues of Economic Integration* 293.

Flynn, L. (2002) 'Coming of Age: the Free Movement Case Law 1993–2002', 39 *Common Market Law Review* 773.

Louis, J.V. (2004) 'The Economic and Monetary Union: Law and Institutions', 41 *Common Market Law Review* 575.

McNamara, K. (2005) 'Economic and Monetary Union', in Wallace, H., Wallace, W. and Pollack, M. (eds.), *Policy-Making in the European Union*, Oxford: Oxford University Press.

Molle, W. (2006) *The Economics of European Integration: Theory, Practice, Policy* (5th edn), Aldershot: Ashgate, chapter 8.

Peers, S. (2002) 'Free Movement of Capital: Learning Lessons or Slipping on Spilt Milk?', in Barnard, C. and Scott, J. (eds.), *The Law of the Single European Market: Unpacking the Premises*, Oxford: Hart Publishing.

Swann, D. (2000) *The Economics of Europe: From Common Market to European Union*, London: Penguin.

## Further Reading cont'd

Usher, J. (2006) 'Monetary Movements and the Internal Market', in Nic Shuibhne, N. (ed.), *Regulating the Internal Market*, Cheltenham: Edward Elgar.

Zilioli, C. and Selamyr, M. (2001) *The Law of the European Central Bank*, Oxford: Hart Publishing.

## Key Websites

The European Commission's website on the euro, the currency of thirteen European Union countries, is available at:
**http://ec.europa.eu/economy_finance/euro/our_ currency_en.htm**

Information related to the enlargement of the Eurozone is available at the Europa website, addressing EU Economic and Monetary Affairs:
**http://europa.eu/scadplus/leg/en/s01050.htm**

The website of the Directorate-General for Economic and Financial Affairs is available at:
**http://ec.europa.eu/economy_finance/index_en.htm**

The European Commission website focusing on the free movement of capital is available at:
**http://ec.europa.eu/internal_market/capital/index_en.htm**

The website for the European Central Bank is available at:
**http://www.ecb.eu/**

The Council Report to the European Council, *Improving the Implementation of the Stability and Growth Pact*, 20 March 2005, Annex II of the Conclusions of the Brussels European Council Meeting, 22–23 March 2005, is available at:
**http://europa.eu/bulletin/en/200503/i1018.htm**

# Chapter 9

# The Common Agricultural Policy

## Introduction

'Today marks the beginning of a new era. European agricultural policy will change fundamentally' [SPEECH/03/326]. So stated the then Commissioner for Agriculture, Franz Fischler, on the occasion of the agreement in Council of a set of revisions to the Common Agricultural Policy (the CAP). The revisions, agreed in June 2003, are the latest to be made to a policy which, for over forty years, has received by far the greatest financial contribution from the EU budget of any policy field (at its height, in 1970, accounting for 87 per cent of the annual budget, and currently running at some 45 per cent, at nearly 45 billion euro), as well as giving rise, year on year, to a vast body of legislation, and a consistently heavy workload for the Court. In addition to its financial and legal significance, the CAP has had, over the EU's history, and continues to have, enormous political significance, both within the European Union and internationally: the EU is the largest importer of agricultural products in the world and the second-largest (to North America) exporter, and is thus a significant player in the World Trade Organisation system. The CAP, which is 'characterised by direct and radical intervention in economic practices concerning the production, processing and marketing of agricultural products' (AG Geelhoed, Case C-228/99 *Silos e Mangimi Martini SpA* v. *Ministero delle Finanze dello Stato* [2001] ECR I-8401 at para. 33), is also unmatched among the Union's activities in terms of its public notoriety.

While the CAP has been evolving, the objectives for it as set out in the Treaty have remained the same, and the Constitutional Treaty foresaw no amendment to them. The first of the objectives listed (at Article 33 EC) is 'to increase agricultural productivity' and, for many, the CAP has been perceived as being directed too much towards quantity over quality. The overproduction stimulated by the production aids available under the CAP memorably resulted in butter mountains, beef mountains, and wine and milk lakes. More recently, links have been suggested between the glut of food crises in the EU such as BSE, dioxins in chicken, and foot and mouth disease, and the agricultural practices and intensive farming techniques which were supported under the CAP. Given recent food scares, it is not surprising to find that according to Eurobarometer figures from 2005, ensuring that agricultural products are healthy and safe and promoting respect for the environment rate in the top three of citizens' objectives for the CAP, along with ensuring a stable income for farmers (Special Eurobarometer 221, Wave 62.2).

While the relevant Treaty articles on the CAP have not been amended or updated to include such objectives, it is the case that these concerns are now very much on the CAP agenda. The changes agreed in 2003 are presented as seeking to incorporate more fully in the CAP environmental issues, issues relating to the safety and quality of food, animal welfare, rural development, as well as broader international trade issues, seeking to counter the previously damaging effects of the CAP on developing nations. In that sense, moreover, this chapter should be read in the light of the relevant sections of Chapters 5, 11, 17 and 19. These changed priorities are being reflected in the complex structure of secondary legislation which operationalises the CAP. The latest reforms were finalised before the 2004 enlargement, although the new Member States were granted observer status at the negotiations. The enlargement to 27 Member States has been seen as presenting critical pressures for the continuation of the CAP, and for the continued coherence of a 'European Model of Agriculture', given the histories of agricultural production in the former Eastern bloc states. The 2004 enlargement to 25 Member States increased the number of farmers in the EU by 57 per cent, from 6.5 million to about 11 million (Kosior, 2005: 568), raising new fears of overproduction and surpluses; however, given the lower productivity levels of the new states owing to structural deficiencies in their agricultural sectors, fears of such oversupply may have been overstated (but see Grant, 2006). As with certain other policy sectors, full and immediate participation on a par with the EU-15 has been deemed impossible for the new states, and a series of transitional measures are in place.

The CAP framework is built on what are now described as its two pillars. The first pillar comprises the longstanding common organisations of the market (COM). Separate markets for different agricultural products (cereals, beef, wine, for example) are established and, in order to achieve the objectives of the CAP (which include increased productivity, a fair standard of living for the agricultural community and stabilised markets), a range of mechanisms are undertaken by public authorities, which insulate the commodity market from the effects of market forces. These mechanisms may include financial aid for production and marketing, and price support, including guaranteed purchase of goods by public authorities. The second pillar is that of support for rural development, and this pillar has been taking on an ever greater significance, politically, legally and financially. Here, the overlap with the materials discussed in Chapter 18 is very important. Funding for activities was, until recently, operated under the European Agriculture Guarantee and Guidance Fund (EAGGF). The distinction between the two sections has been taken further by Council Regulation 1290/2005 (OJ 2005 L209/1) on the financing of the CAP. Under the first pillar, support for the COMs comes from the European Agriculture Guarantee Fund (EAGF) and, under the second pillar, from the European Agriculture Fund for Rural Development (EAFRD, Council Regulation 1698/2005, OJ 2005 L277/1), formerly the Guidance section of the European Agriculture Guarantee and Guidance Fund (EAGGF). Each of the pillars will be examined in this chapter, following a consideration of the legal context of the CAP (including a consideration of its legal significance) and an overview of policy development in this field. The chapter will then move on to consider the intersection between the agricultural sector and other policy sectors, turning finally to an examination of the international trade aspects of CAP, and its relationship with the WTO.

## 9.2  Legal Context

Title II of the EC Treaty is dedicated to Agriculture, and it opens, at Article 32, with the statement that the common market shall extend to agriculture and trade in agricultural products. Agricultural products are defined at 32(1) as 'the products of the soil, of stockfarming and of fisheries, and products of first stage processing directly relating to these products', and Article 32(3) further provides that a list of products is to be found in Annex I to the Treaty. Article 32(2) provides that the rules on the common market shall apply to such products, 'save where otherwise provided by in Articles 33 to 38' (see further 9.7 below). Article 32(4) provides that the common market in agricultural products is to be accompanied by a common agricultural policy.

The objectives of the CAP are set out in Article 33. They are:

'(a) to increase agricultural productivity by promoting technical progress and by ensuring the rational development of agricultural production and the optimum utilisation of the factors of production, in particular labour;
(b) thus to ensure a fair standard of living for the agricultural community, in particular by increasing the individual earnings of persons engaged in agriculture;
(c) to stabilise markets;
(d) to assure the availability of supplies;
(e) to ensure that supplies reach consumers at reasonable prices.'

The CAP is operationalised through a framework of secondary legislation, which, according to Article 37(2), is to be adopted by the Council, on a proposal from the Commission and after consulting the European Parliament. Decision-making is by qualified majority voting (QMV). The change from unanimity was timetabled for January 1966, though in practice delayed through the French government's 'empty chair' policy, and the subsequent agreement of the Luxembourg Accords. Once QMV was operational, legal base challenges began to be raised against legislation introduced under Article 37(2), as with Case 68/86 *United Kingdom* v. *Council (Hormones in Beef)* ([1988] ECR 855), in which the UK argued unsuccessfully that the general law-making basis of Article 94, requiring unanimity, should also have been used as the basis for the adoption of the relevant directive, which sought *inter alia* to harmonise national law in the interests of consumers. The Court, determining the scope of Article 37(2), ruled that where a measure relates to the production and marketing of agricultural products mentioned in Annex I of the Treaty, and the measure contributes to one or more of the objectives set out in Article 33, the appropriate legal basis is Article 37. The fact that the measure takes into account other interests, such as the protection of human, animal or plant health, or consumer protection, does not alter this, and indeed:

'efforts to achieve objectives of the Common Agricultural Policy . . . cannot disregard requirements relating to the public interest . . . [they are] requirements which the community institutions must take into account in exercising their powers' (para. 12).

The subsequent development of Community competence in the sphere of public health has brought some changes, in that Article 152(4) EC provides that the public health basis, requiring Parliamentary co-decision (see 14.8) and QMV, may be used by way of derogation from Article 37, for the adoption of 'measures in the veterinary and phytosanitary fields which have as their direct objective the protection of public health', although the practice has been to introduce such measures on a dual basis (Usher, 2002: 25).

Spinning out from Article 37 is a vast and complex web of legislation which has, among other things, established (and reformed) common organisations of the market in an extensive range of agricultural products, a structural policy and a system of funding. The basic regulations establishing the different elements of the CAP, adopted by the Council in accordance with Article 37(2), generally contain provisions delegating the power to adopt implementing legislation to the Council, or to the Commission. Indeed, the vast majority of agricultural legislation is made by the Commission. Where the degree of discretion afforded to the Commission so demands, it exercises its delegated powers in accordance with the committee procedures, whereby the Commission decides subject to the involvement of a committee of Member State representatives. It was in the agricultural context that this 'comitology' system was first established, and its legality tested, with the Court ruling in Case 25/70 *Einfuhr-und-Vorrasstelle* v. *Köster* ([1970] ECR 1161 at para. 9) that 'without distorting the Community structure and the institutional balance, the management committee enables the Council to delegate to the Commission an implementing power of considerable scope'.

In operationalising the CAP, the Community institutions are recognised as having a wide degree of discretion. There is, as was made clear in Case 5/67 *Beus* ([1968] ECR 83), no clear hierarchy among the objectives listed at Article 33 and, indeed, the objectives are contradictory: as these objectives 'are intended to safeguard the interests of both farmers and consumers, [they] may not all be simultaneously and fully attained' (at p.97). Thus, while 'the Community institutions must secure the permanent harmonization made necessary by any conflict between these aims taken individually' ... they may ... 'where necessary, allow any one of them temporary priority in order to satisfy the demands of the economic factors or conditions in view of which their decisions are made' (Case 5/73 *Balkan Import–Export GmbH* v. *Hauptzollamt Berlin-Packhof* [1973] ECR 1091 at para. 24). The Community institutions' role in legislating for the CAP, as the Court has repeatedly recognised, is a political one, and they are afforded a correspondingly broad discretion in their actions (see, for example, Case C-280/93 *Germany* v. *Council (Bananas)* [1994] ECR I-4973 at para. 47); they may thus take into account a broad range of political, economic, legal and social considerations when legislating, such as development policy for third states, as in the *Bananas* judgment, and consumer protection in *UK* v. *Council (Hormones)*.

The cases establishing the breadth of the institutions' discretion have arisen in the context of challenges being made to the legality of acts adopted under the CAP. Indeed, this policy area has been very heavily litigated, and behind the exceedingly technical language may stand highly politicised challenges. Examples would include Poland's recent and repeated applications to the Court to challenge measures under the CAP which treat the new Member States differently from the EU-15 (T-257/04 *Poland* v. *Commission* (OJ 2004 C251/20), T-258/04 *Poland* v. *Commission* (OJ 2004 C251/21) and T-04/06 *Poland* v. *Commission* (OJ 2006 C74/27). Actions are also very regularly brought by private applicants, which is to be expected given that legislation relating to the COM may determine, *inter alia*, entitlement to quotas for production, import and export, as well as subsidies for production and marketing, and economic interests, indeed livelihoods, may be affected. This litigation has given rise to the development of key principles in the legal order, most obviously in respect to judicial review, and to the non-contractual liability of the community institutions. Thus the test for non-contractual liability (arising in the event of 'a sufficiently flagrant violation of a superior rule of law for the protection of the individual') was originally set by the Court in a case concerning the impact of rules adopted in the context of the sugar COM (Case 5/71 *Aktien-Zuckerfabrik Schöppenstedt* v. *Council* [1971] ECR 975) and litigation over the CAP has dominated its subsequent development. The principles governing the standing of private applicants to bring actions in judicial review have also been set through litigation regarding the CAP, from Case 25/62 *Plaumann* v. *Commission* ([1963] ECR 95), which set the test for direct and individual concern, heavily criticised by some as too restrictive, through Case C-309/89 *Codorniu* v. *Council* ([1994] ECR I-1853), in which a less restrictive approach was adopted, to Case C-50/00P *Unión de Pequeños Agricultores* v. *Council* ([2002] ECR I-6677), which reaffirmed the

*Plaumann* approach and rejected the alternative test of 'substantial adverse impact' advanced by Advocate General Jacobs.

Turning to the substantive grounds on which judicial review is conducted, cases brought in respect to the CAP have been central in recognising fundamental rights in the legal order, such as the right to property (Case 44/79 *Hauer* v. *Land Rheinland-Pfalz* [1979] ECR 3727). They have also given rise to the recognition of various general principles of law against which administrative and legislative legality is tested, such as proportionality (for example, Case 181/84 *R* v. *Intervention Board, ex parte ED and F Man (Sugar) Ltd* [1985] ECR 2889, where a security for an export licence to sell sugar, of over £1,500,000, was lost when paperwork was lodged four hours late), as well as legal certainty, legitimate expectations and non-retroactivity. The prohibition of 'any discrimination between producers or consumers within the Community', which is set out at Article 34(2), is another ground commonly raised in judicial review, and one which the Court has described as 'merely a specific enunciation of the general principle of equality, which is one of the fundamental principles of Community law' (Joined Cases 117/76 and 16/77 *Rückdeschel* v. *Hauptzollamt Hamburg-St. Annen* [1977] ECR 1753, at para. 7). However, while cases in judicial review may be regularly brought, and may have contributed significantly to the development of general principles and fundamental rights in the Community legal order, the incidence of success for applicants is very limited, for, as Barents (1997: 843) has argued, given the scope of discretion afforded to the Community institutions, an:

'essential feature of Community agricultural law is the limited significance of legal review. Only if measures manifestly exceed the wide limits of Article [33] or if they are manifestly incompatible with fundamental rights and general principles does the Court annul acts or declare them invalid.'

With the EU institutions laying down the general principles and basic rules of the CAP, it is in very large part left to the Member States to implement the policy: for example, within the terms of the relevant legislation, Member States may be responsible for granting licences and production quotas, awarding subsidies and intervening through purchasing of products. While direct action against Community institutions as the true authors of an unlawful act are possible (Case 175/84 *Krohn* v. *Commission* [1986] ECR 753), the Court ruled in Case 96/71 *Haegemann* v. *Commission* ([1972] ECR 1005 at para. 7) that 'disputes concerning the levying on individuals of the charges and levies . . . must be resolved, applying Community law, by the national authorities and following the practices laid down by the law of the Member States'. Such actions before national courts may of course involve Article 234 EC references which may give rise to the legality of the underlying Community action being challenged (however, on the limitations inherent in this system, see the opinion of Advocate General Jacobs in *Unión de Pequeños Agricultores*). Expenditure incurred by Member States in the administration of the CAP is chargeable to the EAGF or EAFRD, and reclaimable from the Commission, and this can give rise to another source of legal action before the ECJ, when, during the annual clearance of accounts, the Commission may refuse to reimburse Member States particular sums due to accounting irregularities, or their alleged non-compliance with the terms of the relevant legislation (on the latter see, for example, Case 11/76 *Netherlands* v. *Commission* [1979] ECR 245). More generally, in conformity with the Article 10 EC obligation to act in good faith, the Court has ruled that:

'once the Community has legislated for the establishment of COM in a given sector, Member States are under an obligation to refrain from taking any measures which might undermine or create exceptions to it' (Case 51/74 *Van der Hulst's Zonen* v. *Produktschap voor Siergewassen* [1975] ECR 79 at para. 25).

Indeed, the adoption of legislation in the sphere covered by the COM may be precluded under the doctrine of pre-emption, as the Court has held that 'once rules on the COM . . . may be regarded as forming a complete system, the Member States no longer have competence in that field unless Community law expressly provides otherwise' (Case 16/83 *Prantl* [1984] ECR 1299 at para. 13).

## 9.3  Stages in the Evolution of the CAP

In 1956, an Intergovernmental Committee of Foreign Ministers, headed by the Belgian Foreign Minister, Spaak, delivered the Report which was to provide the basis for the EEC Treaty negotiations. According to the Spaak Report, any attempt to construct a common market which did not include agriculture was inconceivable. It was, it was believed, essential economically, as without a common market in agriculture, the differences in national price levels would undermine the attempts to achieve other aspects of the integration process, and would result in significant competitive advantages for low-price countries (Fennell, 1979: 6). It was also seen as a political necessity, with France unwilling to accept the importation of German industrial products without the concomitant opening of markets for its own agricultural products. It was also clear that the nature of the agricultural sector was such that it would not be politically acceptable simply to open up a common market in agriculture: associated support measures would be required, in the form of a Common Agricultural Policy. Among all the original Member States, there was a strong tradition of state intervention in agriculture, with mechanisms to direct production (needed, of course, over the war years to ensure food supplies) and to protect agricultural incomes (and over 20 per cent of the labour force in the original Member States were, in the late 1950s, employed in agriculture, forestry and fishing). The special nature of the agricultural sector was reflected in the Treaty of Rome, with Article 33(2) declaring that:

'In working out the common agricultural policy and the special methods for its application, account shall be taken of:
(a) the particular nature of agricultural activity, which results from the social structure of agriculture and from structural and natural disparities between the various agricultural regions;
(b) the need to effect the appropriate adjustments by degrees;
(c) the fact that in the Member States agriculture constitutes a sector closely linked with the economy as a whole.'

The Treaty provided for the CAP to be developed gradually, with a first step being the Commission's convening of a 'conference of the Member States with a view to making a comparison of their agricultural policies, in particular by producing a statement of their resources' (Article 37(2)). This took place in Stresa, Italy, in 1958, at which the Member States identified a number of aspects which they regarded as key, including the need for structural adaptations to improve productivity and competitiveness in farming, while at the same time respecting and protecting the overwhelmingly family-based nature of farming. On the back of Stresa the Commission submitted its proposals for legislation which was to form the CAP, and over the course of the first part of the 1960s, the majority of the COMs were established and the financial instruments created (Council Regulation 25/62, OJ 1962 B30/991). This period also saw the setting of three basic principles which have underscored the CAP (Council Resolution, Bull. CE 1/61 p.83). These are market unity, Community preference and financial solidarity. The first, market unity, relates to the establishment of a single market for agricultural commodities under the CAP, extending to a common system of marketing and common prices. From the start, the decision was made to run Community agricultural prices above those on the world market. The Community preference principle relates to the preferential position of Community farmers in comparison with producers from outside the Community, and securing this involved setting quotas and duties on imports into the Community, and subsidies for exports out. The financial solidarity principle relates to the common financing of the CAP by all Member States, which, Fennell argues, in a Community 'committed to a narrowing of the economic gap between regions and member states . . . must of necessity involve the richer countries contributing a disproportionate amount for the benefit of the less fortunate parts of the community' (Fennell, 1979: 14).

By the early 1970s, action had begun in respect of a structural policy for Community agriculture, in the form of a set of directives which concerned, *inter alia*, the modernisation of farms (Council Directive 72/159, OJ 1972 L96/1), the facilitation of early retirement (Council Directive 72/160, OJ 1972 L96/9) and training (Council Directive 72/161, OJ 1972 L96/15). These steps were relatively small scale as compared with the Commission's 1968 Mansholt Plan (COM(68) 1000), which had proposed a structural policy directed to consolidating farms into larger, more efficient units, and which had meet extreme opposition from the farming lobby. The structural policy strand of the CAP was very much secondary to the COM strand, that of markets and prices. With support linked to production, the CAP was certainly proving successful in stimulating production, which was in line with initial policy objectives given the Community's original position as a net importer of agricultural products. However, one of the specificities of the agricultural sector is relatively inelastic demand, that is, demand for agricultural products remains fairly stable. Production increased and soon overtook demand, which resulted in extensive surpluses in a number of commodities. These surpluses placed an enormous financial obligation on the Community budget, whether they were disposed of on the Community market (attracting market and price support payments) or outside the Community (with export subsidies being payable). In 1980, the CAP accounted for some 73 per cent of the Community's budget. By the 1980s, the Commission, convinced that unlimited price guarantees could not continue, sought to restrain support and spending, and limit production. In its 1980 Communication entitled 'Reflections on the CAP' (Bull. Supp. 6/80), the Commission advanced what has come to be regarded as a fourth principle for the CAP, that of 'producer co-responsibility', according to which:

'any production above a certain volume, to be fixed taking into account the internal consumption of the Community and its external trade, should be charged fully, or partially to the producers' (para. 27).

This principle was reflected in measures such as the introduction in 1984 of milk quotas, setting maximum production output thresholds, in excess of which levies would be chargeable. Over the 1980s, a set of further measures to restrict production and spending were taken, including the introduction of the system of 'set-aside', under which compensatory payments were made to farmers taking a proportion of their arable land out of production for a minimum of 5 years. Also, for the first time in 1988, an overall ceiling was placed on agricultural expenditure.

This process of continual, incremental evolution and adaptation took a step change in 1992 with the so-called MacSharry Reforms, named after the then Agriculture Commissioner. The reforms were stimulated in great part by the discussions taking place under the auspices of the GATT, which had opened the Uruguay Round in 1986. This set of negotiations on international trade included for the first time considerations of agricultural trade. The talks, which were timetabled to be concluded by 1990, were derailed when the 'Cairns group' of states, who sought a more liberalised world market in agricultural products, walked out of talks over the Community's refusal to reduce protectionism and move towards a more competitive market-oriented policy. Given the impact a failure to agree would have on all aspects of world trade, the Community recognised its position on agriculture was untenable, and the MacSharry reforms brought an acceptable (if short-term) compromise, making agreement on the Uruguay Round possible in 1994.

The MacSharry reforms included agreement to stage an incremental reduction in Community prices, in respect of certain agricultural sectors (notably cereals and beef), so as to bring them closer into line with world price, and increase access to the Community market. In return for the price reduction, Community producers were offered, in compensation, direct payments, 'decoupled' from production, so as not to stimulate overproduction. The MacSharry reforms also placed a much stronger emphasis than before on structural policy, and a broader focus on rural development. Environmental concerns too were gaining a stronger hold on the policy agenda. In terms of expenditure, however, the market and price support aspects of the CAP far exceeded those on rural development. For example, while the Guarantee section of the EAGGF saw expenditure of some 39,108 million ECU in 1995, in the same year 3,609 million ECU were expended under the Guidance section.

In 1997 the Commission presented its proposals for the next set of reforms, in the shape of the 'Agenda 2000' package (COM(97) 2000), which covered agricultural reform, as well as reform of the structural funds (see further Chapter 18). In addition to the need to respond to continuing pressures from international legal commitments under GATT/WTO, the key policy issue facing agriculture at this time was eastward enlargement. A continuation of the existing policy in an enlarged Union would, it was believed, generate enormous costs, and the application of common prices – which were considerably higher than those within the candidate states – would, it was feared, further contribute to stimulating greater production in the new states, and thus surpluses. A significant reform of the CAP was not forthcoming however, and the agreement reached by the European Council in Berlin in 1999 was in very large measure a continuation of the MacSharry approach of a reduction in prices, a switch to direct compensatory payments and increasing attention paid to rural development, now branded the 'second pillar' of the CAP. The agreement reached in Berlin was in turn translated into legal acts, which included Council Regulation 1268/1999 (OJ 1999 L161/87), which established a fund offering pre-accession aid, SAPARD, the Special Accession Programme for Agriculture & Rural Development. Agreement on support after accession was reached at the Copenhagen European Council in December 2002, with direct payments being phased in over stages, the starting point being 25 per cent of the full rate in 2004.

Also, over this period, the issue of food safety was catapulted onto the policy agenda through, most pointedly, the link made public in 1996 between BSE in cattle and a variant of Creutzfeldt–Jakob disease in humans. The Union's response involved first imposing export bans on UK cattle and cattle products (Commission Decision 96/239 EC, OJ 1996 L78/47), the legality of which was unsuccessfully challenged in Cases C-157/96 *United Kingdom* v. *Commission* ([1998] ECR I-2211) and C-180/96 *United Kingdom* v. *Commission (British Beef Ban)* ([1998] ECR I-2265). This was then followed by the adoption of a comprehensive eradication programme (Commission Decision 96/385, OJ 1996 L151/39), leading to an eventual lifting of the ban, subject to compliance with conditions. A 'date-based export system', applying to animals born after 1 August 1996, fulfilling conditions relating to absence of BSE in dam, the age and the traceability of the animal was introduced by Commission Decision 98/692/ EC, though exports under the system were initially refused entry by France, leading to action before the ECJ (Case C-1/00 *France* v. *Commission* [2001] ECR I-9989).

The most recent set of reforms, resulting from the Mid-Term Review of the Agenda 2000 reforms (COM(2002) 394), were tabled by the Commission in January 2003, with agreement reached in Council in June 2003. The key legislative measure for the Common Organisations of Markets is Council Regulation 1782/2003 (OJ 2003 L270/1). The reforms have been described by the Commission as 'fundamental' and 'landmark', as more market oriented and less trade-distorting. Further, the 'multifunctional' nature of agriculture is emphasised, that is, the 'non-food outputs' of agriculture (Cardwell, 2004: 3) are promoted and supported, and rural development further consolidated and strengthened. Most significantly, the 'decoupling' of support from production which had been partially introduced under the MacSharry reforms is extended, with the new support regime being based upon a single payment scheme, and payments under it made conditional on compliance with compulsory obligations in respect of environmental protection, food security and animal welfare (the Annex III Statutory Management Requirements, Council Regulation 1782/2003), and a general obligation under the regulation to maintain all agricultural land in good agricultural and environmental condition ('cross-compliance', see 9.5). Not all agree that these reforms are as fundamental and radical as presented by the Commission. There is a clear continuation of approach in these reforms to those of previous years. Decoupled support is acceptable under the terms of the WTO, as it is not considered to affect production decisions, and as such it is not subject to a commitment to reduce the levels (under the WTO terminology, it falls within the 'green box', see further 9.8). Under the Mid-Term Review reforms, decoupling, though much increased, is not yet absolute. Further, to the extent that it does occur, the switch to decoupled aid is, as Grant reports, often criticised as a means of 'perpetuating existing agricultural subsidies in a more acceptable form in a liberalised agricultural trade regime' (Grant, 2004). As Cardwell (2004: 20) argues, however, the special treatment afforded to agriculture, its 'exceptionalism' in relation to other sectors of the economy, has a long history and, while:

'the removal of such special treatment may be a simpler matter to advocate than achieve in practice . . . [there is] a shift to a new form of 'exceptionalism', based less upon farmers as providers of food and more upon, *inter alia* notions of rurality, care for the environment and food safety.'

## 9.4 Pillar One: The Common Organisations of Markets

Article 34(1) EC provides that:

> 'In order to attain the objectives set out in Article 33, a common organisation of agricultural markets shall be established. This organisation shall take one of the following forms, depending on the product concerned:
> (a) common rules on competition;
> (b) compulsory coordination of various national market organisations;
> (c) a European market organisation.'

Despite the Treaty offering a range of choices, it has in practice been the third of the alternatives set out in 34(1) which has been adopted – the adoption of separate, common, EU-wide market organisations for different agricultural products. Article 34(2) further provides that the forms of market intervention and management taken under these market organisations (also known as regimes) may include the 'regulation of prices [including a common price policy], aids for the production and marketing of the various products, storage and carryover arrangements and common machinery for stabilising imports or exports'. Transitional measures in respect of the gradual establishment of the first COMs were adopted in 1962, covering cereals, pigmeat, eggs, poultry, fruit and vegetables and wine, with milk, beef and rice following in 1964. Following the end of the transitional stage and the completion of the customs union, these COMs were fully established, and new legislation in the form of basic Council regulations for each product adopted (for example, Council Regulation 120/67 for cereals, OJ English Spec. Ed., 1967, p.33). All of the founding regulations were subject to extensive amendment and have, in time, been revised, reformed and replaced. New COMs have also been subsequently introduced, such as that for sheep and goatmeat (Council Regulation 1837/80, OJ 1980 L183/1) and that for bananas (Council Regulation 404/93, OJ 1993 L47/1). Of them all, it is the cereals COM which is consistently singled out as the 'archetypal' form of COM. It is one of the earliest and most developed COM, employing the greatest range of support mechanisms, and has been used as a template for other COMs. It is also closely linked to the COMs in pigmeat, eggs and poultry, which, because of the use of cereal crops as feeding stuffs, are treated as ancillary to the cereal COM. For these reasons, this chapter will focus on the cereal COM; for detailed descriptions of the other COMs, which follow to a greater or lesser extent the model presented here, the reader is directed to a specialist text, such as Cardwell (2004).

The current basic regulation for the COM in cereals is Council Regulation 1784/2003 (OJ 2003 L270/78), which repealed and replaced Council Regulation 1766/92 (OJ 1992 l181/21), which itself had been repealed and replaced earlier legislation. The basic regulations for each product are complemented by a large body of implementing legislation and administrative acts, as well as a number of broader measures which apply across the different COMs, such as those on financing under the EAGF (Council Regulation 1290/2005) and on direct support schemes (Council Regulation 1782/2003, OJ 2003 L270/1, see further 9.5). According to the original model of the COM in cereals (which includes common wheat, rye, barley and durum wheat), three prices were set for the products covered by the regime: *a target price*, being the price level which it was hoped producers would receive, and which was, from the start fixed above world market rates; *a threshold price*, the minimum price for imports into the Community; and *an intervention price*, the price at which national authorities would be legally obliged to buy in EU crops offered to them. This price would increase progressively over the year to take into account storage costs. The operation of the COM has clearly reflected the principles outlined above, of financial solidarity, market unity and, particularly, Community preference: the COM insulated the Community producer from market forces, by providing a minimum guaranteed income (the intervention price) and, through the threshold price, ensuring that Community-produced goods could compete on price with lower-priced third country goods. This was achieved by requiring import levies to be paid on goods coming into the Community, and by assisting Community exporters by paying them export refunds to cover the difference between the world price and that in the EC. As a result of the Uruguay Round, variable import levies have been replaced by import duties, which are, for the most part, at the rate set under the Common Customs Tariff, though the Basic Regulation provides that there may be derogations to this rule (at Article 10). Although under severe pressure under the Doha Round negotiations, and due to be phased out by 2013, export refunds continue to be available, subject to certain limitations on volume and value (Articles 13–18, 1784/2003). Cereals taken into intervention may be disposed of either on the home market or exported. The former is only available where there is no risk that market prices will be depressed, a decision to be taken by the relevant national intervention agency. For both internal market and export sales, the Commission will invite purchase by tender (in the form of a Regulation published in the OJ). In the case of exports, if the tender is successful (the decision resting with the Cereals Management Committee) a licence will need to be granted to the trader, and deposits lodged by them, as a guarantee that the products are disposed of during the period of the licence's validity. Failure to comply with the terms of the licence will result in the security being lost, save in cases of *force majeure* (Article 9, 1784/2003). The legality of this system was accepted by the Court in Case 11/70 *Internationale Handelsgesellschaft* ([1970] ECR 1125). Intervention purchases and export refunds are financed out of the Guarantee section of the EAGFF, and some 3.4 billion euro were devoted to such expenses in 2001 (8 per cent of this amount in the cereal sector).

The COM in cereals, as with a number of other COMs, is based upon a common price system. Common prices were originally expressed using the 'Agricultural Unit of Account' (AUA), which was initially converted at a fixed rate exchange in respect to each Member State currency. However, by the early 1970s, the system of fixed exchange rates had come to an end, and currency fluctuations meant that agricultural prices as expressed in AUA (and later in ECU) no longer reflected real prices. Further complicating the situation was the political decision to operate a separate agricultural rate of exchange ('green money') for each state, against which the price in AUA/ECU was firstly converted, which could bear little relationship with the actual exchange rate. In response, the Community operated a system of 'monetary compensatory amounts' (MCA), which applied to trade *within* the Community, and which could result in duties being imposed or subsidies paid on goods moving from one state to another, depending on the level at which that state's green rate was set. The legality of MCA was challenged before the ECJ, which found that, although having the effect of partitioning the market, MCA 'have a corrective influence on the variations in fluctuating exchange rates which, in a system of market based on uniform process, might cause disturbances in trade in these products . . . Consequently, these compensatory amounts are conducive to the maintenance of a normal flow of trade in the exceptional circumstances created temporarily by the monetary situation' (Case 5/73 *Balkan Import–Export* [1973] ECR 1091 at para. 29). Despite the exceptional and temporary nature of MCA referred to by the Court, MCA would not be eliminated until 1992 (through Council Regulation 3813/92, OJ 1992 L387/1).

According to the Court: 'The essential aim of the machinery of the common organizations of the market is to achieve price levels at the production and wholesale stages which take into account both the interests of Community production as a whole in the relevant sector and those of consumers, and which guarantee market supplies without encouraging over-production' (Case 297/82 *De Samvirkende Danske Landboforeninger* [1983] ECR 3299 at para. 13). Of course, overproduction was a feature of many COMs over the 1970s and 1980s, and the level at which the common prices have been fixed is thought to have contributed greatly to this outcome. As McMahon argues, 'this may be seen as the inevitable consequence of giving the power to make decisions on the level of prices to a political body, such as the Council, rather than allowing it to remain with the Commission' (2000: 64). By the late 1980s, political agreement was achieved on the need for budgetary discipline and, across the COMs, a greater emphasis came to be placed on balancing supply and demand. In the cereals sector, the MacSharry reforms resulted in both the target and intervention prices being reduced (Council Regulation 1766/92, OJ 1992 L181/21) and, following the conclusion of the Uruguay Round, target and threshold prices were removed altogether (Council Regulation 1528/95, OJ 1995 L148/3). The progressive reduction in intervention prices in the cereals sector was accompanied by the introduction of the Arable Area Payment Scheme (AAPS) (Council Regulation 1765/92, OJ 1992 L181/12), designed to compensate in part for the loss of income from intervention. The level of payment made under the AAPS was determined, *inter alia*, by the area of arable land held by the farm, subject to overall regional base limits. The AAPS was also linked to production control, in that, as a condition of receiving payment under the scheme, a proportion of applicants' farm land was required to be 'set aside', not put to agricultural use, though this requirement did not apply to small farmers under the AAPS.

As a result of the Mid Term Review reforms of June 2003, the intervention price has, for some products in the cereals COM, been maintained, while for others, such as rye, it has been removed altogether. Buying in under intervention is only available during certain periods of the year, and attaining the full intervention price is conditional on the product being of the required standard (Council Regulation 1784/2003, Articles 4 and 5, with Article 6 providing the basis for detailed implementing legislation on these matters to be adopted by the Commission). The reduced importance of intervention and the reliance on guaranteed prices which came with it is replicated across the COMs, however this does not mark the end to financial support to farmers under the CAP. Instead, this support is to come increasingly in the form of direct, decoupled payments.

In December 2006, and in line with the objectives of the Commission's 2005 Communication *Simplification and Better Regulation for the Common Agricultural Policy* (COM (2005) 509 final), the Commission proposed radical simplification of the legal framework underpinning the COMs, by replacing the 41 pieces of legislation that currently establish the 21 different COMs with a single horizontal regulation: the Single COM. The regulation is intended to bring about a purely technical change, rather than bringing any change to the underlying policy of any of the existing COMs.

## 9.5    Decoupling: Single Farm Payments and Cross-Compliance

Council Regulation 1782/2003 on direct support schemes under the CAP is a horizontal regulation, applying across the various COMs. The regulation marks a further and significant shift from the CAP as a system of production support, to a system of producer support. The majority of existing direct payments available under the different COMs are consolidated into one single source of income support for farmers: the 'single farm payment' (SFP). The introduction of the SFP could lead to greater administrative simplification, and reduction in the capacity for fraud which has long featured in the CAP. The Commission has promoted the shift as one that is good for farmers, consumers and tax-payers, offering a policy under which 'farmers will enjoy more income stability, more freedom to produce what the market wants, and a system of support which is much easier to justify from a social point of view' [Fischler, SPEECH/03/326]. The switch to the SFP would also bring these elements of CAP support into the WTO 'green box', a move which may be seen as strengthening the EU's negotiating position in the Doha Round Agriculture talks.

Crucially, payments under the SFP are based on the principle of 'cross-compliance'. Compliance with a set of priority concerns is required for the full entitlement to be paid out. These include a body of 'statutory management requirements', which are a number of existing EC legislative measures in the areas of environmental protection, food safety, animal health and welfare (Article 4, listed in Annex III of Council Regulation 1782/2003). Farmers must also comply with the requirement to maintain the farm in 'good agricultural and environmental condition', the minimum requirements for this to be set by the Member States at national or regional level (Article 5). The regulation further provides for the establishment of national farm advisory systems to be established to offer guidance in respect to matters of cross-compliance. If the cross-compliance requirements are not met, aid may be withdrawn or reduced (Articles 6 and 7), though the new Member States are allowed a transition period during which they are not subject to the full demands of the cross-compliance obligations. Detailed rules on how Member States' authorities are to implement and operate the cross-compliance provisions are set out in Commission Regulation 795/2004 (OJ 2004 L141/1) and Commission Regulation 796/2004 (OJ 2004 L141/18).

The amount awarded to each farmer under the SFP is in principle (for the EU-15 at least, a different system applies for the new Member States) calculated on the basis of the aid received by farmers over 2000–2002, however Member States are afforded a degree of discretion here. As an alternative to individualised payments based on an averaging of farmers' 'historical' entitlements, a flat rate payment for each hectare farmed during 2005 may be made. These alternatives are in fact available on a regional level, as can be seen in the devolved UK, where, for example, Wales has adopted the historical approach, while England operates the flat rate, though opposition from the farming lobby has resulted in a mixed system applying in England for a transitional period. Regardless of the route adopted, direct payments under the SFP are subject to 'modulation', whereby a percentage of the SFP made to those in receipt of over 5000 euro direct aid each year is transferred to regional development measures (see 9.6).

The degree of discretion in the new system goes far beyond mechanisms for calculating the SFP. The introduction of the SFP system may be delayed by two years from the 2005 start date (longer for the new Member States) and, even once the final implementation date has been reached, Council Regulation 1782/2003 provides many opportunities for the continuation of 'coupled' aid, with states being permitted to maintain elements of existing support schemes (sometimes, as in the case of the beef slaughter premium, at up to 100 per cent) at regional or national level (Articles 64 *et seq.*). Some states, such as France, have taken up these opportunities, while others, such as the UK, are favouring the shift to full decoupling. The potential for national variations, which may bring distortions to the market, have led to doubts being voiced as to the continued 'common' nature of the CAP. In March 2007, proposals were introduced to revise the existing regulations, taking into account the lessons learnt during the first years of the system's operation. These include minor revisions allowing states to decide not to pursue very minor infringements of the rules.

## 9.6 Pillar Two: Rural Development

In the Commission's Agenda 2000 proposals, it was observed that EU action in respect to rural development amounted to 'a juxtaposition of agricultural market policy, structural policy and environmental policy with rather complex instruments and lacking overall coherence' (*Agenda 2000*, Vol I, p. 24). Following the outcome of the Berlin Summit 1999 and the adoption of Council Regulation 1257/99 (OJ 1999 L160/80), which allowed support for Rural Development from the 'Guidance' section of what was then the European Agriculture Guarantee and Guidance Fund, the Commission welcomed the laying of foundations for a comprehensive and consistent rural development policy, which henceforth formed the 'second pillar' of the CAP. The starting point for the EU's Rural Development policy was a much narrower concern with improving the structure of agricultural industry. That the CAP should have a structural policy was suggested in the wording of Article 33 EC, although the primary focus of CAP was, and has remained, markets and prices. One early step in the creation of a structural policy came with the splitting of the Guidance and Guarantee Funds through Council Regulation 17/64 (OJ 1964 P34/586), which provided that part funding would be available from the EAGGF/Guidance for a range of structural measures, including the adaptation and improvement of conditions of production in agriculture; and the adaptation and improvement of the marketing of agricultural production. A more ambitious vision for structural development was proposed in the 1968 Commission 'Memorandum on the Reform of Agriculture', the Mansholt plan, which outlined proposals to restructure agriculture by rationalising the use of agricultural land and the workforce, through increasing the size of agricultural holdings, taking land out of production and reducing the agricultural workforce from ten to five million by 1980. Structural reform of the degree proposed in the Mansholt plan proved to be politically unacceptable, though certain of the less controversial aspects of the 1968 plan were to resurface in a trio of directives successfully adopted in 1972. Council Directive 72/159 on the modernisation of farms provided for part funding of farm development measures to enable participating farmers to achieve, over a six year period, a comparable income to local non-agricultural workers. Additional agricultural land for participating farmers could come in part from land released under the operation of Council Directive 72/160, on the cessation of farming and the facilitation of early retirement, through part funding of incentives by EAGGF/Guidance. Council Directive 72/161 concerned information and training for farmers, providing, again, part finance under EAGGF/Guidance.

According to Snyder, 'the 1972 socio-structural directives and related measures were based on the assumptions that western European economies would continue to expand, that people leaving agriculture would continue to find employment in urban industry and that increasing agricultural and food production would continue to be matched by consumer demand' (Snyder, 1985: 170). The oil crisis and recession of the early 1970s undermined these assumptions. Moreover, the Community began to develop regionally specific policies to assist those areas worst affected by the changing economic fortunes of Europe, including, in 1975, the creation of the Regional Development Fund (see further 19.2). In the agricultural context, measures were introduced which reflected this regional concern. Council Directive 75/268, on mountain and hill-farming and farming in less-favoured areas, introduced a range of measures including part financing to achieve the objectives of ensuring the continuation of farming, the maintenance of minimum population level and the conservation of the countryside in less favoured areas. Key elements of these four directives would later feature in Council Regulation 797/85 (OJ 1985 L93/1) on improving the efficiency of agricultural structures, which replaced them in 1985.

The focus on the regional aspect of the developing development policy continued over the late 1970s and 1980s, with the introduction of a number of measures targeted on specific regions, and broadening into concerns beyond agricultural production, such as the Mediterranean (Council Regulations 269/79, OJ 1979 L38/1, and 270/79, OJ 1979 L38/6), the west of Ireland and Northern Ireland (Council Regulations 1942/81, OJ 1981 L197/17, and 1943/81, OJ 1981 L197/23). The focus on the regional dimension was then qualitatively taken further with the formal incorporation of the Community's developing regional policy into the main body of the EC Treaty, through the SEA (see Chapter 18). These provisions were introduced under a new Title on 'economic and social cohesion', now found at Articles 158 *et seq.* EC, and which provides that:

> 'In order to promote its overall harmonious development, the Community shall develop and pursue its actions leading to the strengthening of its economic and social cohesion. In particular, the Community shall aim at reducing disparities between the levels of the development of the various regions and the backwardness of the least favoured regions or islands, including rural areas.'

A key tool in the achievement of these objectives was specified as being the structural funds and, in 1988, the so-called 'Delors I' package of decisions reformed the operational framework for these funds (led by Council Regulation 2052/88, OJ 1988 L185/9 on the tasks of the Structural Funds and their effectiveness and on coordination of their activities between themselves) and also doubled their existing budget. The Structural Funds were subsequently to operate in accordance with four 'implementation principles': concentration of funding, programming, partnership and additionality (see further 18.4 *et seq.*). In accordance with the principle of concentration, funding under EAGGF/Guidance was targeted at two of the newly established priority objective areas. Along with the other structural funds, EAGGF/Guidance would part fund 'Objective 1' measures, which relate to the 'development and structural adjustment of the regions whose development is lagging behind'. In addition, an Objective 5 was created, comprising two parts – (a) speeding up the adjustment of agricultural structures and (b) promoting the development of rural areas. In 1991, the 'LEADER' programme ('Links between Actions for the Development of the Rural Economy') was introduced, as a mechanism for stimulating local responses to rural development with local action groups, and proposing that local action plans would be eligible for part funding under the scheme.

Despite the reference in Council 75/268 on mountain and hill-farming and farming in less-favoured regions to be the objective of the conservation of the countryside, the Community had paid relatively little regard to the environmental consequences of the CAP. Few initiatives were adopted, and of those that were, such as a programme for the protection of environmentally sensitive areas, under Council Regulation 797/85 (OJ 1985 L93/1), the Community committed itself to rather limited expenditure – in this case at a rate of only some 25 per cent, with each Member State providing the rest. The 1992 MacSharry reforms responded to this increasingly unsustainable situation through, on the one hand a 'greening' of the COMs, including initiatives such as the set aside scheme; and on the other, the adoption of accompanying measures, the most significant of which was Council Regulation 2078/92 (OJ 1992 L215/85), on 'agricultural production methods compatible with the requirements of protection of the environment and the maintenance of the countryside'. Funding for initiatives promoting good environmental practices was to be made, this time under the EAGGF/Guarantee section, at a possible rate of up to 75 per cent. Two other accompanying measures, Council Regulation 2079/92 (OJ 1992 L215/91) on early retirement and Council Regulation 2080/92 (OJ 1992 L215/96) on forestry aid, were to be similarly supported. The focus on the environment was carried through into other aspects of Community funding as a result of the 1993 amendment of Council Regulation 2052/88 (OJ 1988 L185/9), which, as well as continuing the priority objectives established in 1988, provided that the tasks of EAGGF/Guidance were to include developing the social fabric of rural areas, safeguarding the environment and preserving the countryside (Council Regulation 2081/93, OJ 1993 L193/5, Article 3).

The Agenda 2000 reforms, which introduced the concept of rural development policy as the 'second pillar' of the CAP, also saw a significant reorganisation and simplification of existing measures, which were brought together into one Rural Development Regulation, Council Regulation 1257/99 (OJ 1999 L160/80). The regulation contributed to an increasing flexibility, and decentralisation of responsibility to the Member States in their Rural Development policies. Under the regulation, Member States drew up, at the most suitable level, rural development plans, selecting from a 'menu' of measures. These included investment in farm businesses, with the aim, *inter alia*, of reducing production costs, improving product quality and increasing diversification; a range of measures on human resources, including support for young farmers, incentives for early retirement, and training; compensatory payments for farming in less-favoured areas; forestry aid; production and marketing aid; as well as broader rural development measures such as promotion for rural tourism, and crafts. Member States selected those measures which were of most relevance to them, although they were obliged to include a range of agri-environmental measures in their programmes. The rural development plans under the regulation covered the period 2000–2006, and required the approval of the Commission. Part funding to operationalise the plans was supplied under EAGGF, with an increasing role for the Guarantee section. In addition to these programmes, Member States could also, if they had eligible regions, submit integrated programmes which could include rural development aspects, under the Structural Funds priority objectives (see 19.4). The existing community instruments, which include LEADER, were also rationalised, though LEADER continued, now in the guise of 'LEADER+'.

The reforms implemented as a result of the mid-term review continue with the programming 'menu' approach, although the amending Council Regulation 1783/2003 (OJ 2003 L270/70) contains a wider range of items on the menu than before. These include support for measures promoting good practice in animal welfare (though assistance to comply with statutory minimums is not available, such costs having to be met by farmers directly); as well as measures on food quality, including incentives for producers to participate in schemes designed to improve the quality of agricultural products, and inform consumers of this, such as the EU system of geographical indications and designations of origins (Council Regulation 510/2006, OJ 2006 L93/12, see further 5.17), as well as the promotion of organic food (Council Regulation 2092/91, OJ 1991 L198/1). Council Regulation 1783/2003 also provides for support to meet the obligations of cross-compliance, including support to attain new standards not already implemented in national legal orders, as well as financial support for the farm advisory services which offer guidance on cross-compliance. As had already been indicated, the mid-term review also introduces for the first time compulsory modulation, under which, eventually 5 per cent of 'first pillar' funds are to be redirected to the second pillar, though Member States may individually decide to increase this amount. At 5 per cent, this has been calculated to bring an additional 1.2 billion euro to the second pillar annually. While the balance between the level of spending under the two pillars has always been massively skewed in favour of the first pillar, this goes only a little way to making a significant impact to this overall balance, which currently sees only some 10 per cent of agricultural spending going on rural development measures.

Further reforms of the rural development policy system were proposed in 2004, and adopted as Regulation 1698/2005 (OJ 2005 L277/1), which will be operational over 2007–2013. Commissioner Fischler introduced the proposals as being geared towards a 'more efficient, coherent and visible rural development policy', the key change being the introduction of one funding and programming instrument for rural development, the European Agriculture Fund for Rural Development (EAFRD), replacing the Guidance section of the EAGGF. Rural Development policy is to be based around four axes, which comprise three objectives, and a suggested approach. The three objectives are first, increasing the competitiveness of the agricultural sector through support for restructuring; second, enhancing the environment and countryside through support for land management; and third, strengthening the quality of life in rural areas and promoting diversification of economic activities. The approach is through the use of bottom-up local development strategies – the LEADER approach. While the 'menu' approach to regional planning remains, flexibility is circumscribed to a greater extent than before, as Member States are to apportion minimum percentages of funding to each of the axes, and to the LEADER initiatives. The proposal also sets out to increase EU funding, to a total EU funding of 13.7 billion euro per year over the period. Despite the continual upgrading of the EU's rural development policy, it does remain very much a junior partner to the first pillar. It has also been bedevilled with accusations of inefficiency and lack of policy effectiveness over its history. Some of these criticisms have focused on the extreme complexity of the system. Certainly the new regulation continues a recent and welcome trend towards greater simplification. However, as Cardwell has observed, simplification of the system at EU level can result, and has resulted, in increasing complexity and detail at national level (and below) (Cardwell, 2004: 218). Other concerns have surrounded the very different responses of the Member States to the take-up of rural development policies and the very different levels of funding received by different states, arguably quite out of line with 'need'. However, as long as support for rural development funding remains partial and reliant on match-funding at the national level (as opposed to the full meeting of costs under the first pillar), this aspect of rural development policy looks set to remain.

## 9.7 Relationship with Other Policy Areas

As will be apparent, the EU's agricultural policy intersects with a wide range of other policy fields, including consumer protection, food safety and food quality, public health, and environmental protection. While the tendencies towards 'quantity over quality' apparent in the CAP in the past could be seen as undermining the attainment of high standards in these policy areas, the more recent orientations of the CAP certainly would seem to seek to reinforce and develop improved standards in these areas. Although the objectives of the evolving CAP are apparently congruent with objectives in these areas, the relationship between the CAP, with its heavy intervention in the operation of agricultural markets, and the general internal market rules on free movement and competition may be perceived as rather less so. As is recognised in Article 32(2) EC, the provisions on the common market have to give way to the *lex specialis* of the CAP in respect to trade in agricultural products. That said, the starting point is the presumption that general rules of the Treaty will apply. As regards the free movement of goods, for example, the Court has established that in the absence of a COM, the provisions on the free movement of goods are fully applicable to agricultural products, thus catching measures taken under national market organisations which have the effect of quantitative restrictions (Case 48/74 *Charmasson* v. *Minister of Economic Affairs* [1974] ECR 1383).

Again in the absence of a COM, Article 38 EC provides that where a national market organisation exists which operates so as to place relevant products at a competitive advantage on the markets of other Member States, 'counterveiling charges' may be imposed to counteract the benefit gained by the supported product. This opportunity, which appears very much like the imposition of something akin to a customs duty, is very infrequently used today, given the fact that national market organisations have for the most part now given way to COMs, which exist in respect of the majority of key agricultural products (except potatoes). As was confirmed by the Court in Case 232/78 *Commission* v. *France (Sheepmeat)* ([1979] ECR 2729), a dispute which arose prior to the introduction of the sheepmeat COM, and concerned French reactions to British aid under its national market organisation, states may not impose counterveiling charges independently – they must be imposed by the Commission.

In respect to products for which COMs do exist, the Court has recognised that 'many mechanisms of the organization of the market, such as price fixing and intervention systems, by organizing and regulating trade involve limitations on free movement' (Joined Cases 80 and 81/77 *Société Les Commissionnaires Réunis SARL* [1978] ECR 927 at para. 18). However, such limitations are chosen by the Community institutions in the setting of COMs under the CAP – the Member States themselves are not extended the same scope to act independently in a way contrary to the internal market. Member States operate within the context of the COM, and are prohibited from applying unlawful tariff and non-tariff barriers to trade. The earliest COMs, adopted before the end of the transitional period and before the common market had come into being, expressly incorporated the free movement rules. COM Regulations no longer contain the text of these provisions, the

Court having held that they automatically apply, thus rendering the practice superfluous (Joined Cases 3, 4 and 6/76 *Kramer* [1976] ECR 1279). To the extent that the COM imposes more specific rules than those in Articles 28–30, these are to take precedence. Thus, as a reading of many of the canonical cases on justifications and mandatory requirements reveals, the Court will consider first the position under the relevant COM, and only where measures are compatible with the COM (or where the matter is unregulated under the COM) will it need to go on to consider whether Articles 28–30 have been breached (see, for example, Case 120/78 *Rewe-Zentrale AG* v. *Bundesmonopolverwaltung für Branntwein (Cassis de Dijon)* ([1979] ECR 649), which begins the 'mandatory requirements' formula with the words 'in the absence of common rules relating to the marketing of the products concerned'; see 5.6). While the free movement provisions will give way to more specialised rules under the COM, the Court has ruled that it is not permissible for Member States to use generalised claims about acting in accordance with the objectives of the CAP so as to justify actions in apparent contravention of the free movement rules (as attempted by France in relation to its prohibition on the sale of substitute milk powder, justified, it argued, on the basis of milk surpluses and the CAP's attempt to stabilise the markets: Case 216/84 *Commission* v. *France* [1988] ECR 793).

Turning to competition law (see Chapter 10), Article 36 EC provides that 'the provisions of the Chapter relating to the rules on competition shall apply to production of and trade in agricultural products only to the extent determined by the council, account being taken of the objectives set out in Article 33'. The decisions taken to respond to this provision resulted in what the Court has termed 'a residual field of competition' applying in relation to the COMs (Joined Cases 40–48 etc./73 *Cooperatiëve Vereniging 'Suiker Unie' UA* v. *Commission* [1975] ECR 1663 at para. 24). Of course, current policy pronouncements are to the effect that the CAP is to admit more open and competitive markets, and it is the case that such exceptions to the application of the competition rules which have existed have been interpreted restrictively. The regime for the application of competition law rules to agricultural products was established under Council Regulation 26/62 (OJ 1962 L30/993), which provides, at Article 1, that Articles 81–88 EC, on restrictive agreements, abuse of a dominant position, mergers and state aids, all apply to agricultural products. Article 2 provides the exceptions, specifically the non-application of Article 81 to agreements, decisions and concerted practices which are an integral part of the national market organisation or needed for the attainment of the objectives of the CAP. More particularly, the Article provides that Article 81(1) does not apply to agreements between farmers and farmers' associations of the same Member State which concern the production or sale of agricultural products or the use of joint facilities for the storage, treatment or processing of agricultural products, which do not impose an obligation to charge identical prices and which do not exclude competition. A clear breach of these conditions resulted in the imposition by the Commission, in 2003, of a fine of 16.7 million euro, where a collection of French farming unions and federations coerced slaughterhouse federations into an agreement to set a minimum price for beef, and to limit or suspend imports (COMP/38.279 – PO/Viandes Bovines Françaises). More generally, if the derogations under Regulation 26/62 are to apply, a number of conditions must be fulfilled. Agreements may only be in respect to those agricultural products specified in 'Annex I'. Additionally, agreements must fulfil all the objectives of the CAP listed at Article 33, or, if those objectives should prove divergent, the Commission is 'able to reconcile those objectives so as to enable that derogating provision, which must be interpreted strictly, to be applied' (Case C-265/97P *VBA* v. *Florimex* [2000] ECR I-2061 at para. 94). The derogations under Regulation 26/62 are applicable only in respect to restrictive agreements; they do not apply to rules on the abuse of dominant positions or mergers.

Finally, the rules on state aids, set out in Articles 87 and 88 EC, apply in the context of COMs, although not to aid paid by states in the way of financial part-contributions which are also receiving support under the structural funds. Aid outside these arrangements will be subject to the usual system of notifications by the Member States, and Commission. Certain types of state aid are explicitly declared not to be prohibited under Article 88 of the EAFRD, including investments in agricultural holdings relating to the protection and improvement of the environment, and the improvement of the hygiene conditions of livestock enterprises and the welfare of animals. A number of recent measures have been adopted which appear to grant Member States more autonomy and room for manoeuvre in respect to state aids. Commission Regulation 1/2004 (OJ 2004 L1/1) introduces a block exemption, an exemption on Member States from obtaining prior clearance for aid, in respect to aids paid to SMEs active in the production, processing and marketing of agricultural products. According to the Commission, given the definition of 'SMEs' (up to 250 employees and 40 million euro annual turnover), almost all farms and agricultural companies are covered. The Commission has also introduced proposals for the introduction of a *de minimis* rule in relation to agricultural state aids, a rule which has not applied in the agricultural sector (confirmed in Joined Cases C-113 and 114/00 *Spain* v. *Commission* [2002] ECR I-7601).

### 9.8   International Dimensions

The CAP's principle of 'Community preference' necessarily seeks to place producers from outside EU at a disadvantage, 'home' producers benefiting from a range of financial subsidies, available for disposal of agricultural goods on both the EU and the world market, as well as from the operation of import quotas. In addition to these measures, which distort the international market for trade in agricultural goods, are measures on health protection and the quality of products for import into the EU, and together these create a significant body of tariff and non-tariff barriers to free international trade. These in turn have led to disputes – economic, political and legal – between the EU and its trading partners within GATT, and now the WTO (see Chapter 11). However, it should be noted that, just as agriculture has traditionally held a special place in the EU system, and has been subject to different rules than industrial products, so there has been a tradition of agricultural exceptionalism in the GATT/WTO system, agricultural products being subject to a series of exemptions and exceptions from the general trade rules. For example, the general prohibition against import quotas in Article XI does not extend to quotas on agricultural imports which may be imposed where there are measures in place to control the domestic production of like products (XI: 2(c)). A further exception to this exception was granted to the US in 1955, the waiver operating to permit import quotas even in the absence of domestic control measures. Similarly, the general prohibition against export subsidies, found in XVI: 4 does not apply to primary products, except to the extent that the operation of subsidies results in that contracting party holding a 'more than equitable share of world trade in the relevant product market' (XVI: 3). Definitional ambiguity and difficulties in determining causation resulted in a relatively toothless regime.

The Uruguay Round was to mark a distinct shift in the treatment of agriculture under the GATT/WTO system. As permitted to do under Article 133 EC (and confirmed in Opinion 1/94 [1994] ECR I-5267), the Commission negotiated on behalf of the Community (guided by directives for negotiation from the Council, which ultimately decides on whether to accept the outcome of negotiations) and these negotiations eventually resulted in the conclusion of a comprehensive 'Agreement on Agriculture' (the AoA), bringing agriculture firmly within the scope of WTO rules. The AoA, which entered into force in 1995, focused on three matters: first, the improvement of market access through, *inter alia*, the reduction of import barriers. This involved a shift towards 'tariffication' of non-tariff barriers, notably with CAP, variable import levies being converted into customs duties (such levies had, in Case 17/67 *Neumann* [1967] ECR 441, been defined as not in fact customs duties but charges regulating external trade connected with the common price policy). A commitment to reduce such tariffs, for developed nations, by an average of 36 per cent was also agreed. Second, the AoA introduced discipline in respect to levels of domestic support, and the introduction of the classification of measures, according to their trade-disorting impact, into three 'boxes'. The first measures, the 'amber box', are trade distorting and are subject to reduction commitments. 'Blue box' measures include partly decoupled subsidies, which while designed to limit production are still linked to production. A 'peace clause' was to apply to these until 2003. Finally, the non-trade-distorting decoupled measures are regarded as 'green box' aid, and may continue. Third, the AoA addressed the particularly contentious issue of export subsidies, resulting in agreement to reduce their levels and scope of application. In 2000, in advance of the main round, and in accordance with the terms of the AoA, further negotiations began on the ongoing reform of agricultural trade. These negotiations were, according to Article 20 AoA, to draw on the experience of implementing the commitments made in the Uruguay Round and take account of non-trade concerns, special treatment for developing countries and the objective of establishing a fair and market-oriented agricultural trading system. The negotiations continued as part of the Doha Development Round and are ongoing, though they came closer to successful completion with the package of agreements in August 2004. Key elements of the agricultural framework agreement include, most significantly, the phasing out of export subsidies (by 2013, as agreed at the Hong Kong Ministerial meeting in December 2005), as well as greater discipline in respect to blue box expenditure and a review of green box expenditure, so as to ensure that they have no, or at most minimal, trade-distorting effects or effects on production. The interpretation of 'trade-distorting' here will undoubtedly be one which will be politically as much as economically determined.

Also introduced as part of the Uruguay Round, though formally falling outside the AoA, were new rules governing trade restrictions imposed to protect human, animal and plant health, in the form of the Sanitary and Phytosanitary Agreement (SPS). Under the SPS, where parties are determining the appropriate level of protection, they may take such measures as are necessary to protect human, animal or plant life or health, which must be based on scientific principles, and must not arbitrarily or unjustifiably discriminate between trading partners. Provisional measures may be adopted where scientific information is still insufficient, provided that a serious attempt is made to establish a more informed basis for action within a reasonable period of time, and prevailing international standards may be exceeded where there is sound scientific justification. The degree of latitude left open to contracting parties to exceed international standards was considered by the WTO Disputes Panel (and subsequently by the Appellate Body) in the *Beef Hormones Dispute*, which arose out of the Community's ban on the marketing of hormone-treated beef on the grounds of consumer safety, and which effectively excluded US and Canadian beef from the EU market. Ultimately, the Community's ban was found against at both instances, as it was found that though a higher level of protection could be imposed if scientifically based, the risk assessment procedures of the SPS agreement had not been followed, the EU's stated reliance on the precautionary principle not being sufficient. Further trade disputes between the EU and the US, notably the 2003 complaint lodged by the US, Canada and Argentina against the operation of the EU's regime on marketing of GM crops, continue to demonstrate the very different regulatory approaches taken towards protecting public health, with, on the one hand, the US favouring a more science-based one, while, on the other, the EU paying regard also to political, ethical and societal considerations (Cardwell, 2004: 379).

The contours of today's CAP have been significantly shaped by the EU's participation in the GATT/WTO order. However, while the political and legislative significance of the GATT/WTO system on the CAP is increasingly marked, the impact of the WTO rules on EC law before the Court of Justice have been less great. The Court has ruled that the WTO rules are not capable of direct effect, and has refused to allow the review of EU legislation in the light of WTO rules, except 'where the Community intended to implement a particular obligation assumed in the context of the WTO, or where the Community measure refers expressly to the precise provisions of the WTO agreements' (Case C-149/96 *Portugal* v. *Council* [1999] ECR I-8395 para. 49, and see also for the refusal to allow individuals to plead the incompatibility of Community legislation with WTO legislation before national courts Case C-377/02 *Van Parys* [2005] ECR I-1465; see further 11.8). Further, and as has been particularly demonstrated in respect to complainants challenging the terms of the COM in bananas, breach of WTO rules by the Community institutions will not, except in these same circumstances, give rise to the non-contractual liability of Community institutions. Thus, even actions in apparent contravention of findings of the WTO Dispute Settlement Body will not give rise to the basis for a claim, unless the Council and Commission 'intended to implement ... specific obligations contained in the WTO Panel report ... or in the DSB decision adopting that report' (Joined Cases T-641 and 65/01 *Afrikanische Frucht-Compagnie GmbH* v. *Council* [2004] ECR II-521) (see also 4.7).

## Summary

1. The Common Agricultural Policy has a fundamental financial, legal and political significance in the EU order.

2. The EU is the largest importer of agricultural products in the world, and the second-largest (to North America) exporter, and is thus a significant player in the World Trade Organisation system. The contours of today's CAP have been significantly shaped by the EU's participation in the GATT/WTO order.

3. The CAP framework is built on two pillars. The first concerns the Common Organisations of the Market (COMs – EU-wide market organisations for different agricultural products), the second being rural development.

## Summary cont'd

4. Funding for the CAP comes from the European Agriculture Guarantee Fund (EAGF) for the first pillar and, under the second pillar, from the European Agriculture Fund for Rural Development (EAFRD).

5. The objectives for the CAP are set out at Article 33 EC. These include: increasing agricultural productivity; ensuring a fair standard of living for the agricultural community; stabilising markets; and ensuring a fair price for consumers. The Court has recognised that these objectives may be mutually incompatible.

6. The CAP is regulated through a large body of legislation and, within this, the Commission holds significant powers to issue delegated legislation. In operationalising the CAP, the Community institutions are recognised as having a wide degree of discretion.

7. The CAP is very heavily litigated, and many key principles of the EU legal order have emerged from this area.

8. The core principles underpinning the CAP are market unity, Community preference, financial solidarity and producer co-responsibility.

9. The CAP has gone through a number of significant revisions. The most recent, of 2003, have sought to make the agricultural sector more market oriented, removing trade-distorting supports, and have also stressed rural development.

10. The 2003 reform marks a significant shift from the CAP as a system of *production* support, which have insulated agriculture from the operation of the market, and in some cases resulted in overproduction, to a system of *producer* support. The majority of existing direct payments available under the different COMs are consolidated into one single source of income support for farmers: the 'single farm payment' (SFP).

11. Payments under the SFP are based on the principle of 'cross-compliance'. Compliance with a set of priority concerns in respect of, among others, environmental protection, animal health and welfare, and food safety, is required for the full entitlement to be paid out.

12. The potential for national variations under the new system has led to doubts being voiced as to the continued 'common' nature of the CAP.

13. The EU's engagement with Rural Development policy began in the 1970s, and has recently taken on a much greater significance.

14. Agricultural policy intersects with a wide range of other policy fields, including consumer protection, food safety and food quality, public health, environmental protection and competition policy.

# Exercises

1. Why has such significance been given to agriculture in the history of the EU?

2. Why have separate Common Organisations of the Market been introduced for agricultural products, rather than making these goods subject to standard EU internal market rules?

3. Critically assess the potential contribution of cross-compliance to the achievement of the objectives and priorities of the CAP.

4. Explain why it is suggested that it is increasingly problematic to describe today's CAP as a 'common' policy.

5. What are the legal implications of the WTO for the CAP?

## Further Reading

Cardwell, M. (2004) *The European Model of Agriculture*, Oxford: Oxford University Press.

Cardwell, M. (2006) 'Current Developments: Agriculture', 55 *International and Comparative Law Quarterly* 467.

Cardwell, M. and Rodgers, C. (2006) 'Reforming the WTO Legal Order for Agricultural Trade: Issues for European Regional Policy in the Doha Round', 55 *International and Comparative Law Quarterly* 805.

Kosior, K. (2005) 'New Stakeholders in the Common Agricultural Policy: A Real Burden to Reform Processes in the Enlarged European Union?', 11 *European Law Journal* 566.

Usher, J. (2002) *EC Agricultural Law* (2nd edn), Oxford: Oxford University Press.

## Key Websites

The Commission's website for agriculture and rural development is at:
**http://ec.europa.eu/agriculture/index_en.htm**

The World Trade Organisation site is at:
**http://www.wto.org/**

Wyn Grant blogs on the CAP at:
**http://commonagpolicy.blogspot.com/**

# Chapter 10

## The Regulation of Anti-Competitive Conduct

**10.1**   Introduction and Basic Concepts

Article 3(1)(g) EC lays down that the activities of the EU shall include the creation of 'a system ensuring that competition in the internal market is not distorted'. Despite the fact that competition (or 'antitrust') law was almost unknown in Europe in the first years after the Second World War (Slot, 2004), competition law and policy have grown into one of the most important areas of EU law and policy in practice, especially in terms of the effects upon both businesses and the conduct of public authorities at the national, regional and local level. It is also one of the most voluminous and complex fields of EU law and policy in terms of secondary legislation adopted by the Council and the Commission, a very substantial case law emanating from the Court of Justice, the Court of First Instance (hereafter referred to as the 'EU courts') and the national courts, general guidelines and policy guidance issued by the Commission to guide business and decision-makers, and last but by no means least individual enforcement decisions adopted by the Commission. The latter institution has had a central steering role in this field, as well as taking on the role as the guardian of the Treaty by pursuing infringements of the competition rules. It can adopt decisions enforcing EU competition law, including the finding of an infringement, the imposition of fines on undertakings for breach of Articles 81 and 82 EC, and the prohibition of a merger under the Merger Control Regulation. As a result of a major legislative reform in 2003, national courts and national competition authorities will have an increasingly important role to play in enforcing many aspects of EU competition law.

Public authorities usually intervene in markets in the name of 'competition law' to correct some 'market failure' and to ensure the proper operation of market forces. In the EU context, competition law and policy are crucial complements to the rules which govern the internal market as a single trading environment in which the free movement of goods, services, persons and capital is ensured (Article 14 EC). It would severely undermine the effectiveness of the internal market project if the conduct of individual companies, or groups of companies, could recreate the obstacles to trade which the Member States, and indeed the EU itself, are prohibited from maintaining. From the very beginning, therefore, the creation of a framework to regulate anti-competitive conduct in the EU has been linked to the internal or single market. In Case 26/76 *Metro-SB-Grossmärkte GmbH & Co.* v. *Commission* ([1977] ECR 1875) the Court stated:

> 'The requirement contained in Articles 3 and [81] of the [EC] Treaty that competition shall not be distorted implies the existence on the market of workable competition, that is to say the degree of competition necessary to ensure the observance of the basic requirements and the attainment of the objectives of the Treaty, in particular the creation of a single market achieving conditions similar to those of a domestic market' (para. 20).

In addition to reinforcing the point that competition policy in the EU context is very much driven by the circumstances of the EU's integration project, this quotation gives a clue that there are different concepts of 'competition' which can inform legal decision-making and policy-making. In strict economic terms, the concept of 'workable competition' referred to in this quotation is itself a rather contested and uncertain term, usually understood in contradistinction to the search for 'perfect competition'. This latter concept is often referred to as the 'Pareto' optimal use of resources, in the sense of an allocation under which no one could be made better off without someone else being made worse off. In this (perhaps idealistic) context we would see consumer welfare maximised, as well as productive efficiency; there is constant pressure on costs, and cost reductions are the only means whereby firms can stay in business and increase profits.

Whatever notion of 'competition' is adopted, of course, efficiency typically lies at the heart of competition policy, or antitrust policy as it is sometimes also called. According to Industry Canada (Anderson and Dev Khasla, 1995: 17):

> 'The role of competition policy in modern capitalist economies is based directly on economists' understanding of the optimizing properties of competitive markets. Specifically, competition ensures that the prices paid by consumers are equivalent to the marginal costs of producing individual goods and services. This facilitates the efficient allocation of resources throughout the economy ("allocative efficiency"). Competition is also generally believed to encourage firms to minimize their costs by adopting the best available technologies and organizational forms. This is sometimes referred to as "X-efficiency". From this perspective, the role of competition policy is to deter or remedy business transactions and practices that undermine efficiency by impeding the competitive process.'

In fact, although it adopted the terminology of 'workable competition' in the *Metro* case, the Court of Justice has not taken up in a consistent way any specific economic ideology in relation to competition policy, and the appropriate goals for public authorities where they seek to promote competition. For a long time, the same could be said for the Commission, which is tasked with the primary role of enforcing the competition rules in the EC Treaty especially in respect of infringements by individual firms or groups of firms. However, in recent years the latter's view of competition policy has been marked by a more rigorous approach to economic analysis. This has been marked, for example, by the appointment of a Chief Economist within the Competition Directorate-General whose role is to ensure that the Commission's competition policies and decisions are backed up by sound economics. Moreover, in addition to concerns with aspects of efficiency, and with internal market questions, both the Court and the Commission have also from time to time been concerned with other recognised aims of competition law, such as protecting consumers and small firms in the marketplace. Here the case for intervention by public authorities is based on the recognition that economic power can be harmful in terms of liberty, and indeed that excessive market power can be a threat to democracy itself.

In sum, in the EU context competition policy pursues a variety of interlinked objectives, and in addition there may be differences of emphasis between the different institutions such as the Court of Justice/Court of First Instance and the Commission. There is no doubt from the system of the Treaty that market integration is a core objective, and must necessarily strongly inform decision-making and policy-making so long as the internal market remains in any respect incomplete (Ehlermann, 1992). This is examined in more detail in 10.3.

## 10.2 Overview of the Competition Rules

The competition rules contained in the actual EC Treaty are somewhat limited. Article 81 EC is the primary weapon for combating anti-competitive behaviour which takes the form of cartels or other types of anti-competitive agreements between firms (or undertakings as they are termed in EU competition law terminology), groups of undertakings, or decisions of associations of undertakings. It provides:

'1. The following shall be prohibited as incompatible with the common market: all agreements between undertakings, decisions by associations of undertakings and concerted practices which may affect trade between Member States and which have as their object or effect the prevention, restriction or distortion of competition within the common market, and in particular those which:

(a) directly or indirectly fix purchase or selling prices or any other trading conditions;

(b) limit or control production, markets, technical development, or investment;

(c) share markets or sources of supply;

(d) apply dissimilar conditions to equivalent transactions with other trading parties, thereby placing them at a competitive disadvantage;

(e) make the conclusion of contracts subject to acceptance by the other parties of supplementary obligations which, by their nature or according to commercial usage, have no connection with the subject of such contracts.

2. Any agreements or decisions prohibited pursuant to this Article shall be automatically void.

3. The provisions of paragraph 1 may, however, be declared inapplicable in the case of:

– any agreement or category of agreements between undertakings;

– any decision or category of decisions by associations of undertakings;

– any concerted practice or category of concerted practices,

which contributes to improving the production or distribution of goods or to promoting technical or economic progress, while allowing consumers a fair share of the resulting benefit, and which does not:

(a) impose on the undertakings concerned restrictions which are not indispensable to the attainment of these objectives;

(b) afford such undertakings the possibility of eliminating competition in respect of a substantial part of the products in question.'

Article 81 EC is discussed in more depth in 10.5 and 10.6.

Article 82 EC is much shorter, and is concerned with the conduct of undertakings which find themselves in 'dominant positions' in the marketplace:

'Any abuse by one or more undertakings of a dominant position within the common market or in a substantial part of it shall be prohibited as incompatible with the common market insofar as it may affect trade between Member States.

Such abuse may, in particular, consist in:

(a) directly or indirectly imposing unfair purchase or selling prices or other unfair trading conditions;

(b) limiting production, markets or technical development to the prejudice of consumers;

(c) applying dissimilar conditions to equivalent transactions with other trading parties, thereby placing them at a competitive disadvantage;

(d) making the conclusion of contracts subject to acceptance by the other parties of supplementary obligations which, by their nature or according to commercial usage, have no connection with the subject of such contracts.'

In other words, Article 82 EC is concerned with what is colloquially often termed 'monopolies', although in strict terms a monopoly would occur when an undertaking has 100 per cent of a market, and 'dominance' in terms of Article 82 can occur where an undertaking has a much lower market share. This provision is discussed in 10.7.

Article 83 EC creates a legal basis for the Council to adopt detailed regulations for the implementation of Articles 81 and 82, acting by a qualified majority on the basis of a proposal from the Commission, after consulting the European Parliament. Article 84 EC gives a residual role to the competition authorities of the Member States in the enforcement of Articles 81 and 82, so long as there are no implementing rules in place, and Article 85 EC confirms the primordial enforcement role of the Commission in investigating suspected infringements. In practice, most cases falling within the scope of the competition rules have also fallen within the scope of a number of implementing regulations, the most important of which in practice was Council Regulation 17 of 1962 (OJ Spec. Ed. 1962, No. 204/62, p.87). As of May 2004, however, that Regulation was replaced by Council Regulation 1/2003, the so-called Modernisation Regulation, on the implementation of the rules on competition laid down in Articles 81 and 82 of the Treaty (OJ 2003 L1/1). The enforcement of the competition rules will be discussed in 10.9, and the primary focus is on the enforcement under Regulation 1/2003, although clearly this Regulation is likely to be interpreted in many areas in the light of the lengthy experiences with Regulation 17. The key elements of the Commission's investigatory and enforcement powers continue to apply, including the power to fine undertakings which infringe Articles 81(1) and 82 EC.

In addition to the enforcement role of the Commission, it should be noted that the Court has long held that Articles 81(1) and (2) and 82 EC have direct effect (Case 127/73 *Belgische Radio en Televisie* v. *SABAM* [1974] ECR 51). That is, they give rise to rights which individuals can enforce in national courts. In addition, since Article 81(2) EC is directly effective, there was no need for a decision of a competition authority such as the Commission to find that an agreement fell under Article 81(1) EC. If Article 81(1) applied to an agreement, then the sanction of nullity applied automatically and *ab initio*. Consequently, undertakings which believe that they are the victims of anti-competitive conduct have a choice of complaining to the Commission, and looking for the Commission to take action, or of beginning an action in the national court and relying upon the direct effect of the competition rules. The evolution of the current system of competition law enforcement in the EU, and the differing and evolving roles of the Commission, the EU Courts, the national courts and the national competition authorities will be addressed in 10.10–10.12. The general theme of these sections concerns how the role of the Commission has evolved into one of coordination and general oversight, with national competition authorities taking on – from 2004 onwards – a much greater role in day-to-day enforcement of competition law.

Until May 2004, and the entry into force of the Modernisation Regulation, the situation with regard to the applicability of Article 81(3) was different from that which applied to Articles 81(1) and (2). The granting of an exemption has the effect of carrying an agreement which *prima facie* breaches Article 81(1) outside the sanction of nullity contained in Article 81(2). The granting of individual exemptions had hitherto been the province of the Commission alone under Regulation 17, on the basis of notifications of agreements made by undertakings. Alternatively, the only other way an undertaking could gain exemption was to bring its agreement within one of the 'block' or 'group' exemptions granted by the Commission on the basis of authority conferred by a series of Council Regulations. Since 1 May 2004, agreements which fall within the scope of Article 81(1), but which fulfil the conditions for exemption laid down in Article 81(3), are valid and fully enforceable without need for the prior decision of a competition authority. In other words, direct effect now applies also to Article 81(3), and it is likely that in the future national courts will be called upon to adjudicate upon the applicability of the conditions set out in Article 81(3) to specific agreements.

The original arrangements for the control of anti-competitive conduct under the EC Treaty did not extend to cover the field of merger control. Consequently, specialised secondary legislation was adopted by the Council in 1989, to set up a procedure for mergers between separate undertakings which have a 'Community dimension' (essentially a test of size and cross-national effects) to be notified to the Commission before they take effect, so that the Commission can exercise a process of review and, if necessary, prohibit such mergers if they are not 'compatible with the common market' (Council Regulation 4064/89, OJ 1990 L257/13). This regulation was replaced in 2004, with Council Regulation 139/2004 (OJ 2004 L24/1), which applies similar principles to the control of mergers, but introduces additional flexibility in relation to the scrutiny of mergers and the rules applied to their control. Merger control is discussed in 10.9 below.

A number of further EC Treaty provisions deal with other aspects of anti-competitive behaviour. Article 86(1) EC extends the competition rules to 'public undertakings and undertakings to which Member States grant special and exclusive rights', although Article 86(2) EC provides that:

> '[u]ndertakings entrusted with the operation of services of general economic interest or having the character of a revenue-producing monopoly shall be subject to the rules contained in this Treaty, in particular to the rules on competition, insofar as the application of such rules does not obstruct the performance, in law or in fact, of the particular tasks assigned to them.'

Finally, Article 86(3) EC gives the Commission the role to ensure the application of Article 86 EC. It should be noted that these provisions have developed not only into a general proposition that the public undertakings should normally be subject to ordinary market disciplines under the competition rules, but also as a more general tool for a policy of market liberalisation, for example in sectors of the economy previously dominated by single monopoly suppliers, such as the public utilities. Telecommunications is one field where the Commission has been most active in relation to market liberalisation. This dimension of competition policy is discussed briefly in 10.8.

The EU competition rules present something of a 'chicken-and-egg' problem in relation to their presentation. What should come first? A presentation of the key elements which make up a breach of the principles and obligations contained in the EC Treaty and in the Merger Regulation, along with an indication of the views on competition policy which have emerged from the key actors, notably the Commission and the EU courts; or a presentation of the systems which provide for the enforcement of these provisions? The choice is made here to set out first the objectives of EU competition policy, and subsequently to elaborate upon the substantive elements of the principles and obligations contained in Articles 81, 82 and 86 EC and the Merger Control Regulation, before presenting the systems of enforcement. However, it is important to note that these elements must be read as a whole to gain a full understanding of how EU competition law and policy actually work in practice. Wherever possible, the presentation will highlight how the substantive policy principles and the systems of enforcement are linked together.

## 10.3 Objectives of EU Competition Policy

The Annual Reports produced by the European Commission on competition policy are perhaps the best source of 'insider' views about what constitute the objectives of EU competition policy. In more recent years, these objectives tend to be put in the widest terms. Thus, in the 2002 Report (SEC(2003) 467 final, p.11), the Commission stated:

> 'The virtues of effective competition on the market in delivering efficient allocation of resources and fostering innovation and technical development are widely recognised throughout the world. However, ensuring or creating the conditions which allow markets to function competitively constitutes an ongoing challenge both as regards the behaviour of actors on these markets and in view of the obstacles created by State measures. Competition policy then serves a twofold aim: addressing market failures resulting from anti-competitive behaviour by market participants and from certain market structures, on the one hand, and contributing to an overall economic policy framework across economic sectors that is conducive to effective competition, on the other.'

The 1999 Final Report (SEC(2000) 720) linked the objectives of EU competition policy more directly to the single market, as well as to competitive markets more generally:

> 'The first objective of competition policy is the maintenance of competitive markets. Competition policy serves as an instrument to encourage industrial efficiency, the optimal allocation of resources, technical progress and the flexibility to adjust to a changing environment . . .
>
> The second is the single market objective. An internal market is an essential condition for the development of an efficient and competitive industry. As the Community has progressively broken down government-erected trade barriers between Member States, companies operating in what they had regarded as 'their' national markets were, and are for the first time, exposed to competitors able to compete on a level playing field. There are two possible reactions to this: either to seek to compete on merit, looking to expand into other territories and benefit from the opportunities offered by a single market, or to erect private barriers to trade – to retrench and act defensively – in the hope of preventing market penetration . . .'

The 1996 Report (COM(97) 628 final) also linked the objectives of competition policy explicitly to other objectives of EU policy-making:

> '1. The aim of competition policy, through its impact on the basic structures of the European economy, is to ensure that markets acquire or maintain the flexibility they need to allow scope for initiative and innovation and to allow an effective and dynamic allocation of society's resources. This structural action means that competition policy interacts with most other broadly based policies such as the development of the internal market, the policy on growth and competitiveness, the policy on cohesion, research and development policy, environmental policy and consumer protection.
>
> 2. Competition policy is thus both a Commission policy in its own right and an integral part of a large number of European Union policies and with them seeks to achieve the Community objectives set out in Article 2 of the Treaty, including the promotion of harmonious and balanced development of economic activities, sustainable and non-inflationary growth which respects the environment, a high level of employment and of social protection, the raising of the standard of living and quality of life, and economic and social cohesion.'

To put it another way, in almost every Annual Report some reference is made to the aims and objectives of competition policy, but in slightly differing terms which stress issues such as allocative efficiency, the single market and – although this issue is not specifically covered in this chapter – the global economy. The extent to which ancillary policies such as those highlighted in the 1996 Report are given a specific mention tends to vary according to the specific 'mix' of political objectives which is dominant at any given time within the Commission. This is affected by political variables such as the identity and ideological approach of the Competition Commissioner and the political make-up of the Commission and the European Parliament.

In sum, competition policy in the EU, although sharing many elements with competition policies which operate at national level, is an enterprise with a number of special features. A quotation drawn from the Europa website which sets out the basics of EU competition policy nicely illustrates how the various strands are woven together:

> 'Competition policy is essential for the completion of the internal market. The *raison d'être* of the internal market is to allow firms to compete on a level playing field in all the Member States, and competition policy sets out to encourage economic efficiency by creating a climate favourable to innovation and technical progress. In a market economy, competition promotes economic success, safeguarding the interests of European consumers and ensuring that European undertakings, goods and services are competitive on the world market.
>
> European competition policy makes it possible to ensure that healthy competition is not hindered by anticompetitive practices on the part of companies or national authorities (restrictive agreements and concerted practices). It attempts to prevent one or more undertakings from improperly exploiting their economic power over weaker companies (abuse of a dominant position). It also seeks to prevent the Member States' governments from distorting competition (state aid)' (**http://europa.eu/scadplus/leg/en/lvb/l26055.htm**)

## 10.4 Common Elements in the Application of the Competition Rules

There are a number of common elements which apply regardless of whether the alleged breach of the competition rules pertains to Article 81 or Article 82 EC. The first is the requirement, under Article 2 of Regulation 1/2003, that any person alleging a breach of Article 81(1) or 82 EC bears the burden of proving that a breach has occurred. Second, the alleged breach must have been committed by one or more undertakings or, in the case of Article 81 EC, an association of undertakings.

An 'undertaking' is an entity engaged in commercial activities. In Case C-41/90 *Höfner and Elser* v. *Macrotron GmbH* ([1991] ECR I-1979), the Court held that 'in the context of competition law . . . the concept of an undertaking encompasses every entity engaged in an economic activity, regardless of the legal status of the entity' (para. 21). This means that a number of public bodies engaged in the provision of commercial activities, such as employment agencies and public service broadcasting organisations, have been held to be undertakings within the meaning of either Article 81 or 82. Particular difficulties have been encountered in relation to entities involved in the health care sector, and the Court has generally made a distinction between bodies operating in competition with commercial entities in relation to the provision of health care services, and those engaged in functions of a purely social nature. However, there is considerable controversy surrounding the extent of application of the competition rules and the issue has been highly politicised in recent years as governments increasingly use market mechanisms to encourage efficiency improvements in public health care systems (Slot, 2003). Further issues regarding the applicability of the competition rules to public undertakings and in highly regulated markets are covered in 10.8. On the other hand, a body performing public functions will not be caught by Article 81 or 82, as was the case with Eurocontrol, which is an international organisation established by international convention entrusted with tasks in relation to the safety of air navigation services, in particular air traffic control in the Benelux and northern Germany (Case C-364/92 *SAT Fluggesellschaft mbH* v. *European Organization for the Safety of Air Navigation (Eurocontrol)* [1994] ECR I-43).

Groups of companies are regarded as a single undertaking, as usually are holding companies and subsidiaries, and principal and agent, if and insofar as the commercial risk falls only upon the principal. In Case C-73/95P *Viho Europe BV* v. *Commission* ([1996] ECR I-5457), the Court found that the arrangements between Parker Pen and its distributors, which were also its subsidiaries, which prohibited the distributors from selling outside their prescribed territories was an intra-group arrangement not caught by Article 81(1) EC. The Court held that 'Parker and its subsidiaries . . . form a single economic unit within which the subsidiaries do not enjoy real autonomy in determining their course of action in the market . . .' (para. 16).

The third requirement is jurisdiction, in the territorial sense. It is not a requirement that an undertaking be based in the EU for the EU competition rules to apply. In the *Woodpulp* cases (Joined Cases 89, 104, 114, 116, 117 and 125–129/85 *A. Ahlström Osakeyhtiö* v. *Commission (Woodpulp)* [1988] ECR I-5193), the Court held that a cartel between non-EU-based undertakings which had been *implemented* within the EU fell under the jurisdiction of the EU in respect of the enforcement of the competition rules. It remains unclear whether a cartel which is formed and implemented outside the EU, but which has effects within the EU, could be caught by Article 81 EC.

Finally, there must be an effect on interstate trade. This is a concept which has been substantially clarified by the practice of both the Commission and the EU courts. Most recently, especially in the context of the reform of the enforcement systems which gives a substantially greater role to the national authorities and national courts, the Commission has issued some Guidelines on the concept (Commission Notice, Guidelines on the effect on trade concept contained in Articles 81 and 82 of the Treaty, OJ 2004 C101/81). Although without prejudice to the case law of the EU courts and not 'binding' as such, these Guidelines are now the most important starting point. Essentially the 'interstate trade' criterion asks whether the agreement is capable of affecting the creation of the single European market, and operates as a jurisdictional criterion determining when EU law bites, as opposed to national competition law (para. 12 of the Guidelines; Joined Cases 56 and 58/64 *Établissements Consten and Grundig* [1966] ECR 429). In addition, the criterion contains a quantitative element, which in essence concerns whether or not there is a sufficiently 'appreciable' effect on trade between Member States:

'The effect on trade criterion confines the scope of application of Articles 81 and 82 to agreements and practices which are capable of having a minimum level of cross-border effects within the Community' (para. 13 of the Guidelines).

The test of 'appreciable effects' was introduced by the Court of Justice. In Case 5/69 *Völk* v. *Vervaecke* ([1969] ECR 295), it held that:

'an agreement falls outside the prohibition in Article [81 EC] when it has only an insignificant effect on the markets, taking into account the weak position which the persons concerned have on the market of the product in question' (p.302).

Thus, much depends upon the market position of the parties in question (para. 45 of the Guidelines).

The EU courts essentially apply two tests to the interstate trade criterion:

▶ the pattern of trade test (most often applied in the context of Article 81); and
▶ the structure of competition test (most often applied in the context of Article 82).

The pattern of trade test was articulated in Case 56/65 *Société Technique Minière* v. *Maschinenbau Ulm GmbH* ([1966] ECR 235):

> '[I]t must be possible to foresee with a sufficient degree of probability on the basis of a set of objective factors of law or of fact that the agreement in question may have an influence, direct or indirect, actual or potential, on the pattern of trade between Member States' (p.249).

Because the reference to 'pattern of trade' is neutral, the interstate trade criterion may apply in fact even where trade is *increased*, as well as where it is restricted or reduced. It is sufficient that the pattern of trade will develop *differently* than how it would otherwise have developed in the absence of the agreement or practice under scrutiny (para. 34 of the Guidelines). Perhaps one of the most common ways in which vertical agreements, such as distribution agreements, affect trade between Member States is by partitioning the internal market, creating segmented national or regional markets. It will be obvious, thereafter, that even agreements with an apparently exclusively domestic remit, applicable to one Member State only, will in fact affect trade between Member States if they foreclose access by suppliers in other Member States to the domestic market.

The structure of competition test focuses in particular on cases where a competitor is liable to leave the market as a result of the anti-competitive conduct. Hence, it is most applicable in cases under Article 82 EC where it is the abuse of a dominant position which must affect trade between Member States (Joined Cases 6 and 7/73 *Istituto Chemioterapico Italiano SpA and Commercial Solvents Corp.* v. *Commission* [1974] ECR 223). In that case, it may not be necessary to look at the pattern of trade in goods and services (see also para. 94 of the Guidelines).

### 10.5  Article 81(1) EC: Anti-Competitive Agreements and Collusive Conduct

In addition to the common elements outlined above, there are two specific elements to proving a beach of Article 81(1) EC:

- the alleged breach must comprise an *agreement* or *concerted practice*, or a *decision* of an association of undertakings; and
- this agreement/concerted practice/decision must *restrict competition* in an *appreciable* way.

For the purposes of Article 81 EC, 'agreements' may be horizontal or vertical in nature. The Court of Justice made this clear in Joined Cases 56 and 58/64 *Établissements Consten SARL and Grundig-Verkaufs GmbH* v. *Commission* ([1966] ECR 299), when it ruled that Article 81:

> 'refers in a general way to all agreements which distort competition within the common market and does not lay down any distinction between those agreements based on whether they are made between competitors operating at the same level in the economic process or between non-competing persons operating at different levels' (p.339).

In addition, agreements may be legally binding or mere arrangements or understandings of reciprocal action. Form is immaterial. For example, a 'gentleman's agreement' (Case 41/69 *ACF Chemiefarma NV* v. *Commission (Quinine Cartel)* [1970] ECR 661) has been treated as an 'agreement' by the Court of Justice. Where there are highly complex arrangements lasting over many years and involving a substantial number of parties, the Commission does not have to show that any individual undertaking participated in all elements of the agreement, but rather treat the conduct – such as a cartel – as a single agreement (see the cases arising out of the *Polypropylene* cartel, for example Case T-1/89 *Rhône Poulenc SA* v. *Commission* [1991] ECR II-867). These principles are particularly important for the Commission, as the pursuit of so-called 'hard core' cartels is a central element of its overall competition policy at the present time.

Particular difficulties arise in distinguishing between 'concerted practices' and the conscious parallelism involved in so-called oligopolies (see also the later discussion of 'collective dominance' in the context of Article 82 EC). The key definition was given by the Court of Justice in the *Dyestuffs Industry* case. It covers:

> 'a form of coordination between undertakings which, without having reached the stage where an agreement properly so-called has been concluded, knowingly substitutes practical cooperation between them for the risks of competition' (Case 48/69 *Imperial Chemical Industries Ltd* v. *Commission* [1972] ECR 619, para. 64).

It is worth noting that in French, the term *'accord'* is used in the context of competition law to cover agreements *and* concerted practices, and draws attention to the fact that there is not necessarily a clear distinction between the two.

Article 81 EC also covers 'unilateral' conduct within a contractual context, such as the application by a supplier of its standard conditions of sale (Case C-277/87 *Sandoz Prodotti Farmaceutici SpA* v. *Commission* [1990] ECR I-45). In principle, a supplier operating a selective distributive system will be in conformity with Article 81(1) EC whenever the supplier ostensibly selects distributors on the basis of objective qualitative criteria. However, the failure to objectively apply such a selective distributive system, and to discriminate among distributors on the basis of non-objective criteria, falls within the scope of the agreement concept (Case 107/82 *AEG Telefunken AG* v. *Commission* [1983] ECR 3151). On the other hand, there has to be some 'concurrence of wills' between at least two parties for there to be an agreement, so where there was no evidence of anything other than unilateral conduct on the part of a supplier seeking, for example, to impose an export ban, Article 81 will not apply (Joined Cases C-2 and 3/01P *Bundesverband des Arzneimittel-Importeure eV and Commission* v. *Bayer AG* [2004] ECR I-23].

Article 81(1) prohibits agreements which have as their *object or effect* the *restriction or distortion* of competition within the common market. It is particularly difficult to define a 'restriction' of competition in any general sense. The Commission and the EU courts have consistently adopted a broad approach to the interpretation of this concept, thus bringing many agreements within the scope of Article 81(1). This is in stark contrast to competition law of the US. Under the Sherman Antitrust Act of 1890, a so-called rule of reason requires that in each individual case a balancing of the pro- and anti-competition effects of an agreement must be undertaken. The broad approach adopted in the EU has, in turn, placed a substantial burden on the Commission over the years, since until very recently all agreements falling within Article 81(1) had to be notified to the Commission under Regulation 17, especially if the parties wished to seek an exemption under Article 81(3). This point is considered in more detail below in 10.10, in the context of the evolution and modernisation of the enforcement of the competition rules under Regulation 1/2003.

The concept of 'object' must first be applied. According to the Court of Justice in

*Établissements Consten and Grundig,* 'there is no need to take account of the concrete effects of an agreement once it appears that it has as its object the prevention, restriction or distortion of competition' (p.342). A further gloss upon this distinction comes from the Court of First Instance judgment in the *European Night Services* case (Joined Cases T-374, 375, 384 and 388/94 *European Night Services Ltd et al* v. *Commission* [1998] ECR II-3141), where it held:

> 'it must be borne in mind that in assessing an agreement under Article [81(1)] of the Treaty, account should be taken of the actual conditions in which it functions, in particular the economic context in which the undertakings operate, the products or services covered by the agreement and the actual structure of the market concerned . . . unless it is an agreement containing obvious restrictions of competition such as price-fixing, market-sharing or the control of outlets . . . In the latter case, such restrictions may be weighed against their claimed pro-competitive effects only in the context of Article [81(3)] of the Treaty, with a view to granting an exemption from the prohibition in Article [81(1)]' (para. 136).

In effect, 'object' and 'obvious' are elided into a single category of agreements which contain provisions which are regarded as particularly dangerous under Article 81(1), and which are treated as *per se* unlawful. A not dissimilar approach comes across in the Commission's Notice on agreements of minor importance which do not appreciably restrict competition under Article 81(1) or the *de minimis* Notice (OJ 2001 C368/07). This mirrors the 'appreciability' test applicable in the context of the interstate trade criterion, except that in the Notice the Commission attempts to place some figures on the market shares below which there will not be an *appreciable* restriction of competition. However, these principles do not apply where certain 'hardcore' restrictions can be found in the agreement in question, such as price-fixing arrangements.

The 'effect' criterion requires extensive market analysis. This is most obvious and most advanced in the context of vertical agreements. The beer supply agreement at issue in the *Delimitis* case provides a particularly good example (Case C-234/89 *Delimitis* v. *Henninger Bräu AG* [1991] ECR I-935). A beer supply agreement normally involves the granting of certain economic and financial benefits to the retailer, such as the letting of premises, in return for a commitment to sell the suppliers' beer and other drinks products in the premises in question. The Court held that:

> 'it is necessary to analyse the effects of a beer supply agreement, taken together with other contracts of the same type, on the opportunities of national competitors or those from other Member States, to gain access to the market for beer consumption or to increase their market share and, accordingly, the effects on the range of products offered to consumers' (para. 15).

The judgment went on to provide not only guidance on determining the relevant market within which such economic analysis must take place (see the Commission Notice on the definition of the relevant market for the purposes of Community competition law: OJ 1997 C372), but also detailed reflections upon the types of opportunities for access to the market which might arise for competitors such as acquisition of a brewery, or the opening of new public houses. This suggests a substantial challenge for any competition authority or court called upon to apply such a test.

Even so, as commentators sometimes note, there has been remarkably little analysis of the concept of 'restriction of competition' in the context of weighing the effects of an allegedly anti-competitive agreement. However, the Court of First Instance has recently made clear that this does *not* involve weighing the pro- and anti-competitive effects of an agreement in order to reach a conclusion under Article 81(1). Pro-competitive effects can only be assessed under Article 85(3) (Case T-328/03 *O2 (Germany)* v. *Commission* [2006] ECR II-1231).

In relation to horizontal agreements between competitors, there have been few difficulties for the Commission or the EU courts when they have been faced with clear cartels between competitors, restricting the effects of the competition. A more problematic type of policy decision involves the treatment of cooperation agreements, such as research and development agreements and various types of joint ventures, especially in the hi-tech fields. Case C-250/92 *Gøttrup-Klim Grovvareforeninger* v. *Dansk Landbrugs Grovvereselskab AmbA* ([1994] ECR I-5641) concerned a requirement imposed by cooperative purchasing associations that members should not participate in other organisations in competition. The requirement was found not to infringe Article 81(1). The Court of Justice held:

> 'The compatibility of the statutes of such an association with the Community rules on competition cannot be assessed in the abstract. It will depend on the particular clauses in the statutes and the economic conditions prevailing on the markets concerned' (para. 31).

In some cases, the Court of Justice has concluded that certain provisions in an agreement are permissible because they are only 'ancillary restraints', for example contained in an agreement for the sale of a business, or because they are 'inherent' in the pursuit of certain objectives. For example, in Case C-309/99 *Wouters* v. *Algemene Raad van de Nederlandse Orde van Advocaten* ([2002] ECR I-1577), the Court had to adjudicate upon the possible anti-competitive effects of a rule of the Dutch Bar Council prohibiting lawyers from entering partnerships with non-lawyers. In the context of this decision of an association of undertakings, the Court felt it necessary to look at the role of the Bar Council in setting rules relating to matters such as professional ethics and qualifications, in the interests of consumers and in the public interest. If some of these rules have 'consequential effects restrictive of competition', are these 'inherent in the pursuit of those objectives' (para. 97)?

An agreement which is found to be in breach of Article 81(1) is null and void *ab initio* under Article 81(2). However, the Court has held that if the nullity only affects certain offending clauses, then, in principle, if those clauses can be severed effectively from the rest of the agreement, the rest of the agreement need not be rendered inapplicable (see Case 56/65 *Société Technique Minière* v. *Maschinenbau Ulm GmbH* [1966] ECR 235). Pursuant to the sanction of nullity and the wording of the provisions of the EC Treaty, the Court of Justice has held that Articles 81(1) and (2) have direct effect in the sense that they can be applied directly by national courts in cases brought seeking the application of the competition rules (Case 127/73 *Belgische Radio en Televisie* v. *SABAM* [1974] ECR 51). This is confirmed by Article 1(1) of Regulation 1/2003.

### 10.6  The Application of Article 81(3): Individual and Block Exemptions

In its recent Notice providing Guidelines on the application of Article 81(3) (OJ 2004 C101/97), the Commission cogently explains the philosophy of Article 81(3) and its interrelationship with Article 81(1):

> 'The aim of the Community competition rules is to protect competition on the market as a means of enhancing consumer welfare and of ensuring an efficient allocation of resources. Agreements that restrict competition may at the same time have pro-competitive effects by way of efficiency gains. Efficiencies may create additional value by lowering the cost of producing an output, improving the quality of the product or creating a new product. When the pro-competitive effects

of an agreement outweigh its anti-competitive effects the agreement is on balance pro-competitive and compatible with the objectives of the Community competition rules. The net effect of such agreement is to promote the very essence of the competitive process, namely to win customers by offering better products or better prices than those offered by rivals. This analytical framework is reflected in Article 81(1) and Article 81(3). The latter provision expressly acknowledges that restrictive agreement may generate objective economic benefits so as to outweigh the negative effects of the restriction of competition' (para. 33).

In sum, under the conditions laid down in Article 81(3), an agreement may enjoy exemption under Article 81(3) if it provides a benefit for the Community as a whole, of which a 'fair share' is enjoyed by consumers, and it satisfies two negative conditions. It must contain no 'indispensable restrictions' and it must not lead to a 'substantial elimination of competition'. The latter condition in particular requires a detailed market analysis, and among the most important factors to take into account are the nature of the agreement and the market position of the parties.

The system relating to the application of exemptions has undergone a complete overhaul as a result of the reforms introduced by Regulation 1/2003 and the replacement of Regulation 17. Previously, the Commission had a monopoly over the granting of exemptions. In the case of *individual* exemptions, this meant that undertakings were required to notify their agreements to the Commission under Regulation 17, and the Commission would investigate the applicability of Article 81(1) and then the case for applying Article 81(3), and the positive and negative conditions which it contains relating to the pro-competitive effects of the agreement. Article 81(3) did not apply automatically, and could not be applied by national courts. The Commission enjoyed discretion in relation to its application of Article 81(3), and the Court of Justice was generally reluctant to interfere with the Commission's exercise of its discretion. However, as the Commission was generally heavily burdened with work under Regulation 1/2003, undertakings which notified their agreements often had to wait many years for a definitive decision from the Commission, or had to make do with an informal settlement termed a 'comfort letter', which had no binding legal effect.

Under Article 1(2) of Regulation 1/2003, a new legal situation is created in respect of Article 81(3). It provides:

'Agreements, decisions and concerted practices caught by Article 81(1) of the Treaty which satisfy the conditions of Article 81(3) of the Treaty shall not be prohibited, no prior decision to that effect being required.'

Furthermore, Articles 4–6 confirm that the Commission, the competition authorities of the Member States and national courts all have the power to apply Article 81 in full. Consequently, all can apply Article 81(3), and the concept of an exemption 'decision' applying to a specific agreement no longer exists, except that the Commission may – of its own initiative – make a finding of inapplicability of the competition rules, either because it finds that Article 81(1) does not apply, or because it finds that the conditions of Article 81(3) are satisfied (Article 10 of Regulation 1/2003). It is not expected that the Commission will make substantial use of this possibility. Since the national authorities and national courts are expected to apply Article 81(3), the Commission has issued the Guidelines referred to above. As with the Notice on the interstate trade criterion, these Guidelines are advisory only, giving the Commission's interpretation of the conditions for exemption. The Guidelines insist on the importance of a non-mechanical and case-by-case application of the principles which it contains (para. 6).

*Block* or *group* exemptions have existed since the late 1960s, as a means of overcoming the backlog of cases before the Commission in certain areas where there were many similar agreements requiring exemption, such as exclusive distribution and purchasing agreements. In other words, block exemptions were precisely a result of the notification system introduced by Regulation 17. Block exemptions apply to categories of agreements which can be defined by reference to objective criteria (e.g. specialisation agreements, research and development agreements). Block exemptions operate on the basis of Commission Regulations which are themselves based on empowering legislation adopted by the Council. The legal framework for a block exemption is an EU regulation. Such a measure applies directly within the laws of the Member States, and consequently an agreement which falls within the legal framework established by the regulation will benefit automatically from the exemption, and the regulation can be interpreted and applied by national courts. The system of block exemptions has survived the legal revolution of Regulation 1/2003, but it has been reformed over the years to make it a more effective system.

Block exemptions are based on a presumption that agreements conforming to that pattern actually fulfil the four conditions contained in Article 81(3). The Commission is empowered to withdraw the benefit of a block exemption if an agreement has effects which are incompatible with Article 81(3) (Article 29 of Regulation 1/2003). Until recently, a block exemption regulation would typically provide 'white' lists of permissible clauses and 'black' lists of prohibited ones. Sometimes, they also contained lists of 'grey' clauses which required further Commission scrutiny. However, in the most recent block exemptions issued by the Commission, there are no longer any white lists as these are thought to be too restrictive for the undertakings. They tend to stultify creativity. The shift has been away from legal formalism and towards economic analysis.

The most important block exemptions are Commission Regulation 2790/99 on vertical agreements (OJ 1999 L336/21), Commission Regulation 1400/02 on distribution agreements for motor cars (OJ 2002 L203/30), Commission Regulation 2658/2000 on specialisation agreements (OJ 2000 L304/3) and Commission Regulation 2659/2000 on research and development agreements (OJ 2000 L304/7). The block exemption on vertical agreements has been in large measure influenced by the Commission's progressive review of its policy on vertical restraints, which included a Green Paper in 1996 (COM(1996) 721) and a Communication in 1998 (COM (1998) 544).

## 10.7 Article 82 EC: The Abuse of a Dominant Position

Article 82 EC is concerned with the unilateral conduct of so-called 'dominant' firms which commit 'abuses'. In addition to the elements outlined in 10.4, 'dominance' and 'abuse' are key elements in the finding of a breach of Article 82. First it is necessary to consider whether one or more undertakings has or have a dominant position. This must be assessed by reference to the definition of the relevant product, geographical and temporal markets, and then by reference to power on that market as so defined. Second, since it is not dominance as such which is objectionable, the question of abuse must be considered separately from the question of dominance.

Article 82 contains no equivalent to the Article 81(2) sanction of nullity, but it can be applied in national courts (Case 127/73 *Belgische Radio en Televisie* v. *SABAM*; Article 1(3) of Regulation 1/2003). Furthermore, it contains no equivalent to the Article 81(3) exemption provision. Unlike Article 81, which has been applied by the Commission in many hundreds, if not thousands, of decisions since the 1960s, Article 82 has been applied by the Commission only in just over 50 decisions since 1971, the date of its first decision. On the other hand, the Court has tackled the market behaviour of some quite substantial enterprises in its case law, such as, for example, IBM, Coca-Cola and, most recently, the US software giant Microsoft (Case COMP/C-3/37.792, Decision of 24 March 2004; COM (2004) 900; Case T-201/04 *Microsoft* v. *Commission*, pending before the Court of First Instance).

In principle, the application of Article 82 should draw heavily upon economics. In particular, it should be the competitive structure of the market which should be at the core of any enforcement process, rather than the fate of (smaller) competitors as such. However, over the years the Commission in particular has faced a good deal of criticism from commentators and practitioners regarding its approach to the application of the prohibition in Article 82, by being too harsh on larger firms which are largely operating within the confines of market forces which demand that they behave efficiently. It seems inimical to the very idea of competition policy if Article 82 can lead to penalties being imposed upon firms simply because they are more efficient (see in particular Whish, 2003: 175–6).

The first step in the process of assessing dominance involves the determination of the relevant market. Here the Commission's Notice on the definition of the relevant market for the purposes of Community competition law (OJ 1997 C372/5) can be helpful, especially in relation to the relevant product and geographical markets:

'A relevant product market comprises all those products and/or services which are regarded as interchangeable or substitutable by the consumer, by reason of the products' characteristics, their prices and their intended use'.

It is useful to consider this by reference to some examples. Case 27/76 *United Brands Company and United Brands Continentaal BV* v. *Commission* ([1978] ECR 207) raised the question whether bananas constitute a separate market, as compared to 'fruit' as a whole, or even 'soft fruit'. The Court stated that:

'For the banana to be regarded as forming a market sufficiently differentiated from other fruit markets it must be possible for it to be singled out by such special features distinguishing it from other fruits that it is only to a limited extent interchangeable with them and is only exposed to their competition in a way that is hardly perceptible' (para. 22).

The Court concluded that the banana constituted a sufficiently distinct market of its own, highlighting that:

'The banana has certain characteristics, appearance, taste, softness, seedlessness, easy handling, a constant level of production which enable it to satisfy the constant needs of an important section of the population consisting of the very young, the old and the sick' (para. 31).

When looking at the substitutability or interchangeability of products, it is essential to look at both whether a producer could easily move into a market to provide a product by a simple and relatively cheap adaptation of their production (Case 6/72 *Europemballage Corporation and Continental Can Co. Inc.* v. *Commission* [1973] ECR 215), as well as whether a customer can adapt its production to use different raw materials to do without a particular product (Joined Cases 6 and 7/73 *Istituto Chemioterapico Italiano SpA and Commercial Solvents Corp.* v. *Commission*).

The test for substitutability, which is emphasised in the Commission's Notice on the definition of the market, is the so-called SSNIP test. This asks whether 'a small (5 to 10 per cent) but significant and non-transitory increase in the price' of one product (A) will cause purchasers to purchase sufficient quantities of another product (B) instead. If it does, then the test indicates that A and B form part of the same product market.

According to the Commission Notice:

'The relevant geographic market comprises the area in which the undertakings concerned are involved in the supply and demand of products or services, in which the conditions of competition are sufficiently homogeneous and which can be distinguished from neighbouring areas because the conditions of competition are appreciably different in those areas.'

This element is combined with the requirement that the dominance be in a 'substantial part of the common market'. In Joined Cases 40–48, 50, 54–56, 111, 113 and 114/73 *Coöperatieve Vereniging 'Suiker Unie' UA* v. *Commission* ([1975] ECR 1663), the Court held:

'For the purpose of determining whether a specific territory is large enough to amount to "a substantial part of the common market" within the meaning of Article [82] of the Treaty the pattern and volume of the production and consumption of the said product as well as the habits and economic opportunities of vendors and purchasers must be considered' (para. 371).

In practice, most Article 82 cases concern a market of at least one Member State, thus quasi-automatically satisfying the 'substantial part of the common market' requirement.

Within the market, once defined, dominance must be assessed. According to the Court in *United Brands*, dominance is:

'[a] position of economic strength enjoyed by an undertaking which enables it to hinder the maintenance of effective competition on the relevant market by allowing it to behave to an appreciable extent independently of its competitors and customers and ultimately of consumers' (para. 65).

In assessing market power, the following factors are most relevant:

- market share;
- statutory monopoly and legal regulation;
- financial and technical resources;
- vertical integration and scale;
- the existence and use of intellectual and industrial property rights; and
- economies of scale.

Market share matters in both an absolute and a relative sense. That is, it matters not only what the market share of the allegedly dominant undertaking is, but also what is/are the market share(s) of any competitor(s). Certainly market shares in excess of 75 per cent will almost always be found to provide evidence of a dominant position (Case 85/76 *Hoffmann-La Roche & Co. AG* v. *Commission* [1979] ECR 461). In Case C-62/86 *AKZO Chemie BV* v. *Commission* ([1991] ECR I-3359), a market share in excess of 50 per cent creates a first presumption of dominance.

As to the other factors, in most cases a finding of dominance will involve a variety of these factors in combination, operating to secure the 'overall independence of behaviour' of the dominant firm (Decision of the Commission in *Continental Can* [1972] JO L7/25, para. 3).

Article 82 refers to 'one or more' undertakings holding a dominant position. From this has grown the concept of 'collective dominance', which offers one of the means whereby the EU competition authorities have sought to control oligopolies. Oligopolistic markets are ones where there are a small number of leading firms, all of which know each others' identities and main characteristics. There is a danger in oligopolistic markets either that the parties may engage in a cartel to maximise profits at the expense of the consumer by controlling prices and removing competition – i.e. through collusive conduct, which is caught by Article 81 – or that other forms of conscious or semi-conscious parallel behaviour may occur. The petrol retail market is a good example, where one supplier's raising of prices is often followed by other suppliers raising their prices. In some circumstances, within oligopolistic markets, the Commission has relied on a concept of collective dominance of the market by several undertakings to find an infringement of Article 82. For example, in Joined Cases T-68, 77 and 78/89 *Società Italiano Vetro SpA et al* v. *Commission (Italian Flat Glass)* ([1992] ECR II-1403), the Court of First Instance determined that the key to collective dominance is 'economic links' (para. 42). These 'economic links' enable the undertakings to 'act independently of their competitors, their customers and their consumers' (Joined Cases C-395 and 396/96P *Compagnie Maritime Belge Transports SA et al* v. *Commission* [2000] ECR I-1365). In other words, the normal concept of dominance is applied, but it is applied to several undertakings. These undertakings may be linked by an agreement, or other legal structures, but these are not decisive. In *Compagnie Maritime Belge Transports*, the applicants were members of a liner conference linking a group of shipowners that had a dominant position on certain shipping routes in Africa. The Court ruled that:

> 'the existence of an agreement or of other links in law is not indispensable to a finding of a collective dominant position; such a finding may be based on other connecting factors and would depend on an economic assessment and, in particular, on an assessment of the structure of the market in question' (para. 45).

Although the concept of abuse is separate from the concept of dominance, the Court has referred to the 'special responsibility' of dominant firms in relation to their conduct on the market. In Case 322/81 *Nederlandsche Banden-Industrie Michelin NV* v. *Commission* ([1983] ECR 3461) the Court held that:

> 'A finding that an undertaking has a dominant position is not in itself a recrimination but simply means that, irrespective of the reasons for which it has such a dominant position, the undertaking concerned has a special responsibility not to allow its conduct to impair genuine undistorted competition on the common market' (para. 57).

Some assistance can be derived from the non-exhaustive list of abuses in Article 82 itself, which refers to matters such as unfair prices, the limiting of production, discrimination and the tying of the conclusion of contracts to supplementary obligations. These are helpful examples of the type of conduct which might be abusive, but do not go to the root of what constitutes an abuse. In Case 85/76 *Hoffmann-La Roche and Co. AG* v. *Commission* ([1979] ECR 461), the Court held:

> 'The concept of abuse is an objective concept relating to the behaviour of an undertaking in a dominant position which is such as to influence the structure of a market where, as a result of the very presence of the undertaking in question, the degree of competition is weakened and which, through recourse to methods different from those which condition normal competition in products and services on the basis of the transactions of commercial operators, has the effect of hindering the maintenance of the degree of competition still existing in the market or the growth of that competition' (para. 91).

Thus, the intention of the undertaking is irrelevant. Furthermore, the undertaking need not be dominant in the market in which it commits the abuse (Case C-333/94P *Tetra Pak*

*International SA* v. *Commission* [1996] ECR I-5951). A broad distinction is drawn between *exploitative* and *anti-competitive* abuses, although in practice the same abuse can constitute both exploitation and anti-competitive behaviour. A good example of this would be discriminatory pricing.

Some typical forms of abuse include excessively high selling prices (Case 26/75 *General Motors Continental NV* v. *Commission* [1975] ECR 1367), predatory pricing (*AKZO Chemie*), discriminatory pricing (*United Brands*), tying (*Tetra Pak*), the abuse of exclusive rights of supply, such as through discounts (*Hoffmann-La Roche*) and refusal to supply (*Istituto Chemioterapico Italiano SpA and Commercial Solvents*). One of the most complex issues arising in relation to the question of abuse has been the determination of whether or not it constitutes an abuse of a dominant position to deny access to so-called 'essential facilities'. This emerged strongly in the *Magill* case (Joined Cases C-241/91 and 242/91P *Radio Telefis Eireann* (*RTE*) *and Independent Television Productions Ltd* (*ITP*) v. *Commission* [1995] ECR I-743) which concerned a television programming guide publisher's access to information about television and radio programmes, and the use of intellectual property rights to protect this information. The Court held that:

> 'the exercise of an exclusive right by the proprietor may, in exceptional circumstances, involve abusive conduct. In the present case, the conduct objected to is the appellants' reliance on copyright conferred by national legislation so as to prevent Magill – or any other undertaking having the same intention – from publishing on a weekly basis information (channel, day, time and title of programmes) together with commentaries and pictures obtained independently of the appellants' (paras. 50–51).

In Case C-7/97 *Oscar Bronner GmbH and Co. KG* v. *Mediaprint Zeitungs- und Zeitschriftenverlag GmbH & Co. KG* ([1998] ECR I-7791), the issue concerned access to a daily newspaper distribution system, without which it was in practice very difficult to gain access to the Austrian newspaper market on a high volume basis. The Court responded cautiously to this contention, by stressing that refusing access, against reasonable remuneration, could only be an abuse if the refusal would be likely to eliminate all competition in the market. In reality, there are other ways of selling newspapers and magazines.

As one element of what is expected to be a long-term and thorough review of its practice under Article 82, the Commission in 2005 issued a discussion paper on the application of Article 82 to exclusionary abuses, by which it means measures taken by dominant firms which are likely to have a foreclosure effect on the market. As Vickers (2005: F244) notes, the treatment of anti-competitive behaviour by firms with market power is:

> 'perhaps the most controversial current issue for competition policy. Lax policy would jeopardise the competitiveness of markets, but rigid policy would chill pro-competitive, pro-consumer conduct.'

## 10.8 Competition Rules, Member States, Public Undertakings and Regulated Markets

Competition rules do not only apply to private undertakings. They do apply, however, in a variety of respects to the conduct of the Member States, to public undertakings, and to undertakings operating within highly regulated markets.

The Court of Justice has read Articles 3(1)(g), 10, 81 and 82 EC in combination in order to hold that Member States have an obligation to abstain from conduct – including the maintaining in force of legislation – which distorts competition. Article 10 EC concerns the duty of Member States in general to abstain from conduct which impairs the achievement of the objectives of the Treaty. It is often termed the 'duty of loyalty' of the Member States. In Case 267/86 *Van Eyke* v. *NV ASPA* ([1988] ECR 4769) the Court held that a Member State would be in breach of Article 10 EC, read in conjunction with Article 81 EC, if it were:

> 'to require or favour the adoption of agreements, decisions or concerted practices contrary to Article [81] or to reinforce their effects, or to deprive its own legislation of its official character by delegating to private traders responsibility for taking decisions affecting the economic sphere' (para. 16).

In more recent cases, the Court has re-emphasised this point by reference to the requirement in the EC Treaty, since the coming into force of the Treaty of Maastricht, that Member States must observe the principle of an open market economy with free competition (Articles 4(1) and 98 EC; see Case C-198/01 *Consorzio Industrie Fiammiferi (CIF)* v. *Autorità Garante della Concorrenza e del Mercato (Italian Matches)* [2003] ECR I-8055). Equally, undertakings may escape penalties in respect of conduct effectively 'forced' by national legislation, both at the hands of the Commission (Joined Cases C-359 and 379/95P *Commission and France* v. *Ladbroke Racing Ltd* [1997] ECR I-6265), and at the hands of the national authorities, including the national competition authorities (*Italian Matches*).

It is clear, pursuant to Article 86 EC, that public undertakings and 'undertakings to which Member States grant special and exclusive rights' are in principle subject to the competition rules, and subject to protection under Article 86(2) EC in respect of the performance, in law or in fact, of the particular tasks assigned to them. In practice, the so-called regulated markets, such as the utilities sectors of post and telecommunications, energy and transport, especially where there are public service obligations imposed by national legislation, have received a very substantial amount of attention under the competition rules. The application of the actual Treaty competition rules has been an important catalyst towards the development of sector-wide liberalisation legislation, in addition to maintaining the principle in Article 16 EC of protecting public service obligations under the heading of 'services of general economic interest'. Article 86(3) entrusts the Commission with primary responsibility for ensuring observance of Article 86, although a substantial amount of liberalising legislation has also been adopted under the legislative procedures involving the Council and the Parliament.

Closely associated with these principles are the procedures laid down in Articles 87–89 EC allowing the Commission to deal with state aid that could distort competition in the common market. Much state aid given to enterprises by Member States is incompatible with the common market, and the Commission has been given the role of policing this prohibition. According to Hansen *et al* (2004: 182):

> 'European Court practice defines state aid in the sense of Article 87(1) EC as: (i) a measure that confers a benefit or advantage, (ii) which is granted by or under instruction of the state and involves state resources, (iii) which favours certain undertakings (often referred to as "selectivity" or "specificity"), (iv) which distorts or threatens to distort competition, and (v) which affects trade between the Member States. Aid must be notified to the Commission before it is granted (the "stand-still" obligation) and the Commission has exclusive competence to find compatibility of aid measures. The Commission applies Articles 87 and 88 through a variety of guidelines, framework programmes, and "block exemptions".'

For example, exemptions are given for certain types of aid, such as aid having a social character granted to individual consumers, and aid to small- and medium-sized enterprises. In 2006, the Commission issued a block exemption regulation covering state aid falling below a threshold beyond which it is not deemed to meet all the criteria under Article 87(1) EC (Council Regulation 1998/2006, OJ 2006 L379/1).

## 10.9  The EU Merger Control System

The final element of the legal framework for competition policy concerns the control of mergers. The original Merger Control Regulation of 1989 is no longer in force, and has been replaced by Council Regulation 139/2004 (OJ 2004 L24/1) as of 1 May 2004. However, in large measure the new Merger Control Regulation (MCR) still preserves the system applied and developed under the 1989 Regulation; consequently, the case law of the Commission and the EU courts will continue to be relevant. The most significant change has been to the actual substantive test which is used to determine the compatibility of a merger, i.e. a concentration – the term used in EU legislation – with the common market.

The concept of merger or 'concentration' covers a wide range of corporate transactions, involving not only the classic situation when two corporate entities merge into one, but also situations in which one company takes control of another, for example through the purchase of shares. Article 3 of the MCR defines a concentration as a 'change of control on a lasting basis', and identifies 'merger' and 'acquisition' as the two means whereby control can be taken. It also includes under the concept of 'acquisition' the creation of a joint venture 'performing on a lasting basis all the functions of an autonomous economic entity' (Article 3(4) MCR). This is a so-called 'full-function' joint venture. Mergers are often not only big business but also big news. Merger with another undertaking is one obvious way in which a business can grow and acquire market share. Merger activity ebbs and flows, but it is significant that in an increasingly global economy, merger activity itself is becoming increasingly transnational and indeed complex. This in turn has placed considerable challenges before public authorities in many states (inside and outside the EU) and within the EU itself to design effective systems of merger control. Although the original EC Treaty competition rules did not provide for merger control, the EU courts as well as the national courts have applied Articles 81 and 82 EC in some measure to merger activity. In Case 6/72 *Europemballage Corporation and Continental Can Co. Inc.* v. *Commission*, the Court of Justice held that strengthening a dominant position through a merger may breach Article 82 EC. In the *Philip Morris* case (Joined Cases 142 and 156/84 *British American Tobacco Co. Ltd and R.J. Reynolds Inc.* v. *Commission* [1987] ECR 4487), the Court subsequently held that Article 81 EC may apply to agreements involving the purchase of shares which bring about structural changes in the market.

The Court's rulings in these cases suggested the possibility of chaotic and disorganised application of the competition rules to merger activity, either by the Commission under its ordinary procedures, or by national courts at the behest of aggrieved applicants complaining of breaches of Article 81 or 82. Moreover, in the late 1980s, following the Single European Act, the European Communities moved into a new stage of development with the December 1992 deadline for the establishment of the single market programme. The adoption of a procedurally effective merger control system became subsumed into that programme of legislative activities, and previous obstacles to agreement in the Council of Ministers disappeared by 1989, with the adoption of a measure which came into force in 1990. At the same time, the Directorate-General IV (now known as DG Comp) established the Merger Control Task Force which is responsible for receiving notifications and conducting the necessary scrutiny of all merger and acquisition activity. This is particularly important because of the need to ensure confidentiality in matters of corporate mergers and acquisitions and because of the potential risks such activity presents to investors in volatile stock markets. In addition to the granting of new resources to the Commission to carry out these tasks, the Merger Control Task Force simply absorbed some of the already scarce resources applied to other areas of DG Comp activity, such as Articles 81 and 82 EC, state aid control and the liberalisation of highly regulated sectors.

The MCR does not simply create a set of tests against which the pro- or anti-competitive effects of mergers can be appraised. It is also a complex set of procedural arrangements creating what amounts to a 'one-stop-shop' giving the Commission competence to appraise all mergers with a 'Community dimension', and to adopt an array of decisions ranging from unconditional and conditional approval to prohibition. The notion of Community dimension is defined in Article 1 of the MCR in quantitative terms, specifically:

- where the combined aggregate worldwide turnover of all the undertakings concerned is more than €5 billion; and
- where the aggregate turnover in the EU of each of at least two of the undertakings concerned is more than €250 million;

unless each of the undertakings concerned generates more than two-thirds of its aggregate EU-wide turnover within a single Member State. Although there are a number of additional alternative ways in which the threshold amounts can be reached, the fact is that the MCR concerns only mergers of a substantial European and indeed global scale in financial terms, which also have a sufficiently transnational element. Of course, even though a merger may lack a Community dimension, it may still need to be notified to one or more national merger control authorities for clearance under their (inevitably differing) interpretations, so Article 4(5) MCR puts in place arrangements for mergers notified at national level within three or more Member States to be referred to the Commission for a single determination. Companies can trigger the referral process. There can also be referral back to the Member States where a merger 'significantly affects, or threatens to affect significantly, effective competition on a specific market within a Member State' (Article 9(2)(a) MCR). Ultimately, experience has shown that it is qualitative rather than quantitative criteria which really determine whether the correct forum for the appraisal of a merger is the national level or the EU level. Consequently reforms of the arrangements have focused on increasing the flexibility within the system of referral rather than tinkering with the turnover thresholds.

The substantive test for compatibility with the common market under the 1989 version of the MCR reads as follows:

'A concentration which creates or strengthens a dominant position as a result of which effective competition would be significantly impeded in the common market or in a substantial part of it shall be declared incompatible with the common market' (Article 2(3) MCR).

In the 2004 MCR, this wording has been reversed, with the emphasis on effective competition rather than the creation or strengthening of a dominant position:

'A concentration which would significantly impede effective competition, in the common market or in a substantial part of it, in particular as a result of the creation or strengthening of a dominant position, shall be declared incompatible with the common market' (Article 2(3) MCR).

A change to the original test was canvassed by the Commission in a pre-reform Green Paper (COM(2001) 745), which suggested the adoption of what is termed the 'substantial lessening of competition' test which is widely applied in the US, Canada, Australia and the UK, as the basis for the appraisal of mergers. The substantial lessening of competition test appears to have been broadly adopted by the Commission although it is worded a little differently (Vickers, 2004). It focuses on the significant impediment to effective competition, with the creation or strengthening of dominance as the primary incidence of this. The reform declined to clarify the concept of dominance, which was the original proposal of the Commission, but which might have the unfortunate consequence of creating a different concept of dominance within the MCR from that applicable under Article 82 EC.

Even prior to merger, firms may approach the Commission for approval of a planned transaction. This is intended to give greater flexibility to firms and to make the system work more effectively and in the interests of markets. Upon notification, the Commission must conduct a first phase, 'light touch' investigation, within twenty-five working days, which may be extended by ten days. It has to decide, of course, whether the merger falls within the scope of the MCR, and then it must decide whether to initiate a more detailed investigation. If it does not, then it will take a decision under Article 8(1) MCR and declare the merger to be compatible with the common market. The merger can then go ahead. If the Commission proceeds with a more in-depth investigation however, it will initiate proceedings under Article 6(1)(c) MCR which must be concluded within ninety working days, although this period can be extended in some circumstances by up to thirty days. This procedure affords the Commission a range of conclusions that it can reach. It can still find a merger compatible with the common market, perhaps after taking into account behavioural or structural commitments from the parties (Article 8(2) MCR), or it can declare the merger to be incompatible with the common market (Article 8(3) MCR). The Commission also has the power to require the dissolution of a merger which has been implemented without approval regardless of the Commission's prohibition. Moreover, the Commission may impose substantial fines, both for procedural offences such as supplying incorrect information, and substantive offences such as implementing a merger without notification (Article 14 MCR). Only a small minority of proposed mergers proceed to the full investigation. If they do, the Commission must observe a number of procedural proprieties under the MCR, including the hearing of the parties to the merger and other interested parties.

Merger control decisions are subject to the powers of judicial review of the EU courts, initially the Court of First Instance and then, on appeal, the Court of Justice. Indeed, during 2002, the Court of First Instance was particularly busy with cases brought by companies which objected to the Commission blocking their mergers. In some cases, the Commission was taken to task by the Court of First Instance because there were serious economic errors in its analysis. However, the cases also demonstrated that the Commission was pushing the 1989 MCR to its limits, and testing out some of the more uncertain concepts within the legislative framework. The reaction of the Court of First Instance to the work of the Commission in the field of merger control contributed in no small way to the process of revision and review of the MCR, with the attempts to invest greater flexibility into the system and to learn from past experience. In one case, in particular, *Tetra Laval*, the world's leading manufacturer of carton packaging, brought an appeal against the Commission's decision prohibiting its merger with a French company, Sidel, manufacturers and distributors of packaging equipment and PET plastic bottles. Among the Commission's difficulties with the case was the centrality of the dominance test within the tools at its disposal to appraise the proposed merger (Case T-5/02 *Tetra Laval* v. *Commission* [2002] ECR II-4381). Consequently, it is hoped that the new test will avoid some of these difficulties in the future.

To complement the new MCR, the Commission has issued a notice on best practice in dealing with merger notifications, as well as guidelines on horizontal mergers between competitors (OJ 2004 C31/5). In the latter area, there is increasing evidence of the globalisation of at least some areas of competition law and policy. Among the results of an enhanced level of cooperation between the Commission and other competition authorities such as the US, Canada and Japan, have been attempts to ensure a more consistent standard of scrutiny for large global-scale mergers.

### 10.10  The Evolution of the System of Competition Law Enforcement

Articles 81 and 82 EC (as they are now numbered) were the only provisions of the original EEC Treaty aimed directly at the conduct of individuals or firms, as opposed to the conduct of the Member States. However, the EEC Treaty did not provide for enforcement mechanisms, although it already gave primary responsibility to both the authorities in the Member States (Article 88 EEC – now Article 84 EC) and the Commission (Article 89 EEC – now Article 85 EC). However, Regulation 17, adopted in 1962, filled many of the gaps by establishing in more detail the Commission's powers of investigation and enforcement in relation to Articles 81 and 82. In many respects, the role of the national authorities was usurped, especially after the judgment of the Court of Justice in Case 14/68 *Walt Wilhelm* v. *Bundeskartellamt* ([1969] ECR 1), in which it was held that the application of national law should:

> 'not prejudice the uniform application throughout the common market of the Community rules on cartels and of the full effect of the measures adopted in implementation of those rules' (para. 4).

The story on the application of competition law by *national* competition authorities is picked up again in 10.12. In relation to Article 81 EC and the competition law of the European Union, Regulation 17 created the system of notification of agreements, which is important not only for those undertakings wishing to seek formal clarification that their agreements fell outside the scope of Article 81 (negative clearance), but especially for those seeking exemption for their agreements under Article 81(3) EC. Not only has Regulation 17 and the notification system given the Commission a monopoly over the application of Article 81(3), but it has resulted also in a huge burden of work, resulting from the immediate and continuing notification of many thousands of agreements. In practice, therefore, it left little space to national authorities for the application of EU competition law.

While it is hard to sum up in a few lines the more than forty years of experience with the application of the competition rules which have elapsed since the adoption of Regulation 17, it is nonetheless clear that a number of crucial developments should be given centre stage in any review.

First, Regulation 17 has provided an enforcement system against a blank canvas of procedural rules, rather than against the background of codes of criminal, civil and administrative procedure, including the rights of the defence, such as would exist at the national level. Thus, many of the most important aspects of the procedures for investigating alleged infringements, fact finding, dealing with complainants, protecting the interests of those under investigation, and developing a system of judicial review have evolved incrementally. This has occurred in part through the case law of the EU courts, but also through the adoption and formalisation of new practices and procedures on the part of the Commission. This has included measures on hearings of parties to competition investigations, on the role of the Hearing Officer, a function established to try to ensure effective and fair hearings, and on the forms available for notifications and complaints. It has also included non-binding notices and guidelines on cooperation between the Commission and national courts/national competition authorities, on processing requests for access to files in competition cases, and on the reduction of fines in cartel cases in response to requests for leniency.

Second, within that overall trend of incremental development, it is clear that one of the dominant themes has been a burgeoning framework of principles and rules on the interaction between competition and human rights/civil liberties, notably rights of the defence. Two primary reasons for this can be discerned. The first is that the trend has been fuelled in no small way by the litigiousness of those who have faced the threat or reality of fines or other infringement actions under the competition rules, and who have unsurprisingly turned to the legal process in order to protect their interests. However, the need to develop the interaction has arisen above all because the Commission has probably been given too many roles in the context of EU competition law enforcement and policy development. It is responsible for much general policy evolution. In addition, however, it is also responsible for the investigation of alleged infringements, *and* it has also been given the power of decision to establish infringements and to punish delinquent enterprises. In most competition law systems, these roles are either split (e.g. in the US where the Federal Trade Commission or the Department of Justice prosecute before a Federal court) or, if they are held jointly, they are at least held by specialised executive agencies which are independent of political control (such as the *Bundeskartellamt* in Germany) (Wils, 2004).

This combination of functions was exacerbated by the slender body of rules laid down in the first instance for the Commission's conduct of investigations. For example, Regulation 17 provided for investigations, including powers on the part of the Commission to request information and to conduct investigations, but it did not lay down the countervailing rights of the defence which would normally protect individuals subject to investigation against the potentially oppressive power of the state (or in this case the EU). The base line for these questions is now the *Stenuit* decision of the European Human Rights Commission in relation to French competition law (*Société Stenuit* v. *France* (1992) 14 EHRR 509). Competition proceedings fall within the scope of Article 6 European Convention on Human Rights (ECHR) since they can lead to the imposition of a fine. Consequently, those subject to such proceedings must be accorded fair and public hearing within a reasonable time by an independent and impartial tribunal. Against this background a substantial case law has developed.

The third theme has been the pressure for what is often termed 'modernisation and decentralisation' in the context of EU competition law enforcement, which in reality combines a number of elements:

- The urgent need for a response to the long-term excessive burden placed on the Commission by the notification system under Regulation 17, and its monopoly on the granting of exemptions.
- The recognition that from the date of enlargement in May 2004 onwards, this was only going to become worse.
- The consequential impact of the role of the Commission upon the roles of national courts and national competition authorities in enforcement:
  - *in relation to the national courts*   although individual complainants have frequently been a useful source of information for the Commission about allegedly delinquent conduct under the competition rules, in reality most complainants have preferred to limit their self-help to a less-costly complaint to the Commission, eschewing potentially much more expensive actions in the national courts; in addition, because of the limitations placed by the monopoly of the Commission over Article 85(1) EC, national courts have been very limited hitherto in the ways in which they can deal with EU competition law;
  - *in relation to national competition authorities*   again they have been constrained by their inability to apply Article 85(3) EC, and furthermore, by the lack of a *culture* of decentralised enforcement.
- The opportunity cost of the current arrangements, in the sense that the Commission has spent too little time pursuing what are perceived to be the core problems of competition policy and competition law enforcement (e.g. cartels, certain types of vertical arrangements which continue to segment the market), and too much time on reacting to notifications and complaints, and dealing with issues which could be effectively delegated to the national authorities or dealt with by national courts, which could then make references to the Court of Justice under Articles 234 EC.
- Overall, moreover, the Commission has had less time than would have been desirable to assimilate the lessons of competition law policy in an emerging and enlarging EU political and economic space, notably the need to bring more and better economic analysis into its decision-making.
- Finally, after forty years of experience, many of those affected by competition law (i.e. undertakings and their advisors) should be moving increasingly towards a self-reliant approach to compliance based on self-assessment and benchmarking, rather than feeling that their reactions to competition law and policy are excessively steered and guided by a formalistic system.

Regulation 1/2003, combined with a range of notices and guidelines issued by the Commission to help make what amounts to a new system work in practice, is the final response to these considerations which emerged out of a dialogue between the Commission, national actors and policy-makers, commentators and those involved in competition law practice (see, for example, Commission White Paper on modernisation of the rules implementing Articles [81] and [82] of the EC Treaty, OJ 1999 C132/1; Ehlermann, 2000). Substantial hopes are invested in the new system (Venit, 2003; Müller, 2004), which may be dashed if, for example, national competition authorities prove unreliable, inconsistent or unwilling to adapt in their work on EU competition law enforcement. This may continue to throw the burden back onto the Commission. There may also be no substantial growth in the private enforcement in national courts, not least because national courts find themselves overwhelmed by the challenge of applying

Articles 81 and 82 EC, and the economic analysis that increasingly comes with them, and so do not offer an attractive forum for the resolution of disputes for individual complainants or applicants (Gilliams, 2003). The Commission has tried and failed in the past to encourage more 'action' at the national level, and to set in place the mechanisms of cooperation. Perhaps Regulation 1/2003 will prove a conclusive break with the past. Whether this will happen is not completely clear. It is worth quoting a practitioner's comment on these matters in detail:

> 'At the end of the day, the Commission's "more efficient and consistent enforcement" prophecy will depend on a triple leap of faith, namely (a) that increased enforcement that the Commission has promised with respect to serious infringements will in fact materialise, (b) that competition authorities, even in delicate cases involving "their" companies, will agree to work in the Community's interest and according to the Commission's directives, and (c) that courts and competition authorities will in fact develop a sufficient degree of expertise and deal with matters in a reasonable period of time so as to close the gap that will be left by the Commission' (Gilliams, 2003: 473).

It is worth adding that the effectiveness of the system of enforcement may also depend upon the way in which practitioners themselves respond to the challenge of a more decentralised system, and whether they encourage undertakings increasingly to incorporate pre-emptive compliance with the competition rules into their corporate strategies.

Finally, the new enforcement system leaves Article 82 EC substantially unchanged, and some have argued that it too cries out for modernisation and reform (Furse, 2004).

## 10.11 The Enforcement of the Competition Rules by the Commission

Even taking into account the abolition of the notification system in Regulation 1/2003, it remains the case that the Commission is, and will continue to be, central to the enforcement of the competition rules. Not the least reason for this will be its overwhelming expertise and experience in the field, and also the fact that it still has far more resources than any other body to ensure effective enforcement.

A Commission investigation into an alleged breach of Articles 81 and 82 may be triggered by a number of events, such as a complaint from a consumer, a tip-off (e.g. by an employee), a press report, information from the national authorities, information derived from an investigation into another matter, formal investigations into specific sectors of the economy (albeit not very common) and Commission enquiries, either formal or informal, into troublesome sectors, such as the chemical or building industries.

If a complaint is made to the Commission, it is obliged to fulfil certain basic obligations to that complainant in relation to investigating the basis of the complaint. However, the Commission is not obliged either to proceed with a formal investigation leading to a finding of infringement, or indeed to take a detailed look into the issues raised by the complaint. It may suggest instead that matters should be taken either to the national authorities, or should be raised in an action before the national courts. This is not because the complaint does not necessarily raise issues of EU law, but simply because it is legitimate for the Commission to prioritise in its allocation of limited resources. The Court of Justice has held, on a number of occasions, that:

> 'The Commission, entrusted by Article 89(1) of the EC Treaty (now, after amendment, Article 85(1) EC) with the task of ensuring application of the principles laid down in Articles 85 and 86 of the Treaty, is responsible for defining and implementing the orientation of Community competition

policy. It is for the Commission to adopt, subject to review by the Court of First Instance and the Court of Justice, individual decisions in accordance with the procedural rules in force and to adopt exemption regulations. In order effectively to perform that task, which necessarily entails complex economic assessments, it is entitled to give differing degrees of priority to the complaints brought before it' (Case C-344/98 *Masterfoods Ltd* v. *HB Ice Cream Ltd* [2000] ECR I-11369, para. 46).

Complaints are now regulated by Commission Regulation 773/2004 (OJ 2004 L123/18) on the conduct of proceedings by the Commission under Articles 81 and 82. Complainants must show a legitimate interest if they wish to make a complaint (Article 5 of Regulation 773/2004). Thereafter, they have certain rights to participate in the proceedings (Article 6), including the right to be heard before the Commission rejects the complaint (Article 7), and certain rights of access to information (Article 9). It is good grounds for the Commission to reject a complaint under Article 13 of Regulation 1/2003 if the matter is being dealt with by a national competition authority. In no small measure, these complex rules on complaints have been brought about as a consequence of a body of case law examining in detail the position of the complainant within competition investigations and the availability of judicial remedies to protect their interests (for example, Case T-64/89 *Automec* v. *Commission (Automec I)* [1990] ECR II-367; Case T-24/90 *Automec* v. *Commission (Automec II)* [1994] ECR II-2223; and Case T-28/90 *Asia Motor France SA* v. *Commission (Asia Motor I)* [1992] ECR II-2285). An extended statement of the Commission's policy can be found in its 2004 notice on the handling of complaints (OJ 2004 C101/65).

If the Commission decides to initiate an investigation into an alleged infringement under Regulation 1/2003, it has a number of powers enabling it to find the necessary evidence in order to establish the facts. These largely replicate, but in some respects enhance, those available under Regulation 17. Consequently, much of the old case law in which the Commission's powers have been constrained within certain bounds, and hedged around by rights of the defence, remains applicable.

Article 18 of Regulation 1/2003 affords the Commission the power to request information, either as a 'simple request' (Article 18(2)), or by means of a decision requiring information (Article 18(3)). Such a decision, like all the decisions taken in the course of an investigation, is itself reviewable by the EU courts. However, the Court of Justice has held that undertakings have an active duty of cooperation with the Commission, although not the obligation to answer leading questions (Case 374/87 *Orkem* v. *Commission* [1989] ECR 3283). Article 19 gives the Commission the new power to take statements in order to collect evidence, but only with the consent of the interviewee. Article 20 gives the Commission powers of inspection. These have been extended to the home and other private premises of the directors and others responsible for an undertaking (Article 21), and the Commission has also been given powers to seal premises, in order to avoid the running of the dreaded shredding machines. Where there is resistance to an inspection, Article 20 has tightened up the arrangements for conducting investigations, in particular in conjunction with the relevant national competition authorities and with judicial authorisation or warrant (Articles 20(7) and (8)). The latter provision sets out the role of the national judicial authority, and represents a codification of the Court of Justice's judgment in *Roquette Frères* (Case C-94/00 *Roquette Frères* v. *Directeur générale de la concurrence, de la consommation et de la repression des frauds* [2002] ECR I-9011). The national court's role is to ensure the authenticity of the request, not to review the circumstances leading the Commission to seek an on-the-spot investigation. Regulation 1/2003 has also increased the level of fines and penalty payments that the Commission may impose under Articles 24(1)(d) and (e) on those who obstruct investigations or supply incorrect information. This is to increase the deterrent effect of the penalty system.

After the fact-finding phase comes an inquisitorial phase, in the sense that the Commission will issue a statement of objections, which must set out in full its case as to the existence of an alleged infringement. The statement of objections is:

> 'a procedural and preparatory document, intended solely for the undertakings against which the procedure is initiated with a view to enabling them to exercise effectively their right to a fair hearing' (Case 60/81 *International Business Machines* v. *Commission* [1981] ECR 2639).

The statement of objections is not a reviewable act and so it cannot be challenged before the Court of Justice. If new facts emerge, a new or supplementary statement of objections may be needed. Thereafter the firm under investigation is given a right of written reply, and an oral hearing will be held before the Hearing Officer (see Chapter V of Commission Regulation 773/2004). The hearing will also include other participants, such as complainants. Commission Decision 94/810 (OJ 1994 L330/67), on the terms of reference of Hearing Officers in competition procedures, will continue to deal with these matters in detail.

There are numerous rights of the defence issues relating to the use and protection of information under the competition rules. These are regulated by Chapter VI of Regulation 773/2004, read in conjunction with earlier Court of Justice case law. It is long established that legal professional privilege governs communications between firms under investigation and their lawyers (but not in-house lawyers) in relation to competition proceedings (Case 155/79 *A.M. & S. Europe Ltd* v. *Commission* [1982] ECR 1575). This principle has recently been applied in interim proceedings before the Court of First Instance, in which the President of the Court of First Instance affirmed once more that the rights of the defence, of which professional privilege is a part, is a fundamental right (Joined Cases T-125 and 253/03R *Akzo Nobel Chemicals Ltd and Akcros Chemicals Ltd* v. *Commission* [2003] ECR II-4771, para. 186). There is no right to withhold documents in the context of investigations just because they constitute business secrets, but of greater significance is the question of what the Commission then does with this information. Article 15 of Regulation 773/2004 now regulates access to the file. This is granted to those to whom a statement of objections has been issued, but access does not extend to business secrets, other confidential information, internal documents of the Commission and the national competition authorities, and correspondence between the Commission and the national competition authorities.

As regards confidentiality and business secrets, the general principles for the EU are laid down in Article 287 EC which provides that:

> 'The members of the institutions of the Community, the members of committees and the officials and other servants of the Community shall be required, even after their duties have ceased, not to disclose information of the kind covered by the obligation of professional secrecy, in particular information about undertakings, their business relations or their cost components.'

Article 28(1) of Regulation 1/2003 specifies that subject to the rules governing the exchange of information (Article 12) and cooperation with national courts (Article 15): 'information collected pursuant to Articles 17 to 22 [i.e. in the course of investigations] shall be used only for the purpose for which it was acquired.' Article 28(2) lays down the general obligation of professional secrecy. Further details are laid down in Article 16 of Regulation 773/2004 regarding the Commission's responsibilities to protect confidential information and business secrets, including a procedure under which undertakings can argue for the protection and non-disclosure of their information.

Chapter III of Regulation 1/2003 establishes the range of decisions which the Commission may take at the conclusion of (or during the course of) an investigation. These include the finding of an infringement and the requirement that it be terminated (Article 7), and in that context the Commission may take commitments from the undertakings concerned (Article 9). In cases of urgency the Commission may adopt interim measures (Article 8). The Commission can make a finding of inapplicability 'where the Community public interest . . . so requires', in relation to both Articles 81 and 82 EC (Article 10). This is the closest equivalent to the old 'negative clearance' issued after notification. The Commission can – and does – impose substantial fines and periodic penalty payments (Articles 23 and 24) in respect of infringements, especially in relation to an intentional or negligent infringement of Article 81 or 82 EC. These can be up to 10 per cent of the total turnover of the undertaking in question during the previous business year. The most substantial fines imposed totalled €855.22 million imposed on eight companies implicated in a cartel in the vitamins market which involved market-sharing and price-fixing. In the Commission's Decision, Hoffmann-La Roche and BASF were subject to particular criticism for their roles and given individual fines of €462 million and €296.16 million respectively. The largest single fine (€497 million) was that imposed on Microsoft in May 2004, in respect of its software bundling and interoperability practices which the Commission found to have been contrary to Article 82 EC, after a lengthy process which will continue for many years in the form of various appeals before the EU courts. In total, during Mario Monti's tenure as Competition Commissioner (1999 – 2004), fines totalling €1.4 billion were imposed on undertakings. However, both the size of the fines imposed and the vigour with which the Commission has been pursuing cartels have been increased, as during one year alone (2006) of Commissioner Neelie Kroes' tenure, fines totalling €1.8 billion were imposed on undertakings.

The Commission has issued Guidelines (most recently in 2006: OJ 2006 C210/2) on the imposition of fines, indicating the factors which weigh heavily in assessing the gravity of the offence. Issues such as duration and the type of infringement (minor, serious or very serious) are taken into account. In relation to the treatment of cartels, which the Commission is particularly anxious to eradicate from the single market, special rules apply. The validity of an earlier 1998 version of these Guidelines, in the light of the European Convention on Human Rights, including their retrospective application, was upheld by the Court of Justice in Joined Cases C-189, 202, 205–208 and 213/02P *Dansk Rørindustri A/S et al* v. *Commission (District Heating Pipes)* ([2005] ECR I-5425). Since 1996, the Commission has had a leniency programme, offering inducements, in particular immunity from fines, to undertakings prepared to provide information about activities such as price-fixing, production or sales quotas, market-sharing, and the restriction of imports and exports (OJ 1996 C207/4). Most recently, it issued a Notice, updated in 2006, on immunity from fines and reduction of fines in cartel cases (OJ 2006 C298/11).

The EU courts play a substantial role in reviewing decisions of the Commission under the competition rules. They are responsible for the scrutiny of policies regarding Articles 81 and 82 EC, for ensuring fairness and observance of rights of the defence in matters of procedure, for protecting the interests of third parties and for protecting the EU public interest. Under Article 229 EC, the EU courts have unlimited jurisdiction which gives them complete power to review fines. Actions are most often brought by aggrieved parties under Article 230 EC for annulment of a decision, but from time to time Article 232 EC, which provides for action against a failure to act on the part of the Commission is invoked, particularly by complainants. Where appropriate the Court can issue interim measures.

## 10.12 The Competition Rules before National Courts and the National Competition Authorities

The role of the national courts and the national competition authorities in relation to the enforcement of the EU competition rules raises specifically the decentralisation dimension of the recent reform programme.

As a matter of general EU law, Articles 81 and 82 have long been held to be enforceable in national courts. This is confirmed by Article 6 of Regulation 1/2003. Thus, they can be invoked either as a 'sword', for example to seek a remedy against an undertaking alleged to be abusing a dominant position, or as a 'shield', for example to resist the enforcement of a contractual obligation on the grounds that the provision in question is null and void under Article 81(2) EC. Furthermore, as the Court of Justice held in Case C-453/99 *Courage Ltd* v. *Crehan* ([2001] ECR I-6297, para. 24), the fact that a person is a party to a contract which infringes Article 81 does not mean that he or she cannot claim damages for loss caused as a result of that infringement. However, so long as there is no harmonisation under EU law, it is national law which will lay down the detailed procedural rules governing such actions, insofar as these respect the principles of equivalence (no less favourable than those governing similar domestic actions) and effectiveness (must not be such as to render practically impossible or excessively difficult the exercise of rights conferred by Community law; e.g. *Courage* v. *Crehan*, para. 29). In referring to a remedy in damages, the Court settled a longstanding uncertainty as to the extent to which EU law imposed on national courts the duty to provide for specific remedies for breach of the EU competition rules. It held:

'The full effectiveness of Article [81] of the Treaty and, in particular, the practical effect of the prohibition laid down in Article [81(1)] would be put at risk if it were not open to any individual to claim damages for loss caused to him by a contract or by conduct liable to restrict or distort competition. Indeed, the existence of such a right strengthens the working of the Community competition rules and discourages agreements or practices, which are frequently covert, which are liable to restrict or distort competition. From that point of view, actions for damages before the national courts can make a significant contribution to the maintenance of effective competition in the Community' (*Courage* v. *Crehan*, paras. 26–27).

The Court reiterated this point in Case C-295/04 *Manfredi* ([2006] ECR I-6619) and added that 'any individual can claim compensation for the harm suffered where there is a causal relationship between that harm and an agreement or practice prohibited under Article 81 EC' (para. 61).

In fact, an action in the national courts is the only way through which aggrieved parties can obtain compensation for any harm they have suffered, since there is no possibility under the procedures operated by the Commission (10.11) for compensation to be paid to a complainant. The provisions of general EU law are now buttressed by Article 1 of Regulation 1/2003 which declares that Articles 81(1), 81(3) and 82 EC operate automatically, 'no prior decision . . . being required'. This means, for example, that if a national court is faced with an agreement which falls within the scope of Article 81(1), but which satisfies the conditions in Article 81(3), it can make a declaration to that effect, since it is simply confirming what constitutes an underlying legal 'fact'. Previously, it would have had to stay proceedings in such a case, and wait for the Commission – if the case were before the Commission – to take a decision on an exemption. This increases the level of legal certainty for individual undertakings, especially those who conclude agreements in the belief that they have brought themselves within the safe haven of Article 81(3).

Overall, although both Regulation 1/2003 and the case law of the EU courts should have eased the road ahead for the private enforcement of the EU competition rules in the national courts, it is not clear that there will be either a substantial increase in reliance on private enforcement, or that all of the major obstacles such as standing, evidentiary questions and causation have been overcome (Woods *et al*, 2004). The Commission has sought to confront these concerns more directly by issuing, in 2005, a Green Paper identifying the main obstacles to a more efficient system for bringing damages claims (or bringing them to effective fruition), such as access to evidence, the existence of national defence arguments that companies claiming damages may have simply passed on any price increases to their own customers and the quantification of damages (COM(2005) 372). The Green Paper forms the basis for a consultation exercise, seeking views on various options to address these problems, options which might in the long term involve legislative action at the EU level (Diemer, 2006). However, the practical obstacles to this occurring are substantial. Moreover, the fear in some quarters is that the more litigious environment surrounding US antitrust law may result from giving too many incentives to private parties to engage in private litigation.

Regulation 1/2003 also deals with the issues of supremacy and pre-emption insofar as they affect the role of the Commission. Article 3(1) Regulation 1/2003 requires national authorities and national courts which apply national competition law to agreements and similar instruments that are covered by Articles 81(1) and 82 EC, to apply the provisions of the EC Treaty:

> 'The application of national competition law may not lead to the prohibition of agreements, decisions by associations of undertakings or concerted practices which may affect trade between Member States but which do not restrict competition within the meaning of Article 81(1) of the Treaty, or which fulfil the conditions of Article 81(3) of the Treaty or which are covered by a Regulation for the application of Article 81(3) of the Treaty' (Article 3(1) Regulation 1/2003).

Member States are not precluded from adopting and applying within their territories stricter national laws which prohibit or sanction unilateral conduct engaged in by undertakings, or from applying national merger laws (subject to the MCR, of course), or relevant provisions of national law that 'predominantly pursue an objective different from that pursued by Articles 81 and 82' (Article 3(3)). For the avoidance of doubt, in order to effect the desired decentralisation of powers to national competition authorities, Article 5 explicitly states that the competition authorities of the Member States have the power to apply Articles 81 and 82 EC in individual cases. They can require an infringement to be brought to an end, order interim measures, accept commitments, impose fines, etc. provided for in national law.

Central to the hoped-for success of the decentralisation scheme is the system of cooperation between the Member States and the Commission (see Chapter IV of Regulation 1/2003). In the first instance, there shall be cooperation within a Network of Competition Authorities. On this matter, the Commission has issued a Notice (OJ 2004 C101/43), which provides for the sharing of work among public bodies responsible for enforcing competition law, the exchange of information, the allocation of jurisdiction and the provision of information specifically on pending cases. To give more institutional effect to the cooperation arrangements, the Commission has created the European Competition Network.

While it is termed cooperation, it amounts to an 'iron fist in a velvet glove' as far as the national courts and competition authorities are concerned, since in the interest of the uniform application of EU competition law, Article 16 requires that national courts and competition authorities, when ruling on alleged infringements which are already the subject of a decision by the Commission, cannot take a decision running counter to the decision taken by the Commission. Furthermore, national courts must also avoid giving decisions which would conflict with a decision contemplated by the Commission, a weighty obligation on any public authority. However, the national court can always make a preliminary reference under Article 234 EC to the Court of Justice. The Commission has also issued a notice on cooperation between national courts and the Commission (OJ 2004 C101/54).

Another mechanism whereby the Commission will seek to reduce the risk of aberrant interpretations of Articles 81 and 82 EC, especially in relation to novel questions, is through the issuing of guidance letters at the request of individual undertakings. Again, it has issued a notice on this matter (OJ 2004 C101/78). Guidance letters are not Commission decisions, and do not bind national courts or competition authorities, but it is open for those bodies to take account of guidance letters as they see fit in the context of any cases before them. In practice, one suspects that the national courts and competition authorities will be strongly encouraged to take notice of such guidance.

## Summary

1. Competition law and policy are central to the EU's activities in the field of economic integration, and the competition rules complement the rules establishing the internal market and the free movement of goods, services, persons and capital. In practice, EU competition policy has not always been consistently driven by the types of economic thinking which informs, for example, US antitrust policy. Competition policy in the EU is closely linked to the project of market integration and liberalisation.

2. Article 81 EC prohibits anti-competitive agreements and collusive conduct which adversely affects trade between the Member States. Certain types of agreements may be permitted exemption from the prohibition under Article 81(3), a provision which balances the anti-competitive effects of an agreement against other benefits. The prohibition in Article 81(1), the sanction of nullity applied to agreements under Article 81(2) and (since May 2004) the exemption provision in Article 81(3) must be applied by national courts in cases brought before them.

3. Article 82 EC prohibits the abuse of a dominant position by one or more undertakings, which affects trade between Member States. The prohibition in Article 82 must be applied by national courts.

4. The Commission has a pre-eminent position in relation to the enforcement of Articles 81 and 82 EC. In more recent years, however, there has been significant encouragement given to aggrieved undertakings which consider themselves to be victims of anti-competitive conduct to bring actions before the national courts, including actions to seek damages for breach of the competition rules. The Court of Justice reviews the legality of enforcement decisions taken by the Commission, which can include the imposition of substantial financial penalties. The Court also receives preliminary references from national courts concerning the interpretation of the competition rules.

## Summary cont'd

5. Since the entry into force of Regulation 1/2003 in May 2004, there have been important changes to the procedures for the enforcement of the competition rules. Much of what is contained in Regulation 1/2003, especially with regard to the enforcement role of the Commission, draws upon the experience with Regulation 17, which dates back to 1962. In addition, Regulation 1/2003 attempts to significantly empower the national competition authorities and national courts in relation to the enforcement of the EU competition rules. It is too early at this stage to conclude whether this attempt at the decentralisation of competition law enforcement, so that the Commission can concentrate on large-scale cases which have a true impact at the EU level, will be successful.

6. Although the competition rules are primarily aimed at undertakings operating in the private sector, they apply both to public undertakings engaged in commercial activities and also to the Member States themselves, which must not adopt legislation or engage in practices which bring about breaches of the competition rules.

7. Merger control was not provided for in the original EEC Treaty, but since the early 1990s, a system enabling the Commission to review large mergers capable of affecting the internal market has been in place, under a Regulation which was reformed and replaced, without substantial changes to the system, in 2004. Proposed mergers between independent undertakings must be notified to the Commission in advance, and may be prohibited if they are not compatible with the common market insofar as they create or strengthen a dominant position held by one of the participants.

# Exercises

1. Why did the original EEC Treaty contain measures on anti-competitive conduct by undertakings? How successful has the EU's competition policy been in the fifty years since its inception?

2. Why is 'market analysis' an increasingly important element in the application of Article 81 EC to agreements?

3. 'Article 82 EC is a very blunt instrument to address the problems of concentrated markets.' Do you agree?

4. To what extent does the Merger Control Regulation succeed in creating the instruments necessary to respond to the structural and other challenges facing the evolving EU economy?

5. 'The role of a properly functioning judicial review system is to ensure that the Commission maintains a high level of quality in its decisions.' What structures and principles operate in EU competition law to enable the achievement of this objective for judicial review?

6. What factors led to the attempted 'modernisation' of the enforcement arrangements for EU competition policy through Regulation 1/2003? Would you expect this reform to be successful in achieving its objectives?

7. Do the procedural rules governing the enforcement of the competition rules by the Commission adequately protect the 'rights of the defence' of undertakings under investigation?

## Further Reading

Bright, C. (1996) 'EU Competition Policy: Rules, Objectives and Deregulation', 16 *Oxford Journal of Legal Studies* 535.

Diaz, F. (2004) 'The Reform of European Merger Control: *Quid Novi Sub Sole?*, 27 *World Competition* 177.

Ehlermann, C.D. (2000) 'The Modernization of EC Antitrust Policy: A Legal and Cultural Revolution', 37 *Common Market Law Review* 537.

Furse, M. (2004) 'On a Darkling Plain: The Confused Alarms of Article 82 EC', 25 *European Competition Law Review* 317.

Gerber, D. and Cassinis, P. (2006) 'The "Modernization" of European Community Competition Law: Achieving Consistency in Enforcement: Part 1', 27 *European Competition Law Review* 10; 'Part 2', 27 *European Competition Law Review* 51.

Komninos, A. (2004) 'Article 234 EC and National Competition Authorities in the Era of Decentralisation', 29 *European Law Review* 106.

Monti, G. (2001) 'The Scope of Collective Dominance under Article 82 EC', 38 *Common Market Law Review* 131.

Monti, G. (2002) 'Article 81 EC and Public Policy', 39 *Common Market Law Review* 1057.

Riley, A. (2003a) 'EC Antitrust Modernisation: The Commission Does Very Nicely – Thank You!: Part One', 24 *European Competition Law Review* 604.

Riley, A. (2003b) 'EC Antitrust Modernisation: The Commission Does Very Nicely – Thank You!: Part 2', 24 *European Competition Law Review* 657.

Slot, P.J. (2004) 'A View from the Mountain: 40 Years of Developments in Competition Law', 41 *Common Market Law Review* 443.

Temple Lang, J. (2004) 'National Measures Restricting Competition, and National Authorities under Article 10 EC', 29 *European Law Review* 397.

Vickers, J. (2004) 'Merger Policy in Europe: Retrospect and Prospect', 25 *European Competition Law Review* 455.

Vickers, J. (2005) 'Abuse of Market Power', 115 *The Economic Journal* F244.

Wilks, S. (2005) 'Competition Policy', in Wallace, H., Wallace, W. and Pollack, M. (eds.), *Policy-Making in the European Union* (5th edn), Oxford: Oxford University Press.

Willimsky, S. (1997) 'The Concept(s) of Competition', 1 *European Competition Law Review* 54.

Wils, W. (2004) 'The Combination of the Investigative and Prosecutorial Function and the Adjudicative Function in EC Antitrust Enforcement: A Legal and Economic Analysis', 27 *World Competition* 201.

Woods, D., Sinclair, A. and Ashton, D. (eds.) (2004) 'Private Enforcement of Community Competition Law: Modernisation and the Road Ahead', *2004 Competition Policy Newsletter*, No. 2, Summer, 31.

## Key Websites

The website for the EU Competition Directorate-General which includes links to comprehensive policy areas as well as to the Annual Reports on Competition Policy is available at:
**http://ec.europa.eu/comm/competition/index_en.html**

The website for the United Kingdom Department of Trade and Industry which addresses competition policy and regulation is available at:
**http://www.dti.gov.uk/bbf/competition/index.html**

The United Kingdom Office of Fair Trading (OFT) serves to enforce competition and consumer protection rules and to deter all forms of anti-competitive behaviour. The OFT website is available at:
**http://www.oft.gov.uk/**

## Key Websites cont'd

The United Kingdom Competition Commission is an independent public body which conducts inquiries into mergers which have been referred to it by the other authorities, including the Office of Fair Trading. The Competition Commission's website is available at:
**http://www.competition-commission.org.uk/**

The United States Department of Justice Antitrust Division serves to promote competition through the enforcement of antitrust laws, often coordinating matters with foreign antitrust enforcement agencies. The Antitrust Division website is available at:
**http://www.usdoj.gov/atr/index.html**

The Bureau of Competition is the United States Federal Trade Commission's antitrust authority and seeks to prevent business practices that restrain competition. The mission of the Bureau of Competition is to investigate alleged violations of antitrust law and, when appropriate, recommend that the Commission take formal enforcement action. The Bureau of Competition website is available at:
**http://www.ftc.gov/bc/index.html**

# Chapter 11

## External Economic Relations

Introduction

This chapter examines the external economic relations of the European Union. The discussion concentrates on the more traditional topics of external trade policy, especially trade with third countries in goods, but the scope of the chapter also extends to trade in services, including the question of transport, as well as other commercial policy issues such as intellectual property and investment. As required, it also refers to circumstances in which there are interactions between external economic relations and other aspects of the EU's external relations, e.g. development policy and foreign and security policy. Trade policy instruments are often the means by which other political objectives in external relations can be achieved (e.g. preferential access to the marketplace for imports from developing countries to facilitate industrial development in such countries or economic sanctions against third states to enforce compliance with international law or United Nations' resolutions).

Under the EU Treaties, the EU has a number of powers to establish contractual relations with third countries and with and within international organisations with a view to establishing the conditions on which, for example, economic operators may import goods into the EU. These powers are concentrated in the EC Treaty – i.e. under the so-called first 'Community' pillar. Some of these contractual relationships are bilateral; others are multilateral, for example within the framework of the World Trade Organisation. International agreements are an important dimension of the EU's external relations powers. The EU also has powers – again primarily under the EC Treaty – to establish unilateral measures which have external effects. For example, in establishing the rules under which banks and credit institutions may benefit from the internal market and provide services or establish themselves in Member States other than the one in which they are based (see Chapter 6), the EU institutions may also choose to regulate the circumstances in which economic operators from third states can benefit from such market liberalisation. It can also take 'defensive' measures in relation to international trade, for example to protect itself against subsidised exports facilitated by third countries, or the so-called 'dumping' of goods. In addition to a number of instances of express competence, the EU also has implied powers in the external sphere. Many of these arose because the original Treaties did not contain extensive rules on external relations; however, the implied powers continue to be significant in the current phase of policy development even though there are now many more examples of express external competences under the Treaties as currently drafted.

The foundation-stone for the regulation of external trade in goods is the customs union. This was examined in Chapter 4. The Common Customs Tariff is one of the best examples of a unilateral EU measure with external effects, in this case governing the customs tariffs to be paid in respect of goods imported from third countries into the territory of the Member States, or the exemptions from such tariffs. However, just as the completion of the internal market required not only the removal of tariff barriers to trade between Member States, but also to non-tariff barriers, including many aspects of domestic regulation (e.g. product composition requirements and rules on market access of products), so the external aspects of the customs union have required the removal of varying national policies on non-tariff barriers to the movement of goods, because variations in non-tariff barriers can be as damaging to the development of the EU as a single internal market as can variations in tariff barriers. There is also an important parallelism between the internal and the external aspects of the internal market, as the continued application of national rules at the external frontier could justify the maintenance of internal frontier controls between the Member States. Consequently, over the years these have been replaced, as required, by common EU-level rules (e.g. on phytosanitary controls and animal health standards).

External relations are one sphere of activity where a strict legal distinction between the European Union and the European Community remains significant. This is because only the European Community in the strict legal sense has international legal personality (Article 210 EC) and therefore the formal capacity to act as an international actor. The European Union does not have formal legal personality, although there is under Article 24 EU a limited power on the part of the EU institutions to conclude international agreements when implementing the Common Foreign and Security Policy. Notwithstanding this important legal distinction between the Union and the Community, this chapter continues the practice of this book of referring wherever possible to the EU and the Union, rather than the Community.

Perhaps more than any other area of EU policy in the socio-economic sphere, external economic relations are inextricably linked to the wider international environment, in this case the burgeoning network of multilateral trade agreements (Cremona, 2001). Article 131 EC commits the Member States to 'the harmonious development of world trade, the progressive abolition of restrictions on international trade and the lowering of customs barriers'. In other words, the project of European integration was conceived from the beginning in the context of global trade relations. Most significantly, as already laid out in the context of tariff reductions in 4.1, since the inception of the European Communities there have been successive rounds of amendments and supplements to the General Agreement on Tariffs and Trade (GATT), which originally dates from 1947, and which focused primarily on tariff questions in international trade in goods. These rounds initially widened the scope of the GATT itself, and then eventually led in the context of the Uruguay Round to the establishment of the World Trade Organisation (WTO), the reworking of GATT to cover domestic regulatory issues such as environmental policies, food safety and animal health issues, and the establishment of new regulatory structures such as GATS (General Agreement on Trade in Services) and TRIPS (Trade-Related Aspects of Intellectual Property Rights) covering services and intellectual property issues. Mostly recently, a wider range of concerns has animated international trade policy-makers, especially since protesters against globalisation mobilised at Seattle against what was seen as the neo-liberal agenda of the WTO. The most recent round of talks (the Doha Round) has had a much broader 'development' agenda, particularly with a view to building the capacity of developing countries to compete effectively in the international trade context, with an emphasis on fair, as well as free, trade; it sought to address, *inter alia*, the sensitive questions of trade in agricultural goods and trade in services. In late 2003, at the WTO ministerial Conference in Cancun in Mexico, this round ran into serious difficulties, and slow progress was made up to and beyond the next ministerial Conference, held in Hong Kong in December 2005. Although the participants set a timetable for 2006, and resolved to complete an agreement by the end of 2006 (having missed the original deadline of 1 January 2005), this never seemed entirely feasible, and the talks continued into 2007 without agreement being reached.

As of January 2007, the WTO comprised 150 members. It operates as a multilateral international organisation, within which an agreed set of rules for international trade to prevent tariff wars and to regulate international trade in a fair and efficient manner can be negotiated. There are around 30 international agreements subsumed under the WTO system. The types of general principles encompassed under the WTO agreements include the requirement that countries must not apply quantitative restrictions or quotas on imports or exports, that an advantage granted to one country must be extended to all WTO members (the 'most favoured nation' principle), and that there should be no discrimination between domestic products and imported products. In addition, the WTO insists on transparency and the making public of all rules and laws affecting trade, on the binding effect of the commitments which member countries make and on the submission of disputes to the (independent) dispute settlement system. Countries are able to protect themselves by taking measures to protect their interests against unfair trading practices, and to protect health and safety standards.

In terms of the EU's participation in the WTO, one of the most important questions concerns whether the EU (and by extension its Member States) will be more effective operators in international trade negotiations if they act through a single spokesperson (i.e. via the European Commission) than if they act separately (even if making broadly the same points). In legal terms, this translates into the question of the scope and nature of the competences of the EU in the external trade arena. These are the issues on which this chapter concentrates. These legal questions are not only dealt with in the Treaties and in various forms of institutional practice, including questions such as how international agreements are negotiated and brought into force within the EU legal order, but they have been extensively interpreted by the Court of Justice in lines of case law which are not always easy to make sense of. Where appropriate, reference is also made to the impact of this case law on institutional practice, such as where the Member States have chosen to acknowledge a more significant external relations role for the Commission as a result of the manner in which the Court of Justice has interpreted the 'state' of the overall competence question.

The scope of *express* external economic relations competences under the EC Treaty is addressed in 11.2, with the focus shifting to the scope of *implied* powers in external economic relations in 11.3. The nature of all of these competences and especially the issues of *exclusivity* and *uniformity* are the focus in 11.4, with the specific issue of the impact of the *Treaty of Nice* on external economic relations dealt with in 11.5. The proposed changes to external relations by the *draft constitutional treaty* are detailed in 11.6. The focus shifts in 11.7 to *institutional* questions, including the duty of cooperation in external relations. The *effects* of international trade agreements in cases brought before the Court of Justice is the subject in 11.8. Finally, 11.9 turns briefly to another dimension of external economic relations, and looks at *defensive measures* and *trade protection*.

## 11.2 The Scope of Express External Economic Relations Competences under the EC Treaty

The original (express) powers under the EC Treaty in the sphere of external economic relations were not extensive. Aside from the Common Customs Tariff (now Article 26),

Article 133 EC (previously Article 113) provides for a common commercial policy (i.e. a common external trade relations policy) 'based on uniform principles'. This builds in turn on the commitment in Article 3(1)(b) EC to the adoption of a common commercial policy (CCP) as one of the activities of the EU. In terms of subject matter, Article 133 refers to 'changes in tariff rates, the conclusion of tariff and trade agreements, the achievement of uniformity in measures of liberalisation, export policy and measures designed to protect trade such as those to be taken in the event of dumping or subsidies', but this is not an exhaustive list. There is no definition of a common commercial policy in Article 133, only examples of what it includes, with a strong focus on trade in goods. In Opinion 1/75 *Local Cost Standards* ([1975] ECR 1355), an opinion adopted on the basis of Article 300 EC regarding the compatibility of a proposed international agreement with the terms of the EC Treaty, the Court indicated that the CCP would contain the same elements as the external trade policy of a state. It elaborated upon this point in Opinion 1/78 *Natural Rubber* ([1979] ECR 2871), when it stated that the CCP may include trade regulation as well as trade liberalisation measures. The Court held:

> 'Although it may be thought that at the time when the Treaty was drafted liberalisation of trade was the dominant idea, the Treaty nevertheless does not form a barrier to the possibility of the Community developing a commercial policy aiming at a regulation of the world market for certain projects rather than a mere liberalisation of trade' (at p.2913).

In Opinion 1/94 *GATT/WTO* ([1994] ECR I-5267) concerning the conclusion by the Community and the Member States of the Uruguay Round Treaties which established the WTO, the Court concluded that goods were not the only subject matter of the CCP. It held that:

> 'Having regard to [the trend in international trade whereby the services sector is the dominant sector of the economy in many developed countries], it follows from the open nature of the common commercial policy, within the meaning of the Treaty, that trade in services cannot immediately, and as a matter of principle, be excluded from the scope of Article [133]' (at para. 41).

However, it went on to restrict the coverage of the CCP under Article 133 to only one of the four modes of supply of services, which are defined by the GATS: the cross-frontier of supply of services. This is where:

> 'the service is rendered by a supplier established in one country to a consumer residing in another. The supplier does not move to the consumer's country; nor, conversely, does the consumer move to the supplier's country. That situation is, therefore, not unlike trade in goods, which is unquestionably covered by the common commercial policy within the meaning of the Treaty. There is thus no particular reason why such a supply should not fall within the concept of the common commercial policy' (at para. 44).

The Court did not extend the reasoning to the other three modes of supply of services, namely 'consumption abroad' which involves the consumer moving to another country in which the supplier is established, 'commercial presence', namely the presence of a subsidiary or branch in the country in which the service is to be rendered, and the presence of natural persons from one country in another in order to supply services. Since they fell outside the scope of Article 133 in the formulation of the time (1994), essentially because they involve the movement of legal or natural persons, a policy which is dealt with separately in Article 3(1) of the EC Treaty, the Court concluded that this part of the agreement should be concluded by *both the Member States and the EU*. It reached a similar conclusion on the TRIPS aspects of the Uruguay Round settlement, with the exception of the provision in TRIPS related to frontier controls on counterfeit goods. This point is discussed in more detail in 11.4, as it pertains to one of the most important features of the CCP, which is its exclusivity. That is, where the EU has competence to conclude an international agreement within the framework of the CCP, this competence is exclusive. It precludes the Member States individually or collectively concluding international agreements, or adopting unilateral measures.

Article 133 has undergone a series of revisions, dating back to the Treaty of Maastricht in 1993. The most recent amendments came into force in 2003 with the Treaty of Nice. They are highly complex and are discussed in detail in 11.5, because in part they can only properly be understood once some of the fundamental principles of the existence and exercise of external economic competence have been understood, notably the concepts of exclusivity and uniformity. In essence, the Treaty of Nice amendments to Article 133 have the effect of extending the CCP expressly to cover all aspects of trade in services and what are termed the 'commercial aspects of intellectual property'. However, it does so in a way which challenges the exclusivity of the CCP.

Article 113 EEC in its original formulation provided for both the conclusion of international agreements and for the adoption of unilateral measures to implement the CCP. What is now Article 300 EC (previously Article 228) governed the respective roles of the institutions in the negotiation and conclusion of international agreements applied (see further 11.7 on institutional arrangements). Qualified majority voting in the Council has applied to measures adopted under the CCP. One notable institutional absentee has remained the European Parliament which has been largely excluded as a matter of law from the negotiation or conclusion process, although as a matter of practice it has often been consulted and involved by both the Commission and the Council.

Aside from the CCP, the EC Treaty also provided for the adoption of 'association agreements' (now Article 310 EC) with third countries and for the maintenance of relations with international organisations such as the United Nations and the GATT (now Articles 302–304 EC). Association agreements involve a more detailed framework of reciprocal rights and obligations, common action and special procedures between the EU (and often its Member States) and a third country, typically a near neighbour or a country in a region where the EU has adopted a specific policy of engagement or integration of markets.

Subsequent amendments to the EC Treaty external relations powers right up to the Treaty of Nice have added a number of new competences in areas which are closely related to the arena of external economic relations. However, unlike the CCP, they are not exclusive powers but rather shared between the EU and the Member States. For example, in the realm of development policy, under Article 181 EC: 'within their respective spheres of competence, the Community and the Member States shall cooperate with third countries and with the competent international organisations.' It goes on to state that any agreements between the EU and third parties 'shall be without prejudice to Member States' competence to negotiate in international bodies and to conclude international agreements'. A similar formulation is used in relation to environmental policy under Article 174 EC. Other references to external relations can be found in the provisions on research and technological development (Article 170 EC) and in the context of complementary powers which the EU has in the fields of education and vocational training (Articles 149 and 150 EC), culture (Article 161), health (Article 152) and trans-European networks (Article 155). There are also external powers in the context of the provisions on Economic and Monetary Union (Article 111), but it is clear that such powers – if they are to be effective – must necessarily be exclusive in nature, since the EU has exclusive competence in relation to monetary matters for those states which have adopted the euro.

## 11.3 Implied Powers in External Economic Relations: The Scope of Competences

Not all EU external competences are expressly stated in the EC Treaty. Since the *ERTA* case (Case 22/70 *Commission* v. *Council* [1971] ECR 263), it has been established that the Community has also had implied powers to conclude international agreements or to adopt unilateral measures in the external relations sphere. *ERTA* is one of the most important examples of the Court's application of a thesis of implied powers as a means of complementing the express provisions of the Treaty. Cases such as this derive their legitimacy from an efficacy argument: if the Communities were given tasks such as those in relation to transport it makes sense for them to have the powers to complete these tasks. The *ERTA* case concerned an international agreement in the field of international transport (European Road Transport Agreement), signed in 1970 within the framework of the United Nations Economic Commission for Europe. The Member States passed a Resolution within the Council of Ministers stating that they, not the Community, would conclude it. The Commission was able to frame an action for annulment against the minutes of the Council under what is now Article 230 EC, because the Court concluded that this Resolution was a reviewable act. This conclusion allowed the Commission then to argue its substantive case, namely that it was the Community which should have concluded the agreement, as competence had passed in the field of transport to the Community.

The Court found that there were no specific provisions in the Treaty relating to the negotiation and conclusion of international agreements in the field of transport policy. It therefore turned to 'the general system of Community law in the sphere of relations with third countries' (para. 12). It held that powers may not only be express, but 'may equally flow from other provisions of the Treaty and from measures adopted, within the framework of those provisions, by the Community institutions' (para. 16). The Court pointed out the parallelism of the internal and external spheres of Community policies, and found that when 'common rules come into being, the Community alone is in a position to assume and carry out contractual obligations towards third countries' (para. 18). Such relevant internal powers existed in relation to transport policy, in what were then Articles 74 and 75 EEC, and specifically the Court found that the subject matter of the ERTA fell within the scope of a 1969 Council Regulation harmonising certain matters relating to road transport, such that the 'Community has been empowered to negotiate and conclude the agreement in question since the entry into force of the . . . Regulation' (para. 30). Significantly, these powers excluded what the Court called 'the possibility of concurrent powers on the part of Member States, since any steps taken outside the framework of the Community institutions would be incompatible with the unity of the common market and the uniform application of Community law' (para. 31). These points have been reiterated frequently by the Court in subsequent cases. In Opinion 2/91 *ILO* ([1993] ECR I-106), the Court summarised the position thus:

'authority to enter into international commitments may not only arise from an express attribution by the Treaty, but may also flow implicitly from its provisions . . . [W]henever Community law [was] created for the institutions of the Community powers within its internal system for the purpose of attaining a specific objective, the Community had authority to enter into the international commitments necessary for the attainment of that objective even in the absence of an express provision in that connection' (at para. 7).

There are two important points coming out of the *ERTA* line of case law. The first concerns the possibility of implied external competence, which arises not only where there are existing EU measures in place, but also where there are none (Opinion 1/76 *European Laying Up Fund for Inland Waterway Vessels* [1977] ECR 754). The second concerns the nature of that competence. In what circumstances will it be an exclusive competence, which pre-empts the powers of the Member States either to adopt unilateral measures, or to participate in the adoption of the multilateral agreement in question? This was not an issue in *ERTA* since it did concern a matter where there was already internal EU legislation in place, and the Court clearly held that the power was *exclusive* in nature. The point is considered in more detail in 11.4.

## 11.4 The Nature of External Relations Competences: Exclusivity and Uniformity

The EU's powers in external relations are either exclusive or shared with the Member States. Exclusivity is a consequence of the supremacy of EU law. Member States would be able to prejudice the operation of EU law if they could enter into external obligations independently. This is most clearly shown in the field of common commercial policy under Article 133. In Opinion 1/75, the Court referred to the rationale of preserving the unity of the EU's position *vis-à-vis* third states and the defence of the 'common interests' of the EU as the basis for the exclusivity of the CCP:

'The common commercial policy . . . is conceived [in Article 133] in the context of the operation of the common market, for the defence of the common interests of the Community, within which the particular interests of the Member States must endeavour to adapt to each other . . . The provisions of [the articles on the CCP] . . . show clearly that the exercise of concurrent powers by the Member States and the Community in this matter is impossible. To accept that the contrary were true would amount to recognizing that, in relations with third countries, Member States may adopt positions which differ from those which the Community intends to adopt, and would thereby distort the institutional framework, call into question the mutual trust within the Community and prevent the latter from fulfilling its task in the defence of the common interest' (at para. B.2).

Notwithstanding the apparently firm line taken by the Court of Justice in such cases on the exclusivity of the CCP, and the extent of uniformity, in fact there remains some scope for national action in relation to the CCP. This is examined in more detail at the final paragraph of this section.

The field of development cooperation is a good example of non-exclusive competence. The second paragraph of Article 181 makes it clear that the EU's competence is 'without prejudice to the Member States' competence to negotiate in international bodies and to conclude international agreements'. In Joined Cases C-181 and 248/91 *Parliament* v. *Council and Commission (Bangladesh Aid)* ([1993] ECR I-3685) the Court held that:

'it should be pointed out that the Community does not have exclusive competence in the field of humanitarian aid, and that consequently the Member States are not precluded from exercising their competence in that regard collectively in the Council or outside it' (at para. 16).

However, even where competences are shared with the Member States (which is the case with the majority of the EU's external powers), it may be that in certain areas the Member States are precluded from entering into international agreements because of the framework of EU law, such that the EU competence is in effect exclusive. The operation of this doctrine is best demonstrated by a detailed study of the Court's most significant recent case on implied external relations competences, the *Open Skies* cases, which are concerned with implied external competences in the air transport field (e.g. Case C-467/98 *Commission* v. *Denmark et al (Open Skies)* [2002] ECR I-9519). With these enforcement actions brought by the Commission against eight Member States, the Commission was seeking to establish the recognition in EU law of an exclusive competence for the EU to negotiate air service agreements with third countries. The actions were brought against the Member States which had, individually and independently, concluded bilateral agreements with the US governing reciprocal access and landing rights. The Commission argued that the Member States had thereby infringed the external competence of the EU, as their powers to conclude such agreements should properly be seen as having been transferred wholly to the EU. As a result, the Commission should negotiate such agreements, on the basis of a mandate conferred by the Council, and such agreements should be concluded by the Council on behalf of the Union. While this exclusive competence is not explicitly set out in the Treaty, the Commission suggested that it was necessary to recognise it in order to attain the objectives of the Treaty, because the introduction of autonomous rules by Member States would lead to distortions of competition, discrimination and disturbance of the EU market.

The Court of Justice did not agree with the Commission on this question, but its conclusions did have enormous significance for the field of external competence in relation to air transport. In the first place, it acknowledged that air transport constitutes an example of implied external competences, based on the parallelism with an existing internal competence (now Article 80 EC). The Court was also called upon to elaborate upon its interpretation of the scope of implied external competences in cases such as Opinion 1/76, where it had held that:

'such competences may exist not only whenever the internal competence has already been used in order to adopt measures for implementing common policies, but also if the internal Community measures are adopted only on the occasion of the conclusion and implementation of the international agreement' (Case C-467/98, para. 56).

Furthermore, as the Court acknowledged in Opinion 1/94, there were cases where the internal competence 'may be effectively exercised only at the same time as the external competence, the conclusion of the international agreement thus being necessary in order to attain objectives of the Treaty that cannot be attained by establishing autonomous rules' (Case C-467/98, para. 57). The Court decided that such a scenario did not apply here, contrary to the argument mounted by the Commission, indicating that this is not a situation where internal competence can only be effectively exercised at the same time as external competence. On the contrary, internal competence had been effectively exercised already. The implication is that the scenario envisaged in Opinion 1/76 will be relatively rare.

On the other hand, the Court did hold by reference to its judgment in the *ERTA* case, that where the EU does have implied external competence where this results from other provisions of the EC Treaty and from measures adopted within the framework of those provisions, there are circumstances where this will preclude autonomous national action. The Court accepted the principle that the Member States are not free to enter into international commitments affecting the common rules adopted on the basis of the relevant internal rules on air transport (Article 80(2) EC), since that would 'jeopardise the attainment of the objective pursued by those rules and would thus prevent the Community from fulfilling its task in the defence of the common interest' (Case C-467/98, at para. 78). In other words, in certain circumstances, depending upon the nature of the internal rules, the competence could be exclusive. This proved to be the legal crux of the case, and involved a scenario in which the EU had already, by virtue of certain internal rules, effectively 'occupied the field'. This was the case in relation to EU legislation on slot allocation, fare-setting and computer reservation systems, and in those limited respects the Court found that the agreements were incompatible with EU law since the Member States could no longer conclude international agreements, even if they tried in good faith to insert provisions in these agreements in order to avoid conflict with EU law. This they had done in relation to the Open Skies bilateral agreements with the US, but to the limited extent that the EU had exclusive competence, to no avail. It is also important that the Court found that certain provisions in the agreements contravened Article 43 EC, which guarantees freedom of establishment. In the standard agreements with the US, the Member States were precluded from designating as entitled to rely upon the reciprocal benefits under the agreements, airlines based, owned and controlled in other Member States. This is not a competence question but a simple application of the free movement rules of the EU. On the other hand, somewhat controversially the Court demonstrated substantial deference to the powers of the Member States in respect of traffic rights. The bilateral agreements gave what are termed 'fifth freedom' rights to carriers designated by the US. This freedom enables airlines to carry passengers to one country, and then to fly them on to another country (rather than back to their own). In other words, US carriers can land initially in the UK, and then fly on, with the same aircraft, and having picked up further passengers, to Germany.

It is relevant to understanding these cases that for many years the Commission had been unsuccessfully seeking a mandate to negotiate external agreements in the air transport field from the Council, as required by Article 80(2) EC. Although the Court's findings on the scope of *exclusive* EU external competence were very limited, they have had a significant impact in this field, especially when combined with the Court's finding on Article 43. One of the major difficulties for the EU in this field is that there is some fundamental asymmetry in relations with the US. Notably, whereas the US has negotiated fifth freedom rights for its carriers, which allow them to carry passengers within the EU, when EU-based carriers land in the US, they cannot pick up new passengers and carry them onto another, final destination, elsewhere in the US, because this is internal air transport, termed 'cabotage', which is excluded from the scope of international air transport agreements. Also, the restrictions on the designation of non-national carriers impacted more heavily upon the EU and EU airlines than on the US. All US airlines can benefit from all US bilateral agreements. Since the Member States were unable to designate airlines to benefit from the bilateral agreements which were not substantially owned and controlled within its territory, only a smaller number of EU airlines could benefit from the various bilateral separate agreements. The capacity of the EU and its Member States to negotiate a more balanced arrangement would be strengthened if the EU were acting with a single voice in this area.

After the judgments were handed down the Commission reiterated its call for a negotiating mandate in a November 2002 Communication (COM (2002) 649). This was not initially granted by the Council, but it was becoming increasingly clear that bilateral arrangements would be less and less attractive for individual Member States if they were precluded from negotiating on vital questions such as slot allocation. Eventually in June 2003, the Council granted two mandates, one specifically concerned with negotiating a 'open aviation area' with the US, and the second to negotiate with all third countries, including the US, to correct the problems identified in the *Open Skies* judgments in the bilateral agreements. These negotiations made slow progress until a breakthrough in November 2005, which outlined an agreement on opening up transatlantic air transport, but was dependent upon the US in turn making a better offer in relation to domestic airline ownership, an area in which it has been notoriously protectionist. Despite this, the finalisation of the agreement proved elusive and it was not finalised until March 2007, mainly because of EU objections to the US insistence on ownership restrictions in relation to US airlines. However, swifter progress was made on other bilateral agreements, such as with Australia and with New Zealand.

As noted above, notwithstanding the exclusive nature of the CCP, there remained – at least until 1994 – considerable scope for national protective measures, especially in relation to rules on imports of goods. In 1994, the Council Regulation on common rules on imports was substantially updated, particularly in order to bring the EU's rules into line with the requirements of the WTO in relation to permissible safeguard measures (Council Regulation 3285/94, OJ 1994 L349/1). The only exclusions from this regulation are textiles, so far as they are not yet integrated into the GATT 1994 arrangements, and a group of non-market economy countries which are not members of the WTO. In essence, for the large bulk of imports the regulation establishes a regime for imports which removes all quotas on imports, subject to the possibility of the EU itself taking the GATT-compatible safeguard measures. However, there are some exceptions, which allow, for example, the Member States to apply the discretion they preserve under Article 30 EC in respect of restrictive measures on the intra-EU movement of goods, in relation to imports from third countries. It has existed in all versions of the Import Regulation thus far, and is paralleled in Article 11 of the Export Regulation, which has been interpreted on a number of occasions by the Court of Justice in the context of the permissibility of national restrictions on the export of dual use goods out of the EU (Case C-70/94 *Fritz Werner Industrie-Ausrustungen GmbH* v. *Germany* [1995] ECR I-3189; Case C-83/94 *Criminal Proceedings against Leifer, Krauskopf and Holzer* [1995] ECR I-2131). Dual use goods are ones which could have both military and non-military applications. Such national rules must meet the normal, classic tests of proportionality and necessity, and must be justified by the Member State. This is because there are no common EU rules on dual use or strategic goods (see generally Koutrakos, 2001).

## 11.5  External Economic Relations after the Treaty of Nice

Article 133 EC has been amended on a number of occasions, most notably in the context of the Treaty of Nice, which introduced some substantial amendments which could affect in significant ways the scope of EU external economic relations. They are one part of the development of a wider, but probably more diffuse, concept of the Common Commercial Policy. It should be recalled that in Opinion 1/94, the Court of Justice held that only a very small segment of trade in services fell within the concept of the CCP as it then applied under what was Article 113, namely the cross-frontier supply of services in which neither the supplier nor the recipient of the services actually moved across the border. Similarly, only one small segment of the WTO deal on intellectual property, namely that concerned with checks at frontiers, fell within the CCP. Since the Treaty of Nice, Article 133(5) now applies the CCP arrangements in Article 133(1)–(4) also to 'the negotiation and conclusion of agreements in the fields of trade in services and the commercial aspects of intellectual property'. This would appear to bring these within the exclusive competence of the Union – but in fact this impression is misleading. The provision does not cover unilateral measures in the external sphere in these fields, and consequently other legal bases in the Treaty would have to be used for these. Moreover, the provision goes on to make it clear that the Council shall – in derogation from the normal arrangements under Article 133 – act unanimously when negotiating and concluding an agreement 'where that agreement includes provisions for which unanimity is required for the adoption of internal rules or where it relates to a field in which the Community has not yet exercised the powers conferred upon it by this Treaty by adopting internal rules'. Finally, and most significantly, the paragraph is expressed not to 'affect the right of the Member States to maintain and conclude agreements with third countries or international organisations in so far as such agreements comply with Community law and other relevant international agreements'.

Article 133(6) goes on to add yet more conditions and limitations, expressly applying to the external sphere the principle of the attribution of competences, providing that 'an agreement may not be concluded by the Council if it includes provisions which go beyond the Community's internal powers, in particular by leading to harmonisation of the laws and regulations of the Member States in an area for which this Treaty rules out such harmonisation'. It seems unlikely that this adds anything to Article 5 EC, which contains the attributed powers' principle, but it certainly provides reassurance for Member States. Finally, agreements relating to trade in cultural and audiovisual services, educational services, and social and human health services are expressly stated to fall within the 'shared competence of the Community and its Member States'. Such agreements therefore require the common accord of the Member States and should be concluded jointly by the Community and the Member States as mixed agreements (see further 11.7). Transport continues to be governed by the existing Treaty provisions on Transport rather than by the general CCP.

Finally, Article 133(7) contains a 'passerelle' clause, allowing the Council, acting unanimously on a proposal from the Commission and after consulting the European Parliament, to extend these Byzantine and complex new rules also to cover international negotiations and agreements on intellectual property which are not covered by the phrase 'commercial aspects'. It has not thus far been used.

Commentators (e.g. Cremona, 2001; Eeckhout, 2004: 52–3) have regretted that the IGC which concluded the Treaty of Nice missed an opportunity to take a substantial step towards giving the EU a more effective and comprehensive external economic relations policy. There are a number of provisions in the new Article 133 which are testimony to the sensitivity of particular Member States, such as the exception in relation to cultural and audiovisual services, which is kept in place specifically for France, with its concerns about the viability of a French language film industry in an increasingly Hollywood-dominated global film market. Some view the new Article 133 as an attempt, in effect, to codify Opinion 1/94 into the Treaty, rather than to use Treaty amendments to overcome some of the unsatisfactory aspects of that judgment. The problems of participation in multilateral trading arrangements under the competence conditions established by Article 133 once the EU has enlarged to include 27 Member States in 2004 and 2007 were bound to become worse. The question was therefore reviewed, once again, in the context of the work of the Convention on the Future of the Union, which drew up the draft Treaty establishing a Constitution for Europe, a draft project which was then put before the IGC which began in October 2003.

## 11.6 The Treatment of External Economic Relations in the Treaty establishing a Constitution for Europe

The field of external relations received a good deal of attention in the Convention on the Future of the Union, and consequently in the draft Treaty establishing a Constitution for Europe, which it submitted to the European Council in June and July 2003 (see generally Krajewski, 2005). As such it is worth paying some attention to these proposed innovations, even though it is unlikely that the Constitutional Treaty as drafted will enter into force in the foreseeable future, if ever. Within the context of the project to simplify the EU, one of the major innovations suggested by the Convention – which proved to be largely uncontroversial and was approved in the final version of the Constitutional Treaty signed in October 2004 – was the effective abolition of the pillar system which characterises the current EU, and the institution of a single legal personality for the EU (Article I-7 CT). This covers all aspects of legal personality, including matters of responsibility in international law, but most significantly it confirms beyond all doubt the power of the EU to conclude binding international agreements in the areas where it has competence. This is formally confirmed in Article III-323 CT:

> 'The Union may conclude an agreement with one or more third countries or international organisations where the Constitution so provides or where the conclusion of an agreement is necessary in order to achieve, within the framework of the Union's policies, one of the objectives referred to in the Constitution, or is provided for in a legally binding Union act or is likely to affect common rules or alter their scope.'

This text appears in an extended Title V of Part III CT covering the Union's External Action. This Title represents the first occasion on which all of the various political and commercial aspects of external relations have been brought together in a single Title, and offers the possibility for more integrated action in the future. It reflects also the fact that scholars of EU law have increasingly begun to look at the EU's external relations as a package (e.g. Eeckhout, 2004; Koutrakos, 2006a,b). However, Part I of the Constitutional Treaty remains important so far as it sets the general parameters for external action, including a general statement of the Union's external relations objectives:

> 'In its relations with the wider world, the Union shall uphold and promote its values and interests. It shall contribute to peace, security, the sustainable development of the earth, solidarity and mutual respect among peoples, free and fair trade, eradication of poverty and protection of human rights, in particular the rights of the child, as well as to the strict observance and development of international law, including respect for the principles of the United Nations Charter' (Article I-3(4) CT).

Article I-13 categorises the Common Commercial Policy and the Customs Union as areas of exclusive competence. The provisions of Chapter III of Title V of Part III then incorporate into the Constitutional Treaty much of what is currently contained in Article 133 EC, in its post-Nice formulation. This reflects the general approach taken to drafting Part III of the Constitutional Treaty, which largely reflects the old EC/EU Treaties. However, Article III-315 CT states specifically that the 'common commercial policy shall be conducted in the context of the principles and objectives of the Union's external action', and the list of illustrative actions in relation to the CCP has been updated to include not only the issues included within the scope of Article 133 by the Treaty of Nice, namely trade in services and the commercial aspects of intellectual property, but also – an innovation – foreign direct investment. However, many of the conditions and qualifying points commented upon in 11.5 are likewise preserved in the new Article III-315. Paragraph 4 preserves the requirement of unanimity for the negotiation and conclusion of agreements in the fields of trade in services involving the movement of persons, the commercial aspects of intellectual property and foreign direct investment, where unanimity is required for the adoption of acts in the internal sphere. The French 'cultural exception' in respect of trade in cultural and audiovisual services is also preserved, for the case 'where these agreements risk prejudicing the Union's cultural and linguistic diversity'. There is also an exception in relation to trade in social, education and health services, where these agreements 'risk seriously disturbing the national organisation of such services and prejudicing the responsibility of Member States to deliver them' (Article III-315(4)(b)).

Article III-315(6) CT provides that the exercise of competences conferred under Article III-315 is without prejudice to the delimitation of internal competences of the Union, and shall not lead to the harmonisation of legislation where this is not otherwise possible under the Constitution. An important innovation of the Constitutional Treaty would be that it does not include the provision which continues to undermine the exclusivity of the CCP as regards the so-called 'new' subjects added by the Treaty Nice, namely the saving provision in respect of the right of the Member States to maintain and conclude agreements with third countries or international organisations, so far as these are compatible with EU law (Article 133(5), fourth paragraph EC).

Overall, these provisions would represent a considerable simplification of the currently cumbersome formulation of Article 133 EC, although the difficulties of managing exclusivity in combination with a requirement of unanimous voting in the Council of Ministers in certain fields could be considerable. Moreover, of considerable significance as a by-product of the general application across the Constitution of a single dominant form of legislative process for European laws and framework laws involving a modified form of Council/Parliament co-decision is that for the first time the Parliament is given a significant role in law-making in relation to the CCP. The CCP must be implemented by laws and framework laws adopted according to the standard law-making process. Although the Parliament remains less involved in matters relating to the negotiation of international agreements, it must be consulted on the question of negotiating mandates, and in future its effective veto over internal implementing rules for international agreements will considerably strengthen its role.

Two other categories of exclusive competence with significant external repercussions are included in Article I-13, namely monetary policy, for those Member States participating in the euro, and the conservation of marine biological resources under the common fisheries policy. The Constitution also attempts to reflect the complex case law of the Court of Justice discussed in this chapter by providing that exclusive competence for conclusion of an international agreement may arise 'when its conclusion is provided for in a legislative act of the Union or is necessary to enable the Union to exercise its internal competence, or insofar as its conclusion may affect common rules or alter their scope' (Article I-13(2) CT). This offers the possibility, undermined by the intense difficulties of expressing a complex case law in simple 'constitutional' language, of a clearer delimitation of the exclusive and shared competences of the EU and the Member States in the external sphere in the future.

As regards other areas of external action with economic implications, such as development cooperation, the Constitution essentially picks up the principles applicable under the Treaty of Nice. Thus in relation to development cooperation, for example, this is a category of shared competence, but the right of the Member States to exercise their own competence, subject to general compliance with the provisions of EU law, is expressly preserved, as it is at present (Article I-14(4) CT).

## 11.7 Institutional Questions

Institutional questions have been referred to on a number of occasions in passing in the previous paragraphs. Of considerable importance here is Article 300 EC, which provides the general principles for the negotiation and conclusion of international agreements by the European Community. This expressly provides for the Commission to negotiate agreements, on the basis of an authorisation by the Council, and in consultation with special committees appointed by the Council to assist it in this task, and within the framework of any mandate set by the Council. Normally, the Council is to act by a qualified majority, except in cases where the agreement covers a field for which unanimity is required for the adoption of internal rules, and in respect of Association Agreements under Article 310 EC. The signing of an agreement is also decided under qualified majority or unanimity, according to the same principles. The European Parliament is merely kept informed on negotiations, although it is consulted on the conclusion of agreements by the Council except in the case of Article 133 EC. The Parliament must, however, give assent to Association Agreements. If an agreement requires modifications to the EC Treaty, then the modifications must first be instituted, in accordance with the procedure laid down in Article 48 EU, including an intergovernmental conference and national ratification.

The European Parliament, the Council, the Commission or a Member State may seek an opinion from the Court of Justice, under Article 300(6) EC, on the compatibility of a proposed agreement with the Treaty. This seems to suggest that the Court can only express an opinion, strictly speaking, on whether or not the agreement is within the scope of the Treaty and so consequently whether it can be approved by the EU itself, or by the Member States, but in practice its opinion is regularly sought on the question of which legal basis ought to be used for the approval of an agreement. Thus the Court frequently adjudicates on whether a measure is within the exclusive or shared competence of the EU (e.g. Opinion 2/00 *Cartagena Protocol on Biosafety* [2001] ECR I-9713). In fact, that has overwhelmingly been the case with the matters referred to the Court of Justice under Article 300(7). As Cremona has commented (1999: 158):

'There has only been one case where the Court held that the EC lacked external competence . . . and this lack could not be "cured" or remedied by shared competence: it was a lack of a different kind, a complete absence of the appropriate legal basis for action, either via Article [308] or via implied powers, which only Treaty amendment could cure. All the cases of shared competence including Opinion 1/78 . . . and Opinion 1/94, have been cases where the sharing arises *not* from any lack on the Community's part, but out of the *retention* of competence by the Member States.'

If an agreement is within the scope of *shared* competence, this does not mean that the EU cannot conclude it *alone*. However, in practice it is frequently the case that Member States will participate in international agreements *as well as* the EU. These are so-called mixed agreements. Participation of the Member States is often required because of financial implications of agreements.

In these circumstances, there is a duty of cooperation between the Member States and the EU. As the Court held in Opinion 1/94:

'where it is apparent that the subject-matter of an agreement or convention falls in part within the competence of the Community and in part within that of the Member States, it is essential to ensure close co-operation between the Member States and the Community institutions, both in the process of negotiation and conclusion and in the fulfilment of the commitments entered into. That obligation to co-operate flows from the requirement of unity in the international representation of the Community' (at para. 108).

## 11.8 International Trade Agreements before the Court of Justice

In its case law the Court of Justice has consistently refused to acknowledge that the provisions of the GATT can have direct effect, and can thus be relied upon by individuals in cases before national courts which themselves concern EU law. This is in contrast to its position on, for example, the provisions of Association Agreements, where it has applied the usual justiciability tests and found that particular provisions can be used by individuals in national courts as giving rise to rights upon which they may rely (Case 104/81 *Kupferberg* [1982] ECR 3641). In Joined Cases 21–24/72 *International Fruit Company NV v. Produktschap voor Groenten en Fruit* [1972] ECR 1219), the Court held that, although the old pre-WTO GATT did 'bind the Community', even so, because of its flexibility in particular in relation to enforcement, its provisions could not have direct effect. The Court has continued this case law in relation to the post-WTO GATT, and other agreements such as TRIPS. On the positive side of the balance sheet in terms of judicial protection, it has confirmed in cases such as Case C-53/96 *Hermès International* v. *FHT Marketing* ([1998] ECR I-3603) that it has jurisdiction to interpret provisions of TRIPS, notwithstanding its status as a mixed agreement. However, since the Member States and the EU have shared competence in relation to TRIPS, it remains a possibility that some national courts may allow nationals to rely upon provisions of the TRIPS before the national courts. This is the case notwithstanding the fact that in Joined Cases C-300 and 392/98 *Parfums Christian Dior* ([2000] ECR I-1137) the Court held, as was expected, that the provisions of TRIPS 'are not such as to create rights upon which individuals may rely directly before the courts by virtue of Community law' (para. 44). If there were direct effect in a national court, this would be by virtue of *national law* and *its* cognisance of international law. On the other hand, the Court did establish a principle of sympathetic interpretation of TRIPS in relation to provisions of EU law in the *Parfums Christian Dior* case, holding that:

'In a field to which TRIPS applies and in respect of which the Community has already legislated, as is the case with the field of trade marks, it follows from the judgment in *Hermès* . . . that the judicial authorities of the Member States are required by virtue of Community law, when called upon to apply national rules with a view to ordering provisional measures for the protection of rights falling within such a field, to do so as far as possible in the light of the wording and purpose of Article 50 of TRIPS' (at para. 47).

In reaching this conclusion, the Court also relied upon its reasoning in a case which, although not directly involved with the question of the direct effect of the post-WTO GATT, effectively settled the point, the so-called *Portuguese Textiles* case (Case C-149/96 *Portugal* v. *Council* [1999] ECR I-8395). In this case, the Court decided that, with few exceptions (related to the possibility that the Community was acting specifically to implement a GATT/WTO obligation), WTO law could not serve as the basis for reviewing the legality of measures of the Community. In its assessment of GATT in this case, it recognised that it had changed considerably as compared to its pre-WTO formulation, but it pointed out that the GATT system overall was characterised by a strong element of negotiation between governments and reciprocity in terms of operation. In concluding that the GATT could not be the basis for legality control of EU acts themselves, this effectively settled the direct effect point as well, and so this has proved as later cases, particularly those involved with the long running saga of challenges to the EU's regime on banana imports, have shown, including recent cases where the applicants have sought to invoke rulings of the WTO's Dispute Settlement Body which declare the EU regime incompatible with the GATT (Case C-377/02 *Van Parys* v. *Belgisch Interventie- en Restitutiebureau* [2005] ECR I-1465).

## 11.9 Defensive Measures and Trade Protection

The EU, like any trading bloc, has the right to defend its industries against unfair trading practices by trading partners. It can make use of three principal sets of defensive measures:

- anti-dumping measures where it applies Council Regulation 384/96 on protection against dumped imports from third countries (OJ 1996 L56/1);
- anti-subsidy rules where it applies Council Regulation 2026/97 on protection against subsidised imports from third countries (OJ 1997 L288/1); and
- protective measures under the Trade Barriers Regulation (Council Regulation 3296/94, OJ 1994 L341/14), which allows measures to be taken in relation to states which set up unfair trade practices which impede market access for EU exporters

The general framework for trade protection is provided by the GATT/WTO, allowing, for example, the taking of safeguard actions under Article XIX of GATT. For example, it allows for the initiation of the dispute settlement procedure under WTO in cases where market access is impeded. Failing compliance with any GATT ruling, retaliatory measures can be adopted against the state impeding access. In the case of subsidised and dumped imports, the EU rules allow for the imposition of countervailing duties which offset the support provided to imports into the EU by third countries, and to create a level competitive playing field for all economic operators.

# Summary

1. The original EEC Treaty contained rather limited coverage of external trade policy, allowing for the adoption of both international agreements and unilateral measures, to complement the customs union provisions and the provisions on internal free movement. These provisions have been developed substantially through treaty amendments, most recently the Treaty of Nice, and also as a result of the development of concepts of implied powers and the exclusivity of EU powers under the common commercial policy under Article 133 EC, articulated by the Court of Justice.

2. The wider context in which the EU's external trade policies have developed has changed dramatically since the inception of the Treaties. The GATT of the 1940s has been replaced and complemented by additional measures regulating trade in services as well as goods, international tariffs between most trading nations have been progressively lowered, and in the 1990s the World Trade Organisation was instituted, as part of a set of moves to improve the enforceability and effectiveness of the GATT/WTO law including a new set of dispute settlement mechanisms. The current round of talks under the aegis of the WTO, the so-called Doha Round, holds out the promise of supporting a broader development agenda of fair, as well as free, trade.

3. The express powers in relation to the development of a common commercial policy under the original EEC Treaty were limited to trade in goods, but were found by the Court of Justice in a series of cases to be exclusive in nature. That is, they precluded both the participation of the Member States in the relevant international agreements, and also the creation or maintenance of separate measures or policies by the Member States individually or collectively outwith the framework of the EU. However, as the WTO agreements of the 1990s included measures relating to services and other matters such as the commercial aspects of intellectual property, these fell into areas where the EU did not have an exclusive competence at the time, and so consequently the EU participated alongside the Member States in the relevant international agreements, which were concluded as mixed agreements.

4. In addition to express powers, the EU also has implied powers in the external sphere. These arise where the Treaty grants the institutions internally the power to adopt measures to attain a specific objective; in this case the EU – or more specifically the European Community which has the relevant international legal personality – has the power to enter into international commitments for the purposes of achieving those objectives. This has been important in areas such as transport.

5. Even implied powers may become exclusive in nature, in certain areas. There are good policy reasons to support such a move, as if the EU negotiates with one voice rather than many it can exercise a great deal more bargaining power in the international sphere. The field of transatlantic aviation, and the negotiation of so-called Open Skies agreements with the US, is a case where the EU has gradually taken on the mantle of negotiating and concluding agreements from the Member States, partly on the basis of interpretations given by the Court of Justice of the nature of the EU's implied external competence in this area and the relationship between internal and external measures.

6. The Constitutional Treaty would, if ratified, introduce important amendments to the sphere of external trade policy, extending the sphere of exclusivity into the area of foreign direct investment; however, the provisions would also include derogations to protect cultural and linguistic interests, and also to protect the integrity of the delivery of public services by the Member States.

## Summary cont'd

7. Although international trade agreements are binding on the EU, and as such constitute part of the EU law as a whole, the Court of Justice has consistently refused to ascribe to allow individuals to invoke GATT or WTO obligations in cases before the national courts in order to challenge the legality of EU measures, or to allow the Member States to use these obligations in order to seek the annulment of EU measures.

# Exercises

1. Why did the Court of Justice develop a theory of implied powers in the external sphere to complement the express powers conferred by the EC Treaty?

2. What has been the impact upon EU external economic relations of the progressive development of the GATT and associated international agreements, and the creation of the WTO?

3. What does it mean to say that certain EU external powers are 'exclusive' in nature?

4. Why does international air transport present such an important challenge to the evolution of the law on external economic relations?

5. What is the meaning and effect of the amendments to Article 133 introduced by the Treaty of Nice? What additional changes would be introduced if the Constitutional Treaty entered into force?

6. Why are 'mixed' agreements important?

7. Why does the Court of Justice refuse to give direct effect to WTO agreements?

## Further Reading

Bernard, N. (2006) 'Internal Market Governance in a Globalised Marketplace: The Case of Air Transport', in Nic Shuibhne, N. (ed.), *Regulating the Internal Market*, Cheltenham: Edward Elgar.

Cremona, M. (2001) 'A Policy of Bits and Pieces? The Common Commercial Policy after Nice', 4 *Cambridge Yearbook of European Law* 61.

Cremona, M. (2002) 'The External Dimension of the Single Market: Building (on) the Foundations', in Barnard, C. and Scott, J. (eds.), *The Law of the Single European Market: Unpacking the Premises*, Oxford: Hart Publishing.

Cremona, M. (2006) 'External Relations of the EU and the Member States: Competence, Mixed Agreements, International Responsibility, and Effects of International Law', *EUI LAW Working Paper 2006/22*, European University Institute, available at **http://www.eui.eu**

Eeckhout, P. (2004) *External Relations of the European Union*, Oxford: Oxford University Press. See especially chapters 2, 3 and 10.

Heffernan, L. and McAuliffe, C. (2003) 'External Relations in the Air Transport Sector: The Court of Justice and the Open Skies Agreements', 28 *European Law Review* 601.

Herrmann, C. (2002) 'Common Commercial Policy after Nice: Sisyphus would have done a better job', 39 *Common Market Law Review* 7.

Holdgaard, R. (2003) 'The European Community's Implied External Competence after the Open Skies Cases', 8 *European Foreign Affairs Review* 365.

Koutrakos, P (2006a) *EU International Relations Law*, Oxford: Hart Publishing.

## Further Reading cont'd

Koutrakos, P. (2006b) 'The External Dimension of the Internal Market and the Individual', in Nic Shuibhne, N. (ed.), *Regulating the Internal Market*, Cheltenham: Edward Elgar. See especially chapters 1, 2 and 3.

Krajewski, M. (2005) 'External Trade Law and the Constitution Treaty: Towards a Federal and More Democratic Common Commercial Policy?', 42 *Common Market Law Review* 91.

Slot, P.J. and De la Rochère, J. (2003) 'Case Note, *Open Skies* cases', 40 *Common Market Law Review* 697.

Woolcock, S. (2005) 'Trade Policy: From Uruguay to Doha and Beyond', in Wallace, H., Wallace, W. and Pollack, M. (eds.), *Policy-Making in the European Union* (5th edn), Oxford: Oxford University Press.

## Key Websites

World Trade Organisation at:
**http://www.wto.org/**

In-depth coverage of the WTO by the *Financial Times* at:
**http://www.ft.com/indepth/wto2005**

DG External Trade at:
**http://ec.europa.eu/trade/index_en.htm**

The EU's portal giving full information on air transport and especially the conclusion of external agreements is available at:
**http://ec.europa.eu/transport/air_portal/index_en.htm**

# Part III

# Citizens and Non-Citizens

# Chapter 12
## EU Citizens in the Internal Market

Introduction – the 'Citizens of the Union'

According to the Court of Justice, 'Union citizenship is destined to be the fundamental status of nationals of the Member States . . .' (Case C-184/99 *Grzelczyk* v. *Centre Public d'Aide Sociale d'Ottignies-Louvain-la-Neuve (CPAS)* [2001] ECR-I 6193, para. 31). This chapter is structured around an assessment of the significance of the provisions on citizenship of the Union (Articles 17–22 EC), which were introduced by the Treaty of Maastricht into the EC Treaty.

The core provisions on citizenship of the Union in the EC Treaty insist upon the centrality of the nationality of the Member States as defining the scope of Union citizenship:

'Article 17
1. Citizenship of the Union is hereby established. Every person holding the nationality of a Member State shall be a citizen of the Union. Citizenship of the Union shall complement and not replace national citizenship.
2. Citizens of the Union shall enjoy the rights conferred by this Treaty and shall be subject to the duties imposed thereby.'

Member States are thus the gatekeepers of Union citizenship, since it is access to Member State nationality which determines the personal scope of Union citizenship. Furthermore, the reference to the rights conferred by the EC Treaty seems to reinforce the complementary nature of the Union citizenship provisions. However, Articles 18–21 EC do contain a number of rights which attach to Union citizenship, although not all of them are confined exclusively to Union citizens. Article 18 confirms the right of free movement of Union citizens:

1. Every citizen of the Union shall have the right to move and reside freely within the territory of the Member States, subject to the limitations and conditions laid down in this Treaty and by the measures adopted to give it effect.
2. If action by the Community should prove necessary to attain this objective and this Treaty has not provided the necessary powers, the Council may adopt provisions with a view to facilitating the exercise of the rights referred to in paragraph 1. The Council shall act in accordance with the procedure referred to in Article 251.
3. Paragraph 2 shall not apply to provisions on passports, identity cards, residence permits or any other such document or to provisions on social security or social protection.

Article 19 EC confers the right on EU citizens resident in a Member State other than the one of which they have the nationality to vote and to stand as a candidate in local elections and elections to the European Parliament, under the same conditions as nationals. Article 20 EC provides that citizens of the Union, when present in the territory of a third state, can enjoy consular and diplomatic protection from the authorities of any Member State, under the same conditions as nationals. Article 21 gives citizens of the Union the right to petition the European Parliament, to apply to the European Ombudsman and to write to the institutions and bodies of the Union in any of the official languages of the Union, and to receive a reply in the same language. Articles 194 and 195 EC, however, establish that the first two rights are also given to 'any natural or legal person established in the Union' – and thus extend to resident third country nationals.

To understand the significance of Union citizenship, and in particular the right of free movement conferred by Article 18, it is essential first to understand the extent of rights to free movement and non-discrimination enjoyed by nationals of the Member States under the original treaties, secondary legislation and case law of the Court of Justice. The citizenship provisions are supplements to, rather than replacements of, the existing provisions on the free movement of persons. Furthermore, Article 18 refers to the free movement of, and right of residence of, Union citizens generally; it remains 'subject to the limitations and conditions laid down in [the EC] Treaty'. In practice this means different rights for different groups of citizens, and their families, in particular by reference to whether they are economically active or not. There is a hierarchy of protection, with the economically active receiving greater protection under the free movement rights than the economically inactive and, in particular, those who are reliant upon the state for welfare benefits for their subsistence. The key provisions are:

- Article 39 EC which provides for the free movement of workers and their families.
- Article 43 EC which provides for the free movement of self-employed persons and their families.
- Article 49 EC which provides for the free movement of those providing and receiving services.
- Three Council Directives introduced in 1990 and 1993 (now repealed and replaced by European Parliament and Council Directive 2004/38 on Citizens' Rights, OJ 2004 L158/77) which provided for the free movement of students, those of independent means, and retired persons.
- Council Regulation 1612/68 on freedom of movement for workers (OJ Spec. Ed. 1968, No. L257/2, p.475) and the Citizens' Rights Directive which amplify the free movement and non-discrimination rights of the different categories of beneficiary.
- Article 12 EC, which prohibits discrimination on grounds of nationality (of the Member States), which remains the 'backstop' provision, underpinning the more specific non-discrimination rights contained in measures such as Regulation 1612/68 and the Citizens' Rights Directive.

In relation to the free movement of persons, two central questions must always be asked:

- Who can benefit from the provisions of EC law?
- And what rights can they derive?

The first part of the chapter is concerned with the different categories of beneficiary, and the focus in the latter part is on the scope of the rights derived.

### 12.2 Free Movement of Economically Active Persons: Workers

The Court of Justice has made it clear that the concept of worker is an EU concept with a single meaning in every Member State. Consequently, it has been the Court itself which has defined who counts as a worker, as the Treaty was silent on the matter. Case 53/81 *Levin* v. *Staatssecretaris van Justitie* ([1982] ECR 1035) concerned a British citizen who wished to reside in the Netherlands, but whose employment paid less than the amount which the Dutch legislation deemed to be the minimum amount of money required for subsistence. Levin supported herself primarily through other means. In these circumstances could she be categorised as a worker, and fall within the scope of Article 39? The Court held that, as the free movement of workers is a fundamental EU right, it should be interpreted as widely as possible and covers all 'effective and genuine activity', excluding only activities which can be regarded as marginal and ancillary. Thus, Mrs Levin's employment qualified her as a worker. Mrs Levin maintained herself by private means, and was thus not a drain on state social security. However, in Case 139/85 *Kempf* v. *Staatssecretaris van Justitie* ([1986] ECR 1741), the same conclusion was reached in the case of a part-time music teacher, who claimed supplementary benefit and subsequently sickness benefit. The Dutch government argued that Kempf, a German national, was doing his music teaching part time in order to be able to claim supplementary benefit and thus avoid working full time, and that this could not be defined as effective and genuine work. The Court made it clear that the source of the supplementary income – private or public funds – is not relevant in assessing whether part-time work is effective and genuine. Significantly, the Court repeated that, because free movement of workers is a fundamental right, it must be interpreted broadly. Both *Levin* and *Kempf* taken together must be read as an attempt by the Court to ensure that as many people as possible fall under the free movement provisions and are able to benefit from EU law rights (and thus, of course, are brought under the jurisdiction of the Court itself).

The Court further clarified its position by setting out a test in Case 66/85 *Lawrie-Blum* v. *Land Baden-Württemberg* ([1986] ECR 2121). A worker, according to the *Lawrie-Blum* test, is someone within an employment relationship, defined as a person 'performing services for and under the direction of another person in return for which he receives remuneration'. Three elements can be discerned from the definition given in *Lawrie-Blum*:

- The employed person must be performing services of economic value. However, the Court added that the services need not be of a *purely* economic nature; Ms Lawrie-Blum was a trainee teacher, which, the Court made clear, is a profession that has an economic value, even though it may not be of a purely economic nature.
- The employed person must be carrying out services for, and under the direction of, another person. This excludes from the category of worker the self-employed, who are covered by other provisions.
- The employed person must receive remuneration, although as *Levin* and *Kempf* had previously made clear, that remuneration need not be sufficient to provide a minimum level of subsistence.

The first element, specifically the distinction between economic value and economic nature, needed some elucidation. It was discussed by the Court in two subsequent decisions. The first (Case 196/87 *Steymann* v. *Staatssecretaris van Justitie* [1988] ECR 6159), concerned a German national who settled in the Netherlands as part of a religious community. As his contribution to the community, he carried out plumbing work (for which he was trained) and did various other jobs as part of the general commercial activity of the community. However, the policy of the community was that members should receive their material needs, and should contribute to the community as much as they were able. There was thus no direct equivalence between the work that he did and what he received. He was not paid in cash, but in food, housing and other basic subsistence needs. The Court considered it important that the community did carry out commercial activities, and on that basis held that Steymann was providing services of economic value. The question of remuneration was not discussed directly, but it may be assumed that the fact that his material needs were being met was considered to be sufficient.

However, the limits of the Court's broad approach can be seen in Case 344/87 *Bettray* v. *Staatssecretaris van Justitie* ([1989] ECR 1621). This concerned a German national who was in the Netherlands for the purpose of attending a drug rehabilitation centre. As part of the Dutch Social Employment provisions, he was given work to do in order to help with his rehabilitation, and was remunerated for that work. The Court held that the fact that the work was fairly unproductive and that the remuneration was provided by public funds was irrelevant. However, because the work was carried out for social, rather than economic, purposes and because the selection of a particular individual to carry out a particular job was made on the basis of the needs of the individual, rather than the ability to carry out that job, the work could not be seen as having economic value and thus did not fulfil the first of the *Lawrie-Blum* criteria. This would seem to suggest that the crucial element in *Steymann* was that the religious community was carrying out commercial activities. This approach was confirmed more recently in Case-456/02 *Trojani* v. *CPAS* ([2004] ECR I-7573) where the Court held that the crucial issue was whether or not the services performed are capable of being regarded as part of the normal labour market, and can be understood as real and genuine.

Thus while the Court has tried to expand the concept of worker as widely as possible, it is still, at heart, an economic concept. A worker is someone who is economically active. The mere fact of carrying out work is not sufficient, the work must be of some (however small or inefficient) economic value. This approach has been criticised as excluding from the scope of the Treaty provisions people such as carers, who carry out work but whose work is perceived as having social, rather than economic, value. The extension of the status of citizenship has meant that such people are granted free movement rights but that those rights can be limited by their access to financial resources.

### 12.3 Free Movement of Economically Active Persons: Job Seekers

Article 39 provides that there should only be free movement between Member States in order to take up offers of employment actually made. This form of words would appear to exclude from its application the case of an individual moving to another Member State in order to seek work. As the Court of Justice pointed out in Case C-292/89 *R* v. *Immigration Appeal Tribunal, ex parte Antonissen* ([1991] ECR I-745), this is a very restricted notion of the free movement of workers which would make it very difficult for any offer of employment to be actually made. Given that Article 39 is to be interpreted broadly as a fundamental freedom, the Court held in that case that job seekers fell within the scope of Article 39. As such, this would suggest that job seekers would fall into the same category as workers.

A better interpretation, however, would be that they fall into a specific sub-category. In *Antonissen*, the Court went on to place a crucial limitation on the rights of job seekers by stating that Member States may prescribe a period of time after which the job seeker may be required to leave the country if he has not found work and if he can provide no evidence that he has a genuine chance of finding work. The Court did not specify what that period of time should be, merely that it should be reasonable; in the case of Mr Antonissen, the Court held that six months appeared to be a reasonable period. Article 14(4)(b) of the Citizens' Rights Directive deals specifically with the right of residence of those Union citizens who have entered the territory of the Member State in order to seek employment. It provides that: 'the Union citizens and their family members may not be expelled for as long as the Union citizens can provide evidence that they are continuing to seek employment and that they have a genuine chance of being engaged.'

A second limitation was placed on the position of job seekers in Case 316/85 *Centre public d'aide sociale de Courcelles* v. *Lebon* ([1987] ECR 2811), where the Court of Justice differentiated between workers and job seekers, limiting the right to equal treatment in social and tax advantages to workers. This point is returned to later, where it will also be considered what impact the decision in Case C-85/96 *Martínez Sala* v. *Freistadt Berlin* ([1998] ECR I-2691) has had in this area.

According to Article 7(3) of the Citizens' Rights Directive, persons who have previously been employed in the host state for more than one year and suffer 'involuntary unemployment' retain the status of worker, provided they register as a job seeker with the relevant authorities. Those who have completed a shorter period of employment before becoming involuntarily unemployed retain the status of worker for at least six months.

## 12.4 Free Movement of Economically Active Persons: The Self-employed

In Case C-55/94 *Gebhard* v. *Consiglio dell'Ordine degli Avvocati e Procuratori di Milano* ([1995] ECR I-4165), a person was said to be established in a Member State if they participate on a stable and continuous basis in the economic life of that State. A self-employed person is one who carries out work of economic value (as a worker does) but who is not acting under the direction of another and who is receiving remuneration, but not in the form of a salary. In Case C-268/99 *Jany* v. *Staatssecretaris van Justitie* ([2001] ECR I-8615), 'window' prostitutes, paying rent to the owners of the premises they worked out of were held to be self-employed, though the Court raised a set of additional criteria to be fulfilled in the light of the vulnerable position of sex workers. These were that the prostitution took place outside any relationship of subordination concerning the choice of that activity, working conditions and conditions of remuneration; that it was under that person's own responsibility; and in return for remuneration paid to that person directly and in full.

In practice, the definitional problems concerning establishment relate to the distinction between an established person and a person merely providing services on a cross-border basis (for more details see 6.2) rather than between a self-employed person and a worker. In essence, self-employed people who are established in another Member State enjoy the same rights and benefits as employed persons or workers.

## 12.5 Free Movement of Economically Active Persons: Service Providers and Recipients

The provision of services involves a temporary presence within a Member State, in order to carry out economic activities. The relevant Treaty provisions address directly only those who travel across a border in order to *provide* services. However, the secondary legislation implies that *recipients* of services are also covered by legislation, and this was confirmed in Joined Cases 286/82 and 26/83 *Luisi and Carbone* v. *Ministero del Tesoro* ([1984] ECR 377). In this case, two Italian citizens wished to travel in order to receive medical services, but were prevented from doing so by currency restrictions which meant that they would be unable to pay for the services. The Court clarified that Article 49 applies not just to providers of services but also to individuals travelling to receive services, and therefore any barrier, either on their travel or on their ability to profit from or pay for services, is *prima facie* unlawful.

This case law was further expanded in Case 186/87 *Cowan* v. *Le Trésor Public* ([1989] ECR 195), a case concerning a British tourist who was mugged and robbed on the Paris underground, and who was initially denied compensation under the French criminal injuries compensation scheme, as he was not a French national. The Court held that the non-discrimination provisions of the Treaty applied, as he was a recipient of services and thus fell within the scope of the Treaty. It acknowledged that the French rule did not act as a barrier to free movement in any substantial sense, but stated instead that non-discrimination in protection from harm must nevertheless be a corollary of free movement. As Advocate General Lenz pointed out in his Opinion, the concept of tourist is a difficult one to define. However, he argued that the best approach was to assume that anyone lawfully travelling in a country for a temporary period would necessarily make use of some services. It was not, however, necessary for an applicant to specify precisely which services he had used. Under that logic, it would appear that any Member State national lawfully visiting another Member State on a temporary basis is covered by Article 49. Advocate General Lenz suggested that this needs to be established on the basis of the status of the individual on entry, rather than on the basis of evidence that economic services were actually used, in the interests of clarity and certainty. Given that it seems almost unimaginable that someone might spend time in a State and not make use of any service at all (for example, buying a cup of coffee or using public transport), his position seems fair. Subsequently, in Case C-215/03 *Oulane* v. *Minister voor Vreemdelingenzaken en Integratie* ([2005] ECR I-1215), the Court ruled that it was appropriate to require nationals from other states to adduce evidence of lawful residence to the authorities of the host state before they could be considered tourists, rather than the state simply having to 'assume' they were tourists and treat them accordingly. For periods under three months, presentation of identity card or passport would be sufficient. Thus anyone travelling on a temporary basis within a Member State which is not their own is considered a recipient of services and thus falls within the economically active category. This, however, applies with one important proviso: they are only entitled to the rights necessary in order to ensure the provision of the service, and their rights subsist for only as long as necessary in order to ensure the provision of the service. The rights granted to service providers and recipients are limited in so far as they are necessary to ensure free movement of services, but, subject to this limitation, the same rights are available to service providers as to workers: in Case 63/86 *Commission* v. *Italy* ([1988] ECR 29), the Court made it clear that, while it will not usually be necessary for a service provider to claim social benefits, if such benefits are necessary to ensure the provision of the service, they must be granted. It seems, however, highly unlikely that a tourist will need to claim social benefits.

The law on free movement of services is one of the areas where more and more Union citizens are being granted basic rights of non-discrimination. In Case C-274/96 *Criminal*

*Proceedings against Bickel and Franz* ([1988] ECR I-7637), two lorry drivers, one Austrian and one German, were arrested while travelling in Northern Italy in the course of the provision of transport services. They were summoned before the courts, and they asked that the trials be conducted in German, as is the right of the German-speaking inhabitants of Northern Italy. The authorities refused, claiming that that right was only held by Italian citizens. The Court of Justice held that Bickel and Franz fell within the scope of the Treaty because of their status as service providers and therefore that the non-discrimination provisions of the Treaty meant that they could not be discriminated against in this way. The scope of Article 49 was broadened even further in Case C-60/00 *Carpenter v. Secretary of State for the Home Department* ([2002] ECR I-6279), where a UK citizen and, in particular, his third country national wife were brought within the scope of protection of EU law by virtue of his business, which involved him in the provision of services in other Member States. Mrs Carpenter had been threatened with deportation from the UK because her previous visa (as a domestic worker) had expired and her situation had not been regularised under UK immigration law, even though she was providing care for Mr Carpenter's children by a previous marriage. The Court invoked the European Convention on Human Rights and Fundamental Freedoms (ECHR) and held that:

> 'The decision to deport Mrs Carpenter constitutes an interference with the exercise by Mr Carpenter of his right to respect for his family life within the meaning of Article 8 [ECHR], which is among the fundamental rights which, according to the Court's settled case-law, restated by the Preamble to the Single European Act and by Article 6(2) EU, are protected in Community law' (para. 41).

Given the expansion of intra-European business in recent years, this has the potential to include a significant proportion of Union citizens. The Court did appear to limit the scope of the judgment by repeatedly referring to the fact that 'a significant proportion' of the services provided by Mr Carpenter were provided on a cross-border basis, presumably in order to place some kind of limit on the numbers of people who can benefit from the judgment. Nevertheless, it is a significant extension.

## 12.6 Free Movement of the Economically Inactive

The Treaty and the original secondary legislation only covered economically active persons, and their dependants (see 12.7). From the 1980s onwards, the situation started to change, through a combination of Court activism and new secondary legislation. Students, retired persons and those of independent means were covered by a series of directives originally enacted in 1990, and now repealed and replaced by the Citizens' Rights Directive:

▶ *Students* An original 1990 Directive, annulled by the Court of Justice because it was based on the wrong provision of the EC Treaty (Case C-295/90 *Parliament v. Council (Students' Rights)* [1992] ECR I-4193), was replaced by Council Directive 93/96 (OJ 1993 L317/59) on the right of entry and residence for student nationals of a Member State who have been accepted onto a vocational training course in another Member State for the duration of the course of study. Spouses and dependent children are also given rights of entry and residence under the same terms. Under Article 1, students had to be able to demonstrate that they had sufficient resources to avoid becoming a burden on the social assistance system of the host Member State and that they had sickness insurance. The directive created no entitlement to maintenance grants. This directive followed the judgment of the Court in Case 293/83 *Gravier* v. *City of Liège* ([1985] ECR 593), where the Court held that access to education does fall within the scope of the Treaty, as a policy on common vocational training was being developed by the Community. Consequently, the Court held, Member State nationals could not be treated in a discriminatory manner if they wished to study in a Member State not their own in relation to the right of residence and the conditions of access to education. While both the directive and *Gravier* used the phrase 'vocational education', that phrase has been interpreted widely to cover university education in general (see Case 24/86 *Blaizot* v. *University of Liège* [1988] ECR 379).

▷ *Retired people* Council Directive 90/365 (OJ 1990 L180/28) deals with the right of residence for employees and self-employed persons who have ceased their occupational activity and provides rights of entry and residence for retired Member State nationals in receipt of a pension sufficient for them to avoid being a burden on the social assistance system of the host Member State. An earlier measure had already allowed Member State nationals who had previously worked in another Member State to stay there after their retirement (see now Article 17 of the Citizens' Rights Directive). The 1990 directive, however, extended the right of free movement to all retired people, provided they are able to support themselves.

▷ *People of independent means* Council Directive 90/364 (OJ 1990 L180/26) on the right of residence (sometimes referred to as the Playboy Directive) granted rights of entry and residence to any Member State national, their spouse and dependants, on the condition that they have sufficient means to avoid being a burden on the social assistance scheme of the host Member State and that they have sickness insurance.

These separate directives have now been repealed and replaced by the Citizens' Rights Directive, which appears at first sight to deal with issues of free movement on the basis of general entitlements of Union citizens, but in practice continues to mirror the layers of entitlement laid down in the previous case law and legislation. Article 7 deals with the right of residence of Union citizens for periods of more than three months. While Article 7(1)(a) deals with the position of workers and the self-employed, Article 7(1)(b) deals with retired persons and those of independent means, providing that: 'all Union citizens shall have the right of residence on the territory of another Member State for a period of longer than three months if they . . . have sufficient resources for themselves and their family members not to become a burden on the social assistance system of the host Member State during their period of residence and have comprehensive sickness insurance cover in the host Member State.' Article 7(1)(c) covers students and gives a right of residence to those who are: 'enrolled at a private or public establishment, accredited or financed by the host Member State on the basis of its legislation or administrative practice, for the principal purpose of following a course of study, including vocational training; and have comprehensive sickness insurance cover in the host Member State and assure the relevant national authority, by means of a declaration or by such equivalent means as they may choose, that they have sufficient resources for themselves and their family members not to become a burden on the social assistance system of the host Member State during their period of residence.'

The extent to which these free movement rights can be combined with the right to non-discrimination, especially in view of the Court's significant case law on Union citizenship since the late 1990s, in particular *Martínez Sala, Grzelczyk* and Case C-209/03 *R* v. *London Borough of Ealing, ex parte Bidar* ([2005] ECR I-2119) will be examined further in 12.16.

## 12.7 Free Movement of Dependants

From the early days of the Community, the dependants of the economically active have been granted rights under secondary legislation. However, these rights can be seen as parasitic rights, in that they only exist by virtue of the relationship between the economically active citizen and the dependant. Traditionally, the following categories of dependants have been covered:

- the spouse;
- children under the age of 21 or who are dependent; and
- dependent relatives in the ascending line of the worker and his or her spouse.

Protection is extended by Article 2(2)(b) of the Citizens' Rights Directive to the Union citizen's partner who is defined as a person 'with whom the Union citizen has contracted a registered partnership, on the basis of the legislation of a Member State, if the legislation of the host Member State treats registered partnerships as equivalent to marriage and in accordance with the conditions laid down in the relevant legislation of the host Member State'. Dependants covered by the Citizens' Rights Directive are given the right to move on the basis of the worker's right to be accompanied by his family. Some attempts have also been made to encourage the Member States to adopt a broad approach to the notion of family reunification. Thus Article 3 of the Citizens' Rights Directive also requires Member States to 'facilitate entry and residence' of 'any other family members, irrespective of their nationality, not falling under the definition in point 2 of Article 2 who, in the country from which they have come, are dependants or members of the household of the Union citizen having the primary right of residence, or where serious health grounds strictly require the personal care of the family member by the Union citizen'. The same duty also applies to 'the partner with whom the union citizen has a durable relationship, duly attested'. The Member State is required to 'undertake an extensive examination of the personal circumstances' and to 'justify any denial of entry or residence to these people'.

This right is given to all such family members, not just those who are Member State nationals. It is thus not restricted to Union citizens. Dependants' rights are the main way in which third country nationals can gain free movement rights within the EU. However, third country nationals do not gain EU rights merely by being dependent upon a Member State national. The Member State national must in addition exercise his or her rights of free movement under EU law. This can involve moving to another Member State to work. It can also, according to the Court in *Carpenter*, involve service providers, where a significant proportion of their services are provided in other Member States, as long as the spouse can be said to facilitate that provision of services (for example, by taking care of the children when the worker goes on business trips). Finally, under the rather specific situation in Case C-200/02 *Zhu and Chen* v. *Secretary of State for the Home Department* ([2004] ECR I-9925), a person with the nationality of one Member State (in this case Irish) who has always lived in another Member State (in this case Britain) may claim EU rights, including dependants' rights, on the basis of nationality alone. Further, as was made clear in Case C-370/90 *R* v. *Immigration Appeal Tribunal and Surinder Singh, ex parte Secretary of State for the Home Department* ([1992] ECR I-4265), if a Member State national leaves her state of origin in order to work in another Member State, and then wishes to return home, her third country national spouse will retain the right of entry and residence to the State of origin. They will not, however, have such a right of entry and residence, if the Member State national has not exercised her free movement rights. In Joined Cases 35 and 36/82 *Morson and Jhanjan* v. *State of the Netherlands* ([1982] ECR 3723), for example, two Dutch nationals of Surinamese origin were held to have no right derived from EU law to bring their dependent parents from Surinam to live in the Netherlands. This limitation makes it clear that the intention behind dependants' rights is not to give specific rights to non-economically active citizens or to third country nationals, but to facilitate the free movement of the economically active. Workers are unlikely to want to move to work in another Member State if they cannot take their families with them (see the remarks of the Court in Joined Cases C-64 and 65/96 *Land Nordrhein-Westfalen* v. *Uecker and Jacquet* [1997] ECR I-3171).

There is a clear overlap here between immigration law and free movement law. The issues which this raises were considered by the Court in Case C-109/01 *Secretary of State for the Home Department* v. *Akrich* ([2003] ECR I-9607). This case concerned a Moroccan citizen who had been deported from UK on a number of occasions. While living clandestinely in the UK, he married a UK citizen, and they moved to Ireland for a while, with the explicit intention of making use of the *Singh* principle to bring themselves into the scope of EU law. He then tried to get a current deportation order on him revoked. The UK government was concerned that he was exploiting the free movement rules to circumvent a national immigration decision and that, if he were allowed to do so, this would render ineffective immigration law when applied to people married to Union citizens. The Court took the view that the intention of the parties was not relevant in deciding whether or not they held EU rights. However the Court did recognise the risk of the abuse of EU law by saying that, if the marriage is a marriage of convenience, EU rights do not apply. Further, the non-EU national spouse must be lawfully resident in one Member State before moving to another, and thus the Akrichs could not, on the face of it, take advantage of EU rights. Here, the Court is concerned to ensure that Member States retain their power to exclude non-EU nationals for good reason, using domestic immigration law. The Court of Justice clarified the effect of its judgment in *Akrich* in Case C-1/05 *Jia* v. *Migrationsverket*, judgment of 9 January 2007, where it held that it was not necessary for a third country national to have been previously resident in another Member State before acquiring a right under EU law. A third country national may, in such circumstances, move directly to the host Member State from a third country.

Being parasitic, these rights are somewhat precarious. In Case 267/83 *Diatta* v. *Land Berlin* ([1985] ECR 567), the Court refused to rule that a spouse separated from the worker was deprived of her EU law rights and stated that the personal scope of those rights must not be interpreted restrictively. Necessary clarification of this point has been brought by the Citizens' Rights Directive. Article 13 states that divorce or annulment of a marriage does not deprive a spouse who is an EU citizen of EU rights. The rights of a spouse who is not an EU citizen are more limited. The right of residence continues if the marriage lasted at least three years, of which one was spent in the host Member State, or where the non-EU spouse has custody of the children, or if the marriage was dissolved because of 'particularly difficult circumstances' (this would seem to refer to domestic violence or abuse). Such spouses must further demonstrate that they have sufficient resources, without drawing on the finances of the host State.

These legislative provisions confirm and complement the case law of the Court of Justice. One of the cases considered (Case C-413/99 *Baumbast and R* [2002] ECR I-7091) involved a divorced couple, a French national and a US national, residing in the UK. After the divorce, the US national was said by the UK authorities to have no right of residence in the UK, as her marriage to an EU citizen had ended. It was held by the Court that the children of the marriage, however, maintained a right of residence and a right of access to education, by virtue of their relationship with their French father. Further, both the spirit of the EU legislation (prior to the Citizens' Rights Directive) and Article 8 of the ECHR (the principle of respect for family life) required that their American mother, who was their primary carer, should also be permitted to remain in the UK. Her right of residence, therefore, was derived from her children's rights and would, presumably, cease once they finished their education or if they decided to move elsewhere (subject to the conditions now laid down in the Citizens' Rights Directive). This was confirmed in *Zhu and Chen*, where it was clarified that this derived right of residence is not a dependant's right, but rather part of the right of a citizen of the EU. Giving a child a right of residence is meaningless unless their parent or other carer also has a right of residence.

As Nic Shuibhne argues, however, the restrictions on dependants' rights are becoming increasingly untenable, given the development of citizenship of the Union and the extent to which EU law can now affect a person's life (Nic Shuibhne, 2002). The judgment in *Carpenter* does have some significance in this regard, extending the rights to a provider of services, which is a far larger category than those who move on a permanent basis, and which potentially opens up the 'slippery slope of service receipt', covering a huge number of Member State nationals (although the way in which the Court appeared to limit *Carpenter* to situations where a significant proportion of services are provided in other Member States would suggest that the Court would not be open to such a move). In addition, the Commission had initially proposed, as part of the Third Country Nationals' Directive, that third country national dependants of all citizens (not just those who have exercised free movement rights) be covered by the free movement legislation. This section was ultimately removed from the directive (Council Directive 2003/109 concerning the status of third country nationals who are long-term residents, OJ 2004 L16/44), but the Commission has stated that 'the alignment of the rights of all Union citizens to family reunification will be reviewed later . . .'. By this means it intends to ensure that the nexus between family reunification and free movement will be removed and that the principle of family reunification will be given independent status under EU law.

The judgment in *Carpenter* indicates that a further basis for the right can be considered. In that case, the Court suggested that Union citizens taking advantage of their free movement rights have a fundamental right to family life (as laid down in Article 8 of the European Convention on Human Rights), which would be breached if, as in the particular case, the third country national spouse was deported.

Until the legislative changes brought about by the Citizens' Rights Directive, which have improved the situation for both heterosexual and homosexual couples who are able to take advantage of the legislative changes at national level to allow registered partnerships, the Court was somewhat restrictive in its definition of dependants, and particularly of spouses. In Case 59/85 *Netherlands* v. *Reed* ([1986] ECR 1283), an unemployed UK citizen resident in the Netherlands argued that she had Community rights of entry and residence by virtue of a long-term cohabiting relationship with another UK citizen working in the Netherlands, which had not been formalised through marriage. The Court rejected this argument, holding that under EU law a spouse is someone who was legally married. It did, however, go on to hold that, under the non-discrimination provisions of the EC Treaty, the worker had the right to equal treatment with other Dutch nationals. If, as was in fact the case, a Dutch national had the right to have a cohabiting relationship legally recognised, without formal marriage, an EU worker must also be given that same right, and it should then be protected as a social advantage within the terms of Regulation 1612/68 (see 12.14). On that basis, the Court held that Ms Reed was entitled to reside in the Netherlands with her partner. Again, however, it will be noted that this reduces the partner to the status of the subject, rather than the object, of EU rights.

Surprisingly, nowhere in the legislation is the notion of 'dependence' defined. In *Jia*, the Court of Justice gave a much needed definition, which draws upon comparisons with the state of origin, rather than the host Member State. A person will be a dependant within the meaning of EU legislation if he or she needs 'the material support' of the EU citizen 'in order to meet their essential needs in the State of origin of those family members or the State from which they have come at the time when they apply to join that Community national'.

## 12.8 The Scope and Nature of the Rights to be enjoyed

As the previous discussion has indicated, a number of different rights are granted to those people who fall within the personal scope of the free movement provisions, and moreover that not all categories of beneficiary enjoy the same rights. These rights will be analysed in the following sections, beginning with the rights which are available to all such citizens (right of entry, residence and work, right of non-discrimination) and going on to discuss the rights which are only available to certain categories of citizens (social benefits).

## 12.9 The Rights of Entry and Residence

According to the preamble to the Citizens' Rights Directive, 'Citizenship of the Union confers on every citizen of the Union a primary and individual right to move and reside freely within the territory of the Member States . . .'. This confirms what was held by the Court of Justice in its judgments in *Baumbast and R* and *Trojani*, that Article 18(1) EC (combined with the secondary legislation) gives EU citizens a general right of residence, which may only be restricted under certain circumstances, and that this right is directly effective and must be upheld by national courts. One reading of Article 18 EC would seem to suggest that all citizens, not merely those covered by the original EC Treaty provisions and secondary legislation, should be able to move and reside freely throughout the Member States. However, in a report issued shortly after the adoption of the Maastricht Treaty, the Commission stated that, as far as it was concerned, no further legislation was required in order to give effect to Article 18 EC (Report from the Commission on the Citizenship of the Union (COM(1993) 702)). This clearly suggested a view of free movement, or indeed of citizenship, so limited as to bear very little resemblance to Article 18 EC on paper. At its inception, therefore, Union citizenship appeared to be of a mainly symbolic nature, and rights of free movement and residence were to be derived from prior legislation and case law, most of which was focused on the economically active. However, the judgments of the Court of Justice in *Baumbast and R* and *Trojani* seem to indicate that the Court has done what the Commission refused to do and given an independent meaning to Article 18, at least in the context of Union citizens who are already lawfully resident in other Member States. This is one of the main contributions of the notion of EU citizenship and the rights enshrined in Articles 17–22 EC to the further development of the free movement rights of the nationals of the Member States beyond where they stood when the Treaty of Maastricht was concluded.

Other than the public interest exceptions detailed below in 12.10, any restrictions placed by Member States are likely to relate to the recognised need to prevent an unreasonable burden being placed on the public finances of Member States, and will usually require that citizens do not claim assistance from public funds (Nic Shuibhne, 2006: 208–26). This seeks to remove the risk of social or 'welfare' tourism, where citizens might be motivated to move to the Member State which has the most beneficial social security provisions, and such provisions are considered necessary unless and until Member State social security systems can be harmonised. However, the Court of Justice has clarified that the source of the personal resources on which the citizen will draw is irrelevant. In Case C-408/03 *Commission* v. *Belgium* ([2006] ECR I-2647) it suggested that a non-notarised and non-binding undertaking by a spouse to support the non-national citizen could be sufficient to justify a claim for residence. Notably, in para. 47 of the judgment, the Court acknowledged that '(t)he loss of sufficient resources is always an underlying risk, whether those resources are personal or come from a third party, even where that third party has undertaken to support the holder of the residence permit financially'.

Under the Citizens' Rights Directive all EU citizens and their family members have a right of residence for up to three months without any need to acquire any form of residence permit (Article 6). This is subject only to the requirement that they should not 'become an unreasonable burden on the social assistance system of the Member States' (Article 14(1)). Member States, therefore, are not permitted to restrict entry and are not permitted to require visas of citizens who have EU rights to enter and reside. They are, however, allowed to require that citizens show passports or other identity documents at the border, in order to prove that they have entitlement to the right of free movement (see Case C-378/97 *Criminal Proceedings against Wijsenbeek* [1999] ECR I-6207, and Article 5 of Directive 2004/38). They are also permitted to require EU citizens on their territory to produce evidence of their citizenship, but only if similar identity checks are required of their own citizens, and there is thus no discrimination (Case C-215/03 *Oulane* v. *Minister voor Vreemdelingenzaken en Integratie* [2005] ECR I-1215). Family members who are not nationals of any Member State may be required to obtain entry visas; however, Article 5(2) of the Citizens' Rights Directive states that Member States should accord to such people every facility for obtaining visas by means of an accelerated procedure. The Court of Justice made it clear in Case C-459/99 *Mouvement contre le racisme, l'antisémitisme et la xénophobie ASBL (MRAX)* v. *Belgian State* ([2002] ECR I-6591) that the purpose of permitting the Member States to maintain a visa requirement in this case is to allow Member States to investigate thoroughly whether the person concerned has the requisite family ties to be able to take advantage of EU rights, and to ensure that there are no good public policy reasons for excluding them (see 12.10). Member States cannot therefore turn back or deport family members for failure to obtain a visa if they can prove that they are entitled to be there under EU law. In Case C-503/03 *Commission* v. *Spain* ([2006] ECR I-1097), the Court clarified the relationship between the powers of the Member States and the arrangements for the exchange of information about third country nationals under the

Schengen Information System (a computerised system for sharing information between states relevant to immigration and asylum requests; see further 13.2). It held that if a Member State wishes to refuse a visa to the third country national spouse of an EU citizen availing herself of the right of free movement, it could not simply rely upon the presence of an 'alert' under the Schengen Information System, without further satisfying itself that the person in question represented 'a genuine, present and sufficiently serious threat affecting one of the fundamental interests of society' (para. 59). In *Wijsenbeek* it was further pointed out that these internal checks are allowed because there is, as yet, no common regime for external border controls. Where there is such a common regime developed and in operation, any internal border controls should become superfluous and will no longer be permitted (see Chapter 13).

After three months, there is a right of residence under Article 7 of the Citizens' Rights Directive, for workers, the self-employed, and those satisfying the requirements laid down for students and those of independent means (including those who are retired), detailed in 12.6. After three months, Member States may impose registration requirements, including a requirement that entitlement to EU rights be proved. EU citizens may not be required to hold a residence card or permit, but family members who are third country nationals may be so required. Once EU citizens and third country national family members have been lawfully resident in another Member State for more than five years, they may obtain the right of permanent residence (Article 16); or an even shorter period of time for those reaching retirement age or who stop working because of permanent incapacity, and for frontier workers who start to work in a third Member State (Article 17). The right of permanent residence is an important innovation of the Citizens' Rights Directive.

## 12.10 Derogations from the Rights of Free Movement and Residence

Both the Treaty and the secondary legislation set out certain grounds on which Member States are entitled to refuse entry and residence to people who would otherwise have EU rights. Article 39(3) EC allows limitations to free movement of workers on the grounds of 'public policy, public security and public health'. This is repeated in Article 46, concerning freedom of establishment, which also applies, by virtue of Article 55, to freedom to provide services. The Citizens' Rights Directive clarifies the extent of these provisions, largely repeating the provisions of Council Directive 64/221 (OJ 1964 Spec. Ed. No. 850/117, now repealed) on the coordination of special measures concerning the movement and residence of foreign nationals which are justified on grounds of public policy, public security and public health, but also building upon the provisions of Directive 64/221 in important ways, not least by bringing in a number of principles already established in the case law (see Nic Shuibhne, 2006: 191–2). The public health derogation has been rarely applied and is of considerably less significance than the derogations on grounds of public policy and public security, which – to a great extent – overlap.

Article 27 of the Citizens' Rights Directive states that public policy and public security relate only to the personal conduct of the individual concerned, and not to wider, more general questions of policy (for example, a policy decision to exclude certain categories of individuals because of a perception that this category poses particular security risks). However, in Case 41/74 *Van Duyn* v. *Home Office* ([1974] ECR 1337), the Court of Justice did allow that active association with a suspect group (in that instance, the Church of Scientology) could constitute personal conduct and thus fall within the scope of the exception. Article 27(2) adds to this by stating that previous criminal convictions cannot by themselves justify exclusion (see also Case 67/74 *Bonsignore* v. *Oberstadtdirektor der Stadt Köln* [1975] ECR 297). However, if the criminal convictions form part of the evidence to suggest that an individual is a present security risk (Case 30/77 *R* v. *Bouchereau* [1977] ECR 1999), and if it is clear that that judgment is based on current evidence and not solely on the existence of previous criminal convictions, they may be taken into consideration in taking a decision to exclude an individual. The thrust of the legal provisions and case law leads to the conclusion that each decision to exclude an EU citizen on grounds of public policy or public security must be examined on its facts; Member State authorities may not fetter their discretion by setting out categories of individuals who must be excluded. The same is true for the case of non-EU citizens who have a right of residence under EU law because of their family ties (*Commission* v. *Spain*, above).

The decision to deport or to refuse entry on grounds of public policy and public security provides one of the few instances where Member States are entitled to discriminate against EU citizens of a different nationality. However, the question has been posed as to the extent of this permitted discrimination. May Member States deport non-nationals in circumstances where nationals would not be penalised? Generally speaking, the answer is 'no'. The question was asked in *Van Duyn*, where it was argued on behalf of Mrs Van Duyn that the fact that the UK government tolerated the Church of Scientology and did not ban it meant that they could not justifiably refuse her entry to work for the Church. The Court replied that there was no need to ban the Church, and indeed appeared to accept that to do so would be an infringement of freedom of religion. However, it stated that Member State authorities must have 'clearly defined their standpoint as regards the activities of a particular organisation and . . . taken administrative measures to counteract these activities . . .' (para. 19). Thus the Member State must have taken some measures against the organisation or activity. This was further discussed in Joined Cases 115 and 116/81 *Adoui and Cornuaille* v. *Belgium* ([1982] ECR 1665), where the Court said that, in the case of refusal of a residence permit on the grounds of suspected prostitution, the activities concerned must give rise to repressive measures if carried out by Member State nationals. Therefore, there must be some level of penalty or control of the activities; States may not deport or refuse entry to nationals of other States for activities or conduct which would attract no sanctions or official disapproval if carried out by their own nationals.

The rise in importance of fundamental rights within the EU legal order has had a further impact on the right to deport. Specifically, a public policy justification may only be successful if it takes account of fundamental rights. Particularly important in this field is the right to respect of family life, which may affect the right of a Member State to deport an individual in a way which separates them from their family (Case C-441/02 *Commission* v. *Germany* [2006] ECR I-3449). Article 28(1) of the Citizens' Rights Directive provides that: 'before taking an expulsion decision on grounds of public policy or public security, the host Member State shall take account of considerations such as how long the individual concerned has resided on its territory, his/her age, state of health, family and economic situation, social and cultural integration into the host Member State and the extent of his/her links with the country of origin.' Article 28(2) provides special protection for Union citizens and their family members, who have the right of permanent residence, limiting expulsion decisions only to '*serious* grounds of public policy or public security'.

Even more limited is the recourse against Union citizens who have resided in the host Member State for the previous ten years, or are a minor; such expulsion decisions may only be based on '*imperative* grounds of public security' (Article 28(3)).

The Citizens' Rights Directive also gives consideration to the question of procedure. Article 31 provides that persons affected by an expulsion decision must have access to judicial and, where appropriate, administrative redress procedures in the host Member State to appeal against the decision. The proportionality of the decision, especially in view of the considerations stated in Article 28 about permanent and long-term residents, is one of the specific questions that must be looked at on appeal. Automatic permanent expulsions for life are also not permitted. This was established by the Court of Justice in Case C-348/96 *Criminal Proceedings against Calfa* ([1999] ECR I-11), and is dealt with explicitly in Article 32 of the directive. Persons against whom an expulsion decision has been made may submit an application for its lifting after a reasonable period. The objective is to avoid punitive expulsions, and to ensure that they are only taken on the grounds of a present threat to public order or public security.

## 12.11　Free Movement and Enlargement

The right to move freely around the territory of the Union, to enter and reside in other Member States and to take up employment have raised particular issues in the light of the recent enlargements of the EU. Ten new Member States joined the EU in May 2004 and two further states joined in January 2007, bringing the total population of the European Union very close to 500 million. The implications for the free movement of persons of these two enlargements are very significant, given the substantial differences in the level of incomes and gross national product between most of the states in the 'old' and the 'new' European Union, and given that rates of unemployment are very high, in particular in the ten states of central and eastern Europe which had planned economies until the 1990s. Significant issues arise for all of the Member States, both 'new' and 'old'. Firstly, in some Member States, specifically Germany and Austria, there was a fear that a significant and disproportionate increase in migration from the new Member States might distort the employment market. While it is unclear whether this fear is realistic, and indeed the Commission suggested that some increased migration might be necessary in some Member States (such as Germany) to combat an aging population, the unevenness of new migration flows and their impact on public opinion could not be ignored. Secondly, a sudden and uneven increase in migration towards more prosperous Member States could have a detrimental impact on the labour forces of the new States, who would need to sustain their economic growth. The same factors do not exist in the context of free movement of goods, and indeed freedom of establishment and the free movement of services, all of which are generally in place in advance of accession, as a consequence of association agreements with candidate states. It is also worth mentioning that the potentially disruptive effects of the free movement of persons following accession had been recognised in the context of earlier enlargements; Greece, Spain and Portugal were all subject to transitional periods before the provisions on the free movement of workers were fully activated.

The Treaty of Accession signed in 2003 with the ten Member States which acceded in 2004 allowed the fifteen 'old' Member States to impose transitional restrictions on the free movement of workers as against eight of those ten states (Cyprus and Malta were excepted). No transitional restrictions are placed upon freedom of establishment or freedom to provide services. Only Ireland, Sweden and the United Kingdom chose not to invoke the possibility of imposing transitional restrictions and opened their labour markets to what were termed A8 (i.e. Accession 8) nationals, although since 2006 a number of the other Member States, such as Spain and Italy, have opened their labour markets. With regard to the 2007 accession of Bulgaria and Romania, transitional restrictions on the free movement of labour were also made possible by the Treaty of Accession signed in 2005, and these were invoked by a different set of Member States. For example, reflecting a growing negativity within some sections of public opinion at the large numbers of, in particular, Polish workers who had taken advantage of the opportunity to work in the United Kingdom and Ireland, these two Member States chose to impose restrictions on Bulgarian and Romanian workers. However, other Member States of the EU-25 (i.e. those states already members before Bulgaria and Romania joined) allowed immediate full market access, such as Denmark (although it kept a work permit regime in place) and Poland, which itself has suffered a skills and labour drain since 2004 and for whom workers from Romania can, therefore, represent an important resource. The situation is, of course, quite fluid, and the transitional restrictions can only be kept in place normally until 2009, and exceptionally if serious disturbances of the labour market can be shown, until 2011 in respect of the Member States acceding in 2004. A similar set of arrangements applies to the 2007 enlargement, which must end by 2014 at the latest. By that stage, the economies of all of the new Member States can be expected to be closer to the EU average for GDP, and indeed Slovenia had already passed the point of being 75 per cent of EU-27 average by 2007, with states such as Estonia not far behind. On the other hand, with the restrictions that have been in place, which have effectively continued the division between 'old' Europe and 'new' Europe after accession, an important distinction has been drawn between those who are fully privileged as citizens of the Union and those who are not (Carrera, 2005). In view of the geopolitical importance of the post-2004 enlargements, which are related to the political and economic changes resulting from the end of the Cold War, the effects of these distinctions so far as they continue to divide Europe in two have been rather negative.

## 12.12  Non-Discrimination and Equal Treatment for Migrants

All of the provisions of the EC Treaty and secondary legislation require that EU citizens must be able to exercise their free movement rights without discrimination on grounds of nationality. Moreover, the judgment in Case C-224/98 *D'Hoop* v. *Office National de l'Emploi* ([2002] ECR I-6191) confirmed discrimination on the grounds that a person has exercised his or her free movement rights is also prohibited. This case concerned a Belgian citizen who, having received her secondary education in France, was refused an unemployment benefit, on the grounds that her secondary education had not been received in Belgium. The Court preferred to analyse this situation as one of discrimination against movers, rather than as an example of an obstacle to free movement which should be removed (Iliopoulou and Toner, 2003). In his opinion in Case C-190/98 *Volker Graf* ([2000] ECR I-493), Advocate General Fennelly argued that the case law of the Court has created a principle of non-discrimination on grounds of migration, which sits alongside the principle of non-discrimination on grounds of nationality. This seems to have been confirmed in Case C-224/02 *Pusa* ([2004] ECR I-5763), where the Court made it clear that

EU law precludes discrimination based on the fact of a citizen having exercised their fundamental right of free movement. Throughout this section, for simplicity's sake, references to discrimination on grounds of nationality should be understood as including discrimination on grounds of migration.

The concept of non-discrimination can thus be seen as increasingly important in free movement law. It is an expression of the general principle of non-discrimination contained in Article 12 EC. It applies, here, to entry, residence and work (both in terms of job offers and in terms of working conditions). The non-discrimination obligation is imposed on Member States and, unlike the other free movement provisions, also horizontally, to cover, for example, employers (see Case C-281/98 *Angonese* [2000] ECR I-4139). It also extends, as we shall see in the following paragraphs, to many social and welfare benefits. In the Citizens' Rights Directive, the prohibition on discrimination is rephrased in more positive language as the right to 'equal treatment' (Article 24). It is unclear as yet whether this will affect the scope of the entitlements given to non-nationals.

The prohibition on discrimination covers both direct and indirect discrimination. Direct discrimination is discrimination which explicitly treats non-nationals less favourably than nationals, and is prohibited unless it can be saved by reference to the derogations contained in Article 39(3) or Article 46 (discussed in 12.10). Indirect discrimination exists where a condition or criterion applies without regard to nationality, but where, in reality, the great majority of those affected are, in fact, non-nationals, or where non-nationals may find it more difficult to comply with the condition or criterion than nationals. Article 3 of Regulation 1612/68 states that provisions are unlawful 'where, though applicable irrespective of nationality, their exclusive or principal aim or effect is to keep nationals of other Member States away from the employment offered'.

One example of an indirectly discriminatory measure may be a requirement that all employees have a university degree or qualification from a particular Member State. This does not directly concern nationality, but in fact nationals of that Member State are significantly more likely to have the required degree or qualification. Another example might be a language requirement, which would significantly advantage nationals of the Member State where that language is spoken. However, Article 3 of Regulation 1612/68 goes on to state specifically that it does not apply to 'conditions relating to linguistic knowledge required by reason of the nature of the post to be filled'. This provision can be interpreted widely: in Case 397/87 *Groener* v. *Minister of Education* ([1989] ECR 3967), the Court held that a requirement that a primary school teacher in Ireland be able to speak Irish was allowable, even though teaching and all other activities of the school took place in English, as a legitimate part of cultural policy.

In Case C-237/94 *O'Flynn* v. *Adjudication Officer* ([1996] ECR I-2617), the Court specified that the requirement for a disparate impact means that there must be the potential for such an impact. It is not necessary to prove that there is in fact a disparate impact. This is similar to the *Dassonville* formula which applies to the free movement of goods, in that it covers potential as well as actual discrimination.

Objective justification is central to the concept of indirect discrimination. According to the Court in *O'Flynn*, such discrimination is unlawful unless it is justified by objective conditions independent of nationality and it is proportionate to the legitimate aim pursued by national law. In relation to the free movement of services, according to Case C-288/89 *Gouda* ([1991] ECR I-4007), the space for justification appears to be somewhat narrower, as the requirements imposed must be justified by an overriding aim of public interest.

Article 39(4) EC provides for a further exception to the non-discrimination principle, in that it permits Member States to reserve positions in the public service for their own nationals. This is intended as a defence of traditional notions of sovereignty, in that it is felt that many public service positions are only appropriate for people with loyalty and citizenship ties with the State. However, the Court of Justice has interpreted the provision strictly. First, the Court asserts the right to determine whether a particular job falls within the public service exception; this is not a conclusion which can be reached by the Member State authorities (Case 152/73 *Sotgiu* v. *Deutsche Bundespost* [1974] ECR 153). This makes sense, as the traditions of Member States vary considerably as to the extent of the public service and the exceptions should apply in broadly the same way throughout the EU. Second, the Court interprets the exception narrowly. In Case 149/79 *Commission* v. *Belgium* ([1980] ECR 3881), the Belgian government argued that, in the Belgian system, all employees of national and local authorities and publicly-owned undertakings are classified as working in the public service, and all such jobs should be reserved to Belgian nationals. The Court rejected this interpretation of Article 39(4). It stated that employment in the public service involves 'direct or indirect participation in the exercise of powers conferred by public law and duties designed to safeguard the general interest of the State or of other public bodies' (at para. 10). This kind of work can properly be reserved for people with a tie of allegiance with the state. However, such a tie is not necessary for people working, for example, as cleaners or low-grade administrative staff.

The educational sphere has provided a particular focus for Article 39(4) litigation, with the Court holding that teachers (*Lawrie-Blum*; Case C-4/91 *Bleis* v. *Ministère de l'Education nationale* [1991] ECR I-5627) and university foreign language assistants (Case 33/88 *Allué and Coonan* v. *Università degli Studi di Venezia* [1989] ECR 1591) do not fall within the exception.

In respect of freedom of establishment and the freedom to provide services, Article 45 EC provides that these freedoms do not apply 'to activities which in [a Member State] are connected, even occasionally, with the exercise of official authority'. This provision has not precluded the substantial liberalisation of many aspects of the commercial provision of lawyers' services. Professional contact with a national court does not, as such, fall within the official authority exception (Case 2/74 *Reyners* v. *Belgium* [1974] ECR 631, para. 51).

## 12.13 The Right of Access to Economic Activity

The Court of Justice has, however, moved beyond the concepts of direct and indirect discrimination to address more generally the notion of a right of access to economic activity. For example, in Case C-464/02 *Commission* v. *Denmark* ([2005] ECR I-7929) it stated that:

'the provisions of the Treaty on freedom of movement for persons are intended to facilitate the pursuit by Community citizens of occupational activities of all kinds throughout the Community, and preclude measures which might place Community citizens at a disadvantage when they wish to pursue an economic activity in the territory of another Member State ... Provisions which preclude or deter a national of a Member State from leaving his country of origin in order to exercise his right to freedom of movement therefore constitute an obstacle to that freedom even if they apply without regard to the nationality of the workers concerned ... However, in order to be capable of constituting such an obstacle, they must affect access of workers to the labour market' (paras. 34–36).

Chalmers *et al* (2006: 705) indicate the Court is now moving towards 'developing an explicit overarching right to take up and pursue an occupation in another Member State, which encompasses and structures both Articles 39 and 43.

The leading case in relation to the free movement of workers is Case C-415/93 *Union Royal Belge des Sociétés de Football Association* v. *Bosman* ([1995] ECR I-4921). *Bosman* concerned a Belgian footballer, contracted to a Belgian club, who wished to leave and join a French club. His club refused to agree a transfer with the French club, and thus Bosman was not able to take up employment with the French club. Bosman challenged this decision, and the Court of Justice ruled that the transfer rules which prevented him from moving clubs were contrary to EU law, as they 'directly affect players' access to the employment market in other Member States and are thus capable of impeding freedom of movement for workers', despite the fact that they were also applicable to players wishing to move clubs within one Member State. The Court therefore stated that any rule which hinders free movement of workers falls, in principle, within the scope of Article 39. The *Bosman* judgment had a huge impact on the world of football, forcing UEFA and FIFA to change their transfer rules and leading to a wider discussion of the applicability of internal market rules to sport (see, for example, the Commission discussion document 'The European Model of Sport', published in November 1998, and the Helsinki Report on Sport (COM(1999) 644 final)). Its significance in free movement law is also great although, given the unique nature of the employment conditions of footballers, it has not had the impact of its equivalent judgments (*Dassonville* and *Cassis*) in the field of free movement of goods. The *Bosman* case law was not taken to the extreme that the *Cassis* case law went to. In Case C-190/98 *Volker Graf* ([2000] ECR I-493), for example, the Court stated that Article 39 did not apply in cases where the potential impediment to freedom of movement was too uncertain and indirect. For this reason, perhaps, the Court has not felt it necessary to restrict the impact of *Bosman* in the way that it did in the *Keck* judgment on free movement of goods. Barnard, indeed, sees *Graf* as fulfilling the same function as *Keck*, in that it 'stem(s) the flow of cases that seek to challenge key pillars of national welfare and social provision internal to the Member States which were never intended to interfere with free movement' (Barnard, 2001).

The equivalent cases in the field of establishment are Case 107/83 *Ordre des Avocats* v. *Klopp* ([1984] ECR 2971) and *Gebhard*. In *Klopp*, a requirement imposed by the Paris Bar that all advocates wishing to be registered as advocates in Paris must register exclusively with the Paris Bar was held to contravene Article 43, as it rendered secondary establishment impossible and thus ran contrary to the objective of freedom of establishment. This was the case even though the Paris Bar's rules applied also to advocates wishing to practise in more than one region of France. In *Gebhard*, the court stated that 'national measures liable to hinder or make less attractive the exercise of fundamental freedoms guaranteed by the Treaty must fulfil four conditions' in order not to breach Article 43:

'they must be applied in a non-discriminatory manner; they must be justified by imperative requirements in the general interest; they must be suitable for securing the attainment of the objective which they pursue; and they must not go beyond what is necessary to attain it' (para. 37).

This rule, which moves away from thinking about obstacles to free movement in terms of different categories of discrimination and towards a purposive, market access approach, has much in common with the Court's approach in the law relating to goods and services.

Barnard (2001) has proposed a move away from the discrimination approach for all categories, and towards a simple market access test. This would eliminate the complexities inherent in the categories of discrimination, and make for a simpler, more effective, approach.

## 12.14 Access to Social and Welfare Benefits: The Principle of Equal Treatment

Traditionally, access to social and welfare benefits on the part of non-nationals resident in the host Member State has been restricted to those who are economically active, and their families. This is regulated expressly for workers and their families, who are granted the right under Article 7(2) of Regulation 1612/68 to enjoy the 'same social and tax advantages as national workers'. It is therefore unlawful for Member States to discriminate in the awarding of 'social advantages' either against other Union citizens on grounds of nationality, or against their own nationals on the grounds that they have previously lived in another Member State (Case C-18/95 *Terhoeve* v. *Inspecteur van de Belastingdienst Particulieren/Ondernemingen Buitenland* [1999] ECR I-345). Historically, there was no equivalent provision in EU law for self-employed persons, whether established in another Member State or operating as a service provider, but they are indubitably covered by the right to equal treatment in Article 24 of the Citizens' Rights Directive. Article 24(1) provides:

> 'Subject to such specific provisions as are expressly provided for in the Treaty and secondary law, all Union citizens residing on the basis of this Directive in the territory of the host Member State shall enjoy equal treatment with the nationals of that Member State within the scope of the Treaty. The benefit of this right shall be extended to family members who are not nationals of a Member State and who have the right of residence or permanent residence.'

In any event, in Case 197/84 *Steinhauser* v. *City of Biarritz* ([1985] ECR 1819), the Court had already held that to refuse a self-employed person access to social advantages would be to hinder the right of establishment, and in Case 63/86 *Commission* v. *Italy* ([1988] ECR 29), the Court held that access to social advantages must be available on a non-discriminatory basis to service providers if to deny the benefit would hinder the freedom to provide services. In this sense, the directive consolidates the previous law. However, the reference in Article 24(1) to other 'specific provisions' is important, because under EU law not all categories of migrants, and their families, have been able to access 'social advantages'. Indeed, Article 24(2) itself highlights restrictions on access to what it terms 'social assistance' for certain categories of migrants and to certain benefits for students, which Member States may impose, notwithstanding the equal treatment principle. However, before considering in more detail the layers of entitlement in EU law in a field which has been especially fluid since the establishment of the legal rights of EU citizenship in the 1990s and the associated case law which has resulted from this, it is important to review in more detail the concepts of 'social advantages' and 'social assistance' in order to ascertain what is covered.

## 12.15 Social Advantages: What is covered

The definition of the term 'social advantages' has proved controversial. Early on, the Court of Justice appeared to take the view that Article 7(2) of Regulation 1612/68 was intended to ensure that workers from other Member States were not discriminated against in the context of their work. Thus, in Case 76/72 *Michel S* v. *Fonds National de Reclassement Handicapés* ([1973] ECR 457), it was held that the only benefits available under Article 7(2) were those directly connected to employment, and therefore granted only to workers and not to their families, although other benefits might be available through the application of other provisions (notably Article 12 of Regulation 1612/68 on children's right to access to education). However, in Case 32/75 *Fiorini* v. *SNCF* ([1975] ECR 1085), the Court backtracked from this position, holding that Article 7(2) should not be interpreted in such a restrictive manner, as its goal was to achieve general equality of treatment. Therefore, Article 7(2) should be held to cover 'all social and tax advantages, whether or not attached to the contract of employment'. In Case C-310/91 *Schmid* v. *Belgian State* ([1993] ECR I-3011), the definition was clarified to include:

> 'all rights which are generally granted to national workers because of their objective status as workers or by virtue of the mere fact of their residence on the national territory, and whose extension to workers who are nationals of other Member States therefore seems likely to facilitate the mobility of such workers within the Community' (para. 18).

It also includes rights with a link to the status of worker, even if the claimant no longer has the status of worker (for example, because they have been made redundant (Case 39/86 *Lair* v. *Universität Hamburg* [1988] ECR 3161; Case C-57/96 *Meints* v. *Minister van Landbouw, Natuurbeheer en Visserij* [1997] ECR I-6689)). Also covered are advantages granted to the families of workers (*Lebon*) and self-employed people, including dependent adults who need access to disability benefits (Case 63/76 *Inzirillo* v. *Caisse d'Allocations Familiales de l'Arrondissement de Lyon* [1976] ECR 2057). However, those advantages must be construed as, in some way, providing an advantage to the worker, however indirect. This construction was achieved in *Inzirillo* by stating that failure to grant the benefit would induce the worker not to remain in the Member State where he was working in order to ensure that his dependent adult offspring would gain full access to the necessary benefits (para. 17). This approach has proved to be fairly flexible. The Court held that advantages were available to family members even in a situation where the self-employed person, although established in one Member State, maintains residence in the Member State of which he is a national and where the dependant (in this case, the child) remains resident in the Member State of which she and her parent are nationals (Case C-337/97 *Meeusen* v. *Hoofdirectie van der Informatie Beheer Groep* [1999] ECR I-3289). This judgment was decided on the basis of the principle of non-discrimination, in so far as no residence requirements were placed on children who were citizens of that Member State (the Netherlands). While the Court referred briefly to the necessity of ensuring that freedom of establishment is not hindered, it is difficult to see why preventing the child of a Belgian national, resident in Belgium but established in the Netherlands, from having access to study finance provided by the Netherlands, would hinder the Belgian national from becoming established in the Netherlands. The situation would be different if the family had moved to the Netherlands.

The *Meeusen* judgment suggests that the Court is becoming less concerned with ensuring that the advantage will, in the specific case, facilitate free movement and more concerned with the application of the principle of non-discrimination, either on grounds of nationality or on grounds of migration (although it continues to use the language of the facilitation of free movement in its judgment). This seems consistent with the rise in the status of citizenship, and the suggestion that citizenship rights are rights in themselves, rather than rights intended to facilitate the free movement of workers. It has however refused to go so far as to allow for the continuation of rights after the worker has returned to his state of origin, requiring that the migrant worker must be exercising an activity in the host Member State in order to receive social advantages from that State (Case C-33/99 *Hassan Fahmi and Esmoris Cerdeiro-Pinedo Amado* v. *Bestuur van de Sociale Verzerkeringsbank* [2001] ECR I-2415).

## 12.16 Access to Benefits for Non-Economically Active Persons

Until the judgment of the Court in *Martínez Sala*, it was clear that social advantages were not available to job seekers, the retired, the economically self-sufficient and students. Since that judgment and the judgment in *Grzelczyk*, the question has been less clear, in that both judgments stated that all EU citizens lawfully resident in a Member State other than their own must be treated in a non-discriminatory fashion, even in the matter of access to social advantages.

The Court's judgment in *Martínez Sala* marked the start of a process in which it has explored the limits of the right to non-discrimination on grounds of nationality, contained in Article 12 EC, when it is read in combination with the citizenship provisions, notably Article 17(2) which states that 'Citizens of the Union shall enjoy the rights conferred by this Treaty and shall be subject to the duties imposed thereby'. Maria Martínez Sala was a Spanish citizen living in Germany, having moved there as a child with her parents long before Spanish accession to the European Union. She was not employed, but was caring for her child, and her residence status was in some doubt, as she had been issued over the previous few years with acknowledgements that her application for residence was being dealt with, rather than a full residence permit. She applied for a child-raising allowance and was turned down, as she was unable to produce the necessary documents. As a non-national she was required to produce certain documents, notably a residence permit, in order to access the benefit, whereas such formalities were not required of nationals. The Court of Justice relied on Article 17(2) and argued that because Martínez Sala was a citizen of the Union, lawfully resident in a Member State other than her own, she had the right not to be discriminated against in the field of social security. Unfortunately, the Court did not rule on the question of whether she derived her underlying right of residence from EU law or German law, since it noted that the right of residence had in practice been conceded by the German Government. Martínez Sala therefore counted as a national of a Member State lawfully resident in another Member State, who was entitled to equal treatment under Article 12 EC. It can be argued that the judgment opens the door to 'something close to a universal non-discrimination right including access to all welfare benefits . . . as a consequence of the creation of the figure of the Union citizen' (Fries and Shaw, 1998). Jacqueson argues that the impact of *Martínez Sala* was that the principle of equal treatment was no longer regarded as a means to an end (the end being the achievement of free movement and the internal market) but as a goal of the Union itself (Jacqueson, 2002).

The judgment in *Martínez Sala* was reinforced by the subsequent judgment in *Grzelczyk* which concerned access to benefits by a student. Grzelczyk was a French student studying in Belgium who found, towards the end of his studies, that he was no longer able to support himself; he consequently sought to claim the Belgian *minimex*, a universal minimum income benefit. He was refused, on the grounds that he was not a Belgian national and that previous Court of Justice case law had held that students' free movement rights do not extend to the right to claim financial support from the state in which they are studying. The Court pointed out that since the earlier case law (e.g. Case 197/86 *Brown* [1988] ECR 3205) Member States had amended the EC Treaty, through the Treaty on European Union, or the Treaty of Maastricht, in order to introduce citizenship of the Union and, moreover, had adopted Council Directive 93/96 on the right of residence for students. While Member States may make entry to study conditional on the existence of sufficient resources to do so and states may require students to make a declaration of sufficient resources (both under Directive 93/96 at that time and now under Article 7 of the Citizens' Rights Directive), this did not mean that students would for ever be prohibited from applying for welfare benefit support. As the Court noted, 'a student's financial position may change with the passage of time for reasons beyond his control. The truthfulness of a student's declaration is therefore to be assessed only as at the time when it is made' (para. 45). The Court emphasised the point that the applicant was lawfully resident in Belgium under EU law (thus suggesting that the solution for Member States would be to withdraw residence rights from students whose financial resources run out); it also stated that withdrawal of residence rights should not be the automatic consequence of the student's recourse to social assistance, particularly if the lack of funds is likely to be temporary. Withdrawal of residence rights is justified when a student becomes an 'unreasonable' burden on State funds, and the Court refers to the acceptance of 'a certain degree of financial solidarity' between the Member States in respect of the entitlements of EU citizens (para. 44).

The Court developed this point further in Case C-209/03 *R* v. *London Borough of Ealing, ex parte Bidar* ([2005] ECR I-2119) when considering the availability of subsidised loans to students in higher education in the United Kingdom. Bidar was not a student who moved in order to study in a different state, but a French national who was residing with his grandmother in the United Kingdom who completed his secondary education in the United Kingdom. However, although he had achieved a high degree of integration within the host society, he nonetheless did not satisfy the ordinary residence test applied by the UK authorities in order to qualify for access to subsidised loans as a student of higher education. The Court referred again to the 'certain degree of financial solidarity' to be expected between the Member States under the citizenship provisions, and combined this with the non-discrimination provision: 'a citizen of the Union who is not economically active may rely on Article 12 EC where he has been lawfully resident in the host Member State for a certain period of time or possesses a residence permit' (para. 56). It remains a little difficult (see Dougan, 2006) to reconcile the rights which the Court appears to give Union citizens in *Grzelczyk* and *Bidar* with Article 24(2) of the Citizens' Rights Directive, which contains the clearly expressed legislative 'will' of the Member States:

> 'By way of derogation from paragraph 1 [the right to equal treatment], the host Member State shall not be obliged . . . prior to acquisition of the right of permanent residence, to grant maintenance aid for studies, including vocational training, consisting in student grants or student loans to persons other than workers, self-employed persons, persons who retain such status and members of their families.'

The situation of work seekers has also evolved as a consequence of the innovation of Union citizenship, the case law of the Court of Justice and the provisions of the Citizens' Rights Directive. Article 24(2) provides that 'the host Member State shall not be obliged to confer entitlement to social assistance during the first three months of residence or, where appropriate, the longer period provided for in Article 14(4)(b) . . .'. Nonetheless in *Trojani*, the Court held that social assistance *does* fall within the scope of the EC Treaty, and a national of a Member State who is not economically active can rely upon the equal treatment principle in order to access a social assistance benefit (in this case, as in *Grzelczyk*, the Belgian *minimex*), provided that he or she has been lawfully resident for some time in the host state. On the other hand, while the equal treatment principle may apply, there may also be scope in relation to social assistance for Member States to apply objective justification in relation to access to social assistance benefits, in particular where the distinction is drawn not on the basis of nationality as such, but rather the residence or – to use the UK terminology – *habitual* residence of the claimant. In Case C-138/02 *Collins* v. *Secretary of State for Work and Pensions* ([2004] ECR I-2703), the Court of Justice made it clear that job seekers were not to be understood as falling into the same category as workers. Member States may place restrictions on their right to claim any social benefit related to their status as job seekers (in this case, the UK Jobseeker's Allowance), even if those restrictions discriminate on grounds of place of habitual residence, given that the restrictions can be justified in order to maintain integrity of the labour market. The period of residence required under national law must not, however, exceed what is necessary in order for the national authorities to be able to satisfy themselves that the person concerned is genuinely seeking work in the employment market of the host Member State (para. 72) (see also Case C-406/04 *De Cuyper* v. *Office National de l'Emploi* [2006] ECR I-6947).

## 12.17  Mutual Recognition of Qualifications – A Move towards Positive Integration?

Thus far what has been discussed is a form of negative integration – the removal of barriers to free movement. Rules have been enacted to remove physical barriers (border controls – see Chapter 13), administrative and legal barriers (requirements for residence and work permits) and discrimination against non-nationals in the employment market. There have, however, been moves towards more positive integration, in the form of more complex harmonisation of regulations which restrict access to occupations and professions. This is not unproblematic. While cultural and contextual barriers are by no means unknown in the harmonisation of regulations concerning goods or services, they are more prevalent when it comes to regulations concerning people, who are essentially cultural beings. Thus, cultural differences can prove to be barriers to free movement which are not easily overcome.

A failure to recognise qualifications obtained in another Member State is one of the most tangible barriers to migration for the purposes of employment. It was suggested in 12.12 that to restrict employment to people with degrees from certain Member States would be an example of indirect discrimination on grounds of nationality and would thus only be permissible if objectively justified. This can be seen as a first step on the road to the removal of barriers, but it allows for objective justification on the grounds of consumer protection, among other things. However, in certain fields, the EU has moved further by setting out rules for the mutual recognition of qualifications. This could be seen as a precursor to the possible harmonisation of professional qualifications, in the context of an EU educational and vocational training policy. The starting point is that, in the absence of harmonisation of professional qualifications, states are free to regulate access to trades and professions in whatever way they choose, as long as they comply with the fundamental principles of the EU (Case C-108/96 *Criminal Proceedings against Mac Quen et al* [2001] ECR I-837; Case C-58/98 *Corsten* [2000] ECR I-7919). In particular, they must regulate in a non-discriminatory fashion and the regulations must comply with the *Gebhard* conditions (12.13). This requirement is not too onerous, as it can usually be argued that regulation of qualifications is in the interests of consumer protection.

However, the EU has established rules concerning the mutual recognition of qualifications, and has taken some steps towards the harmonisation of qualification frameworks. Within much current EU policy-making, harmonisation is less of a priority than the development of a system of mutual recognition, facilitated by increased transparency. In this way, different cultures and traditions can be respected. Armstrong (2002) has distinguished two types of mutual recognition, as it exists within the EU framework. Passive mutual recognition is a system whereby an agreed list of equivalent qualifications exists, and states merely need to note, and formally recognise, that an individual holds a qualification deemed to be equivalent to the relevant local qualification in order to allow them to carry out their profession. It is thus necessary that states be able to trust in the regulatory systems of the other Member States. Active mutual recognition is a system where states are required to investigate whether a particular qualification is equivalent to the relevant local qualification, and to allow individuals to carry out their profession if their qualification is found to be equivalent. This therefore allows Member States more control over what they choose to accept. Armstrong further suggests that active mutual recognition facilitates the process of communication (which is also being undertaken in other contexts) which will give Member States trust in each others' standards and make passive mutual recognition more feasible. In practical terms, if there is passive mutual recognition there is no need, as far as the internal market is concerned, to harmonise further, although it might be desirable in the context of education and vocational training policy.

The EU's legislative structures for facilitating the national recognition of the individuals qualified (and practising in one Member State) who wish to work or establish themselves in another Member State have evolved incrementally. In 2005, the system was rationalised by the adoption of European Parliament and Council Directive 2005/36 on the recognition of professional qualifications (OJ 2005 L255/2) to be implemented by October 2007. This does not replace the variety of different systems for the recognition of professional qualifications used hitherto, but it consolidates the legislative framework. The basic principle is stated in Article 4(1):

> 'The recognition of professional qualifications by the host Member State allows the beneficiary to gain access in that Member State to the same profession as that for which he is qualified in the home Member State and to pursue it in the host Member State under the same conditions as its nationals.'

However, in practice how this is achieved varies from profession to profession. The earliest system was that used for a list of specified professional qualifications, in particular doctors, nurses responsible for general care, dentists, vets, midwives, pharmacists and architects. The system consists of the automatic recognition of training qualifications (passive mutual recognition) combined with limited harmonisation in the form of setting minimum standards and training conditions. Thus, for each profession, there exist two directives, one of which lays out minimum standards and training conditions, and the other of which requires mutual recognition and lists the equivalent qualifications.

A second system is similar, but focuses on a set of industrial, craft and commercial activities, where not all Member States may require formal qualifications. It requires the automatic recognition of qualifications attested by professional experience, thus allowing experience to be used as an equivalent to a qualification. These regulations were originally set out in separate directives for each activity, but many of them were consolidated by a 1999 directive, which has now been repealed by Directive 2005/36.

Finally, there is a general system applying to any profession or situation not falling within the first two categories. This general system was initiated in two directives: Council Directive 89/48 on higher education diplomas (OJ 1989 L19/16) (which applied to everyone who has completed at least 3 years of tertiary education and is not covered by one of the sectoral directives) and Council Directive 92/51 on other educational diplomas (OJ 1992 L209/25). These have now been replaced by Directive 2005/36. The basic principle of the general system is active mutual recognition, whereby Member States are required to investigate the equivalence of qualifications and experience. Mutual recognition may be dependent on the application of compensatory measures – usually an aptitude test or adaptation period – in cases where the Member State feels that there are substantial differences between the training acquired by the migrant and the training required in the host Member State.

The general system can be seen as a legislative application of the principle underlying the line of case law which started with the Court of Justice's judgments in Case 222/86 *UNECTEF* v. *Heylens* ([1987] ECR 4097) and Case C-340/89 *Vlassopoulou* ([1991] ECR I-2357). In these cases the Court, while starting from the principle that Member States are entitled to regulate access to an occupation in the absence of harmonisation, continued to argue that such regulation must take into consideration both qualifications and experience gained in another Member State. This is the case, following the judgment in Case C-238/98 *Hocsman* v. *Ministre de l'Emploi et de la solidarité* ([2000] ECR I-6623), even if a sectoral directive exists in the field, if that directive does not precisely cover the particular situation concerned. This also applies, to some extent, to qualifications obtained outside the Community, where the individual has carried out their activity within a Member State. While the directives do not cover non-Member State qualifications, and thus passive mutual recognition will not apply (Case C-154/93 *Tawil-Albertini* v. *Ministre des Affaires Sociales* [1994] ECR I-451), the fact that a qualification obtained outside a Member State has enabled the person to practise and gain experience within a Member State must be taken into consideration in applying the *Vlassopoulou* principle (Case C-319/92 *Haim* [1994] ECR I-425; see also *Hocsman*). This applies, however, only to EU citizens who have obtained qualifications in non-Member States. Non-EU citizens do not have the right to mutual recognition of qualifications (even if they were obtained within the EU), just as they do not have free movement rights more generally.

The goal of Directive 2005/36 is simplification and consolidation, and the need to allow space for flexibility, both in terms of developing educational systems and in terms of the needs of enlargement. Some minor changes are made to the general system (for example, compensation periods may still apply when there is a question about the content of training, but not when the duration is seen as insufficient). It will also apply to service providers, who would be entitled to provide services in another Member State under their own professional title, subject to verification by the host state, but not subject to specific rules of recognition. If a service provider who is entitled to carry out his activity in his home Member State does not have a qualification which may be required in a more regulated host state, two years' experience in the field would be sufficient.

An exception to this endeavour is provided by the measures relating to lawyers. A distinction there is made between qualification and authority to practise. Lawyers' qualifications have been covered by a sectoral directive, and are now covered by Directive 2005/36. Authority to practise is dealt with separately, and that separate system remains in force. This is because of the importance that lawyers practising within a jurisdiction would normally be expected to know the law of that jurisdiction, and Member States have a legitimate interest in ensuring that that will be the case. The Lawyers' Services Directive (Council Directive 77/249, OJ 1977 L78/17) was one of the earliest mutual recognition directives. This allows lawyers to provide legal services in other Member States. They must use their home state title (e.g. *solicitor* if they are UK qualified, *avocat* if they are French qualified, etc.), in order to make it clear that they are only providing services on a temporary basis. They must comply with all host state rules, except for any concerning residence and registration. Host states may require that, in the case of lawyers involved in litigation, they be formally introduced by a local lawyer to the judge or Bar, or that they work with a local lawyer. Host states may also request proof of qualification. They may not, however, require registration.

Provisions on the establishment of lawyers in the host state were adopted much later, as they require a much greater level of mutual recognition and trust. Initially, the establishment of lawyers was dealt with under the general Higher Education Directive (Directive 89/48) now replaced by Directive 2005/36. This gave lawyers qualified to practise in one Member State the right to establish themselves in another Member State by being registered in that state. If they wished to use the host state title (e.g. *solicitor* in the UK; *avocat* in France; *Rechtsanwalt* in Germany) they could be required, under Directive 89/48, either to take an aptitude test or to acquire the appropriate knowledge of the national law and legal system. It was for the host state to decide whether they required an aptitude test or not, and most Member States did require such a test. In practice, this proved to be a significant barrier to the mobility of lawyers. Consequently, European Parliament and Council Directive 98/5 (OJ 1998 L77/36) was adopted. This measure, dubbed the Lawyers' Home Title Directive, removed the requirement for an aptitude test, and extended the opportunities for lawyers to practise under their home state title in other Member States, assuming that with experience and practice, lawyers will assimilate the law and practice of that other state. Once a lawyer has spent three years effectively and regularly practising law in the host state, he or she may apply to join the legal profession of the host state without being subjected to an aptitude test (the option of an aptitude test remains open for those who do not want to wait three years). In its first judgments on the effects of the Lawyer's Home Title Directive (Case C-506/04 *Wilson* [2006] ECR I-8613 and Case C-193/05 *Commission* v. *Luxembourg* [2006] ECR I-8673), the Court confirmed that Member States may impose restrictions on the right to practise by reference to professional ethics requirements, but that they may not impose additional requirements not mentioned in the directive, such as linguistic requirements.

In sum, for lawyers, whether they wish to provide services in another Member State or establish themselves there, there is a system of passive mutual recognition, combined with a practical requirement to acquire, by whatever possible means, knowledge of the legal system in which they are operating if they wish to join the legal profession of the Member State where they are practising.

# Summary

1. The law governing free movement of persons was originally based on Articles 39, 43 and 49, which were to be found in the original Treaty of Rome, and in some early legislation. It became a very well-established area of law, as one of the so-called four freedoms.

2. The creation of Union citizenship under Article 17 EC, and the various rights granted to citizens of the Union, notably the right of free movement and residence under Article 18, have had a significant effect on this area of law, as the Court of Justice has used it to expand the scope of free movement rights to most Union citizens and to guarantee non-discrimination on grounds of nationality under Article 12 EC to all Union citizens, subject only to certain proportionate limitations imposed by the Member States.

3. The most privileged category of people under EU law are workers. The concept of worker has been interpreted widely and is defined as a person performing services of economic value under the direction of another for remuneration.

4. Work seekers are also given the right to move and reside, for a limited time, in another Member State in order to look for work.

5. The self-employed and service providers may also move in order to carry out their business. Free movement rights are also granted to those who travel in order to receive services.

6. Union citizens who exercise their free movement rights have the right to take their dependants with them when they migrate.

7. The Court of Justice refers increasingly frequently to the principles of family reunification and the right to a family life in cases concerning dependants, and no longer focuses exclusively on strictly economic justifications.

8. Students, retired people and people with independent means are also given free movement rights, but their ability to rely upon the welfare systems of the host state are much more limited.

9. The Citizens' Rights Directive streamlines some aspects of the law on the free movement of persons, and it relies more heavily on the status of Union citizen and extends their rights; however, the case law of the Court of Justice hints that there may be some tension in the future between some of the legislative restrictions imposed in the directive and the Court's increasingly broad interpretation of the rights of Union citizens.

10. Free movement rights include the right of entry into and residence in Member States. Member States are not permitted to restrict entry to Union citizens covered by the legislation, but may impose border controls and controls intended to verify that the conditions of entitlement to the right are fulfilled.

11. Member States may restrict rights of entry or residence in the case of a threat to public policy, public security or public health.

12. Direct and indirect discrimination on grounds of nationality or migration are prohibited. The exception to this is that Member States may reserve positions in the public service for their own nationals, but the concept of public service is narrowly interpreted by the Court.

13. Migrants have the right to non-impeded access to economic activity throughout the EU.

14. Economically active migrants have access to a range of social advantages, but access to these benefits is more restricted in respect of job seekers, students, the retired or people with independent means.

15. An important step in facilitating the free movement of persons is the developing framework of mutual recognition of qualifications.

# Exercises

1. What has been the impact of the judgment in *Martínez Sala* on the law of free movement of persons?

2. How does the Court of Justice define a 'worker'? What is meant by 'work of economic value'?

3. Who is classified as a 'dependant' under EU law? What is the nature of their rights?

4. What substantive rights are given to the following categories: (a) workers; (b) job seekers; (c) service recipients; and (d) the children of migrant workers?

5. On what grounds, and under what conditions, can a Union citizen be deported from a Member State?

6. What was the impact of the judgment in *Bosman* on the law governing the free movement of persons?

7. What is classed as a 'social advantage' and who can access such benefits?

# Workshop

1. To what extent do you think the law of free movement of persons is moving away from an emphasis on economic activity?

2. Consider the application of EU law to the following situation:

   Jens is a Danish citizen. When travelling around Italy, he meets and joins a group known as the Children of St Francis. They require him to renounce all his possessions and work within the community, where he will be supported. His particular skill is gardening and he works in the community garden producing fruit, flowers and vegetables to be used within the community and sold outside.

   After being there for two years, he comes to realise, however, that he is slowly being brainwashed by the group. He makes contact with an organisation called Europeans Against Cults (EAC) and they manage to get him out of the community. He goes to live in EAC's safe house in Florence. Because he is psychologically and emotionally damaged from the experience of brainwashing, he is unable to work, and is supported by the funds of the EAC. He wants to claim disability benefit. Although the Italian authorities acknowledge that he is lawfully resident in Italy, they refuse to give him the benefit.

   While in Florence, Jens meets and falls in love with Iva, a Croatian national who has been rescued from a cult in Sicily. They decide to set up home together in Siena and get married. Jens finds work, and Iva becomes pregnant and decides to become a full-time mother. Unfortunately, Jens remains troubled, and soon becomes hooked on heroin. He is violent towards Iva and she leaves him. He is then convicted of dealing in illegal substances and serves a two year prison sentence. The Italian authorities want to deport him.

## Further Reading

Barnard, C. (2001) 'Fitting the Remaining Pieces into the Goods and Persons Jigsaw', 26 *European Law Review* 35.

Carrera, S. (2005) 'What does Free Movement Mean in Theory and Practice in an Enlarged EU?', 11 *European Law Journal* 699.

Dougan, M. (2006) 'The Constitutional Dimension to the Case Law on Union Citizenship', 31 *European Law Review* 613.

Ellis, E. (2003) 'Social Advantages: A New Lease of Life?', 40 *Common Market Law Review* 639.

Fries, S. and Shaw, J. (1998) 'Citizenship of the Union: First Steps in the Court of Justice', 4 *European Public Law* 533.

Mather, J.D. (2005) 'The Court of Justice and the Union Citizen', 11 *European Law Journal* 722.

Nic Shuibhne, N. (2002) 'Free Movement of Persons and the Wholly Internal Rule: Time to Move On?', 39 *Common Market Law Review* 731.

Nic Shuibhne, N. (2006) 'Derogating from the Free Movement of Persons: When can EU citizens be deported?', 8 *Cambridge Yearbook of European Legal Studies* 187.

O'Leary, S. (1999) 'The Free Movement of Persons and Services', in Craig, P. and de Búrca, G. (eds.), *The Evolution of EU Law*, Oxford: Oxford University Press.

Reich, N. in collaboration with Harbacevica, S. (2003) 'Citizenship and Family on Trial: A Fairly Optimistic Overview of Recent Court Practice with Regard to Free Movement of Persons', 40 *Common Market Law Review* 615.

White, R. (2005) 'Free Movement, Equal Treatment and Citizenship of the Union', 54 *International and Comparative Law Quarterly* 884.

## Key Websites

While the free movement of persons, as such, should be regarded as a facet of the internal market, and therefore under the domain of DG Internal Market, at:
**http://ec.europa.eu/internal_market/index_en.htm**

the free movement of workers is dealt with by Commission DG Employment and Social Affairs, at:
**http://ec.europa.eu/employment_social/free_ movement/index_en.htm**

The Commission maintains a website specifically providing citizens with information about living and working in the internal market, at:
**http://ec.europa.eu/youreurope/nav/en/citizens/index.html**

The Citizens' Signpost Service is intended to provide solutions for citizens encountering mobility problems in the Union, at:
**http://ec.europa.eu/citizensrights/front_end/index_en.htm**

However, the notion of EU Citizenship as such is the responsibility of DG Justice and Home Affairs, at:
**http://ec.europa.eu/justice_home/fsj/citizenship/fsj_citizenship_intro_en.htm**

Questions related to the single market in sport are dealt with under a dedicated website, at:
**http://ec.europa.eu/sport/sport-and/markt/markt_overview_en.html**

This is part of a wider set of websites dedicated to the interface between sport as commercial and leisure activity, at:
**http://ec.europa.eu/sport/index_en.html**

# Chapter 13

# Towards an Area of Freedom, Security and Justice without Internal Frontiers

## 13.1 Introduction

The creation of an Area of Freedom, Security and Justice (AFSJ) has become one of the core projects of the EU and the rate of legislative activity on the part of the EU institutions, under both the First Pillar provisions governing visas, asylum, immigration and other policies related to free movement of persons (Title IV of Part III of the EC Treaty) and under the Third Pillar provisions governing police and judicial cooperation in criminal matters (Title VI of the Treaty on European Union), has been consistently high since the entry into force of the Treaty of Amsterdam. The Area of Freedom, Security and Justice or – to put it another way – law and policy on justice and home affairs (JHA) in its broadest sense was one area where the provisions of the Constitutional Treaty, had it been duly ratified, would have made a substantial difference to the conditions under which substantive law-making is undertaken and, to a more limited extent, the scope of EU competences. Moreover, it would have fully 'mainstreamed' this field of law-making alongside more traditional 'Community' policies, such as the internal market and competition law. The phrasing of Article I-3(2) of the Constitutional Treaty is revelatory in this context. It states:

> 'The Union shall offer its citizens an area of freedom, security and justice without internal frontiers, and an internal market where competition is free and undistorted.'

This is slightly different in tone and emphasis from Article 2 EU, which currently provides that the Union shall set itself the objective:

> 'to maintain and develop the Union as an area of freedom, security and justice, in which the free movement of persons is assured in conjunction with appropriate measures with respect to external border controls, asylum, immigration and the prevention and combating of crime.'

The notion of an 'area of freedom, security and justice' needs unpacking, if its scope and the coherence of the diverse issues of law and policy which are contained within it are to be fully understood.

Firstly, the notion of an 'area' suggests a geographical space, within which people move, reside and live their lives. JHA policy thus requires not only specific rules about the rights and status of those people, but also rules about where the boundaries of the geographical space are, how they are to be policed and who is, and is not, to be entitled to enter into the AFSJ. This field of policy and regulation can be understood as a corollary of the internal market and the free movement provisions. In his Opinion in Case C-109/01 *Secretary of State for the Home Department* v. *Akrich* ([2003] ECR I-9607), Advocate General Geelhoed described the current situation as follows:

> 'Immigration legislation makes entry into the Member States of the European Union subject to rules. Those rules are becoming more and more stringent. EC legislation in regard to freedom of

movement for persons seeks to liberalize movement to and residence in other countries. The right to remain in another Member State is becoming increasingly more complete' (para. 59).

'In themselves these are not necessarily opposing developments. It is even unavoidable that development of the substantive law in both areas of competence should become more and more divergent. For since the European Union is more and more becoming an area within which persons may move with unrestricted freedom, it is necessary to exercise control at the point of entry to that area' (para. 60).

It is important to note also that while the AFSJ is avowedly about the EU offering 'its citizens freedom, security and justice', in practice this means a disproportionate emphasis upon measures aimed at non-citizens, that is, third country nationals, in particular in relation to the issue of crossing the external borders of the Member States and residence within the territory of the Member States.

Secondly, within the AFSJ, there is an expressed commitment to preserving the values of freedom, security and justice by means of excluding from the area those who would threaten those values, setting up legal frameworks to treat fairly those who are able to remain within the area, and maintaining common and safe rules to enforce those values. Criticisms have been made in the past that the values of security and justice have been given priority over the value of freedom. In its Final Report, Working Group X of the Convention on the Future of Europe, which dealt with the Area of Freedom Security and Justice, stated that:

'(the) policy should be rooted in a shared commitment to freedom based on human rights, democratic institutions and the rule of law . . . [I]t is important that the citizens feel that a proper sense of "European public order" ["*ordre public européen*"] has taken shape and is actually visible today in their daily lives . . . The establishment of a European Area of Freedom, Security and Justice is also closely linked with respect of the rights of citizens and the principle of non-discrimination' (CONV 426/02).

Finally, and most responsively, much of JHA law and policy is based on the fact that the creation of this geographical space where people adjudged to be non-threatening are able to move more freely necessarily creates increased risk of cross-border crime and cross-border private law disputes, notably consumer law and family law disputes. Consequently, measures need to be taken to address that risk and provide specific rules for dealing with cross-border disputes. Again, according to Working Group X:

'The battle against crime is an area in which the European Union can demonstrate its relevance to its citizens in the most visible way' (CONV 426/02).

The law and policy relating to the AFSJ have evolved dramatically since it was first formally introduced into the structures of the EU legal order by the Treaty of Maastricht (although the origins of JHA policies lie in much earlier examples of intergovernmental cooperation between the Member States which date back to the 1960s and 1970s). Indeed, since the 1990s, JHA law and policy have evolved and changed perhaps more than any of the other fields discussed in this book. The narrative of that change has a number of important and interrelated features. First, the evolution of law and policy-making on JHA reflects significant institutional change within the European Union itself. JHA policies were largely rooted in the original post-Maastricht Third Pillar of the EU (Justice and Home Affairs) and thus all the advantages and difficulties of the 'pillar system' as conceived by the Treaty on European Union were visible in the lack of progress on the Union's objectives after the entry into force of that Treaty in 1993. However, the Treaty of Amsterdam brought about an important 'communitarisation' of those parts of JHA law and policy which are concerned with the free movement of persons and immigration and asylum questions. This has resulted in a substantial acceleration in the pace of policy-making, especially when it is viewed in conjunction with the incorporation into the EU system of the Schengen Agreements, originally agreed between a limited number of Member States in the 1980s with a view to creating the area without internal frontiers, which was already identified as an objective of European integration in the Single European Act of 1986. However, the incorporation of the Schengen Agreements within the EU legal order has perpetuated a scenario of 'variable geometry', as the UK, Ireland and Denmark all have a variety of 'opt-outs' in relation to the development of law and policy on the free movement of persons, visas, immigration and asylum.

Furthermore, JHA law and policy have been very substantially affected by significant external events, above all the terrorist attacks in the US on 11 September 2001 (and the subsequent bombings in Madrid in March 2004 and in London in July 2005). While the securitisation narrative was clearly visible in the rhetoric of EU policy-making on JHA before 9/11, thereafter there was a significant acceleration in policy-making, despite the institutional limitations of the residual Third Pillar on police and judicial cooperation, which requires all significant measures to be adopted by a unanimous vote of the Member States.

## 13.2 The Origins of Justice and Home Affairs Policy

The origins of this policy area lie in a number of informal mechanisms of cooperation between national ministers, the best example of which was the 'Trevi group'. From 1976 onwards this group of Member State ministers concerned with anti-terrorism and policing met regularly in order to discuss cooperation in terms of policy and the sharing of information. However the approach was piecemeal and informal.

During the mid-1980s certain aspects of this policy area began to be more central to the European integration project. If, as the Single European Act stated, an internal market was to be defined as an area without internal frontiers, allowing for free movement of persons between Member States, the question of security and security cooperation became more serious. The 1985 Schengen Agreement, followed by the 1990 Schengen Convention, was an attempt by some Member States to begin the process of the abolition of the internal physical borders within the territory of the Community. The agreement was so named because it was signed in the village of Schengen, on the borders of France, Germany and Luxembourg. It was originally signed by five Member States – France, Germany, the Netherlands, Luxembourg and Belgium – and was an intergovernmental agreement, outside the structures of the EC as it then was, intended to begin the process of the abolition of physical internal borders, through the mechanism of compensatory measures, including a common approach to the external frontier and the creation of necessary internal measures, such as the exchange of information, which would allow for the removal of internal frontier controls. Thus, the agreement recognised that there was a need for common rules concerning external border controls to be set out in order to give states the confidence to abolish internal borders without risking their own internal security. Harmonised visa policies were required, with lists of third states whose nationals should and should not be required to obtain a visa in order to enter the territory of the signatory states, and with the goal of moving towards a common visa. Common rules concerning the management of external border controls were to be set up, so that the level of security did not depend on which Member State actually controlled the border. Finally, rules concerning the movement of non-nationals were necessary, giving those with residence permits in one signatory state the right to free circulation in other states. The 1990 Schengen Convention, which was eventually signed by thirteen Member States, as well as by Norway and Iceland, set out details on visa rules, border controls and rules for dealing with requests for asylum. It also set up the Schengen Information System – a computerised system for sharing information between states relevant to immigration and asylum requests. The UK and Ireland did not sign the Schengen Convention.

## 13.3  The Creation of the Third Pillar under the Treaty of Maastricht

The Treaty of Maastricht brought about the partial incorporation of the issues dealt with by the Schengen Convention into the legal order of the new European Union, in particular through the creation a Third Pillar, known as Justice and Home Affairs. The JHA pillar, dealt with by Title VI EU, listed nine common concerns of the Member State:

1. Asylum policy.
2. Rules governing the crossing by persons of the external borders of the Member States and the exercise of controls thereon.
3. Immigration policy and policy regarding nationals of third countries:
   - conditions of entry and movement by nationals of third countries on the territory of Member States;
   - conditions of residence by nationals of third countries on the territory of Member States, including family reunion and access to employment;
   - combating unauthorised immigration, residence and work by nationals of third countries on the territory of Member States.
4. Combating drug addiction in so far as this is not covered by points 7 to 9.
5. Combating fraud on an international scale in so far as this is not covered by points 7 to 9.
6. Judicial cooperation in civil matters.
7. Judicial cooperation in criminal matters.
8. Customs cooperation.
9. Police cooperation for the purpose of preventing and combating terrorism, unlawful drug-trafficking and other serious forms of international crime, including if necessary certain aspects of customs cooperation, in connection with the organisation of a Union-wide system for exchanging information within a European Police Office (Europol).

The nature of the competences conferred under the pillar was very limited. Decisions taken in accordance with Article K2 EU would not be held to affect Member State action in the fields of law and order and internal security. Decision-making was intergovernmental in nature, in that the Council would only adopt measures if there was unanimous agreement from all members. Depending on the field, either Member States or the Commission were given the right to propose decisions, and the Commission was said to be 'fully associated' with the process of policy-making under the Third Pillar. Article K4 set up a committee of civil servants, known as the K4 committee, to work with the Committee of Permanent Representatives in assisting the Council in its decision-making. The Court of Justice had no mandatory jurisdiction, although it could be called upon to settle matters if required.

Furthermore, Article K9 of the Treaty set up mechanisms, known as *passerelles*, under which decisions on the first six areas of concern listed above could be transferred to the First Pillar and added to the very limited list of JHA issues included in what was then Article 100c EC. This provision only applied to the adoption of measures determining the third countries whose nationals must be in possession of a visa when crossing the external borders of the Member States. Such a transfer would have meant that these matters could be decided using the procedures laid down in Article 100c (which provided for decision-making by unanimity until 1996, and by qualified majority thereafter), and that any binding legislation passed would fall under the jurisdiction of the Court of Justice in the usual way. A *passerelle* could only be activated if the Council decided unanimously that it wished this to happen, and in any event, as a mini-amendment to the Treaties, this would require the unanimous ratification of all of the Member States in accordance with their respective constitutional requirements. In reality, this *passerelle*, in common with others which have been included in the EU Treaties over the years, was never activated. However, its inclusion signalled the need – when a broader-based Treaty-amendment process was due – to reconsider the Treaty basis for policy-making in this field. This happened, in due course, with the Treaty of Amsterdam.

### 13.4 Freedom, Justice and Security, and the Treaty of Amsterdam

A further significant milestone in the evolution of JHA law and policy was the 1997 Treaty of Amsterdam. A number of developments occurred in this treaty. First, to the list of objectives of the Union set out in Article 2 EU was added the aim of creating an area of Freedom, Security and Justice. This gave a constitutional frame of reference to JHA policy. Furthermore, Article 61 EC recognised the task of *progressively* establishing an area of freedom, security and justice, seeking the achievement, within five years of the entry into force of the Treaty of Amsterdam (i.e. 2004), of the objectives relating to the free movement of persons enshrined in Article 14 EC. Second, in order to achieve these objectives, the Treaty of Amsterdam 'communitarised' a substantial part of policy-making on JHA, in particular that concerned with the free movement of persons. Competences in this field were transferred from the Third Pillar to the First Pillar, and – with some qualifications, exceptions and transitional period – made subject to a version of the usual Community legislative procedures and scrutiny mechanisms, such as the jurisdiction of the Court of Justice and the role of the European Parliament. There were, however, some limitations to this. For the first five years after the coming into force of the Treaty, decisions were to be reached unanimously, using the consultation procedure, and Member States shared the right to propose legislation with the Commission. After this transitional period, the Council was given the role, under Article 67(2) EC, of taking a unanimous decision with a view to changing the legislative procedure in all or some of the areas covered in the Title to that laid out in Article 251 EC (co-decision). After that transitional period, the right of Member State initiative ends, but the Commission must receive and consider any requests made by Member States for new proposals to be put forward. The exception to these transitional provisions was the field of visas. During the transitional period, legislation was to be passed using the consultation procedure, but was voted on in the Council using qualified majority voting, and the move to the co-decision procedure took place automatically after five years. The reason for this exception is straightforward: visa regulations never fell under Pillar Three competence, as the Treaty of Maastricht had already created a legal basis for action under Article 100c EC.

Communitarising these issues should have the effect of giving the Court of Justice full jurisdiction over legislation and its interpretation. However, special provisions dealt with the role of the Court of Justice in this field. As regards preliminary references, a slightly modified regime was created. Rather than permitting all national courts to make references, Article 68(1) EC limits the right of reference to courts of last resort, who are required to make references when the question of law raised is necessary to decide the case before them. Secondly, there is no judicial review in relation to measures adopted using Article 62(1) EC, in so far as these measures relate to the maintenance of law and order and the safeguarding of internal security (Article 68(2)).

Not all of the Maastricht Third Pillar was communitarised and the remainder of the pillar was retitled Police and Judicial Cooperation in Criminal Matters. Changes to that pillar were made in order to increase the power of the institutions, as opposed to Member States, and to allow the Court of Justice to make preliminary rulings on Pillar Three issues, but only once the Member States had made a declaration accepting the jurisdiction of the Court of Justice. Not all Member States have made such a declaration. For example, the UK has chosen not to. The new Third Pillar provides for the adoption of a new type of legal instrument, the Framework Decision, which 'shall be binding upon the Member States as to the result to be achieved but shall leave to the national authorities the choice of form and methods. They shall not entail direct effect.' Despite these limitations, in Case C-105/03 *Pupino* ([2005] ECR I-5285) the Court held that, notwithstanding the absence of an equivalent to Article 10 EC in the Third Pillar (Article 10 upholds the duty of 'Community loyalty'), national courts are nevertheless under the obligation, when considering the effects in national law of a Framework Decision, to interpret national law in the light of relevant EU law (in that case, the Framework Decision on the victims of crime). The *Pupino* judgment is one of a number handed down by the Court of Justice in which it has begun to import into the Third Pillar some of the core constitutional principles of the First Pillar which underpin the relationship between EU law and national law (e.g. Case 354/04 *Gestoras Pro Amnistía* v. *Council*, judgment of 27 February 2007). However, no amount of constitutional activism on the part of the Court of Justice can overcome some of the specific institutional weaknesses of the Third Pillar, such as the absence of any provision which is equivalent to Article 226 EC, which allows the Commission to bring Member States defaulting on their obligations under the EC Treaty before the Court of Justice. Where Member States fail to implement and properly enforce Framework Decisions, the most that the Commission can do in order to try to bring about compliance is to issue reports and seek the 'naming and shaming' of the Member States in question.

Third, the rules and measures which comprised the Schengen Agreement and Convention and their implementing measures, collectively known as the Schengen *acquis*, were incorporated into the Treaty structures, with the various elements of the *acquis* to be allocated to the First and the Third Pillar, as appropriate. In order to address the fact that the UK and Ireland had not signed up to the Schengen Convention, and that Denmark did not wish to see the Schengen *acquis* given the force of Community law, a set of opt-outs was agreed to suit these individual positions. The protocols setting out the UK and Irish opt-outs make it possible for the UK and Ireland to opt back into various aspects of Schengen-related matters, such as the Schengen Information System, and also other measures adopted under Title IV. As Norway and Iceland had signed the Schengen Convention without being Member States of the EU, measures have likewise been taken to make it possible for them to continue to be members of the Schengen area.

## 13.5    Post-Amsterdam Developments in Freedom, Justice and Security

The pattern of policy development in the JHA area since the Treaty of Amsterdam has been marked, from a structural point of view, by the role of programmes, action plans and scoreboards, which have sought to create aims and objectives and to identify benchmarks for progress; such an approach can be significant in areas where Member States often display considerable sensitivities about intrusions into national sovereignty, not least because it brings into the foreground the institutional role of the European Council. At the same time, as noted in 13.1, exogenous factors, notably terrorist attacks and US-led military action in Iraq and Afghanistan, have restructured the conditions which underpin the need for an EU-level policy on internal security.

The 1998 Vienna Action Plan, drawn up by the Council and the Commission, outlined how that process should be undertaken, both in terms of setting certain policy objectives and also of assessing how inter-institutional cooperation and the principle of subsidiarity should be applied. It was a relatively conservative document, which limited itself to setting out strategies to achieve what was required by the Treaty of Amsterdam. In this respect, the Conclusions of the October 1999 Tampere European Council meeting were something of a milestone, in that they placed, explicitly, the creation of an area of Freedom, Security and Justice at the heart of the EU project. They stated in particular that the freedom which the EU was trying to achieve for its citizens should not be limited only to citizens, but should be made accessible to immigrants and asylum seekers, through common policies of asylum and immigration, and moves to facilitate the integration of third country nationals resident in the EU. The conclusions went on to outline a number of policy goals, some of which will be explored in more detail in the next section, in three main fields: the development of a common migration and asylum policy; access to justice and the mutual recognition of decisions; and the fight against organised and trans-national crime. On the face of it, therefore, the Tampere Conclusions seemed to be attempting to draw a line under Fortress Europe, where the benefits created by the EU were available only to citizens, and to extend the rights of non-EU citizens.

The conclusions of the Seville European Council, less than three years later in 2002, had a different emphasis. While welcoming the developments in the common immigration and asylum policy, the Heads of State and Government were at pains to note the need to balance integration for lawfully resident third country nationals and an asylum policy conforming to international standards, with action to combat illegal immigration. This marked the beginnings of an explicit rhetoric at EU level about the need to combat illegal immigration, justified in the name of the limited reception capacity of the European Union and its Member States. However, it is impossible to dissociate this change of heart with the events of 11 September 2001, and the pressure which these events placed on the creation of an Area of Freedom, Security and Justice. Tougher anti-terrorism rules, with associated strictures placed upon immigration and asylum, became commonplace in the West as a response to the attacks in New York and Washington DC, and the response of the EU was that very limited progress could be seen on the range of legislation which had been in the pipeline on immigration and asylum. Members of the Council were unwilling to engage in further harmonisation at a time when public sensibility about immigration and asylum rules was particularly acute.

Nevertheless, harmonisation was facilitated by the adoption of Council Decision 2004/927 under the Dutch Presidency; this provides for certain areas of Title IV of Part Three of the Treaty establishing the European Community to be governed by the procedure laid down in Article 251 of that Treaty (OJ 2004 L 396/45). This decision, despite its rather technical-sounding title, mostly fulfils the task given to the Council under the Treaty of Amsterdam to adjust the decision-making processes in relation to measures relating to the free movement of persons. In tandem with other provisions, including amendments inserted by the Treaty of Nice which came into force in 2003 (new Article 67(5) EC) and a Protocol appended to the Treaty of Nice affecting Article 66 EC, this Decision ensures that all measures adopted under Title IV, with the exception of those related to legal migration into the EU and its Member States, will be adopted under Article 251, involving co-decision with the European Parliament and a qualified majority vote in the Council of Ministers. Peers has raised the possibility that this procedural change could lead to a more liberal policy in this area, as it removes the option for individual Member States to block legislation and thus avoids the problem of legislation and policy conforming to the lowest (i.e. more restrictive) common denominator (Peers, 2005). However, initial experience with the Schengen Borders Code, adopted by co-decision, did not seem to suggest that this would necessarily be the outcome (Council Regulation 562/2006, OJ 2006 L105/1).

The Dutch Presidency of the second half of 2004 also saw the approval by the European Council of a further programme of action for the JHA field, the Hague Programme. In a Communication issued in 2004 (COM(2004) 401), the Commission declared the programme of work under the Tampere Conclusions to be essentially complete, and it was invited to prepare a programme of work for the next five years. This was approved in broad outline by the European Council in November 2004 (OJ 2005 C53/1), and a detailed programme was approved in May 2005 (COM(2005) 184, *The Hague Programme. Ten Priorities for the Next Five Years*). Although the programme was formulated in the shadow of the ratification process of the Constitutional Treaty, it was emphasised by both the Commission and the European Council that the implementation of the Hague Programme *did not* require the Constitutional Treaty to be ratified. Hence, although the 'loss' of the Constitutional Treaty through non-ratification does constitute a cost in terms of the evolution of the area of freedom, security and justice, it has not been constructed – in institutional discourse at least – as central to the success of the policy area. The key objectives of the Hague Programme are to reinforce the principle of mutual recognition, which has become central to the development of policy in relation to police and criminal justice cooperation, the establishment and evolution of cross-border police cooperation, especially in relation to access to information and what is termed the 'principle of availability' in this field, and the acceptance of the idea that the internal security and public order of one Member State is a matter of concern to all the other Member States.

It is important finally to mention what is colloquially known as 'Schengen III', or the Treaty of Prüm, an intergovernmental agreement originally concluded between Belgium, Germany, Spain, France, Luxembourg, Netherlands and Austria. It is termed Schengen III because its conclusion outside the EU framework mirrors the original Schengen Agreement and Convention (Schengen I and II), as a laboratory to foster more intensive cooperation between the Member States concerned. In this case, the cooperation concerns, in particular, cross-border cooperation between law enforcement agencies with a view to combating terrorism, cross-border crime and illegal migration. What also mirrors Schengen have been the attempts initiated by the German Presidency in early 2007 to bring about the incorporation of the Prüm *acquis*, including a substantial annex comprising an operational manual, within the framework of the Third Pillar, by means of a Framework Decision. This will signify a considerable intensification of the level of cross-border cooperation, for example opening up the DNA records of the national law enforcement agencies to the authorities of the other Member States.

## 13.6　The Constitutional Treaty and the Issue of Fundamental Rights Protection

Just as previous Treaties have made particularly significant changes to this field of action, so the Constitutional Treaty would have had a significant impact in relation to the institutional basis for JHA law and policy-making, including the nature of the instruments that could be adopted, the legislative processes for adopting those instruments, and related issues such as parliamentary accountability and judicial review. However, it is not clear that the institutional changes proposed would have necessarily changed the balance between freedom, security and justice as it stands at the present. On the other hand, the formal removal of the 'pillar' divide, with the creation of a single set of provisions dealing with JHA matters (Articles III-257 to III-277), could have lent a coherence to the policy field which is lacking at the present, especially if the requisite political will had been forthcoming from the Member States. However, the inclusion of a specific provision in Part I of the Constitutional Treaty addressing certain particularities of the policy field (such as a continued partial sharing of the right of initiative for legislation between the Member States and the Commission in relation to police and judicial cooperation in criminal matters) continues to reinforce the unwillingness of the Member States wholly to assimilate JHA to the mainstream of EU cooperation and integration.

The incorporation of the European Charter on Fundamental Rights, concluded in 2000 (OJ 2000 C364/1) into Part II the Constitutional Treaty, thus making it a legally binding element of the EU's constitutional framework, would have added weight to the 'freedom' and 'justice' dimensions of the policy area and could have had an effect in ensuring that measures comply with human rights standards. The policy objectives laid out for FSJ were also widened by the Constitutional Treaty. In particular, there was an increased emphasis on solidarity and burden-sharing between Member States. Use of the default co-decision procedure could also improve the efficiency of the legislative process, although it should be noted that some areas of FSJ policy, notably measures relating to family law and aspects of criminal procedure, would have retained the requirement for a unanimous vote. The Constitutional Treaty therefore gave a great deal of scope for increased action in this important policy area, while recognising the sensitivities of the Member States.

Thus the reluctance of Member States and their electorates to accept Europe-wide measures in issues which are seen to affect national security was recognised. Particular care was taken to ensure that the principles of subsidiarity and proportionality are respected, and that national parliaments should be accorded a full role. Furthermore, concerns from some states, notably the UK and Ireland with their common law traditions, that moves towards harmonisation in some aspects of criminal procedure could lead to the dilution of national legal traditions and systems, had to be taken seriously. Provisions were inserted explicitly in order to protect the differences between national legal traditions and systems. It should also be noted that the various opt-outs negotiated by the UK, Ireland and Denmark were maintained under broadly the same terms as they exist at present.

### 13.7 Title IV: Visas, Asylum, Immigration and Other Policies related to Free Movement of Persons – The Scope of Coverage

The following elements make up the objective set under Article 61 EC of achieving that part of the internal market objective in Article 14 EC which is concerned with the free movement of persons:

- policies on the crossing of internal borders between the Member States, specifically to remove internal frontiers;
- policies on the crossing of the external borders of the Member States, covering the checks carried out at borders, the rules on rules (who requires them; procedures and conditions for issue of visas; uniform format, etc.);
- conditions under which third country nationals can travel between the Member States for periods of no more than three months;
- measures on the treatment of those seeking asylum, refugees and displaced persons, including measures on burden-sharing between the Member States;
- measures on the conditions of (lawful) entry and residence of third country nationals into the Member States, including long-term visas and residence permits and family reunification issues;
- measures on illegal immigration and residence, including repatriation of illegal residents;
- measures defining the rights and conditions under which third country nationals resident in one Member State may reside in other Member States.

As noted above, different (and evolving) institutional arrangements have applied over the period since the entry into force of the Treaty of Amsterdam in relation to these various matters; the exercise of these competences is regulated by the complex provisions of Articles 62 and 63 EC. Moreover, the Member States have shown variable levels of enthusiasm for adopting legislative measures in relation to the different headings. Although the Commission has consistently sought to persuade the Member States of the need to develop a common approach to the question of what types of immigration are required from a labour market perspective within the European Union, it has not been successful, and there are so far *no EU-level measures* on the arrangements for *first entry* into the Union by prospective immigrants, except in the case of family reunification. These questions are discussed below (13.9) under the heading of 'fair treatment' for nationals of third countries, which was one of the themes of the Tampere Conclusions. There exists, however, a substantial corpus of measures relating to border controls, visas and illegal immigration; some of that corpus of measures comprises legislative measures, requiring the harmonisation of national laws, some of it comprises the creation of autonomous EU-level institutions such as the External Borders Management Agency *Frontex*, and some of it requires administrative cooperation between the Member States provided for under Article 66 EC.

## 13.8　Border Controls, Visas and Illegal Immigration

Measures on border controls, visas and illegal immigration can be considered together. The Schengen Agreements and Convention secured the removal of internal frontiers within the Member States, based on the creation of a common set of external border controls, including common rules on visas. The requirement for such 'positive' measures was emphasised by the judgment of the Court of Justice in Case C-378/97 *Criminal Proceedings against Wijsenbeek* ([1999] ECR I-6207), where the Court of Justice held that it was permissible for Member States to continue requiring of those travelling within the European Union to show a document proving their identity and nationality when crossing an internal frontier. The incorporation of the Schengen *acquis* into the European Union achieved that objective from the perspective of EU law, at least for those states which are not covered by an opt-out, namely the UK and Ireland (the Danish opt-out is different and Denmark is still part of the Schengen area, albeit on a different legal basis from the other Member States). Since the incorporation of Schengen, and the creation of the legal bases in Articles 62 and 63 EC to deal with the regulation of borders and the securitisation of movement, a substantial body of EU measures has been adopted. Part of the process has been about consolidation of the Schengen *acquis* and its readoption in an EU legislative form. The Schengen Borders Code, which provides a complete code for Member States on dealing with the regulation of internal and external borders, is an important example of such measures (European Parliament and Council Regulation 562/2006 establishing a Community Code on the rules governing the movement of persons across borders, OJ 2006 L105/1).

Article 6 of the Border Code is significant, insofar as it states certain basic principles in a clear and transparent manner:

'Conduct of border checks
1. Border guards shall, in the performance of their duties, fully respect human dignity. Any measures taken in the performance of their duties shall be proportionate to the objectives pursued by such measures.
2. While carrying out border checks, border guards shall not discriminate against persons on grounds of sex, racial or ethnic origin, religion or belief, disability, age or sexual orientation.'

Common visa policy is an area with a longer history than other aspects of the regulation of borders. Some aspects of visa policy were placed within the First Pillar by the Treaty of Maastricht (Article 100a EC, now incorporated into Article 62 EC), and so certain legislation was adopted at an early stage of the development of JHA policy. In 1995, the Council adopted Regulation 1683/95 (OJ 1995 L164/1), laying down a uniform format for visas, and Regulation 2317/95 (OJ 1995 L234/1), setting out a 'negative list' of countries whose nationals should be required to have a visa to enter the EU. The political controversy and negotiations around the area, and the disputes as to which states should be included in the list, meant that these provisions were fairly limited (they did not, for example, require Member States to recognise visas granted by other Member States) and little progress has been made. After the Treaty of Amsterdam, all other areas of visa policy were brought under Article 62 EC. In 2001, the Council adopted a Regulation setting out both a 'negative list' and a 'positive list' – countries whose nationals should be required to have a visa and countries whose nationals should be exempt from the requirement to have a visa (Council Regulation 539/2001, OJ 2001 L081/1). This is regularly updated. Visas also have a uniform format, with an identical sticker which is secure and is recognised by the other states allowing travel throughout the Schengen area without further frontier controls. Accessing these multi-state visas currently occurs on the basis of the Common Consular Instructions elaborated as part of the Schengen *acquis,* which works as a result of cooperation between the national consular authorities and because of the availability of information within the Schengen Information System. This operates a system of alerts against individuals who have come to the attention of national authorities and to whom visas should not be issued. A visa information system, based on a Council Decision adopted in 2004 (Council Decision 2004/512, OJ 2004 L213/5), now means that cooperation in the future will be enhanced since information about visas issued is now coordinated on the basis of a single database of information accessible to all consular authorities. However, the visas issued are still strictly speaking national visas, even though they are referred to as 'Schengen visas'. A Community Code on visas, paralleling the Border Code, has been proposed by the Commission (COM(2006) 403), and the Commission is also proposing the updating and upgrading of the EU measures in relation to the use of biometric identifiers in this area (proposal for a European Parliament and Council Regulation on biometric identifiers, COM(2006) 269).

This is the heading under which issues of visa policy, information policy, cooperation between border controls and the fight against illegal immigration can be considered. Given the increased concern in Member States about securitisation, this is an important area of action, but also an area where it is difficult to find agreement. Post-Seville, this has been a priority area of action of the EU, and the Commission produced a communication in 2002 on the integrated management of external borders (COM(2002) 233), emphasising the importance of strengthening the external frontiers of the EU, which requires a common policy. However, because of different perceptions of risk and different processes and administrative structures, border control policy varies throughout the Member States. The Commission proposed the setting-up of a common coordination and operational cooperation mechanism, which would involve the cooperation of those involved in border control, combined with some common surveillance and inspection mechanisms and a common integrated risk-analysis procedure. This would involve harmonisation of the factors used in risk assessment, so that Member States would agree on what threats exist, where they may come from and what the appropriate and proportionate action to take would be. In turn, this would have an important policy-harmonisation effect.

In the long term, it has been suggested that there should be a European Corps of Border Guards to control external borders. This proposal is obviously controversial and, in the interim, a number of joint operations at external borders were undertaken by groups of Member States. Monar (2000) suggested that these joint operations, while often successful, tend to be uncoordinated, with differential levels of commitment from Member States. The Commission therefore proposed the creation of an external Border Management Agency, to enhance and structure this cooperation. Frontex, which is based in Warsaw and headed up by senior officers from the Finnish border guard, was established by a Council Regulation of 2004 (Council Regulation 2007/2004, OJ 2004 L349/1) and began work in 2005. The task of Frontex is to enhance external border security by carrying out risk analysis, coordinating operational cooperation between the Member States, assistance to Member States on training border guards, developing research, assisting Member States where they require specific support on a short-term basis, and supporting Member States where they require this for organising joint return operations repatriating those found on the territory without lawful permission. In the early years, the management of the European Union's southern maritime border has been a particular concern.

More generally, illegal immigration has been the focus of a number of EU initiatives. Illegal immigration involves not only the problem of people entering the territory of one of the Member States illegally (often with the help of human traffickers or people smugglers), but also the problem of those persons who overstay their entry permits or visas. After the conclusions of the Seville European Council in June 2002, which concentrated in particular upon the issue of illegal immigration, the Commission has issued many plans and communications which concentrate upon this question. Already in 2001, the Member States had adopted a Directive on the mutual recognition of each others' expulsion decisions (Council Directive 2001/40, OJ 2001 L149/34), and since that date the Member States have reached decisions on the organisation of joint flights for the removal of persons against whom expulsion decisions have been taken (OJ 2004 L261/28), and they have also adopted a number of readmission agreements with third countries. A draft directive on common standards and procedures for returning illegally overstaying third country nationals has yet to be adopted by the Council (COM(2005) 391).

## 13.9    Third Country Nationals under Title IV and the Case for 'Fair Treatment'

The provisions of the EC Treaty on the free movement of persons apply only to citizens of the Union, who are defined as nationals of Member States; third country nationals only fall within the scope of these provisions where they are members of the family of a citizen of the Union. This means that third country nationals lawfully resident in a Member State, who may indeed have been given certain rights under the immigration laws of that state, may not benefit from EU free movement or from non-discrimination rights, even though they may have lived within the Union for many years. It is significant that for the first time the provisions of Title IV gave a competence to the EU institutions to adopt measures harmonising national laws governing the treatment of third country nationals, both in relation to conditions of entry and conditions of residence, albeit that this competence must be exercised by unanimity in the Council of Ministers. In addition, the legal bases contained in Articles 63(3)(a) and 63(4) EC must be read in conjunction with Article 137(1)(g) EC, which refers to the role of the Community in supporting and complementing the activities of the Member States in relation to the 'conditions of employment for third-country nationals legally residing in Community territory'. Here too, the Council must act unanimously, after consulting the European Parliament (Article 137(2) EC).

Building on the measures included in the Treaty of Amsterdam, the Tampere Conclusions of 1999 engaged in some detail with the status of third country nationals:

'The European Union must ensure fair treatment of third country nationals who reside legally on the territory of its Member States. A more vigorous integration policy should aim at granting them rights and obligations comparable to those of EU citizens. It should also enhance non-discrimination in economic, social and cultural life and develop measures against racism and xenophobia . . .' (para. 18).

'The legal status of third country nationals should be approximated to that of Member States' nationals' (para. 21).

However, the only substantial step which has been taken towards achieving the objective of fair treatment is Council Directive 2003/109 (OJ 2004 L16/1), concerning the status of third country nationals who are long-term residents. This measure was substantially watered down, so far as concerned the rights of third country nationals already legally resident in the Member States, during the course of the negotiation processes which preceded its adoption. It requires Member States to confer a right of permanent residence on long-term resident third country nationals who have resided legally and continuously for a period of five years in that state. This applies also to dependent family members. Following from this, Member States must provide equal treatment for third country nationals in relation to many aspects of residence in the host state, including tax benefits, access to employment and access to education and vocational training. However, it does not require equal treatment in relation to access to welfare benefits. There are limited facilities under the directive allowing third country nationals to move to other Member States, but these do not approximate to the free movement rights of EU citizens. Finally, there are provisions governing the conditions under which Member States may expel otherwise lawfully resident third country nationals from their territory, and it is evident from the text that the directive reflects some of the concerns of the Member States about possible security risks posed by third country nationals in the wake of the terrorist attacks of 11 September 2001 in the US, in the way in which it treats public security issues. The UK and Ireland have opted out of this directive, by virtue of the arrangements created by the Treaty of Amsterdam.

This directive is solely concerned with third country nationals whose residence is lawful on the basis of national immigration law, and it does not establish any grounds on which third country nationals may access the territory of the Member States for the first time. A proposal for a Council Directive on the conditions of entry and residence of third country nationals for the purpose of paid employment and self-employed economic activities (COM(2001) 386) never received substantial support from the Member States, and was eventually withdrawn by the Commission in 2005. The Member States are reluctant to cede control over the question of which third country nationals (and how many of them) may access the national territory. Thus, in this area, very few EU measures have been adopted, and thus far the Commission has been restricted to adopting a Green Paper on Managing Migration (COM(2004) 811) and subsequently a Policy Plan on Legal Migration (COM(2005) 669).

The specific case of family reunification was dealt with in a Directive adopted by the Council (Council Directive 2003/86, OJ 2003 L251/13); this is another directive from which the UK and Ireland have opted out. The terms of this directive were exceptionally controversial, to the extent that it was unsuccessfully challenged by the European Parliament before the Court of Justice on the grounds that its terms failed to comply with Article 8 of the European Convention on Human Rights and Fundamental Rights regarding the protection of family life (Case C-540/03 *Parliament* v. *Council* [2006] ECR I-5769). The Parliament's contentions concerned, in particular, the treatment of children under the directive. From the point of view of the evolution of EU law, the case is interesting because in the course of its conclusion, the Court of Justice referred for the first time, as one of the bases for its conclusions, to the text of the Charter of Fundamental Rights, even though it remains a declaratory text. The Council has also adopted directives dealing with the specific cases of admission of third country nationals for the purposes of scientific research (Council Directive 2005/71, OJ 2005 L289/15) and on the conditions of admission of third country nationals for the purposes of studies, pupil exchange, unremunerated training or voluntary service (Council Directive 2004/1114, OJ 2004 L375/12).

A less controversial piece of legislation under this agenda has been Council Regulation 859/2003 (OJ 2003 L124/1), extending the provisions of the existing social security Regulations (1408/71 and 574/72) to third country nationals. However, this was adopted not under the provisions of Title IV but under Articles 42 and 308 EC, and Regulation 1408/71, as amended, has now been replaced by a single piece of codifying and consolidating legislation (European Parliament and Council Regulation 883/2004, corrected version published at OJ 2004 L200/1).

It is also important to note, in relation to the issue of 'fair treatment', developments concerning racism, xenophobia and non-discrimination. Article 29 EU gives the EU the objective of 'preventing and combating racism and xenophobia'. Article 13 EC introduced a legal basis for the Council to adopt measures to combat discrimination based on six specified grounds, including racial or ethnic origin, and religion.

As Monar pointed out, the acknowledgment of racism and xenophobia as a serious problem necessitating Union action has only become apparent over the past decade or so (Monar, 2000). This development had started prior to the Tampere Conclusions, with the European Year Against Racism in 1997 and the establishment in 1998 of the European Monitoring Centre of Racism and Xenophobia (EUMC), which was given the mandate of researching and monitoring racism in the various Member States. As of 2007, the EUMC was superseded by a more broadly based EU Fundamental Rights Agency (Council Regulation 168/2007, OJ 2007 L53/1). Perhaps the most significant legal development in the field of anti-racism policy is Article 13, with the adoption of Council Directive 2000/43 (OJ 2000 L180/22), implementing the principle of equal treatment for persons irrespective of racial or ethnic origin. This directive specifically excludes from its scope differential treatment on the basis of *nationality* (Article 12 EC covers only the nationality of the Member States), but does provide a concrete example of action against racism. It is discussed in more detail in Chapter 15. In addition, a proposal for a Framework Decision on racism and xenophobia was produced (COM(2001) 664), which suggested further harmonisation of the procedures and criminal processes used by national legal systems to deal with racism, by encouraging the criminalisation of incitement to racial hatred, public threats towards racial groups, the condoning or trivialising of genocide and the distribution of racist material, and the consideration of racist motives as an aggravating circumstance in other crimes. This proposal remained stalled in decision-making processes for many years until its adoption was made a priority by the German Presidency in the first half of 2007.

Although the Tampere Conclusions referred to the question of integration into the Member States, there is no clear competence in the EC Treaty in relation to the issue of the integration of immigrants. Even the Constitutional Treaty did not substantially change this position, although it does refer specifically to the issue of integration:

'European laws or framework laws may establish measures to provide incentives and support for the action of Member States with a view to promoting the integration of third-country nationals residing legally in their territories, excluding any harmonisation of national laws and regulations of the Member States' (Article III-267(4) CT).

In terms of positive integration measures which could be adopted under the EC Treaty, in Joined Cases 281 etc./85 *Germany et al* v. *Commission (Migration Policy)* ([1987] ECR 3203) the Court acknowledged that within the framework for the development of EU social policy as it then existed before the Single European Act (Article 118 EEC), the Commission had a limited power to request information from the Member States regarding the integration into the workforce of third country nationals within their territories. Since that time, the issue of the integration of immigrants at the national level has become significant, not least as a result of the recognition that the EU Member States have become, or in some cases are in the process of becoming, states of immigration, with substantial populations of resident third country nationals.

After the Tampere Conclusions, the Commission argued in a Communication on a Community integration policy (COM(2000) 757) for the legal status granted to third country nationals to:

> 'be based on the principle of providing sets of rights and responsibilities on a basis of equality with those of nationals but differentiated according to the length of stay while providing for progression to permanent status. In the longer term this could extend to offering a form of civic citizenship, based on the EC Treaty and inspired by the Charter of Fundamental Rights, consisting of a set of rights and duties offered to third country nationals.'

More recent documents issued by both the Commission and the European Council have focused on the security dimension rather than the fairness dimension of integration. Unintegrated migrants are posited as a problem for the host society, although the Common Basic Principles for Integration adopted in the form of Council Conclusions in November 2004 refer to integration as a two-way process, involving adjustment on the part of both the host society and the immigrants. Only very weak instruments are available to the EU institutions in this field. The Commission has sought to lead a process of national benchmarking against standards, with the exchange of good practices through national contact points, with the relevant national ministries meeting regularly to discuss integration issues.

## 13.10  Towards a Common European Asylum System?

An important goal set out in the Tampere Conclusions was that of establishing a common asylum system throughout the Member States; this system would determine which state would be responsible for decisions on individual cases, set out common standards and minimum conditions of reception, and harmonise both the process for according and the content of refugee status. Given the increasing attention on refugees and asylum seekers by some political groups and by the media, this is an important area of action and one in which some legislative progress has been achieved, although in many cases the measures adopted have been highly controversial.

The goal of a common asylum system can be understood as having two aspects. First, the EU has shown its commitment to the rules of the 1951 Geneva Convention on the status of refugees, most notably by including the right to asylum in the 2000 Charter of Fundamental Rights; consequently, at least rhetorically, it is committed to high standards of human rights protection for asylum seekers and refugees, in particular the principle of non-refoulement, which prohibits states from returning persons who have sought protection to a state where they may face persecution. A common asylum policy should be seen as enforcing those rules and standards. Second, a common asylum policy will minimise movement of asylum seekers between Member States, by removing the temptation for them to congregate in the state which has the most favourable conditions for them. This second aspect is in fact closely connected to the first; a state with higher standards may be tempted to lower them if it finds that it is attracting more asylum seekers than it can cope with. The best way of ensuring high standards of treatment and protection is to implement a common policy. It is equally possible, however, that a common policy will institutionalise a lower standard of protection than has been available hitherto in some Member States, in the name of burden-sharing (Rogers, 2002; Juss, 2005).

The first important action of the Member States in this field was the Dublin Convention, drawn up in 1990 and signed and ratified in 1997. This Convention, like the Schengen Convention, was agreed outside the formal EU structures and thus has the status of an international treaty. It was originally agreed by twelve Member States, joined by Austria, Sweden and Finland shortly afterwards. Its goal was to establish common rules determining which Member State is responsible for an asylum application. This should eliminate the problem of applications being made to two or more Member States, which might then make conflicting determinations, and the problem of no Member State accepting responsibility for an application. The Convention contained a list of rules stating which state should be responsible for an asylum application, based on factors such as point of first entry, family connections with resident refugees, residence and, by default, the place of first application. All Member States should apply these rules. Therefore, asylum seekers in the EU should have their application considered by one state only, and if that application is refused no further application within the EU can be made. States may also determine that a third country should be responsible.

The success of the Dublin Convention was mixed. Originally, it was not used as much as had been hoped. Over 1998 and 1999, it was found that, of applications lodged with a Member State, in only 6 per cent of cases was a request made to another state to take responsibility for the application. It seems unlikely that 94 per cent of asylum applicants choose the correct state under the Convention rules, and thus this suggests that the rules were not being applied by Member States (Evaluation of the Dublin Convention – SEC (2001) 756). Further, even when another state agreed under Convention rules to take responsibility for an application, the application was only in fact transferred in 40 per cent of cases. The Commission took the view that this was due partly to the large number of asylum seekers without documents (meaning that the evidence is not available to apply the Convention rules) and partly to the administrative burden of making requests. A further important issue has been conflicts over the interpretation of the Convention, owing to the vagueness of certain terms and perceived gaps. The external nature of the Dublin Convention was also an issue. Following the inclusion of asylum issues in the EC Treaty, as a result of the Treaty of Amsterdam, Regulation 343/2003 (known as the Dublin II Regulation) (OJ 2003 L50/1) was adopted by the Council to perform the same function as the Dublin Convention. It also addressed some of the issues raised in the 2001 evaluation. The broad system, however, remains the same. This Regulation forms one of the building blocks for the common asylum system envisaged in the Tampere Conclusions, and it is complemented by the Council Regulation establishing the EURODAC fingerprint database, which allows the identification of asylum seekers across the Member States (Council Regulation 2725/2000, OJ 2000 L316/1). This has been criticised as imposing an unprecedented degree of physical control upon the bodies of asylum seekers, including children (Guild, 2006).

Four further instruments comprise the rest of the first phase of measures taken to implement a common policy:

- Council Directive 2001/55 on minimum standards for giving temporary protection in the event of a mass influx of displaced persons (OJ 2001 L212/12);
- Council Directive 2003/9 on minimum standards of reception for asylum seekers (OJ 2003 L31/18);
- Council Directive 2004/83 on minimum standards for the qualification and status of third country nationals or stateless persons as refugees or as persons who otherwise need international protection and the content of the protection granted (OJ 2004 L304/12);
- Council Directive 2005/85 on minimum standards on procedures in Member States for granting and withdrawing refugee status (OJ 2005 L326/13).

The latter three measures are the key measures, establishing the duties of the Member States in relation to asylum seekers, including matters relating to housing, education and health (Reception Directive), laying down a clear set of criteria for qualifying either for refugee or subsidiary protection status and setting out what rights are attached to each status (Qualifications Directive), and ensuring that throughout the EU the same procedures are used for the determination of refugee status (Procedures Directive). The Qualifications Directive was particularly controversial. The difficulty lay in reaching political agreement on a list of safe third countries to which asylum seekers may be deported. In the final version of the directive, the idea of such a list is abandoned; instead, criteria are set for Member States to use in deciding which states can be considered safe (Annex II) and Member States are required to report periodically to the Commission as to the states to which they apply this concept (Article 27). Article 29 further gives the legislative institutions the power to adopt a minimum list of safe third countries.

   This group of instruments are very much minimum measures, although in relation to some Member States they do represent an improvement in comparison to previous measures. The likelihood of these measures being interpreted extensively by the Court of Justice is restricted by the provision in Article 68 EC, which restricts the scope of Article 234 EC by allowing only courts or tribunals against which there is no judicial remedy under national law to make a reference to the Court of Justice. The financial stringencies of asylum seekers, who are often denied legal aid, make it particularly difficult for them to take any appeal to the highest national court.

## 13.11   The External Dimension of EU Policies

As well as addressing migrants coming to the EU, the Tampere European Council placed a priority on working with the countries of origin of migrants and refugees in order to limit migration at source. The focus here is on encouraging the fight against poverty, the improvement of economic conditions, and supporting democracy and promoting human rights, in such a way as to minimise the need for migration, whether economically motivated or otherwise. However, there are also moves to limit illegal immigration by controls in the states of origin. To some extent, this area of policy overlaps with EU development cooperation policy, in that both have as their goals the improvement of the economic and political conditions within certain third countries (see Chapter 19). This is particularly evident from the Commission 2006 Communication on the Global Approach to Migration (COM(2006) 735).

In this field, soft law measures are the most prominent. Action plans have been drawn up for a number of states: Afghanistan, Morocco, Somalia, Sri Lanka, Iraq and Albania – all states which provide a large percentage of immigrants and asylum seekers in the EU. These action plans include the promotion of democratisation and human rights, social and economic development, and conflict prevention. However, more concrete financial support is provided by the programme set up by Council Regulation 491/2004 (OJ 2004 L80/1), establishing a programme for financial and technical assistance to third countries in the areas of migration and asylum. This programme, known as the AENEAS programme, allows for the grant of financial assistance to states who sign cooperation agreements with the EU which include an undertaking for the joint management of migration flows and compulsory readmission of illegal immigrants. Its legal basis is found in the development cooperation provisions, rather than the AFSJ provisions, and is justified explicitly by the need to control the migration of skilled nationals from developing countries. This programme is due to last for four years, from 2004 to 2008, and has a budget of €250 million.

## 13.12 Police Cooperation and the Development of a European Criminal Law

Internal security policy is an essential part of the Area of Freedom, Justice and Security, and the EU has adopted what it refers to as a Union-wide fight against crime. Article 29 EU states that an objective of the Union is to 'provide citizens with a high level of safety within an area of freedom, security and justice'. This covers both police cooperation and judicial cooperation (13.14). This policy was launched in a public way with the Treaty of Maastricht, with the inclusion, in the Third Pillar of provisions intended to encourage and facilitate police cooperation for the purposes of preventing and combating terrorism, of unlawful drug trafficking and other serious forms of international crime. However, its origins lie further back, with both operational cooperation among national law enforcement agencies, and cooperation in bodies such as Trevi between national governmental officials. Police cooperation was mainly focused on cross-border crime, especially organised crime and, more recently, terrorism.

Under the Third Pillar, as amended at Amsterdam, the emphasis was essentially combative – the 'fight' against crime and the role of the police forces in pursuing and apprehending criminals. However, in the Tampere Conclusion an emphasis was placed on the integration of crime prevention as well as crime fighting into the policy. In 2000, the Commission in a Communication stated that crime prevention could include reducing the opportunities that make crime easier, improving the social factors that foster crime, and informing and protecting victims (COM(2000) 786). No concrete actions are proposed to improve social factors beyond the statement that crime prevention is a new Union policy. In a 1998 Resolution (OJ 1998 C408/1) on the prevention of organised crime, the Commission was invited to reassess Community policies in the light of crime prevention – a possible step towards a mainstreaming approach, looking at social policy, regional policy, and economic and financial policies. This is far more appealing than the quick-fix approaches which could lead to the appearance of a police state. However, as experience in other areas, notably the environmental sphere, has shown, mainstreaming is a complex and long-term solution. As a result of this, a European Crime Prevention Network has been set up (see Decision 2001/427, OJ 2001 L153/1). The goal of this is to facilitate the kinds of cooperation and exchanges of information which were envisaged by the Commission.

The crime prevention strategy is carried out through soft-law measures intended to facilitate cooperation. However, in some fields binding legislation has been passed. This is particularly the case for financial crime: money laundering and counterfeiting. A directive was passed as early on as 1991 (Council Directive 91/308, OJ 1991 L166/77) to address the question of the use of financial systems for money laundering, and the question of money laundering was emphasised in the Tampere Conclusions as an area of special concern, as it is seen as being at the heart of all forms of organised crime. The Council called, as well as for the full application of the directive, for the harmonisation of laws relating to money laundering around the EU and the adoption of common standards of treatment of corporations registered outside the EU which may be used for money-laundering purposes. In 2001, part of the legislative package introducing the euro was a Regulation addressing the protection of the euro against counterfeiting (Council Regulation 1338/2001, OJ 2001 L181/6). This was then extended to cover the whole of the EU, not just Euroland (the territory of the Member States who participate in the single currency) by Council Regulation 1339/2001 (OJ 2001 L181/11). Another important domain in which the EU has adopted legislation shaping the body of national criminal law is the field of terrorism (Council Framework Decision 2002/465, OJ 2002 L164/3). Member States are bound to legislate to create terrorist offences covering certain defined types of behaviours. The two interests in financial crime and terrorism converge in European Parliament and Council Directive 2005/60 on the prevention of the use of the financial system for the purposes of money laundering and terrorist financing (OJ 2005 L309/15).

A further important EU strategy, and one which has been in force since 1992, is that of police cooperation and joint operations. The Schengen Convention, as incorporated into the First Pillar, allows for certain situations where the police forces of one state are able to operate in other Member States, notably when in 'hot pursuit' of a suspect where there is no time to inform the local authorities and in order to carry out surveillance operations, which can give rise to joint operations. The improvement of police cooperation was a further priority set out at Tampere. Joint operations had been successfully run prior to this time, and organised through the establishment of a procedural handbook, setting out how the operations should be run. In June 2002, a legally binding measure was passed, in the form of a Framework Decision on joint investigation teams (OJ 2002 L162/1). This allows the authorities of two or more Member States to set up joint teams to investigate cross-border crimes or crimes in different Member States which are connected, and sets out the ways in which those investigation teams can be run.

Another strategy is information-sharing. Two main information-sharing databases exist: the Schengen Information System (SIS), which contains information intended to inform individual decisions about immigration and asylum by warning Member States about individuals who are, or who are suspected, of being involved in serious criminal activity; and the Customs Information System which contains information about customs violations. The SIS has a dual purpose: to assist in the fight against crime; and to help promote free movement. This is brought into focus by Council Regulation 2424/2001 setting up the Schengen II system (OJ 2001 L328/4), which will upgrade the SIS to manage enlargement and which states in the preamble that its legislative basis is both Article 66 EC and Articles 30(1)(a) and (b), 31(a) and (b) and 34(2)(c) EU. SIS II is not yet in operation. At issue since the Hague Programme was adopted in 2004 has been the implementation of the 'principle of availability' covering information held by national law enforcement agencies (Proposal for a Council Framework Decision on the exchange of information under the principle of availability, COM(2005) 490). The fact that information is held in another state should never be a barrier to it being made available to those who need the information. This has serious civil liberties' implications as the Member States have not been able to adopt, thus far, a comprehensive set of rules on data protection in the Third Pillar domain. A 2005 Commission proposal in this area has not been adopted (COM(2005) 475). Data protection is achieved through *ad hoc* rules, which are included in respect of each legal instrument adopted. Nonetheless the Member States are pressing ahead with important new instruments, such as the Council Framework Decision 2006/960 on simplifying the exchange of information and intelligence between the law enforcement authorities of the Member States (OJ 2006 L386/89). In this context, the developments related to the incorporation of the Treaty of Prüm and its *acquis* into the framework of the Third Pillar are an equally important initiative, once again offering only piecemeal protection in relation to personal data (see 13.5).

A final element of police cooperation in the EU is Europol. Europol has its roots in the European Drugs Unit agreed under the aegis of the Treaty of Maastricht negotiations. However, in October 1998 the Europol Convention was agreed (OJ 1995 C316/2), and Europol came into operation in July 1999. Europol covers cross-border organised crime in the fields of illicit drug-trafficking, illicit immigration networks, trafficking in human beings, trafficking in vehicles, terrorism, money laundering and forgery. It is intended to share intelligence between Member States in this field, and a database is in the process of development. As such, it has been subject to criticism in that it is not properly used and Member States are often unwilling to share their intelligence. There is also a serious lack of accountability, which is problematic given the power and information which Europol potentially have at its disposal. In 2006, the Commission proposed that the Council should adopt a Decision giving a legal basis to Europol under the Third Pillar (COM(2006) 817). One objective of this measure is to give a more robust basis for parliamentary accountability of Europol, which is very weak at the present time (Den Boer, 2002; Fijnaut, 2004).

## 13.13 Judicial Cooperation in Civil and Criminal Matters

The area of Freedom, Security and Justice involves two types of judicial cooperation: civil and criminal. To some extent these are quite separate, and judicial cooperation in criminal matters is best understood in relation to police cooperation. In terms of Treaty basis, civil and criminal cooperation are distinct, judicial cooperation in criminal matters falling, with police cooperation, under the Third Pillar while judicial cooperation in civil matters has been consolidated by the Treaty of Amsterdam as a competence of the European Community under Article 65 EC. As this provision is included in Title IV covering visas, immigration and asylum, etc., the UK and Ireland have the possibility to opt out from new measures which are adopted in the form of Community instruments, such as regulations. The UK is opting out of new measures relating to judicial cooperation in relation to family law. However, its participation in the core measures regarding the mutual recognition of civil and commercial judgments is fully secured (e.g. Council Regulation 44/2001 on jurisdiction and the recognition and enforcement of judgments in civil and commercial matters, OJ 2001 L12/1, which is the successor instrument to the Judgments Convention).

Although there are separate legal bases for judicial cooperation in civil and criminal matters, a European Judicial Network has been created covering both civil and criminal matters (OJ 2001 L174/25), recognising that judicial cooperation shares basic principles in both contexts. In both criminal and civil matters, judicial cooperation tends to be limited to the mutual recognition and enforcement of decisions and judgments, and to information-sharing. In criminal matters some progress has been made in putting forward proposals aimed at the harmonisation of criminal law process for the purposes of fighting cross-border fraud. However the proposal to create a European Public Prosecutor for these matters, which was raised during the drafting of the Constitutional Treaty, proved controversial because of the risks to national criminal procedure which might thereby be created. The solution in the final draft was to create a legal basis to create a European Public Prosecutor, but to require that Member States vote unanimously if that legal basis were to be exercised (Article III-274 CT).

In civil law, a number of projects have been produced considering the possibility of a European civil code, but other than that European rules tend to be limited to mutual recognition. Harmonisation of laws and procedures is treated with some suspicion.

## 13.14 Judicial Cooperation in Criminal Matters and the Principle of Mutual Recognition

Judicial cooperation in criminal law is closely related to police cooperation, in that it has its origins in the fight against cross-border crime (which had been rendered easier following the relaxation of border controls and controls on the movement of capital). More recently, it has been the imperative of combating, preventing and detecting terrorist offences which has been the most significant external driver of EU law-making. To some extent the principle of the mutual recognition of judgments is similar to that in civil matters; criminal judgments handed down in one Member State should be recognised in all other Member States. In some ways, moreover, it is akin to the principle of mutual recognition operating in the internal market sphere (3.8). The principle of mutual recognition did not appear in the Treaty of Amsterdam, but made its first appearance in the Tampere Conclusions. It has shaped the various measures adopted under the Third Pillar in relation to judicial cooperation (Mitsilegas, 2006). However, the idea of mutual recognition in criminal matters now goes further than just a narrow focus on judgments, and encompasses also the more general idea that there should be mutual trust (and presumably understanding) between the criminal laws and procedures of the Member States. Here EU law is carried into very challenging territory.

The significance of the principle of mutual recognition is clearly evident in the most far-reaching measure which has been adopted under the Third Pillar thus far, that concerning the so-called European Arrest Warrant (Framework Decision on the European arrest warrant and the surrender procedures between Member States, OJ 2002 L190/1). In essence, this allows the Member States to depart from the historically cumbersome and discretionary processes of extradition in order to seek the surrender of a person from the territory of another Member State. Subject to very few exceptions stated in the Framework Decision, Member States must arrest and surrender to another Member State any individual, including a national, in respect of whom a surrender request is made. There have been substantial difficulties with the practical implementation of the European Arrest Warrant at the national level, as several Member States have previously had constitutional prohibitions on the extradition of nationals. National legislation implementing the Framework Decision was struck down, for example, in Germany, by the Federal Constitutional Court.

Some of the difficulties encountered with the European Arrest Warrant have made the Member States more cautious when negotiating, for example, a draft Framework Decision on the European Evidence Warrant for obtaining objects, documents and data for use in criminal proceedings (COM(2003) 688) and on the organisation and content of the exchange of information extracted from criminal records between the Member States (COM(2005) 690). These negotiations illustrate that whatever might be stated rhetorically by the EU institutions, the requisite degree of mutual trust between the Member States needed to make mutual recognition work in practice, without undermining guarantees within the criminal process, is not yet fully present.

Significant difficulties have also been encountered in the negotiations on the draft Council Framework Decision on certain procedural rights in criminal proceedings throughout the European Union (COM(2004) 328). Clearly, all Member States are bound by the underlying guarantees offered by Article 6 ECHR in relation to the criminal process, but it was nonetheless considered important by the Commission that measures taken in relation to facilitating the cross-border detection and prosecution of crime should be complemented by a measure harmonising certain minimum rights which are particularly important in a multilingual single market, such as linguistic rights during a criminal trial. However, thus far agreement has not been reached, even on a significantly watered-down proposal.

Mutual trust has also been a significant theme in relation to the one field of judicial cooperation in criminal matters where a modest body of case law is beginning to accumulate. This concerns the application of the principle of *ne bis in idem*, or double jeopardy. This principle protects those wishing to take advantage of their free movement rights, since it assures them that they cannot be prosecuted twice in respect of the same facts in different Member States, where the matter has been finally disposed of. In Joined Cases C-187 and 385/01 *Gözütuk and Brügge* ([2003] ECR I-1345), the Court of Justice held that Articles 54–58 of the Convention implementing the Schengen Agreement do not require any harmonisation of the national laws in order to take effect. In fact, it follows instead that there is a 'necessary implication that the Member States have mutual trust in their criminal justice systems and that each of them recognises the criminal law in force in the other Member States even when the outcome would be different if its own national law were applied' (para. 33). In *Gözütuk and Brügge* and subsequent cases (e.g. Case C-469/03 *Miraglia* [2005] ECR I-2009 and Case C-467/04 *Gasparini* [2006] ECR I-9199), the Court has taken a broad approach to determining when national courts must accept that a particular case has been finally disposed of, in respect of the same facts, in another Member State, thus allowing the defendant to invoke the *ne bis in idem* principle.

A further significant step in cooperation in criminal matters has been the establishment of EUROJUST. This was proposed at the Tampere European Council in the following terms:

'To reinforce the fight against serious organised crime, the European Council has agreed that a unit (EUROJUST) should be set up composed of national prosecutors, magistrates, or police officers of equivalent competence, detached from each Member State according to its legal system. EUROJUST should have the task of facilitating the proper coordination of national prosecuting authorities and of supporting criminal investigations in organised crime cases, notably based on Europol's analysis, as well as of co-operating closely with the European Judicial Network, in particular in order to simplify the execution of letters rogatory' (para. 46).

Council Decision 2002/187 established EUROJUST with a view to reinforcing the fight against serious crime (OJ 2002 L63/1). By that stage, EUROJUST had been given a firmer legal basis in the EU by the Treaty of Nice, which had been signed but had not yet entered into force. Amendments incorporating EUROJUST were introduced to Articles 29 and 31 EU. EUROJUST has a very light structure, aimed more at information-sharing than anything else. According to Article 3, EUROJUST's task is:

'(a) to stimulate and improve the coordination, between the competent authorities of the Member States, of investigations and prosecutions in the Member States, taking into account any request emanating from a competent authority of a Member State and any information provided by any body competent by virtue of provisions adopted within the framework of the Treaties;

(b) to improve cooperation between the competent authorities of the Member States, in particular by facilitating the execution of international mutual legal assistance and the implementation of extradition requests;

(c) to support otherwise the competent authorities of the Member States in order to render their investigations and prosecutions more effective.'

In the future, EUROJUST may evolve into a more proactive rather than a responsive body, but the obstacles to such developments in criminal process at the EU level are well illustrated by the difficulties faced among the Member States in reaching agreement over a European Public Prosecutor.

## Summary

1.  The development of the internal market and the consequent removal of internal borders within the EU necessitates, in turn, increased cooperation in the field of immigration, asylum and security policy.

2.  Justice and Home Affairs policy was formalised under the Third Pillar of the Treaty on European Union and covers a broad substantive area of policy. However, the level of action permitted was restricted so as not to interfere with national sovereignty in matters of internal security, and the decision-making process remained intergovernmental.

3.  Under the Treaty of Amsterdam, the achievement of an area of Freedom, Security and Justice became a central objective of the Union, and the Third Pillar was communitarised.

4.  The development of Freedom, Justice and Security policy has been subject to national political sensitivities in the field of immigration and asylum.

5.  Concerns have been expressed regarding the lack of human rights input into Freedom, Security and Justice policy.

6.  A Directive grants rights to third country nationals who are long term residents in the EU. These rights are less extensive than those held by citizens of the Union.

7.  The fight against racism and xenophobia must remain central to EU immigration and asylum policy.

8.  The legislative institutions are moving towards the goal of a common asylum policy and procedure.

## Summary cont'd

9. It has proved difficult to reach agreement in the field of migration management, owing to different national opinions and traditions on border control and risk.

10. The sharing of information to aid crime prevention and crime fighting is increasingly important, in particular when dealing with cross-border, organised crime. The EU has passed stronger, legally binding measures concerning the fight against organised crime.

11. There has been some limited cooperation in judicial matters, where there is a cross-border element to the dispute.

# Exercises

1. Why did a common policy on justice and home affairs become necessary?

2. What was the practical significance of the communitarisation of justice and home affairs policy in the Treaty of Amsterdam?

3. What developments are taking place in the law relating to third country nationals?

4. Why is a common asylum policy seen as being necessary?

5. What is the difference between a 'negative list' and a 'positive list' in visa policy?

6. What are the elements of the 'Union-wide fight against crime'?

7. What is the potential impact of judicial cooperation in civil and criminal matters?

## Further Reading

Den Boer, M. (2002) 'Towards an Accountability Regime for an Emerging European Police Governance', 12 *Policing and Society* 275.

Chalmers, D. *et al* (2006) *European Union Law*, Cambridge: Cambridge University Press, chapter 14 'EU Law and Non-EU Nationals'.

Fijnaut, C. (2004) 'Police Co-operation and the Area of Freedom, Security and Justice', in Walker, N. (ed.), *Europe's Area of Freedom, Security and Justice*, Oxford: Oxford University Press.

Groenendijk, K. (2001) 'Security of Residence and Access to Free Movement for Settled Third Country Nationals under Community Law', in Guild, E. and Harlow, C. (eds.), *Implementing Amsterdam: Immigration and Asylum Rights in EC Law*, Oxford: Hart Publishing.

Guild, E. (2002) 'The Single Market, Movement of Persons and Borders', in Barnard, C. and Scott, J. (eds.), *The Law of the Single European Market: Unpacking the Premises*, Oxford: Hart Publishing.

Guild, E. (2006) 'The Bitter Fruits of an EU Common Asylum Policy', in Balzacq, T. and Carrera, S. (eds.), *Security Versus Freedom? A Challenge for Europe's Future*, Aldershot: Ashgate.

Halleskov, L. (2005) 'The Long Term Residents Directive: A Fulfilment of the Tampere Objective of Near-Equality?', 7 *European Journal of Migration and Law* 181.

Juss, S. (2005) 'The Decline and Decay of European Refugee Policy', 25 *Oxford Journal of Legal Studies* 749.

Kostakopoulou, T. (2002) ' "Integrating" Non-EU Migrants in the European Union: Ambivalent Legacies and Mutating Paradigms', 8 *Columbia Journal of European Law* 181.

Kuijper, P.J. (2004) 'The Evolution of the Third Pillar from Maastricht to the Constitutional Treaty: Institutional Aspects', 41 *Common Market Law Review* 609.

## Further Reading cont'd

Lavenex, S. and Wallace, W. (2005) 'Justice and Home Affairs. Towards a "European Public Order"', in Wallace, H., Wallace W. and Pollack, M. (eds.), *Policy-Making in the European Union* (5th edn), Oxford: Oxford University Press.

Lööf, R. (2006) 'Shooting from the Hip: Proposed Minimum Rights in Criminal Proceedings throughout the EU', 12 *European Law Journal* 421.

Mitsilegas, V. (2006) 'The Constitutional Implications of Mutual Recognition in Criminal Matters in the EU', 43 *Common Market Law Review* 1277.

Monar, J. (2001) 'The Dynamics of JHA: Laboratories, Driving Factors, Costs', 39 *Journal of Common Market Studies* 747.

Peers, S. (2004) 'Implementing Equality? The Directive on Long Term Resident Third Country Nationals', 29 *European Law Review* 437.

Peers, S. (2005) 'Transforming Decision-making in EC Immigration and Asylum Law', 30 *European Law Review* 285.

Peers, S. (2006) *EU Justice and Home Affairs Law*, Oxford: Oxford University Press.

Rogers, N. (2002) 'Minimum Standards for Reception', 4 *European Journal of Migration and Law* 215.

Walker, N. (2004) 'In Search of the Area of Freedom, Security and Justice: A Constitutional Odyssey', in Walker, N. (ed.), *Europe's Area of Freedom, Security and Justice*, Oxford: Oxford University Press.

Wasmeier, M. and Thwaites, N. (2006) 'The Development of *ne bis in idem* into a Transnational Fundamental Right in EU Law: Comments on Recent Developments', 31 *European Law Review* 565.

## Key Websites

DG Freedom, Security and Justice at:
**http://ec.europa.eu/justice_home/index_en.htm**

Frontex at:
**http://www.frontex.europa.eu/**

Europol at:
**http://www.europol.europa.eu/**

EUROJUST at:
**http://www.eurojust.europa.eu/index.htm**

Fundamental Rights in the European Union at:
**http://ec.europa.eu/justice_home/fsj/rights/fsj_rights_intro_en.htm**

Statewatch, an NGO active in the field of civil liberties across Europe, which also provides extensive coverage of EU legislation on JHA and other activities, including depositories of documents and several important 'Observatories' of EU policies such as data protection, is located at:
**http://www.statewatch.org/**

Presidency Conclusions, Tampere European Council, 15 and 16 October 1999, available at:
**http://europa.eu.int/council/off/conclu/oct99/oct99_en.htm**

Crime Prevention network at:
**http://www.eucpn.org/**

# Part IV

# The Social Dimension

# Chapter 14

## The Development of a
## Social Dimension

14.1 Introduction

This part of the book focuses on the range of policies which together form the social dimension to the European integration project. Subsequent chapters will focus on equality, employment law and policy, environmental law, social cohesion and regional policy, and development policy. The latter two chapters represent interesting cases, offering both the internal and the external dimensions of the EU's redistributive policies. The present chapter serves a number of functions. Acting as an introduction to the social dimension, it accounts for action in the social policy field by examining the rationales for intervention by the European Union: it sketches the competences held by the Union, and it charts the evolution of the social dimension. In addition, it examines in some detail specific policy fields within the social dimension to which a separate chapter has not been devoted, namely social protection, health, consumer protection and cultural policy.

A social dimension to EU integration has always existed, and it has become more entrenched and established as the years have progressed. It has been variously presented as supplementing, complementing, counterbalancing or, increasingly, underpinning the Union's core economic project. Certainly the political rhetoric employed throughout the EU's existence has been careful to stress the equal status of the social and economic dimensions of integration. As early as 1958, the Commission, in its *First General Report on the Activities of the Community*, stated that 'the objectives of a social character are placed on the same footing as those of an economic character' (1958: para. 102). A similar message was delivered by the Heads of State and Government at the October 1972 Paris Summit, when they declared they attributed 'the same importance to energetic proceedings in the field of social policy as to the realisation of the economic and financial union'. More recently, the Working Group on Social Europe submitted in its report to the Convention on the Future of Europe, which drafted the Treaty Establishing a Constitution for Europe, that the 'affirmation of social objectives as equivalent, not subordinate, to economic objectives constitutes an integral part of the spirit in which the European Union was conceived and of the direction in which it develops' (CONV 516/1/03 REV 1: 8).

However, this longstanding rhetoric of the equivalent status of social and economic concerns has not been reflected in policy outputs. There has always been, as Scharpf terms it, a 'constitutional asymmetry' between the EU's economic and social policies (2002: 645). This is felt both at the supranational level, where the central mission of economic integration has tended to dominate and frame social policy interventions, and also at national level, where Member States are increasingly constrained in what they can achieve through their own social policies, given the hard legal obligations and budgetary strictures imposed by economic integration. While social goals and values have been anchored increasingly firmly within the Treaty framework, and while a steadily growing body of 'social' legislation undoubtedly exists, the social policy field has by necessity been a test-bed for alternatives to traditional hard law regulatory measures, in many respects as a consequence of ongoing political disputes about whether and to what extent the EU should engage with social policy matters.

## 14.2 Rationales for the European Union's Social Dimension

The celebrated social policy scholar T. H. Marshall has defined social policy as the use of 'political power to supersede, supplement or modify operations of economic systems in order to achieve results which the economic system would not achieve on its own . . . guided by values other than those determined by market forces' (Marshall, 1975: 15). While national variations in approach exist, over the course of the twentieth century, states became increasingly involved in providing for the social needs of their citizens, through the public provision of health care, education, public housing and income support for those unable to maintain a liveable income through work. The adoption of legislative guarantees to equality and to rights to fair treatment for those in employment further contributes a 'social' counterbalance to the 'economic' concerns of the market. According to Streeck, such social policies are essentially 'market correcting, generating entitlements for workers [and others] that the market would not provide on its own' (1995: 398).

Why did nation states develop such social policies? Three groups of reasons tend to be advanced for these regulatory and redistributive policies, which see resources redistributed from one section of society to another. The first of these is efficiency grounds. If market forces alone are relied on to deliver social services, gaps in provision are expected to arise which will have a knock-on effect for the economic wellbeing of society as a whole. Healthy stable economies require healthy, well-trained workers, and consumers to purchase the products of the economy. Education, health and social security policies and the like can thus be justified on economic efficiency grounds. The second group of reasons is based more on notions of social justice; these are equity-based arguments that resources and opportunities should be shared fairly among the members of a society. Finally, social policies may be justified on the grounds that they contribute to, and arise from, a sense of solidarity, as a means to generate or reinforce a sense of community and identity within a society, and in order to protect the society from the negative consequences of social dislocation or exclusion (Kleinman, 2002: 4).

If these are the possible justifications for nation state engagement in the field of social policy, what are the possible rationales for EU intervention? According to Streeck (1995), the EU developed a social dimension for 'market-making', rather than 'market-correcting' reasons. A social dimension to integration evolved as it was seen as a necessary component in the economic integration process. Social policy was, at first, 'decoupled' from the European project (Joerges, 2005: 463) and left to be addressed at the national level. However, social policy issues subsequently took their place on the EU policy agenda through their linkage with the market-making project. This can be seen as conforming with the prognosis of policy 'spill over' advanced by neofunctionalist theory (on neofunctionalism, see Rosamund, 2005). The harmonisation of divergent national standards in relation to equality legislation, working conditions and environmental regulation, for example, was seen as necessary for the equalisation of costs and the creation of a level playing field for economic operators. The imposition of minimum social standards from above could also stand in the way of potential 'social dumping' – a national 'race to the bottom' where Member States remove costly social entitlements in an attempt to gain a competitive advantage in the market (Barnard, 2000a).

Of course, a market-correcting argument could also be advanced for the adoption of minimum standards legislation and for the EU's engagement in the social dimension more generally – that these measures promote social justice and respect for the individual citizen. Indeed, for some participants in the EU law-making process, these reasons have always been to the fore, though this conceptualisation has not been universally shared. However, as Maduro (2000) states, as the European project moves further towards the goal of political integration and beyond economic integration, questions about the nature and scope of the EU's social dimension, about the EU's 'social identity', become ever more pressing. Maduro argues that further political integration will require a fundamental shift in the conceptualisation of the EU's role in the social sphere – one which breaks with the market-creating rationale and which is based instead on notions of distributive justice, solidarity and cohesion among European citizens. By working towards a more just division between citizens of the benefits of economic integration, the *social* legitimacy of the *economic* integration project may be enhanced and ensured. The development of a strong supranational social policy competence may be linked to the idea of the EU as an emerging polity which goes beyond an economic project. A strong social dimension also feeds into, and gives substantive content to, the evolving concept of EU citizenship, with the EU standing in direct relation to its citizens.

In delivering its social policy, the Union uses very different tools from those traditionally employed at the level of the nation state. The Union has only a limited (albeit highly politically significant) role in operating redistributive policies, through the Structural Funds. Redistribution takes place at the regional and Member State level, and not at individual or group level, as operates within nation states. The Union has an established regulatory role in certain social policy fields – most notably employment rights and environmental protection. In those fields most closely related to 'social policy' as it is defined at national level, such as social assistance, public health care and education, soft law is the primary policy tool available to the EU.

## 14.3   Overview of Current Competences

The tasks of the Community, set out in Article 2 EC, include the promotion of 'a high level of employment and of social protection, equality between men and women, . . . a high level of protection and improvement of the quality of life of the environment, the raising of the standard of living and quality of life, and economic and social cohesion and solidarity among Member States'. The articles providing the EU with the competence to contribute to the achievement of these tasks are scattered throughout the Treaty. Specific Titles, granting legislative powers, exist on the Environment (Title XIX, Articles 174–176 EC), Economic and Social Cohesion (Title XVII, Articles 158–162 EC) and Social Policy, Education, Vocational and Youth (Title XI, Articles 136–145 EC). Under this latter title, hard legislative powers are by and large reserved for the field of workers' rights. Article 137 EC is the relevant basis here, providing for the introduction of directives on working conditions, information and consultation of workers, and equality at work between men and women. The combating of social exclusion and the modernisation of social protection systems are also included at Article 137, however the introduction of directives in these areas is explicitly excluded, and alternative, soft law techniques must be used. Limitations on legislative competence also operate in other areas. For example, in the field of public health, there is, outside certain narrowly drawn areas, an explicit prohibition against the

EU introducing legislation which substitutes or harmonises national laws. Instead, the EU is limited to adopting 'incentive measures' (Article 152 EC). Similar prohibitions against harmonising legislation apply in other areas of 'supporting' competence, where the EU's role is one of encouraging cooperation between the Member States to find policy solutions to common issues – such as the employment-generating measures taken under the auspices of the European Employment Strategy (Article 129 EC), education (Article 149 EC), vocational training (Article 150 EC) and culture (Article 151 EC).

Other provisions of a social nature which provide a basis for the introduction of legislation can be found in the early part of the Treaty. In the opening 'Principles' Title, and reflecting the constitutional significance of the non-discrimination principle, Article 13 EC, introduced by the Treaty of Amsterdam, provides for legislative action to combat discrimination 'based on sex, racial or ethnic origin, religion or belief, disability, age or sexual orientation'. Measures taken to complete the internal market can also have a clear social dimension. An obvious example would be Article 42 EC, which provides for Council legislation on social security in order to facilitate the free movement of workers and their families. A rather less obvious example of the social dimension to the internal market relates to the free movement of goods. Title XIV (Article 153 EC) on Consumer Protection, for example, recognises an explicit, positive competence for the EU to ensure the protection of the health, safety and economic interests of consumers when introducing harmonising measures under Article 95 EC.

When adopting certain social measures, the option exists for rule-making by the representatives of the two sides of industry, management and labour, whose agreements may then be given the force of law through Council decision (Articles 138–139 EC). This 'social dialogue' route was introduced by the Treaty of Maastricht, and has been keenly advocated, particularly by the Commission (see further 16.5). The 'social' dialogue is however available only in respect of employment law-related matters. A similar 'privatisation' of the policy process has not occurred in other areas of the social dimension, though the Commission funds, and meets twice yearly to discuss policy issues with a 'Social Platform' involving over thirty NGOs operating in the social policy field.

Finally, in furtherance of the goal of 'economic and social cohesion' between the regions of the EU, and its peoples, the EU operates a series of redistributive policies through its Structural Funds: most notably the European Regional Development Fund (Articles 158–162 EC) and the European Social Fund (Articles 146–148 EC), which is involved in the operation of the European Employment Strategy and, through its contribution to improved employment opportunities, in combating social exclusion. 'Incentive measures' envisaged in areas such as education and health may also carry with them elements of financial support, which can act as a stimulant to policy convergence.

## 14.4 Negative Harmonisation

The review in 14.3 outlined the areas in which legislative action may be taken by the EU, which can have a direct impact on national social systems. These systems may also be subject to a process of 'negative' integration. For example, the demands of operating within a competitive market economy may create deregulatory pressures on these systems, leading to a national 'race to the bottom' as Member States reduce or remove their social and employment protection measures in an attempt to gain a competitive advantage and thereby attract capital investment. The response of firms which move their operations to countries with lower standards is described as 'social dumping' (Barnard, 2000a: 26).

Further pressures on national social policy arrangements may come in the guise of formal legal challenges to national measures on the basis that they present unjustified obstacles to the exercise of the economic freedoms guaranteed within the internal market. National employment protection measures have been challenged on the grounds that they restrict the free movement of goods and services. Good examples are provided by Case 155/80 *Oebel* ([1981] ECR 1993), concerning a limitation on night work in German bakeries, and Case C-113/89 *Rush Portuguesa Lda* v. *Office Nationale d'Immigration* ([1990] ECR I-1417), concerning French legislation requiring its own, higher level of employment protection to be applied to workers temporarily posted to France by companies based in other states with lower standards of employment protection. Challenges have also been made to aspects of national social protection systems, on the basis of their possible incompatibility with the Treaty rules on competition and state aids. The examples here include Joined Cases C-159 and 160/91 *Poucet and Pistre* v. *AGF and Cancava* ([1993] ECR I-637), concerning the operation of occupational sickness and maternity insurance funds, and Case C-67/96 *Albany International BV* v. *Stichting Bedrijfspensioenfonds Textielindustrie* ([1999] ECR I-5751), concerning pension funds, where, in both cases, membership of a particular fund was compulsory, thus removing the possibility of competition in the market for these services.

The prevalence of such challenges is growing as alternatives to direct state provision of these services develop, in response in large measure to the financial pressures on national systems, and as service providers increasingly seek access to this market. The cross-border provision of social policy-related services in this increasingly market-driven arena became a contentious focal point in the discussions leading to the adoption of the Services Directive (European Parliament and Council Directive 2006/123, OJ 2006 L 376/36); see 6.13). The directive seeks to open up the market in services across the EU, with the operation of a general principle of home state control. Ultimately, health and social services were excluded from the directive; their inclusion had been met with considerable opposition, and the fears of social dumping generated by them were undoubtedly one factor behind the 'no' votes against the proposed Constitution, particularly in France, where concerns over the privileging of economic interests over social concerns gained especial political salience. In response to such pressures, and the view of the European Parliament, the Commission in April 2006 proposed excluding these sectors, and will bring forward a separate initiative in the field of health services (on the rights of citizens to move to receive health services, see 14.8).

It should be noted, however, that in the case law of the Court, countervailing social 'constraints' do challenge the dominance of the liberalising tendencies of the market. In the legal challenges to national social measures, the Court has, by and large, sought to avoid disrupting national arrangements. Thus, in the employment law examples above, the national rules were deemed either to fall outside Articles 28–29 EC, or to constitute justifiable restrictions to the free movement rules. In the competition law cases meanwhile, the Court has developed the concept of 'social solidarity' which it applies as a protective shell around certain national arrangements for social welfare provision. For this 'buttress against internal market law' (Hervey, 2000b) to be available, the national arrangements need to correspond with a range of conditions: they must fulfill a social, not economic objective, operate on a not-for-profit basis, and be based on the principle of solidarity between all workers, membership on comparable terms being open and compulsory for all whether young or old, good or bad risks. In *Poucet*, these factors were enough to remove the relevant public sector organisation outside the reach of competition law entirely, as it was not to be regarded as an 'undertaking' (see also C-218/00 *Cisal* v. *INAIL* [2002] ECR I-691).

In *Albany*, however, despite being a not-for-profit body exhibiting significant solidarity characteristics, the Court held that the pension fund was to be considered an undertaking for the purposes of competition law. Here, the incidences of solidarity were limited. The Court focused in particular on the operation of the capitalisation principle – that levels of benefits payable were determined by the results of the financial investments made by the fund. The fund was regarded as an undertaking engaged in an economic activity in competition with insurance companies. Nevertheless, the Court went on to rule that there was no breach of the competition law rules in cases where undertakings were given exclusive rights, where such a monopoly was regarded as necessary for 'the performance of a particular social task of general interest' (at para. 98).

## 14.5 Ebbs and Flows

The evolution of the social dimension has not been smooth. Political tensions between the Member States as to the proper role for EU social policy, and as to the correct balancing between economic and social objectives, have been a constraining factor in the evolution of the social dimension, particularly as unanimity was required for decision-making for a lengthy stretch of the EU's history. While the Member States have continued to dominate policy development in the social arena, any account of its evolution must acknowledge the significant role played by the Commission, which has tended to pursue a broadly expansionist agenda in this field, operating as a 'purposeful opportunist', working behind the scenes to ensure that when policy windows open and opportunities for action present themselves, it is ready to put forward developed proposals (Cram, 1997). Of comparable significance has been the role of the European Court of Justice, which likewise has pursued a generally pro-social dimension agenda, regularly delivering expansive interpretations of primary and secondary legislation, taking these measures beyond their economic aims, and the impact intended by their authors.

The early phase has been described as one of benign neglect (Mosely, 1990). While a specific title on Social Policy was included in the EEC Treaty, this has been described as being 'generally exhortatory' (Barnard, 2006: 4), containing statements of political intent, rather than direct entitlements for citizens, or any specific law-making competence for the Community. Outside the field of the free movement of workers, few policy initiatives were taken in the social policy arena. By the early 1970s, however, pressures had begun to mount on the Community in favour of a more interventionist approach to social policy. The assumption that the functioning of the common market would automatically, and fairly swiftly, bring about a general, Community-wide improvement in living and working conditions had proved misplaced. Economic growth had come at a price – there were losers as well as winners, 'and the readiness of the average European citizen to pay the price was rapidly diminishing' (Shanks, 1977: 3). Facing an economic downturn, and fearing repeats of the civil and industrial unrest which had spread across mainland Europe in the later 1960s, the Council of Ministers meeting in Paris in 1972 declared their commitment to 'vigorous action in the social sphere' (Bull. EC 10/1972). In response to the call from the Paris Summit, the Commission drew up its first Social Action Programme (Bull. EC Supp. 2/74). This outlined three key objectives for the Community – the attainment of full and better employment; the improvement of living and working conditions; and the increased involvement of the 'social partners' (the EU-level representatives of employers and employees) in decision-making, at the level both of the Community and the undertaking.

The policies of the first Social Action Programme (SAP) were not fully brought to fruition, and only a handful of these proposed measures reached the stage of adoption. The significant success stories of the 1970s were directives on sex equality at work, a limited programme of employment protection directives, and health and safety measures (see Chapters 15 and 16). The Court of Justice was also contributing to the temporary upturn in activity in the social sphere, most significantly in its decisions in respect of the direct effect of the sex equality at work provision in Article 141 EC (former Article 119 EEC). After 1974, however, a combination of economic recession and a lack of political will in the Council of Ministers effectively destroyed the SAP as the basis for a comprehensive Community social policy.

Prospects for social Europe appeared more optimistic over the second half of the 1980s. The vision of a strong social dimension to the rejuvenated internal market project, advanced by the newly installed Commission President Delors, garnered enough support to bring about a range of additions to the EEC Treaty through the Single European Act, and relaunch social Europe once more. Economic and social cohesion was introduced into the Treaty as a policy goal and, for the first time, a dedicated legal basis for the introduction of social provisions was introduced into the Treaty title on social policy. Building on one of the few successes of the SAP, this legal basis was available for the introduction of health and safety measures. The adoption of measures outside this apparently narrow area continued to face the obstacle of unanimity requirements, as only the general law-making powers in Articles 94 (100) EC and 308 (former 235) EC were available. Other developments at this time include a move towards greater involvement of the social partners in the policy-making process. This had already been referred to in the 1974 SAP, and was reflected in the SEA's introduction of an obligation on the Commission to develop the social dialogue between the two sides of industry. The 1980s also saw the launch of a more extensive Community vocational training policy, building on the initial impetus given by the Court, as well as a restructuring of, and substantial increase in, the budget for the Regional Development and the Social Fund (see Chapter 18). In 1989, all Member States bar the UK adopted the non-binding Community Charter of Fundamental Rights of Workers. A new Action Programme was drawn up by the Commission containing a wide range of measures which were intended to contribute to the attainment of the Charter rights. The operationalisation of this legislative programme was again significantly obstructed by a lack of political will, in particular the intransigence of the UK which was firmly attached to a deregulatory agenda in social matters, a situation which was exacerbated by the narrow grounds on which measures could be adopted by quality majority voting (QMV).

A new phase in EU social policy was subsequently brought about by the Treaty of Maastricht, which, while introducing into the EC Treaty a number of emerging policy fields including culture, public health and consumer protection, also institutionalised the UK's opposition to social Europe. A stronger role, greater competence and more qualified majority voting than under the existing social policy title were envisaged. However, the UK was unwilling to agree to this enhanced social policy title. A compromise was wrought, under which enhanced and extended social policy provisions and legal bases were to be placed outside the main body of the EC Treaty, in the form of a Social Protocol and an annexed Social Policy Agreement. Recourse by all other states to this 'Social Chapter' allowed UK intransigence to policy development in the social sphere to be overcome, though measures adopted in this way would have no legal effects on the UK. The Social Chapter also saw a qualitative advance in the involvement of the social partners in policy-making, through the introduction of the social dialogue law-making route. This allows the two sides of industry to adopt agreements which could be given the force of law.

The UK's opt-out continued until the election of the UK Labour government in 1997, when it agreed to be bound by the strengthened Social Chapter. The Chapter was subsequently inserted into the main body of the EC Treaty through the Treaty of Amsterdam, replacing the existing Social Policy Title and bringing the 'twin track' approach (Shaw, 1994) to an end. However, while the Treaty of Amsterdam brought the Member States back together under a common framework, with common objectives and legal bases for the introduction of legislative measures that will apply to all states, this phase saw little in the way of new legislative measures in the social field, apart from some subsequent notable exceptions in the field of equality and non-discrimination (see 15.14 and 15.15). Developments here include the adoption in 2000 of the directives on equal treatment between people irrespective of racial or ethnic origin (Council Directive 2000/43, OJ 2000 L180/22) and on a general framework for equal treatment in employment and occupation (Council Directive 2000/78, OJ 2000 L303/16). Equality issues also featured in the revisions to the EC Treaty brought by the Treaty of Amsterdam, with the 'mainstreaming' of equality between men and women across all policy activities: 'in all the activities referred to [in Article 3 EC], the Community shall aim to eliminate inequalities, and to promote equality, between men and women' (Article 3(2) EC). A similar 'mainstreaming' commitment was also made in respect of environmental protection (Article 6 EC).

The Treaty of Amsterdam also introduced into the EC Treaty a new Title on employment, and provided a new structure for the coordination of Member States' employment policies in the drive to combat unemployment, in the form of the European Employment Strategy (Title VIII, Articles 125–130). Increasing employment and promoting 'social inclusion', which embraces but goes beyond reducing poverty, have become the dominant policy preoccupations of this phase, and feature prominently in the policy objectives of the Commission in the Social Policy Agenda (SPA), adopted to support the Lisbon strategy, in 2000 (COM(2000) 379). The Agenda states that it 'does not seek to harmonise social policies' (p.7) but instead seeks to promote coordination of social and employment policies, presenting social, employment and economic policies as mutually interdependent and reinforcing. The primary role for social policy is as a productive factor, with social expenditure (on health, education and the like) presented as an investment in human capital, facilitating the entry, and continued participation of individuals in the employment market. These national social protection systems, through which such expenditure is managed and delivered, and which together reflect a common 'European social model', require 'modernising', owing *inter alia* to pressures caused by demographic shifts. The EU's role in social policy is one of developing coordination between Member States as they face common challenges.

For Szyszczak, the 2000 SPA represents 'a series of policy aspirations lacking a legislative backbone', and the subsequent Nice Treaty, which saw little development of the social provisions, as a sign that the EU had 'run out of ideas and ambition for any further development of social policy' (2003: 320). Certainly, there were few hard legislative proposals in the 2000 SPA, or in its follow-up Agenda running from 2005 to 2010 (COM(2005) 33). The policy preoccupations of the current phase have seen a definitive shift in social policy, away from the EU's traditional concern with workers' rights, where legislative competence is clear. This shift is understandable. As was stated in the Report to the Commission by the *High Level Group on the future of social policy in an enlarged European Union* (2004), 'legislative action is more behind us than before us' (p.71). This is for a variety of reasons: no major legislative gaps are seen in respect to workers' rights and, more pragmatically, rather than introduce new legislation, a period of consolidation is needed during which the new Member States fully transpose and implement the existing *acquis*, a process which is seen as particularly underdeveloped in respect of health and safety and equal treatment. Further, rather than legislation, the current policy objectives demand alternative means of intervention, and soft law, the open method of coordination and the use of the European Structural Funds are particularly identified.

Little change was foreseen in respect of the existing social provisions in the Constitutional Treaty, which identifies social policy; economic, social and territorial cohesion; the environment, consumer protection and certain public health matters, as areas of shared competence (Article I-14). Despite making new commitments to the objectives of promoting a social market economy, full employment and social progress (Article I-3), for many voters in the referenda held over 2005, the Constitution was perceived as giving insufficient guarantees to social concerns. The Constitution would have given legal force to a body of fundamental rights, including social rights, adopted in 2000 as the non-binding Charter of Fundamental Rights of the European Union (OJ 2000 C364/1).

## 14.6  Social Rights as Fundamental Rights?

In international and domestic human rights instruments, a distinction is generally seen between, on the one hand, civil and political rights, and, on the other, social and economic rights. The latter are less likely to be considered justiciable fundamental rights, being seen more as programmatic aspirations, demanding costly positive interventions from states. Many civil and political rights meanwhile rest instead on non-interference from the state in the public and private lives of individuals. While this distinction has been challenged, mainly by social rights' advocates as overly simplistic, civil and political rights certainly have a more entrenched position in human rights systems and instruments. Conversely, in the EU order, civil and political rights have not had such privileged status. No explicit provision was made in the original Treaty for mechanisms protecting against the infringement of civil and political rights. While such protections have evolved through case law and Treaty revision, the system has, from the start, appeared to privilege economic rights, affording these a fundamental, constitutional status, as is reflected in the terminology of the 'fundamental freedoms' and in the case law of the Court. Economic rights have dominated, and a similar privileging of social rights has not been a feature of the EU order. While it was recognised in 14.4 that social considerations may be taken into account to defend national practices challenged as being hindrances to the operation of the internal market, Bernard has pointed out that these considerations 'are not conceptualised as rights, but rather as derogations from (economic) rights. As such this places social considerations in a more fragile position since derogations from fundamental internal market freedoms are to be interpreted narrowly according to the case law of the Court' (Bernard, 2003: 253).

By recognising and giving effect to a body of fundamental social rights within the EU order, something of a recalibration of the constitutional balance may take place. In practical terms, such rights would not necessarily automatically trump economic rights if both were regarded as fundamental, but a shift in perception in the status of social concerns, by the Courts, by the legislature and by individuals could prove significant in engendering further support for the integration project.

Given that social rights inevitably carry significant costs, and that it would be the individual Member States rather than the EU institutions which would have to stand as provider of these rights, it is unsurprising that there has been limited enthusiasm from the Member State governments for the adoption of a body of fundamental social rights that would be enforceable at national level. The first references to fundamental rights in the EU social order came with a declaratory statement in the preamble to the Single European Act of the significance of fundamental rights, including social rights contained in the Council of Europe's European Social Charter, as an inspiration for the EU's activities. Subsequently, and serving a similar purpose, the social policy Title of the EU treaty was amended by the Amsterdam Treaty to include reference to social rights' instruments. These include the European Social Charter, and also a specific social rights' instrument proclaimed by 11 of the then 12 Member States (the UK dissenting) – the 1989 Community Charter of Fundamental Social Rights of Workers. This Charter significantly was less ambitious in its scope than the *citizens'* charter initially proposed by the Commission, with the rights it contains limited to those in work. The Charter is also non-binding, and essentially programmatic, setting out principles to be attained by Member States and, within the limits of its competence, the Union. As Kenner (2003a: 10) shows, while the Charter is without legally binding force, it is not without legal consequences. *Inter alia*, it was drawn on by the Commission in a linked Social Action Programme, giving rise to a number of legislative proposals and 'often serving to reinforce an otherwise shaky legal foundation' for legislative intervention. It has also been regularly referred to by Advocates General and the Court in its judgments, serving as an aid to interpretation of existing legislative provisions. The Charter rights have been particularly influential in the field of working time for example, with a broad interpretation of key concepts in the directive being presented on the basis of the significance of certain rights' fundamental status (Case C-84/94 *United Kingdom* v. *Council* [1996] ECR I-5755; Case C-173/99 *R* v. *Secretary of State for Trade and Industry, ex parte BECTU* [2001] ECR I-4881).

A broader set of social rights, including, but going beyond, rights at work were included in the 2000 Charter of Fundamental Rights of the European Union. The Union institutions, and the Member States, when implementing EU law are called upon to 'respect the rights, observe the principles and promote the application thereof in accordance with their respective powers and respecting the limits of the powers of the Union'. Social rights feature predominantly in the solidarity title, and include workers' rights to information and consultation, fair and just working conditions, the right to legal, economic and social protection of the family, entitlement to social security benefits and social services, to social and housing assistance, and access to preventative health care. The potential influence of the Charter on citizens' legal heritage has been much debated (Hervey and Kenner, 2003; Peers and Ward, 2004). At the very least, O'Leary submits, it should have a 'standstill' effect, 'preventing any regression from the level of social rights protection already achieved' (2005: 87). The Charter remains non-legally binding, and grants no new enforceable rights to citizens – there is repeated reference to the rights in the solidarity Title applying 'in accordance with national laws and practices'. In terms of generating a dynamic to new legislative proposals, some rights clearly fall outside the legislative competence of the Union.

Nevertheless, it cannot be ruled out that the Court of Justice will start to draw upon the social rights expressed in the Charter in future judgments in a similar way to its use of the 1989 Charter, although it has been slow to take this step. Its first reference to the Charter came in the context of a challenge by the Parliament to the Family Reunification Directive (Council Directive 2003/86, OJ 2003 L251/13) in Case C-540/03 *Parliament* v. *Council* ([2006] ECR I-5769; see 13.9), where it dismissed the Parliament's arguments based on the Charter and other instruments. It has yet to use the Charter in such a way as to change the outcome which it would otherwise have reached using a combination of the instruments to which it would commonly refer, such as the two Social Charters and the ECHR.

## 14.7 Social Protection

Social protection systems are a fundamental feature of all Member States' national social policy regimes. Social protection has been defined as 'all the collective transfer systems designed to protect people against social risks' (Commission Communication *The Future of Social Protection: A Framework for a European Debate*, COM(95) 466, p.1). Social protection systems generally incorporate elements of *social security*, under which the employed and self-employed insure themselves against a set of risks, including illness, old age and injury, as well as *social assistance*, a safety net of cash payments and benefits in kind, including health care services available to those in need. While variations exist between the states' systems, sufficient commonalities exist for a distinctive 'European' approach to social protection to be identified. 'Europe's' commitment to social protection and to the principles of solidarity underpinning it are differentiated from the rather more privatised US model in which social inequality is accepted (Vos, 2005). This contributes to a vision of a specific European Social Model, defined at the Barcelona Summit (2002) as being 'based on good economic performance, a high level of social protection, education and social dialogue'.

The organisation and financing of social protection systems remain the responsibility of the Member States, and this point has been made repeatedly by the Court of Justice (e.g. Case 238/82 *Duphar* [1984] ECR 523; Case C-70/95 *Sodemare* [1997] ECR I-3395; Case C-385/99 *Müller-Fauré* [2003] ECR I-4509). It has also been incorporated into the EC Treaty, which provides at Article 137 EC that provisions adopted under that Article 'shall not affect the right of Member States to define the fundamental principles of their social security systems and must not significantly affect the financial equilibrium thereof'. Nevertheless, the EU engages in, and impacts on, the operation of these regimes in a variety of ways and, while it may not directly provide social protection, the EU has become 'a partial guarantor of welfare rights for EU citizens' (de Búrca, 2005: 2).

The first thread of EU action on welfare policy is the adoption of coordinating legislation, primarily under Article 42 EC which provides for the adoption of 'such measures in the field of social security as are necessary to provide freedom of movement to workers'. The key measure here has been Council Regulation 1408/71 (OJ 1971 L149/2), which was designed to ensure that workers and the self-employed exercising their free movement rights were not disadvantaged by the operation of the different systems of social security that they might encounter when moving from state to state. Intended to cover contributory social security schemes only, the Regulation allowed periods of employment and insurance in more than one state to be taken into account when calculating entitlement to benefits, and also for the export of certain social rights by the claimant, from the home to the host state. This Regulation was amended many times over the years, including the 1992 revision (Council Regulation 1247/92, OJ 1992 L136/1), which saw the Council overturning the European Court's controversial interpretation of the Regulation which permitted apparent non-contributory, social assistance-type measures to be exported (Joined Cases 379, 380, 381/85 and 93/86 *Caisse régionale d'assurance maladie Rhône-Alpes* v. *Giletti* [1987] ECR 955). The Regulation was recently revised and replaced by European Parliament and Council Regulation 883/2004 (OJ 2004 L166/1), which covers all insured migrants, not just the economically active, and which has seen some extension in the range of benefits which is covered.

Moving on from this coordinating 'de-territorialising' legislation, which has been subject to myriad Court interpretations over the years, has been the process of 'denationalisation' of social protection (Sindbjerg Martinsen, 2005), whereby national benefits are made available to resident non-nationals. Both contributory and non-contributory benefits have been made available to migrants, initially on the basis of their economic activity, though ultimately on the basis of their status as EU citizens. This process, in which the Court has taken a key role, has been extensively detailed in Chapter 12.

Moving outside the free movement aspects of social protection, more recently, demographic shifts, increasing international competition and declining economic growth have been among the factors which have placed significant pressures on the sustainability of existing national social protection systems. The Treaty of Nice introduced a competence for the EU to support and complement the activities of the Member States in modernising their social protection systems (Article 137(1)(k) EC). Soft coordinating measures designed to stimulate policy convergence predated this Treaty change by nearly a decade (Council Recommendation 92/422 (OJ 1992 L245/49) on the convergence of social policy objectives and policies). Following the introduction of the policy task by the Nice Treaty, and repeated calls for action at successive European Summit meetings, soft law remains the key policy tool, as the use of directives is explicitly excluded (Article 137(2) EC).

Instead of hard legislation, the convergence and modernisation of national systems are to take place under the Open Method of Coordination (OMC; see 2.5), and with the involvement of the Social Protection Committee, established in 2000 (see now Article 144 EC). Four strands of OMC were initially envisaged: a social inclusion OMC (see further Chapter 18); one on pensions; one on health and long-term care; and, finally, 'making work pay' (making social protection systems more employment-friendly), with the former being the most developed. In 2003, the Commission first proposed rationalising and simplifying the existing processes (COM(2003) 261, *Strengthening the social dimension of the Lisbon strategy: Streamlining open coordination in the field of social protection*). From 2006, an overarching OMC on social protection and social inclusion exists, with three separate policy strands: the eradication of poverty and social exclusion; the provision of adequate and sustainable pensions; and ensuring accessible, high-quality and sustainable healthcare and long-term care (COM(2005) 706, *Working Together, Working Better: A new framework for the open coordination of Social Protection and Inclusion Policies in the European Union*). Common overarching objectives are supplemented by more specific objectives, all of which should be factored in to national policy plans. These plans are then monitored and evaluated at EU level, and examples of best practice exchanged. Rather than dismissing it as simply 'the European emperor's newest clothes' (2005: 227), Zeitlin submits that the OMC process in the social field has, to date, succeeded in raising the salience of certain issues at national level, and has contributed to broad shifts in national policy orientations, although he concedes there are methodological difficulties in demonstrating the policy impacts of the OMC.

The process of 'modernising' national systems, given the pressures they are under, and the additional financial strictures imposed by the requirements of economic and monetary union, may suggest that states would be under considerable pressure to reduce or scale back entitlements, or find alternatives to public provision. Arguably this could conflict with the commitments of the Community to promoting a 'high level of social protection' (Article 2 EC) and of the Member States and the Community to guaranteeing 'proper social protection' (Article 136 EC Treaty). It would be very bold of the European Court to read these commitments as anything other than political rhetoric, or give an expansive reading to the rights relating to social protection contained in the EU Charter (and the draft constitution), all of which are declared to operate 'in accordance with Union law and national law and practice'.

## 14.8  Health

Another key aspect of national welfare systems is health care services. These include emergency hospital care, as well as primary health care services, which cover non-emergency consultations with family practitioners, opticians and dentists. Secondary health care services cover those received following referrals to medical specialists, usually based in hospitals. In addition, there are home nursing and occupational health services. Among the Member States, differences exist in the range of services which are provided by the state, rather than, or in addition to, the market. Differences also exist in the extent to which the service is free, at the point of delivery, to the patient. The area of health care services is one which the Member States have tried to carefully delineate off from EU intervention (Hervey, 2002; Hervey and McHale, 2004a). Article 152(5) EC provides 'Community action in the field of public health shall fully respect the responsibilities of the Member States in the organization and delivery of health services and medical care'. This was repeated and developed in the provisions of the Constitutional Treaty, which further provides, at Article III-278(7) that 'the responsibilities of the Member States shall include the management of health services and medical care and the allocation of the resources assigned to them'. However, as a result of the Court's interpretation of the free movement provisions, Member States have seen their autonomy in the operation of their health services compromised, as case law opens up national systems to citizens moving from one country to another to receive medical treatment. In their review of the different areas in which EU law may impact on national health systems, Hervey and McHale submit that 'deregulation, through private litigation, has the potential to have the most destabilizing effects on national health law' (2004b: 243).

Traditionally, the health systems of the EU Member States have been organised around the principle of territoriality: that citizens are restricted to making use of the public health services located in their state of residence. Beyond this common principle, the EU health systems are by and large separated into two main models. The first, as seen in the UK, Ireland, Spain and Denmark, is based on a system of universal coverage of health service provision, which is free at the point of delivery, and funded through general taxation. The second is a social insurance system, under which insurance payments are made to sickness insurance funds which then fund treatment. Two main forms of social insurance systems exist. Under the first, the 'benefits in kind' system, the sickness insurance fund provides funding to contracted health providers directly, entitling the patient to receive medical services without charge made to themselves (as seen in Germany and the Netherlands for example). Under the second, as seen in France, Luxembourg and Belgium, the insurance fund provides reimbursement to the patient who has paid the service provider upfront for treatment.

Access to emergency health care services in another EU state is guaranteed for EU citizens as a result of Regulation 1408/71, on the coordination of social security schemes (OJ 1971 L149/2, as amended, now replaced by the 'modernised and simplified' Regulation 883/2004, OJ 2004 L166/1). Article 22(1)(a) of the existing Regulation (and Article 19 of the new Regulation) provides for access to care 'which becomes necessary on medical grounds during a stay in the territory of another Member State, taking into account the nature of the benefits and the expected length of the stay'. The European Health Insurance Card (the successor to the E111 certificate) provides confirmatory evidence of this right to treatment. Depending on the nature of the system in the destination state, treatment may be free to the patient, or may require payment, which will be reimbursed by the home state, to the level that residents of the destination state would be reimbursed.

This system of emergency medical treatment does not however cover the position of those who have travelled to another state in order to receive medical treatment. The social security Regulation provides that patients may travel to receive treatment 'appropriate' to their condition, on the condition that it has been authorised by the competent institution in the home state. Authorisation and – with it – payment for services by the home state institution must be granted where, first, the treatment requested is among the benefits provided for by the legislation of the home state, and, second, treatment in the home state is not available 'within the time normally necessary for obtaining the treatment . . . taking account of his current state of health and the probable course of the disease'.

In addition to these well-established provisions entitling patients to cross-border public health care, recent years have witnessed a significant development in the recognised legal basis for entitlement to cross-border treatment. Petitioned by a number of patients who had travelled to receive medical care either without having first requested the authorisation required under Regulation 1408/71 or who had applied for it but had it refused by the competent institution, the Court of Justice has recognised that Article 49 EC, the general provision on the free movement of services, may be a source of rights for those wishing to travel for medical purposes. Having already identified this provision as a source of rights for those travelling to receive *private* health care in Joined Cases 286/82 and 26/83 *Luisi and Carbone* ([1984] ECR 377), the Court has subsequently extended it to cover *public* health care (see 6.7). In so doing, and by opening up the possibilities for patient mobility under public health systems beyond those tightly drawn under the secondary legislation as adopted by the Member State government, the Court has aroused considerable concerns in some quarters. These concerns centre on the financial viability of the new 'open' systems, of resourcing implications and the potentially damaging unsettling of careful planning of health service provision. Rather than a carefully considered balanced legislative response, a patient-driven, Court-led response has been made, which may be seen as failing to fully accommodate the policy imperatives of this area. Nonetheless, patients' rights to access public health services in other Member States are certainly not absolute, and the Court has recognised that access may be prevented in the interests of the continuance of efficient health service planning.

The break-through case on patient mobility under national health systems came in the 1998 case of *Kohll* (Case C-158/96 *Kohll* v. *Union des Caisses de Maladie* [1998] ECR I-1931). Mr Kohll, a Luxembourg national, arranged for orthodontic treatment for his daughter, to take place in Germany. The prior authorisation requirement, which was necessary if the Luxembourg insurance fund was going to pay for the services, was successfully challenged as unreasonable restriction on the Article 49 EC Treaty freedom to provide (and receive) services. Case C-385/99 *Müller-Fauré* ([2003] ECR I-4509), concerning a Dutch woman receiving dental treatment in Germany, subsequently extended this principle to cover home states which operate a benefit in kind system, in addition to the reimbursement-type system operating in Luxembourg in the *Kohll* case. Reimbursement under Article 49 will be at home state rates, rather than those of the host state, which is the situation under the Regulation.

While prior authorisation is no longer required for non-hospital treatment, the Court has held that it may be necessary in the case of hospital treatment, to enable Member States to maintain a 'rationalised, stable, balanced and accessible supply of hospital and medical services' (Case 157/99 *Geraets-Smits and Peerbooms* [2001] ECR I-5473, at para. 81). Mrs Geraets-Smits' treatment outside the Netherlands for her Parkinson's disease at the expense of the Dutch health system was, according to the Netherlands authorities, only possible if the treatment was normal in the professional circles concerned, and medically necessary: that is, that timely and adequate treatment was not available in the Netherlands. The Court declared that in defining 'normal', consideration had to be given to international medical practice and opinion, and not simply national practices, as 'to allow only treatment habitually carried out on national territory and scientific views prevailing in national medical circles to determine what is or is not normal will not offer those guarantees and will make it likely that [national] providers of treatment will always be preferred in practice' (at para. 96). The Court also declared that prior authorisation could be refused on the grounds of a lack of medical necessity only if 'the same or equally effective treatment can be obtained without undue delay at an establishment having a contractual arrangement with the insured person's sickness insurance fund' (at para. 108). Subsequently, in Case C-372/04 *Watts* v. *Bedford Primary Health Case Trust and the Secretary of State for Health* ([2006] ECR I-4325), which established that the UK's National Health Service was also caught by Article 49, the Court ruled that the fact that treatment was available in the home state within the time specified under the system of national waiting lists did not mean that it was necessarily available 'without undue delay'. As Kaczorowska warns, the implications of the free movement cases may be particularly acute for the new Member States, where a greater instance of poor health and under-investment in health systems may result in a potential patient movement that 'may well be catastrophic' for the national security systems of new Member States (2006: 367).

This spill-over from the free movement field into a highly sensitive area of national policy has been described by Greer as 'uninvited europeanization' (2006). The extent to which Member States have formally and explicitly 'invited' the EU into the field of health service provision is extremely limited – providing for 'cooperative exchange' of best practices through the operation of the open method of coordination, in the process of modernising national health and long-term care systems. This was proposed in Commission Communication *Modernising social protection for the development of high-quality, accessible and sustainable health care and long-term care: support for the national strategies using the open method of coordination* (COM(2004) 304) and is still in its very earliest stages; now it will take place in the context of the streamlined, overarching social protection and social inclusion OMC.

Outside the area of health service provision, the Member States have recognised a number of competences for the Union. One of the most well-established fields is that of occupational health and safety, though as Greer shows (2006: 140–2), the operation of measures adopted with this objective may have significant impacts on the organisation and resourcing of national health systems. The extension of the Working Time Directive to junior doctors in 2000 (European Parliament and Council Directive 2000/34 (OJ 2000 L295/41), amending Council Directive 93/10 (OJ 1993 L307/18) and now consolidated by European Parliament and Council Directive 2003/88, (OJ 2003 L299/9), limited the number of hours junior doctors can be required to work and has potentially enormous implications on health service staffing, training and financing (see 16.10).

In addition to occupational health, the area of public health is also one that Member States have granted competence to the EU, recognising the added value of a transnational approach to public health promotion and protection. Article 152 EC provides that 'a high level of human health protection shall be ensured in the definition and implementation of all Community policies and activities'. While the Treaty of Maastricht introduced a competence for the EU to take supporting action in the public health field, giving rise to a number of action programmes (for example, on AIDS and other communicable diseases; European Parliament and Council Decision 647/96, OJ 1996 L 95/16), the introduction of harmonising legislation was explicitly excluded. This remains the situation, though Article 152(4) EC recognises legislation is permissible in regard to certain defined topics, including the safety and quality of organs and blood, and health protection measures in the veterinary and phytosanitary field. As the Court of Justice's ruling striking down the Tobacco Advertising Ban Directive shows (European Parliament and Council Directive 98/43, OJ 1993 L307/18), attempts to circumvent this restriction by the use of the internal market basis for the introduction of measures which have an overriding public health dimension will be unsuccessful (Case C-376/98 *Germany* v. *European Parliament and Council (Tobacco Advertising)* [2000] ECR I-8419). However, as was later ruled in the Tobacco Control Directive case, the fact that the protection of public health is a 'decisive factor in the choices to be made' is not enough to remove the measure from the lawful ambit of the internal market legal basis, so long as the measure was intended, and had the object of facilitating free movement (Case C-491/01 *R* v. *Secretary of State for Health, ex parte BAT and Imperial Tobacco* [2002] ECR I-11453; see also Case C-380/03 *Germany* v. *European Parliament and Council* [2006] ECR I-11573).

## 14.9  Consumer Protection

The field of Public Health is intimately connected with that of Consumer Protection, with the two sharing a Directorate-General (DG SANCO), and – until January 2007 – a Commissioner. Indeed, in 2005, the Commission proposed that the formally separate Action Plans adopted in each area should be brought together under one common *Programme for Health and Consumer Protection* (COM(2005) 115). The Programme, running from 2007 to 2013, is based around three common objectives: first, to 'protect citizens from risks and threats which are beyond the control of individuals and that cannot be effectively tackled by individual Member States'; second, to 'increase the ability of citizens to take better decisions about their health and consumer interests'; and third, to 'mainstream health and consumer policy objectives across all Community policies'.

In many respects, the evolution of the EU's role in consumer protection mirrors that of many other policy sectors in the social dimension. From a position of, at best, marginal significance and no policy mandate, the process of policy spill-over from market integration brought matters of consumer protection onto the legislative agenda. This has now led on to a position where there is, to some degree, the development of an autonomous policy field, with its own guiding principles, policy priorities and legal base for action. The role of the consumer in the EU may, as with the role of the individual and citizen more generally, be perceived as undergoing a process of evolution from a passive to an active subject: from a position of the consumer being the 'passive beneficiary', the unwitting recipient of a consumer policy writ large – that of the market integration process which was to bring in its wake consumer benefits (Weatherill, 1999: 693), to the consumer being a subject of law with enforceable protections, and rights to active participation in policy-making.

The beginnings of the EU's engagement with consumer protection began, as with so many of the flanking policies, with pronouncements at the 1972 Paris Summit, the Heads of State and Government calling upon the institutions of the Communities to strengthen and coordinate measures for consumer protection. This was followed by a 1975 Council Resolution on consumer protection and information policy (OJ 1975 C92/1), which outlined a preliminary programme in the field, and identified a set of concerns around which consumer policy was to be developed. These were: the protection of the health, safety and economic interests of consumers; the right of redress; the right to information and education; and the right to representation. These same concerns are now to be found set out in the dedicated Treaty provision on consumer protection, which was introduced under the Maastricht Treaty (current Article 153 EC). This provision recognises the legislative competence of the Community to act in respect of these issues, in the promotion of the interests of consumers and of ensuring a high level of consumer protection. Two bases for legislative action are recognised: first, Article 95 EC, in the context of the completion of the internal market; and second, Article 153 itself, which provides for the introduction, under co-decision, of 'measures which support, supplement and monitor the policy pursued by the Member States' (Article 153(3b)) and which, according to Article 153(5), may be supplemented by (notified) national legislation setting higher standards of consumer protection.

While the Treaty of Maastricht introduced the first specific legal basis for consumer protection, a body of legislation had already been developed through the Articles 94 and 95 EC general internal market legal bases. Measures had been adopted both in the field of the protection of consumer health and safety (for example, Council Directive 88/378 (OJ 1988 L187/1) concerning the safety of toys) and in the interests of the protection of consumers' economic interests (e.g. Council Directive 84/450 (OJ 1984 L250/17) concerning misleading advertising). In 1989, and coming after two further Council resolutions on the direction of consumer policy (OJ 1981 C133/1 and OJ 1986 C167/1), the Council issued a Resolution on future priorities for relaunching consumer protection policy (OJ 1989 C294/1), which identified the integration of consumer protection and promotion of consumer interests into the other common policies as key priority, and in response to which the Commission introduced the first of a series of three year action plans (COM(90) 98; COM(93) 378; COM(95) 519), and a continued legislative programme, which, despite the introduction of the more specific Article 153(3b) EC legal base, was developed primarily through Article 95 EC, a situation which still persists today.

The Action Plan submitted in 1999, for implementation over the period 1999–2001, was to be fundamentally superseded by events in the area of food safety. Precipitated by the mounting food scares of the 1980s and 1990s, the field of food safety branched off from 'general' consumer protection, to have its own legislative agenda and set of institutional actors. A new legal framework, developed on the back of the White Paper on Food Safety (COM(1999) 719), has been in evolution, central to which is the role of the independent advisory committee, the European Food Safety Authority (European Parliament and Council Regulation 178/2002, OJ 2002 L21/1).

Subsequent Action Plans and Programmes (Action Plan 2002–2006, COM(2002) 208, Council Resolution OJ 2003 C11/1, and the Action Programme 2007–2013, Decision of the European Parliament and Council 1926/2006, OJ 2006 L404/39) for the most part propose a revision and consolidation of existing measures, rather than the introduction of new legislative measures. Legislation is just one technique proposed under the current approach, and soft law techniques are increasingly championed. However as Howells and Wilhelmsson argue, such non-legislative trends discernible under the agenda present challenges from a consumer protection perspective. Co-regulation, for example, proceeds through framework directives where the detail is left to be agreed upon by industry and consumer organisations working together, though difficulties surround it, given 'industry domination and the problems of organising the consumer voice at the European level, even with some institutional support' (2003: 387). Self-regulation is at least as problematic, for 'it is one thing to advocate soft law in a context where business expects to follow such rules and consumers are conscious of their value and quite another if in some countries such rules will simply be ignored because of unfamiliarity or contempt for self-regulatory controls' (2003: 388).

## 14.10 Cultural Policy

Cultural policy is receiving an increasingly high profile within the EU order, with policy rhetoric emphasising the contribution cultural policy can play to promote EU citizenship and integration (Craufurd Smith, 2007). With a specific legal base for cultural policy measures (Article 151 EC Treaty) introduced by the Treaty of Maastricht, funded programmes such as Culture 2007 (Decision No. 1903/2006 of the European Parliament and of the Council of 12 December 2006 establishing the Culture Programme (2007–2013), OJ 2006 L378/22), and an increasingly coherent policy agenda, cultural policy has developed significantly from the early days of the Community. The only real inclusion of cultural matters in the original Treaty of Rome was the inclusion in Article 30 EC (former Article 36) of the protection of national treasures possessing artistic, historical or archaeological value as a ground for the maintenance of barriers to the free movement of goods, and Article 182 EC (former Article 131) on Community contributions to the cultural development of third countries.

In line with other developments in the social dimension, the 1970s witnessed some first steps by the institutions in the development of new policy fields. Calls for a wider cultural policy came, for example, in the 1974 Parliamentary resolution calling for Community action on culture (OJ 1974 C62/5). In 1977, the Commission produced a Communication on Community action in the Cultural Sector (EC Bull. Supp. 6/77) which, while recognising that the specific characteristics of workers and goods in the cultural sector may need to be taken into account, proposed that the standard rules on free movement should apply. This was confirmed by the Court of Justice in its 1968 judgment in Case 7/68 *Commission* v. *Italy (Italian Art)* ([1968] ECR 423), where it held that art treasures are defined as goods, and are thus included within the rules relating to financial barriers to free movement.

The idea of a wider cultural policy, however, was seen as beyond the competence of the Community. Nevertheless, some cooperation activities began to develop. The Stuttgart European Council, which met in 1983, declared that there was a need to promote 'closer co-operation on cultural matters in order to affirm the awareness of a common cultural heritage as part of a European identity'. The question of European identity was becoming an important political issue around this time: the second Adonnino report on a People's Europe produced proposals for the improvement of the image and identity of Europe among its citizens, in order to promote the European ideal (EC Bull. Supp. 7/85). This need to promote European identity was a new driving force behind activity in the cultural sphere. In 1984, the first formal meeting of Ministers of Cultural Affairs within the Council took place, and this prompted a number of developments in the form of resolutions, such as a European sculpture competition (OJ 1985 C153/3), creating special conditions of admission for young people to museums and cultural events (OJ 1985 C348/2), the protection of European cultural heritage (OJ 1986 C320/1), the promotion of the translation of European works (OJ 1987 C309/3) and the setting-up of the European City of Culture project (OJ 1985 C153/2), now renamed the European Capital of Culture (OJ 1999 L166/1) – the competition for this title is often heated, and it can provide a boost for the city chosen, as well as positive publicity for the EU's cultural goals.

For its part, the Court of Justice trod extremely reluctantly around the cultural sphere. As its case law on free movement of goods developed, the Court was asked to consider whether a non-discriminatory barrier to trade could be justified by a cultural objective: the protection of the French film industry (see Joined Cases 60 and 61/84 *Cinéthèque SA* v. *Fédération Nationale des Cinémas Français* [1985] ECR 2605). The Court refused to say that cultural protection, in general terms, could constitute a mandatory requirement under the *Cassis de Dijon* principles (see Chapter 5), presumably because cultural policy as a concept is very broad. It restricted itself instead to the unexplained assertion that the French legislation was justified by an appropriate objective, without stating what that objective was. Equally, in Case C-379/87 *Groener* v. *Minister for Education* ([1989] ECR 3967), the Court held that an Irish measure which discriminated indirectly against non-Irish citizens could be justified by means of a policy intended to protect the Irish language, but did not say anything which would imply that cultural policy more broadly could justify any such measure. The Court thus took a cautious approach to culture, refusing to refer to it in more general terms. This is perhaps to be understood, as cultural policy is a broad and nebulous concept, which could be used by Member States to justify a wide range of restrictive policies. A general declaration by the Court that the protection of national and regional cultures could justify discriminatory measures or barriers to trade could well have created far too wide an exception.

By the mid-1980s, some piecemeal legislation with connections to cultural policy had been introduced (such as Council Directive 77/486 on the education of children of migrant workers (OJ 1977 L199/32)) but, by and large, the institutions proceeded cautiously with cultural policy, introducing some limited measures of intergovernmental cooperation, while recognising the cultural dimension of the internal market. In 1987, however, the Commission produced a document entitled 'A Fresh Boost for Culture in the European Community' (EC Bull. Supp. 4/87, p.5). This document represented a move, following the Adonnino report, towards cultural policy understood as a political necessity for the development of European identity and the success of the European project. The essence of the document was that existing action should be continued, but that it should be coordinated by the Commission, in order to create a more visible, defined policy. Five fields of activity were set out:

- creation of a European cultural area;
- promotion of the European audiovisual industry;
- improvement of access to cultural resources;
- improvement of training in the cultural sector; and
- promotion of cultural dialogue with the rest of the world.

These fields were to be the locus of action, albeit limited, in the cultural sphere over the next five years. Resolutions were passed on matters such as the promotion of books and reading (OJ 1989 C183/1), the training of arts' administrators (OJ 1991 C188/1) and the development of European cultural networks (OJ 1991 C314/1). Hard legislative measures included the 1989 Television without Frontiers Directive (Council Directive 89/552, OJ 1989 L293/23) and, closely connected with the internal market project, Council Regulation 3911/92 on the export of cultural goods (OJ 1992 L395/1) and Council Directive 93/7 of 15 March 1993 on the return of cultural objects unlawfully removed from the territory of a Member State (OJ 1993 L74/74). However, as McMahon points out, the field did not expand significantly during this period. He suggests that this may have been due to the reticence of the Court of Justice, and the fact that other bodies such as the Council of Europe were also active in the cultural sector (McMahon, 1995: 158).

Cultural matters were, however, incorporated into the framework of the Treaties by the Treaty of Maastricht. Under Article 3 EC, the activities of the Community are to include contributions towards 'a flowering of the cultures of the Member States'. Second, under Article 151 EC (former 128) the Community has competence to 'contribute to the flowering of the cultures of the Member States, while respecting their national and regional diversity and at the same time bringing the common cultural heritage to the fore'. EU action is to be aimed at:

- improvement of the knowledge and dissemination of European history and culture;
- conservation and safeguarding of cultural heritage of European significance;
- non-commercial cultural exchanges;
- artistic and literary creation, including in the audiovisual sector.

The emphasis of Article 151 EC is on subsidiarity, cultural diversity and decentralisation. A mainstreaming clause has been introduced, with Article 151(4) requiring the Community to 'take cultural aspects into account in its action under other provisions of this Treaty, in particular in order to respect and promote the diversity of culture'. Further, Article 151(5) EC explicitly excludes the harmonisation of national policies. Nonetheless, action by the EU has been criticised as encouraging homogeneity by prioritising the common cultural heritage, and doing little for minority cultures (i.e. cultures which are not the 'national' culture of a Member State) (Barber, 2002).

Since 2000, the previously diverse patchwork of individual programmes in spheres such as cooperation in the arts, literary fields and field of heritage has been replaced by an umbrella project, first Culture 2000, now replaced by Culture 2007, which runs until 2013. The Culture programme offers support to cultural projects, institutions and studies which promote at least two of the following objectives: transnational mobility for people working in the cultural sector; transnational circulation of artistic and cultural works and projects; and intercultural dialogue. Depending on the nature and amount of funding sought, the minimum number of states involved range upwards from three. The link between cultural policy and a specifically European citizenship has been made explicit: the Commission saying of the Culture Programme that it will 'actively contribute to the bottom-up development of a European identity, by giving cultural operators and citizens more opportunities to create networks, to implement projects, to be more mobile and to enhance cultural dialogue' (COM(2004) 154).

In addition to the funding available under Culture 2007 (some 400 million euro), funding is also available through the structural funds, in recognition of the role that culture can play in regeneration of areas and job creation. With funding from structural funds generally needing to be matched by national funding, it is important that EU competition law provides scope for national actions, as well as for stand-alone state intervention. Thus, Article 92 (now Article 87) on state aids, allows as compatible with the common market the provision of state aids to promote culture and heritage conservation.

Culture and cultural discourse are thus becoming an increasingly important part of EU policy-making and identity-building. However, both within the Court of Justice and within constitutional development, a great deal of caution has been exercised in keeping culture outside tight legal frameworks. Culture is a vague term, and an explosive one. Cultural policy has been seen as a means by which European identity and the European project can be strengthened. Many of the fears of Eurosceptics are centred on the spectre of a homogenising EU destroying national and regional cultures. The Constitutional Treaty would have contributed to this view by a new emphasis on *Europe's* cultural heritage, and profound concerns were raised by the attempts to include a reference to Christianity in the Constitutional Treaty. While EU cultural policy does contain much that can be supportive of national and regional cultures, EU authorities have had to be somewhat cautious about its potential.

## 14.11 Conclusion

The EU's social dimension is often characterised as being 'underdeveloped' when compared with its economic project. Certainly, it has not developed a social dimension which is comparable to that of a nation state in terms of the functions it plays. While some may argue for the development of a supranational welfare state, complementing, if not replacing, national welfare states (Blackburn, 2005), these views are very much in the minority. Steps in this direction would certainly encounter opposition on the basis that the EU would be overreaching itself. Majone (1996b) and Scharpf (2002), for example, have both argued that, while an effective regulatory entity, the EU lacks the credentials to become a locus of welfare provision: there is insufficient social solidarity between the citizens of Europe, and a lack of the essential demos – and democracy – needed to underpin such a system.

While not state-like in its reach, a significant social dimension to integration has evolved. The EU has developed policy competences over a broad range of social matters, and has made a significant contribution to citizens' legal heritage, most clearly, but not exclusively, in the field of gender equality (see Chapter 15). The exercise of economic rights must also increasingly be shown to be consistent with a range of social concerns. Nonetheless, as the recent national ratification processes of the Constitutional Treaty demonstrate, there remains a high degree of public disenchantment with the status of the social dimension. A stronger social dimension is increasingly seen as essential to the success of the European Union. This is also the message from the EU institutions, with the vision of mutually reinforcing social, employment and economic policies which is currently being advanced. The greater focus on social rights as reflected in the EU's Charter of Fundamental Rights, and its subsequent attempted incorporation in the Constitutional Treaty, may contribute to an upgrading of the concerns of the social dimension. Somewhat paradoxically, however, and as the discussion of the areas of social protection, health and consumer protection shows, at the same time as this increase in rights-talk, soft law techniques and other alternatives to standard regulation are increasingly being turned to. These trends, and the tensions they generate, are replicated across the social dimension, as subsequent chapters demonstrate.

## Summary

1. According to the EU institutions' political rhetoric, social considerations have always been expressed as being as important as economic ones, however the EU's social dimension is generally regarded as not being as firmly entrenched as the economic project. The perceived weakness of the social dimension may have contributed to the rejection of the Constitutional Treaty.

2. Welfare provision is a key feature of national social policies, whereby the redistribution of resources takes place from one sector of society to another. The EU has extremely limited redistributive powers. Instead, its interventions in the social dimension are largely regulatory.

3. A social dimension to integration may be justified from a market perspective, as well as on the grounds of social justice, and as a means of generating a sense of solidarity among the peoples of the European Union.

4. A 'European Social Model' is perceived to exist, which is distinguishable by its emphasis on 'a high level of social provision, education, and social dialogue'.

## Summary cont'd

5. Within the social dimension, the EU's most well-established competences lie in the areas of workers' rights, non-discrimination and the environment. In some areas, legislative activity by the EU is explicitly excluded (e.g. the modernisation of social protection systems and the harmonisation of public health matters).

6. Alternatives to the standard Community method of law-making are key features of the EU's social dimension. These include the social dialogue and the open method of coordination. The current Social Policy Agenda foresees little in the way of the introduction of new legislation.

7. The national social policy choices of the Member States are increasingly constrained through EU membership. The financial parameters that states participating in the euro must work within may have some impact, as may the implications of the operation of the principle of non-discrimination on the grounds of nationality in relation to access to various aspects of their social systems.

8. The Commission and the Court of Justice have played crucial roles in the evolution of the social dimension, often in the face of recalcitrance on the part of some Member States.

9. The status of the social dimension may be enhanced following the adoption of the EU Charter of Fundamental Rights, which includes many social rights, despite the fact that it remains without direct legal effects.

10. While the organisation and financing of social protection and health systems remain the responsibility of the Member States, EU law impacts on their operation in a variety of ways.

11. The evolution of the EU's role in respect of consumer protection is emblematic of policy development in many areas in the social dimension. From a position of no explicit policy mandate, the policy field came onto the EU's agenda through spill-overs from the market project, and has now resulted in the emergence of an autonomous policy field.

12. Amendments to the EC Treaty introduced by the EU Treaty empower the EU to contribute to the flowering of cultures in the Member States and to bring the common cultural heritage to the fore. Recent policy developments have connected explicitly European culture with European citizenship.

# Exercises

1. Why does the EU have a social dimension?

2. Is the EU's social dimension underdeveloped in comparison to its economic dimension? What is the evidence for your view?

3. How significant has the role of the Court of Justice been in the development of the social dimension?

4. What contribution may the EU Charter of Fundamental Rights make to the status of the social dimension?

5. Does the EU provide individual welfare benefits? Should it?

6. Under what circumstances will an EU citizen have the right to access public health services in another Member State, with the cost met by their home state system? Is the Court's jurisprudence on this matter appropriate?

## Further Reading

Barnard, C. (2000) 'Social Dumping and the Race to the Bottom: Some Lessons for the European Union from Delaware?', 25 *European Law Review* 57.

de Burca, G. (ed.) (2005) *EU Law and the Welfare State: In Search of Solidarity*, Oxford: Oxford University Press.

Craufurd Smith, R. (2007) 'From Heritage Conservation to European Identity: Article 151 EC and the Multi-faceted Nature of Community Cultural Policy', 32 *European Law Review* 48.

Daly, M. (2006) 'EU Social Policy After Lisbon', 44 *Journal of Common Market Studies* 461.

Dougan, M. and Spaventa, E. (eds.) (2005) *Social Welfare and EU Law*, Oxford: Hart Publishing.

Hervey, T. and Kenner, J. (eds.) (2003) *Economic and Social Rights under the EU Charter of Fundamental Rights: A Legal Perspective,* Oxford: Hart Publishing.

Hervey, T. and McHale, J. (2004a) *Health Law and the European Union*, Cambridge: Cambridge University Press.

Hervey, T. and McHale, J. (2004b) 'Law, Health and the European Union', 25 *Legal Studies* 228.

Howells, G. and Wilhelmsson, T. (2003) 'EC Consumer Law: Has it Come of Age?', 28 *European Law Review* 370.

Joerges, C. (2005) 'What is left of the European Economic Constitution? A Melancholic Eulogy', 30 *European Law Review* 461.

Scharpf, F. (2002) 'The European Social Model: Coping with the Challenges of Diversity', 40 *Journal of Common Market Studies* 645.

Shaw, J. (ed.) (2000) *Social Law and Policy in an Evolving European Union*, Oxford: Hart Publishing.

Vos, K. (2005) 'Americanisation of the EU social model?', 21 *International Journal of Comparative Labour Law and Industrial Relations* 355.

Weatherill, S. (2005) *EU Consumer Law and Policy*, Cheltenham: Elgar European Law.

## Key Websites

The website of the EU Commission's Directorate-General for employment, social affairs and equal opportunities is at:
**http://ec.europa.eu/employment_social/index_en.html**

The social protection and inclusion process is detailed at:
**http://ec.europa.eu/employment_social/social_inclusion/index_en.htm**

The Commission's site on health is at:
**http:/ec.europa.eu/health-eu/index_en.htm**

Information from the Commission on consumer policy is at:
**http://ec.europa.eu/consumers/index_en.htm**

The Commission's Europe and Culture website is at:
**http://ec.europa.eu/culture/eac/index_en.html**

The website of the European Foundation for the Improvement of Living and Working Conditions is at:
**http://eurofound.europa.eu/**

The website of the Social Platform of European NGOs, which seeks to lobby the Commission and the other EU institutions on social policy matters, can be found at:
**http://www.socialplatform.org/**

# Chapter 15

# Equality Law and Policy

## 15.1 Introduction: What is Equality?

EC law on equality between men and women is complex and well developed, and, more recently, the scope of equality law has expanded to cover other types of inequality. Before going into details of the specific legislation and policy, it is useful to begin with a few remarks about the nature of equality law generally, and what it is intended to achieve. Many people would say that the meaning of equality is straightforward. It means treating people the same and not discriminating, or making differences between them. This approach, however, can create problems, if we try to apply it to some concrete examples, taken from the sphere of equality between men and women. What does it mean to treat men and women equally in the casting of a play? Should a man and a woman be treated the same when they are auditioning for the part of Lady Macbeth? Most people would say clearly not. What does it mean to treat a man and a woman equally when the woman is pregnant? Should the woman be given special treatment because of her pregnancy? Many people would say 'yes', within reason. What does it mean to treat a man and a woman who are applying for a job in a male-dominated profession, such as engineering, equally? Should the woman be given preference in the application procedure or when it comes to promotion? This is an issue on which opinion is more likely to be divided.

Treating everyone the same, then, is too simplistic a solution. To take the second example, treating a pregnant woman the same as a man might mean asking the woman to do things that would be physically dangerous for her or her unborn child. Aristotle proposed a different solution. He argued that equality means treating people the same when they are the same, and treating different people differently in proportion to their 'difference'. This approach allows us to decide the situations in which people should be treated the same, and when, and how, they should be treated differently. However, it is not unproblematic. At the most extreme end of the debate, it has been argued that equality, understood in this way, is meaningless. In order to apply the principle of equality, it is necessary to rely on external standards in order to decide when people are to be treated the same and when, and how, they should be treated differently. According to this argument, the principle of equality is of no help at all in deciding how people should be treated and is just empty rhetoric. Feminists argued that the Aristotelian approach leads to the setting-up of a man as 'default', and then judging women's rights and needs in terms of whether they are the same as or different from a man. An approach based on equal respect, rather than sameness/difference equality, might achieve a more equitable result.

The achievement of equality, then, is about more than treating people the same. A number of legal strategies can be used to achieve equality. A non-discrimination strategy involves legislation prohibiting any discrimination between categories of people. Here, the definition of discrimination can become complex, as the discussion of the concepts of direct and indirect discrimination in 15.7 and 15.8 below suggests. A positive action strategy is one which aims at ensuring substantive equality by, in some contexts, permitting positive discrimination in favour of members of disadvantaged groups. More recently, some discussion has focused on diversity strategies (Barmes with Ashtiany, 2003), which involve proactive policies intended to enhance inclusiveness of different social groups within the labour force or in other contexts such as education. In the context of the EU, most legislation concerned with equality issues has deployed an anti-discrimination strategy, combined with creating some space for other strategies such as positive action. Indeed, as will be seen throughout this chapter, the weaknesses of the anti-discrimination principle in achieving equality mean that other strategies have also been used, or at least permitted.

A further question is that of the particular inequalities which are to be challenged, and therefore the grounds of discrimination which are to be prohibited. In fact, equality policies do not aim at the overall equality between all human beings, but rather at eliminating specific inequalities affecting particular (historically or otherwise) disadvantaged groups. Thus, equality policies address equality between men and women, equality between people of different ethnic origins or different religions, equality between people with disabilities and able-bodied people, equality between people of different sexual orientations, equality between people of different ages, etc. It is generally recognised that different strategies or combinations of strategies are required to address different inequalities. In addition, however, a coherent equality policy needs an overall strategy to address the question of whether or not some inequalities are to be considered more problematic than others and what is to be done about clashes between equality rights. Such a policy must also address the issue of multiple inequalities; the experience of a black woman, for example, is different both from that of a black man and of a white woman. As will become apparent from this chapter, it is a significant flaw of EU equality policy that such an overall, coherent strategy does not really exist (Costello, 2003). There is unevenness in the way in which different inequalities are addressed and the issues of rights' clashes or multiple inequalities are not addressed. To some extent, this can be seen to be a consequence of the dominance of gender equality policy, which drives the agenda to the detriment of other inequality issues.

## 15.2 The Development of EU Equality Policy

The primary focus of EU equality policy has been equality between men and women. Despite a more recent expansion in the competences conferred under the EC Treaty, gender equality measures continue to dominate. In part, this is because the legal measures have, as the first part of this chapter will demonstrate, become so well developed as almost to take on a life of their own. The maintenance of a legal structure which divides gender equality from other non-discrimination issues has been the focus of effective lobbying at the EU level, notably by the European Women's Lobby. For example, a case was made for the Constitutional Treaty to retain the division to be found in the EC Treaty between provisions focusing specifically on gender equality issues (e.g. Article I-2 (Union's values), Article I-3 (Union's objectives), Article III-116 (elimination of inequality between men and women), Article III-214 (equal pay and equal treatment for men and women)) and provisions which focus on equality and non-discrimination issues more generally (e.g. Article III-118 (elimination of discrimination based on sex, racial or ethnic origin, religion or belief, disability, age or sexual orientation) and Article III-124 (competence to enact measures to combat discrimination based on sex, racial or ethnic origin, religion or belief, disability, age or sexual orientation)). Furthermore, equality between men and women continues to be dealt with by a separate unit with DG Employment and Social Affairs in the Commission. It is also important to recognise the continued economic drive behind the development of this policy area. The original impetus behind the inclusion of very limited non-discrimination provisions in the Treaty of Rome was economic. In the 1950s, France was the only European country to have any kind of equal pay legislation for men and women. The French government feared that this would place their businesses at a competitive disadvantage in a common market, and so pushed for a similar provision to be included within the Treaty (Article 119 EEC; now Article 141 EC). In more recent years, the continued emphasis on the significance of women in the labour market and the negative impact which discrimination against women has on economic productivity make a priority for gender equality easier to argue for within the context of the so-called 'Lisbon' agenda to make the European Union 'the most competitive and dynamic knowledge-based economy in the world capable of sustainable economic growth with more and better jobs and greater social cohesion'.

This has tended to mean that, while EU rhetoric now emphasises the importance of a general principle of equality, in practice there is a hierarchy of equalities, with gender equality being seen as the most significant. Indeed, in the preamble to the general Framework Equality Directive (Council Directive 2000/78, OJ 2000 L303/16; 'FED'), one of the explanations given for expanding the prohibited grounds of discrimination is that women often suffer multiple discrimination. This implies that gender equality remains the first priority and the reasoning behind expanding the grounds is that women are often disadvantaged by further types of discrimination.

Article 141 EC requires men and women to be paid the same for doing the same work. For the first twenty years of the existence of the European Community, it was a neglected provision. However, an important step was taken in Case 43/75 *Defrenne* v. *SABENA (No. 2)* ([1976] ECR 455). Two significant points were made by the Court in its judgment here. Firstly, it declared that equal treatment of men and women is a fundamental principle of EC law. Article 141 should not be treated simply as an aspect of the single market. It has a separate social policy goal. This statement by the Court of Justice reflected the 1972 Paris Summit declaration and the general move towards bringing social policy objectives to the forefront of the European Community's concerns. It was also strengthened by the passing in 1975 of the Equal Pay Directive (Council Directive 75/117, OJ 1975 L45/19; 'EPD'), which clarified some points relating to the application of Article 141, and in 1976 of the Equal Treatment Directive (Council Directive 76/207, OJ 1976 L39/40; 'ETD'), which expanded the equality principle to employment conditions other than pay.

Secondly, in *Defrenne* the Court held that Article 141 has direct effect and can thus be relied upon by individuals in national courts. This important step must be understood in the context of the issue of equality between men and women becoming, in many Member States in the 1970s, an important political and social issue. Campaigners for the feminist cause saw developing Community competence as an invaluable tool in the struggle for equal rights. This led, in some Member States such as the UK and Germany, to a concerted and well-organised litigation strategy. In the UK this was spearheaded by the newly formed Equal Opportunities Commission. A large number of practically significant cases were referred to the Court of Justice by the national courts before which these cases came (Alter and Vargas, 2000; Kilpatrick, 2001).

All of these developments mean that, in a relatively short space of time, the law governing equal treatment between men and women became the most well-developed element of EU social policy. The legislation adopted in the 1970s has been supplemented and updated, in ways which will be discussed throughout the chapter, to cover access to and supply of goods and services (Council Directive 2004/113 of 13 December 2004, OJ 2004 L373/37) and to consolidate and recast most (but not all) of the legislative texts in a single legislative measure (European Parliament and Council Directive 2006/54, OJ 2006 L204/23; 'recast directive'). This latter measure built upon an earlier measure bringing EU equal treatment legislation substantially into line with Court of Justice case law (European Parliament and Council Directive 2002/73, OJ 2002 L269/15; Equal Treatment Amendment Directive or 'ETAD'). Although the recast directive now means that most EU gender equality legislation is to be found in a single text, it remains important to bear in mind the terms of the original measures, not least because they remain in force until 2009. Furthermore, because of the specificities of the regime of judicial protection in relation to EU rights, it is of considerable significance whether a particular equality right stems from the treaty itself (equal pay: Article 141), or whether it is based on a legislative measure such as a directive. In addition, in 2007 the EU established the European Institute for Gender Equality (European Parliament and Council Regulation 1922/2006, OJ 2006 L403/9) in order to support legislative and policy efforts, at the EU and the national levels, aimed at achieving gender equality.

In the context of a broadening EU social policy, gender equality law has maintained its place as a central pillar. Indeed, the Court of Justice regularly reaffirms that the principle of equality between men and women forms one of the foundations of the EU (e.g. Case C-381/99 *Brunnhofer* v. *Bank der Österreichischen Postsparkasse* [2001] ECR I-4961 at para. 28). Moreover, this judgment was also grounded in a general principle of equality 'which prohibits comparable situations from being treated differently unless the difference is objectively justified'. In furtherance of this principle, in recent case law the Court has adopted a broader approach. Referring to Article 13 EC, which was introduced by the Treaty of Amsterdam as a legal basis for the adoption of measures to combat discrimination based on sex, racial or ethnic origin, religion or belief, disability, age or sexual orientation, and which has been used both for the FED as well as a specific directive dealing with discrimination on grounds of race (Council Directive 2000/43, OJ 2000 L180/22; Race Equality Directive or 'RED'), the Court has held that it is not these directives which lay down the principle of equal treatment in the field of employment and occupation. In relation to the FED, it held in Case 144/04 *Mangold* v. *Helm* ([2005] ECR I-9981) that:

> '. . . in accordance with Article 1 [of the directive], the sole purpose of the directive is "to lay down a general framework for combating discrimination on the grounds of religion or belief, disability, age or sexual orientation", the source of the actual principle underlying the prohibition of those forms of discrimination being found, as is clear form the third and fourth recitals to the preamble to the directive, in various international instruments and in the constitutional traditions common to the Member States.'

The nature and extent of such a principle, and its likely effects in EU law now that it has been recognised by the Court of Justice, remain uncertain.

Finally, it needs to be recalled that under Article 2 EC, as amended by the Treaty of Amsterdam, equal treatment of men and women has been 'constitutionalised' as a general objective of the Union. Article 3(2) EC introduced at the same time the principle that 'in all the activities referred to in this Article [i.e. the list of the activities of the Community], the Community shall aim to eliminate inequalities, and to promote equality, between men and women'. This can be said to bring a principle of 'gender mainstreaming' into the EU framework. Accordingly, the Framework Strategy on Gender Equality (2001–2005) (COM(2000) 335 final) proposed a dual track approach to the achievement of gender equality within the EU – gender mainstreaming, and specific actions in favour of women; this approach was explicitly maintained in the 2006–2010 Roadmap for equality between men and women (COM(2006) 92). In terms of scope, the Roadmap identifies six areas for priority action:

- equal economic independence for women and men;
- reconciliation of private and professional life;
- equal representation in decision-making;
- eradication of all forms of gender-based violence;
- elimination of gender stereotypes;
- promotion of gender equality in external and development policies.

Gender mainstreaming is defined as 'the (re)organisation, improvement, development and evaluation of policy processes, so that a gender equality perspective is incorporated in all policies at all levels at all stages, by the actors normally involved in policy-making' (Council of Europe, 1998: 15). It was adopted as an approach by the Commission in 1996 (see COM(96) 67). Pollack and Hafner-Burton have argued that gender mainstreaming has been a successful and efficient strategy of incorporating gender issues into a much wider framework than the employment sphere. They went as far as to argue that the EU is 'gradually emerging as one of the most progressive polities on earth in its promotion of equal opportunities for women and men' (Pollack and Hafner-Burton, 2000: 452). Not all evaluations have been so positive. Stratigaki (2005) has suggested that gender mainstreaming has mainly been used as an alibi to justify neutralising positive action measures in favour of women.

## 15.3 Equal Pay: Article 141

In 1957, when the Treaty of Rome was signed, unequal pay between men and women was, in many Member States, the rule, rather than the exception. France was the only state which forbade explicit differentiation between men and women in salary scales. Inequalities were justified by the assumption that men had a family to support, whereas women worked only for pocket money. Fifty years later, although the principle of equal pay is ingrained into national legal structures throughout Europe, disparities still exist. According to the Roadmap on gender equality in 2006, women still earn 15 per cent less than men, and this gap is only very slowly being closed. The reason for this is not explicitly unequal pay scales, but differences in the kinds of work that men and women do, and the relative economic value which is placed on that work. Legislation and case law on equal pay have had to adapt and develop in order to try to address these facts.

According to Article 141, pay is the:

'ordinary basic or minimum wage or salary or any other consideration, whether in cash or in kind, which the worker receives, directly or indirectly, in respect of his employment from his employer.'

The Court of Justice has interpreted the legislative provisions very widely. Limits have been placed on it, however, at the intersection with social security, which is covered by different legislation. It was the distinction between pay and social security which led to the first *Defrenne* case (Case 80/70 *Defrenne* v. *Belgian State* [1971] ECR 445). The payment under discussion was a retirement pension, financed by the employer, the employee and the state, and linked directly to the salary. According to the Court of Justice, a payment only counts as 'pay' if it is a result of an agreement between the worker and the employer, or the worker and a particular occupational organisation. Schemes that are set up by means of legislation are not covered by Article 141, because they are not part of the employment relationship, and are dealt with under separate provisions.

If a payment results from the employment relationship, it is covered by Article 141. The following are covered:

▷ non-financial benefits in kind for family, attached to employment (Case 12/81 *Garland* v. *British Rail Engineering Ltd* [1982] ECR 359);
▷ statutory sick pay (Case 171/88 *Rinner-Kühn* [1989] ECR 2743 – demonstrating once more the fine line between social security and pay);
▷ maternity pay (Case C-342/93 *Gillespie* v. *Northern Health and Social Services Board* [1996] ECR I-475 – although, as will be seen later, it is subject to different rules);
▷ compensation for unfair dismissal (Case C-167/97 *R* v. *Secretary of State for Employment, ex parte Seymour-Smith* [1999] ECR I-623 – it must, however, be distinguished from the separate remedy of reinstatement rights, which have been covered by the Equal Treatment Directive);
▷ seasonal bonuses (Case C-333/97 *Lewen* v. *Lothar Denda* [1999] ECR I-7243).

It is in the area of pensions that the distinction between pay and social security has had most effect. In *Defrenne* v. *Belgian State*, statutory pension schemes were held not to be covered by Article 141 because they were not part of the employment relationship. They were, instead, covered by Council Directive 79/7 (OJ 1979 L6/24) on the progressive implementation of the principle of equal treatment for men and women in matters of social security, which covered state pension schemes. However, in Case 170/84 *Bilka Kaufhaus* v. *Weber von Hartz* ([1986] ECR 1607), it was held that supplementary pension schemes (i.e. additional to the basic state pension) were covered because they formed part of the employment relationship. This decision appeared to conflict with the existence of Council Directive 86/378 (OJ 1986 L225/40) on the application of the principle of equal treatment for men and women in occupational social security schemes which removed these schemes from the ambit of Article 141 and set out a separate legal regime. Indeed, the existence of separate regimes for statutory and occupational pension schemes was the consequence of a conscious decision taken by the Council and necessitated by the difficulty of reaching political agreement. The sensitive nature of national social security systems meant that Member States were unwilling to be committed to a wholesale reorganisation of those systems, and instead agreed to legislation requiring a progression towards equality and allowing for significant exemptions (see Hervey, 1998: 87–8). This conflict between the Court and the legislative institutions was brought to a head in one of the most controversial and far-reaching decisions of the Court of Justice: Case C-262/88 *Barber* v. *Guardian Royal Exchange* ([1990] ECR I-1889).

The decision in *Barber* was about occupational pension schemes which are contracted out by the employer, and which replace the statutory scheme. It was held that such schemes constitute pay, because they are agreed and entirely financed by the employer, they are not compulsorily applied to certain categories of employers, and they can go further than the statutory requirements and cover supplementary schemes as well. The impact of this judgment was huge. Under Directive 86/378, pension schemes are exempt from the principle of equal pay. However, if they fall to be considered solely under Article 141, they must comply with the principle of equal pay. *Barber* meant that a radical and fundamental change in the organisation of pension schemes was required. All occupational pension schemes needed to be overhauled to check their compatibility with Article 141. Even worse, the spectre of massive compensation claims stretching back decades loomed large, although the Court of Justice had already sought to limit the temporal effects of its judgment by holding that benefits payable under occupational social security schemes are not to be considered as remuneration insofar as they are attributable to periods of employment prior to the date of the judgment (17 May 1990). Furthermore, the Member States added the so-called 'Barber Protocol' to the EC Treaty by the Treaty of Maastricht, in order to reinforce the temporal limitation. In addition, Council Directive 96/97 (OJ 1997 L46/20) amended Directive 86/378 to bring it in line with the *Barber* decision and with subsequent decisions (e.g. Case C-132/92 *Birds Eye Walls Ltd* v. *Roberts* [1993] ECR I-5579; Case C-109/91 *Ten Oever* v. *Stichting Bedrijfpensioenfonds voor het Glazenwassers- en Schoonmaakbedrijf* [1993] ECR I-4879). This is reflected in Article 5 of the recast directive.

## 15.4  Equal Pay for Work of Equal Value

The 1975 EPD was primarily intended to clarify certain points about Article 141. Its main significance was that it made explicit the fact that equal pay is also required for work of equal value, as well as for the same work. This is important. It is not enough to say that people doing the same job must be paid the same. A major cause of the gender pay gap is the existence of perceived 'men's jobs' and 'women's jobs'. If equal pay is only available for the same work, employers can avoid equal pay claims by only employing one sex for one type of work, or by paying less for work that is perceived as 'women's work'. Equal value claims can go some way, although not all the way, to alleviating this problem. Equal value is now enshrined in the amended version of Article 141(1) EC, and in Article 4 of the recast directive.

The difficulty remains of how to work out whether work is of equal value. This question has generally been left to the national courts by the Court of Justice. However, in Case C-400/93 *Royal Copenhagen* ([1995] ECR I-1275), the Court has given some indications as to the way in which the national court should be approaching the decision. The court should ascertain whether, taking into account a number of factors such as the nature of the work, the training requirements and working conditions, the employees can be considered to be in a comparable situation. In *Brunnhofer*, the Court emphasised that the simple fact that two employees were on the same job scale does not mean that they are doing equal work or work of equal value. What must be examined is the actual work carried out by the employees. Finally, for work of equal value to be shown, there must be a single source which is responsible for the unequal pay and which could restore the equal treatment. It is not necessarily the case that the complainant must be working for the same employer as the comparator, but there must be one body which is responsible for the unequal treatment and which could rectify the situation (Case C-320/00 *Lawrence* v. *Regent Office Care* [2002] ECR I-7325; see also Case C-256/01 *Allonby* v. *Accrington and Rossendale College* [2004] ECR I-873). The controversial and, some would argue, highly damaging (Barnard,

2006: 354) 'single source' requirement was not included in the final version of the recast directive, having been included in the draft, as the Commission accepted the argument that the Court was likely to continue to refine its case law on this matter. The alignment of the equal pay and equal treatment provisions through the recast directive may, however, make it easier to argue for hypothetical comparators to be used in certain equal pay cases, as a single definition of direct discrimination is given in Article 2(1)(a). Direct discrimination arises 'where one person is treated less favourably on grounds of sex than another is, has been or would be treated in a comparable situation'.

## 15.5 Equal Pay and Collective Agreements

Collective bargaining agreements raise a particular problem when dealing with pay. Collective bargaining is a kind of industrial democracy, where pay scales are not imposed by employers or by legislation, but are negotiated between the employer(s) and employees' representatives. Collective bargaining agreements apply either within individual organisations or, often, throughout particular sectors, particularly in the public service. In many Member States collective bargaining plays a key role in industrial relations but sometimes, as is the case within the UK, collective agreements are not held to be legally binding and are therefore not controlled by employment legislation.

Nevertheless, under the equal pay legislation and according to the Court of Justice, collective agreements must comply with the principle of equal pay. In Case 165/82 *Commission* v. *United Kingdom (No. 2)* ([1983] ECR 3431) it was made clear that EC law applies to collective agreements, and that they must not discriminate unlawfully (see also Case C-33/89 *Kowalska* v. *Freie- und Hansestadt Hamburg* [1990] ECR I-2591). As the Advocate General noted in Case C-127/92 *Enderby* v. *Frenchay Health Authority* ([1993] ECR I-5535), the collective bargaining process is by no means immune from discrimination on grounds of sex, and there is therefore no justification for using collective agreements as a way of avoiding anti-discrimination law.

## 15.6 Proving Unequal Pay

One major practical difficulty for litigants of equal pay claims is the difficulty of proving their case. Pay scales often lack transparency, and it can be hard to see whether, if there is a difference in pay between a man and a woman, this difference is due to unlawful discrimination or to other factors. This problem was first recognised by the Court of Justice in Case 109/88 *Danfoss* ([1989] ECR 3199). There, it was held that, if there is *prima facie* evidence that one sex is being paid less than another for work of equal value, and if the pay scale lacks transparency, the burden of proof shifts to the employer to demonstrate that the pay differential is in fact due to reasons other than gender. Effectively, this forces an employer to render the pay scale transparent.

Notwithstanding this decision, the Court and the Commission continued to be concerned about the continuing existence of non-transparent pay scales, and the difficulties which this causes. As a consequence, Council Directive 97/80 (OJ 1998 L205/66) on the burden of proof in cases of discrimination based on sex was passed. This directive consolidated the case law on proof, confirming that a worker should not be denied a remedy because lack of transparency means that they cannot prove that they have been unlawfully discriminated against. Under Article 4 of the directive, in cases where the establishment of the facts is down to the plaintiff, rather than to the court, all the plaintiff has to do is establish facts from which it may be presumed that there is unlawful discrimination. Once that is done, it is for the respondent employers to prove that there has been no unlawful discrimination in fact. This has been superseded by Article 19 of the recast directive.

Article 21(4) of the recast directive encourages employers to make available to employees and/or their representatives, at appropriate regular intervals:

> 'appropriate information on equal treatment for men and women in the undertaking. Such information may include an overview of the proportions of men and women at different levels in the organisation; their pay and pay differentials; and possible measures to improve the situation in cooperation with employees' representatives.'

Although only an advisory provision, this represents an important step towards encouraging transparency in remuneration for all employees, which may operate for the benefit of women.

## 15.7  Direct Discrimination

The preceding discussion has dealt with pay and pay structures, and considered what it means to say that there is discrimination in pay and how to prove it. The second important question, however, is to deal with the question of whether that discrimination is unlawful. A distinction has been developed between direct discrimination and indirect discrimination. In EU law, that distinction was originally developed in the law relating to equal pay, but it applies in all matters of discrimination on grounds of gender.

The legislation makes it clear that anti-discrimination law applies equally whether a man or a woman is being discriminated against. For ease of language, this chapter refers to the person being discriminated against in the feminine – this being by far the most common situation. However, it should be borne in mind that cases can be brought by men as well. Indeed, discrimination against men, for example in cases of maternity pay and benefits, can be caused by the same assumptions which lead to the unequal treatment of women.

Direct discrimination is relatively easy to understand. It exists where a woman is treated less favourably than a man because of the difference in sex, as Article 2(1)(a) of the recast directive makes clear. Direct discrimination is always unlawful in matters of equal pay. The sex-based nature of the discrimination need not be made explicit by the employer, or even be intended by the employer. It is not limited to situations like pay scales, which existed in the UK prior to the 1970 Equal Pay Act, which have separate rates of pay for women, or to employers who act according to conscious prejudices. There must, however, be a relationship of causation between the sex of the applicant and her lower rate of pay.

The way in which this is shown in practice is by introducing a comparator. This is a worker of the opposite sex, who is in no material way, other than sex, different from the applicant, but who is paid more. One of the major issues in direct discrimination is the identification of an appropriate comparator. Usually, it would be someone doing the same work or work of equal value. In Case 129/79 *McCarthys Ltd* v. *Smith* ([1980] ECR 1275), the Court of Justice held that it was also possible to compare the applicant with her predecessor in the post. This avoids the risk of an employer sacking a man and taking on a woman purely in order to reduce the wages bill. As noted in 15.4, the recast directive allows for hypothetical comparators, because of the use of the term 'would be' in Article 2(1)(a).

## 15.8 Indirect Discrimination

Indirect discrimination is rather more complicated. Women are often discriminated against, not simply because they are women, but rather because of other characteristics more often possessed by women than by men. These characteristics may be physical – strength or height, or socially constructed – women are more likely to be single parents, or to have other caring responsibilities. This form of discrimination is termed indirect discrimination. More specifically, according to the leading cases (Case 96/80 *Jenkins* v. *Kingsgate (Clothing Productions) Ltd* [1981] ECR 911; Case 170/84 *Bilka Kaufhaus* v. *Weber von Hartz* [1986] ECR 1607), there is indirect discrimination if there is less favourable treatment on grounds that are apparently objective, but which apply to a significantly larger proportion of one sex than another. In practice, the majority of cases brought before the Court of Justice have been concerned with part-time workers, the vast majority of whom are women in every Member State, and who have typically suffered substantial pay discrimination. EU law has led to significant improvements in the situation of part-time workers, but initially this was through judicial developments in the interpretation of Article 141, which did not specifically deal with the issue of indirect discrimination. Cases have dealt with overtime pay, age bars, requirements that employees be able to work anywhere in the country, shift work and the length of time an employee has been with the company, among other matters, cutting across both equal pay and equal treatment more generally. More recently, Council adopted legislation specifically addressing discrimination against part-time workers (Council Directive 97/81, OJ 1998 L131/10). Using the length of service with an employer as a criterion for giving rewards to employees has also been a particular issue for female employees. In Case C-17/05 *Cadman* v. *Health and Safety Executive* ([2006] ECR I-9583), the Court of Justice held that in normal circumstances an employer does not have to provide special justification for having recourse to the criterion of length of service as the basis for reward, for in general 'length of service goes hand in hand with experience, and experience generally enables the worker to perform his duties better' (para. 35). However, it went on to suggest that there may be situations:

'in which recourse to the criterion of length of service must be justified by the employer in detail. That is so, in particular, where the worker provides evidence capable of giving rise to serious doubts as to whether recourse to the criterion of length of service is, in the circumstances, appropriate to attain [the legitimate objective of pay policy of rewarding workers for undertaking their work to a higher standard]' (paras. 37 and 38).

While indirect discrimination was originally a judicial development, it has subsequently been defined by legislation. A number of different definitions have been deployed in the gender equality field and in relation to the other equality grounds, but the recast directive confirms that there is now a single definition of indirect discrimination which applies to equal pay and equal treatment issues, and in respect of all the protected equality grounds. Article 2(1)(b) states that indirect discrimination is:

'where an apparently neutral provision, criterion or practice would put persons of one sex at a particular disadvantage compared with persons of the other sex, unless that provision, criterion or practice is objectively justified by a legitimate aim, and the means of achieving that aim are appropriate and necessary.'

This confirms that an earlier definition in the Burden of Proof Directive, which referred to criteria or practices which disadvantaged a 'substantially higher proportion' of the members of one sex, is now displaced. Already the ETAD had used the formula of 'particular disadvantage' which is now used in the recast directive, but the importance of the latter instrument is that it confirms that the EU now has a single definition of indirect discrimination across all grounds and in respect of both equal treatment and equal pay. However, none of these measures specifies how 'particular disadvantage' is to be established. Burrows and Robison (2007: 200) comment:

> 'while it is to be expected that statistical factors will continue to remain an element of the test, statistics will not be deemed necessary to establish particular disadvantage. Clearly this clarity on the question of the use of statistics is an important one for the individual seeking to prove indirect discrimination.'

The only real guidance on statistics has been that given in *Enderby*, where the Court said the statistics must cover sufficient individuals, must not relate to purely fortuitous or short-term circumstances, and must be statistically significant. This requires a level of scientific validity, which would suggest that the analysis needs to be carried out by statisticians, and presented as evidence, rather than assessed by the court.

## 15.9  Objective Justification

A further, important factor differentiates direct and indirect discrimination. Direct discrimination, it will be recalled, is always unlawful unless it falls within a statutory exception or derogation. Indirect discrimination is only unlawful if it cannot be objectively justified by the employer. This allows employers more leeway to make decisions that genuinely need to be made for business reasons. It also allows the justification of national legislation which is indirectly discriminatory on economic or social grounds. The Court of Justice is trying to balance the right of women to equal treatment against the needs of the employers and the state. The way it tends to express it is that indirect discrimination gives rise to a shift in the burden of proof. Once a disparate impact or 'particular disadvantage' has been identified, it is for the employer to justify that impact. Otherwise, it is assumed that men and women should receive the same treatment, and that the disparate impact is evidence of discriminatory practice.

In *Jenkins*, the first case to discuss indirect discrimination, the possibility of objective justification was simply stated. More detail was given in *Bilka*, where the Court articulated a proportionality test. For an objective justification to be acceptable, the measures taken must:

- respond to a real need on the part of the undertaking;
- be appropriate for achieving that need; and
- be necessary for that need.

This set of conditions referred specifically to employers' choices. In *Rinner-Kühn*, however, the litigation concerned German legislation which excluded part-time workers from sick pay provisions, on the ground that part-time workers are insufficiently integrated within a company. Although the applicant brought the case against her employer, the German court referred a question specifically about the legislation. No issue about the responsibility of the employer for the consequences of the legislation was raised. In its decision, the Court of Justice made two important points. Firstly, the justification given for the legislation was insufficient, because it relied on generalisations about a particular class of worker. The Court takes the view that such generalisations should not be made. This is an appropriate policy, bearing in mind that, at its most basic level, discrimination is caused by generalisations made about one sex or another. Secondly, contrary to the rather conservative argument of the Advocate General, the *Bilka* conditions were applied to legislation in the same way as to employers' policies, and Germany was required to justify that legislation.

It sought to do so on grounds of social policy, and there is no indication that this would be unacceptable in principle, had the justification offered been sufficient in practice. Case C-226/98 *Jørgensen* v. *Foreningen af Speciallæger and Sygesikringens Forhandlingsudvalg* ([2000] ECR I-2447) looked at the possibility of economic justifications for social policy. This is a case concerned with equal treatment, rather than equal pay, issues, but the principles are identical, especially now that there is a single definition of indirect discrimination. Dr Jørgensen was a Danish GP who complained about a reorganisation of the system for her recovery of fees from the national health insurance scheme, on the grounds that it discriminated against her, and other women, who had chosen to spend less time at work and more time caring for her family. Denmark argued that this reorganisation was purely due to budgetary considerations, and thus objectively justified. The Court of Justice disagreed. It stated that budgetary grounds cannot be used by states to justify discriminatory measures and practices. If they could, the application of the general principle of equality would vary according to the financial position of the state concerned. In contrast, however, justifications based on the need for the sound management of public expenditure can succeed.

## 15.10 Equal Treatment

Discrimination in matters of employment and occupation, but in relation to non-pay issues, has been governed by the ETD, as amended by the ETAD, and is being subsumed, as with equal pay, into the recast directive. Non-pay issues were not dealt with in the original EEC Treaty, and hence have been developed through legislative means, and also some modest amendments to the EC Treaty. These include, in particular, the insertion of a new Article 141(3) EC, which gives a legal basis for the adoption of measures in the field of equality between men and women, on the basis of co-decision between the European Parliament and the Council. Article 141(3) is the legal basis for both the ETAD and the recast directive. The objective of the ETAD was to bring the legislation into line with the case law of the Court of Justice, in particular by providing legislative definitions of direct and indirect discrimination. However, an important impact is a legislative recognition that sexual harassment is a form of discrimination. This obliges employers to provide a workplace that is free of harassment. Instruction to discriminate is also a form of discrimination. It is significant that these forms of discrimination are now explicitly extended also to the equal pay field, under Article 2(2) of the recast directive.

Some of the concepts of equal pay, particularly the distinction between direct and indirect discrimination, are also applicable in this field. Indeed, some of the cases discussed above, such as *Jørgensen*, are equal treatment cases. However, the legislation on equal treatment raises a number of specific issues. For example, Article 2 ETD included a list of derogations from the general principle of equality. These statutory exceptions apply both to direct and indirect discrimination, and should not be confused with the objective justification of indirect discrimination. It was made clear in Case 222/84 *Johnston* v. *Chief*

*Constable of the RUC* ([1986] ECR 1651) that these exceptions must be interpreted restrictively. Each of these derogations is now reproduced in the recast directive.

Article 14(2) of the recast directive provides that:

'Member States may provide, as regards access to employment including the training leading thereto, that a difference of treatment which is based on a characteristic related to sex shall not constitute discrimination where, by reason of the nature of the particular occupational activities concerned or by the context in which they are carried out, such a characteristic constitutes a genuine and determining occupational requirement, provided that its objective is legitimate and the requirement is proportionate.'

This provision recognises that, in a few cases, jobs are inherently male or female. However, there are very few such jobs. In Case 61/81 *Commission* v. *United Kingdom (No. 1)* ([1982] ECR 2601) it was held not to be unlawful to restrict the profession of midwife to women. However, it is thought that the Court of Justice was influenced in its decision by the fact that the UK itself had expressed its intention to change the law on this matter. In Case 312/86 *Commission* v. *France (No. 1)* ([1988] ECR 6315), prison warders in single-sex prisons were held to fall under para. 2.

More controversial questions have been raised under what was then Article 2(2) ETD concerning employment in the armed forces and security forces. An early case on the matter was *Johnston* v. *RUC*, concerning the policy of the Royal Ulster Constabulary not to give weapons to women, which restricted the functions that women could perform. The RUC argued that there was a higher likelihood that armed women would be abducted or assassinated, and that public opinion was hostile to the idea of women carrying arms. The Court held, first, that the ETD did apply to the RUC, and to all armed and security forces, notwithstanding its public security role. Second, while the first justification may be allowed, depending on the circumstances, the second was not sufficient. The matter must be kept under review, and decisions taken according to the principle of proportionality. More recently, in Case C-273/97 *Sirdar* v. *The Army Board and Secretary of State for Defence* ([1999] ECR I-7403), a female catering officer in the British Army was refused a transfer from the Royal Artillery to the elite Royal Marines. The Marines' principle of interoperability meant that all members of the Marines must be capable of front line action, and women, in the British Army, are not allowed on the front line. The Court of Justice confirmed that the *Johnston* principles apply and, if they are properly applied, the ban could be allowed. However, the national court must make a proper investigation. In Case C-285/98 *Kreil* v. *Bundesrepublik Deutschland* ([2000] ECR I-69), on the other hand, the limits of the discretion allowed to the armed forces are shown. German law banned all women from military posts involving the use of arms which, in practice, meant from virtually all military posts. The Court held that that rule was too broad. A ban on women serving is only allowable if it is applied to specific functions.

A second exception to the principle of equal treatment concerning measures taken for the protection of women, particularly as regards pregnancy and maternity, is now dealt with in Article 28(1) which provides that: 'This Directive shall be without prejudice to provisions concerning the protection of women, particularly as regards pregnancy and maternity.' In practice, the application of this provision has been limited to the area of pregnancy and maternity, and in *Johnstone* it was made clear that it relates only to the biological condition of women and the relationship between a mother and her child. Other protective legislation, such as French legislation prohibiting women from working at nights, is not covered and thus unlawful. The provision which appeared in the original

ETD should be seen as first tentative step towards dealing with the tricky questions surrounding pregnancy and maternity, and the equality issue which was referred to at the start of the chapter. It allows certain national measures to be taken. In more recent years, EU law has also addressed the question of pregnancy and maternity in a more positive form, and the relevant body of law will be discussed in more detail later.

## 15.11 Positive Action

The final derogation from the principle of equal treatment concerns positive action. The derogation, now contained in Article 3 of the recast directive, permits Member States to maintain or adopt measures 'within the meaning of Article 141(4) of the [EC] Treaty with a view to ensuring full equality in practice between men and women in working life'; this raises the difficult question of the relationship between 'equal treatment' and 'equality'. On one reading the text certainly seems to allow discrimination in favour of the less favourably treated sex, in order to help them to catch up. Where the recast directive differs from earlier versions is in its reference back to the text of Article 141(4) EC, a paragraph which was included in the EC Treaty by the Treaty of Amsterdam, in order to give explicit constitutional approval to the notion of positive action, where previously the only reference had been in the ETD.

This is a highly contested issue. Fredman has outlined a spectrum of responses to the question of whether such positive action should be allowed (Fredman, 1997):

▷ On one side is the *symmetric view*, according to which any use of sex as a criterion for making a decision is wrong. Proponents of this view believe that equality cannot be achieved unless the law is completely neutral. The value of equal treatment is seen as ensuring that an individual is not discriminated against.

▷ On the other side is the *substantive justice view*, according to which discrimination to benefit a historically disadvantaged group is qualitatively different from discrimination against that group. It should be allowed in order to right the balance and end the disadvantage, and the state has a duty to ensure that that happens. This view holds that what is important is that groups within society are equal.

▷ Between these two perspectives lies an *equal opportunities approach*, which mixes aspects of the two more extreme views. The aim of this approach is to equalise the starting points of individuals, while recognising that the law is not neutral, and any assumption that it is can be damaging for individuals.

Article 141(4) EC and Article 3 of the recast directive seem to suggest a move away from the pure symmetric view, in that some measures have been allowed that run contrary to the principle of equal treatment. The controversy has been about the kinds of measures which are allowed. Burrows and Robison (2007: 197) have argued that the inclusion of Article 141(4) and now Article 3 of the recast directive indicate 'a shift in the underlying conception of equality law at the Community level away from a symmetrical and formal model towards one which accommodates measures that are aimed at remedying disadvantage and achieving substantive equality'. They also include more recent case law as evidence of this shift; however, this has been quite a long and difficult road in terms of the approach which the Court of Justice has taken to this question.

The first case in which the Court of Justice had to deal with this question was Case

C-450/93 *Kalanke* v. *Frei Hansestadt Bremen* ([1995] ECR I-3051). This was a decision about a public sector recruitment policy which stated that if, in any particular sector, there was less than a particular proportion of one sex employed, that sex was to be given automatic preference in recruitment. The Court held that such a policy is unlawful, in that it guarantees absolute and unconditional priority for one sex in those circumstances, and this goes beyond what was permitted by what was then Article 2(4) ETD. What should be done is to take steps to achieve equality of opportunity, rather than substitute for these steps a rather mechanistic system to achieve equal representation. The individualism of this decision is particularly noticeable. What is important is not a perfect balance of men and women in a particular sector, but equality of opportunity for individuals.

This decision caused a great deal of consternation among Member States. The *Kalanke* ruling appeared to be blanket condemnation of positive discrimination policies which existed in some Member States. In a Communication (COM(96) 88), the Commission stated that its interpretation of *Kalanke* was that it affected only the kind of policy which required absolute and unconditional priority to be given to one sex. A more nuanced policy, according to the Commission, need not be covered.

A further case was brought to test this interpretation: Case C-409/95 *Marschall* v. *Land Nordrhein-Westfalen* ([1997] ECR I-6363). This concerned a policy that was like that in *Kalanke*, except for the existence of a 'saving clause,' whereby women are not to be given priority if reasons specific to an individual male candidate tilt the balance in his favour. In this case, the Court gave much clearer support for the principle of positive action, confirming that a saving clause was what was necessary to bring the policy within the ambit of Article 2(4) ETD. The decision represents a clear endorsement of the equal opportunities position. Therefore, it looks as though all that is required to render a positive action policy lawful under EU law is the insertion of a 'saving clause'.

Matters, however, were complicated again by Case C-158/97 *Badeck* v. *Hessischer Ministerpräsident* ([2000] ECR I-1875). This and later cases were decided after the entry into force of Article 141(4), and this appears to have made no difference to the Court's approach. The judgment in *Badeck* concerned a far more complex regime of positive action, involving targets and action plans for particular sectors of employment in higher education. This kind of regime, according to the logic of *Kalanke* and *Marschall*, ought not to be approved, given that it aims at a specific quota of women within sectors, rather than at equal opportunity for the individual. Nevertheless, despite stating as a clear rule that policies are compatible with EU law if they give no automatic and unconditional preference, and require an objective assessment allowing for consideration of personal circumstances, the Court allowed the quota schemes in *Badeck*, and ignored arguments that they go too far in the way of a collective approach. However, the limits of the Court's flexibility have been seen in Case C-407/98 *Abrahamsson and Anderson* v. *Fogelqvist* ([2000] ECR I-5539), where it was held that positive discrimination cannot be used to justify the appointment of a woman over a more highly qualified man. In Case C-476/99 *Lommers* v. *Minister van Landbouw, Natuurbeheer en Visserij* ([2002] ECR I-2891) the Court approved a scheme under which nursery childcare places are made available to staff, but with a certain number of places reserved for female staff, with provision, in exceptional cases, for male staff. Burrows and Robison (2006: 30) conclude that the Court has approved a range of 'purposefully inclusionary policies', outreach measures and preferential treatment, but outlawed a number of forms of preferential treatment which are rigid. They conclude that the EU measures have moved substantially towards giving recognition to the difficulties faced by women in reconciling work and care, and in achieving a work–life balance.

## 15.12    Pregnancy and Parenthood

The question of how to deal with pregnancy, motherhood and parenthood has always been a vexed one for all legal systems. Any coherent equality policy needs to have a way of dealing with a situation, such as pregnancy, where men and women are inherently different and have different needs. There is, however, a need to go beyond pregnancy and look at the whole question of parenthood. Should all parents be treated equally, or should we recognise that women often, in practice, carry a heavier burden of childcare responsibilities and can suffer physical difficulties and complications as a result of pregnancy and childbirth? These are issues which the EU has tried to confront. It will be recalled that the first step was Article 2(3) ETD, which allowed states to take protective measures, which is reproduced once more in Article 28(1) of the recast directive. The limits of this provision were in evidence in Case 184/83 *Hofmann* v. *Barmer Ersatzkasse* ([1984] ECR 3047), which concerned provisions allowing mothers but not fathers to take paid parental leave. According to the Court, in a formula which has been repeated in a number of cases: '(t)he Directive was not designed to settle questions concerned with the organisation of the family, or to alter the division of responsibility between parents.' Given that it is often the organisation of the family and the division of responsibility between parents that can lead to discrimination, this shows a remarkable lack of ambition. Case C-218/98 *Abdoulaye* v. *Regie National des Usines Renault SA* ([1999] ECR I-5723), which held that a one-off payment made to mothers was permissible, for the purposes of compensating for the disadvantages of having to take maternity leave, demonstrates that special treatment for mothers is still permitted under Article 2(3).

Article 28(1), however, merely permits states to take action. What has been needed was a EU-wide law, binding on Member States, forcing them to respect the rights of pregnant women and mothers. A first step towards that was taken by the Court of Justice in Case C-177/88 *Dekker* v. *Stichting Vormingscentrum voor Jong Volwassenen* ([1990] ECR 3941). The Court held that a woman, refused employment because she was pregnant, had been *directly* discriminated against. The finding did not, however, depend upon proof that she had been less well treated than a similarly situated man, because, as the Court said, there is no man who is similarly situated to a pregnant woman. All discrimination on grounds of pregnancy is *per se* direct discrimination. This has been held to be the case even if legislation makes it impossible for a pregnant woman to carry out the work for which she would be employed, at least when employed on an indefinite contract, on the grounds that the pregancy would only affect her work for a limited period of time (Case C-207/98 *Mahlburg* v. *Land Mecklenburg-Vorpommern* [2000] ECR I-549).

The radical nature of this decision was somewhat tempered by another decision published on the same day, Case C-179/88 *Handels- og Kontorfunctionærenes Forbund I Danmakr (acting for Hertz)* v. *Dansk Arbejdsgiverforening (acting for Aldi)* ([1990] ECR I-3979), which concerned dismissal on grounds of pregnancy-related illness. *Hertz* made it clear that the rule in *Dekker* applies during the period of pregnancy and maternity leave, as set out in the law of the individual Member States, and therefore that a woman cannot be dismissed for pregnancy-related illness during this time. Beyond that time, periods of leave, even if the sickness is directly attributable to pregnancy, are treated in the same way as ordinary sick leave, and a woman can be dismissed for such absence as long as it cannot be shown that a man absent for a similar period on sick leave would be treated better.

There has been some confusion as to the application of the provision. In Case C-400/95 *Larsson* v. *Føtex Supermarket* ([1997] ECR I-2757), the Court of Justice held that, when calculating the amount of time a worker had been absent on sick leave, in order to justify dismissal, illness during maternity leave could be taken into consideration. However, soon after, the Court explicitly overruled itself, and held that illness during maternity leave should not be counted (Case C-394/96 *Brown* v. *Rentokil Ltd* [1998] ECR I-4185). Finally, the Court has held that the protection afforded by *Dekker* does not apply when the absence from work was caused not by incapacity from work but by routine complaints, or for absences recommended medically, which are aimed at protecting the unborn child, but which is not related to an actual pathological condition or increased risk (Case C-66/96 *Pedersen* v. *Kvickly Skive* [1998] ECR I-7327).

A second, more positive, clarification of the *Dekker* decision came from the important decision in Case 32/93 *Webb* v. *EMO Air Cargo* ([1994] ECR I-3567). That decision makes it clear that any discrimination on any grounds relating to pregnancy is unlawful, notwithstanding the possible existence of a comparator. Pregnancy cannot be compared to anything else. Effectively, after *Webb*, the only way a pregnant woman can be dismissed, or not employed, is if the employer can prove that the treatment is totally unrelated to the pregnancy. The Court confirmed this in Case C-320/01 *Busch* v. *Klinikum Neustadt* ([2003] ECR I-2041), holding that it was direct discrimination on grounds of sex to refuse to allow a woman to return to work before the end of her parental leave on the grounds that she was once again pregnant.

The *Webb* case, however, was further complicated by the fact that, when it was decided, the Pregnant Workers Directive (Council Directive 92/85, OJ 1992 L348/1) had been passed but had not yet come into force. This directive was not adopted under the equality provisions, but under the health and safety provisions of the EC Treaty. It is thus explicitly directed towards the protection of the *health* of the women concerned during pregnancy and breastfeeding, rather than towards the achievement of equality in the workplace. As a consequence, it does not cover the original employment of a pregnant woman, because health and safety reasons cannot be given for insisting that someone be appointed to a job. Refusal to employ is therefore still covered by the equality legislation (i.e. now Article 14 of the recast directive) and the *Dekker* case law.

Under the Pregnant Workers Directive standards of minimum protection of pregnant women are set, protecting them from exposure to hazardous and stressful situations and from night work, giving them time off to attend medical examinations, requiring the setting of a period of maternity leave, prohibiting their dismissal for reasons related to their pregnancy, and requiring that they receive some sort of allowance during maternity leave.

Subsequent case law has clarified the position on pay. Women on maternity leave are not entitled to equal pay to other employees, but simply to an adequate allowance (*Gillespie*). The Pregnant Workers Directive was not intended to create a right to equal pay (Case C-411/96 *Boyle* v. *Equal Opportunities Commission* [1998] ECR I-6401), but only to a level of subsistence sufficient to allow a woman to take time off work. While bonuses count as pay, they can be refused to pregnant women if they relate specifically to periods of employment where the woman was on maternity leave (*Lewen*). However, the limits seem to have been drawn in Case C-136/95 *CNAV* v. *Thibault* ([1998] ECR I-2011), where a refusal to promote a woman because of her pregnancy-related absences, where otherwise she would have received automatic promotion, was declared unlawful. Article 15 of the recast directive now provides that:

> 'a woman on maternity leave shall be entitled, after the end of her period of maternity leave, to return to her job or to an equivalent post on terms and conditions which are no less favourable to her and to benefit from any improvement in her working conditions to which she would have been entitled during her absence.'

Furthermore, Article 2(2)(c) explicitly states that discrimination under the recast directive includes 'any less favourable treatment of a woman related to pregnancy or maternity leave within the meaning of [the Pregnant Workers Directive]'. However, the relationship between the recast directive, the Pregnant Workers Directive and the relevant case law will continue to be uncertain, as the latter directive was *not* included in the recasting process, and thus Article 28(2) of the recast directive provides that it (i.e. the directive) is 'without prejudice to the provisions' of the Pregnant Workers Directive. It is also without prejudice to the provisions of the Parental Leave Directive, which is discussed in the next few paragraphs.

It was pointed out at the start of this section that a problem with the law relating to parenthood is that it often gives rights and opportunities to women, but not to men. As the *Hofmann* case demonstrates, this can often mean that the core facets of the organisation of domestic life go unaffected, women are confirmed in their role of primary caregiver, and the perception that they will be less committed to their employment continues. Indeed, the failure to address discrimination against men in matters of parenting means that people are obliged to conform to traditional patterns of the organisation of family life.

This is an issue that the EU has taken the first step towards addressing, by means of the Parental Leave Directive (Council Directive 96/34, OJ 1996 L145/4). This directive has enormous symbolic significance, in that it recognises for the first time that men have a role to play in parenting, and that the law should be supportive of that role. Unfortunately, however, its practical impact is limited. It entitles all parents to three months' parental leave, which can be taken at any time during the first eight years of the life of the child. However, Member States are entitled to set reasonable conditions as to the availability of that right, such as a length of service requirement. It also entitles all parents to time off work for unforeseen and urgent reasons related to the family. Its major weakness is that the right to time-off is not accompanied by a right to be paid during that leave. This, for a large proportion of workers, effectively strips the provisions of all practical utility. Having a new baby is an expensive business, and the mother on maternity leave is not entitled to full pay, so it may not be financially viable for the father to take unpaid leave at that time.

Therefore, there persists significant differentiation between the treatment given to fathers and that given to mothers. Some of that differentiation may be justified by the different physical roles that each parent plays in the process. However, as McGlynn has argued, the Court of Justice has maintained the difference between fathers and mothers by means of the acceptance and reinforcement of a particular ideology of motherhood, which can have the effect of disadvantaging mothers, but not fathers, within the workplace (McGlynn, 2000). Article 16 of the recast directive addresses the issue of parental leave and requires that those Member States which do recognise rights to paternity and/or adoption leave must take the necessary measures to protect working men and women against dismissal due to exercising those rights, and ensure that they return to work to the same or an equivalent post, under the same conditions.

The failure to include the Pregnant Workers Directive and the Parental Leave Directive in the recast directive highlights a continuing tension between whether EU law provides a special rights' regime or an attempt to guarantee substantive equality (Burrows and Robison, 2007: 195).

## 15.13   Beyond Gender?

In more recent years, the question has been raised as to whether gender equality law can be grounded in a more general principle of non-discrimination. The judgment in Case 13/94 *P* v. *S and Cornwall County Council* ([1996] ECR I-2143) seemed to suggest that it could. This was a case concerning a worker who had been employed as a man. After taking the decision to undergo gender reassignment therapy, she informed her employers that, as part of that therapy, she would be living and working as a woman. Her employer dismissed her. In many ways, *P* v. *S* was the perfect sex discrimination case. *P* argued that she had been dismissed on grounds of her sex, and proposed that the appropriate comparator to use to demonstrate this was herself, when she had been employed as a man. The only difference between her at the time of the sacking and her previously was her apparent sex. The Court of Justice agreed that there had been discrimination. In its judgment, it pointed out that discrimination is usually caused by stereotypes that are held about men and women, and argued that the role of equality law is to challenge those stereotypes. This statement has enormous potential to be extended to a general principle of non-discrimination, which prohibits making decisions based on anything other than the personal abilities of the individual. Any decisions based on groups that the individual belongs to, be they gender, race, religion, age or anything else, are based on stereotypes and should be outlawed.

The decision in *P* v. *S* gave hope to a number of longstanding anti-discrimination campaigns, and particularly to those challenging legal discrimination against lesbians and gay men. Case C-249/96 *Grant* v. *South West Trains* ([1998] ECR I-621) was brought in order to test whether the principle could be stretched to cover discrimination on grounds of sexual orientation. Lisa Grant was an employee of a train company, which granted free rail passes to spouses and long-term heterosexual partners of employees, but refused to grant one to Lisa Grant's partner, on the grounds that it was a same-sex relationship. It was argued that this constitutes sex discrimination, given that, had Grant been male, her female partner would have been entitled to a pass. It was also argued that this constituted discrimination on stereotypical grounds, rather than a decision made on an individual basis.

The Court, to the surprise of many commentators, found that there was no discrimination. It stated that the ETD could not be stretched far enough to cover discrimination on grounds of sexual orientation. There are a number of probable reasons for this decision:

▶ While, in some Member States, lesbians and gay men have been granted equal legal rights, in others it is still considered acceptable, and indeed morally justified, to discriminate. For the Court (as opposed to the EU legislature) to impose a solution where there was so much division would have been highly controversial, and it may well not have wanted to have taken the risk.

▶ The economic implications of a decision to outlaw discrimination would have been huge. The situation in *P* v. *S* affects a relatively small number of people. However, discrimination against lesbians and gay men covers areas such as spousal benefits, pensions and other financial services, and the cost of creating equality could be considerable. By itself, of course, this is not a particularly persuasive argument, given the financial pressures that the Court was prepared to impose in its *Barber* judgment.

▶ A final, and probably pivotal, reason lies in the amendment to the EC Treaty by the Treaty of Amsterdam giving rise to the new legal basis in Article 13 EC, allowing for the adoption of anti-discrimination legislation across six prohibited grounds: sex, racial or ethnic origin, disability, age, religion or belief, and sexual orientation. The Court stated that, given that the Member States now had competence in the area, it felt that it was inappropriate to substitute its decision for that of the states.

The position taken by the Court, that the legislation on equal treatment between men and women does not apply in cases where the discrimination is in fact on the grounds of sexual orientation, was confirmed in Joined Cases C-122 and 125/99P *D and Sweden* v. *Council* ([2001] ECR I-4319).

The unanimity requirement in Article 13 EC suggested that it would be hard to envisage much binding legislation being produced. However, the inclusion of Article 13 coincided with two factors. First, as a negative factor, the arrival in coalition government of the far right and populist Freedom Party in Austria gave rise to fears of a far right revival more generally and a desire to legislate to secure certain fundamental rights to non-discrimination. A more positive impulse stems from the good fit between the new competence and the drive towards the creation of a fundamental rights core for the EU, including an emphasis on citizenship and constitutionalism. As a consequence, four key measures have been adopted which, taken together, significantly have expanded the scope of EU equality law, moving it beyond the workplace and giving it a wider effect in European society. A wider range of grounds of discrimination are prohibited. However, the relationship between the different discrimination grounds continues to be uncertain, and a number of scholars have written of a hierarchy of prohibitions, with gender and race jostling for position as the most significant prohibition, with the widest range of protections (e.g. Waddington and Bell, 2001; Howard, 2006).

## 15.14　Race Equality

Perhaps the most radical piece of legislation passed under Article 13 is the Race Equality Directive (RED). This represents a new step forward in two ways. First, it is the first piece of binding legislation adopted by the EU to tackle the increasing problem of racism, and cuts across the fields of social policy and freedom, security and justice policy (see Chapter 13). Secondly, while it covers the employment relationship, its scope is extended to social rights, education, access to goods and services and cultural activities, taking it well beyond the ambit of the single market. Only in 2004 was gender equality law extended, also on the basis of Article 13, to cover access to goods and services (Directive 2004/113, see 15.2; Caracciolo di Torella, 2006). Chalmers has argued that this directive is the most powerful basis for the development of a truly multicultural polity within the EU (Chalmers, 2001).

The directive begins by prohibiting discrimination, both direct and indirect, on racial or ethnic grounds. Indirect discrimination is defined by reference to the 'particular disadvantage' terminology now used in the recast directive for gender equality (Article 2(2)(b)). It is worth noting that this approach mirrors the test used for nationality discrimination (see Case C-237/94 *O'Flynn* v. *Chief Adjudication Officer* [1996] ECR I-2617), in being aimed not at provisions which do in fact disadvantage certain groups, but provisions which are liable to disadvantage those groups. This avoids the need for complex statistical proof of disparate impact. As well as the provisions for justification of indirect discrimination, any discrimination can be justified as a 'genuine and determining occupational requirement' (Article 4). Article 5 allows Member States to implement positive action measures to prevent or compensate for existing inequality.

To this extent, therefore, the RED reflects the same pattern as is found in existing gender discrimination law (especially after the recast directive), in that it combines an anti-discrimination model with provision permitting positive action. However, a third, non-legislative, equality strategy is used. States are required, under Article 13, to set up independent bodies to deal with complaints, to investigate discrimination and to make reports and recommendations. This directive could have an important impact on EU life and policy, and particularly, as Bell points out, on the position of third country nationals within the EU (Bell, 2000). Hence the directive should also be taken into account in the context of the development of the EU as an area of freedom, security and justice (see Chapter 13). Although the explanatory notes make it clear that the directive does not prohibit discrimination on grounds of nationality, nationality and race are often closely connected. In addition, discrimination on grounds of nationality can be conceptualised as indirect racial discrimination, and would then need to be objectively justified.

In addition, attempts have made to introduce mainstreaming in the area of race equality. Decision 2000/75 establishing an EU action programme to combat discrimination (OJ 2000 L303/23) allows for the funding at national level of projects intended to encourage equality mainstreaming. A focus on anti-racism has been particularly apparent in the section of DG Education and Culture addressing youth policy. However, it is notable that anti-racism mainstreaming and other types of policy activity have not been nearly as prominent or as widespread as activities in gender equality policy (see also 18.12 where issues of inequality are reconsidered in the context of EU policy on cohesion and regional development).

## 15.15 The Other Grounds

The second directive passed under Article 13 EC was the Framework Equality Directive. Despite the name, this is another anti-discrimination directive, expanding the grounds on which discrimination is prohibited to include age, disability, sexual orientation and religion or belief. Unlike the race and sex directives, it takes a horizontal approach, covering a number of different grounds in one instrument. However, certain specific provisions demonstrate that different types of discrimination need to be dealt with in different ways. This is particularly notable in the field of disability discrimination, where the approach used is a requirement for employers to make reasonable accommodation for employees with disabilities, as long as this does not impose a 'disproportionate' burden, and does not affect health and safety requirements. This is very different from the standard non-discrimination approach which is used for the other grounds, and recognises in particular the need to adapt the physical environment in order to remove the disadvantage experienced by people with disabilities. Despite the origins of the notion of reasonable accommodation in the US law on religious discrimination, the directive does not extend the use of the concept to the other prohibited grounds. The other provisions mirror those of the sex equality legislation, and the definition of indirect discrimination used is the same as that in the RED.

A notable absence from both the FED and the RED is any definition of the prohibited grounds of discrimination. This omission appears likely to keep the Court of Justice busy for some time to come. While the preamble to the RED rejects a biological concept of race, and further distinguishes race from nationality, the relationship, for example, between race discrimination and the denial of minority rights is not always clear. This becomes significant since the enlargement of the EU in 2004 and 2007, when, as the recent Equality Green Paper suggests, the Roma have become the largest minority group within the EU (*Equality and Non-discrimination in an enlarged European Union*, DG Employment and Social Affairs, 2004, p.20). The link between race discrimination and religious discrimination is equally unclear and the FED provides no guidance as to how a religion should be defined, and whether, and how, a religion should be distinguished from a cult or an ideology. It is not clear whether disability includes long-term illnesses such as cancer, or conditions such as multiple sclerosis or chronic depression, and it is equally uncertain the extent to which carers of people with disabilities could be covered by the legislation. The concept of sexual orientation is sometimes controversial, and arguably the flames of this controversy are fanned by the assertion in the Commission's proposal that the prohibition relates to sexual orientation rather than sexual behaviour. There are legitimate concerns that the legislation should not be expressed in such a way as to cover paedophilia. Nevertheless, if this interpretation is adopted by the Court, it could legitimise discrimination against people on the grounds of their private sexual relationships.

The inclusion of sexual orientation as a prohibited ground of differentiation has been controversial and provides a good illustration of the way in which the directive attempts to deal with clashes between the prohibited grounds. Many religious groups hold same-sex sexual relationships to be wrong and some religious employers have argued in favour of their right not to employ people in same-sex sexual relationships, in order to maintain the particular character of their organisation. The way in which the directive addresses this is complex. Article 4 of the directive deals with occupational requirements, and in Article 4(2), one of the more opaque provisions within the legislation, the right of religious organisations to make employment decisions based on the religion of the applicant is preserved in those Member States where it already exists. However, Article 4(2) does not operate to permit such a right in Member States where it has not previously existed. The reason for this unevenness is the significant diversity of practice among Member States. Further, Article 4(2) explicitly states that it should not justify discrimination on another ground. Therefore, Article 4(2) permits, for example, a Christian organisation to refuse to employ someone who is not a Christian, but excludes any right to refuse to employ someone in a same-sex relationship. This poses more questions than it answers. How, for example, would the Court respond to an organisation which defined its religious allegiance as conservative evangelical Christian (and thus theologically opposed to same-sex sexual relationships) and which refused to employ a liberal Christian who disagreed with that position and in fact lives in a same-sex sexual relationship?

So far, the Court of Justice has only been called upon to consider the con 'disability' under the FED. It held in Case C-13/05 *Chacón Navas* v. *Eurest Colectivid* ([2006] ECR I-6467), that the concept of disability required 'an autonomous and uniform interpretation throughout the Community' (para. 40), but that this concept did not automatically cover 'sickness'. Disability is a condition which, at the very least, it must be probable will last for a long time.

The preamble to the directive explicitly recognises individuals may face discrimination on multiple grounds. However, there is little within the text of the directive itself which addresses this issue. While the directive takes a horizontal approach, it does not require Member States to do so. Some Member States have, in order to implement the provisions of the directive, launched a full-scale horizontal reform of their discrimination framework, but others, such as the UK, have simply added that which was considered necessary and the field remains fragmented. The 2004 Green Paper expressed concern that a number of Member States had not yet taken steps to implement the provisions, and it is as yet too early at the time of writing to make an assessment of the impact of the directive on anti-discrimination provision within the Member States.

## 15.16 Conclusion: Equality as a Fundamental Principle of EU Law

The EU's Charter of Fundamental Rights, signed at Nice in 2000, contains a chapter on equality. It also contains a bewildering array of different equality strategies. Article 20 is the type of provision traditionally in civil liberties instruments, guaranteeing 'equality before the law' for all people. Article 21 prohibits discrimination on a wide range of grounds in an explicitly non-exclusive list. Further articles make more specific statements about cultural, religious and linguistic diversity, and the cases of men and women, children, the elderly and persons with disabilities. While discrimination on grounds of sexual orientation is prohibited under the general Article 21, no more specific provisions on sexual orientation or transgendered people are included. The scope of the Charter is significantly wider than that of most EU legislation (with the exception of the RED and now, since 2004, gender equality law), in that it covers all aspects of life, rather than just employment. However, the current status of the Charter is of a non-binding declaration, although it was proposed for inclusion in the Constitutional Treaty as Part II.

Since the judgment of the Court of Justice in *Mangold* (15.2), it is appropriate to ask whether – even without a legally binding charter – EU law is moving towards the recognition of a general principle of equal treatment, if not necessarily substantive equality. However, caution needs to be exercised, in the context of the likely broader reception of *Mangold*. Not only has it been widely questioned in the literature (e.g. Krebber, 2006; Jans, 2007), but it was also doubted on the first occasion that it came up for serious judicial consideration by Advocate General Mazák in Case C-411/05 *Palacios de la Villa* v. *Cortefiel Servicios SA*, Advocate General's Opinion of 15 February 2007. He argued that:

'As I read the judgment [in *Mangold*], the Court did not therefore accept that Directive 2000/78 has horizontal direct effect; rather, it bypassed the lack of it by ascribing direct effect to the corresponding general principle of law. In adopting that approach the Court set foot on a very slippery slope, not only with regard to the question whether such a general principle of law on the non-discrimination on grounds of age exists, but also with regard to the way it applied that principle' (paras. 132 and 133).

In the light of such reservations, which have yet to be further considered by the Court of Justice, it would be unwise to make firm predictions about the fate of a possible general principle of non-discrimination in EU law, at least above and beyond the very well-established field of gender equality.

## Summary

1. Gender discrimination law and policy have been part of the Community legal order since its inception, and have developed from a few legal principles expressed in the EC Treaty into a set of wider legal principles underpinned by a constitutional framework in the EC Treaty, the EU Treaty and the Charter of Fundamental Rights.

2. In addition to securing non-discrimination through Treaty provisions and legislative measures, EU law and policy also recognise the role of positive action and mainstreaming instruments (especially gender mainstreaming) in achieving more substantive equality objectives.

3. A central pillar of EU gender discrimination law is the principle of equal pay for work of equal value. The concept of pay has been interpreted broadly, although the line between pay and social security is often hard to draw.

4. EU law prohibits both direct and indirect discrimination. Direct discrimination is discrimination which is directly based on sex. Indirect discrimination is treatment or behaviour which appears neutral on its face, but in fact places the members of one group at a particular disadvantage. While direct discrimination is always unlawful, indirect discrimination can be objectively justified by reference to a proportionality test.

5. EU law requires equal treatment between the sexes in employment. This can be derogated from in cases where special treatment is required to protect the condition of pregnant women and women who are breastfeeding, or in cases where Member States choose to allow positive action measures.

6. Separate legislation exists prohibiting discrimination against pregnant women and women who are breastfeeding. However, the question of parental rights and the reconciliation of work and family life remains a difficult one.

7. Gender discrimination legislation has been extended by the Court of Justice to cover discrimination against transsexuals, but not to cover discrimination on grounds of sexual orientation.

8. However, the new competence introduced by the Treaty of Amsterdam in the form of Article 13 EC has provided the basis on which the EU legislature has adopted far-reaching legislation addressing discrimination on grounds of race or ethnic origin, age, religion or belief, disability and sexual orientation.

## Exercises

1. How has the Court of Justice defined pay, and what is the difference between pay and social security?

2. On what grounds can measures which are (a) directly discriminatory and (b) indirectly discriminatory, be allowed?

3. What kinds of justifications may constitute an objective justification?

Exercises cont'd

4. Under what conditions does the Court of Justice allow Member States to engage in positive action in favour of women?

5. For what period of time is a woman protected by the *Dekker* case law and by Directive 92/85?

6. How did the Court justify applying gender discrimination legislation to the situation in *P* v. *S*?

7. Which groups are now beneficiaries of EU anti-discrimination legislation, and would it be true to say that they benefit from a hierarchy of different levels of protection against discrimination?

# Workshop

Eatwell Ltd is a large supermarket chain. Three of their employees, Ophelia, Cordelia and Juliet, have approached you with complaints about their conditions of work. Advise them as to whether Eatwell Ltd has fully complied with its obligations under EU law.

Ophelia is the manager of the staff canteen. Following a job evaluation exercise, she was placed on the same grade as the manager of the warehouse. However, she has since discovered that, while they are paid the same gross salary, he receives a series of performance bonuses, including cash payments but also tickets to theme parks and shopping vouchers. When she approached the human resources department, they explained to her that this was because his job occasionally makes extra demands on him, which they believe should be compensated.

Cordelia works in the accounts department. She has just given birth to her first child. She has requested that she be allowed to adopt a more flexible pattern of working, in order to enable her to take care of her child, as her husband does shift work. The human resources department has refused her request, saying that flexible working hours are not available within the company.

Juliet works in the customer relations department. She has also recently had a child. During her maternity leave, she suffered serious complications, which led to her being hospitalised for four months. Since she returned to work three months ago, she has had to take on average one day off per week, as her difficult pregnancy has left her in a weakened state. However, her condition is improving, and her doctors state she should be fully fit in another three months. The human resources department have written to her, stating that they are terminating her contract because of her ongoing illness.

# Further Reading

Barmes, L. with Ashtiany, S. (2003) 'The Diversity Approach to Achieving Equality: Potential and Pitfalls', 32 *Industrial Law Journal* 274.

Barnard, C. (2006) *European Employment Law* (3rd edn), Oxford: Oxford University Press, chapters 6 10.

Bell, M. (2000) 'Equality and Diversity: Anti-Discrimination Law after Amsterdam', in Shaw, J. (ed.), *Social Law and Policy in an Evolving European Union*, Oxford: Hart Publishing.

Burrows, N. and Robison, M. (2007) 'An Assessment of the Recast of Community Equality Laws', 13 *European Law Journal* 186.

Caracciolo di Torella, E. (2006) 'The Principle of Gender Equality, the Goods and Services Directive and Insurance: A Conceptual Analysis', 13 *Maastricht Journal of European and Comparative Law* 339.

## Further Reading cont'd

Caracciolo di Torella, E. and Masselot, A. (2001) 'Pregnancy, Maternity and the Organisation of Family Life: An Attempt to Classify the Case Law of the Court of Justice', 26 *European Law Review* 239.

Chalmers, D. (2001) 'The Mistakes of the Good European?', in Fredman, S. (ed.), *Discrimination and Human Rights. The Case of Racism*, Oxford University Press: Oxford.

Costello, C. (2003) 'Gender Equalities and the Charter of Fundamental Rights of the European Union', in Hervey, T. and Kenner, J. (eds.), *Economic and Social Rights under the EU Charter of Fundamental Rights*, Oxford: Hart Publishing.

Howard, E. (2006) 'The Case for a Considered Hierarchy of Discrimination Grounds in EU Law', 13 *Maastricht Journal of European and Comparative Law* 445.

Jans, J. (2007) 'The Effect in National Legal Systems of the Prohibition of Discrimination on Grounds of Age as a General Principle of Community Law', 34 *Legal Issues of European Integration* 53.

Kilpatrick, C. (2001) 'Gender Equality: A Fundamental Dialogue', in Schiarra, S. (ed.), *Labour Law in the Courts: National Judges and the European Court of Justice*, Oxford: Hart Publishing.

McGlynn, C. (2000) 'Ideologies of Motherhood in European Community Sex Equality Law', 6 *European Law Journal* 29.

More, G. (1999) 'The Principle of Equal Treatment: From Market Unifier to Fundamental Right?', in Craig, P. and de Búrca, G. (eds.), *The Evolution of EU Law*, Oxford: Oxford University Press.

Pollack, M.A. and Hafner-Burton, E. (2000) 'Mainstreaming Gender in the European Union', 7 *Journal of European Public Policy* 432.

Stratigaki, M. (2005) 'Gender Mainstreaming vs Positive Action. An Ongoing Conflict in EU Gender Equality Policy', 12 *European Journal of Women's Studies* 165.

Waddington, L. and Bell, M. (2001) 'More Equal than Others: Distinguishing European Union Equality Directives', 38 *Common Market Law Review* 587.

## Key Websites

Commission website on gender equality at:
**http://ec.europa.eu/employment_social/gender_ equality/index_en.html**

Commission website on anti-discrimination on other grounds including race discrimination, at:
**http://ec.europa.eu/employment_social/fundamental_ rights/index_en.htm**

Website of the European Fundamental Rights Agency at:
**http://www.eumc.europa.eu/eumc/index.php**

The UK Commission for Equality and Human Rights, which is described as 'an independent influential champion whose purpose is to reduce inequality, eliminate discrimination, strengthen good relations between people and protect human rights', brings together the Equal Opportunities Commission, the Commission for Racial Equality and the Disability Rights Commission in one body, and extends their remit to cover all the Article 13 grounds, as required by the relevant EU legislation. It combines this with a mission to champion human rights in the UK. Its website is at:
**http://www.cehr.org.uk/**

# Chapter 16
## Employment Law and Policy

Introduction

This chapter focuses on both employment *law* and employment *policy*. Employment law refers to the collection of individual and collective rights that EU law has granted to workers – rights protecting their employment status, their health and safety and general wellbeing, and rights enabling them to participate, collectively, in the decisions which affect them at work. Employment policy meanwhile refers to policy interventions (generally non-legislative) which seek to generate employment and combat unemployment. While the EU has long played a role in respect of employment law, its explicit role in respect of employment policy has been more recently acquired, formalised in the EC Treaty through the Treaty of Amsterdam, and operationalised through the European Employment Strategy concerned with the reform of labour markets among other matters, to which we turn briefly at the end of the chapter.

This recent focus on employment policy at EU level might have brought with it renewed constraints and limitations on EU employment law, as their goals are sometimes presented as irreconcilable. According to this conflict model, protective employment legislation imposes burdens on labour markets which are at best ineffective, at worst, inefficient, costly and anti-competitive. Employment protection measures have been blamed for introducing rigidities into the labour market which prevent employers from responding swiftly and effectively to fluctuations in demand, and for contributing to higher unemployment, as new entrants and returners to the labour market are excluded, their route blocked by the (too) well protected. While this neoclassical economic critique of employment protection legislation is by no means universally accepted, it lay behind the deregulatory agenda of the UK Conservative governments of 1979–1997 and, in turn, given the unanimity requirements for employment law decision-making at EU level for most of this period, for what could be seen as the arrested development of EU employment legislation.

This combination of unanimity requirements and political opposition meant that the Commission has needed to be inventive and opportunistic in getting employment law matters on the legislative agenda, and this has resulted in a somewhat idiosyncratic mix of employment law measures, which has lacked coherence and a common, consistent rationale. Variously, EU employment law measures have been justified on the grounds that some (partial) harmonisation of measures is required to equalise costs on employers and create a level playing field between Member States, as well as on the basis that minimum (rather than equal) standards are required to avoid social dumping and the 'competitive deregulation' of national employment protection measures (Deakin and Wilkinson, 1994). These 'market-making' rationales are complemented, though not wholly replaced, by arguments for EU intervention based on justice, equity and solidarity.

The traditional requirement for employment law measures to be attached to, and be in support of, the market integration project resulted, according to Davies, in a body of subordinate, 'hobbled' laws (1992: 347). That said, the Court of Justice in its interpretation of employment law measures has often taken an approach that is expansive, employee-protective and, for some, overly paternalistic (Bogg, 2006), 'freeing' employment law measures from the straitjacket of the market-making approach. In addition, recent Treaty amendments, coupled with the human rights rhetoric of the 2000 EU Charter, which includes a range of employment-related rights, may suggest that employment legislation based on a clearer, more autonomous social rationale could emerge.

The current dominant depiction of the relationship between employment law and employment policy, presented in documents such as the Lisbon Council Presidency conclusions and the Commission's 2005 *Social Policy Agenda* (COM(2005) 33), is that they are to be seen as mutually reinforcing: in short, enhanced and improved conditions at work may contribute to employment growth and productivity. The promotion of 'Quality in Work' has been identified as a core policy principle for the European Employment Strategy, and its pursuit is recognised as having positive connections with the drive to full employment, higher productivity and greater social cohesion (Commission Communication, *Improving Quality in Work: A Review of Recent Progress* (COM(2003) 728)). The definition of 'quality in work' provided by the Commission is that of sustainable jobs which invest in the individual. Factors which are seen as making for quality jobs include: improved health and safety at work; enhanced social dialogue and the involvement of the social partners (the representatives of employers and employees); and the balancing of 'flexibility', of both different forms of work such as part-time work and fixed-time work, and working time, with a degree of employee-friendly 'security', so countering the potentially precarious nature of such employment relationships. The EU's role in respect to such matters will be dealt with below, first in a general account of the trends in employment law over the EU's history (16.2 and 16.3), and then, following a closer look at the law-making process in this area (16.4 and 16.5), through a review of the key legislative and judicial pronouncements in respect of specific areas, covering employment protection, working conditions and collective labour law. The operation of the European Employment Strategy is addressed in 16.16.

## 16.2　Trends in the Evolution of EU Employment Law and Policy

The history of the EU's engagement with employment law and policy may be separated into a number of phases, each with its own set of policy priorities, and policy tools, which are in turn reflected in legislative output. If we leave aside the employment-related non-discrimination measures (as between men and women, and nationals and non-national migrant workers) provided for in the Treaty, it took almost twenty years for the first employment law measures to be adopted. While original Article 117 EEC set out that 'Member States agree upon the need to promote improved working conditions and an improved standard of living for workers', the tools for realising this improvement were, according to that Article, first and foremost, the functioning of the market itself.

The 'inaction' of this first phase may thus be explained on the basis of this reliance on the market for the achievement of social goals, coupled with the belief that the integration process did not require the harmonisation of national labour standards, as it was considered that differences in costs reflected different productivity rates. This assumption is generally seen to be behind the lack of any express legislative power to introduce employment legislation under the Treaty's social policy title.

By the early 1970s, the reliance on the market was replaced by a more proactive approach, leading to the adoption of the 1974 *Social Action Programme* (OJ 1974 C13/1). In addition to policy activity in respect of equality between men and women, and development of the European Social Fund, the programme led to a focus on two key areas of employment law – employment protection and employee participation. While separate employee participation measures were proposed over this period, none were to be adopted, although participation was to be a feature of broader employment protection measures. The focus on employment protection is explicable when placed against the wave of industrial restructurings which were taking place across Europe, as the economic and industrial implications of the common market project played themselves out. Three related messages were adopted over a five year period. The first of these, the 1975 Collective Redundancies Directive (Council Directive 75/129, OJ 1975 L48/29) (subsequently amended by Council Directive 92/56 (OJ 1992 L248/3) and now consolidated by Council Directive 98/59 (OJ 1998 L225/16)), set out a framework of basic procedural guarantees, requiring employers to inform and consult with workers when proposing restructuring entailing large-scale redundancies. The 1977 Acquired Rights Directive (Council Directive 77/197, OJ 1977 L61/26) (amended by Council Directive 98/50 (OJ 1998 L201/88) and consolidated by Council Directive 2001/23 (OJ 2001 L82/16)) meanwhile was designed to offer protection to workers when the undertakings they worked for were transferred, resulting in them having a new employer, as may result, for example, from a merger of two different companies. Again, this protection included information and consultation rights but, in addition, involved the guarantee of certain substantive rights – including protection against dismissal in a transfer situation (unless for an economic, technical or organisational reason), and the automatic continuance of their existing terms and conditions (their 'acquired rights') with the new employer. The third of the employment protection measures, the 1980 Insolvency Directive, places an obligation on Member States to establish 'guarantee institutions' to meet the otherwise unmet and outstanding claims of workers when their employer was in a state of insolvency (Council Directive 80/987, OJ 1980 L283/23, amended by Council Directive 2002/74, OJ 2002 L270/10).

All three directives were introduced under the general legislative basis of what is now Article 94 EC (former Article 100), though reference was also made to former Article 117 EEC and Article 2 EEC on the general objectives. Article 94 EC is available for the introduction of measures which remove obstacles that directly affect the establishment or functioning of the common market. The 'obstacles' here were the differences in Member State approaches to these issues. By the time of the introduction of the employment protection directives, the first wave of enlargement had taken place, resulting in three distinct families of industrial relations and employment law being represented among the Member States: the Anglo-Irish, Nordic and Romano-Germanic. Each of these has dominant characteristics in respect of such matters as the role played by the state, and by the two sides of industry, and the relative significance of legislation and collective agreements. In the Nordic system for example, there is relatively little state intervention or legislation, as the regulation of industrial relations has traditionally been left to the social partners, through the setting of legally enforceable collective agreements, which by and large cover all the workforce. The Romano-Germanic tradition sees a less important role for the social partners, but far greater state intervention and legislation, including constitutional guarantees of certain employment rights. The Anglo-Irish system meanwhile is historically one of limited state intervention, the employment contract being of primary importance. Specific legislation has been limited (though there has been a trend to more legislative intervention in respect of individual employment rights) and collective agreements limited in coverage, and not legally enforceable. Within each of these families, further differences exist, resulting in a diverse set of responses to common questions – such as what rights do employees have when the company they work for is taken over, and a new employer arrives?

Such different responses were thus presented as obstacles to the completion of the market, as they gave rise to possible distortions of competition. However, rather than introducing a standard set of rules which would apply across the Member States without distinction, the approach taken was more one of 'partial harmonisation', which fixed a set of minimum standards, but which allowed Member States to offer further protections, and which also granted further flexibility, in that many of the directives' key terms were not uniquely fixed, but open to definition in the light of the Member States' industrial relations and employment law traditions.

As Davies notes, while the economic justifications put forward for the adoption of the measures were weak, it was legally and politically necessary to cast employment law measures in this way if they were going to be able to be adopted under the market-related former Article 100 EEC (1992: 330). However, even dressed up in this way, it became clear that the combination of economic recession and the political intransigence of some states meant that the necessary unanimity for the adoption of further employment law measures would not be forthcoming. The area of health and safety presented something of an exception to this situation. While there had been some limited action in this field (resulting in two Action Programmes covering 1978–82 (OJ 1978 C165/1) and 1982–6 (OJ 1984 C67/02), and a small body of legislation), law-making in this area took off in the latter part of the 1980s. On the domestic level, the UK already had a significant body of health and safety measures (with a focus particularly on industrial accidents and occupational diseases) and so developments at the EU level were more politically acceptable, so much so that it proved possible to introduce through the Single European Act the first dedicated employment law legal basis into the EEC Treaty. Article 118a EEC enabled the Council to adopt, by qualified majority voting, directives 'imposing minimum requirements for gradual implementation' to encourage 'improvements, especially in the working environment, as regards health and safety of workers'.

## 16.3 The SEA and Beyond

Facilitated by new Article 118a, the late 1980s and early 1990s saw the adoption of a significant body of health and safety legislation, heralded by the Third Action Programme (COM(87) 520) and including the centrepiece 1989 Framework Directive (Council Directive 89/391, OJ 1989 L183/1), which imposed a duty on employers to ensure the safety and health of workers in every aspect related to their work, and which was to spawn a body of 'daughter' directives covering specific risks relating to the workplace, work equipment and dangerous substances. Importantly, not all of the measures adopted under Article 118a could be classified as 'traditional' health and safety measures, dealing with immediate physical hazards to health. Adopting a broad notion of health and safety which draws on the World Health Organisation's definition of health as 'a state of complete psychic, mental and social well-being [which] does not merely consist of absence of disease or infirmity', the Commission took the opportunity to avoid the unanimity requirement, and push through under Article 118a EEC a number of protective measures including the Working Time Directive, introduced despite the abstention of the UK (Council Directive 93/104, OJ 1993 L307/18, amended by European Parliament and Council Directive 2000/34, OJ 2000 L295/41 and consolidated by European Parliament and Council Directive 2003/88, OJ 2003 L299/9), the Young Workers Directive (Council Directive 94/33, OJ 1994 L216/12) and the Health and Safety of Atypical Workers Directive (Council Directive 91/383, OJ 1991 L206/19).

The immediate impetus for these measures lay in the non-binding 1989 Community Charter of Fundamental Social Rights for Workers (from which the UK abstained), which included references to rights for all workers to a weekly rest period and an annual period of paid leave, the protection of children and adolescents, and the protection of health and safety at work. The Charter gave rise to an Action Programme (COM(89) 568), and the majority of legislative proposals made under this programme were to be introduced under Article 118a. Again, a 'minimum standards' approach was adopted in this legislation – rather than setting one harmonised, uniform standard, a minimum floor of rights was imposed, over and above which individual Member States were permitted to go. Notably, the flexibility found in earlier employment protection directives is much greater. The measures adopted during this period often contain broad general principles, leaving the detail to be filled in at Member State level, and often by the social partners. Further, as notoriously demonstrated by the Working Time Directive, derogations from protections afforded by the directive are available.

The use of Article 118a EEC for the adoption of this body of legislation was not universally accepted. Chief among the opponents was the UK government, which brought a legal challenge against the legality of the Working Time Directive, on the basis that Article 118a should not have been used for its introduction (Case C-84/94 *United Kingdom* v. *Council (Working Time Directive)* [1996] ECR I-5755). The UK government argued that the link between working time and health and safety was not sufficiently made, and so the directive could not properly be seen as a health and safety measure, and should have been introduced under one of the general legal bases, requiring, of course, unanimity. The Court of Justice, in the first case explicitly to give priority to rights also set out in the 1989 Social Charter over economic considerations, rejected the UK's challenge, and, employing the broader definition of health offered by the WHO, adjudged the directive to be principally a health and safety measure, and correctly introduced under Article 118a, although the specification of Sunday as the weekly day of rest was struck down, the 'health and safety' case for this day rather than any other day of the week being the rest day not being made out.

Undeniably, the Working Time Directive can be linked with policy discourses outside the area of health and safety. Indeed, the issue of working time had been addressed in earlier, soft law measures from the perspective of job creation and the reduction of unemployment. The reorganisation of working time (through the reduction of an individual's hours of work) can bring with it a redistribution of the work to be done across a wider workforce, while flexibility in working time (as well as flexibility in the number of workers employed, the nature of their contracts and the skill sets they hold) enables employers to better utilise their resources as and when demand requires. These concerns of employment generation and enhancing flexibility have dominated the agenda in the post-Maastricht period. They have been particularly visible in documents such as the 1997

Green Paper *Partnership for a New Organization of Work* (COM(97) 128) and the follow-up Communication *Modernising the Organization of Work – A Positive Approach* (COM(98) 592). While there has been widespread concern that 'flexibility' in its many forms will impact negatively on the position of workers, Commission documents stress that the flexibility that firms need has to be balanced with security for workers. However, the Commission sees employment 'security' as being something different from that guaranteed by the earlier employment protection directives, in that 'the concept of security of workers has been reformulated, focusing more on security based on employability in the labour market, rather than security in a specific job' (Commission, *An Employment Agenda for the Year 2000: Issues and Policies*, COM(97) 479).

This particular focus suggests a greater emphasis on employment policy and training policies, and a more limited role for employment law. Few measures were adopted in the period between the Maastricht Treaty and the Amsterdam Treaty, and those that were (such as Council Directive 94/45 on European Works Councils (OJ 1994 L254/64) and Council Directive 96/34 on Parental Leave (OJ 1996 L145/4) made use of the Social Policy Agreement (SPA). The SPA was appended to Protocol 14 of the Maastricht Treaty, which was itself in turn appended to the EC Treaty. The SPA provided new, extended legal bases for the introduction of social policy measures for application in all Member States apart from the UK. Directives adopted under it were later readopted to cover the UK (Works Councils Directive 97/74, OJ 1997 L10/22; Parental Leave Directive 97/75, OJ 1997 L10/24). Following the 'opting-back-in' to these broader social policy competences by the UK in the Amsterdam Treaty, the new, broader employment-related social policy provisions (see especially Articles 136–139 EC), applying to all Member States, have been used to adopt a small number of legislative measures, most notably in the area of collective labour law. This area has seen something of a breakthrough, and a bucking of the trend away from legislation towards more soft law measures, resulting in Council Directive 2001/86 on Employee Involvement in the European Company (OJ 2001 L294/22) and Directive 2002/14 (OJ 2002 L80/29) on a General Framework for Improving Information and Consultation Rights of Employees. In addition to developing participation of the two sides of industry within enterprises, in the post-Maastricht era, space is being created for ever greater involvement of the social partners in the processes of governance (Barnard, 2002). The greatest innovation is the role now granted to the social partners in the making of EU employment law, through the social dialogue (16.5).

The most recent Social Policy Agendas, of 2000 (COM(2000) 379) and 2005 (COM(2005) 33), are explicitly tied to contributing to the achievements of the Lisbon Agenda, and foresee little in the way of new legislation, apart from some revision of existing measures as part of a modernisation programme of labour law. More generally, it proposes a strengthened role and greater autonomy for the social partners, and a focus on alternatives to legislation. These include a greater focus on the use of the European Funding, such as the role of the European Social Fund, as a means to support active employment-generating measures. Political agreement was reached in December 2005 on a European Globalisation Fund, to assist workers made unemployed through 'changing global trade patterns'. Also highlighted are voluntary initiatives in the field of Corporate Social Responsibility, both internal to the EU and externally, targeting companies operating in developing nations and encouraging respect for basic labour standards. This latter focus reflects a growing concern with the external dimension of the EU's social dimension, as seen in the 2001 Commission Communication *Promoting Core Labour Standards and*

*Improving Social Governance in the Context* (COM(2001) 416). In November 2006, the Commission initiated a process of review of existing and future EU labour law interventions with the publication of the Green Paper *Modernising Labour Law to Meet the Challenges of the 21st Century* (COM(2006) 708). Specifically, it asks how labour law could be refashioned to better support the achievement of the Lisbon objectives.

## 16.4  Making Employment Law

Articles 137–139 EC deal with the making of employment *law*, while the procedures for developing employment *policy* find their basis in Articles 125 *et seq*. EC. Employment policy-making will be examined in a separate section on the European Employment Strategy (16.16), while this section will focus on employment law-making, both through traditional legislative means as well as through the social dialogue route.

Under Articles 137–139, law-making starts with the Commission's consultation of the EU-level representatives of the two sides of industry, the social partners, over the possible direction of EU action. Should the Commission decide to move forward with a proposal after this first consultation, it will then return to the social partners, to seek their views on the content of the envisaged proposal (Article 139 EC). It is after this point that the law-making process can split into two routes: either the social partners indicate to the Commission that they wish to negotiate and reach agreement on the subject themselves, or the standard legislative route is followed. The legislative route is also used as a fall-back, should the social partners' negotiations subsequently break down (as with the negotiations on working conditions for temporary workers in 2002), or, indeed, if they never get off the ground (as was the case with the first attempt to use the social dialogue route in 1993, in relation to European Works Councils). This use of the standard legislative route as a fall-back, in deference to social partner decision-making, is described by the Commission as 'a practical application of the principle of social subsidiarity' (Commission, *The European Social Dialogue, a Force for Innovation and Change*, COM(2002) 341, at p.8).

The standard legislative route is set out in Article 137 EC. It provides for the introduction of minimum standards directives by the co-decision of the Council and the European Parliament, with qualified majority voting operating in respect of health and safety and the working environment, working conditions, information and consultation, the integration of those excluded from the employment market, and equality between men and women. In a range of more politically sensitive areas (social security and social protection, the protection of workers on the termination of their contracts, the representation and collective defence of the interests of workers and employers, and employment of third country nationals), decision-making is to be through the consultation route and subject to unanimity in Council. Provision is also made for law-making in the final three of these areas to be transferred, following a unanimous vote in favour, to the co-decision/qualified majority voting route. Under both the consultation and the co-decision tracks, the Economic and Social Committee and the Committee of the Regions must also be consulted.

In addition to the general requirements of respecting the principles of proportionality and subsidiarity (and compliance with these principles has often been challenged in this area, sometimes legally, as with the Working Time Directive), legislative proposals in the employment law field must also 'take account of the diverse forms of national practices', as well as the 'need to maintain the competitiveness of the European economy' (Article 136 EC). Article 137 EC further provides that particular attention must be paid, when introducing directives, to avoiding 'administrative, financial and legal constraints in a way which would hold back the creation and development of small and medium sized enterprises'. Even where the standard legislative route rather than the social dialogue route to law-making is used, opportunities exist for social partner involvement in the legislative process. Under Article 137 EC, Member States may, in response to the joint request of the national-level social partners, entrust to them the implementation of directives, though the state itself remains under an obligation to ensure that the rights under the directive are in fact being given effect. This may require the state to adopt legislation to protect those who are not covered by the collective bargaining system. Increasingly, and an example of the rather more 'flexible' measures currently being adopted in the employment law field (Barnard, 2000a, b), the social partners are involved in standard-setting *within* measures adopted through the legislative route, as with the provisions in the Working Time Directive enabling the social partners, at national level and below, to determine such issues as the duration of rest breaks.

## 16.5 The Social Dialogue Route

Operating as an alternative to the standard legislative procedure, the social dialogue route was first introduced into the EU machinery through the Maastricht Treaty's Social Policy Agreement. The concept of the social dialogue was already a familiar one in the EU system, with the Single European Act having introduced an obligation on the Commission to endeavour to develop the dialogue between the two sides of industry (former Article 118b EEC). The inclusion of this Treaty article marked a formal recognition of a practice of dialogue within the Community context, which had started with the 1985 Val Duchesse talks. The social dialogue contained in the SPA, and now in the main body of the EC Treaty, is qualitatively different from that under Article 118b, in that EU-level agreements reached by the social partners can set EU-wide standards, which may be given legal force.

The bare bones of the social dialogue process are set out in Articles 138 and 139 EC. Having informed the Commission of their intention to commence the dialogue following the second consultation phase, the social partners then have a nine month period – which may be extended with the agreement of the Commission – to undertake negotiations 'which may lead to contractual relations, including agreements' (Article 139(1) EC). These agreements are then either transposed into legislation through the adoption, by the Council, of a directive, or may be left to be implemented directly by the social partners themselves, in accordance with the procedures and practices specific to management and labour and the Member States' (Article 139(2); see Smismans, 2007). To date, three agreements have been reached by the cross-industry, intersectoral social partners, which have been adopted as Directives (on Parental Leave, Part Time Work (Council Directive 97/81, OJ 1997 L14/9) and Fixed Term Work (Council Directive 99/70, OJ 1999 L175/43)). Negotiations between organisations operating in specific sectors (the sectoral social dialogue) have themselves led to directives which have application for those sectors alone (such as Council Directive 1999/63 on the Agreement on the Organisation of Working Time of Seafarers (OJ 1999 L167/33) and Council Directive 2000/79 on the Agreement on the Organisation of Working Time of Mobile Workers in Civil Aviation (OJ

2000 L302/57)). Among the measures which are to be implemented by the social partners themselves, without the intervention of the Community legislature, are the 2002 Framework Agreement on Telework and the 2004 Framework Agreement on Work Related Stress. As the Commission identifies is its 2004 Communication *Partnership for change in an enlarged Europe – enhancing the contribution of European social dialogue* (COM(2004) 557), there are other forms of 'autonomous agreements' reached between the social partners which are more 'process oriented', setting out recommendations for the social partners within the Member States to follow up, and these include the 2002 Framework of Actions on the Lifelong Development of Competencies and Qualifications.

While the output of the social dialogue route may be seen as both quantitatively and qualitatively disappointing (see further on the minimalism of the agreements, Kenner, 2003b), the process continues to be strongly championed by the Commission. In its Communication *The European Social Dialogue, a Force for Innovation and Change* (COM(2002) 341), the social dialogue is described as being 'at the centre of the European social model' and as a 'key to better governance of the enlarged Union'. While the process is thus highlighted as a positive example of the techniques of governance, serious concerns have been raised about the democratic legitimacy of the social partner route, particularly as it removes the European Parliament from the law-making process altogether. The most often raised counter to this challenge is that although the social partners are not able to represent the peoples of Europe as a whole, they are nevertheless ideally placed to represent the interests of those most closely affected by the measures being adopted. But are these legitimacy claims satisfied? Who are the social partners, and how representative are they of management and labour across Europe?

The basic model of law-making under the social partner route was first set out in a 1991 agreement made between three organisations – for employers, UNICE, the Union of Industrial and Employers Confederations of Europe, and CEEP, the European Centre of Enterprises and Public Participation; and for employees, ETUC, the European Trades Union Confederation. This agreement fed into the Maastricht IGC process. These three organisations have continued to dominate the intersectoral social dialogue process. More organisations are eligible to participate, and eligibility is determined by the Commission in accordance with a set of criteria first set out in its 1993 Communication on the *Application of the Protocol on Social Policy* (COM(93) 600). These criteria include: first, the requirements that the organisations are organised on a cross-industry basis, or relate to specific sectors, and are established at European level; second, that they are composed of organisations which themselves are an integral part of Member State social partner systems, are representative of all Member States and have an effective mandate from members; and third, they must possess an appropriate structure to conduct negotiations. However, while those on the Commission's list are *eligible* to participate, their involvement is also subject to the agreement of the other partners to involve them in negotiations. The sidelining of one of the cross-industry social partners, UEAPME (which represents small- and medium-size employers – SMEs), in the negotiations leading to the adoption of the Parental Leave Directive resulted in UEAPME's challenge to the Directive's legality before the Court of First Instance (Case T-135/96 *UEAPME* v. *Council* [1998] ECR II-2335).

The case centred around the issue of the admissibility of the action. As a 'non-privileged' actor seeking to bring an action under Article 230 EC, the CFI proceeded on the basis that UEAPME would need to have specific rights which had been infringed if it were to have the necessary direct and individual concern to bring an action in annulment.

This hinged on whether the Commission and Council had correctly discharged their obligation to ensure that the participating bodies were 'sufficiently representative', or was it in fact the case that UEAPME's involvement would be necessary for the parties involved to be regarded as sufficiently representative of management and labour. The CFI ruled that it was not, and that the Commission and Council had properly discharged their role. The particular constituency represented by UEAPME, the management of small- and medium-sized enterprises, was adequately represented by UNICE, which had a general cross-industry mandate representing the management of all categories of undertakings.

Not everyone is convinced by the CFI's assessment of representativity. Bernard (2000: 288), for example, has argued that the Court did not address the point that while both UNICE and UEAPME represented SME undertakings, the latter's 'voice' in the process would be different from UNICE's, in that UEAPME exists exclusively to represent the interests of SMEs. More generally, concerns about the claims of the representativity of *any* of the social partners have been raised, particularly in relation to issues which most affect those traditionally under-represented by any union, such as atypical workers and women workers (Schmidt, 1999). On a more conceptual level, commentators such as Bernard (2000) have further argued that attempts to found the legitimacy of the process on the idea of representative democracy are bound to fail, and alternative models, such as participative and associative democracy, should be considered.

For the Commission, the legitimacy of the social dialogue continues to rest on the representativeness of the social partners (COM(2002) 341, at p.9). In its 2004 Communication (COM(2004) 557), the Commission commits to supporting more research on the issue, which has been made more pressing by expansion of the EU to include a number of states with, at best, a nascent social partner tradition. While it remains committed to greater autonomy for the social partners, the Commission identifies a number of weaknesses which need addressing, which include: the need for more detail in the Framework Agreements, which it says are too often imprecise and vague; more effective follow-up procedures; greater transparency; and stronger links between the different levels at which the Social Dialogue operates.

## 16.6 Employment Protection

The three employment protection measures adopted on the back of the 1974 Social Action Programme (on Collective Redundancies, Transfers of Undertakings, and Insolvency) were adopted under a common legal basis (the 'market-making' Article 94 EC (former 100 EEC)) and with common, dual objectives. These objectives were to facilitate the widespread industrial restructurings which were occurring as a necessary component of further economic integration, and also to respond to the negative social impacts that such restructuring had for the workers involved (Barnard, 2006: 619). Some had expected these selective interventions in the field of employment protection to be swiftly accompanied by a more general measure on individual dismissal (Hepple, 1977). No directive on individual dismissal is yet to materialise, although the 2000 EU Charter of Fundamental Rights includes at Article 30 the right to protection against unfair dismissal (Hunt, 2003).

The first of these measures to be adopted, the Collective Redundancies Directive, has provided relatively little work for the Court of Justice, and relatively little in the way of effective rights and substantive protections. The directive provides information and consultation rights for workers' representatives, which are triggered when the contemplated number of redundancies reaches the minimum thresholds set out in Article 1(1). This Article provides two alternative thresholds from which the Member States can choose when implementing the directive, either 20 redundancies over 90 days, or, depending on the size of the workforce, between 10 and 30 redundancies over a period of 30 days. For the purposes of the directive, dismissals taking place for any reason 'not related to the individual workers concerned' are considered relevant redundancies. Workers' representatives are to be informed of a range of issues, including the reasons for the contemplated redundancies, the number of those to be affected and the period over which redundancies are to be effected. Additional issues were introduced through the revision of the directive in 1992, namely the criteria for selection and the method for calculating redundancy payments.

Moving qualitatively beyond information rights, the directive provides for consultation between the employer and workers' representatives on, at the minimum, means to avoid or reduce redundancies and, where redundancies must take place, to mitigate their consequences, for example through providing for redeployment and retraining of those affected. These consultations are to proceed 'with a view to reaching agreement' and 'in good time'. As with all the employment protection legislation, national law and practice are deferred to for the identification both of 'workers' to be protected by the legislation (which contrasts sharply with the definition of worker developed by the Court in the area of the free movement of workers) and of workers' representatives, although the UK's practice of only allowing recognised trade unions to be consulted was rejected in Case C-383/92 *Commission* v. *United Kingdom* ([1994] ECR I-2479). The Court has however offered a single EU definition of the concept of 'redundancy', being the point at which the employer declares his or her intention to terminate the employment contract, rather than, as in the German practice, the date of actual cessation of work (Case C-188/03 *Junk* v. *Kühnel* [2005] ECR I-885).

In a further attempt to bolster the effectiveness of the directive, and reflecting the increasingly transnational nature of corporate restructuring which is resulting in an ever greater concentration of company ownership, the amended directive makes clear that an employer's obligations to inform and consult apply not only where the decision to dismiss is taken by the employer, but also when that decision is taken by an undertaking controlling the employer. Despite the apparent 'upgrading' of the directive, limitations in its protective potential remain. Some are apparently of the Court's making – for example, in Case 284/83 *Dansk Metalarbejderforbund* v. *Nielsen* ([1985] ECR 553), the Court of Justice was asked whether the directive applies not only where the employer contemplated redundancies, but also where the employer *ought* to have contemplated redundancies but failed to do so. According to the Danish Supreme Court, if this were not the case, the effectiveness of the directive would be impaired, however the Court of Justice ruled that there is no implied obligation under the directive to foresee collective redundancies. Other limitations have been shown to arise from the lack of effective enforcement mechanisms and adequate sanctions at national level in the event of non-compliance with the directive, and while this is by no means specific to this particular directive, these limitations were particularly visible in the high-profile and unexpected closure of the Renault plant in Vilvoorde, Belgium, in 1997, which proceeded without consultation. While a Belgian tribunal found against Renault, it imposed no sanctions against it (Kenner, 2003b: 364).

## 16.7    The Acquired Rights Directive

A far more controversial directive, and one which has generated far greater activity before the Court of Justice, is the Acquired Rights Directive. As with the Collective Redundancies Directive, the ARD provides (at Article 7) for the information and consultation of workers' representatives in the event of corporate restructuring (here the transfer of one undertaking to another), but goes further, adding substantive protections including the automatic transfer to the new employer of the employment relationship, along with a maintenance of existing terms and conditions (Article 3), as well as terms contained in collective agreements (though only, in the case of transfer to an employer not participating in collective bargaining, for the life of the collective agreement existing at the time of transfer; Case C-499/04 *Werhof* v. *Freeway Traffic Systems* [2006] ECR I-2397). Further, the worker is protected from transfer-related dismissal, subject to an exception for 'economic, technical or organisational' reasons (Article 4), though this protection may not, it appears, prevent or render ineffective termination, rather it renders it unfair (Case C-425/02 *Boor* v. *Ministre de la Fonction Publique* [2004] ECR I-10823). The directive's politically controversial status came with the Court of Justice's endorsement of its application to new forms of transfers not envisaged at the time of its initial adoption. These new forms of transfer include, most notably, contracting-out – where services previously provided in-house are delivered instead by outside operators. Over the last two decades, contracting-out has become increasingly prevalent in both the private and public sectors in many Member States, for reasons which tend to centre on greater efficiency and cost-effectiveness. This practice became particularly associated with the UK Conservative government, which had pursued a comprehensive policy of opening up local and central government services to contracting-out. However, the ability of outside contractors to offer services at lower costs was to be greatly constrained following the decisions of the Court of Justice which indicated that the protection of the directive applied in respect of contracting-out, which would therefore require contractors to take existing staff on, maintaining their terms and conditions.

In the early 1990s, the Commission embarked on a revision of the 1977 Directive, which was initially approached as a straightforward 'housekeeping' measure, expected to bring the directive into line with changes made to its sister Collective Redundancies Directive. However, the revision process became an increasingly politicised battle, with the lines drawn over the issue of contracting-out (Hunt, 1999). The result of the revision process, Directive 98/50 (both Directives now consolidated into 2001/23), has failed to stem the tide of references to the Court of Justice which continue to seek guidance on the issues of the circumstances in which a transfer may be said to have occurred. Further revisions of this, and the other employment protection measures, are envisaged under the 2005 Social Policy Agenda, as part of an agenda of modernising labour law.

Article 1(1) establishes that the directive applies to 'any transfer of an undertaking, business, or part of an undertaking or business to another employer as a result of a legal transfer or merger'. A first consideration is thus whether the transfer event may be classed as a 'legal transfer or merger', this is then followed by a consideration of whether, given the circumstances of the case, an undertaking has in fact been transferred.

The Court of Justice has taken a very broad approach to its interpretation of legal transfer, looking not at the nature of the commercial transaction behind the transfer, but at the question of whether, 'in the context of contractual relations', there is a change in the identity of the employer. Further, it is not necessary for direct contractual relationship to exist between the transferor and the transferee. As a result, the directive has been applicable in a wide variety of circumstances, including leasing and the rescission of a lease (Case 287/86 *LO* v. *Ny Mølle Kro* [1987] ECR 5465), contracting-out (Case C-209/91 *Rask and Christiansen* v. *ISS Kantineservice A/S* [1992] ECR I-5755), second round contracting-out (C-13/95 *Süzen* v. *Zehnacker Gebäudereinigung Gmbh Krankenhausservice* [1997] ECR I-1259) and subcontracting (Case C-51/00 *Temco* v. *Imzilyen et al* [2002] ECR I-969).

In relation to the assessment of whether, on the facts, a transfer of an undertaking has occurred, the initial guidance offered to the national courts by the Court of Justice directed them to look at whether there is the transfer of an undertaking which 'retains its identity in as much as it is transferred as a going concern', as would be suggested by the continuation of 'the same or similar activities' (Case 24/85 *Spijkers* v. *Gebroeders Benedik Abattoir* [1986] ECR 1119). The Court of Justice took an ever-expanding, flexible and employee-friendly view of what was to be considered an undertaking – and suggested very clearly that a company's ancillary activities, such as the running of its canteen (as in *Rask*) or operation of its cleaning service could be considered undertakings – even where that cleaning operation consisted of one solitary employee (Case C-392/92 *Schmidt* v. *Spar- und Leihkasse der früheren Ämter Bordesholm, Kiel und Cronshagen* [1994] ECR I-1311). Following this ruling in *Schmidt*, the Court of Justice came under fire for what was seen by some as an overextensive interpretation of an undertaking, under which an undue and commercially unrealistic emphasis was being granted to the protection of employees. The Court subsequently responded by tightening up both its test for an undertaking (which has to be more than simply an activity – it has to be a stable economic entity, defined as 'an organized grouping of persons and assets facilitating the exercise of an economic activity' (*Süzen*, para. 15, and subsequently codified in Article 1(1)(b) of the new directive)), as well as the factors to take into account when considering whether that undertaking had transferred. Following *Süzen*, the resumption of the same or similar activities is not enough, instead this has to be accompanied by the transfer of the 'stable economic entity which retains its identity' – as would be suggested if, for example, the assets – tangible and intangible – of the entity were transferred. According to the Court of Justice, in some labour-intensive sectors, where there may be little in the way of tangible assets, and the 'economic entity' comprises mainly the workforce, the necessary retention of the entity's identity would require the transfer of a significant proportion of the workforce (Joined Cases C-127, 229/96 and 74/97 *Hernandez Vidal* v. *Perez and Contratas y Limpiezas SL* [1998] ECR I-8179). This test is problematic however, as, by making the application of the directive and its protection dependent on the transfer of the workforce, employers in labour-intensive sectors are offered a mechanism to avoid the directive's application by simply refusing to take over the staff, jeopardising the protective impact of the directive for those who are arguably most in need of it.

The case of *Abler* (Case 340/01 *Abler* v. *Sodexho MM Catering* [2003] ECR I-14023), however, may now suggest that the Court is shifting back towards a broader, more employee-protective interpretation of the concept of a transfer of an undertaking. *Abler* concerned the transfer, from one catering company to another, of a contract to provide hospital catering services. The new service providers, Sodexho, used the hospital facilities to perform the contract, as the previous contractor, Sanrest, had done, but Sodexho had refused to take over the previous contractor's materials, stock and employees. Asserting that it had not taken over any of Sanrest's tangible or intangible assets, Sodexho regarded the situation as falling outside the scope of the directive's protection, and as such it had no obligation to Mr Abler or any other of Sanrest's staff previously employed on this contract. The Advocate General in his opinion agreed: this was a case of a reassignment of a contract for services, and no stable economic entity had transferred. The Court however found otherwise. It stated that 'catering cannot be regarded as an activity based essentially on manpower since it requires a significant amount of equipment'(para. 36). Finding that the tangible assets had transferred, being 'premises, water and energy and small and large equipment', it ruled that a transfer of an undertaking had occurred. It would appear that when a contract for services involving the use of the client's site and equipment is reassigned, a transfer for the purposes of the directive can be assumed: the Court will now no doubt be faced with questions seeking to establish whether this applies only in 'non-labour-intensive' services and, if so, where the line falls on what is to be considered 'labour-intensive'.

## 16.8    Insolvency

In recognition of the special considerations surrounding insolvency, Article 5 of the Acquired Rights Directive provides that Member States may elect not to apply the directive in such circumstances and, where they do, limitations may be placed on the protection offered to workers. These provisions are designed to facilitate the selling-off of viable parts of the undertaking, and ultimately the preservation of jobs. For those whose jobs are not maintained in this way, some protection is offered through the third of the employment protection directives, on insolvent companies. The directive, first adopted in 1980 (Directive 80/987), and most recently amended in 2002 (Directive 2002/74), obliges Member States to put in place systems to guarantee that outstanding claims that employees may have against their insolvent employer are met, and provide that benefit entitlements, based on employer contributions, are not adversely affected. As with the other employment protection directives, Member States have a considerable degree of flexibility in determining the nature of these systems and the principles by which they will operate – the systems may, for example, be funded by employers or by public authorities, or both (Article 5), though ultimately the state stands as guarantor for the claims to be met. States may themselves determine the trigger factors which end the period in respect of which claims may be made (Article 3), may place a limit on the amount able to be claimed (Article 4, subject to the amount being compatible with the social objective of the directive) and may exclude the claims of certain categories of employee.

The most recent amendments provide some clarification and upgrading of the protections offered by the directive. It makes clear, for example, that part-time, fixed-term or temporary workers may not be excluded, and it also introduces guidance (Article 8) on which country's guarantee institution will be responsible where the employees involved work for an undertaking which has a presence in more than one Member State, filling a gap previously encountered in Case C-117/96 *Mosbæk* v. *Lønmodtagernes Garantifond* ([1997] ECR I-5017) and Case C-198/98 *Everson* v. *Secretary of State for Industry* ([1999] ECR I-8903). Finally, any discussion of the Insolvency Directive must make reference to perhaps the most significant non-implementation of a directive, namely that of Italy, which resulted in the *Francovich* litigation and the establishment of the principle of state liability for breaches of Community law (Joined Cases C-6 and 9/90 *Francovich and Bonifaci* v.

*Italian Republic* [1991] ECR I-5357). Over fifteen years on, the UK's failure to properly implement the directive was at the heart of Case C-278/05 *Robins et al* v. *Secretary of State for Work and Pensions*, judgment of 25 January 2007. The Court ruled that, under the directive, where the employer is insolvent and the assets of the supplementary company or intercompany pension schemes are insufficient, accrued pension rights need not necessarily be funded by the Member States themselves or be funded in full. While finding that the UK's own system for protecting pension rights did not go far enough to comply with the directive, it suggested that this failure on the part of the state was not such as to render them liable in damages under the Francovich principles, owing in part to the lack of clarity in the relevant provisions of the directive.

## 16.9  Working Conditions

The EU has long been committed to the promotion of fair and just conditions at work and, indeed, rights to fair and just working conditions are included in the 2000 EU Charter (OJ 2000 C364/1), and in turn the Constitutional Treaty. Article 31 EU Charter contains a collection of specific rights, which, for the most part, reflect measures already adopted by the EU. These include, first, the right of every worker to working conditions which respect his or her health and safety. Mention has already been made to the extensive body of health and safety legislation adopted by the EU, including notably the Framework Directive 89/391, which, from a perspective of risk prevention, places a series of general obligations on both employers and employees to encourage improvements in workers' health and safety. This directive, along with its more specific daughter directives, filling in the detail on particular risks, has however been the source of a steady stream of enforcement actions before the Court of Justice. A recent string of cases for example has focused on Member States' incomplete transposition of the requirements of Article 7 on 'Protective and Preventative Services', which, *inter alia*, obliges employers to designate, and provide support for, qualified employees (or where not available, external services) to have responsibility for health and safety activities in the workplace (see Case C-49/00 *Commission* v. *Italy* [2001] ECR I-8575; Case C-441/01 *Commission* v. *Netherlands* [2003] ECR I-5463; Case C-335/02 *Commission* v. *Luxembourg* [2003] ECR I-5531). Previous actions, such as Case C-5/00 *Commission* v. *Germany* ([2002] ECR I-1305), dealt with the state's failure to respond fully to the Article 9 requirement that *all* employers have available a documentary assessment of the risks to safety and health at work.

It now appears that the period of intensive regulation in this sector is at an end, replaced by the general trend towards greater intervention through 'persuasive policy making' (Smismans 2003: 55), using 'soft law' mechanisms, most clearly signalled by the *Fourth Action Programme on Safety Hygiene and Health at Work* (COM(95) 282). As Smismans outlines, there have been significant difficulties in realising this soft law agenda. This he says is a result in large part of a lack of policy coherence and of a downgrading of the priority afforded to this policy area, which has seen significant funding redirected from DG EMPL to the Bilbao-based European Agency for Safety and Health Protection at Work (established by Council Regulation 2062/94, OJ L216/1). The Agency has a role in information-gathering and dissemination, and operates separately from the Commission. Perhaps significantly, the Agenda covering 2002–2006 (*Adapting to Change in Work and Society, A New Community Strategy on Health and Safety*, COM(2002) 118) promoted the mainstreaming of health and safety issues across other policy sectors, as financing and support for a separate unit dwindled. The strategy focuses on soft law procedures, as well as on improving the implementation of existing law. It declares that it places at its centre a 'global approach to well being at work', which includes a focus on risks of a 'psycho-social' nature, including harassment, stress and bullying, which feeds into the EU's contribution to generating conditions for the respect of another of the Charter's Rights, that of dignity at work (Article 31 Charter). This shift away from hard law interventions is continued in the Commission's Communication *Improving Quality and Productivity at Work: Community Strategy 2007–2012 on Health and Safety at Work* (COM(2007) 62).

## 16.10  Working Time

Article 31 of the EU Charter also provides that every worker has the right to a limitation of maximum working hours, daily and weekly rest periods, and to an annual period of paid leave. Each of these rights is contained in the provisions of the Working Time Directive, introduced in 1993, and amended in 2000 (Directive 2000/34) so as to cover previously excluded sectors and activities, including doctors in training, and transport workers, though a distinction in the levels of the protections for mobile and non-mobile workers in those sectors will remain. In principle, the directive provides for a daily rest period of 11 hours (Article 3), a weekly rest break of 24 hours, following on without interruption from the daily break (Article 5), a maximum 48 hour working week (Article 6), and four weeks' paid annual leave (Article 7). There are also special provisions concerning night work, shift work and patterns of work. The directive, notoriously, is riddled with exceptions and derogations, allowing Member States to derogate, in principle, from all but the Article 7 right to annual leave. This can be seen in Article 17(1) in respect of workers engaged in work the duration of which is not measured or predetermined, such as managing executives and family workers, as well as in Article 17(3), through the agreement of national- or regional-level social partners. Most remarkably, Article 18(1)(b) provides that the 48 hour maximum working week may be waived if the employer is able to gain the employee's express and freely given individual consent (agreement through collective agreement not being, by itself, sufficient: Joined Cases C-397–403/01 *Pfeiffer et al* v. *German Red Cross* [2004] ECR I-8835). Initially, only the UK made general use of this opt-out, though they were joined by Cyprus and Malta on their accession.

The continued existence of the opt-out is the most controversial of the matters being examined under the review of the directive, which began in 2004. Also under consideration is the issue of reference periods, which currently allow the 48 hour week total to be averaged over a four month period, as well as the concept of 'working time' itself. This last issue has come onto the agenda following a line of cases which have considered the issue of time spent on call, which is not explicitly addressed in the directive. The Court's response has generated serious difficulties in the field of health services, and has given rise to France, Germany and Spain operating the opt-out in this field.

The first of these cases (Case C-303/98 *SIMAP* v. *Conselleria de Sanidad y Consumo de la Generalidad Valenciana* [2000] ECR I-7963) concerned the interpretation of the directive's inclusion in its definition of working time – 'time spent at the employer's disposal'. Did this then cover time spent 'on call'? The Court ruled that if the on-call worker was required to be 'on site', then that on-call period should be counted as working time. If however the on-call period could be spent away from the place of work, this should not be counted as working time, but as rest time (the two being mutually exclusive), albeit that the worker has to remain contactable and ready to respond if called in. As Case C-151/02 *Landeshauptstadt Kiel* v. *Jaeger* ([2003] ECR I-8389) demonstrates, however, this approach has not been welcomed by the German system, and the Court was given the opportunity to revisit its test and exclude 'inactive' time spent on site and on call from the definition of working time. The Court was not prepared to accept this interpretation, ruling that the decisive factor in determining whether time on call is working time is whether workers are required to be present at the place determined by the employer and available to the employer in order to be able to provide their services immediately in case of need.

The proposed amendments (COM(2004) 607, and amended proposal COM(2005) 246) adopt this definition of on-call work, as the 'period during which the worker has the obligation to be available at the workplace to intervene, at the employer's request, to carry out his activity or duties'. The inactive part of on-call time will not constitute working time within the meaning of the directive, unless Member States, under national law or by agreement between the two sides of industry, elect otherwise. The Parliament, in its report from May 2005 (A6-0105/2005), indicated concerns about the impact on the health and safety of workers regularly on call, and further called for the phasing out of the individual opt-out. As of June 2007, agreement had still not been reached.

The Court has also been given a number of opportunities to rule on the issue of the right to annual leave. In Case C-124/05 *Federatie Nederlandse Vakbewegig* v. *Netherlands* ([2006] ECR I-3423), the Court ruled that leave cannot be replaced by payment in lieu for holiday that has not been taken. The purpose of annual leave is to contribute to the health and safety of the worker, by allowing for actual rest, and while it recognised that carrying over holiday entitlement into future years did not allow for the full protective effect of this provision to be deployed, the Court ruled that carrying over holidays to future years was permissible. Similarly, a concern with ensuring that actual rest is taken led the Court to find the practice of 'rolled-up' holiday pay incompatible with the directive. This refers to the practice of incorporating pay for periods of leave into workers' hourly or daily rate. Under this system, no wages are payable over the period that the worker is taking leave, a situation which may lead workers not to take the leave due to them (Joined Cases C-131 and 257/04 *Robinson-Steele* v. *R.D. Retail Service Limited* [2006] ECR I-2531).

In Case C-173/99 *R* v. *Secretary of State for Trade and Industry, ex parte BECTU* ([2001] ECR I-4881), the broadcasting union BECTU sought to challenge the UK's requirement that a thirteen week qualification period be worked with the same employer before the right to annual leave began to accrue. Many workers in this sector, employed on a succession of short-term contracts with different employers, were simply unable to qualify for paid annual leave. While Article 7(1) of the directive establishes that this right is to be provided in accordance with national law and practice, the national legislative qualification in this case was deemed to constitute an unlawful derogation from 'a particularly important principle of Community social law', a phrase it repeated in Case C-124/05 *Federatie Nederlandse Vakbewegig*. While not explicitly using the language of fundamental rights, it would appear that the Court was influenced by the opinion of Advocate General Tizzano, who turned to Article 31 of the EU Charter for 'the most reliable and definitive confirmation' that the right to annual leave is a 'fundamental social right', which must not be negated. Qualifications to this 'fundamental social right' were however in evidence in Case C-133/00 *Bowden* ([2001] ECR I-7031). While non-mobile transport workers were formally excluded from the protection of the directive under (former) Article 1(3) of the directive, the applicants (office workers employed in the road transport sector) and the national referring court, inspired by the human rights rhetoric in *BECTU* sought a 'just and purposive construction' of the directive, seeking to give effect to the fundamental right of every worker to annual paid leave, and avoid the 'significantly destructive' effect of the exemption. The opportunity to extend judicially the scope of the directive was rejected by both the Advocate General and the Court. Kenner has submitted that the judicial reluctance in this case stems from its respect for the Community legislator, which it was not prepared to override (2003b: 179). Far from being 'universal and automatic', the right to paid annual leave was thus time-limited by a narrow reading of the scope of Community legislation.

## 16.11  Atypical Work

As well as linking with the developing human rights discourse, over the course of the 1990s, the area of working time also became associated with the employment creation debate. According to a view already clearly apparent in the 1993 White Paper *Growth, Competitiveness and Employment* (COM(93) 700), by making available more flexible ways of organising working time and patterns of work, greater efficiency, productivity and competitiveness would be expected to result. Responding to the view that the 'flexibility' required by employers has to be balanced with 'security' for employees, the area of 'flexible' or 'atypical' work became a focus for legislative intervention.

Atypical work may be defined as employment falling outside the 'norm' of the open-ended, permanent contract, and would include part-time, fixed-term, temporary, seasonal and home work. The interest shown in atypical work by EU during the 1990s was by no means unprecedented. With the majority of workers in at least some of these categories being women, some engagement with atypical workers' rights was already occurring through the law on equality and non-discrimination. A series of proposals over the 1980s had sought to reduce recourse to atypical work forms, ostensibly from the perspective of preventing abuse of the workers involved (Jeffery, 1995). By the end of the decade, however, atypical work was becoming increasingly 'normalised' (Murray, 1999) and accepted. Again, attempts to introduce legislation were made, though this time the protections they offered were watered-down versions of previous attempts. A set of three related proposals was introduced on the back of the 1989 Community Charter, though only one, on non-discrimination in respect of the health and safety of temporary and part-time workers (Directive 91/383, OJ 1991 L206/19), was successfully adopted. The other measures, of which the proposal in COM(90) 228 was, in relative terms, the most ambitious, seeking equivalence for atypical workers across working conditions and social security protection, were blocked, the necessary unanimity proving impossible to attain (Jeffery, 1995).

This deadlock was in time overcome with the use of the social dialogue route to legislation. A first round of consultations on part-time, fixed-term and temporary work was held in 1995, by which time the debate was dominated by the link with employment creation (SEC(95) 1540/30). In turn, framework agreements on part-time and fixed-term work were concluded, and introduced as directives. These directives seek to establish the 'general principles and minimum requirements' which should apply to atypical work. A core principle common to both is that of non-discrimination in comparison with standard employees in respect to working conditions, though objectively justified differences in treatment would be permissible. Some additional protection is offered under the fixed-term directive, which seeks to prevent the abuse and overuse of such contracts of employment; however, as Murray submits, rather than offering real, enforceable protections, this provision 'is little more than a platform for national level bargaining' (Murray, 1999: 275). The Court's interpretations of the directive to date offer conflicting evidence of its protective potential. In Case C-144/04 *Mangold* v. *Held* ([2005] ECR I-9981; see also 15.2) the Court ruled that the directive's provisions, including the need to objectively justify the use of a fixed-term contract would not apply to the *first* fixed-term contract, concluded between worker and employer. In Case C-212/04 *Adeneler et al* v. *ELOG* ([2006] ECR I-6057), meanwhile, the Court's approach to the directive has been characterised as one that 'refuse[s] the language of employment policy . . . the Court does not seem willing to interpret the Fixed-Term Work Directive in the light of the employment objectives of adaptability and flexicurity' (Zappala, 2006: 440–1). Declaring that 'the benefit of stable employment is viewed as a major element in the protection of workers' the Court stated that 'it is only in certain circumstances that fixed-term employment contracts are liable to respond to the needs of both employers and workers'. The 'objective reasons' which must be advanced to justify the use of successive fixed-term contracts must thus relate to 'precise and concrete circumstances characterising a given activity'.

The third of the envisaged measures, on temporary work by agency workers, remains unadopted, following the breakdown in 2001 of social partner negotiations. The sticking point for the social partners was the identity of the comparator, the employers refusing to accept that terms and conditions of the temporary agency worker should be compared with those of a comparable worker in the host undertaking (Sargeant, 2002). Despite the Commission introducing a revised proposal for a Directive in 2002 (COM(2002) 701), support from the social partners has proved elusive, as has agreement between the states.

Finally, Directive 91/533 (OJ 1991 L288/31) provides that all workers with an employment contract or an employment relationship are to be supplied with a written statement of the terms and conditions applicable to their employment. According to the preamble of the directive, such transparency is designed to ensure that workers are in a better position to be able to identify possible infringements of their employment rights. Such protection, limited though it may be, may be excluded entirely for certain particularly vulnerable groups of workers, including casual workers, and those working less than one month or less than eight hours a week.

## 16.12　Posted Workers

With the opening-up of a free market for the provision of services, workers may find that they are temporarily posted to other states by their employers, to complete contracts for works. Cross-border contracting and subcontracting, and, with them, the posting of workers, are a particular feature of the construction industry (Cremers, 2006), but is also present in many other sectors. Directive 96/71 (1996 OJ L18/1), the Posted Workers Directive, aims to facilitate the cross-border provision of services while at the same time safeguard the rights and interests of the workers involved. The core principle is one of host state control – service providers may use their own workforce to complete contracts (as already established in Case C-113/89 *Rush Portuguesa Lda* v. *Office Nationale d'Immigration*

[1990] ECR I-1417) but must comply with the employment law operating in the host state where the contract is being performed.

The directive was adopted under Articles 47 and 55 EC, provisions on free movement, rather than under the employment law title of the Treaty. Article 3 of the directive sets out the terms and conditions which must be guaranteed in accordance with the host state provisions when employees are temporarily posted outside the country in which they are habitually employed. These terms and conditions include working time, paid leave, non-discrimination, health and safety, and minimum rates of pay. Member States may implement these employment rights by law, regulation or administrative provision (Article 3), or, as regards the construction industry, through collective agreement. More favourable terms and conditions than the minima are not precluded.

The directive provides that certain payments should be excluded from consideration in calculating the minimum wage (including overtime payments and contributions to supplementary occupational pension schemes, Article 3(7)). In Case C-341/02 *Commission* v. *Germany* ([2005] ECR I-2733) the Court held that Germany had unlawfully excluded certain other allowances payable by the employer posting the workers from its calculations of whether the minimum pay rates were being met. Thus the 'minimum wage' payable by employers for these workers would be higher than the German minimum wage. At issue in Case C-60/03 *Wolff and Müller* v. *Pereira Felix* ([2004] ECR I-9553), meanwhile, was national legislation which made the local undertakings receiving posted workers guarantors for the pay due to these workers. Assessments of the value of the guarantor scheme are mixed; while they may offer some protection, they do require a worker who has most likely returned to the home state to bring an action in the host state. Further, the German rules, rather than being aimed at protecting posted workers, were stated as having the objective of making it more onerous to enter into contracts with 'cheap-labour' countries. The obligations imposed under the guarantor system were challenged as being incompatible with Article 49 EC Treaty. The Court of Justice highlighted the significance of the Posted Workers Directive, and particularly Article 5 thereof, which provides that 'adequate procedures are available to workers and/or their representatives for the enforcement of obligations under this Directive'. It ruled that the guarantor system was not precluded by the directive as it could be a meaningful mechanism for enforcement.

Not all countries provide for a statutory minimum wage. In Sweden, for example, wages are set by industry-wide collective agreement. In the construction industry, this main agreement is between the trade union, Byggnads, and the Swedish Construction Federation on the employers' side. For employers who are not members of the Construction Federation, including many foreign employers, individual 'application agreements' are signed with the union. In Case C-341/05 *Laval un Partneri Ltd* v. *Svenska Byggnadsarbetareforbundet*, judgment pending, the Latvian company posting workers to Sweden to complete a building contract, Laval, had not signed an application agreement, and were not paying their workers in line with Swedish collectively agreed rates. As is the norm – and entirely lawful – under the Swedish system, the failure to sign an application agreement or to meet Swedish wage standards resulted in a series of industrial actions by Swedish unions. The *Laval* action considers the Swedish implementation of the directive and its apparent failure to give full effect to the minimum wage requirements, and, more fundamentally, questions the lawfulness of the industrial action in the light of EU law on provisions of services and the Posted Workers Directive.

Woolfson and Sommers report that the Latvian workers involved in the *Laval* action were receiving roughly twice the pay that they would have been in Latvia, in addition to receiving their meals and accommodation. This was still substantially less than Swedish workers were receiving (2006: 54). Significant wage differentials exist between the old and new Member States, and some in the EU-15 have been concerned that measures such as the Posted Workers Directive are insufficiently robust to ensure that their domestic undertakings and workers are not priced out by the new Member States. Two Member States, Austria and Germany, have put in place transitional provisions, which place restrictions on the ability of service providers from the new states to post workers. The restrictions are particularly severe in respect of the construction industry. Permits for workers to be posted will only be issued once a series of conditions have been met. These include the target company in the host state demonstrating that economic and employment market reasons mean that no local workforce is available, and that the posting of workers will not affect the salary and working conditions of local workers.

Assessments of the directive are not altogether positive: as Barnard submits (2006: 288–9), if the measure is supposed to facilitate free movement, the principle of host, rather than home state control imposes a set of additional burdens on service providers. If its aim is to harmonise costs and avoiding social dumping, the setting of terms and conditions at minimum levels renders this unlikely. Barnard concludes that the directive is rather more successful as an employment protection measure. However, as the Commission has reported, there have been significant problems with monitoring and enforcing the directive, which has resulted in the directive's effectiveness being somewhat limited. Rather than amending the legislation, however, the Commission proposes a stronger emphasis on monitoring and information provisions (Commission, 2006, *Commission's services report on the implementation of Directive 96/71 concerning the posting of workers in the framework of the provision of services*, SEC(2006) 439).

## 16.13   Collective Labour Law

Traditionally, the Member States of the European Union have shown a remarkable diversity in their approaches to collective labour law, that is, of their mechanisms for the representation, promotion and defence of the interests of workers as a collective body, within the enterprise in which they work. In some states, for example, worker representatives have a place within the management structures of the company, as with the two-tier board system of the German co-determination model, which sees worker representatives sitting on a supervisory board, overseeing the work of a management board. In addition to such board-level participation, workers' interests may also be represented through unions and other representative institutions, such as works councils. Through these various mechanisms, the representatives of workers may engage in industrial relations with management and employees, involving, at one end of the spectrum, the receipt of information and consultation, negotiation, and on to involvement more usually undertaken by trades union, such as bargaining, and the collective defence of workers' interests by means of strike action (see further Barnard, 2006).

The Commission in particular has long professed its support for the increased involvement of workers and their representatives in the decision-making processes in undertakings; indeed, this was one of the objectives of the 1974 Social Action Programme. However, very few of the legislative proposals issued in the 1970s were successfully adopted. A divergence in the approaches taken to worker involvement proposals was already apparent at that time. On the one hand are measures which are more 'company law' in nature, which seek to determine the balance of power between the organs of the enterprise – between management, shareholders and workers, and establish a role for the latter in the corporate structure which is not formally recognised in all Member States. This type of involvement is generally referred to as *participation*. On the other hand are 'employment law'-type measures, which do not seek to fundamentally reorder corporate structures or to challenge the managerial decision-making prerogative, but which seek nonetheless to provide for worker involvement through *information and consultation* rights exercised through unions, works councils and the like (Kenner, 2003b: 64). While both models were being pursued through a range of proposals over the 1970s and 1980s, only the employment law approach saw the successful adoption of legislation, in the form of the information and consultation provisions of the Collective Redundancy Directive and the Acquired Rights Directive.

## 16.14    European Works Councils Directive

Following the Community's initial incursion into the area of worker involvement, there was then a prolonged period during which a number of proposals, such as the 1980 Vredeling proposal for information and consultation processes for those working in subsidiaries of multinational companies, were blocked by the unanimity requirement in Council. The same concern for the possible remoteness of workers from increasingly transnational corporate decision-making which lay behind the Vredeling proposal was to resurface, this time with some success, in the proposal for a Directive on European Works Councils. Previously stalled in Council, the EWC Directive proposal was to be the first measure considered under the newly minted social dialogue route of the Maastricht Social Policy Agreement; however, little common ground could be found between the two sides of industry and the proposal fell. It was reintroduced under the legislative route of the SPA and adopted by qualified majority voting in 1994 (94/45, OJ 1994 L254/64), and then readopted to cover the UK in 1997 (97/74, OJ 1997 L10/20), following its decision to 'opt-back-in'. The EWC Directive applies to 'Community-scale undertakings', that is, undertakings (and groups of undertakings) which have operations employing at least 1000 workers across the EU, and with a presence in at least two Member States, with at least 150 workers in each. In Case C-62/99 *Works Council of Bofrost\* v. Bofrost\** ([2001] ECR I-2579) , the Court ruled that the directive requires all undertakings in a group to supply workers with the necessary information about employee numbers in other parts of the group, to enable them to determine whether there are sufficient numbers for the establishment of a EWC. In Case C-440/00 *Central Works Council of Kühne and Nagel v. Kühne and Nagel* ([2004] ECR I-787) it was further held that where central management is located outside the geographical coverage of the directive (in this case, in Switzerland), the EU/EEA-based undertaking which operates as 'deemed central management', and thus legally responsible for the EWC process, must provide the information necessary for the opening of negotiations for a EWC, such as total number and geographical distribution of employees, the corporate structure of the undertakings, and the names and addresses of employee representatives. If 'true' central management refuses to provide this information to 'deemed' central management, the latter must request this information directly from each EU/EEA-based undertaking in the group, and these are under an obligation to respond.

Where the necessary thresholds are met (and where no existing transnational information and consultation procedure exists), a special negotiating body will be convened from the workers' representatives of the different establishments, which may, in agreement with central management, determine the composition of the Works Council, its scope, function, and the processes for information and consultation. The directive contains a set of default provisions which will apply should agreement not be reached. According to these, at least once a year the Works Council, comprising between 3 and 30 members, should be consulted by central management on issues relating to the undertaking's business and its prospects. In 'exceptional' situations, including relocations, restructurings and redundancies, the Works Council has the right to be informed, and to meet with central management. However, as the directive states, 'this meeting shall not affect the prerogatives of central management'. Indeed, recent research has revealed that in a majority of multinationals surveyed that consulted their EWC on restructurings, the impact of the process of consultation was described by central management as 'low to non-existent' (*ORC European Works Councils Survey 2002*). Of course, the absence of a quantifiable impact on the outcomes should not be taken as a 'failure' of the EWC, as there is undoubtedly a real value in workers and their representatives being kept informed of company developments which may affect them. However, it is reckoned that only 40 per cent of the 1800 companies or groups which are of a size to fall within the scope of the directive have Works Councils, and even among those that do, too often there have been high-profile cases of the EWC requirements being ignored altogether, as with Vilvoorde, and the ABB-Alstom closures, which both feature in a Report and Resolution from the European Parliament (A5-0282/2001) which calls on the Commission to take swift action to tighten up the requirements of the directive, a call echoed by the ETUC. The Commission began the first stages of consultation on the revision of the directive in April 2004, having elected to hold back action in this area until after the successful adoption of a number of related proposals, although support for legislative revision from UNICE has not been forthcoming.

**16.15   Other Collective Law Measures**

One of the related proposals, which may be regarded as the national-level sister to the EWC, is Council Directive 2002/14 (OJ 2002 L80/29) establishing a general framework for informing and consulting employees. The directive requires all undertakings with at least 50 employees, or establishment with 20, to put in place and operate systems of worker information and consultation, covering such issues as business operations, employment trends and changes in work organisation. The directive is in no way prescriptive about the form, composition or procedures of these systems, leaving the practical arrangements 'to be defined and implemented in accordance with national law and industrial relations practices' (Article 1(2)). The directive does not explicitly specify that information and consultation must take place in advance of any decision, only that timing, as well as method and content, must be 'appropriate' (Article 4(4)). The directive will be of most significance to those countries without a general, permanent system of worker information and consultation – in short, the UK and Ireland, who have negotiated a staggered implementation date, allowing them until 2009 to fully comply with the directive's requirements.

A similar light touch and flexibility in approach also made possible the adoption of more company law-based worker involvement measures. One of these, the European

Company Statute, was finally adopted in 2001, thirty years after the original proposal was made. One of the sticking points for the 'European Company' had been the issue of worker involvement, and strong opposition from some quarters to the requirement for a two-tier board with mandatory worker participation along the lines of the German model. The deadlock was finally broken following the separating out of the employee involvement provisions into a separate directive (Council Directive 2001/86, OJ 2001 L294/22), which offers Member States a rather complex range of options, extending from full worker participation on a two-tier or unitary board, through to no worker participation at all, if that was the system under which the companies coming together to create a new 'European Company' operated (for more detail see Edwards, 2003; P. Davies, 2003). While worker participation in the company law sense may be absent, worker involvement in the information and consultation sense is required, either in a form negotiated by management and a SNB, or through a EWC, or by means of the relevant national arrangements. Certain of the standard provisions, such as that on the definition of consultation, appear more demanding than those in the existing EWC, and may in turn come to form part of the revised EWC. Nonetheless, the provisions have been viewed by some as offering prospects for employee participation which are 'cosmetic rather than real' (Villiers, 2006: 186). The same basic approach of the worker involvement provisions of the European Company Statute has also been followed in the recently adopted measures on a European Cooperative Society.

From this upsurge in activity in the field of worker involvement, and with recent soft law measures such as the strategies on corporate social responsibility (COM(2002) 347), the message from the Commission seems clear. Employees have a key role to play as one of the stakeholders of the company, employers have a social responsibility to them, and at core is the promotion of the idea of partnership – for both social and economic wellbeing. In terms of transferring these ideas into legal obligations, the Commission has had to be pragmatic and respond to what is both legally and politically possible. It should be pointed out that certain collective labour law issues remain explicitly excluded from Community competence, particularly those which are closely associated to the operation of trades union, such as the right of association and the right to strike (Article 137(6) EC Treaty). This situation may seem paradoxical given the significant role afforded to unions in the social dialogue process and, indeed, the inclusion of these rights in the 2000 EU Charter of Fundamental Rights (Articles 12 and 28) (and, in turn, the Constitutional Treaty), albeit subject to the usual rider of being in accordance with Community law and national laws and practices (Ryan, 2003) (see Case C-341/05 *Laval un Partneri Ltd*, discussed at 16.12).

### 16.16    Employment Policy

By the mid-1990s, the issue of unemployment had moved centre stage. The proportion of the working age population in employment had dropped to around 60 per cent, some 14 per cent behind that of the US. Such a situation impacts negatively on social cohesion, it brings increasing pressures onto national welfare systems, and the combined pressures could bring insuperable problems for the successful operation of EMU. Thus the EU had a clear interest in involving itself in policies to generate employment growth. The EC already had some policy tools at its disposal to do this – in the form of the structural funds and, in particular, the European Social Fund which continues to support vocational training programmes and other 'supply' side employment policies. As Barnard and Deakin report, there was some discussion about adopting a demand-side approach to employment creation, through the centralised funding of public works which would create new employment opportunities, however the necessary political and, importantly, financial support from the Member States was not forthcoming (1999: 356).

Instead, the approach adopted has been one of the coordination of Member States' own employment policies around a set of commonly agreed objectives. This process, referred to as the European Employment Strategy (or the Luxembourg process, after the site of the 1997 Summit meeting at which the Strategy was launched), has attracted considerable academic interest, as much for the technique of governance employed here as for substantive policy content. The EES is seen as the archetypal form of the Open Method of Coordination – 'radical subsidiarity' in action (Hodson and Maher, 2001: 719), multi-level governance by persuasion, without legal sanctions for non-compliance. For some, it is a breakthrough approach in which otherwise intractable problems may be addressed and solutions found (de la Porte, 2002). For others, the soft law approach is at best unlikely to bring about real change and, at worst, a dangerous precedent which threatens the continuation of the European social model (Degryse and Pochet, cited in Mosher and Trubek, 2003: 64). The direct origins of the EES can in fact be traced back to the 1994 Essen Summit, where a number of common objectives were first set, and the Commission assigned an annual monitoring role. The more structured and formalised EES is now contained in the EC Treaty, at Articles 125–130 EC.

The coordination process under the EES is directed to the goal of developing a high level of employment (Article 127 EC) and, in particular, promoting a 'skilled, trained and adaptable workforce and labour markets responsive to economic change' (Article 125). Article 128 EC sets out the framework for its operation: Employment Guidelines are set at the EU level, on the basis of which Member States draw up their National Action Plans for Employment. Performance in achieving the aims of the National Action Plans is reported to, and reviewed by, the Commission and Council in their Joint Employment Report. This report feeds into the next set of Guidelines, which include benchmarking targets and indicators, and the Council may also issue non-binding Recommendations to individual Member States.

Initially the Guidelines were set annually and, by 2002, after a Commission review of five years of the EES operation (COM(2002) 487), the timing of the process was brought into line with the economic policy coordination process, operating through the Broad Economic Policy Guidelines. This coordinated process is designed to be less short-term in its focus, and more stable and predictable. It was taken a stage further following the 2005 relaunch of the Lisbon Process, with its renewed refocus on employment and economic growth. From 2005, the guidelines for the EES and the BEPG were issued as an integrated package, and operate over a three year period. The key objectives for the EES are first, full employment, second, quality and productivity at work, and finally, cohesion and inclusion (Council Decision 2005/600, OJ 2005 L205/21). The inclusion of the second objective of *quality* work may be seen as crucial from the perspective of reconciling employment law and employment policy. As was initially pointed out by commentators, the EES, subordinated under Article 127 EC to the economic process, was more concerned with quantity, not quality of work (Ball, 2001). The initial Guidelines had been focused on four 'pillars': improving employability, developing entrepreneurship, encouraging adaptability and equal opportunities. The Guidelines' concern with increasing flexibility and adaptability arguably paid insufficient regard to the need to ensure security for workers. Thus, it could be suggested that the EES provided limited space and support for the development of protective employment law. The clear articulation of the 'quality in work' agenda, a central component of the Social Policy Agendas from 2000 (see further Kenner, 2003b: 491) in respect of the EES, provides a signal that normatively there is support for a balanced reconciliation between the goals of employment law and employment policy.

## Summary

1. Employment *law* refers to the collection of individual and collective rights granted to workers; employment *policy* refers to policy interventions (generally non-legislative) which seek to generate employment and combat unemployment. The EU has a role to play in both.

2. While the original Treaty of Rome mentioned improvement of working conditions, it was assumed that the functioning of the market would deliver this and legislative intervention would not be required. No specific legal bases for the introduction of employment law measures were set out in the original Treaty.

3. The 1974 Social Action Programme instigated a legislative programme which used the general law-making bases of Articles 94 and 308 for the introduction of measures. Early directives included protective measures and information and consultation rights in the event of company restructurings.

4. The Member States have very different industrial relations and employment law traditions. This has been a factor in the rather limited development of both individual and collective law measures.

5. The first specific legal base for the introduction of employment law measures was introduced by the Single European Act amendments. It allowed for the adoption of health and safety measures by qualified majority voting. As well as allowing for a significant body of 'traditional' health and safety measures, this base has also been used for the adoption of measures whose direct connection with health and safety has been contested, notably the Working Time Directive.

6. The European-level representatives of the two sides of industry – the social partners – are involved in the law-making process. Indeed, they may reach agreements as an alternative to the introduction of standard legislative measures.

7. An extensive range of employment law rights are contained in the 2000 EU Charter. The European Court, while generally providing a strongly employee-protective interpretation of employment law provisions, has yet to explicitly use the Charter.

8. The employment law field has been at the vanguard of the move towards alternative, non-legislative forms of governance.

9. Enlargement poses particular issues for European employment law. The countries of central and eastern Europe have distinctive employment law traditions, and have a less developed framework for the involvement of social partners.

10. The European Employment Strategy, formalised by the Amsterdam Treaty amendments, provides a framework for the coordination of Member States' employment policies.

# Exercises

1. Why does the EU have competence in the field of employment law? Trace, and account for, the evolution of EU competences in this area, from the original EEC Treaty to the present day.

2. Outline the different ways in which EU employment law can be made. Assess these routes in terms of their democratic legitimacy, and any other standard(s) you believe is/(are) important for law-making to respect. Should the social dialogue route become the standard law-making route in this area?

3. Distinguish between 'individual' and 'collective' employment law. In which area has the EU had greatest impact? Why?

4. How have the different EU human/fundamental rights documents dealt with employment law issues? What are the possible implications of this 'fundamental rights' dimension for the development of employment law?

5. What are the tensions between the objectives of employment law and employment policy? Are they reconcilable?

## Further Reading

Ball, S. (2001) 'The European Employment Strategy: The Will but not the Way?', 30 *Industrial Law Journal* 353.

Barnard, C. (2002) 'The Social Partners and the Governance Agenda', 8 *European Law Journal* 80.

Barnard, C. (2006) *EC Employment Law* (3rd edn), Oxford: Oxford University Press.

Hervey, T. and Kenner, J. (eds.) (2003) *Economic and Social Rights under the EU Charter of Fundamental Rights: A Legal Perspective*, Oxford: Hart Publishing.

Kenner, J. (2003) *EU Employment Law: From Rome to Amsterdam and Beyond*, Oxford: Hart Publishing.

Mosher, J. and Trubek, D. (2003) 'Alternative Approaches to Governance in the EU: European Social Policy and the European Employment Strategy', 41 *Journal of Common Market Studies* 63.

Shaw, J. (ed.) (2000) *Social Law and Policy in an Evolving European Union*, Oxford: Hart Publishing.

Smismans, S. (2007) 'The European Social Dialogue between Constitutional and Labour Law', 32 *European Law Review*, forthcoming.

Woolfson, C. and Sommers, J. (2006) 'Labour Mobility in Construction: European Implications of the *Laval un Partneri* Dispute with Swedish Labour', 12 *European Journal of Industrial Relations* 49.

## Key Websites

The website of the relevant Directorate-General, DG EMPL, contains labour law documentation, including texts of legislative measures, implementation reports and commission communications:
**http://ec.europa.eu/employment_social/index_en.html**

For health and safety at work issues, visit the website of the Bilbao-based European Agency for safety and health at work:
**http://osha.europa.eu/OSHA**

## Key Websites cont'd

The European Foundation for the Improvement of Living and Working Conditions' mission is to provide information, advice and expertise for key actors in the field of EU social policy on the basis of comparative information, research and analysis. Its site is at:
**http://www.eurofound.europa.eu**

The European Foundation's European Industrial Relations Observatory provides information on labour law and industrial relations developments at EU and national level, and features comparative reports on specific topics:
**http://eurofound.europa.eu/eiro**

# Chapter 17

# Environmental Law and Policy

Introduction

The year 2007 not only marked the fiftieth anniversary of the Treaty of Rome, but also thirty-five years of a European Union environmental policy. The starting point was the call from the Heads of State and Government at the 1972 Paris Summit to embark on action in the environmental sphere, as part of its more general emphasis on broadening out the integration process beyond economic concerns (Bull. EC 10-1972). This led in 1973 to the adoption of the First of the Environmental Action Programmes which establish the Union's policy priorities. In 2002 the Sixth and most recent of the Action Programmes was adopted, which sets the framework for action until 2012. Over the intervening years, the EU has witnessed the development of a significant body of environmental legislation, ranging over fields such as air quality and climate change, industrial accidents, noise pollution, water quality, waste management, nature protection and animal welfare. Treaty competences for environmental law and policy have been introduced, strengthened and expanded over successive Treaty revisions; an extensive body of case law has been built up; and Article 6 EC provides as a constitutional principle that environmental protection requirements must be integrated into the definition and implementation of all Community policies, in particular with a view to promoting sustainable development.

The original Paris Summit's call, and much action since, has been in response to international developments and commitments. The immediate impetus to the actions of the early 1970s was the 1972 United Nations Conference on Human Environment in Stockholm. Over the years, the EC has participated in negotiations and entered into, as a party or a signatory, a range of agreements at global level (multilateral agreements agreed under the auspices of the UN), regional level (in the context of the United Nations Economic Commission for Europe) and subregional level (relating to the management of seas and transboundary rivers). Notable measures would include the UN Framework Convention on Climate Change (1992), the Kyoto Protocol (1997), the Aarhus Convention (1998) on Access to Environmental Information, Public Participation in Decision Making and Access to Justice in Environmental Matters, and the Rio Convention on Biological Diversity (1992) and the Cartagena Biosafety Protocol (2000). Such measures, on which the EC has sometimes taken the lead, have had a significant influence on the contours of EU environmental policy.

With the EU an increasingly important international actor in environmental matters, and playing a critical role in Member States' own environmental policies through a range of legal and non-law interventions, environmental law and policy could be seen as one of the EU's success stories. According to the European Environment Agency's Report *The European Environment – State and Outlook 2005*, much has been done to improve the EU's environment. Ozone-depleting CFCs have been phased out, lead removed from petrol, waterways are recovering from pollution through increasing treatment of urban waste water, and ecosystems are being maintained through the protection of natural areas.

However, there is limited cause for celebration. Key environmental challenges remain, and the progress that has been made in terms of legislative responses has not always resulted in effective improvements on the ground. While many hundreds of pieces of legislation have been adopted in the field of the environment, there remains a stubborn implementation gap. This is reflected in the fact that over 20 per cent of all direct enforcement actions brought by the Commission under the Article 226 procedure in 2005 were in respect of environmental law, and by the end of that year, 77 cases against Member States were open for non-compliance with a previous judgment of the Court (Commission, *Seventh Annual Survey on the implementation and enforcement of EU environmental law*, SEC(2006) 1143). The Commission does not simply look to better enforcement and implementation however. Instead, as with employment law and social policy, the environmental sphere is one where there has been a shift to alternatives to traditional top-down regulation. The search for more effective measures has involved the design and deployment of an innovative array of governance tools.

The objectives of EU environmental policy are set out in Article 174(1) EC Treaty. These are:

▷ preserving, protecting and improving the quality of the environment;
▷ protecting human health;
▷ prudent and rational utilisation of natural resources; and
▷ promoting measures at international level to deal with regional or worldwide environmental problems.

Article 175 EC provides the main legal bases, both for the adoption of the Action Programmes (Article 175(3)) and for legislation. Co-decision is the standard law- making route, except for certain areas listed in Article 175(2), including provisions primarily of a fiscal nature, and measures affecting town and country planning. Article 176 EC provides that Member States may maintain or introduce more stringent protective measures than those introduced under Article 175. The current priorities outlined in the Sixth Action Programme (Parliament and Council Decision 1600/2002, OJ 2002 L242/1) are tackling climate change; action in the field of nature and biodiversity; action on environment and health and quality of life; and action on the sustainable use and management of natural resources and wastes. The implementation of the programme is supported by a financial instrument for the environment (LIFE) first introduced in 1992, and new refocused and rebranded as LIFE+ for the period 2007–2013. LIFE+ supports co-financing projects in Member States which address aspects of environmental policy development, implementation, monitoring, evaluation and communication.

This chapter will begin with a presentation of the historical development of EU environmental protection (17.2–17.5), and then turn to an examination of the core principles which underpin activity in this sphere (17.6–7.10) and the integration of concerns with the environmental dimension of sustainable development across the other policy areas, and the interface of these policy areas with environmental law (17.11). An overview of the tools of governance used in environmental policy is provided in 17.12 and 17.13, while 17.14 and 17.15 discuss implementation and enforcement issues, and the chapter closes at 17.16 with a consideration of public participation in environmental law governance.

## 17.2　Stages in the Development of EU Environmental Law

While the Paris Summit of 1972 is generally marked as the start date of the EU's engagement with environmental policy, the Community had in fact already introduced its first pieces of legislation with an environmental dimension by this date: Council Directive 67/548 on classification, packaging and labelling of dangerous substances (OJ 1967 L196/1) and Council Directive 70/220 on air pollution by emissions from motor vehicles (OJ 1970 L76/21). However, 1972 is the date when the first attempts at creating a coherent policy on the environment were made. The early measures were closely linked with the market project, with the objective of standardising national rules in the interests of market integration. For example, Council Directive 70/220 can be justified in these terms as differences between Member States on permissible emission levels from vehicles which could result in a barrier to trade. This market focus would dominate the first decade or so, as a reflection of the political will of the states and institutions, and of the legal bases available. With no explicit Treaty-based competence in environmental matters, these were the internal market base of Article 94 EC and the general catch-all Article 308 EC, both requiring unanimity.

Covering the years 1973–1976, the First Environmental Action Programme (1973 OJ C122/1) was expressed in general terms, defining principles and policy objectives. The principles enunciated in this programme have continued to have a powerful influence over action in this policy sphere, and beyond. The Action Programme principles include an expression of the subsidiarity principle – that action should be taken at the most appropriate level – which would later be incorporated in the EC Treaty as a constitutional principle applying to all EC activity (Article 5 EC). The choice of the appropriate level of action in environmental protection may be crucial. It is often the case that international action is vital in order to provide the most effective remedy against environmental damage: pollution, as the truism goes, does not respect borders. However, local knowledge or expertise is often critical in order to solve particular environmental problems, localised habitats in particular. In addition, as Scott highlights, environmental protection, particularly when it is perceived as standing in the way of economic development and job creation, can prove to be a significant flashpoint for local disagreements (Scott, 1998a: 3). These need to be treated sensitively, and the apparent imposition of rulings from 'Brussels' can raise important questions of legitimacy. Other principles in the Programme would later find their way into the Environmental Title of the EC Treaty: the preventive principle; the principle that damage should be rectified at source; and the principle that the polluter should pay. These are now to be found at Article 174(2) EC, along with the precautionary principle, and the principles that Community policy shall aim at a high level of protection, taking into account the diversity of situations in the various regions of the Community (see 17.6–17.10). Other principles in the Programme included that scientific knowledge should be improved to enable action to be taken, and that environmental policy must take into account the interests of developing nations.

The Second Environmental Action Programme (OJ 1977 C139/1), again covering a relatively short time span (1977–1981), was in many ways a continuation of the first. The concern with market integration and the elimination of trade barriers continued, although directives with less explicitly economic objectives were also passed. Council Directive 78/659 (OJ 1978 L222/1), the Freshwater Fish Directive, was based on Articles 94 and 308

EC, the recourse to Article 308 reflecting its broader objectives, and Council Directive 79/409 (OJ 1979 L103/1), the Wild Birds Directive, based on Article 308 EC alone. Both focused on the need to protect the habitats of certain species, particularly rare or endangered species. Council Directive 75/440 (OJ 1975 L194/26), the Drinking Water Directive (now replaced, see 17.12) and the Bathing Water Directive (Council Directive 76/160, OJ 1976 L031/1, see also European Parliament and Council Directive 2006/7, OJ 2006 L64/1), were both based on Articles 94 and 308 together, and were concerned with the control of water pollution.

Over the 1970s, the environmental movement was beginning to establish itself as a political force, and reflections at the supranational level included the Commission's support for the establishment of a peak-level environmental interest group, the European Environmental Bureau, an umbrella group covering environmental NGOs. The EEB began and continues to play an important lobbying function, alongside the various producer and industry groups, as well as a role in monitoring and reporting infringements of environmental law.

The 1980s witnessed an important evolution in EU environmental policy. The decade began with the launch of the World Conservation Strategy, prepared by the world's leading conservation agencies. It identified three main priorities: maintaining Earth's ability to support life; preserving genetic diversity by preventing the extinction of species; and ensuring sustainable utilisation of species and ecosystems. Again, such international developments were to have an impact on the policy priorities of the EU, and with the Third Action Programme, covering 1982–1986 (OJ 1983 C46/1), there came a new focus on conservation of resources. The early 1980s also witnessed an increased presence and growing influence of environmental interests within the institutions. Environmental matters had been dealt with since the 1970s by a 'service' of the Commission; this was now incorporated into a separate Directorate-General and became better resourced. Growing public awareness and concern with environmental matters saw the arrival in the European Parliament of the first green party members, and the European Court, in 1985, took the opportunity in Case 240/83 *Procureur de la République* v. *Association de défense des brûleurs d'huiles usagées (ADBHU)* ([1985] ECR 531) to declare that environmental protection was 'one of the Community's essential objectives.'

## 17.3 The Single European Act: A Self-Standing Environmental Competence

Chalmers (1999: 666) points to the emergence during the 1980s of an environmental law community, whose academic work in the area impacted on the development of the definition of a separate politico-legal identity for the policy area. In combination with the other pressures growing over the decade, this contributed to the incorporation of a self-standing competence in environmental matters for the EC, brought about by the Single European Act. The revised EC Treaty contained a separate legal base for environmental protection matters, and made it an objective in its own right, rather than an add-on to the single market. Current Articles 174, 175 and 176 EC were introduced as Articles 130r, s and t. Law-making was, at this stage, to be by unanimity in Council. This development, however, was not welcomed unreservedly. Chalmers has criticised the existence of a separate Title for Environmental Policy on the grounds that environmental policy can only be effective if it is integrated with other policies, such as economic and industrial policies.

The creation of a new Title could have the effect of isolating environmental policy, when it really should be operating within the context of the internal market (Chalmers, 1995). Such concerns about the integration of environmental interests across all policy domains are a continuing theme, and surfaced immediately in the Fourth Action Programme (1987–1992, OJ 1987 C328/1).

The Fourth Action Programme refined and developed the work done in the previous three Programmes. It made clear that environmental policy must play a part in as many areas of EC activity as possible, and it drew particular attention to the increasing problem of defective implementation by Member States, and of the difficulties faced by new members of the Community in conforming to the increasingly strict standards that were being set. With the emphasis of the SEA being on the completion of the internal market by the target date of 1992, it is unsurprising that the Fourth Programme retained a clear link with the market project, and environmental policy was presented as contributing to the economic success of the EC. This market link meant that there was scope for measures to continue to be introduced under the market-making general bases, rather than under the new specific base in Article 130s. The SEA had introduced a new general legal base, formerly Article 100a, now Article 95 EC, applying to measures with the object of establishment and functioning of the internal market, and requiring only a qualified majority in the Council for legislation to be passed. As a result, the Commission adopted a tactic of proposing environmental measures, wherever possible, based on Article 100a rather than on Article 130s, to overcome the latter's unanimity requirement. This tactic was challenged in the *Titanium Dioxide* case (Case C-300/89 *Commission* v. *Council* [1991] ECR I-2867). Council Directive 89/428 (OJ 1989 L201/56), on the harmonisation of the programmes for treatment of waste from the titanium dioxide industry, was originally proposed under Article 100a, but the Council forced a change in legal base to Article 130. The Commission then challenged the validity of the directive under the (current) Article 230 EC judicial review procedure, arguing that the directive should have been passed under Article 100a. The Court agreed. As Scott shows, the Court makes a good case for using Article 100a as a base for environmental action, but not for the necessity of using it in preference to the *lex specialis* of Article 130 (Scott, 1998a: 8–9). The decision in *Titanium Dioxide* has generally been interpreted as a pragmatic decision of the Court, demonstrating a clear commitment by the Court of Justice to move environmental policy forward.

By the end of the 1980s, according to some reckonings, around 200 pieces of legislation had been adopted. Some focused on market integration, others responded to environmental issues that had caught the public imagination, such as measures on air quality in response to acid rain (Council Directive 88/609 on limitation of emissions from large combustion plants OJ 1988 L336/1, see now European Parliament and Council Directive 2001/80, OJ 2001 309/1) and, following a massive release of toxic dioxins from an industrial plant at Seveso near Milan in 1978, the Major Accidents Directive (Council Directive 82/501 OJ 1982 L230/1, now replaced by Council Directive 96/82, OJ 1997 L10/13). The first Environmental Impact Assessment (EIA) Directive was adopted during this decade (85/337, OJ 1985 L175/40). The directive (later amended by Council Directive 97/11, OJ 1997 L73/5, and European Parliament and Council Directive 2003/35, OJ 2003 L156/17) requires an examination of the environmental effects of a wide range of infrastructural, industrial, mineral extraction works and other projects before work is permitted to take place. For some projects, such as the building of dams or motorways,

EIA is obligatory. EIAs are to take into account the impact of proposed works on human beings, fauna and flora, on soil, water, air, climate and the landscape, and on material assets and the cultural heritage. The directive also provides for public information and consultation over these matters, and these aspects in particular have been strengthened over the years. The directive has proved a significant source of litigation, both in terms of Commission enforcement proceedings under Article 226 and before national courts.

## 17.4 Environmental Policy after Maastricht

In terms of environmental policy, the first notable event of the 1990s was the 1990 Declaration by the Dublin European Council on the Environmental Imperative (Bull. EC 6-1990, 17). The European Council recognised the ongoing and increasing threats being posed to the state of the environment, and indeed to the continuation of life. A commitment to intensify efforts to 'protect and enhance the natural environment and of the Community itself and the world of which it is part' was made, through a policy developed on a coordinated basis, and on the principles of sustainable development and preventive and precautionary action. The possibility of interventions other than traditional 'command and control' regulatory approaches were highlighted, especially economic and fiscal measures, and a call was made for the forthcoming Intergovernmental Conference to address ways to accelerate decision-making processes in the field. The amendments brought about to the EC Treaty by the Maastricht Treaty and the Fifth Environmental Action Programme (1993–2000, OJ 1993 C138/1) are a clear response to the Dublin Summit Declaration.

The Maastricht Treaty saw the environmental provisions in the EC Treaty amended and strengthened. The legal base in Article 130s was now to operate under the cooperation procedure, and by qualified majority voting in Council. Unanimity was reserved for some new fields, including measures relating to fiscal matters. This would lay the basis for the introduction of 'green taxes', the placing of taxes on non-renewable energy sources such as oil, gas and coal. Legislative breakthrough in what proved to be a highly politically contentious area would be a long time coming (Council Directive 2003/96, Restructuring the Community Framework for the Taxation of energy products and electricity, OJ 2003 L283/51). The Treaty also incorporated the subsidiarity principle as a cross-cutting horizontal principle, and inserted the precautionary principle among those already specified in the environment provisions (see further 17.6–17.10). This principle had been advocated by the 1992 United Nations Conference on Environment and Development, the Rio Earth Summit, which had also witnessed the increasing importance of the concept of sustainability, earlier defined in the 1987 Bruntland Commission Report (Report of the UN World Commission on Environment and Development) as 'development which meets the needs of the present without compromising the ability of future generations to meet their own needs'. Sustainable growth was inserted as a task of the Community in Article 2 EC. The Fifth Action Programme, entitled *Towards Sustainability*, reflected all these core concerns.

Other key developments during the first half of the 1990s include the coming into being of the European Environment Agency, established by Council Regulation 1210/90 (OJ 1990 L120/1), and which started work in Copenhagen in 1993. Formally independent of the EU institutions, the EEA has no regulatory or enforcement function, and its central role is information-gathering and dissemination, as well as developing expert opinions to feed into the policy process. Its first pan-European state of the environment report, the *Dobris Assessment*, was published in 1995. In the same year, expansion of the EU to include Austria, Finland and Sweden brought in new states who already had an established and developed track record on environmental matters, and who could be regarded as potential policy leaders.

This period saw the adoption of an increasingly diverse set of actions. Some continued familiar themes and approaches, such as the Habitats Directive, which seeks to promote the maintenance of biodiversity through the designation of protected 'special areas of conservation', networked together by 'Natura 2000' (Council Directive 92/43, OJ 1992 L206/7). The Air Quality Framework Directive (Council Directive 96/62, OJ 1996 L296/55) meanwhile set basic principles on how air quality was to be assessed and managed, and later spawned a number of 'daughter' directives dealing with specific pollutants. Other measures demonstrated a move away from traditional instruments to innovative schemes such as those on eco-labelling and eco-auditing (see 17.13); and some measures were of a more mixed nature, a fusion of the traditional command and control approach, with apparently more flexible, decentralised measures. The Integrated Pollution Prevention and Control Directive (IPPC) (Council Directive 96/61, OJ 1996 L257/26), for example, requires that operators of certain industrial and agricultural installations obtain permits from state authorities to operate, and the issuance and validity of these permits is tied to the operator meeting certain conditions relating to the prevention and control of pollution. Permits must take into account the whole environmental performance of the plant, covering emissions to air, water and land, generation of waste, use of raw materials, energy efficiency, noise, prevention of accidents, and restoration of the site upon closure. This is the 'integrated' aspect of the directive. In determining permit conditions, the relevant authority may take into account the technical characteristics of the installation, its geographical location and the local environmental conditions, hence introducing an element of flexibility and decentralisation into the process. Local participation by interested stakeholders is foreseen. Permitted emission levels are determined in the light of the Best Available Techniques (BAT), a reflexive standard, which allows industry- or plant-specific differentiation, and for technological advances to be incorporated into the regime without the need for constant re-regulation. Article 2 of the directive gives more guidance on the meaning of BAT – 'best' refers to the most effective for a high level of environmental protection, while the notion of 'available' allows costs and advantages to be taken into account when considering what is available to the plant. However, standing against this apparent flexibility are the BAT Reference (BREF) notes, guidance documents issued by the European IPPC Bureau in Seville, which indicate BAT for particular sectors or issues, and which have come to be regarded by the policy community as important points of reference. Additionally with any relevant EU emissions, legislation will act as a backstop from which no derogation is permitted, thus it is clear to see why some commentators have branded the EU's commitment to flexibility and decentralisation in this directive as 'equivocal' (Scott, 2002: 266; Lee, 2005: 166–71).

## 17.5  Amsterdam and Beyond: Taking Sustainability Seriously?

The Amsterdam Treaty amendments were notable for their inclusion into Article 6 EC of the 'integration principle' – that environmental protection requirements must be integrated into the definition and implementation of all Community policies and activities, in particular with a view to promoting sustainable development. The integration principle has been developed through, *inter alia*, the 'Cardiff Process' initiated by the European Council Summit of 1998. This has required a range of sectors, including agriculture, transport and energy to develop appropriate environmental strategies (see 17.11). Sustainable development meanwhile has become an increasingly significant concept in EU policy circles, albeit one that is provoking concern for environmental considerations.

The European Council in Gothenburg in 2001 launched the Sustainable Development Strategy, adopting the Commission Communication *A Sustainable Future for a Better World: A European Strategy for Sustainable Development* (COM(2001) 264). The Sustainable Development Strategy is described as a third, environmental dimension to the Lisbon Strategy of economic and social renewal. These two strategies are presented as complementary by the European Council: the Lisbon Strategy focuses on growth and jobs, while the Sustainable Development Strategy gives a qualification to the kind of growth to be pursued. Economic, social and environmental policies are presented as mutually reinforcing. The Sixth Action Programme (2002–2012), *Environment 2010: Our Future, Our Choice*, forms the basis for the environmental dimension of the Sustainable Development Strategy. However, as Lee warns, poverty and social exclusion, which contribute to a weakening of social cohesion, are identified as threats to sustainable development (see further Chapter 18) and there is a 'danger that the recently discovered primacy of social development within the sustainable development agenda will squeeze out environmental protection' (Lee, 2005: 35).

The Sixth Environmental Action Programme sets out four priority areas for action: climate change; nature and biodiversity; environment and health; and natural resources and waste. To achieve progress in these areas, five main approaches are to be used:

- ensuring the implementation of existing environmental legislation – here a focus on consolidation rather than expansion can be clearly seen;
- integrating environmental concerns into all relevant policy areas;
- working closely with business and consumers to identify solutions – this suggests a focus on market-oriented, rather than command and control approaches;
- ensuring better and more accessible information on the environment for citizens; and
- developing a more environmentally conscious attitude towards land use.

The EAP is generally strategic in nature, and has been criticised for containing too few clear and attainable objectives and time frames. It certainly appears to reflect an approach to regulation which is more focused on cooperation and agreement and less on centralised enforcement. This approach can also be seen in the Declaration on Article 175 EC attached to the Treaty of Nice, which affirms the commitment of the Member States to environmental protection, but demonstrates a clear preference for market-oriented measures rather than legal enforceable measures. However, a large corpus of measures which demand legal implementation and enforcement exist and, in respect to these, there remains a critical need to find new mechanisms to reduce the 'implementation gap' and ensure timely and effective enforcement. One such proposal has been for the creation of criminal liability for breaches of environmental law which involve the illegal emission of hazardous substances, the illegal shipment of waste, or illegal trade in endangered species, and that cause serious, or are likely to cause serious harm to persons or the environment. Introducing a standardised approach across the Member States of the Union, where currently a very diverse range of approaches exist, could contribute to a significant enhancement in the effectiveness of EU environmental law. However, attempts to introduce such a regime resulted in a constitutional review before the European Court of Justice, when the Commission's own proposal, to be introduced under Article 175 EC (COM(2001) 139), was overtaken by the adoption of Council Framework Decision 2003/80 under the Police and Judicial Cooperation in Criminal Matters pillar of the EU Treaty (see Chapter 13).

Following an application by the Commission, supported by Parliament, the Court of Justice annulled the Framework Decision, on the grounds that, given that its objective was environmental protection, the action should have been based on Article 175 EC (Case C-176/03 *Commission* v. *Council (Environmental Crimes)* [2005] ECR I-7879). It held (paras. 47 and 48):

> 'As a general rule, neither criminal law nor the rules of criminal procedure fall within the Community's competence . . .
>  However, the last-mentioned finding does not prevent the Community legislature, when the application of effective, proportionate and dissuasive criminal penalties by the competent national authorities is an essential measure for combating serious environmental offences, from taking measures which relate to the criminal law of the Member States which it considers necessary in order to ensure that the rules which it lays down on environmental protection are fully effective.'

In February 2007, the Commission reintroduced its Proposal for a Directive on Environmental Crimes under Article 175 EC (COM(2007) 51). Not all are convinced of the effectiveness of this approach, submitting that rather than apply the full force of the criminal law, authorities may seek ways to avoid its application, with further negative implications for implementation (Faure, 2004).

Thus, with its implementation gaps and fears of it losing significance against other policy objectives, EU environmental policy during the first decade of this century could be seen as a field under pressure, and this pressure has been amplified by the recent enlargements. According to Lee once more, while 'it would be wrong to characterise all new entrants from central and eastern Europe as lacking either environmental consciousness or effective structures for environmental protection . . . EC environmental policy is expected to become more conservative, as the influence of the traditional policy leaders in both Council and Parliament is diluted and the new Member States ally themselves with the environmental "laggards" of the existing fifteen' (Lee, 2005; 21–2). It was thus with a certain relief that, while the Treaty establishing a Constitution for the European Union introduced a new set of objectives for the Union (that it should work for 'a Europe of sustainable development based on balanced economic growth, a social market economy, highly competitive and aiming at full employment and social progress, and with a high level of protection and improvement of the quality of the environment'), it left the core environmental policy provisions untouched.

## 17.6  Environmental Principles

As was seen above, beginning with the first Environmental Action Programme, the EU has recognised certain core principles which underpin policy activity in the environmental field. Subsidiarity of course is a general constitutional principle, and one which has been subject to intensive academic comment (e.g. in an environmental context,

Wils, 1994; Golub, 1996; Jordan and Jeppesen, 2000). The following sections consider the principles set out at Article 174(2) EC (former Article 130r): that Community policy shall aim at a high level of protection, taking into account the diversity of situations in the various regions of the Community; the precautionary principle; the preventive principle; the principle that environmental damage should be rectified at source; and the principle that the polluter pays. The broader 'integration' principle set out at Article 6 EC is considered in 17.11. The Article 174(2) EC principles, as will be seen, have influenced the nature and content of the policy tools which the EU has adopted. However, their impact goes beyond this. Case C-318/98 *Criminal Proceedings against Fornasar* ([2000] ECR I-4785) demonstrates that the principles may be used as an interpretive aid: in this case, a directive on hazardous waste was interpreted with reference to the preventive and precautionary principles. More significantly, while in Case C-379/92 *Peralta* ([1994] ECR I-3453) the Court ruled that Article 174 should not be interpreted as requiring the Council to act, in Case C-341/95 *Bettati* v. *Safety Hi-Tech* ([1998] ECR I-4355) it established that acts of the EU institutions could be reviewed for their compatibility with the Article 174(2) principles. The case involved a challenge to the legality of a Council Regulation on substances that deplete the ozone layer, which arose out of proceedings at national level involving a trader whose products were no longer lawfully marketable under the terms of the regulation. The regulation went beyond the international obligations which it was meant to give effect to. The Court ruled that, in its actions, the Council had complied with the principle of ensuring a high level of environmental protection and the measure was lawful. The Court made clear that this does not mean however that it is always the *highest* level of environmental protection technically possible that must be reached in EU legislation. It also established that review is limited to ensuring no manifest errors have been made:

'. . . in view of the need to strike a balance between certain of the objectives and principles mentioned in Article 130r and of the complexity of the implementation of those criteria, review by the Court must necessarily be limited to the question whether the Council, by adopting the regulation, committed a manifest error of appraisal regarding the conditions for the application of Article 130r of the Treaty' (para. 35 of the judgment).

## 17.7    The Preventive Principle

The preventive principle has underpinned many EU initiatives. Its meaning is straightforward: wherever possible, preventive action should be taken to stop environmental damage from happening in the first place, rather than clean it up once it has happened. In short, prevention is better than cure. The Environmental Impact Assessment regime (including the Strategic Environmental Assessment Directive, European Parliament and Council Directive 2001/42, OJ 2001 197/30) is a clear example of this principle in legislative form, albeit one that is regularly the source of actions brought at national level against decisions to undertake works (and, unsuccessfully, at EU level, see Case C-321/95P *Stichting Greenpeace Council* v. *Commission* [1998] ECR I-1651; see further 17.16), and the basis for Commission enforcement actions against Member States for imperfect implementation and operation. A Commission report on the *Application and Effectiveness of the EIA Directive* in 2002 noted the slow responses in some states to incorporate the changes made to the original 1985 directive by Council Directive 97/11, which strengthened and clarified certain core concepts, and extended the scope of the directive in terms of the projects covered. Among the most recent of the regular stream of

226 actions, for example, is Case C-486/04 *Commission* v. *Italy* ([2006] ECR I-11025), involving Italy's unlawful exemption of certain projects from EIA, and, in July 2006, the Commission opened enforcement actions against ten Member States for their failure to properly implement the EIA. Other examples of the preventive principle in action include measures which impose responsibility on producers to reduce potential environmental waste, such as the Packaging and Packaging Waste Directive, which seeks, by imposing obligations on producers to reduce packaging and increase reuse and recycling (European Parliament and Council Directive 94/62, OJ 1994 L365/10). This approach was recently taken further by European Parliament and Council Directive 2000/53 (OJ 2000 L269/34) on End of Life Vehicles, and European Parliament and Council Directive 2002/96 (OJ 2002 L37/24) on Waste Electrical and Electronic Equipment. Producers should recover end of life products, reuse and recycle them where possible, and limit the use of hazardous materials in manufacture (see further Kroepelien, 2000).

## 17.8  The Proximity Principle

The principle that damage should be rectified at source, also known as the proximity principle, has arisen in a number of cases in respect to the free movement of goods. In the *Wallonian Waste* case (Case C-2/90 *Commission* v. *Belgium* [1992] ECR I-4431), a ban ordered by a region of Belgium on the transport of (among other things) non-hazardous waste into the region was challenged, on the grounds that it was a hindrance to trade, discriminating between national and non-national goods. The Court cited the principle that environmental damage should be rectified at source as evidence for the fact that the ban was compatible with EU law. The Court struggled to overcome the absence of a broad enough environmental ground in Article 30 EC on which discrimination on the grounds of nationality could be justified (Article 30 permitting proportionate derogations which protect the health and life of humans, animals and plants) by refusing to find discrimination in this case. Discrimination was found in Case C-379/98 *PreussenElektra* v. *Schleswag* ([2001] ECR I-2099), which concerned a national law that placed an obligation on energy providers to source a proportion of their supplies from local renewable energy installations. Nevertheless, the Court justified the measure on environmental grounds. This was controversial given the formal structure of the Articles 28–30 regime (see Chapter 5, especially 5.17). However, as Advocate General Jacobs pointed out in his opinion, reserving the use of the ground of protection of the environment to indistinctly applicable, non-discriminatory measures is highly problematic as: '[n]ational measures for the protection of the environment are inherently liable to differentiate on the basis of the nature and origin of the cause of harm, and are therefore liable to be found discriminatory, precisely because they are based on such accepted principles as that "environmental damage should as a priority be rectified at source" (Article 130r(2) of the EC Treaty). Where such measures necessarily have a discriminatory impact of that kind, the possibility that they may be justified should not be excluded.'

## 17.9  The Polluter Pays Principle

The Commission has defined the polluter pays principle as meaning that:

'... natural or legal persons governed by public or private law who are responsible for pollution must pay the costs of such measures as are necessary to eliminate that pollution or to reduce it so as to comply with the standards or equivalent measures which enable quality objectives to be met or, where there are no such objectives, so as to comply with the standards or equivalent measures laid down by the public authorities' (Communication annexed to Council Recommendation of 3/3/1975 regarding cost allocation and action by public authorities on environmental matters).

In Case C-293/97 *R* v. *Secretary of State, ex parte Standley and Metson* ([1999] ECR I-8033), the Court ruled that there are two aspects to the principle:

'it must be understood as requiring the person who causes the pollution, and that person alone, to bear not only the costs of remedying pollution, but also those arising from the implementation of a policy of prevention. It can therefore be applied in different ways. Thus, it may be applied either after the event or preventively before the harm occurs' (paras. 93–95).

In many ways, the polluter pays principle is the original economic instrument, in that it aims to minimise pollution by making that pollution expensive for the polluter rather than the tax payer, known as 'cost internalisation'. It is true that many polluters, particularly those involved in manufacturing or the service industry, will in fact pass the cost on to tax payers (in their *alter ego* of consumer). However, the cost will be identified with the polluter, rather than being a general societal cost and, at least in theory, a manufacturer with high pollution costs may become less economically competitive than one with lower pollution costs. Examples of legislation giving clear effect to the polluter pays principle include the eco-tax measures, the proposed measure on criminal liability (which provides that Member States have to ensure that particularly serious environmental crimes are punishable by a maximum of at least 5 years' imprisonment and fines for companies of at least €750,000) and the recent Directive on civil liability (European Parliament and Council Directive 2004/35 on environmental liability with regard to the prevention and remedying of environmental damage, OJ 2004 L143/56). The directive creates strict liability, subject to certain exemptions and defences, for environmental damage caused by activities judged to pose a potential or actual risk to humans and the environment (listed in an Annex), and fault-based liability for damage to natural resources caused by activities which are not inherently dangerous. The opening preamble states that the:

'fundamental principle of this directive . . . [is] . . . that an operator whose activity has caused the environmental damage or the imminent threat of such damage is to be held financially liable, in order to induce operators to adopt measures and develop practices to minimise the risks of environmental damage so that their exposure to financial liabilities is reduced' (see Betlem and Brans, 2005).

## 17.10    The Precautionary Principle

The precautionary principle, introduced by the Maastricht Treaty, has been subject to intense academic comment, and also to testing before the Courts (for example, Fisher *et al*, 2006; Marchant and Mossman, 2004; de Sadeleer, 2006, 2007). As Lee laments: '[a]ttempting to define the precautionary principle in such a way that it could be simply and comprehensively applied to give answers in any particular case is a thankless and probably pointless task' (2005: 98). It is a significant principle of international as well as EU law and, as the discussion in 5.12 demonstrated, its reach has extended beyond the field of the environment. In general terms, it can be summed up by the idea that 'it is better to be safe than sorry'. The 1992 Rio Declaration defined it in the following terms:

'Where there are threats of serious or irreversible damage, lack of full scientific certainty shall not be used as a reason for postponing cost-effective measures to prevent environmental degradation.'

The determination of whether a threat is real enough to warrant a response is complicated by myriad factors. Scientific opinion may well be divided and, more fundamentally, there is what Lee refers to as the 'we don't know what we don't know' problem, for example, 'nobody initially thought to investigate the impact of CFCs on stratospheric ozone, and who knows what we are currently failing to investigate?' (2005: 97). At what point should the law step in to regulate or perhaps prohibit activities? Would an over-precautionary approach not stifle innovation? (Sunstein, 2003). Can and indeed should any activity ever be 'proved' to be risk-free? The Commission has offered a structured approach to the principle's application in its *Communication on the Precautionary Principle* (COM(2000) 1). It divides risk analysis into three stages: risk assessment, risk management and risk communication. Risk assessment is presented as a technical, scientific process, while risk management allows political choices to be exercised in how that risk is handled, although this approach is prone to criticism as being overly simplistic (Lee, 2005: Chapter 4). The limits of these political choices have been tested before the Courts. In Case C-180/96 *United Kingdom* v. *Commission* ([1998] ECR I-2265), involving the Commission's ban on the export of British beef on the grounds there was a risk that it could be contaminated with BSE, the Court ruled:

'[w]here there is uncertainty as to the existence of risks to human health, the institutions may take protective measures without having to wait until the reality and seriousness of those risks become fully apparent' (at para. 99).

As the Court of First Instance has recognised in Case T-13/99 *Pfizer Animal Health* v. *Council* ([2002] ECR II-3305) (concerning the banning of certain antibiotics in animal feed), the institutions enjoy a wide discretion in respect of their choice of response to possible threats, and while the institutions need not wait for adverse risks to materialise before they act, equally they cannot require proof that activities are absolutely safe for them to be permitted. The institutions' responses to threats of serious harm must not be arbitrary. Nor must they be based on a 'purely hypothetical approach to risk founded on mere conjecture which has not been scientifically verified' (para. 143); instead, preventive measures may be taken 'only if the risk, although the reality and extent thereof have not been fully demonstrated by conclusive scientific evidence, appears nevertheless to be adequately backed up by the scientific data available at the time when the measure was taken' (para. 144) (see also Case T-70/99 *Alpharma* v. *Council* [2002] ECR II-3495).

## 17.11 The Integration Principle

Article 6 EC Treaty sets out the principle that:

'[e]nvironmental protection requirements must be integrated into the definition and implementation of all Community policies and activities . . ., in particular with a view to promoting sustainable development.'

The 2002 Sustainable Development Strategy established the vision of the economic, social and environmental dimensions of development as being mutually reinforcing. A sustainable development approach goes beyond the view that growth should not be at the cost of environmental degradation. Rather, it posits that growth that erodes the resource base is, in the long term, impossible to sustain. The Strategy gives the example of climate change. Greenhouse gas emissions resulting from industrial activity cause global warming, which will have severe implications for infrastructure and health, and in turn the potential for economic growth. The Strategy calls for a careful assessment of the full effects of policy proposals, including estimates of their economic, social and environmental impacts, both outside and inside the EU. In 2005 the Presidency Conclusions of the Brussels European Council gave further support to a sustainable development approach and, in response to the concerns about environmental concerns being 'squeezed out', appeared to give greater emphasis to these: environmental protection and 'breaking the link between economic growth and environmental degradation' is listed as the first of the priority objectives, and in relation to economic prosperity, the task is to promote a prosperous, innovative, knowledge rich, competitive and eco-efficient economy. The year 2006 saw Council approval of a Commission Review of the Strategy, and the development of clearer targets and actions to be taken in fields such as tackling climate change, sustainable transport, and sustainable consumption and production (Council, 10117/06). The 2006 Review continues to require an approach to policy-making introduced under the original Strategy, which requires the Commission to submit each new policy proposal to an Impact Assessment (IA) procedure, which assesses the economic, social and environmental impacts of the proposal.

Arguably, this sustainable development approach, which has been in the process of development over the past few years, goes further than the Article 6 integration principle, if the focus of the latter is the integration of environmental policy concerns into other policy fields. Sustainable development is a more holistic notion and a particularly difficult one to pin down in concrete policy terms. Any ability to assess its success in terms of substantive output is still very unclear. The requirement to take environmental concerns into account in other policy fields is of much longer standing, appearing in the first Environmental Action Programmes, though, as Lenschow explains, it has taken many years for the principle to attain the status as 'an autonomous normative principle . . . with procedural and substantive consequence' (2002: 24). Indeed, this status may not yet be fully established. Despite the rhetoric, for many years 'progress in the environmental field [has been] counteracted in other policy fields. In the EU . . . sectoral policies such as agricultural policy, transport policy, energy policy, cohesion policy, fiscal policy and so on [have been] formulated in disregard of their environmental impact. In other words, environmental policy [has not] been treated as a horizontal policy feeding into all relevant policy decisions' (Lenschow, 2002: 19–20). Attempts to incorporate environmental concerns across critical and connected policy fields were often partial and limited. A renewed drive to achieve greater effectiveness came with the launch of the Cardiff Process in 1998. The European Council Summit called on all councils to develop environmental strategies, with certain fields being identified as priorities, including agriculture, transport and energy. In 2004, the Commission presented its review, *Integrating Environmental Considerations in Other Policy Areas – A Stocktaking of the Cardiff Process* (COM(2004) 394). While the process was seen as having succeeded in raising the profile of environmental integration and had resulted in concrete improvements in some sectors, a number of weaknesses were identified. These included a lack of consistency of strategies across Council formations, and a need for better practice in terms of the strategies' content and implementation. Meanwhile, the Commission has itself been developing linkages between the different Commission directorates, a process it began in the 1990s.

Away from the level of policy formulation, linkages regularly emerge across policy fields in the day-to-day decision-making of the Courts. Indeed, these are more often policy clashes rather than linkages. These clashes are most clear in the field of the internal market, where environmental interests may operate as barriers to market access.

Originally, EU environmental legislation was an attempt to resolve this tension, by setting standards at EU level, so that they do not constitute a barrier to trade. By legislating at EU level, the market can be equalised without necessitating a ban on environmental protection and a 'race to the bottom' in environmental terms. However, for the tension to be truly resolved, environmental standards would need to be harmonised throughout the EU. This is not what has happened. Where harmonisation has occurred, Article 176 EC Treaty allows Member States to maintain more stringent measures for the protection of the environment, provided that they are notified to the Commission. In addition, Article 95, which authorises the approximation of laws aimed at the achievement of the single market, specifically permits Member States to maintain national provisions which are necessary for the purposes of environmental protection, provided that those provisions are notified to the Commission. Therefore, where environmental protection requires it, states are entitled to disrupt the internal market by imposing particular requirements.

As has been seen in the discussion on the proximity principle in 17.8, in the absence of specific harmonising legislation, the standard Articles 28–30 EC regime applies. Environmental interests may trump the free movement imperative, subject to the operation of the principle of proportionality – measures must go no further than is necessary to attain their objective. This is seen in *PreussenElektra*, *Wallonia Waste* and also in the *Danish Bottles* case (Case 302/86 *Commission v. Denmark* [1988] ECR 4607), which concerned Danish rules on the recycling of containers for beers and soft drinks, requiring drinks to be marketed in approved reusable containers. Foreign manufacturers were however allowed to use non-metal, reusable but not approved containers for a limited amount of product, provided that a deposit and return system was established. The Commission argued that these rules constituted a barrier to trade under Article 28 EC, in that they made it more difficult for foreign manufacturers to market their products in Denmark. The Court held that environmental protection could operate as a mandatory requirement, and that the deposit and return system was a lawful, proportionate measure. However, the restriction on the quantity of products that could be marketed in non-approved containers by foreign manufacturers was disproportionate. The Court's reliance on the proportionality principle demonstrates an attempt to balance, wherever possible, the two interests. This balancing act was referred to by Advocate General Leger in Case C-371/98 *R v. Secretary of State for the Environment, Transport and the Regions, ex parte First Corporate Shipping Ltd* ([2000] ECR I-9235), which concerned the process of designating sites under the Habitats Directive:

> 'The concept "sustainable development" does not mean that the interests of the environment must necessarily and systematically prevail over the interests defended in the context of the other policies pursued by the Community in accordance with Article 3 of the EC Treaty. On the contrary, it emphasises the necessary balance between various interests which sometimes clash, but which must be reconciled.'

The process of reconciliation of these interests then is sometimes a task for the Courts. Further examples of reconciling economic and environmental interests in a manner that allows the latter to prevail may be drawn from the field of competition law. In Case C-513/99 *Concordia Bus Finland v. City of Helsinki* ([2002] ECR I-7213), the Court ruled that, while such criteria were not specified in the public procurement directives, Article 6 EC should be read across to allow environmental criteria to be used in the award of tenders, provided such criteria are linked to the subject matter of the contract, do not confer an unrestricted freedom of choice on the authority, are expressly mentioned in the contract documents or the tender notice, and comply with all the fundamental principles of Community law, in particular the principle of non-discrimination. Thus provisions on noise levels and emissions relating to bus service contracts would be permissible. In Case T-210/02 *British Aggregates* v. *Commission*, judgment of 13 September 2006, meanwhile, it was argued that by excluding certain products from a tax imposed on aggregates in the UK, the UK was granting an unlawful state aid to certain operators. The action was brought by British Aggregates against the Commission for its failure to proceed against the UK. The purpose of excluding certain products from the scope of the tax was, according to the UK authorities, to encourage their use as construction materials and reduce the need for unnecessary extraction of virgin aggregate, thereby encouraging resource efficiency. The Court of First Instance accepted the environmental justifications, and dismissed the applicant's action. Finally, the *Pfizer* case (Case T-13/99) is a rather different example of the integration principle in action, in that it saw the transposition of a principle holding in the environmental sphere – the precautionary principle – into another policy sphere – agriculture. The precautionary principle is integrated across EU policy activity generally which involves the assessment of risk and scientific uncertainty.

## 17.12 Governance Tools in Environmental Law and Policy: Command and Control

According to Scott, command and control regulation consists of 'legally binding standards which prohibit, constrain and direct the conduct of activities within the Member States' (Scott, 1998a: 24). Such regulation generally establishes basic levels of environmental protection, which are often necessary in order for the EU to comply with its international commitments, and this baseline-setting preserves the integrity of the internal market, where all are treated equally (subject to the ability of the state to impose higher standards). Scott shows that command and control regulation encompasses three main types of legislation: target standards, performance standards and specification standards. Each will be addressed in turn. It should be noted that within this apparently 'traditional' approach to governance, there are some measures which demonstrate a move away from a top-down imposition of regulatory requirements, and which instead, operating in accordance with the subsidiarity principle, open space for more decentralised solutions.

Target standards are standards setting the amount of a given pollutant that can be present in a given medium. Examples of this type of legislation include the Directive on Drinking Water Quality (see Council Directive 98/83, OJ 1998 L330/32), which requires Member States to lay down and enforce quality values for different types of drinking water, and the Air Quality Framework Directive and its daughter directives. The advantage of this regularly used approach is that it deals with the basic problem that there is pollution in a particular medium, and simply requires that pollution be limited, by whatever means are deemed appropriate. It carries with it the possibility of flexibility, given that Member States are usually given the discretion, within fixed limits, to set the appropriate target standard in accordance with local conditions. It does, however, require significant monitoring in order to be enforced.

While target standards control the amount of a pollutant present in a medium, performance standards control the amount allowed to enter that medium. Examples of this kind of regulation include Council Directive 70/220 (OJ 1970 L42/1) and subsequent updating and amending directives, which lay down standards for the amount of certain pollutants (unburned hydrocarbons and carbon dioxide) which may be emitted from motor vehicles. Performance standards, particularly those involving discharge authorisations, are relatively straightforward to monitor and enforce. They place specific requirements on individuals, who can be proceeded against if they violate the rules. However, these types of standards, also known as 'end of pipe' solutions, may be criticised for not addressing the real cause of pollution. In many cases they allow a polluter to buy the right to pollute, either by paying for a discharge authorisation or by violating the standard and paying a fine.

Specification standards are standards which control the kind of technology or processes that can be used in particular types of industry. They focus not on the amount of pollution that is produced but on the way in which industrial processes are carried out, in order to avoid or limit pollution in the first place. Examples of these kinds of standards are Council Directive 94/67 (OJ 1995 L251/43 Sup 45), which requires the issuing of permits for the incineration of hazardous waste, and requires that those permits only be issued if the incineration is carried out according to procedures and methods set out within the directive, and Council Directive 93/12 (OJ 1993 L74/81) and subsequent directives, which control the quality of petrol and diesel fuels. These types of standards seem to be the most in harmony with the preventive principle, and the principle that damage should be rectified at source. They are, however, very prescriptive and do not take into consideration either variations in pollution levels in different Member States, or variations in available technology and economic power. Some Member States can more easily afford to use cleaner technology than others. Affording some degree of flexibility and decentralisation to process specification standards is the IPPC Directive with its BAT approach (see 17.4).

Straddling the different regulatory approaches is the EU's new regime on water policy. The Water Framework Directive (European Parliament and Council Directive 2000/60, OJ 2000 L327/1) expands the scope of protection to all waters, surface waters and groundwater. Along with the main Framework Directive, a number of daughter directives have been passed and others are foreseen (e.g. European Parliament and Council Directive 2006/118 on Groundwater, OJ 2006 L372/19). The aim is to achieve 'good status' for all waters by a set deadline, with regard to both the chemical quality and ecological quality of the water. A combined approach of emission limit values and quality standards is employed: as well as source-based controls, further standards for reducing the levels of pollutants present in water are to operate. An EU-wide minimum ecological quality threshold cannot, unlike the chemical standard, be expressed in an absolute way – the distinctions across the different waterways, at different points, within the EU being too great for any such common standard to be expressed. Because of such ecological variability, the controls are specified as allowing only a slight departure from the biological community which would be expected in conditions of minimal impact from human interference. As well as operating at a decentralised, localised level, the directive also calls for cooperation and coordination between states, as it operates according to a river basin management approach, that is, according to the natural geographical and hydrological unit – instead of according to administrative or political boundaries, requiring joint objective-setting across Member State borders.

## 17.13 Alternatives to Command and Control Approaches

Although command and control has formed, and continues to form the backbone of EU environmental action, a range of variations and alternatives to this approach have been advocated. Many of these variations have already been outlined so far, such as elements of the Water Framework Directive and the IPPC Directive, the Liability Directives, and the extended Producer Responsibility Directives. Command and control approaches do have disadvantages – they can be too prescriptive and too inflexible. The coercive use of standards may not change trends or attitudes, and can lead to hostility on the part of some parties to environmental protection. For a number of years, the EU has been advocating the use of alternative approaches. This section outlines three main types of economic instruments: eco-taxes, the emissions trading system, and the eco-labelling approach.

Economic instruments are often seen as the brightest hope for EU environmental protection. As they tend to be based around the market and around competition, they fit in well with the economic basis of the EU. Furthermore, and as Lee observes, 'by placing a cost on pollution or a benefit on its abatement, economic instruments can be designed to create a constant incentive to reduce pollution, by contrast with direct regulation and its generally fixed environmental standards . . . [in addition] . . . by allowing the regulated party to make decisions based on the relative costs and benefits of pollution and pollution abatement, economic instruments harness the information capacities of the regulated industry' (2005: 187). However, Lee also warns against too easy a reliance on these measures, as 'the impact of many such instruments on environmental quality is unpredictable, depending on uncertain economic calculations and on polluters behaving in economically rational ways. Whatever their benefits, they cannot be presumed to be the preferred solution in every case' (2005: 186).

Fiscal measures, such as tax on petrol or on carbon dioxide emissions, make it more expensive in tax terms to use environmentally unfriendly substances or practices. Although potentially helpful, their utility is limited at EU level, because it has traditionally been difficult to gain agreement between Member States to fiscal harmonisation. In addition, as the protests around Europe against rising fuel prices in 2000 demonstrated, high taxation is unpopular and can create hostility, particularly when not accompanied by visible benefits, such as significant improvements in public transport. The distributive aspects of taxation are also an important consideration, as taxation on domestic consumption of essential products, such as fuel, may impact disproportionately on poorer households (Lee, 2005: 195). As seen in 17.4, in 2003, agreement was finally reached on a Directive Restructuring the Community Framework for the Taxation of energy products and electricity. Setting minimum rates of tax for a range of fuels while granting favourable rates to more environmentally friendly sources, the resulting measures are so beset with derogations and staged implementation that their effectiveness may be called into question. Further exemptions and reductions were subsequently agreed for the acceding Member States.

Under the Kyoto Protocol to the UN Framework Convention on Climate Control (UNFCCC), industrialised countries have committed to collectively reduce their greenhouse gas emissions by 5.2 per cent by 2012, as compared to the 1990 levels. The EU, meanwhile, is committed to achieving at least an 8 per cent reduction in these levels during the period 2008–2012. A key strategy in achieving this target is the EU-wide scheme on Emissions Trading (ETS), established by European Parliament and Council Directive

2003/87 (OJ 2003 L275/32). Under the scheme, overall caps, at EU level and national level, are set on the level of carbon dioxide emissions that can be released by industry. Permits to emit are issued, in accordance with each state's own National Allocation Plan (NAP), and then a market in these permits is created, allowing industrial operators to trade their unused permit allowance, or to go above their originally issued allowance by purchasing from other operators. During the first phase of the scheme's operation, running until the end of 2007, 95 per cent of allowances are to be allocated 'free of charge', this level dropping during the second phase, 2008–2012, when 10 per cent of permits may be auctioned. The deadline for approval of the first-phase NAPs was during 2004, and most missed the deadline. Many of the NAPs finally submitted were rejected or needed amendment by the Commission, generally for excessive allocation. This has given rise to legal challenges against the Commission before the Court of First Instance (e.g. Case T-178/05 *United Kingdom* v. *Commission* [2006] ECR II-4807). Operators are obliged to monitor emissions, and penalties are imposed for their non-compliance with allowance levels, at a rate which increases to €100 per tonne of carbon dioxide by the second phase. Operators may not be the only actors interested in trading permits; traders may move in, speculation may occur and, additionally, as allowances may be cancelled by their owners, environmental NGOs may decide to purchase and 'retire' allowances. There are plans to extend the ETS approach to additional greenhouse gases, and also for it to cover the air transport industry, which is a significant source of greenhouse gas emissions.

Finally, mention should be made of the scheme which enables consumers to assess the environmental-friendliness or otherwise of products and services, and make their purchasing choices accordingly. The Eco-Labelling Regulation (first introduced as Council Regulation 880/92, OJ 1992 L99/1, revised by European Parliament and Council Regulation 1980/2000, OJ 2000 L237/1), promotes 'green' products and services by allowing manufacturers to fix a label of approval on their products. It is a voluntary scheme which is intended to give a competitive advantage to participants. Criteria for award of the Eco-label are drawn up under the comitology system, by the EU Eco-Labelling Board, with standards being set for particular product groups in fields as diverse as clothing, household appliances and tourism. Despite widespread marketing, the scheme still suffers from a lack of visibility and many competing labels exist, which do little to clearly inform the consumer.

## 17.14  Enforcement

Mention has already been made of the implementation gap which exists in respect of environmental law. Member State non-transposition, incomplete transposition and a failure to implement environmental directives in practice are too regular a feature of this field, and although the Court of Justice's Annual Reports have, over recent years, begun to show a reduction in the proportion of cases before it concerning state breach of environmental law, the number of cases remains high. These are caused by a number of factors, such as the complexity of the law, its increasing reliance on decentralisation within the state in environmental legislation, internal institutional and administrative structures of Member States, particular transposition techniques, difficulties with particularly sensitive areas of activity and a lack of coordination within Member States. The Treaty charges the Commission with the task of ensuring that EC law is applied (Article 211 EC), and the Articles 226–228 EC procedure provides the route for Commission enforcement of EC law, where necessary, resulting in an action against the Member State before the Court of Justice for non-compliance. This standard enforcement approach applies to environmental law. The Commission has no direct power of inspection, investigation or enforcement, and nor does the EEA. It learns about infringements primarily through the non-reporting of implementation of directives, and from complaints from NGOs and individuals. Non-compliance with environmental legislation by public authorities and private operators should of course properly be responded to by the state or private litigants within the state, using the national legal order, though in the case of the former, and perhaps in the latter case too, if the state can be regarded as having countenanced non-respect for the law, responsibility may be imputed to the state (as has been seen in respect to the free movement of goods, 5.3).

The familiar concerns with the operation of the Article 226 EC procedure, that it may lack a strategic and coherent focus, and that it may be prone to politicisation in terms of the cases the Commission chooses to pursue within its wide scope of discretion, resurface here. As Hattan reports, during the 1970s and early 1980s, the Commission focused less on enforcement and more on the creation of new environmental tools. Following the Seveso incident however (17.4), the Parliament issued a Resolution condemning the Commission for 'failing to perform fully and properly its function as guardian of the Treaties' (Hattan, 2003: 276). The past two decades have witnessed an increasing concern on the part of the Commission on enforcement matters, reflected in the priorities identified in successive Action Programmes. In 1996, the Commission issued a Communication, *Implementing Community Environmental Law* (COM(96) 5000), in which it set out its approach to enforcement, and stated that it would concentrate on responding to cases of non-transposition, or faulty transposition of directives, rather than pursuing cases of non-application. However, as Hattan shows, in practice the Commission has continued to pursue non-application cases, such as those involving Member States' failure to designate sufficient and appropriate sites under the Habitats Directive, and for poor application of the EIA Directive, for example in terms of the projects selected for assessment.

The Commission now presents annual surveys on the implementation and enforcement of EU environmental law. In its Seventh Annual Survey, covering 2005, it reported that it now groups together cases which have to do with the same policy area. In addition, it was able to report that its intervention has proved a spur for Member States to take remedial action, and that this was the case in almost 90 per cent of the infringement cases it decided to close in 2005. Many cases do progress to Court hearing however, 42 environmental cases were brought before the Court in 2005 for 'bad implementation', and 77 remained open for not complying with a previous judgment of the Court. In respect of these latter cases, the EC Treaty has, since the Maastricht amendments, provided for the possibility of a second action before the Court, leading to the imposition of a financial penalty. It was an environmental case which led to the first ever imposition by the Court of a fine under Article 228 EC (Case C-387/97 *Commission* v. *Greece* [2000] ECR I-5047) and this power has been repeatedly used (e.g. Case C-278/01 *Commission* v. *Spain* [2003] ECR I-14141; Case C-304/02 *Commission* v. *France* [2005] ECR I-6263). In addition to such approaches to stimulating proper implementation, 'softer', more collaborative mechanisms exist, such as the network for the Implementation and Enforcement of Environmental Law (IMPEL), an informal network of national environmental authorities created to act as an informational resource where exchanges between national authorities can take place, providing examples of best practice in implementation.

**17.15**  Enforcement in the National Courts

When fully and properly implemented into national law, EU environmental law should, depending on the nature of the measure in question, be enforceable before national courts. In those situations where national law and its interpretation do not fully comply with the original directive, and the way they are interpreted by the Court of Justice, the full enforceability of the EU law before national courts will depend on whether the measure can be regarded as having direct effect. It will be recalled that, in order for any measure to have direct effect, it must be sufficiently clear and precise, and must not require any further implementation by the Member State. Furthermore, the Court refuses to recognise full horizontal direct effect for directives, meaning that, although national law is incomplete or incorrect, the directive may not be used in an action between private individuals.

Many environmental directives, because of the need to fit the law to local conditions, require Member States to take action, by setting standards, by designating protected areas, or by setting up procedures. Joined Cases 372–374/85 *Ministère Public* v. *Traen and others* ([1987] ECR 2141) illustrate this situation. In the context of criminal proceedings, a Belgian court questioned the compatibility of national legislation with Council Directive 75/442 (OJ 1975 L194/39) on waste and, more specifically, whether provisions from that directive impose obligations directly on operators. In addition to the general point that the directive may not as such impose obligations upon an individual, the Court pointed out that the implementation of the relevant provisions requires the Member State to set up or designate a competent authority, therefore requiring further implementation and, in consequence, denying direct effect. No direct effect was possible either in Case C-236/92 *Comitato di Coordinamento per la Difesa della Cava* v. *Regione Lombardia* ([1994] ECR I-483). In this case, the question was posed to the Court in terms of whether the Waste Directive creates subjective rights. The Court stated that the relevant provisions merely set out a framework for the actions of Member States concerning the treatment of waste and do not require the adoption of specific measures. They are therefore neither unconditional nor sufficiently precise.

*Traen* indicates a further problem. Many environmental provisions, particularly those of a command and control type, are enforced by means of criminal procedure. In Case 168/95 *Criminal Proceedings against Arcaro* ([1996] ECR I-4705), it was held that directives cannot be relied on to impose, or to render more serious, criminal liability. This has the effect of ruling out the direct effect of many environmental directives (and will also, presumably, rule out the direct effect of the proposed criminal liability directive). Furthermore, by their very nature, environmental protection directives may not give rise to the sort of 'rights' that can be exercised by individuals. Indeed, it can be argued that it is in the nature of environmental law not to be about individual rights but rather to focus on the rights of humanity as a whole, on the rights of all inhabitants of Earth, or on the 'rights' of Earth itself. Where however there are economic rights which can be shown to have been affected, courts have shown themselves more able to recognise direct effect than in cases where broader, diffuse environmental interests are at stake (see, for example, from the English Court of Appeal, *Bowden* v. *South West Water Authority* [1998] 3 CMLR 330).

There have, however, been cases where the Court has been prepared to find direct effect for environmental law directives. Notably, in Case C-72/95 *Aannemersbedrijf P.K. Kraaijeveld BV e.a.* v. *Gedeputeerde Staten van Zuid-Holland* ([1996] ECR I-5403), concerning the Environmental Impact Assessment Directive, the Court of Justice held that two situations must be distinguished. If a Member State is acting within the limits of the discretion granted by the legislation, the directive is insufficiently precise to have direct effect. However, if the Member State is acting outside those limits, there may be a case for the directly effective application of the directive against the Member State. Subsequently, in another EIA case (Case C-201/02 *R* v. *Secretary of State for Transport, Local Government and Regions, ex parte Wells* [2004] ECR I-723), the Court indicated that direct effect would not be available: 'where it is a matter of a state obligation directly linked to the performance of another obligation falling, pursuant to that directive on a third party. On the other hand, mere adverse repercussions on the rights of third parties, even if the repercussions are certain, do not justify preventing an individual from invoking the provisions against the Member State concerned.' The Court has interpreted the circumstances in which direct effect will be permissible in a robust manner. In Case C-127/02 *Waddenvereniging and Vogelbeschermingsvereniging* ([2004] ECR I-7405), two nature protection associations brought an action before the national court to challenge the award of permits to fish for cockles in an area protected under the Habitats Directive, on the grounds of the environmental damage caused by such fishing. Under Article 6(3) of the directive, an 'appropriate assessment' was first required before permits could be issued. This provision had not been transposed into national law, and no assessment had been made. Despite the fact that relying on the directive to ensure an assessment was carried out would have potentially adverse repercussions, both short, and potentially long term for cockle fishers, the Court found that Article 6(3) could have direct effect. As Verschuuren (2005: 282) notes, 'one wonders whether there is any environmental directive for which the *Wells* considerations are applicable?'

The problem of identifying 'rights' under environmental law may also pose difficulties for the application of the principle of state liability, first set out by the Court of Justice in Joined Cases C-6 and 9/90 *Francovich and Bonifaci* v. *Italian Republic* ([1991] ECR I-5357). It will be remembered that three conditions must be fulfilled if the Member State is to be held liable for damage caused to an individual because of a breach of EU law. The law breached must be intended to confer rights upon individuals, those rights must be clearly identifiable, and there must be a relationship of causation between the breach and the damage. One environmentally related case where state liability was successfully invoked was Case C-5/94 *R* v. *Ministry of Agriculture, Fisheries and Food, ex parte Hedley Lomas* ([1996] ECR I-2553), which was one of the first cases dealt with by the Court of Justice applying the principle of state liability. The case concerned the restriction placed by the UK government on the export of live animals for slaughter elsewhere in the EU. The exporter argued that this restriction was contrary to the principles of freedom of movement. This argument was upheld, and it was further held that the UK was liable to compensate the exporter for their losses in not having been able to carry out that part of its trade. Therefore, the UK was liable for breach of the free movement rules. However, if the situation is reversed, problems begin to be seen. Assume that the UK were to be found to have violated, not the free movement rules, but an animal protection measure such as, for example, Council Directive 99/74 (OJ 1999 L203/53) on the protection of laying hens. In such a case, no compensation would be payable. The damage done would be done to the animals themselves, who cannot be compensated, and, in a more abstract sense, to humanity as a whole (by allowing inhumane behaviour).

## 17.16   Public Participation in the Operation of Environmental Law

In the opening paragraphs of this chapter, reference was made to the 1998 Aarhus Convention on Access to Environmental Information, Public Participation in Decision Making and Access to Justice in Environmental Matters as an international commitment that has implications for EU environmental governance. The Aarhus Convention establishes a number of rights of the public with regard to the environment, organised around three pillars: first, the right of everyone to receive environmental information that is held by public authorities, including information on the state of the environment, and on policies or measures taken; second, the right to participate in environmental decision-making, enabling environmental NGOs and the affected public to comment on, for example, proposals for projects, plans and programmes affecting the environment, and these comments to be taken into account in decision-making; and, finally, the right to review procedures to challenge public decisions that have been made without respecting the first two rights or environmental law in general.

While the EU initially placed the emphasis on the Member States at national level to respond to these commitments (and many directives provide for public participation, including the IPPC Directive, the EIA and SEA Directives, and the Water Framework Directive), there has been growing evidence of a commitment to incorporating these principles in EU activity. In 2006, the Parliament and Council adopted Regulation 367/2006 on the application of the provisions of the Aarhus Convention to Community institutions and bodies (OJ 2006 L264/13). The regulation extends the already existing regulation on access to information (European Parliament and Council Regulation 1049/2001, OJ 2001 L145/43), and requires the institutions and relevant bodies to provide for public participation in the preparation, modification or review of 'plans and programmes relating to the environment'. Significantly, the regulation also enables environmental NGOs meeting certain criteria (under Article 11 of the regulation, they must be recognised legal persons, established for over two years and pursuing the primary objective of the protection of the environment) to request an internal review under environmental law of acts adopted, or omissions, by Community institutions and bodies. However, the 'Access to Justice' right in Article 10 of the regulation refers only to the review of administrative acts. While the regulation is a positive step forward, it does nothing to assist the applicant wishing to bring an action challenging a general legislative measure. These continue to be governed by the restrictive regime under Article 230 EC Treaty.

The standing rules under the Article 230 EC action in annulment have been the subject of fierce debate over recent years, with pressure mounting on the Court to apply a less stringent test to standing for 'non-privileged' applicants, who include individuals and NGOs. Applicants must show that they have direct and individual concern in an EU measure for them to have standing. Attempts by pressure groups, Advocates General (see Advocate General Jacobs' opinion in Case C-50/00P *Unión de Pequeños Agricultores (UPA)* v. *Council* [2002] ECR I-6677) and indeed the Court of First Instance (Case T-177/01 *Jégo-Quéré* v. *Commission* [2002] ECR II-2365, overturned on appeal to the Court of Justice) to convince the Court of Justice to introduce a more flexible interpretation of the standing rules have been rejected, the Court stating that any change is properly for the Member States to undertake through Treaty revision (*UPA*, and Case C-263/02P *Jégo-Quéré* [2004] ECR I-3425). The restrictive rules on standing in an environmental context can be clearly seen in the *Greenpeace* actions. Before the Court of First Instance (Case T-585/93 *Stichting Greenpeace Council* v. *Commission* ([1995] ECR II-2205), Greenpeace, along with a number of individuals who lived and worked on the Canary Islands, sought to challenge a Commission decision to grant assistance from the European Regional Development Fund to build two power stations on the Islands. Standing, however, was not granted. The Court of First Instance made it clear that no special rules were to be applied in the case of environmental issues, and that the normal rules on standing applied. The Court reiterated the general principle that interest groups may not bring actions when their members individually would not have standing. Furthermore, the individual applicants did not have standing because they could not be distinguished in any way from other residents or workers on the Islands – the individual concern test. The fact that everyone living and working in the Islands would be affected by the power stations was the obstacle to granting some residents standing. The appeal by Greenpeace was subsequently rejected by the Court of Justice (Case C-321/95P *Stichting Greenpeace* v. *Commission* [1998] ECR I-1651). The restrictive approach of the European Courts is out of line with the approach of certain Member States, for example, in the English Divisional Court decision in *R* v. *Inspectorate of Pollution, ex parte Greenpeace (No. 2)* [1992] 4 All ER 329, the court held that the fact that many members of Greenpeace were residents of the area around the Sellafield nuclear plant was relevant, and granted standing, even though most residents were not members of Greenpeace. The approach of the Court of Justice which denies NGOs access to justice is difficult to square with the rhetoric of the EU's commitments to the Aarhus principles.

# Summary

1. The starting point for an EU environmental policy was the call from the Heads of State and Government at the 1972 Paris Summit to embark on action in the environmental sphere, as part of a more general emphasis on broadening out the integration process beyond economic concerns.

2. The Commission responded with the First of the Environmental Action Programmes in 1973. These establish the Union's policy priorities for a given period. The current, Sixth Action Programme runs from 2002 to 2012.

3. The objectives of EU environmental policy are set out in Article 174(1) EC Treaty. These are: preserving, protecting and improving the quality of the environment; protecting human health; prudent and rational utilisation of natural resources; and promoting measures at international level to deal with regional or worldwide environmental problems.

4. International environmental law developments have had a significant impact on the policy priorities of the EU.

5. Many of the early measures in this field focused on bringing Member States' environmental laws into line in the interests of market integration. Since the SEA, the EC Treaty has contained a separate legal base for environmental protection matters and made it an objective in its own right, rather than an add-on to the single market.

6. The mutual interdependence of economic, social and environmental interests is at the heart of the EU's Sustainable Development Strategy.

## Summary cont'd

7. The core principles which underpin policy activity in the environmental field are: subsidiarity; that Community policy shall aim at a high level of protection, taking into account the diversity of situations in the various regions of the Community; the precautionary principle; the preventive principle; the principle that environmental damage should be rectified at source; and the principle that the polluter pays.

8. The integration principle (Article 6 EC) means that environmental protection requirements must be integrated into the definition and implementation of all Community policies and activities, in particular with a view to promoting sustainable development.

9. 'Command and control' regulation has traditionally been the dominant policy tool, though there are many examples of more innovative and flexible tools. In particular, the EU is making use of economic instruments, including eco-taxes and the emissions trading system, and the eco-labelling approach.

10. There is a significant implementation gap which exists in respect of environmental law, which has severe implications for the effectiveness of EU policy.

11. Enforcement of environmental law is a source of significant activity on the part of the Commission, and there is no EU-level environmental inspectorate.

12. The application of the principles of direct effect and state liability can be problematic in the environmental field.

13. The EU is required to provide opportunities for public and NGO access to environmental information, participation in decision-making and access to justice in environmental matters in line with the Aarhus Convention.

# Exercises

1. Do you think that the internal market project could have survived without a European environmental policy?

2. Critically assess the strengths and weaknesses of command and control approaches to environmental regulation.

3. In what ways can the subsidiarity principle be seen in action in the EU environmental law field?

4. Should a central EU body be created with powers to investigate and enforce environmental law?

5. Should environmental NGOs be given the power to challenge EU environmental legislative acts?

## Further Reading

Betlem, G. and Brans, E. (eds.) (2005) *Environmental Liability in the EU – The 2004 Directive compared with US and Member State Law*, London: Cameron May.

Chalmers, D. (1995) 'Environmental Protection and the Single Market: an unsustainable development. Does the EC treaty need a title on the environment?', 1 *Legal Issues of European Integration* 65.

Chalmers, D. (1999) 'Inhabitants in the Field of EC Environmental Law', in Craig, P. and de Búrca, G. (eds.), *The Evolution of EU Law*, Oxford: Oxford University Press.

## Further Reading cont'd

Faure, M. (2004) 'European Environmental Criminal Law: Do We Really Need It?', 13 *European Environmental Law Review* 18.

Fisher, E., Jones, J. and von Schomberg, R. (eds.) (2006) *Implementing the Precautionary Principle: Perspectives and Prospects*, Cheltenham: Edward Elgar.

Hattan, E. (2003) 'The Implementation of EU Environmental Law', 15 *Journal of Environmental Law* 273.

Kramer, L. (2006) *EC Environmental Law* (6th edn), London: Sweet & Maxwell.

Kroepelien, K. (2000) 'Extended Producer Responsibility – New Legal Structures for Improved Ecological Self-Organization in Europe?', 9 *Review of European Community and International Environmental Law* 165.

Lee, M. (2005) *EU Environmental Law: Challenges, Change and Decision Making*, Oxford: Hart Publishing.

Lenschow, A. (2002) 'New Regulatory Approaches to "Greening" EU Policies', 8 *European Law Journal* 19.

Macrory, R. (ed.) (2006) *Reflections on 30 years of EU Environmental Law – A High Level of Protection?* Groningen: Europa Law Publishing.

Marchant, G. and Mossman, K. (2004) *Arbitrary and Capricious: The Precautionary Principle in the European Union Courts*, Washington DC: AIE Press.

de Sadeleer, N. (2006) 'The Precautionary Principle in European Community Health and Environmental Law', 12 *European Law Journal* 139.

de Sadeleer, N. (ed.) (2007) *Implementing the Precautionary Principle: Approaches from the Nordic Countries, EU and USA*, London: Earthscan.

Scott, J. (1998) *EC Environmental Law*, Harlow: Longman.

Scott, J. (2000) 'Flexibility, "Proceduralization" and Environmental Governance in the EU', in de Burca, G. and Scott, J. (eds.), *Constitutional Change in the EU: From Uniformity to Flexibility?*, Oxford: Hart Publishing.

Sunstein, C. (2003) 'Beyond the Precautionary Principle', 151 *University of Pennsylvania Law Review* 1003.

Verschuuren, J. (2005) 'Shellfish for Fishermen or for Birds? Article 6 Habitats Directive and the Precautionary Principle', 17 *Journal of Environmental Law* 265.

## Key Websites

The website of the Commission's Environment DG is at:
**http://ec.europa.eu/environment/index_en.htm**

The European Environment Agency's site is at:
**http://www.eea.europa.eu/**

IMPEL, the European Union Network for the Implementation and Enforcement of Environmental Law, has its site at:
**http://ec.europa.eu/environment/impel/index.htm**

The United Nations Environment Programme site is at:
**http://www.unep.org/**

A useful resource on EU environmental law is available at:
**http://www.eel.nl/index.asp**

The European Environmental Bureau is a federation of 140 NGOs focused on protecting and improving the environment:
**http://www.eeb.org/**

# Chapter 18

# Economic and Social Cohesion

Introduction

The promise of prosperity has been a powerful factor in securing and maintaining support for the European integration project. However, as was recognised at the time of drafting of the original Treaty of Rome, the pace of economic and social development generated by the construction of the internal market would not be the same across the regions of the European Community. Peripheral regions, and those disadvantaged by underdeveloped infrastructures, could be less likely to see the benefits of economic integration. Indeed, the disparities between the economic fortunes of such 'backward' regions and the more developed, more prosperous regions could be exacerbated as the latter flourished, better able to attract inward investment and profit from the opportunities presented by the single market.

Just as economic integration was going to benefit certain regions more than others, so it was that the operation of the market would bring more immediate, more tangible benefit to certain groups in society – most obviously, trained, adaptable, mobile members of the workforce. Those excluded from participating in the market, through, for example, disability, old age or family responsibilities, were effectively sidelined from the economic project of European integration.

According to the Commission, such imbalances and inequalities across regions and social groups are potentially damaging for the Union and those within it:

> 'Imbalances do not just imply a poorer quality of life for the most disadvantaged regions and the lack of life chances open to their citizens, but indicate an under-utilisation of human potential and a failure to take advantage of economic opportunities which could benefit the Union as a whole' (Commission, *First Cohesion Report*, COM(96) 542 at p.11).

EU action designed to reduce such disparities has, since the SEA in 1986, taken place within the context of the policy objective of promoting 'economic and social cohesion'. According to the Commission, 'cohesion policy is the way the EU expresses solidarity and shows that it is not just a large market but also the guardian of a particular model of society' (Commission, *First Progress Report on Economic and Social Cohesion*, COM(2002) 46 at p.17). A range of policy fields and techniques are involved in generating cohesion across the EU. Disparities in levels of economic and social development between *geographical regions* are addressed through the EU's *regional development policy*. The objectives of this policy are set out in Article 158 EC:

> 'In order to promote its overall harmonious development, the Community shall develop and pursue its actions leading to the strengthening of its economic and social cohesion.
>
> In particular, the Community shall aim at reducing disparities between the levels of the development of the various regions and the backwardness of the least favoured regions or islands, including rural areas.'

The most recent enlargements have increased disparities – economic, social and territorial – between the Member States of the EU and the regions within them to an unprecedented level. The *per capita* GDP of some regions in Romania and Bulgaria, for example, are at around 25 per cent of the EU average, while Brussels, the Duchy of

Luxembourg and Inner London have a GDP of between 250 and 300 per cent of the EU average. Central to the policy objective of strengthening cohesion between regions have been the Structural Funds. The Funds operate on the basis of policy co-responsibility between the EU institutions and the Member States, and according to multi-annual programming periods, the current one running from 2007 to 2013. The most significant of the Funds, in terms of available resources, is the European Regional Development Fund (ERDF, European Parliament and Council Regulation 1080/2006, OJ 2006 L210/1). This focuses on redressing the main regional imbalances in the Union, for example by providing financial assistance for infrastructure development, the promotion of job-creating investment and providing support for local businesses. In addition to the ERDF, there is the European Social Fund (ESF, European Parliament and Council Regulation 1081/06, OJ 2006 L210/12) which is targeted at improving employment opportunities, for example through training and support to enable the (re)entry into the workplace of unemployed and disadvantaged groups. The third key Fund, the Cohesion Fund (European Parliament and Council Regulation 1084/2006, OJ 2006 L210/79) directs aid to the poorest Member States, and provides funding for Trans-European Networks and environmental projects. These three together are the central cohesion funds. In addition, the European Solidarity Fund, established after the devastating floods of 2002, provides emergency relief funding following major (natural) disasters (Council Regulation 2012/2002, OJ 2002 L311/3). Pre-accession aid is granted to candidate and potential candidate Member States though the Instrument for Pre-Accession Support (Regulation 1085/2006, OJ 2006 L210/82; see also 19.3), which replaces a range of instruments which applied to the 2004 and 2007 accession countries (SAPARD, dealing with agricultural and rural development; PHARE, on institution building and economic development; and IPSA, funding environmental and transport projects). Other funds now operating outside the formal cohesion policy framework are the European Agricultural Guarantee Fund (EAGF) and the European Agricultural Fund for Rural Development (EAFRD, see Chapter 9), and the Financial Instrument for Fisheries Guidance (FIFG), which provides support for activities promoting the sustainable operation of the fisheries sector.

These cohesion funds, and in particular the ERDF, provide a route for the *redistribution* of wealth across the EU, with roughly one-third of the current EU Budget (raised in part from Member State contributions) being directed to regions identified as being in need, including poorer, 'lagging' regions, and those whose main industries are being lost.

As well as seeking to promote and strengthen economic and social cohesion *between* the regions of the EU (a task which Article 159 EC also envisages as involving the full range of the Community's market-related policies, and the Member States' economic policies), the EU is also involved in attempts to reduce the inequalities in the economic and social situation of disadvantaged groups *within* regions and, ultimately, across the EU. According to the Commission, the greatest threat to social cohesion is poverty and social exclusion. Social exclusion is defined as the state where:

> 'people are prevented from participating fully in economic, social and civil life and/or when their access to income and other resources (personal, family, social and cultural) is so inadequate as to exclude them enjoying a standard of living and quality of life that is regarded as acceptable by the society in which they live' (Council and Commission, 2001, *First Joint Report on Social Inclusion*, p.11).

The dominant philosophy reflected in current EU policy discourse is that the most effective safeguard against such social exclusion is through participation in employment.

A key policy focus is therefore on the improvement of the employment opportunities of potentially (economically) vulnerable and excluded *groups*. Social exclusion policy could clearly also embrace such issues as ensuring access to social assistance, to adequate health services, to adequate housing, to services of general economic interest and to cultural resources. These areas are, in the main, areas of political and economic sensitivity which the Member States have been reluctant to relinquish responsibility for. The EU, and especially the Commission, has an established role in these fields as an information expert (Hervey, 1998: 166), sponsoring research programmes, establishing monitoring centres and observatories, and providing for exchanges of information between Member States. It has not however developed much in the way of standard-setting, or rights-granting legislative competence in these fields. Nevertheless, the EU's involvement in relation to this broader view on social inclusion was taken a stage further following the conclusions of the March 2000 Lisbon Presidency, where it was agreed that the open method of coordination would be applied to this area.

This chapter considers, in turn, the role of the EU's regional policy and the structural funds, and then its policies on combating poverty and social exclusion, to the strengthening of cohesion within and across the EU.

## 18.2 The Development of the Structural Funds

Despite the commitment made in the preamble to the original Treaty of Rome to 'reduce the differences existing between the various regions and backwardness of the less favoured regions', the EEC Treaty itself initially provided little in the way of tools specifically directed to the development of such 'less favoured regions', other than the general measures for establishment and operation of the common market (Evans, 1999). Preferential-rate loans were (and continue to be) available from the European Investment Bank to facilitate, *inter alia*, 'projects for developing less developed regions' (Article 267, former Article 198 EC), but there was no distinct Community 'regional policy' in the sense of there being any coherent political strategy, legal framework or the necessary tools to redress regional imbalances through the promotion of economic development in the 'lagging' regions. The European Social Fund, provided for in the Treaty (former Article 123 EC), and formally operational from 1960, was difficult to characterise fully as a tool of regional policy, as it focused more on moving workers to work, and providing incentive measures for unemployed workers to move to areas of demand, rather than the bringing 'work to the workers' approach typical of regional policies (Anderson, 1995: 126). Established in 1962, the Agricultural Fund was split into two sections in 1964, Guidance and Guarantee, and these measures placed a heavy and enduring emphasis on market- and price-support measures (out of the larger Guarantee section) over structural development measures, which are supported primarily through the Guidance section (now through the EAFRD). Again, this system was not particularly well attuned to reducing regional disparities, as assistance tended to be directed to better farming regions (Fennell, 1979: 196).

By the early 1970s it had become clear that a more proactive, interventionist response to regional disparities was required. The proposed move to EMU, along with the accession of new Member States (including the UK, which sought some form of recompense for what it perceived as a net loss from the CAP), were key push factors behind the establishment of the ERDF, with also a link to the momentum generated in the early 1970s to give the integration process a more human face. The ERDF was instituted by a Regulation (Council Regulation 724/75, OJ 1975 L73/1) adopted under Article 308 (former Article 235) EC. The purpose of the Fund was to assist in the correction of the principal regional imbalances within the Community, and particularly those which were most likely to hinder further economic integration. At this stage, allocations under the Fund were made on the basis of pre-agreed national quotas, though the size of the fund has been described as 'too small to have a significant impact on regional disparities' (Allen, 2000: 247). The 1970s meanwhile witnessed the first major reform of the ESF, with the beginnings of a clearer regional focus, and a particular emphasis on certain categories of workers: for example, unemployed young people, those with disabilities and women, with the majority of funding being directed towards vocational training and educational projects. A similar concern with regional issues was also beginning in the area of agriculture, with a number of measures specifically directed at particular regions being adopted, beginning with the 1975 Directive on mountain and hill farming, and farming in less favoured areas (Council Directive 75/268, OJ 1975 L128/1).

The 1986 Single European Act formally incorporated the Community's developing regional policy and the ERDF into the main body of the EC Treaty. These provisions were introduced under the new Title on 'economic and social cohesion', now found at Articles 158 et seq. EC Treaty. In addition to introducing (though not defining) the cohesion concept into the Treaty, the SEA amendments also provided a new framework for the reform of the structure and operation of the existing structural funds, seeking to create closer coordination between them. In 1988, the so-called 'Delors I' package of decisions reformed the operational framework for these funds (led by Council Regulation 2052/88, OJ 1988 L185/9), and also doubled their existing budget. The Structural Funds were subsequently to operate in accordance with four 'implementation principles': concentration of funding, programming, partnership and additionality. As with the initial decision to establish the ERDF, the main motivations behind the changes of the late 1980s can again be linked to pressures arising both from enlargement and from the decision to move to a new stage in economic integration – in this case, the completion of the single market.

Further changes were brought about with the decision to progress towards EMU. Increased spending under the Structural Funds was agreed as part of the 1993 'Delors II' package deal, and revisions to the existing regulations made, including the splitting off of a separate Fisheries Fund (the FIFG) from the EAGGF (Council Regulation 2080/93, OJ 1993 L193/1). In addition, following the ratification of the Maastricht Treaty, the Cohesion Fund was established as a means to provide additional support for the poorer countries of the EU (Spain, Portugal, Greece and Ireland) (Council Regulation 1164/94, OJ 1994 L130/1). This Fund financed specific projects relating to the improvement and protection of the environment and transport infrastructure, up to a limit of 85 per cent of the projects' total costs. The redistribution of resources from the richest Member States to the 'cohesion countries', which have an average GDP of less than 90 per cent of the EU average, has enabled these poorer states to embark upon much needed structural development without incurring large public spending debts which would endanger their prospects of meeting the EMU convergence criteria.

The framework for the next programming period, covering the years 2000–2006, was adopted at the 1999 Berlin Summit as part of the *Agenda 2000* programme, and incorporated a package of decisions including the General Regulation 1260/99 (OJ 1999 L161/1). The key themes of this period were employment, with the ESF specifically charged with supporting the European Employment Strategy, effectiveness, and, of course, enlargement. The move to the EU of 27 has presented a widening of regional and territorial disparities on a scale without precedence in any previous enlargement. In the light of the great demands that will be placed on the Funds, steps were taken to try to enhance the effectiveness and efficiency of the fund, through greater concentration of funding and more rigorous management processes.

Some 22 billion euro was earmarked for the new states under the funds, running from the date of accession to the end of the 2006 funding period. In order to participate in and benefit from the operation of the funds, Member States have needed to ensure that they have in place adequate national and regional administrative structures for the definition of regional development plans, their implementation, monitoring and evaluation. However, for many of the new Member States, with their histories of centralised planning arrangements, there is little experience of decentralised, regional policies and structures, and concerns have surrounded the weak and insufficiently defined implementation and monitoring systems in some states.

While the new Member States were pushing forward in putting these structures in place and drawing up their development plans, crucial questions about the post-2006 programming period were being raised. A continued application of the existing eligibility criteria into the next funding period would see many regions in the existing EU states lose their entitlement for funding, with funding redirected mainly, if not wholly, to regions in the less developed new Member States. The negotiations leading to the final adoption of the financial budget and the relevant regulatory measures were fraught and long drawn out. The budget finally agreed by the Council in December 2006 is less than that envisaged by the Commission in its proposals from 2004 (COM(2004) 492). The Regulatory framework was adopted in 2006, and it takes further the drive towards greater effectiveness, increased streamlining and simplification of the operation of the funds, and a handing back to the Member States from the Commission of a large measure of responsibility for the operation and management of the Funds. Strategic Guidelines, outlining the policy priorities of the cohesion policy for the current period, were subsequently adopted by the Council in October 2006 (Decision 2006/702, OJ 2006 L291/11). In short, the core priorities are: first, improving the attractiveness of Member States' regions and cities by improving accessibility, ensuring adequate quality and level of services, and preserving their environmental potential; second, encouraging innovation, entrepreneurship and the growth of the knowledge economy; and third, creating more and better jobs by attracting more people into employment.

## 18.3 The Legal Context of the Structural Funds

Analyses of the operation of its redistributive policies are often absent from 'legal' accounts of the EU (see Scott, 1995; Hervey, 1998; Evans, 1999). This arises not least from the fact that this area differs from 'mainstream' areas of EU activity, which more often centre around a 'package of individual rights which are readily enforceable within national courts' (Scott, 1995: xii). The notion of 'rights' in relation to cohesion policy is not at all developed. There is no general exercisable 'right' to benefit from the operation of the structural funds, nor has the concept of 'economic and social cohesion' been seen to create of itself a catalogue of justiciable rights, which must be protected by the courts (Evans, 1999).

While there may be little in the way of actionable 'rights' in this area, there are clearly defined primary and secondary legislative instruments which provide the regulatory framework within which cohesion policy plays out. Article 2 EC Treaty now lists the promotion of economic and social cohesion as a task of the Community, and the strengthening of cohesion is recognised as a Community activity, set out at Article 3(k) EC. In the Treaty establishing a Constitution for Europe meanwhile, Article I-3 recognises among the Union's objectives the promotion of 'economic, social and territorial cohesion and the solidarity among Member States'. The current title on Economic and Social Cohesion in the EC Treaty (Title XVII) provides a more detailed set of policy commitments and indicates the tools to be used in realising these objectives, which include Member State economic policies, the implementation of the internal market and the use of the structural funds.

Article 161 EC provides the legal base for the adoption of the overarching General Regulation, which defines common principles, rules and standards for the implementation and management of the three cohesion instruments (the ERDF, the ESF and the Cohesion Fund). The General Regulation is adopted by the Council, having received the assent of the Parliament, and the same procedure is used for the adoption of the Cohesion Fund Regulation. Both the ERDF and the ESF are adopted according to the co-decision procedure, under, respectively, Articles 162 and 148 EC. A further regulation, the Implementing Regulation, which sets out more detailed rules on how the funds will be managed, is adopted by the Commission. The current Implementing Regulation (Commission Regulation 1828/2006, OJ 2006 L371/1) replaces the numerous separate implementing regulations which existed in previous programming periods, reflecting the streamlining and simplification that have been underway at EU level. Within the current legislative frameworks, powers are delegated to the Commission to enable it to undertake its functions in relation to the implementation and administration of the structural funds. In accordance with the 'comitology' system, the Commission exercises these powers in conjunction with committees of national representatives, chaired by a Commission representative.

There is also a preponderance of 'soft law' in this area. Guidelines, notices and framework documents are all policy tools used by the Commission which are of indeterminate legal status. This reliance on soft law raises the possibility that the regularity of many acts taken in the context of the administration of the structural funds may not be easily amenable to judicial oversight and control. For example, a Commission 'information note', clarifying its interpretation and application of the Funds, was deemed incapable of being challenged as it was not intended to have legal effects (Case C-301/03 *Italy* v. *Commission* [2005] ECR I-10217). Difficulties in challenging decisions taken in this area are also exacerbated by the profoundly 'multi-levelled' nature of governance operating within this policy sector (Hooghe, 1996; Scott, 1998b; Sutcliffe, 2000). As the applicants in *An Taisce and WWF(UK)* v. *Commission* found before both the CFI (Case T-461/93 [1994] ECR II-711) and the ECJ (Case C-325/94P [1996] ECR I-3727), in cases concerning the Cohesion Funds 'the line between Community law and domestic law is surprisingly difficult to draw' (Scott, 1995: xii). The applicants in this case, both environmental organisations, sought to challenge by means of an Article 230 EC action in annulment the part-funding through allocations under the Structural Funds of the construction of a visitors' centre in an area of outstanding natural beauty located in County Clare, Ireland. The General Regulation in place at the time required all operations of the Funds to be 'consistent with other Community policies and operations, in particular in the areas of . . . environmental protection' (this obligation has been strengthened in the current General Regulation, which provides, at Article 17, that 'the objective of the Funds shall be pursued in the framework of sustainable development and the Community promotion of the goal of protecting and improving the environment'). The substance of the applicant's action was that the project contravened certain requirements of EU environmental law. Neither the CFI nor the ECJ got as far as reviewing the substance of the case, as both rejected the action on admissibility grounds, on the basis that there was no *Community* legal act authorising payment for the project which was open to review.

The outcome in *An Taisce* results from the manner in which the decisions to allocate funding operate. While the reforms of 1999 and, in turn, those for the 2007–2013 period went some way to streamline processes, decision-making is 'shared' between the Commission, the relevant Member State, and a range of regional and local bodies. Decisions on specific projects and their operation are taken at the national level, or below, within a broader framework set by the Commission (see further 18.5). Attempting to locate, within this complex web of interactions, a *Community* legal act in relation to the funding of the contested project which would be amenable to review is not easy. The applicants in *An Taisce* approached the issue by seeking to impute to the Commission a decision not to withdraw or suspend funding once the environmental concerns surrounding the project had come to light. Neither Court accepted that any such a decision could be identified. As this case reveals, despite the detailed regulatory framework, there has been something of a 'legal vacuum' in relation to programme implementation (Scott, 1998a: 137). The 1999 reforms sought to go some way towards filling this vacuum by more clearly delineating (and also reducing) the areas of responsibility held by the Commission, a process continued in the 2007–2013 proposals. For example, Article 60 of the current General Regulation declares that the (national or subnational) managing authorities shall be responsible for the management and implementation of the programmes financed under the Funds, in accordance with the principle of sound financial management. In comparison, the equivalent provision in the regulations for the pre-1999 programming period places this responsibility on the 'Member States and Commission'.

Even where a reviewable Community act can be identified, routes for a more pluralist participation in the oversight of operation of the structural funds are limited by the restrictive rules on standing before the Courts. In Case C-321/95P *Stichting Greenpeace Council and others* v. *EC Commission* ([1998] ECR I-1651), the ECJ declared inadmissible the applicants' challenge to the legality of the disbursement of monies under the ERDF. The funding was directed towards the construction of power stations on Gran Canaria and Tenerife, and the Commission had released a number of tranches of money for the project (each decision to disburse being classified as a reviewable act), despite certain alleged irregularities with the environmental impact assessment. The applicant's action in *Greenpeace* failed on the grounds of a lack of individual concern.

## 18.4   Concentration of Funding

The 1988 reforms introduced a number of key principles which govern the manner in which the Structural Funds are operated. The first of these is the principle of concentration of funding. This is designed to ensure that structural funding is directed to areas most in need. For the 2000–2006 period, three priority objectives were identified, a reduction from the six operating previously. The 2007–2013 period sees the maintenance of three broad objectives, though with a degree of reorientation and refocusing.

Under the 2000–2006 system, some 70 per cent of all available funding was directed to so-called *Objective 1* regions. These regions are those with a GDP of under 75 per cent of the EU-wide average. Objective 1 funding was targeted at assisting the development of 'lagging' regions, through the development of infrastructure and the promotion of economic activity. The task of drawing up the list of Objective 1 was, before 2000 (when the Commission became responsible), conducted by the Council of Ministers, and amidst much political bargaining. Given the financial priority given to Objective 1, Member States traditionally fought very hard to obtain, and retain, Objective 1 status for their regions. The results of such negotiations on occasion appeared out of line with the technical, legal criteria for eligibility (Peterson and Bomberg, 1999: 157). *Objective 2* funding was similarly geographically defined, and supports economic and social conversion in areas which are facing economic crisis due to structural change. The ERDF and the ESF operated in relation to this objective. In contrast with the 'zoning' approach of Objectives 1 and 2, *Objective 3* was more 'thematically' defined, and was devoted to the modernisation of training systems and of promoting employment throughout the Union. This objective was funded through the ESF, and priorities were tied into the aims of the European Employment Strategy and reflecting the Employment Guidelines (see Chapter 16).

Of the remaining 6 per cent of funding not directed towards the priority objectives, the vast majority was channelled into support for 'Community Initiatives', which sought common solutions to specific problems. For 2000–2006, these initiatives were: Interreg II, concerned with cross-border, transnational and interregional cooperation; Urban II, directed to the sustainable development of cities and declining urban areas; Leader+, which focused on rural development through local initiatives; and Equal, which focused on transnational cooperation in combating discrimination and inequalities in access to work. The rest went on Commission own-initiative 'Innovative measures', which sought to develop strategies for the exchange of experience and cooperation between those involved in regional policy across the EU.

The scheme for 2007–2013 again identifies three priority objectives, though these are now reformulated as, first, the *Convergence* objective, which is in effect a continuation of Objective 1, being targeted at speeding up convergence of the least developed Member States and regions, by improving conditions for growth and employment (General Regulation, Article 2(2)(a)). This objective attracts around 80 per cent of the available resources, some €282.8 billion from a total of €308 billion (General Regulation, Article 18). The general criteria for eligibility are set out in Article 5 of the General Regulation, those regions fulfilling the criteria are then identified by the Commission. Of the 27 Member States, a majority, 17, have regions which qualify for funding under the convergence criteria, which are those with a GDP per inhabitant of less than 75 per cent of the EU average. These include the whole territories of some of the new States, such as Bulgaria, Estonia and Poland; in the UK, it covers Cornwall and the Scilly Isles, West Wales and the Valleys, and the eligible French regions are the overseas regions of Guadeloupe, Guyane, Martinique and Réunion. Funding for the convergence regions comes from all three of the Structural Funds. A politically necessary move is to afford further 'phasing out' funding to regions which would have been eligible under the criteria if these were calculated on an EU-15 basis (General Regulation, Article 8). The new *Regional Competitiveness and Employment* objective is directed at strengthening regions' competitiveness and attractiveness, and employment growth, and it applies across all EU territory not covered by the convergence objective (General Regulation, Article 2(2)(b)). Urban and Equal are brought to an end and subsumed within this new objective. Nineteen Member States have eligible regions, and the total budget is some €55 billion, drawn from the ERDF and ESF. Finally, the Interreg Community Initiative is upgraded to an objective in its own right, the *European Territorial Cooperation* objective. The aims of this objective are to strengthen cross-border cooperation through joint local and regional initiatives, transnational cooperation aiming at integrated territorial development, and interregional cooperation (General Regulation, Article 2(2)(c)). Some €8.7 billion is available, drawn from the ERDF. This objective is further supported by the possibility of local and regional authorities establishing European Groupings of Cross Border Cooperation, legal entities which can oversee and manage projects under the cooperation objective (European Parliament and Council Regulation 1082/2006, OJ 2006 L210/19).

## 18.5  Programming

Assistance under the Funds is granted not to individual projects, but is tied to multi-annual programmes (General Regulation, Article 10) which may incorporate a range of projects and initiatives and draw from one or more of the Funds. The Commission originally had a more hands-on role in project selection but, since the 1988 reforms, this role and management more generally have been progressively handed over to the Member States. The 2007–2013 Regulations have introduced a more simplified framework for the development of programmes, at least at the level of the interface of the Member States and the EU institutions. With the institutions having agreed the budget, set out the core regulations and developed (in close discussion with the Member States) the strategic guidelines, the next stage in the process is for the Member States to draw up their *National Strategic Reference Framework* (NSRF) (General Regulation, Article 27). This is done in consultation with the Commission, and in the light of the strategic guidelines. The NSRF defines the strategy chosen by the Member State and proposes a list of operational programmes (OPs) that it hopes to implement for each of the objectives it is eligible for (General Regulation, Article 32). The OPs present the priorities of the Member State and the way in which it will lead its programming. These require adoption by the Commission, and it is expected that some 450 OPs will be adopted over the 2007–2013 period. The Commission then commits the expenditure for the OPs, and the Member States and its regions then implement them, selecting thousands of projects which will be funded, and, through management authorities, monitoring and assessing their operation and results, feeding back to the Commission, who will pay the certified expenditure. Ongoing reporting is required from both Member States and the Commission (General Regulation, Articles 28 and 29).

## 18.6  Multi-Level Partnerships

The principle of partnership is designed to promote the full involvement of those 'on the ground' in the operation of the Funds. General Regulation, Article 11 recognises a range of actors who may have a role to play in the operation of programmes: regional, local and urban authorities, the economic and social partners and other relevant bodies representing civil society, the environmental partners, NGOs and bodies promoting equality between men and women. 'Partnership' between these local and regional actors, the central administration of the Member State concerned and the Commission is intended to operate at every stage of the programming cycle, covering the preparation, implementation, monitoring and evaluation of assistance (Article 11(2)).

The possibility for the direct involvement of these subnational bodies in the policy process has formed the empirical basis for the development of the model of multi-level governance in the EU (Hooghe, 1996) as the monopoly of power held by central governments is challenged. Some authors are however sceptical of the claims of the multi-level governance advocates, arguing that the partnership principle is perhaps more illusory than real, and that the dominance of central government in the policy process has not been unduly threatened by the operation of the partnership principle in its current form (Allen, 2000). There is certainly evidence to support the contentions of the intergovernmentalist camp: regional and local actors have no *independent* right to participate in the processes surrounding the operation of the Funds. Instead, the regulation provides that it is for the Member State to control the involvement of such actors, designating the regional and local partners 'within the framework of its current national rules and current practices' (Article 11(1)). The European Anti-Poverty Network, a grouping of NGOs, has reported on the failures to date of effective partnership, and has identified the possibility of the Commission refusing to adopt Operational Programmes which fail to fully respect the partnership principle. Further, it has called on interested parties who consider themselves to have been sidelined to raise a formal complaint with the Commission for a Member State's failure to observe the partnership principle (Harvey, 2006: 29–30).

The legal position of subnational actors before the European Courts is also problematic. In Case C-417/04P *Regione Siciliana* v. *Commission* ([2006] ECR I-3831), the Commission argued that an action by the Sicilian regional authority to challenge a decision ordering repayment of monies paid under the ERDF to fund a dam project that was not completed must fail on the grounds of a lack of direct concern on the part of the applicant. The Commission argued that only the Member State would have direct concern, as it was the Member State alone which was responsible for implementing policy and formed a 'screen between the Commission and the final beneficiary'. The Court agreed.

The respect for national constitutional traditions has led to differentiation in the scope and depth of subnational actor involvement across the Member States. For example, while the German *Länder* are particularly well entrenched in the policy process, regions in more centralised states are often less so. As Scott observes, partnership, 'though a child of community law, remains ultimately a substantive expression of domestic constitutional arrangements' (1998b: 183). There are concerns surrounding the coherence of a regional policy essentially operated 'for regions, by the regions', which may lead to great variation in the definition of both development problems and their solutions (Allen, 2000: 260).

### 18.7 Additionality of EU Funding

Rather than replacing national expenditure, assistance granted under the Structural Funds is designed to complement, and be additional to, national cohesion efforts. National contributions are determined in consultation with the Commission under the NSRF (General Regulation, Article 15). In this way, the effectiveness of Union assistance should be enhanced. Some commentators have doubted whether the Commission has been granted a wide enough set of formal powers to monitor the operation of the additionality principle (Sutcliffe, 2000), which has not always been fully respected by all Member States (Mitchell and McAleavey, 1999). However, rather than increase its powers in this regard under the 2007–2013 system, the management, monitoring and evaluation are increasingly decentralised to the Member States and designated authorities within them. Some role in monitoring and evaluation for the Commission certainly still exists, though this is to be exercised in accordance with the principles of subsidiarity, and proportional intervention: that the financial and administrative resources employed in the operation of the Funds should be proportional to the amount of expenditure allocated under the OP (General Regulation, Article 13).

## 18.8 Relationship with Other Policy Areas

The Structural Funds Regulations provide that the operation of the Funds should be consistent with other EU policies and operations (General Regulation, Article 9(2)). The operation of the Funds is tied to achieving the objectives of the Lisbon agenda, and also to the European Employment Strategy. The Regulation also refers to two horizontal, cross-cutting policy areas, which have been mainstreamed into all EU activity – the promotion of sustainable development, protection of the environment (General Regulation, Article 17) and equality between men and women (General Regulation, Article 16). Cohesion policy must both be consistent with the legal requirements in these fields and actively promote the achievement of these policy goals. As seen above, the General Regulation provides that bodies promoting sex equality and environmental organisations should be considered for participation in partnership, and that the composition of monitoring committees shall promote the balanced participation of women and men.

Despite these stated commitments, in practice potential policy conflicts undoubtedly arise. As Scott has demonstrated in relation to the sometimes deleterious environmental impacts of activities financed under the Funds, the Commission's powers to oversee Member States' compliance with environmental norms at the level of programme and project implementation may be considered as too limited, and to too great an extent dependent on the good faith of the Member States (Scott, 1995: chapter 4). The 2007–2013 Regulations seek to ensure that there are robust monitoring and evaluation procedures in place, though the Commission's role is increasingly reduced to one of checking on Member States' own internal checking systems.

A more fundamental conflict arises in relation to competition policy. Structural interventions of the sort brought about under the Funds are 'anathema to established free market principles' (Frazer, 1995). The granting of assistance under the Funds in order to develop lagging regions, accompanied as it is by Member State contributions in accordance with the principle of additionality, may have the effect of distorting competition. Funding is explicitly designed to favour national (regional) producers and manufacturers, albeit in an attempt to generate conditions of fair competition, through the removal of competitive inequalities. As such, however, Member State contributions may fall foul of the Treaty prohibition against State Aids (Article 87 EC), as may any support granted independently of EU funding initiatives, under *national* regional polices. Indeed, national regional aid programmes far exceed EU interventions both in terms of the extent of financial resources deployed and of the regional coverage of aid.

Aid generally may be exempted from the state aid prohibitions under Article 87(3) EC Treaty. Article 87(3)(a), for example, exempts regional aid for the promotion of the economic development of areas where the 'standard of living is abnormally low or there is serious underemployment'. As seen under the previous programming period, this was interpreted in line with the criteria for eligibility under Objective 1 (Structural Funds Regulation 1260/99, and Commission Guidelines on National Regional Aid, OJ 1998 C74/06). Article 87(3) further provides for the possibility of allowing aid granted for economic purposes and for the purposes of the conservation of culture. While the Regional Policy DG has been seeking for some time to bring into line the areas eligible under EU Funding programmes and those in receipt of funding under internal, national programmes, disparities and a certain degree of incoherence between them remain (Wishlade, 1998; Commission, *Second Report on Economic and Social Cohesion*, COM (2001) 24).

## 18.9 Assessment of Regional Policy and the Structural Funds

Assessments of the Structural Funds' contribution to achieving economic and social cohesion are varied. Not least, there is dispute as to whether in fact the Structural Funds have in any significant way contributed to reducing disparities between states and regions. While the Commission points to successes such as Ireland, which has received substantial cohesion funding and in terms of *per capita* GDP now is the second most prosperous EU country after Luxembourg, disparities between states and regions remain signficant, and of course have been substantially increased following enlargement (*Third Progress Report on Cohesion*, COM(2005) 192). Evans (2003), meanwhile, suggests that the Funds may have been used more to reduce disparities between Member States than between regions. Ingham *et al* (2003), assessing the economic impact of the Funds pre-2004, note that while some degree of convergence in terms of *per capita* output has occurred, there is no conclusive evidence that this has resulted from the operation of the EU's regional policy and its structural funds. De Rynck and McAleavey, meanwhile, have attacked criteria for determining cohesion as being insufficiently precise, allowing cohesion policy and the Structural Funds to be reduced to tools to achieve 'acceptable levels of inequality', a concept which itself will be open to variation 'according to political ideology and change over time' (de Rynck and McAleavey, 2001: 541). It has been suggested that the Funds have simply been spread too thinly across the EU to make a significant impact.

Further, the thrust of cohesion policy, with its traditional focus on *regional development*, has failed to significantly address the disparities in income and opportunities faced by particular *groups* within society. It has been demonstrated that pockets of economic and social disadvantage can be 'hidden' within a region with a relatively high GDP (de Rynck and McAleavey, 2001: 544). The tools of the Structural Funds, dominated as they are by the European Regional Development Fund and insofar as they operate along a geographical dimension, are ill-equipped to reduce disparities between vulnerable groups in society. That is not to say that there are not significant efforts being taken to address the exclusion of disadvantaged groups: thematic programmes funded by the ESF, initiatives under the European Employment Strategy and the EU's policies on poverty and social exclusion are all directed at reducing economic and social disadvantage faced by vulnerable groups.

## 18.10    Combating Poverty and Social Exclusion

From the figures produced by EUROSTAT in 2005, some 16 per cent of the population of the EU-25 live below the poverty line (EUROSTAT, Poverty and Social Conditions, 2005). The definition of 'poverty' is now expressed as a percentage of households with a disposable income of less than 60 per cent of the national median in each Member State. This definition is, of course, relative. Those at risk of poverty in a richer Member State may, in income terms, be relatively well-off in a poorer state. The 2004 and 2007 accessions have intensified this disparity. Calls for measures of poverty based on EU-wide thresholds have been made, which could incorporate 'indicators of objective living conditions and subjective feelings of deprivation' (Fahey, 2007: 35), though these have not as yet been taken up. Those living below the poverty line are less likely to have access to – and be able to benefit from – the full range of economic, social and cultural opportunities available in the community in which they live, and may thus be considered potentially 'excluded' from multiple aspects of life in the community. In this way social exclusion goes wider than poverty, which is generally defined as a lack of material resources. The societal inequalities faced by those disadvantaged in this way places great strain on cohesion within a society. In the face of the 'unacceptable' number of people living below the poverty line and in exclusion in the EU, the 2000 Lisbon Presidency Conclusions proposed a strategy for combating social exclusion as part of its 'employment, economic reform and social cohesion' strategic goal. The combating of social exclusion also feeds into the broader theme of the promotion of solidarity, which was also found among the EU's objectives set out in the Constitutional Treaty.

Concerns with issues of social cohesion and exclusion have been heightened with the enlargement to 27 Member States, and the accession of new states with very different welfare traditions from the already diverse systems represented among the 'old' states. The capacity of all states to meet their welfare commitments to their citizens is, of course, facing significant challenges, and the EU is engaged in assisting the Member States to identify and manage suitable responses to these pressures and, more generally, to the process of combating social exclusion. In so doing, EU action draws on a number of interrelated fields within the social dimension, making use of a range of policy tools, key among which is the 'new governance' technique of the Open Method of Coordination (OMC).

The EU's concern with poverty and social exclusion in fact dates back to the 1970s, and to the 1972 Paris Summit meeting, at which the Heads of State and Government had announced their attachment to 'the same importance to energetic proceedings in the field of social policy as to the realisation of the economic and financial union'. The Summit itself was followed by the 1974 Social Action Programme, which contained proposals for 'the implementation, in co-operation with Member States, of specific measures to combat poverty by drawing up pilot schemes'. The following year saw the adoption of the first of a succession of Anti-Poverty Programmes (Council Decision 75/458, OJ 1975 L1999/34) under the catch-all Article 308 EC, which had the primary focus on conducting research into the causes of poverty. The second programme was adopted ten years later (Council Decision 85/8, OJ 1985 L2/24) and the third in 1989 (Council Decision 89/457, OJ 1989 L224/10). Accompanying the third Anti-Poverty Programme was a Resolution on combating social exclusion (OJ 1989 C277/01), in which the Council and Member States' Social Affairs Ministers in Council set out an understanding of social exclusion as going beyond poverty:

'social exclusion is not simply a matter of inadequate resources, and that combating exclusion also involves access by individuals and families to decent living conditions by means of measures for social integration and integration into the labour market.'

Social exclusion, according to the Resolution, was spreading, 'affecting various individuals and groups of people in both rural and urban areas', and combating it was to be regarded as an important part of the social dimension of the internal market. The Resolution called on the Member States to 'implement or promote measures to enable everyone to have access to education, by acquiring proficiency in basic skills, training, employment, housing, community services, and medical care', though, of course, this request had no legally binding force. The Resolution further called on the Commission to study, and to report on the measures being taken by Member States to combat, social exclusion, the Member States being asked to 'pool their knowledge and assessments of the phenomena of exclusion'. In turn, in 1990 the research and monitoring Observatory on National Policies to Combat Social Exclusion was established, the relevant Directorate-General in the Commission, DG EMPL, initiated and funded the coordination and lobbying European Anti-Poverty Network, and direct funding of action research and pilot projects by the Commission grew.

With the coming to the end of 'Poverty 3', the Commission continued to fund pilot projects, despite the fact that the Council had failed to adopt the Commission's Proposal for 'Poverty 4' (COM(93) 435). While provision had been made for such payments in that year's budget, in the absence of an enabling provision of secondary legislation, these payments would be unlawful and beyond the Commission's powers, unless they could be considered 'non-significant'. The Court of Justice refused to find that they could be classified as non-significant expenditure, and further spending was halted, although none of the already allocated funding was to be recalled (Case C-106/96 *United Kingdom, supported by Germany, the Council and Denmark v. Commission* [1998] ECR I-2729). The failure to adopt Poverty 4 (which also led to the disbanding of the Observatory) resulted from the refusal of certain Member States, particularly Germany and the UK, to accept that the EU should have competence to act in the area of social exclusion and poverty beyond a research coordination role. A change of government in the UK and strategic manoeuvring by the Commission (Bauer, 2002) facilitated the adoption, through the Amsterdam Treaty, of provisions now found in Articles 136 and 137 EC Treaty, which have gone some way to fill the gap in EU competence. Article 136 EC lists combating social exclusion as an social objective for action, while Article 137(2) EC specifically charges the EU with the task of encouraging cooperation between Member States through initiatives aimed at 'improving knowledge, developing exchanges of information and best practices, promoting innovative approaches and evaluating experiences in order to combat social exclusion'.

As will be examined below, this Article has provided the legal basis for the adoption of measures under the Social Inclusion OMC. This OMC now takes its place alongside the many other policies which, directly or indirectly, assist in combating social exclusion. These policies clearly include active labour market policies and the operation of the European Employment Strategy (see Chapter 16) (after all, 'the best safeguard against social exclusion is a job' according to the Lisbon Presidency Conclusions). Also included are the Structural Funds, especially the ESF, vocational training and education policies, and non-discrimination policies. Indeed, there is a very high degree of overlapping of policy objectives, goals and strategies taking place around social exclusion, and many of the operative concepts – exclusion, inclusion and cohesion – are somewhat amorphous and diffuse. This has been presented as both a strength and a weakness (Mayes, 2001: 4). On the one hand, the imprecision allows them to offer 'something for everyone', on the other hand, Member States may find they can get away with not doing very much over and above their already existing actions. Stronger obligations could include the adoption of rights-based minimum standards guarantees in terms of access to social welfare systems, or an approach requiring states to meet quantifiable levels of 'inclusion', rather than simply charting inputs. Of course, there would be no real likelihood of getting Member State support for such politically controversial measures, though there have been some soft law developments in this area. These have included Recommendation 92/441 (OJ 1992 L245/46) which called on Member States to 'recognise the basic right of a person to sufficient resources and social assistance to live in a manner compatible with human dignity', and, more recently, the 2000 Charter of Fundamental Rights of the European Union (OJ 2000 C364/01) contains the provision, at Article 34(4), that 'in order to combat social exclusion and poverty, the Union recognises and respects the right to social and housing assistance so as to ensure a decent existence for all those who lack sufficient resources, in accordance with the rules laid down by Union law and national laws and practices'.

## 18.11   The Social Inclusion OMC

While there appears to be much activity as regards employment-related measures to inclusion, the Commission recognised in its communication *Building an Inclusive Europe* (COM(2000) 79) that 'employment is only a partial solution' to combating social exclusion. Since 2000, the EU has provided a broader strategy for social exclusion to be addressed, and this has taken place through the open method of coordination, under the perhaps more politically acceptable title of the 'Social Inclusion' Process.

The Social Inclusion Process takes forward the policy coordination role given to the Commission under Article 137(2) EC Treaty. The role of the EU institutions is not one of standard-setting or rights-granting legislative intervention, but of a 'softer' management of responses to common policy concerns within the framework of a set of overarching, commonly agreed objectives. Biannual National Action Plans (NAPs) on Social Inclusion are drawn up by each state in the light of these objectives, and these are then reviewed by the Commission and Council, who present a Joint Report, though no provision is made for the delivery of recommendations to specific Member States, as is available under the EES.

The EU-wide objectives for the Social Inclusion Process were first established at the 2000 Nice Summit, and subsequently revised in the light of experience in 2002. These included: facilitating participation in employment and access by all to resources, rights, goods and services; and mobilising all relevant bodies in the fight against exclusion. The first NAPs on Social Inclusion were submitted in June 2001, and the Commission and Council's first Joint Report from December that year contained extensive examples of Member State actions, but declared it impossible to identify 'best practices' in the absence of commonly agreed indicators for measuring the incidence of exclusion, and the success or otherwise of policies to combat it. A set of common indicators for measuring exclusion and monitoring was subsequently agreed upon on the basis of work undertaken by the Social Protection Committee. These indicators (including low-income rate after transfers, long-term unemployment rate, incidence of early school leavers not in education or training, and life expectancy at birth) started appearing in the 2003 second-generation NAP on Social Inclusion, and those presented by the new states following accession in 2004.

In 2006, the Social Inclusion Process was brought together with two other social OMCs – on pensions and health care (see Chapter 14) – under a new umbrella framework: the Social Protection and Inclusion Process. The intention to bring together the separate OMCs, all at very different stages of development, was met with concern from both NGOs and the Social Protection Committee, which, while recognising the benefits of streamlining and rationalising the often overlapping aspects of the different OMCs, was concerned to ensure that 'the identity and achievements of the social inclusion and pensions processes can be preserved, can continue to have visibility, and can be further developed in the future' under the new approach (Opinion of the SPC, 12909/03 Annex).

In response to these concerns, the new framework establishes three common overarching objectives across the three OMCs:

(a) social cohesion, equality between men and women and equal opportunities for all through adequate, accessible, financially sustainable, adaptable and efficient social protection systems and social inclusion policies;
(b) effective and mutual interaction between the Lisbon objectives of greater economic growth, more and better jobs and greater social cohesion, and with the EU's Sustainable Development Strategy (see further 17.5 and 17.11);
(c) good governance, transparency and the involvement of stakeholders in the design, implementation and monitoring of policy.

Separate objectives, to be responded to in the National Action Plans, are then provided for each of the three strands. For the Social Inclusion strand, Member States have the objective of making a decisive impact on the eradication of poverty and social exclusion, by ensuring:

(a) access for all to the resources, rights and services needed for participation in society, preventing and addressing exclusion and fighting all forms of discrimination leading to exclusion;
(b) active social inclusion of all, both by promoting participation in the labour market and by fighting poverty and exclusion;
(c) that social inclusion policies are well coordinated and involve all levels of government and relevant actors . . . and are mainstreamed into all relevant public policies.

Within the scope of these objectives, in their drawing up of NAPs, states may be influenced by a range of factors – identifying, on the basis of their performance against the commonly agreed indicators, areas of limited progress, national policy priorities or *ad hoc* policy directions given from the European Council, such as its call in 2006 for states to address child poverty. In its First Report on the new integrated OMC, the Commission was able to report that the vast majority of states had prioritised the area of child poverty, acknowledging a wide range of responses, which included increasing family income, improving access to services, decent housing and protecting children's rights (Joint Report on Social Protection and Social Inclusion 2007, submitted by the Commission and adopted by the Council in February 2007).

Supporting the OMC is a Community Programme for Employment and Social Solidarity – 'Progress' (European Parliament and Council Decision 1672/2006, OJ 2006 L315/1). With a higher profile and better funded than the previous Poverty Programmes, the Programme places a continued emphasis on the EU's role in information-gathering, analysis and dissemination. Inclusion is just one strand of Progress, with the others being: employment and support for the EES; working conditions; anti-discrimination and diversity; and gender equality.

The critical question of the effectiveness of the OMC in terms of influences on national policies and reductions in poverty and exclusion also remains, at best, open, and difficulties clearly surround assessing whether any progress made at national level could be traced back to the operation of the OMC. The first Joint Inclusion Report highlighted that, by and large, the NAPs contained reports of initiatives which were already underway. The Second Report in 2004 was able to report that there was evidence from many states of a strengthening of their institutional arrangements for mainstreaming poverty and social inclusion into national policy-making. Further, the national target-setting for the reduction of poverty and social exclusion, which was introduced with the second round of NAPs on Social Inclusion, may stimulate greater focus and concentration on addressing the issue of exclusion.

According to the Commission, the primary motivation for streamlining the social OMC was to strengthen the social dimension of the Lisbon strategy Commission Communication *Working together, working better: proposals for a new framework for the open co-ordination of social protection and inclusion policies* (COM(2005) 706). The Lisbon strategy, it is to be recalled, includes promoting economic and employment growth, as well as social cohesion. Indeed, the three dimensions of the strategy – economy, employment and social policy – are seen as mutually reinforcing. However, concerns may be expressed as to the status of the social dimension of this strategy. As Armstrong explains (2003: 179), the social inclusion process (and the social dimension generally) operates within the constraints of both the Broad Economic Policy Guidelines (coordinating economic and fiscal policies) and the European Employment Strategy. The social OMCs are considerably 'softer' than the BEPG process, and the EES, in terms of the powers of the EU institutions (e.g. to issue recommendations) and the requirements made on Member States. At worst, one may say that they occupy a space left by these, taking second place to them and the realisation of their objectives. The streamlining of the social OMC will, in turn, allow for a stronger coordination between the economic, employment and social dimensions of the Lisbon agenda, though this comes with no guarentees of an 'upgraded' status for the social dimension.

## 18.12 Targeting 'Vulnerable' Groups

Certain 'vulnerable' groups are regarded as being more at risk from social and economic exclusion, including the long-term unemployed, the elderly, ethnic minorities and people with disabilities. At the EU level, specific programmes and measures have been devised to target these at-risk groups. Such programmes have, in the main, sought to promote policies which enable people to stay in or return to employment, in line with the mantra that the best safeguard against social exclusion is a job. Overlaps with the OMCs in the social protection field are emerging here also, as well as with the EES. The employment-focused approach can be seen, for example, in respect of the Community's policy on older people. The history of the Community's engagement with the position of the elderly dates back to at least 1974, when the Social Action Programme encouraged measures to 'seek solutions to the employment problems confronting certain vulnerable categories of persons (the young and the aged)' (Commission, 1974: 8). Most recently, the Commission has delivered two communications which set out the contours of its current elderly policy, a policy which is centred on 'active ageing' (Commission, 1999, *Towards a Europe of All Ages, Promoting Prosperity and Intergenerational Solidarity*, COM(1999) 221; Commission, 2002, *Europe's Response to World Ageing*, COM(2002) 143). Given the dramatic demographic shift towards an ever-greater proportion of older people in society, the Commission suggests that Member States facilitate and promote later retirement, and more 'gradual' retirement. Lifelong learning is emphasised too, as it can enable workers to re-skill and adapt to the changing nature of work, rather than exit the market. Further, pension systems should be revised to ensure that they are not operating as disincentives against workers remaining in the labour market. Such a concentration on the labour market participation policies as the key to inclusion may be criticised, not least in respect of those for whom participation in the employment market is simply not viable. The employment focus is also somewhat out of step with the much broader vision of inclusion contained within the 2000 EU Charter, which lists age under the general non-discrimination principle at Article 21, and also provides at Article 25 that 'the Union recognises and respects the rights of the elderly to lead a life of dignity and independence, and to participate in social and cultural life'. Bell warns of the risk that, under the EES, 'older people become a labour market commodity to be managed rather than a group of people who are able to participate and shape the policy choices affecting their future'. While Article 25 is a useful corrective to this view, 'it lacks substantive gurantees' (Bell, 2003: 107).

Action in respect of people with disabilities also dates back to at least the 1974 SAP and, while the focus here has again been on labour market participation, a rather broader agenda has been presented, including the consideration of housing needs, of mobility and accessibility, of mainstream schooling for children with disabilities, and of the integration into the community of the severely disabled. A number of formal action programmes have been operated, beginning in 1981 (Resolution 1981, C 347/1). By 1993, the third Action Programme, HELIOS-II (Handicapped People in the European Community Living Independently in an Open Society, 1993, OJ 156/30), had been adopted, which marked, according to Mabbett (2005), 'a significant evolution in the Commission's approach'. Stakeholder involvement rather than the dominance of professionals in the field began to be promoted, and resulted in the creation of the European Disability Forum. As with ageing, policy interventions in this field have tended to be in the nature of soft law non-binding guidelines, research programmes and funded informational services. For example, 2003 was declared European Year of People with Disabilites, and a range of activities, at EU national and local level, were staged which sought to raise awareness about disability issues and disability rights, and to provide a new impetus for action to achieve equality (Commission Communication on *Implementation, results and overall assessment of the European Year of People with Disabilities*, COM(2005) 468). In 2003, the Commission issued a Communication, *Equal Opportunities for people with disabilities: A European Action Plan* (COM(2003) 650), which set out a vision of action in the field running up to 2010. Particular focus was placed on the place of disability issues under the European Employment Strategy and the Social

Inclusion Process. Disability issues are also to be mainstreamed across 'relevant' policy areas.

Amidst the soft law, some hard legal rights are emerging. While remaining legally unenforceable as it stands, the EU's Charter of Fundamental Rights (OJ 2000 C364/1) does include, as well as disability being a protected ground from discrimination under Article 21, the statement that 'the Union recognises and respects the right of persons with disabilities to benefit from measures designed to ensure their independence, social and occupational integration and participation in the life of the community' (Article 24). If the Constitutional Treaty is adopted, a mainstreaming provision will be introduced (Article III-118: elimination of discrimination based on sex, racial or ethnic origin, religion or belief, disability, age or sexual orientation). Focusing in on the specific, however, the 2000 Framework Directive establishing a general framework for equal treatment in employment and occupation (Council Directive 2000/78, OJ 2000 L303/16; see 15.15) offers an important rights' framework covering disability issues. The directive of course applies only in respect of employment, and it is reported to have led to only minor change at Member State level and not, as yet, stimulating an EU-wide adoption of national disability discrimination legislation (Waddington, 2005).

While the elderly and people with disabilities are without legal protection outside the field of employment, the 2000 Race Equality Directive (Council Directive 2000/43, OJ 2000 L180/22; see 15.14) is of immense significance in that its scope of coverage lies in, and also beyond, this field. Its scope extends to more 'social' concerns: 'social protection, including social security and health care, social advantages, education, access to and supply of goods and services which are available to the public, including housing'. The directive takes its place among the anti-xenophobia and anti-rascism programmes which the EU has operated since the mid-1980s (Hervey, 2000b). The field of discrimination on the grounds of race or ethnicity is one that has seen limited intervention, although events of recent years, including enlargement and with it the incorporation of the Roma population, numbering some several million and who face significant, multiple barriers to inclusion, have placed the matter more firmly on the EU's agenda. An EU-wide monitoring unit, now re-established as the Fundamental Rights Agency, monitors racism, xenophobia and anti-Semitism, and provides assistance and expertise to the EU institutions and Member States. The 'Progress' Community Programme for Employment and Social Solidarity includes a strand on anti-discrimination and diversity, which aims to support the effective implementation of the principle of non-discrimination and to promote its mainstreaming in all EU policies. In respect to Roma issues, an Inter-Service Group has been established, chaired by the Employment, Social Affairs and Equal Opportunities DG, which coordinates the different policies and programmes tackling such issues. Buttressing the rights-based approach of Directive 2000/43 meanwhile is the general non-discrimination principle, applying *inter alia* to race, colour, ethnic origin, language, religion or belief, and membership of a national minority (Article 21 of the EU Charter), and Article 22, which provides that the Union shall respect cultural, religious and linguistic diversity (Article 22). This combination of legal protections and action programmes would appear to provide a potentially valuable addition to the Member States' own inclusion policies. However, do they perform the function of reflecting or generating a sense of solidarity across the peoples of Europe? Worryingly, while the directives extend their protection to third country nationals, they appear to exclude application to discrimination based on nationality of third country nationals. As such, there is the risk that divisions between the citizens and non-citizens of the EU may be deepened. Cohesion and solidarity would appear to be pursued more actively between some groups than others.

## Summary

1. Regional Policy addresses the economic, social and territorial disparities existing between the regions of the EU.

2. The most recent enlargements have increased these disparities to an unprecedented level.

3. The Structural, or Cohesion, Funds have a central role to play in addressing regional disparities. These are the European Regional Development Fund, the European Social Fund and the Cohesion Fund.

4. The Structural Funds operate in accordance with four 'implementation principles': concentration of funding, programming, partnership and additionality.

5. The principle of concentration is designed to ensure that structural funding is directed to areas most in need. For 2007–2013, there are three objectives on which funding is concentrated: convergence; regional competitiveness and employment; and European territorial cooperation.

6. Assistance under the Funds is tied to multi-annual programmes, the broad dimensions of which are drawn up by the Member States and then approved by the Commission. Member States are responsible for choosing individual projects to fund. The principle of partnership is designed to promote the full involvement of those.

7. Member State activity should be based on the principle of partnership, and involve a range of actors, including regional, local and urban authorities, the economic and social partners, and other relevant bodies representing civil society. There is significant diversity in the way 'partnership' works across the Member States.

8. Rather than replacing national expenditure, assistance granted under the Structural Funds is additional to national cohesion efforts.

9. The operation of the Funds should be consistent with other EU policies and operations. Particular difficulties arise in relation to competition law and state aids.

10. There is dispute as to whether the Structural Funds have in any significant way contributed to reducing disparities between Member States and regions.

11. The EU is also involved in attempts to reduce the inequalities in the economic and social situation of disadvantaged groups *within* regions and, ultimately, across the EU.

12. The EU's concern with poverty and social exclusion dates back to the 1970s. Today, action is mainly through the OMC, though it is buttressed by activities in a range of other policy fields.

13. Certain 'vulnerable' groups are regarded as being more at risk from social and economic exclusion, including the long-term unemployed, the elderly, ethnic minorities and people with disabilities. Increasingly, rights-based approaches are being taken in these areas.

# Exercises

1. Why does the EU have a regional cohesion policy?

2. How decentralised should the spending decisions under regional policy be?

3. What is the definition of 'poverty' used by the EU? What are its limitations?

4. How does the OMC work in the field of social inclusion?

5. Are there adequate rights' protection to non-discrimination for people with disabilities in the EU?

## Further Reading

Armstrong, K. (2003) 'Tackling Social Exclusion Through OMC: Reshaping the Boundaries of European Governance', in Börzel, T. and Cichowski, R. (eds.), *The State of the European Union: Law, Politics, and Society*, Oxford: Oxford University Press.

Bauer, M. (2002) 'Limitations to Agency Control in European Union Policy Making: The Commission and Poverty Programmes', 40 *Journal of Common Market Studies* 381.

Bell, M. (2002) *Anti-Discrimination Law in the EU*, Oxford: Oxford University Press. See especially chapter 3, 'Racial Discrimination'.

Bell, M. (2003) 'The Right to Equality and Non-Discrimination', in Hervey, T. and Kenner, J. (eds.), *Economic and Social Rights Under the EU Charter of Fundamental Rights: A Legal Perspective*, Oxford: Hart Publishing.

Evans, A. (1999) *The EU Structural Funds*, Oxford: Oxford University Press.

Evans, A. (2003) 'Evolutionary Problems of EU Law: The Case of the Union Funds', 30 *Legal Issues of European Integration* 201.

Hepple, B. (2004) 'Race and Law in Fortress Europe', 67 *Modern Law Review* 1.

Hervey, T. (1998) *European Social Law and Policy*, Harlow: Longman.

Hooghe, L. (ed.) (1996) *Cohesion Policy and European Integration: Building Multi-level Governance*, Oxford: Oxford University Press.

Mabbett, D. (2005) 'The Development of a Rights-based Social Policy in the EU: The Example of Disability Rights', 43 *Journal of Common Market Studies* 43.

de Rynck, S. and McAleavey, P. (2001) 'The Cohesion Deficit in Structural Fund Policy', 8 *Journal of European Public Policy* 541.

Scott, J. (1995) *Development Dilemmas in the European Community: Rethinking Regional Development Policy*, Buckingham: Oxford University Press.

Scott, J. (1998) 'Law, Legitimacy and EU Governance: Prospects for "Partnership"', 36 *Journal of Common Market Studies* 175.

Waddington, L. (2005) 'Implementing the Disability Provisions of the Framework Employment Directive: Room for National Discretion', in Lawson, A. and Gooding, C. (eds.), *Disability Rights in Europe: From Theory to Practice*, Oxford: Hart Publishing.

## Key Websites

The Commission DG for Regional Policy's site is at:
**http://ec.europa.eu/regional_policy/index_en.htm**

The Commission DG for Employment, Social Affairs and Equal Opportunities' site is at:
**http://ec.europa.eu/employment_social/index_en.html**

A separate Commission site on Social Inclusion is at:
**http://ec.europa.eu/employment_social/social_inclusion/index.html**

The European Social Fund has its own website:
**http://ec.europa.eu/employment_social/esf/index_en.html**

The Progress Programme for Employment and Social Solidarity has its site at:
**http://ec.europa.eu/employment_social/progress/index_en.html**

Further information on living and working conditions in the EU is available from the Eurofound site, the European Foundation for the Improvement of Living and Working Conditions:
**http://eurofound.europa.eu/**

The European Agency for Fundamental Rights' website is at:
**http://eumc.europa.eu/eumc/index.php**

## 19.1 Introduction

This chapter complements Chapter 11 on external trade policy by looking at a different field of EU external relations. EU development policy consists of a range of policies and instruments, aimed at delivering external assistance to states on the OECD's list of Official Development Assistance (ODA) recipients. According to the 2006 European Consensus on EU Development Policy, agreed between the Council, the representatives of the Member States meeting in Council, the Commission and the European Parliament (OJ 2006 C46/1):

> 'The primary and overarching objective of EU development cooperation is the eradication of poverty in the context of sustainable development, including pursuit of the Millennium Development Goals (MDGs).'

The eight MDGs, agreed at the United Nations General Assembly in September 2000 with a target date of 2015, are to:

- eradicate extreme poverty and hunger;
- achieve universal primary education;
- promote gender equality and empower women;
- reduce the mortality rate of children;
- improve maternal health;
- combat HIV/AIDS, malaria and other diseases;
- ensure environmental sustainability; and
- develop a global partnership for development.

More than perhaps any other EU policy, apart from external trade policy (see Chapter 11), EU interventions in the field of development policy have been consistently shaped by global multilateral frameworks, such as those provided by the UN (especially the MDGs), the G8 (especially the agenda on debt relief), the WTO and the OECD (especially its Development Assistance Committee or DAC). In the context of the UK's presidencies of both the G8 and the EU in the latter half of 2005, the EU and its Member States committed themselves to raising the level of aid to 0.56 per cent of GNI by 2010 and 0.7 per cent of GNI by 2015.

Between them, the EU and the Member States deliver annually nearly €50 billion in external assistance, amounting to more than 55 per cent of global aid. This is at present around 0.42 per cent of GNI. The EU alone disburses more than €10 billion annually, through a combination of aid channelled through the EU budget itself and aid channelled through the European Development Fund. This makes the EU itself the third or fourth largest donor in the world, and therefore a significant international actor in this context. Within the EU there are differences in how much the EU Member States contribute. The 'old' pre-2004 Member States have set, and generally meet, higher GNI targets, albeit within a substantial range. Sweden already commits over 1 per cent of GNI to aid, but the southern European states of Greece, Italy and Portugal lie well behind at around 0.20 per cent.

Under the EU treaties, development policy is not at present a shared competence of the EU and the Member States, but an area where EU action is intended to be *complementary* to the action of the Member States. This means that, as well as EU-level agreements and policies, Member States maintain their own development agreements and relationships. This is clear from the text of Article 177 EC, which introduces Title XX of Part Four of the EC Treaty. It provides:

'1. Community policy in the sphere of development cooperation, which shall be complementary to the policies pursued by the Member States, shall foster:
  ▶ the sustainable economic and social development of the developing countries, and more particularly the most disadvantaged among them;
  ▶ the smooth and gradual integration of the developing countries into the world economy;
  ▶ the campaign against poverty in the developing countries.
2. Community policy in this area shall contribute to the general objective of developing and consolidating democracy and the rule of law, and to that of respecting human rights and fundamental freedoms.
3. The Community and the Member States shall comply with the commitments and take account of the objectives that have been approved in the context of the United Nations and other competent international organisations.'

This is reinforced by Article 180 EC, which requires coordination in development cooperation policy between the EU and Member States. The complementarity of the national and the EU policies is such that the two are often considered together in practice. Thus the European Consensus on Development quoted above states that 'EU Development Policy' in this context includes the policies of both the Member States and the European Community. Hence both the EU institutions and the Member States themselves were involved in the process of drawing up, and signing up to, the consensus, which contains both an EU vision of development and details of the European Community development policy itself.

In practice, development policy is not contained within one single part of the EC Treaty or encapsulated by any single type of legal instrument, nor is the policy as a whole dealt with, or indeed coordinated, by one distinct section of the Commission. This can make it a rather confusing policy area. There are important links between EU development policy and other policies such as external trade (Chapter 11), internal security policy under the aegis of the area of freedom, security and justice (Chapter 13), and the common foreign and security policy more generally (which is not specifically discussed in this book). In addition, the EU has made extensive use of external assistance instruments in the context of enlargement to support a range of states under pre-accession programmes, and more generally to support other 'near neighbour' states under the European Neighbourhood Policy, especially with a view to fostering stability and security at the borders of the EU. It is therefore clear that development policy has a role to play not only in the overall context of the EU's external relations (whether economic or political in nature), but also in the context of some of its internal policies. Policies such as those on immigration and multiculturalism are strongly affected by development policies both at the national and the EU level.

The whole field of development policy is highly contested, not only in the EU and its Member States, but also on a global basis. For example, a crisis of faith has been identified within development cooperation generally and therefore within EU policy. The effectiveness of development aid in improving the living conditions of the people in developing countries is being queried more and more frequently. Despite years of aid to sub-Saharan Africa, very little in the way of clear, permanent improvements in the living conditions of the majority of people can be identified. Therefore, there is a need to identify whether current systems are flawed and whether anything can be done about it. One potential reason for the lack of effectiveness of development aid has been that the difficulties within the developing countries have less to do with the provision of resources and more to do with political corruption, the absence of good and effective governance, and the absence of human rights protection. One response to this has been to link cooperation on these issues to aid, a policy known as conditionality. This means that any aid granted is linked to achievement in these fields and can be withdrawn if progress is not satisfactory. It has, however, been a controversial policy, in that it is seen as imposing 'European values' on non-European states. Further, its implementation has been patchy and inconsistent.

More recently, security issues have also come to the fore. The broadly altruistic intention to assist development in the developing world through the delivery of aid has been combined with a more interventionist desire on the part of the EU and its Member States, like other donor states, to transmit 'the political values, norms and securitized approaches of the donor in order to influence Third World governance' (Hadfield, 2007: 39). At the same time, reinforcing what Hadfield calls the 'Janus-face' of EU development policy, the Consensus on Development also reiterates the point that developing states remain primarily responsible for their *own* development. Hence, development policies should not be seen as something done *to* them, but rather something done in partnership *with* them.

Finally, as will be seen, the origins of much EU development policy can be found in the particular relationships between some Member States and those countries with which they have prior colonial relationships. As a consequence, it is often argued that such states continue to enjoy priority over other states, even if the objective case for supporting them in particular is not so clear. This prioritisation has been justified by the continued responsibility of former colonial powers to help countries integrate independently into world affairs. However, this approach has been challenged. It can be argued that policy priorities should be refocused to give countries priority on the basis of need rather than on the basis of prior historical connections.

## 19.2  The Evolution of EU Development Policy

The current format of EU development policy, in terms of the institutions involved and the instruments used, can only be understood in a historical context.

While the original Treaty of Rome made relatively little provision for development cooperation, it did lay the foundations for the subsequent evolution of policy. It contained provisions dealing specifically with territories and countries which already had existing links with the Member States. These provisions were incorporated at the request of France, who wanted to make sure that its colonies would be properly considered in the context of the evolution of European integration. The original treaty made provision not only for association agreements in general (now Article 310 EC), but also for association agreements with the non-European countries and territories (overseas countries and territories: OCTs) which have special relations with certain states (now Denmark, France, the Netherlands and the UK: see Articles 182–188 EC).

Meanwhile, Article 310 has been used to conclude increasingly broad-based partnership agreements with the so-called ACP (African, Caribbean and Pacific) states which are linked to the Member States, most recently the Cotonou Partnership Agreement of 2000 (OJ 2000 L317/3). These combine trade policy and development policy provisions, and – more recently – have included elements concerned with human rights, good governance and security issues.

However, from 1971 onwards, the Commission began to propose a wider policy, covering states other than those linked to the Member States in these ways. In any event, there was to be an expansion of the countries associated with the Community, because the UK's membership required provision to be made for the Commonwealth. However, what was proposed by the Commission was a wider involvement. The breakthrough document was the Commission's 1971 Memorandum on a Community Policy for Development Cooperation (SEC(1971) 2700). This new approach was accepted by the Member States at the Paris Summit in 1972. It was recognised that there was a need for a Community role in aid and development. The goal was to set up a worldwide policy, but give preference to countries with which the Community already has special relations. There was also to be a clearer elaboration of Community policy. Policy should relate to both trade and aid. A trade preference system was to be set up for the import of goods from outside the Community. Commodity agreements were to be promoted, and more official development assistance was to be provided. Nevertheless, no political element was envisaged.

This policy met with limited success. Subsequent policy documents therefore set out as an objective the promotion of self-reliant and sustainable development through proper development programmes, rather than simply short-term aid. It prioritised the promotion of international economic cooperation, rather than making states dependent on bilateral agreements with the Community. From the 1970s onwards thought was given to introducing political elements into the successive Lomé Conventions (the predecessors of the Cotonou Agreement), but this was not achieved until after 1986 when the Single European Act gave the European Parliament the right of assent in relation to Association Agreements. The European Parliament made it clear that it would not assent to the Lomé IV Convention in 1989 without a human rights clause in place.

McMahon has argued that over time three very different types of measures have been given priority. Firstly, food policy, in the form of food aid and food security through agricultural development, was emphasised. Secondly, alongside the increased interest in environmental policy within the Community, the improvement of the environment became an important priority within development policy. Finally, the Community became particularly involved in measures focused on the improvement of the empowerment of women in developing countries (McMahon, 1998b).

Such measures as were introduced above and beyond the arrangements for the ACP states rested on a flimsy constitutional foundation within the EU legal order. Article 308 EC (then Article 235 EEC) was used, for example, as a legal basis for measures aimed at delivering humanitarian aid. The flimsiness of the legal basis in the EC Treaty is evident, argues Eeckhout, from a close reading of two important Court of Justice judgments on external aid matters, dating from the mid-1990s (Eeckhout, 2004: 107). In Joined Cases C-181 and 248/91 *Parliament* v. *Council and Commission (Bangladesh Aid)* ([1993] ECR I-3685), the Parliament sought the annulment under Article 230 EC of a decision to grant special aid of a humanitarian nature to Bangladesh. The Parliament objected to a situation in which aid was to be granted as part of EU policy towards that country either by the Member States directly, or via an account administered by the Commission. The issue underpinning the Parliament's objection was that it thereby lost out in terms of the budgetary powers and powers over financial regulations which it would otherwise exercise. Essentially, the Court's judgment approved the mixed arrangements involving the Member States and the Commission, making a number of comments which stand as good law in general terms, notwithstanding subsequent treaty developments which have extended the Community's competence and added new legal bases.

For example, it held that:

'the Community does not have exclusive competence in the field of humanitarian aid, and . . . consequently the Member States are not precluded from exercising their competences in that regard collectively in the Council or outside' (para. 16).

It is the capacity of the Member States effectively to 'borrow' the Council and indeed certain budgetary arrangements that is crucial. As Koutrakos puts it (2006a: 158):

'The significance of this statement for the exercise of the competence shared by the Member States with the Community may hardly be overstated: Community institutions, procedures and forms of action are available to the Member States in addition to the intergovernmental forms of cooperation to which they may decide to have recourse.'

He goes on to quote extensively from the judgment (2006a: 158):

'In terms of the involvement of Community institutions in the implementation of such policies, Community law "does not prevent the Member States from entrusting the Commission with the task of coordinating a collective action undertaken by them on the basis of an act of their representatives meeting in the Council" ' (para. 20).

'In terms of the mode of implementation of such policies, "nothing in the Treaty precludes the Member States from making use outside the Community context of criteria taken from the budgetary provisions for allocating the financial obligations resulting from decisions taken by their representatives" ' (para. 22).

It is significant, suggests Eeckhout (2004: 108), that neither the Court of Justice nor the Advocate General suggested a specific legal basis in the EEC Treaty as it then stood for humanitarian aid policy. On the other hand, the Court's solution – although problematic from the perspective of the Parliament – could be seen as pragmatic in terms of the freedom which it gave to Member States to agree humanitarian aid packages.

The Parliament was also knocked back in a second action it brought in respect of the financial arrangements for funding the aid elements of the Lomé IV Convention with the ACP states. The ACP–EU Conventions have always been funded (and still are) by means of provisions on a European Development Fund (EDF) set up for each convention by means of an internal agreement between the representatives of the Member States, on each occasion establishing a multi-annual financial framework (EDF 10 for 2008–2013: OJ 2006 L247/32). This in turn is based on the ACP–EU agreement itself, the overall financial framework for the European Union for the relevant period, and a Decision of the ACP–EU Council of Ministers (EDF 10: OJ 2006 L247/22). These are in turn implemented by Financial Regulations adopted by the Council, which mimic the arrangements for disbursing from the EU's own budget, but which are institutionally separate from the budget and the financial regulations passed under Article 279 EC. In Case C-316/91 *Parliament* v. *Council (Lomé IV)* ([1994] ECR I-625), the Parliament challenged essentially identical arrangements in place for the predecessor agreement, Lomé IV, again objecting to its exclusion from budgetary arrangements and arrangements for financial regulations, which would have given it at least the right to be consulted. Although the ACP–EU agreements are association agreements under Article 310 EC, they have always been concluded as mixed agreements (see 11.7 for more details in the external trade context), agreed by both the Member States and the European Community, especially as regards their provisions on development aid. Echoing its judgment in the *Bangladesh Aid* case, the Court held that as regards financial aid given to the ACP states:

> 'The Community's competence in that field is not exclusive. The Member States are accordingly entitled to enter into commitments themselves *vis-à-vis* non-Member States, either collectively or individually, or even jointly with the Community' (para. 26).

The Convention gives rise to obligations on the part of the Member States, the EU and the ACP states. As regards the Member States and the EU, it is a matter for these parties to settle how they fulfil the financial aspects of these commitments, and it is permissible that the Member States may determine that the expenditure was not Community expenditure, even though the EU institutions are associated with the administration of the expenditure.

The Treaty of Maastricht introduced a new title into Part Four of the EC Treaty (Title XX). Not only does this Title set out a coherent statement of the policy for the first time (see Article 177 EC as set out in 19.1 above), but it also introduces the legal bases needed to adopt a range of instruments to support the achievement of the key objectives of supporting sustainable development and eradicating poverty. Significantly, Article 178 EC recognises the multi-textured nature of development policy, by mainstreaming development issues into other policies which affect developing countries:

> 'The Community shall take account of the objectives referred to in Article 177 in the policies that it implements which are likely to affect developing countries.'

However, the attempts to address the issue of mainstreaming development policy by integrating policy objectives into the other policies of the EU have not been very successful. Integration with the Common Agricultural Policy (see Chapter 9) has been particularly difficult. Activities such as the subsidised export, or 'dumping', of surplus EU beef in West Africa, thus undermining the competitive advantage of local producers, do nothing to encourage local trade and production. This has led to accusations of hypocrisy by organisations such as Oxfam.

Title XX gives an explicit legal basis for development policy measures, specifically Article 179 in respect of unilateral measures and Article 181 in respect of cooperation agreements concluded with third parties. Initially, the cooperation procedure was used for measures adopted under Article 179, but since the Treaty of Amsterdam this has been replaced by the co-decision procedure. The scope of the competences conferred by Title XX was questioned by Portugal in a challenge to the Cooperation Agreement between the EU and India (Case C-267/94 *Commission* v. *Portugal* [1996] ECR I-6177). This agreement was concluded by the Community alone under Article 181 EC (and also Article 133 EC in respect of trade aspects), excluding the Member States. The agreement stated that human rights were an essential element of the relationship and it also included matters, such as measures taken against drug abuse, which are outside the competence of the Community, even if they are not outwith the competence of the Union as a whole (compare Article 29 EU dealing with drug trafficking). The Court held that human rights are an important part of development policy as a whole, drawing on Article 177(2) EC to reach that conclusion, and therefore that any competence to sign development cooperation agreements includes competence to include human rights aspects within that policy. Further, as long as the agreements are focused on the general objective of development policy, any areas which contribute to that objective are within the competence conferred by Title XX.

Eeckhout (2004: 117) suggests that 'the Court's rather restrictive approach in *Portugal* v. *Council* may be one of the causes of the insertion into the EC Treaty of a further title on "Economic, Financial and Technical Cooperation with Third Countries", as part of the amendments introduced by the Treaty of Nice'. Article 181a EC provides:

'1. Without prejudice to the other provisions of this Treaty, and in particular those of Title XX, the Community shall carry out, within its spheres of competence, economic, financial and technical cooperation measures with third countries. Such measures shall be complementary to those carried out by the Member States and consistent with the development policy of the Community.

   Community policy in this area shall contribute to the general objective of developing and consolidating democracy and the rule of law, and to the objective of respecting human rights and fundamental freedoms.

2. The Council, acting by a qualified majority on a proposal from the Commission and after consulting the European Parliament, shall adopt the measures necessary for the implementation of paragraph 1. The Council shall act unanimously for the association agreements referred to in Article 310 and for the agreements to be concluded with the States which are candidates for accession to the Union.

3. Within their respective spheres of competence, the Community and the Member States shall cooperate with third countries and the competent international organisations. The arrangements for Community cooperation may be the subject of agreements between the Community and the third parties concerned, which shall be negotiated and concluded in accordance with Article 300.

   The first subparagraph shall be without prejudice to the Member States' competence to negotiate in international bodies and to conclude international agreements.'

This provision has avoided recourse to Article 308 EC for the conclusion of cooperation agreements with those states which do not fall within the ambit of Title XX, and it has also significantly reinforced the general objective 'of developing and consolidating democracy and the rule of law, and to the objective of respecting human rights and fundamental freedoms'. This strongly confirms the encroachment of the EU into the political sphere. The legislative process for the adoption of measures involves merely consultation with the European Parliament, although the Council acts by a qualified majority unless it is concluding an association agreement under Article 310 EC.

The Constitutional Treaty would have brought relatively few innovations in the field of development policy. Under Article I-14 CT it was designated a *shared* rather than a *complementary* competence, although with the specific rider (Article I-14(4)) that:

'in the areas of development cooperation and humanitarian aid, the Union shall have competence to carry out activities and conduct a common policy; however, the exercise of that competence shall not result in Member States being prevented from exercising theirs.'

Policy coherence in the external sphere under the Constitutional Treaty benefited, however, from there being a single provision (Article III-292(2)) under which the EU's objectives would be gathered together, including objectives relating to fostering 'the sustainable economic, social and environmental development of developing countries, with the primary aim of eradicating poverty' (point (d)), alongside external economic objectives and more traditional foreign policy objectives such as the preservation of peace and the prevention of conflict. A single chapter of the Constitutional Treaty also dealt with cooperation with third countries and humanitarian aid, putting the arrangements for humanitarian aid on a somewhat firmer legal basis than before with a specific new provision (Article III-321 CT).

### 19.3 Current Basic Instruments and Institutional Arrangements

The Commission plays a central role in the practical delivery of the EU's objectives in relation to development cooperation. It now operates under a clearer legal framework, given the Treaty developments detailed in 19.2. The year 2006 saw the adoption of an important set of Regulations establishing a number of key thematic instruments aimed at the achievement of the objectives set out in the Consensus on Development. The instruments are based on a mixture of legal bases. These comprise:

▷ European Parliament and Council Regulation 1905/2006 (OJ 2006 L378/41) establishing a financing instrument for development cooperation (based on Article 179(2) EC);

▷ European Parliament and Council Regulation 1889/2006 (OJ 2006 L386/1) on establishing a financing instrument for the promotion of democracy and human rights worldwide (based on Articles 179(1) and 181a(2) EC);

▷ European Parliament and Council Regulation 1717/2006 (OJ 2006 L327/1) establishing an instrument for stability (based on Articles 179 and 181a EC);

▷ Council Regulation 1934/2006 (OJ 2006 L405/41) establishing a financing instrument for cooperation with industrialised and other high-income countries and territories (based on Article 181a EC);

▷ European Parliament and Council Regulation 1638/2006 (OJ 2006 L310/1) laying down the basic provisions for a European Neighbourhood Policy instrument (based on Articles 179 and 181a EC);

▷ Council Regulation 1085/2006 (OJ 2006 L210/82) establishing an instrument for pre-accession assistance (based on Article 181a EC).

These operate in addition to the Cotonou arrangements, based on the agreement of 2000 (OJ 2000 L317/3), as updated in 2005 (OJ 2005 L209/27), which are multilateral in nature (see 19.7). The current arrangements for the association of the OCTs date from 2001 and take the form of a Council Decision adopted under Article 187 EC (OJ 2001 L314/1). Humanitarian aid is based on a Regulation dating back to 1996, giving a mandate to ECHO (see below). The Regulation is based on Article 179 (Council Regulation 1257/96, OJ 1996 L163/1). A separate Rapid Reaction Mechanism (Council Regulation 381/2001, OJ 2001 L57/5), based on Article 308 EC, allows for the financing of civilian crisis management operations, in the context of crises arising in third countries where the EU's action can contribute to conflict prevention or reduction. This is an example of a measure taken under the EC Treaty in order to facilitate the achievement of foreign policy goals identified under the EU Treaty, but it has clear ramifications for the delivery of EU development policy.

One mechanism by which these frameworks are then operationalised is by means of individual cooperation agreements with particular countries. However, such development cooperation agreements can also exist without any particular framework agreement. They contain a wide variety of provisions, including trade preferences, financial support and aid, and technical development assistance. On top of these kinds of agreements, the EU also operates trade preference systems which are applied on a country-by-country and a product-by-product basis. Humanitarian aid is operationalised through partnerships with NGOs and other international organisations. Since 2001, the

EU has followed up OECD initiatives on the 'untying' of aid. Aid is 'tied' where rules applied by the public authorities of a donor state or international organisation granting bilateral development aid to a third state require the public authorities of the donee state to procure, in whole or in part, goods or services to be purchased pursuant to the grant of aid, from undertakings established in the donor. Measures adopted in 2005 open up access to aid on the part of a wider range of organisations and firms (European Parliament and Council Regulation 2110/2005, OJ 2005 L344/1; Council Regulation 2112/2005, OJ 2005 L344/23). According to the preambles to these measures:

> 'The practice of tying the granting of aid, directly or indirectly, to the purchase of goods and services procured by means of that aid in the donor country reduces its effectiveness and is not coherent with a pro-poor development policy. The untying of aid is not an aim in itself, but should be used as a tool to cross-fertilise other elements in the fight against poverty, such as ownership, regional integration and capacity building, with a focus on empowering local and regional suppliers of goods and services in developing countries.'

Most aid projects are financed either through the EU budget and the European Development Funds (ACP and OCT), and are managed by various services of the Commission. The European Parliament continues to be excluded from the establishment of budgetary arrangements for those parts of Community aid policy funded out of the European Development Funds (ACP and OCT).

Since 2000, the Commission has worked on concentrating the delivery of aid through two bodies: the EuropeAid Cooperation Office with responsibility for development aid and ECHO, the EU's humanitarian aid office. Humanitarian aid is distinguished from development aid in that it is a response to particular crisis situations, aimed at short-term solutions. Furthermore, it is not affected by political or trading considerations, because it is considered as aid given to the population, rather than aid given to governments. EuropeAid has a decentralised delivery system bringing in the Commission's delegations in the partner states as key actors. Political responsibility is more diffuse, and somewhat confusing. Both EuropeAid and ECHO fall under the responsibilities of the Commissioner for Development and Humanitarian Aid, who also has responsibility for DG Development. The remit of DG Development covers the ACP (Africa, Caribbean, Pacific) agreements and the OCTs. However, DG External Relations deals with the framework agreements and other cooperation agreements with third countries other than the ACP countries, such as European states covered by the European Neighbourhood Policy, the Mediterranean region, Latin America and Asia. DG Enlargement deals with the current candidate states, and those designated as prospective candidate states. The Commissioner for Development and Humanitarian Aid is therefore only one of several Commissioners responsible for external relations and development issues generally, including the Commissioner for External Relations, the Commissioner for Enlargement and the Commissioner for External Trade. Thus DG Enlargement and DG Trade share some responsibility with the other Directorates-General and offices for the delivery of development policy, using the instruments listed here.

Three core themes can seen coming through the EU's development policy: policies concerned directly with the delivery of aid, especially for the purposes of delivering the MDGs and the eradication of poverty; policies which complement aid delivery through political objectives, especially those concerned with human rights; and policies relating aid to trade.

### 19.4    Aid-related Policy

While early cooperation agreements tended to focus on trade provision, more recent agreements have involved a more explicit aid dimension, with the reduction of poverty being seen as a separate goal of development policy, especially under the framework provided by the MDGs. As the Commission stated in the context of an important review of policy in 2000 (COM(2000) 212 at p.5):

> 'The overarching objective is to refocus the Community development policy on poverty reduction and on aligning the policy framework in different regions. The method would be to support action that would enable developing countries to fight poverty themselves.'

There are two types of aid. Programmable aid is non-repayable aid given to countries as part of traditional development programmes. Non-programmable aid is given to countries on a more conditional basis and can be withdrawn if progress is not satisfactory. Most aid is programmable but the use of non-programmable aid is increasing. Particular efforts to channel aid effectively have been made in relation to water resources, energy resources, infrastructure, education, health issues (especially HIV/AIDS) and food security.

### 19.5    Democracy, Good Governance and Human Rights

It has long been recognised that the political and human rights situation within a country has an important impact on the poverty of its inhabitants. Furthermore, there are particular concerns in the EU at present with conflict prevention, security and the position of so-called 'fragile states' in the difficult international relations' circumstances that have pertained especially after the terrorist attacks in New York on 11 September 2001, and the US-led invasions of Afghanistan and Iraq.

In the EU development policy context, the earliest important statement about the human rights dimension of EU development policy can be found in the Declaration attached to Lomé III in 1985, emphasising that the signatory states maintained an attachment to the value of human dignity. This was incorporated within the Convention itself in 1990, by means of a provision stating that development is centred on humans and thus entails respect for human rights.

A watershed was a 1991 Council Resolution on human rights clauses in cooperation agreements (Bull. EC 11/1991 at p.122). This resolution put good governance and human rights at the centre of the development agenda. It advocated a carrot and stick approach. The carrot takes the form of financial resources made available to beneficiary states in order to encourage democracy and human rights. Any number of subsequent general provisions can be used to illustrate the operation of this carrot. A good example is that the focus on the position of women within developing countries was continued. This was continued through Council Regulation 2836/98 on the integrating of gender issues in development cooperation (OJ 1998 L354/5), which supported the mainstreaming of gender analysis within development policy, allows for the support and facilitation of action to address gender imbalances within developing countries, and gives support for the development and promotion of facilities for working on the gender issue within developing countries. A subsequent 2004 Council Regulation is repealed and subsumed into the general development cooperation instrument (European Parliament and Council Regulation 1905/2006; see 19.3), as gender equality continues to be mainstreamed throughout development policy (see also COM(2007) 100 on gender equality in development). More generally, Council Regulation 975/99 laid down the requirements for the implementation of development cooperation operations which contribute to the general objective of developing and consolidating democracy and the rule of law and to that of respecting human rights and fundamental freedoms (OJ 1999 L120/1), and dealt with the general question of the promotion of human rights and democracy. This provided for technical and financial aid for the promotion and defence of human rights and fundamental freedoms, for support of the processes of democratisation (elections and popular participation in decision-making) and for dealing with internal conflict. The Regulation, however, provided for significant controls to be exercised by the Commission over how the money is spent and what it does. If the money was not spent in a way of which the Commission approves, it could be withdrawn. This Regulation expired at the end of 2006, and was duly replaced by European Parliament and Council Regulation 1889/2006 (see 19.3) for the next period of 2007–2013. It is designed along similar lines, continuing the European Initiative for Democracy and Human Rights, which in 2006, for example, disbursed almost €35 million to support 14 electoral observation missions.

Such positive measures tend to be preferred by the governments receiving aid for a number of reasons. They involve less infringement on national sovereignty, in that they encourage governments to take decisions and make improvement, and they do not further impoverish the innocent victims of undemocratic and corrupt governments. However, they do have their limitations. In particular, they only work when the government concerned is willing to improve governance within the state (Simma *et al*, 1999).

The stick, on the other hand, takes the form of measures which should be taken in the case of violations of human rights and which can lead to the suspension or withdrawal of aid until the situation is improved. This was confirmed in the revised Lomé IV Agreement of 1995, where it was made clear that failure to respect human rights, democracy and rule of law can lead to the retrieval of allocated funds. This is known as the principle of conditionality. This principle is repeated in new cooperation agreements. Since 1995, all cooperation agreements have had to include such a human rights clause (Horng, 2003).

Such measures have in fact been taken against some states, in particular against certain African states, but also against some Mediterranean states. A number of different reasons are cited for different measures, such as warfare, institutionalised violations of human rights or the failure to conduct multi-party elections. Thus, it is only major violations, by the government, of human rights or of the principles of democracy which give rise to measures in the context of cooperation agreements. However, the failure of governments to act according to the principles of democracy and human rights is not the only factor leading to the adoption of punitive measures. Another important factor is the nature of the economic relationship between the state concerned and the EU. It is difficult for such punitive measures to be really effective in the case of some countries in South East Asia, for example, because those countries are economically on a broadly equal level to the EU and therefore there is no relationship of dependence with the EU which can be exploited in order to force the respect of democracy and human rights. In addition, some Member States have commercial interests, such as involvement in arms trading, which may play a role in some of the internal problems within some states and they may not therefore have the moral authority to force the states to change their behaviour.

The policy of human rights conditionality was institutionalised by Article 11 EU. One of the objectives of the Common Foreign and Security Policy is to 'develop and consolidate democracy and the rule of law, and respect for human rights and fundamental freedoms'. Furthermore, we have already noted the references to human rights and democracy in Articles 177 and 181a EC. These provisions demonstrate what Simma *et al* have identified as a problem in this area. Human rights tend to be subsumed within the areas of democracy and the rule of law. However, human rights are in fact needed as a corrective to democracy, particularly in so far as they protect the rights of a minority (Simma *et al*, 1999). It is perhaps significant that the EU's human rights dimension is particularly weak when it comes to protecting minority rights.

A second weakness lies in the very real potential for accusations of hypocrisy on the part of the EU. It can be argued that the EU has very little moral authority to insist on democratic structures and full transparency of decision-making processes, given the genuine concerns expressed by many about the democratic deficit and the lack of transparency within certain policies, including development policy. Internal mechanisms of control are still lacking. The role of the Treaty of Amsterdam in reinforcing the provisions on fundamental rights, democracy and the rule of law in the Treaty on European Union may have gone some way towards dealing with this problem, as did the signature of the Charter of Fundamental Rights of the European Union (OJ 2000 C364/1). While the creation of the European Union Agency for Fundamental Rights in 2007, as successor to the European Union Monitoring Centre for Racism and Xenophobia (Council Regulation 168/2007, OJ 2007 L53/1), also highlights a mounting concern with fundamental rights issues within the EU, it has very limited powers in relation to the monitoring of possible fundamental rights' violations by the Member States outside the scope of the competences covered by the EC Treaty. It does not cover, for example, most of the internal security questions covered by the third pillar, where fundamental rights' violations on the part of the Member States might be most likely to occur (see Chapter 13).

## 19.6 Trade-related Policy

It is perhaps unsurprising that the earliest policy approach taken by the EU to the question of development involved trading assistance. The core liberal free market perspective led to the assumption that free trade was a solution to the problem of poverty and that trade agreements promote positive development. This, however, proved not to be the case. It is not so much import tariffs that affect the economic competitiveness of a particular country as a lack of investment in its economic and social infrastructure. However, trade-related development policy has remained a key aspect of development cooperation, particularly in the context of individual cooperation or association agreements. The EU view seems to be that trade policy is essential, but not sufficient, to support developing countries. Trade-related policy should be understood in the context of the wider EU competence in external economic relations, outlined in Chapter 11.

To complement individual agreements, the EU has established the Generalised System of Preferences (GSP), set up in 1971. This system gives import advantages to lesser developed countries, whether or not there is a cooperation and framework agreement. The GSP is based on three central principles:

▶ *non-reciprocity* means that the trade preference is a benefit conferred by the EU, rather than a bilateral agreement;

▶ *autonomy* means that the trade preference is not dependent on any other system or any other set of rules;

▶ *graduation* means that the preference granted will decrease as the state becomes more economically advanced or as particular products become more competitive.

The system originally functioned by means of tariff suspensions or reductions on certain industrial and agricultural products and with fixed quotas and tariff ceilings. After the major reforms to the system in 1995, quotas and ceilings were replaced by modulated preferential duties within the GSP. The preferences are granted on a country–product basis. This means that both the situation of the country and the competitiveness of the particular product are taken into consideration and therefore that a country could benefit from the GSP for some products but not for others. The GSP was further modified in 2001, incorporating the Everything But Arms Initiative. This grants duty- and quota-free access to the EU market to all products other than armaments coming from the 49 recognised Least Developed Countries. The most recent GSP Regulation dates from 2005 (Council Regulation 980/2005, OJ 2005 L169/1).

As well as the GSP, individual cooperation agreements also contain trade preferences. The maintenance of two separate systems of trade preferences could be said to lead to them cancelling each other out. In particular, questions have been raised as to the effect that the GSP has on the trade advantages given to the poorer African, Caribbean and Pacific states. This has been seen as a significant difficulty. The GSP means that the advantages granted to the ACP in terms of free access to the EU market are much reduced if the competition is increased through the GSP. The ACP countries do benefit from a wider coverage of preferences than that offered by the GSP and the tariff cut is deeper. Nevertheless, the problem of so-called preference erosion by means of the GSP still continues. The benefits granted by the Everything But Arms Initiative have been seen as adding to this problem, which particularly affects states with non-diversified economies, heavily dependent on one or two exports.

The policy is nevertheless defended by the EU. In a speech in 2003, Pascal Lamy, then the Commissioner responsible for external trade, argued that trade barriers are not always the decisive factor in development issues, and that the goal of development should not be to make developing countries dependent on favourable trading relationships with the EU, but rather to encourage economic development within developing regions. The Cotonou Agreement (see 19.7), signed in 2000, sees the end of trade preferences, pursuant to a deal made between the EU and its partners within the WTO, to make the ACP–EU relationship WTO-compliant. It provides for the negotiation of Economic Partnership Agreements, setting up free trade areas between the EU and the six ACP geographical regions, in order to encourage the ACP states to integrate within the world economy and to promote trade within the ACP regions, as well as between individual ACP states and the EU. These agreements are premised on the same arguments about regional economic cooperation driving economic development through the integration of markets, which have been the foundation-stones of the European Union itself. The evolution of the trade–aid relationship also needs to be seen in the light of the continuing Doha Development round of trade talks within the WTO context which are aimed at building the capacity of developing countries to compete effectively in the international trade context, with an emphasis on fair, as well as free, trade (see Chapter 11).

In order to pull together some of the ideas in this chapter, in 9.7 a more detailed discussion is offered of the evolution of the most complex set of development policy relationships which the EU and its Member States have with third countries, namely the EU–ACP partnership.

**19.7** ## Relations with the ACP States

It is important to give some background context to the evolving relationships between the EU and the ACP. The framework cooperation agreement between the EU, its Member States and the ACP states has been updated, and indeed transformed, on many occasions. The agreement has until now always included, and must be replaced by, regionally based Economic Partnership Agreements. However, the ACP–EU framework covers other matters as well, including aid and governance issues. It leads to further bilateral agreements between the EU and the ACP states. It was the earliest forum for development policy, and remains one of the most complex.

The ACP agreements have their origins in the responsibilities of France towards its dependent territories in Africa. Article 131 EEC (now Article 182 EC) allowed for an original convention between the Community and the Overseas Countries and Territories (OCTs), then defined as 'non-European countries and territories which have special relationships with Belgium, France and the Netherlands'. This original convention was signed for five years. It gave to the OCTs preferential access to the EEC market, which meant that, from the perspective of trade, they were effectively treated in the same way as the Member States. Member States were also to contribute to investment within the OCTs.

The successor to this original convention was the Yaoundé Convention of 1963, updated in 1968. This was signed between the EEC and a group called the Associated African and Malagasy States, which comprised 18 countries. It was essentially a continuation of the policies of the original convention, although exceptions to free access in the case of the application of the Common Agricultural Policy were allowed. It contained provisions of both trade preferences and the provision of aid. The Yaoundé Convention, however, included recognition of the fact that many of the OCTs were no longer overseas territories of the Member States, but had gained their independence.

The accession of the UK to the EEC raised certain issues for development policy. It became necessary to expand trade preference to the Commonwealth, with which the UK maintained special trading relationships. The decision taken was that many Commonwealth states would join the Associated African and Malagasy States to form the ACP – African, Caribbean and Pacific states. Some states, such as those on the Indian subcontinent, did not join the ACP, and agreements with them will be considered later in this chapter. In 1975, the First Lomé Convention was signed, between the EEC, its Member States and the ACP states. It consisted of a set of non-reciprocal trade preferences granted to ACP states, combined with separate trading protocols on sugar, beef, veal and bananas. The Second Lomé Convention, in 1979, maintained this basic framework.

The Third Lomé Convention, in 1984, represented a fundamental shift in development policy, in that a move from a simple focus on trade towards the human dimension of development policy can be seen. The agreement focused in particular on self-sufficiency and food security and recognised that, while trade is an important element in eradicating poverty, the problem of poverty needs to be addressed head-on. It also declared a number of basic principles on which relations between the EEC and the ACP should be based: equality, respect for the sovereignty of the states, working towards the mutual interests of the states and interdependence. It made it clear that ACP states had the right to determine their own policies and that they also needed security of relations between them and the EEC in order to make progress. These principles represented recognition of the growing independence and confidence of some ACP states. There was an attempt to make the ACP–EEC convention an agreement between equals and to escape from the patronising post-colonial attitude of the EEC in trying to control the activities of the ACP countries. Aid should not be dependent on the recipient states doing what they are told.

Lomé IV, on the other hand, signed in 1990, with its inclusion of a declaration on human rights and democracy, may have seemed a step backwards in that regard. That agreement contained provisions, not only on human rights, democracy and good governance, but also on the position of women within the states and on the protection of the environment. On top of that, however, the emphasis on increasing regional cooperation was intended to enable the ACP states to lose their relations of dependence on the EC.

The Lomé Agreements can be seen as having achieved a limited success. In 1998, the ACP countries received 43 per cent of the EC aid budget. However, in 1988 the figure had stood at 69.4 per cent. This significant decrease in the proportion of aid given to the ACP countries can perhaps be put down to the perception that aid has not been effective, particularly in sub-Saharan Africa, where conditions have in many cases not improved during the period of the Lomé Conventions. As a response to the perceived ineffectiveness of Lomé, particularly in Africa, a completely new agreement, known as the Cotonou Agreement, was signed between the EU and the ACP in 2000, to replace the Lomé Agreements (OJ 2000 L317/3). This new generation *partnership* agreement was signed for twenty years, with provision made for its revision every five years (see OJ 2005 L209/27), leading to increasing stability in relations between the EU and the ACP countries.

The Cotonou Agreement consists of five pillars (Dearden and Salama, 2002; Hurt, 2003). Firstly, it has a comprehensive *political dimension*, which allows for dialogue between states, and the involvement of the EU in conflict prevention. The policies of human rights and democracy conditionality are maintained, and good governance is to be encouraged. Secondly, *participatory approaches* are to be taken in encouraging development, in particular giving information and allowing for the involvement of actors other than the state. Thirdly, the focus on *poverty reduction* is strengthened. The Cotonou Agreement sets out a general framework for poverty reduction and advocates an integrated approach to poverty reduction strategies, encouraging economic and social development and regional cooperation. The cross-cutting themes of gender balance, environmental sustainability, institutional development and capacity building should be in evidence throughout the whole poverty reduction strategy. Fourthly, the Cotonou Agreement sets out a new framework for *economic and trade cooperation*. New trading agreements will encourage trade liberalisation. Economic cooperation will be linked to human and social development policies and to the strengthening of institutions, and, more generally, include aid policy. In particular, there are proposals to improve the situation for the least developed countries by giving them free access to the EC trading area. Finally, the Cotonou Agreement contains important reforms of *financial cooperation*. States are to be given more responsibility for the money that they are given in aid. Financial aid will be more flexible, in that it will not be attached to specific purposes. However, the agreement moves away from the idea of aid entitlements. No state will be entitled to a particular amount of aid. Their performance will be monitored and either rewarded or punished. It is hoped that this will help to deal with the problem of corruption, when money is absorbed by the government and not used for the purposes of development.

It is still rather too early to say whether the new Cotonou Agreement will succeed where Lomé failed, even after the 2005 revision. Cotonou does seem to respond to the concerns of the ACP states that they were not given sufficient autonomy, although the emphasis on human rights and democracy conditionality and performance-related financial aid both suggest that the ACP countries will need to conform to certain basic standards in order to benefit from development aid. This tension became apparent during negotiations surrounding the first five-year review of the Cotonou Agreement. The EU wished to incorporate into the agreement provisions concerning adherence to international agreements on the non-proliferation of weapons of mass destruction. Many ACP states objected to this, on the grounds that such agreements are not relevant to the development objectives of the Cotenou Agreement and that the EU is using its development policy to achieve political goals. There was also an attempt to deal with the problem of preference erosion, particularly in the case of the least developed states. Hadfield (2007: 65) concludes that:

> 'The political symbolism of Cotonou as a platform of EC external action now outweighs its original geographic or economic objectives.'

She also concurs that the addition of security-based provisions, including provisions effectively imposed in the 2005 revision on weapons of mass destruction, has had a damaging effect on the EU's overall development objectives, 'but arguably adds to the robustness (if not the coherence) of overall EU foreign policy, toughening it up in an increasingly challenging world' (Hadfield, 2007: 66). Increasingly, therefore, EU development policy needs to be seen in the context of the maturing of the EU's wider foreign policy. To that end, a fuller review of the effects of EU development policy would need to consider also the Euro–Med partnership, the European Neighbourhood Policy aimed at the EU's southern and eastern European neighbours, relationships with Latin American states and relationships with Asian states. The latter two cases are particularly interesting as they, like some of the African countries, are increasingly experimenting with forms of regional economic and even political integration which draw heavily upon the experience of the European Union itself. However, development policies aimed at these states, like those of the ACP, are weighed down by frequently contradictory objectives, posing questions regarding policy coherence for which there are – as elsewhere in the context of EU policy-making – no simple answers.

## Summary

1. EU development policy is one of the EU's most important external policies. It combines economic, social and political elements.

2. The objective of EU development policy is the eradication of poverty in the context of sustainable development.

3. EU development cooperation policy consists of a complex structure of multilateral framework agreements, bilateral agreements, trade preference systems and humanitarian aid instruments.

## Summary cont'd

4. While some cooperation mechanisms have existed since the Treaty of Rome was first signed, the early 1970s saw a move towards an explicit EEC role in development cooperation. The amendments to the EC Treaty introduced by the Treaty of Maastricht, in the form of a set of specific provisions and legal bases comprising Title XX of Part Four of the EC Treaty, set out an explicit and relatively coherent field of competence for the Union.

5. The Treaty of Nice introduced an important provision enabling economic, financial and technical cooperation with third countries not covered by Title XX. The Constitutional Treaty, were it to enter into force, would not substantially change the scope of development policy, but lends additional coherence to its provisions.

6. Recent years have seen a substantial overhaul of the basic instruments for the delivery of aid policy, both in respect of the ACP–EU relationship, and also the wider provision of external assistance to third countries.

7. Trade-related policy has always been a central feature of EU development cooperation policy. However, trade preference systems are now understood as being necessary, but not sufficient, to encourage development. Moreover, they are problematic under the WTO. It is seen as equally important to encourage regional economic development, rather than dependence on the EU.

8. Conditionality is an approach whereby development policy is used to promote democracy, good governance and human rights. 'Carrots' are provided to reward good practice, and 'sticks' are used to take action against states violating fundamental principles.

9. The relationship with the African/Caribbean/Pacific states, now based on the Cotonou Agreement, is the longest-standing framework agreement. It has developed from a system of non-reciprocal trade preferences towards having a focus on the promotion of both economic and political development more broadly. The ACP states are negotiating Economic Partnership Agreements with the EU based on the reciprocal guaranteeing of free trade and fostering economic integration between groups of ACP states.

# Exercises

1. What form did the initial interest of what was then the EEC and its Member States in development cooperation with third states take?

2. Why has the European Parliament challenged the legal basis of EU measures supporting development cooperation with third states before the Court of Justice on several occasions, and what important conclusions has the Court of Justice reached?

3. What are the advantages and disadvantages of a trade-based approach to fostering economic development in less-well-developed states, and in what way is the EU well equipped to deliver such an approach from a legal perspective?

4. Can the EU be successful in exporting its values, principles and policies through its development policy?

5. What are the principal problems which currently mark the ACP–EU relationship, as based on the Cotonou Agreement?

6. What are the main differences between the EU's (external) development policies and its (internal) regional development policies?

## Further Reading

Arts, K. and Dickson, A. (eds.) (2004) *EU Development Cooperation: From Model to Symbol*, Manchester: Manchester University Press.

Dearden, S. and Salama, C. (2002) 'The New EU ACP Partnership Agreement', 14 *Journal of International Development* 899.

Eeckhout, P. (2004) *External Relations of the European Union. Legal and Constitutional Foundations*, Oxford: Oxford University Press. See especially pp.103–19 and chapter 13.

Hadfield, A. (2007) 'Janus Advances? An Analysis of EC Development Policy and the 2005 Amended Cotonou Partnership Agreement', 12 *European Foreign Affairs Review* 39.

Horng, D. (2003) 'The Human Rights Clause in the European Union's External Trade and Development Agreements', 9 *European Law Journal* 677.

Hurt, S. (2003) 'Cooperation or Coercion? The Co-Operation Agreement between the European Union and ACP States and the End of the Lomé Convention', 24 *Third World Quarterly* 161.

## Key Websites

EU in the world; portal website at:
**http://ec.europa.eu/world/index_en.htm**

Individual Directorates-General in the 'Relex Family' are at:

*External Relations*
**http://ec.europa.eu/external_relations/index.htm**

*DG Development*
**http://ec.europa.eu/development/index_en.cfm**

*EuropeAid, which coordinates most of the EU's external aid*
**http://ec.europa.eu/europeaid/index_en.htm**

*ECHO, which deals specifically with humanitarian aid*
**http://ec.europa.eu/echo/index_en.htm**

*European Neighbourhood Policy*
**http://ec.europa.eu/world/enp/index_en.htm**

*European Initiative for Democracy and Human Rights*
**http://ec.europa.eu/europeaid/projects/eidhr/index_en.htm**

The EU's websites on trade issues also discuss development questions:

General principles governing EU policy on the intersection of trade and development:
**http://ec.europa.eu/trade/issues/global/development/index_en.htm**

Negotiation of regional Economic Partnership Agreements with the ACP countries to replace the Cotonou Agreement trade chapters:
**http://ec.europa.eu/trade/issues/bilateral/regions/acp/regneg_en.htm**

The Secretariat of the ACP group of countries, carrying up-to-date details of negotiations:
**http://www.acpsec.org/**

The Organisation for Economic Cooperation and Development, based in Paris, groups together 30 Member Countries interested in promoting development and economic cooperation multilaterally.

It publishes authoritative statistics and reports on topics such as development, and brings together the major donor countries and organisations under the umbrella of the DAC (Development Assistance Committee):
**http://www.oecd.org/**

Details of the UN Millennium development goals are available at:
**http://www.un.org/millenniumgoals/**

## Key Websites cont'd

Oxfam's website, discussing fair trade and development and containing some critiques of EU policy is at:

**www.oxfam.org.uk**

CONCORD is the European NGO Confederation for Relief and Development. Its 19 international networks and 22 national associations from the European Member States and the candidate countries represent more than 1600 European NGOs *vis-à-vis* the European Institutions. The main objective of the Confederation is to enhance the impact of European development NGOs *vis-à-vis* the European Institutions by combining expertise and accountability. Its website is at:

**http://www.concordeurope.org/**

# Bibliography and References

Ackers, H. and Stalford, H. (2003) *A Community for Children? Children, Citizenship and Migration in the European Community*, London: Ashgate.

Adenas, M. and Wincott, D. (eds.) (2003) *Accountability and Legitimacy in the European Union*, Oxford: Oxford University Press.

Allen, D. (2000) 'Cohesion and the Structural Funds: Transfers and Trade Offs', in Wallace, H. and Wallace, W. (eds.), *Policy-Making in the European Union* (4th edn), Oxford: Oxford University Press.

Alter, K. and Vargas, K. (2000) 'Explaining Variation in the Use of European Litigation Strategies: European Community Law and British Gender Equality Policy', 33 *Comparative Political Studies* 452–82.

Anderson, J. (1995) 'Structural Funds and the Social Dimension of EU Policy: Springboard or Stumbling Block?', in Leibfried, S. and Pierson, P. (eds.), *European Social Policy: Between Fragmentation and Integration*, Washington DC: Brookings Institute.

Anderson, R. D. and Dev Khosla, S. (1995) 'Competition Policy as a Dimension of Economic Policy: A Comparative Perspective', *Occasional Paper Number 7*, Industry Canada, May 1995. Available online only at:
**http://strategis.ic.gc.ca/epic/internet/ineasaes.nsf/vwapj/op07e.pdf/$FILE/op07e.pdf**

Armstrong, K. (1999) 'Governance and the Single European Market', in Craig, P. and de Búrca, G. (eds.), *The Evolution of EU Law*, Oxford: Oxford University Press.

Armstrong, K. (2002) 'Rediscovering Civil Society: The European Union and the White Paper on Governance', 8 *European Law Journal* 102.

Armstrong, K. (2003) 'Tackling Social Exclusion Through OMC: Reshaping the Boundaries of European Governance', in Börzel, T. and Cichowski, R. (eds.), *The State of the European Union: Law, Politics, and Society*, Oxford: Oxford University Press.

Arts, K. and Dickson, A. (eds.) (2004) *EU Development Cooperation: From Model to Symbol*, Manchester: Manchester University Press.

Ball, S. (2001) 'The European Employment Strategy: The Will but not the Way?', 30 *Industrial Law Journal* 353.

Barber, N. (2002) 'Citizenship, Nationalism and the European Union', 27 *European Law Review* 241.

Barents, B. (1990) 'The Community and the Unity of the Common Market: Some Reflections on the Economic Constitution of the Community', 33 *German Yearbook of International Law* 9.

Barents, R. (1997) 'Recent Developments in Community Case Law in the Field of Agriculture', 34 *Common Market Law Review* 811.

Barmes, L. with Ashtiany, S. (2003) 'The Diversity Approach to Achieving Equality: Potential and Pitfalls', 32 *Industrial Law Journal* 274.

Barnard, C. (2000a) 'Social Dumping and the Race to the Bottom: Some Lessons for the European Union from Delaware?', 25 *European Law Review* 57.

Barnard, C. (2000b) 'Flexibility and Social Policy', in de Burca, G. and Scott, J. (eds.), *Flexible Governance in the EU*, Oxford: Hart Publishing.

Barnard, C. (2001) 'Fitting the Remaining Pieces into the Goods and Persons Jigsaw', 26 *European Law Review* 35.

Barnard, C. (2002) 'The Social Partners and the Governance Agenda', 8 *European Law Journal* 80.

Barnard, C. (2004) *The Substantive Law of the EU: The Four Freedoms*, Oxford: Oxford University Press.

Barnard, C. (2006) *EC Employment Law* (3rd edn), Oxford: Oxford University Press.

Barnard, C. and Deakin, S. (1999) 'A Year of Living Dangerously? EC Social Rights, Employment Policy and EMU', 30 *Industrial Relations Journal* 355.

Barnard, C. and Deakin, S. (2002) 'Market Access and Regulatory Competition', in Barnard, C. and Scott, J. (eds.), *The Law of the Single European Market*, Oxford: Hart Publishing.

Barnard, C. and Scott, J. (eds.) (2002) *The Law of the Single European Market: Unpacking the Premises*, Oxford: Hart Publishing.

Bauer, M. (2002) 'Limitations to Agency Control in European Union Policy Making: The Commission and Poverty Programmes', 40 *Journal of Common Market Studies* 381.

Behrens, P. (2006) 'Case Note: Case C-411/03 *SEVIC Systems AG* [2005] ECR I-10805', 43 *Common Market Law Review* 1669.

Bell, M. (2000) 'Equality and Diversity: Anti-Discrimination Law after Amsterdam', in Shaw, J. (ed.), *Social Law and Policy in an Evolving European Union*, Oxford: Hart Publishing.

Bell, M. (2002) *Anti-Discrimination Law in the EU*, Oxford: Oxford University Press.

Bell, M. (2003) 'The Right to Equality and Non-Discrimination', in Hervey, T. and Kenner, J. (eds.), *Economic and Social Rights under the EU Charter of Fundamental Rights: A Legal Perspective*, Oxford: Hart Publishing.

Berends, G. and Carreno, I. (2005) 'Safeguards in Food Law – Ensuring Food Scares are Scarce', 30 *European Law Review* 386.

Bernard, N. (1996) 'Discrimination and Free Movement in EC Law', 45 *International Comparative Law Quarterly* 82

Bernard, N. (2000) 'Legitimising EU Law: Is the Social Dialogue the Way Forward?', in Shaw, J. (ed.), *Social Law and Policy in an Evolving European Union*, Oxford: Hart Publishing.

Bernard, N. (2003) 'A "New Governance" Approach to Economic, Social and Cultural Rights in the EU Charter', in Hervey, T. and Kenner, J. (eds.), *Economic and Social Rights under the EU Charter of Fundamental Rights: A Legal Perspective*, Oxford: Hart Publishing.

Bernard, N. (2006) 'Internal Market Governance in a Globalised Marketplace: The Case of Air Transport', in Nic Shuibhne, N. (ed.), *Regulating the Internal Market*, Cheltenham: Edward Elgar.

Betlem, G. and Brans, E. (eds.) (2005) *Environmental Liability in the EU – The 2004 Directive compared with US and Member State Law*, London: Cameron May.

Blackburn, R. (2005) 'Capital and Social Europe', 35 *New Left Review* 87.

Den Boer, M. (2002) 'Towards an Accountability Regime for an Emerging European Police Governance', 12 *Policing and Society* 275.

Van den Bogaert, S. (2002) 'Horizontality', in Barnard, C. and Scott, J. (eds.), *The Law of the Single European Market: Unpacking the Premises*, Oxford: Hart Publishing.

Bogg, A. (2006) 'The Right to Paid Annual Leave in the Court of Justice: The Eclipse of Functionalism', 31 *European Law Review* 892.

Bright, C. (1996) 'EU Competition Policy: Rules, Objectives and Deregulation', 16 *Oxford Journal of Legal Studies* 535.

de Búrca, G. (1998) 'The Principle of Subsidiarity and the Court of Justice as a Constitutional Actor', 36 *Journal of Common Market Studies* 155.

dc Búrca, G. (2000) 'Differentiation within the "Core"? The Case of the Internal Market', in de Búrca, G. and Scott, J. (eds.), *Constitutional Change in the EU. From Uniformity to Flexibility?*, Oxford: Hart Publishing.

de Búrca, G. (2003) 'The Constitutional Challenge of New Governance in the European Union', 28 *European Law Review* 814.

de Búrca, G. (ed.) (2005) *EU Law and the Welfare State: In Search of Solidarity*, Oxford: Oxford University Press.

de Búrca, G. and Scott, J. (eds.) (2000) *Constitutional Change in the EU. From Uniformity to Flexibility?*, Oxford: Hart Publishing.

Burrows, N. and Robison, M. (2006) 'Positive Action for Women in Employment: Time to Align with Europe?', 33 *Journal of Law and Society* 24.

Burrows, N. and Robison, M. (2007) 'An Assessment of the Recast of Community Equality Laws', 13 *European Law Journal* 186.

Caracciolo di Torella, E. (2006) 'The Principle of Gender Equality, the Goods and Services Directive and Insurance: A Conceptual Analysis', 13 *Maastricht Journal of European and Comparative Law* 339.

Caracciolo di Torella, E. and Masselot, A. (2001) 'Pregnancy, Maternity and the Organisation of Family Life: An Attempt to Classify the Case Law of the Court of Justice', 26 *European Law Review* 239.

Cardwell, M. (2004) *The European Model of Agriculture*, Oxford: Oxford University Press.

Cardwell, M. (2006) 'Current Developments: Agriculture', 55 *International and Comparative Law Quarterly* 467.

Cardwell, M. and Rodgers, C. (2006) 'Reforming the WTO Legal Order for Agricultural Trade: Issues for European Regional Policy in the Doha Round', 55 *International and Comparative Law Quarterly* 805.

Carrera, S. (2005) 'What does Free Movement Mean in Theory and Practice in an Enlarged EU?', 11 *European Law Journal* 699–721.

Cecchini, P. (1988) *The Economics of 1992*, Oxford: Oxford University Press.

Cecchini, P. *et al* (1988) *The European Challenge: 1992, the Benefits of a Single Market*, Aldershot: Gower.

Chalmers, D. (1995) 'Environmental Protection and the Single Market: An Unsustainable Development. Does the EC Treaty Need a Title on the Environment?', 1 *Legal Issues of European Integration* 65.

Chalmers, D. (1999) 'Inhabitants in the Field of EC Environmental Law', in Craig, P. and de Búrca, G. (eds.), *The Evolution of EU Law*, Oxford: Oxford University Press.

Chalmers, D. (2001) 'The Mistakes of the Good European?', in Fredman, S. (ed.), *Discrimination and Human Rights. The Case of Racism*, Oxford: Oxford University Press.

Chalmers, D. (2003) ' "Food for Thought": Reconciling European Risks and Traditional Ways of Life', 66 *Modern Law Review* 532.

Chalmers, D. and Szyszczak, E. (1998) *EU Law: Towards a European Polity?*, Aldershot: Ashgate.

Chalmers, D. *et al* (2006) *European Union Law: Text and Materials*, Cambridge: Cambridge University Press.

Costello, C. (2003) 'Gender Equalities and the Charter of Fundamental Rights of the European Union', in Hervey, T. and Kenner, J. (eds.), *Economic and Social Rights under the EU Charter of Fundamental Rights: A Legal Perspective*, Oxford: Hart Publishing.

Craig, P. (2002) 'The Evolution of the Single Market', in Barnard, C. and Scott, J. (eds.), *The Law of the Single European Market: Unpacking the Premises*, Oxford: Hart Publishing.

Craig, P. and de Búrca, G. (eds.) (1999) *The Evolution of EU Law*, Oxford: Oxford University Press.

Craig, P. and de Búrca, G. (2003) *EU Law: Text, Cases and Materials* (3rd edn), Oxford: Oxford University Press.

Cram, L. (1997) *Policy Making in the EU: Conceptual Lenses and the Integration Process*, London: Routledge.

Craufurd Smith, R. (2004) *Culture and European Union Law*, Oxford: Oxford University Press.

Craufurd Smith, R. (2007) 'From Heritage Conservation to European Identity: Article 151 EC and the Multi-faceted Nature of Community Cultural Policy', 32 *European Law Review* 48.

Cremers, J. (2006) 'Free Movement of Services and Equal Treatment of Workers: The Case of Construction', 12 *Transfer* 167.

Cremona, M. (1999) 'External Relations and External Competence: The Emergence of an Integrated Policy', in Craig, P. and de Búrca, G. (eds.), *The Evolution of EU Law*, Oxford: Oxford University Press.

Cremona, M. (2001) 'A Policy of Bits and Pieces? The Common Commercial Policy after Nice', 4 *Cambridge Yearbook of European Law* 61.

Cremona, M. (2002) 'The External Dimension of the Single Market: Building (on) the Foundations', in Barnard, C. and Scott, J. (eds.), *The Law of the Single European Market: Unpacking the Premises*, Oxford: Hart Publishing.

Cremona, M. (2006) 'External Relations of the EU and the Member States: Competence, Mixed Agreements, International Responsibility, and Effects of International Law', *EUI LAW Working Paper 2006/22*, European University Institute, available at **http://www.eui.eu**

Crosby, S. (1991) 'The Single Market and the Rule of Law', 16 *European Law Review* 283.

Daintith, T. (1994) 'The Techniques of Government', in Jowell, J. and Oliver, D. (eds.), *The Changing Constitution* (3rd edn), Oxford: Clarendon Press.

Daly, M. (2006) 'EU Social Policy After Lisbon', 44 *Journal of Common Market Studies* 461.

Daniele, L. (1997) 'Non-Discriminatory Restrictions on the Free Movement of Persons', 22 *European Law Review* 191.

Davies, G. (2003) *Nationality Discrimination in the European Internal Market*, The Hague: Kluwer Academic Publishers.

Davies, G. (2005) 'Can Selling Arrangements be Harmonised?', 30 *European Law Review* 371.

Davies, G. (2006) 'The Process and Side Effects of Harmonisation of European Welfare States', *Jean Monnet Working Paper*, 02/06.

Davies, P. (1992) 'The Emergence of European Labour Law', in McCarthy, W. (ed.), *Legal Intervention in Industrial Relations*, *Gains and Losses*, London: Blackwell.

Davies, P. (2003) 'Workers on the Board of the European Company?', 32 *Industrial Law Journal* 75.

Deakin, S. and Wilkinson, F. (1994) 'Rights versus Efficiency? The Economic Case for Transnational Labour Standards', 23 *Industrial Law Journal* 289.

Dearden, S. and Salama, C. (2002) 'The New EU ACP Partnership Agreement', 14 *Journal of International Development* 899.

Degryse, C. and Pochet, P. (2000) 'The Likely Impact of the IGC on European Social Policy': **IGC Info, http://ciginfo.net/CIGinfo/files/igcinfo3en.pdf**

Diaz, F. (2004) 'The Reform of European Merger Control: *Quid Novi Sub Sole*?', 27 *World Competition* 177.

Diemer, C. (2006) 'The Green Paper on Damages Actions for Breach of the EC Antitrust Rules', 27 *European Competition Law Review* 309.

Dougan, M. (2000) 'Minimum Harmonization and the Internal Market', 37 *Common Market Law Review* 853.

Dougan, M. (2006) 'The Constitutional Dimension to the Case Law on Union Citizenship', 31 *European Law Review* 613–41.

Dougan, M. and Spaventa, E. (eds.) (2005) *Social Welfare and EU Law*, Oxford: Hart Publishing.

Doukas, D. (2005) 'The Frailty of the Stability and Growth Pact and the European Court of Justice: Much Ado about Nothing?', 32 *Legal Issues of Economic Integration* 293.

Editorial (2006) 'The Services Directive Proposal: Striking a Balance between the Promotion of the Internal Market and Preserving the European Social Model', 43 *Common Market Law Review* 307.

Edwards, V. (2003) 'The European Company – Essential Tool or Eviscerated Dream?', 40 *Common Market Law Review* 443.

Eeckhout, P. (2004) *External Relations of the European Union*, Oxford: Oxford University Press.

Ehlermann, C. (1987) 'The Internal Market following the Single European Act', 24 *Common Market Law Review* 361.

Ehlermann, C. (1992) 'The Contribution of EC Competition Policy to the Single Market', 29 *Common Market Law Review* 257.

Ehlermann, C. (2000) 'The Modernization of EC Antitrust Policy: A Legal and Cultural Revolution', 37 *Common Market Law Review* 537.

El-Agraa, A. (2004) *The European Union: Economics and Politics* (7th edn), Cambridge: Cambridge University Press.

Emiliou, N. and O'Keeffe, D. (eds.) (1996) *The European Union and World Trade Law*, London: Wiley.

Europe, Council of (1998) 'Gender Mainstreaming: Conceptual Framework, Methodology and Presentation of Good Practices', *EG-S-MS (98) 2 rev.*

Evans, A. (1999) *The EU Structural Funds*, Oxford: Oxford University Press.

Evans, A. (2003) 'Evolutionary Problems of EU Law: The Case of the Union Funds', 30 *Legal Issues of European Integration* 201.

Fahey, T. (2007) 'The Case for an EU-wide Measure of Poverty', 23 *European Sociological Review* 35.

Faure, M. (2004) 'European Environmental Criminal Law: Do We Really Need It?', 13 *European Environmental Law Review* 18.

Federal Trust (2005) *Flexibility and the Future of the European Union*, October 2005: A Federal Trust Report.

Fennell, R. (1979) *The Common Agricultural Policy of the European Community*, London: Granada.

Fijnaut, C. (2004) 'Police Co-operation and the Area of Freedom, Security and Justice', in Walker, N. (ed.), *Europe's Area of Freedom, Security and Justice*, Oxford: Oxford University Press.

Fisher, E., Jones, J. and von Schomberg, R. (eds.) (2006) *Implementing the Precautionary Principle: Perspectives and Prospects*, Cheltenham: Edward Elgar.

Flynn, L. (2002) 'Coming of Age: the Free Movement Case Law 1993–2002', 39 *Common Market Law Review* 773.

Frazer, T. (1995) 'The New Structural Funds, State Aids and Interventions in the Single Market', 21 *European Law Review* 3.

Fredman, S. (1997) *Women and the Law*, Oxford: Oxford University Press.

Fries, S. and Shaw, J. (1998) 'Citizenship of the Union: First Steps in the European Court of Justice', 4 *European Public Law* 533.

Furse, M. (2004) 'On a Darkling Plain: The Confused Alarms of Article 82 EC', 25 *European Competition Law Review* 317.

Gerber, D. and Cassinis, P. (2006) 'The "Modernization" of European Community Competition Law: Achieving Consistency in Enforcement: Part 1', 27 *European Competition Law Review* 10; 'Part 2', 27 *European Competition Law Review* 51.

Gilliams, H. (2003) 'Modernisation: From Policy to Practice', 28 *European Law Review* 466.

Gillingham, J. (2003) *European Integration 1950–2003: Superstate or New Market Economy?*, Cambridge: Cambridge University Press.

Golub, J. (1996) 'Sovereignty and Subsidiarity in EU Environmental Policy', 44 *Political Studies* 686.

Gormley, L. (1996) 'Consolidation, Codification and Improving the Quality of Community Legislation – The Community Customs Code', in Emiliou, N. and O'Keeffe, D. (eds.), *The European Union and World Trade Law*, London: Wiley.

Gormley, L. (2006) 'The Internal Market: History and Evolution', in Nic Shuibhne, N. (ed.), *Regulating the Internal Market*, Cheltenham: Edward Elgar.

Grant, W. (2004) 'Is CAP going to become less green?', 6 April 2004: **http://members.tripod.com/~WynGrant/WynGrantCAPpage.html**

Grant, W. (2006) 'Grain Mountain Growing', 30 January 2006: **http://commonagpolicy.blogspot.com**

Greer, S. (2006) 'Uninvited Europeanization: Neofunctionalism and the EU in Health Policy', 13 *Journal of European Public Policy* 113.

Groenendijk, K. (2001) 'Security of Residence and Access to Free Movement for Settled Third Country Nationals under Community Law', in Guild, E. and Harlow, C. (eds.), *Implementing Amsterdam: Immigration and Asylum Rights in EC Law*, Oxford: Hart Publishing.

Guibernau, M. (ed.) (2006) 'Governing Europe: The Developing Agenda', Milton Keynes: Open University Press.

Guild, E. (2001) Immigration Law in the European Community, The Hague: Kluwer Law International.

Guild, E. (2002) 'The Single Market, Movement of Persons and Borders', in Barnard, C. and Scott, J. (eds.), The Law of the Single European Market: Unpacking the Premises, Oxford: Hart Publishing.

Guild, E. (2006) 'The Bitter Fruits of an EU Common Asylum Policy', in Balzacq, T. and Carrera, S. (eds.), Security Versus Freedom? A Challenge for Europe's Future, Aldershot: Ashgate.

Hadfield, A. (2007) 'Janus Advances? An Analysis of EC Development Policy and the 2005 Amended Cotonou Partnership Agreement', 12 European Foreign Affairs Review 39.

Halleskov, L. (2005) 'The Long Term Residents Directive: A Fulfilment of the Tampere Objective of Near-Equality?', 7 European Journal of Migration and Law 181.

Handler, M. (2006) 'The WTO Geographical Indications Dispute', 69 Modern Law Review 70.

Hansen, M., van Ysendyck, A. and Zuhlke, S. (2004) 'The Coming of Age of EC State Aid Law: A Review of the Principal Developments in 2002 and 2003', 25 European Competition Law Review 202.

Harvey, B. (2006) Manual on the Management of the European Union Structural Funds, European Anti-Poverty Network.

Hattan, E. (2003) 'The Implementation of EU Environmental Law', 15 Journal of Environmental Law 273.

Hatzopoulos, V. (2000) 'Recent Developments of the Case Law of the ECJ in the Field of Services', 37 Common Market Law Review 43.

Hatzopoulos, V. (2002) 'Killing National Health and Insurance Systems but Healing Patients? The European Market for Healthcare Services after the Judgments of the ECJ in Vanbraekel and Peerbooms', 39 Common Market Law Review 683.

Hatzopoulos, V. and Do, T. (2006) 'The Case Law of the ECJ Concerning the Free Provision of Services, 2000–2005', 43 Common Market Law Review 923.

Hedemann-Robinson, M. (1990) 'Indirect Discrimination: Article 95 EC Back to Front and Inside Out?', 1 European Public Law 439.

Heffernan, L. and McAuliffe, C. (2003) 'External Relations in the Air Transport Sector: The Court of Justice and the Open Skies Agreements', 28 European Law Review 601.

Hepple, B. (1977) 'Community Measures for the Protection of Workers Against Dismissal', 14 Common Market Law Review 489.

Hepple, B. (2004) 'Race and Law in Fortress Europe', 67 Modern Law Review 1.

Herrmann, C. (2002) 'Common Commercial Policy after Nice: Sisyphus would have done a better job', 39 Common Market Law Review 7.

Hervey, T. (1998) European Social Law and Policy, Harlow: Longman.

Hervey, T. (2000a) 'Putting Europe's House in Order', in O'Keefe, D. and Twomey, P. (eds.), Legal Issues of the Amsterdam Treaty, Oxford: Hart Publishing.

Hervey, T. (2000b) 'Social Solidarity: A Buttress Against Internal Market Law?', in Shaw, J. (ed.), Social Law and Policy in an evolving European Union, Oxford: Hart Publishing.

Hervey, T. (2002) 'Mapping the Contours of European Union Health Law and Policy', 8 European Public Law 69.

Hervey, T. and Kenner, J. (eds.) (2003) Economic and Social Rights under the EU Charter of Fundamental Rights: A Legal Perspective, Oxford: Hart Publishing.

Hervey, T. and McHale, J. (2004a) Health Law and the European Union, Cambridge: Cambridge University Press.

Hervey, T. and McHale, J. (2004b) 'Law, Health and the European Union', 25 Legal Studies 228.

Heywood, P., Jones, E. and Rhodes, M. (eds.) (2002) Developments in West European Politics 2, Basingstoke: Palgrave Macmillan.

Hilson, C. (1999) 'Discrimination in Community Free Movement Law', 24 *European Law Review* 445.

Hodson, D. and Maher, I. (2001) 'The Open Method as a New Mode of Governance: The Case of Soft Economic Policy Co-ordination', 39 *Journal of Common Market Studies* 719.

van der Hoek, M. (2003) 'Tax Harmonization and Competition in the European Union', 1 *eJournal of Tax Research* 19.

Holdgaard, R. (2003) 'The European Community's Implied External Competence after the Open Skies Cases', 8 *European Foreign Affairs Review* 365.

Hooghe, L. (ed.) (1996) *Cohesion Policy and European Integration: Building Multi-level Governance*, Oxford: Oxford University Press.

Horng, D. (2003) 'The Human Rights Clause in the European Union's External Trade and Development Agreements', 9 *European Law Journal* 677.

Howard, E. (2006) 'The Case for a Considered Hierarchy of Discrimination Grounds in EU Law', 13 *Maastricht Journal of European and Comparative Law* 445.

Howells, G. (2005) 'The Potential Limits of Consumer Empowerment by Information', 32 *Journal of Law and Society* 349.

Howells, G. and Wilhelmsson, T. (2003) 'EC Consumer Law: Has it Come of Age?', 28 *European Law Review* 370.

van Huffel, M. (2006) 'The Legal Framework for Financial Services and the Internet', in Nic Shuibhne, N. (ed.), *Regulating the Internal Market*, Cheltenham: Edward Elgar.

Hunt, J. (1999) 'Success at Last? The Amendment of the Acquired Rights Directive', 24 *European Law Review* 215.

Hunt, J. (2003) 'Fair and Just Working Conditions', in Hervey, T. and Kenner, J. (eds.), *Economic and Social Rights under the EU Charter of Fundamental Rights*, Oxford: Hart Publishing.

Hurt, S. (2003) 'Cooperation or Coercion? The Cooperation Agreement between the European Union and ACP States and the end of the Lomé Convention', 24 *Third World Quarterly* 161.

Iliopoulou, A. and Toner, H. (2003) 'A New Approach to Discrimination against Free Movers?, *D'Hoop v. Office National de l'Emploi*', 28 *European Law Review* 389.

Ingham, M., Ingham, H. and MacQuaid, R. (2003) 'Regional Development and EU Enlargement', in Ingham, M. and Ingham H. (eds.), *EU Expansion to the East: Prospects and Problems*, Cheltenham: Edward Elgar.

Jacqueson, C. (2002) 'Union Citizenship and the Court of Justice: Something New under the Sun? Towards Social Citizenship', 27(3) *European Law Review* 260.

Jans, J. (2007) 'The Effect in National Legal Systems of the Prohibition of Discrimination on Grounds of Age as a General Principle of Community Law', 34 *Legal Issues of European Integration* 53.

Jeffery, M. (1995) 'The Commission's Proposals on Atypical Work', 24 *Industrial Law Journal* 269.

Joerges, C. (2005) 'What is left of the European Economic Constitution? A Melancholic Eulogy', 30 *European Law Review* 461.

Jordan, A. and Jeppesen, T. (2000) 'EU Environmental Policy: Adapting to the Principle of Subsidiarity?', 10 *European Environment* 64.

Jovanovic, M. (1997) *European Economic Integration: Limits and Prospects*, London: Routledge.

Juss, S. (2005) 'The Decline and Decay of European Refugee Policy', 25 *Oxford Journal of Legal Studies* 749.

Kaczorowska, A. (2006) 'A Review of the Creation by the European Court of Justice of the Right to Effective and Speedy Medical Treatment and its Outcomes', 12 *European Law Journal* 345.

Kenner, J. (2003a) 'Economic and Social Rights in the EU Legal Order: The Mirage of Indivisibility', in Hervey, T. and Kenner, J. (eds.), *Economic and Social Rights under the EU Charter of Fundamental Rights: A Legal Perspective*, Oxford: Hart Publishing.

Kenner, J. (2003b) *EU Employment Law: From Rome to Amsterdam and Beyond*, Oxford: Hart Publishing.

Kilpatrick, C. (2001) 'Gender Equality: A Fundamental Dialogue', in Schiarra, S. (ed.), *Labour Law in the Courts: National Judges and the European Court of Justice*, Oxford: Hart Publishing.

Kleinman, M. (2002) *A European Welfare State? European Union Social Policy in Context*, Basingstoke: Palgrave Macmillan.

Komninos, A. (2004) 'Article 234 EC and National Competition Authorities in the Era of Decentralisation', 29 *European Law Review* 106.

Kosior, K. (2005) 'New Stakeholders in the Common Agricultural Policy: A Real Burden to Reform Processes in the Enlarged European Union?', 11 *European Law Journal* 566.

Kostakopoulou, T. (2002) '"Integrating" Non-EU Migrants in the European Union: Ambivalent Legacies and Mutating Paradigms', 8 *Columbia Journal of European Law* 181.

Koutrakos, P. (2001) *Trade, Foreign Policy and Defence in EU Constitutional Law*, Oxford: Hart Publishing.

Koutrakos, P. (2006a) *EU International Relations Law*, Oxford: Hart Publishing.

Koutrakos, P. (2006b) 'The External Dimension of the Internal Market and the Individual', in Nic Shuibhne, N. (ed.), *Regulating the Internal Market*, Cheltenham: Edward Elgar.

Krajewski, M. (2005) 'External Trade Llaw and the Constitution Treaty: Towards a Federal and More Democratic Common Commercial Policy?', 42 *Common Market Law Review* 91.

Kramer, L. (2006) *EC Environmental Law* (6th edn), London, Sweet & Maxwell.

Krebber, S. (2006) 'The Social Rights Approach of the European Court of Justice to Enforce European Employment Law', 27 *Comparative Labour Law and Policy Journal* 377.

Kroepelien, K. (2000) 'Extended Producer Responsibility – New Legal Structures for Improved Ecological Self-Organization in Europe?', 9 *Review of European Community and International Environmental Law* 165.

Kuijper, P. J. (2004) 'The Evolution of the Third Pillar from Maastricht to the Constitutional Treaty: Institutional Aspects', 41 *Common Market Law Review* 609.

Laffan, B., O'Donnell, R. and Smith, M. (2000) *Europe's Experimental Union*, London: Routledge.

Lavenex, S. and Wallace, W. (2005) 'Justice and Home Affairs. Towards a "European Public Order"', in Wallace, H., Wallace, W. and Pollack, M. (eds.), *Policy-Making in the European Union* (5th edn), Oxford: Oxford University Press.

Lavranos, L. (2005) 'The Communitarisation of WTO Dispute Settlement Reports: An Exception to the Rule of Law', 10 *European Foreign Affairs Review* 313.

Lee, M. (2005) *EU Environmental Law: Challenges, Change and Decision Making*, Oxford: Hart Publishing.

Leibfried, S. and Pierson, P. (eds.) (1995) *European Social Policy: Between Fragmentation and Integration*, Washington DC: Brookings Institute.

Leibfried, S. and Pierson, P. (2000) 'Social Policy', in Wallace, H. and Wallace, W. (eds.), *Policy-Making in the European Union* (4th edn), Oxford: Oxford University Press.

Lenschow, A. (2002) 'New Regulatory Approaches to "Greening" EU Policies', 8 *European Law Journal* 19.

Lintner, V. (2001) 'The Development of the EU and the European Economy', in Thompson, G. (ed.), *Governing the European Economy: A Framework for Analysis*, London: Sage.

Littler, A. and Fijnaut, C. (eds.) (2007) *The Regulation of Gambling: European and National Perspectives*, Leiden/Boston: Martinus Nijhoff Publishers.

Lööf, R. (2000) 'Shooting from the Hip: Proposed Minimum Rights in Criminal Proceedings throughout the EU', 12 *European Law Journal* 421.

Louis, J. (2004) 'The Economic and Monetary Union: Law and Institutions', 41 *Common Market Law Review* 575.

Lyons, T. (2001) *EC Customs Law*, Oxford: Oxford University Press.

Mabbett, D. (2005) 'The Development of a Rights-based Social Policy in the EU: The Example of Disability Rights', 43 *Journal of Common Market Studies* 43.

MacMaoláin, C. (2001) 'Free Movement of Foodstuffs, Quality Requirements and Consumer Protection: Have the Court and the Commission Both Got It Wrong?', 26 *European Law Review* 413.

MacMaoláin, C. (2003) 'The New Genetically Modified Food Labelling Requirements: Finally a Lasting Solution?', 28 *European Law Review* 865.

Macrory, R. (1999) 'The Amsterdam Treaty: An Environmental Perspective', in O'Keefe, D. and Twomey, P. (eds.), *Legal Issues of the Amsterdam Treaty*, Oxford: Hart Publishing.

Macrory, R. (ed.) (2006) *Reflections on 30 Years of EU Environmental Law – A High Level of Protection?*, Groningen: Europa Law Publishing.

Maduro, M. (2000) 'Europe's Social Self: The Sickness unto Death', in Shaw, J. (ed.), *Social Law and Policy in an Evolving European Union*, Oxford: Hart Publishing.

Maher, I. (1994) 'National Courts as European Community Courts', 14 *Legal Studies* 226.

Maher, I. (1995) 'Legislative Review by the EC Commission: Review without Radicalism', in Shaw, J. and More, G. (eds.), *New Legal Dynamics of European Union*, Oxford: Clarendon.

Majone, G. (1996a) 'A European Regulatory State?', in Richardson, J. (ed.), *European Union: Power and Policy-making*, London: Routledge.

Majone, G. (1996b) *Regulating Europe*, London: Routledge.

Majone, G. (2005) *Dilemmas of European Integration. The Ambiguities and Pitfalls of Integration by Stealth*, Oxford: Oxford University Press.

Marchant, G. and Mossman, K. (2004) *Arbitrary and Capricious: The Precautionary Principle in the European Union Courts*, Washington DC: AIE Press.

Marshall, T. (1975) *Social Policy in the Twentieth Century* (4th edn), London: Hutchinson.

Mayes, D. (2001) 'Introduction', in Mayes, D., Berghman, J. and Salais, R. (eds.), *Social Exclusion and European Policy*, Cheltenham: Edward Elgar.

McCormick, J. (2001) *Environmental Policy in the European Union*, Basingstoke: Palgrave Macmillan.

McCormick, J. (2005) *Understanding the European Union* (3rd edn), Basingstoke: Palgrave Macmillan.

McGlynn, C. (2000) 'Ideologies of Motherhood in European Community Sex Equality Law', 6 *European Law Journal* 29.

McIntyre, O. (1994) 'The Guiding Principles of European Community Environmental Law-making', *European Environment* 26.

McMahon, J. (1995) *Education and Culture in European Community Law*, London: Athlone Press.

McMahon, J. (1998a) 'The EC Banana Regime, the WTO Rulings and the ACP: Fighting for Economic Survival?', 32 *Journal of World Trade Law* 101.

McMahon, J. (1998b) *The Development Co-operation Policy of the EC*, Kluwer: London.

McMahon, J. (2000) *Law of the Common Agricultural Policy*, London: Longman.

McMahon, J. (2005) 'International Trade; Customs; European Union; Food "The Longstanding Banana Saga" – Towards an Acceptable Solution: Part 1', 11 *International Trade Law and Regulation* 181.

McNamara, K. (2005) 'Economic and Monetary Union', in Wallace, H., Wallace, W. and Pollack, M. (eds.), *Policy-Making in the European Union*, Oxford: Oxford University Press.

Mitchell, J. and McAleavey, P. (1999) 'Promoting Solidarity and Cohesion', in Cram, L., Dinan, D. and Nugent, N. (eds.), *Developments in the European Union*, Basingstoke: Palgrave Macmillan.

Mitsilegas, V. (2006) 'The Constitutional Implications of Mutual Recognition in Criminal Matters in the EU', 43 *Common Market Law Review* 1277.

Molle, W. (2006) *The Economics of European Integration: Theory, Practice, Policy* (5th edn), Aldershot: Ashgate.

Monar, J. (2000) 'The EU's Role in the Fight Against Racism and Xenophobia: Evaluation and Prospects after Amsterdam and Tampere', 22 *Liverpool Law Review* 7.

Monar, J. (2001) 'The Dynamics of JHA: Laboratories, Driving Factors, Costs', 39 *Journal of Common Market Studies* 747.

Monar, J. (2004) 'Maintaining the Justice and Home Affairs *Acquis* in an Enlarged Europe', in Apap, J. (ed.), *Justice and Home Affairs in the EU: European Liberty and Security Issues after Enlargement*, Cheltenham: Edward Elgar.

Monti, G. (2001) 'The Scope of Collective Dominance under Article 82 EC', 38 *Common Market Law Review* 131.

Monti, G. (2002) 'Article 81 EC and Public Policy', 39 *Common Market Law Review* 1057.

More, G. (1999) 'The Principle of Equal Treatment: From Market Unifier to Fundamental Right?', in Craig, P. and de Búrca, G. (eds.), *The Evolution of EU Law*, Oxford: Oxford University Press.

Mortelmans, K. (1998) 'The Common Market, the Internal Market and the Single Market, What's in a Market?', 35 *Common Market Law Review* 101.

Mortelmans, K. (2002) 'The Relationship between the Treaty Rules and Community Measures for the Establishment and Functioning of the Internal Market – Towards a Concordance Rule', 39 *Common Market Law Review* 1303.

Mosely, H. (1990) 'The Social Dimension of European Integration', 129 *International Labour Review* 147.

Mosher, J. and Trubek, D. (2003) 'Alternative Approaches to Governance in the EU: European Social Policy and the European Employment Strategy', 41 *Journal of Common Market Studies* 63.

Müller, F. (2004) 'The New Council Regulation (EC) No. 1/2003 on the Implementation of the Rules on Competition', 5 *German Law Journal* 721.

Murray, J. (1999) 'Normalising Temporary Work: The Proposed Directive on Fixed Term Work', 28 *Industrial Law Journal* 269.

Nic Shuibhne, N. (2002) 'The Free Movement of Goods and Article 28 EC: an Evolving Framework', 27 *European Law Review* 408.

Nic Shuibhne, N. (ed.) (2006) *Regulating the Internal Market*, Cheltenham: Edward Elgar.

O'Keeffe, D. and Twomey, P. (eds.) (1994) *Legal Issues of the Maastricht Treaty*, London: Wiley Chancery Law.

O'Keeffe, D. and Twomey, P. (eds.) (2000) *Legal Issues of the Amsterdam Treaty*, Oxford: Hart Publishing.

O'Leary, S. (1999) 'The Free Movement of Persons and Services', in Craig, P. and de Búrca, G. (eds.), *The Evolution of EU Law*, Oxford: Oxford University Press.

O'Leary, S. (2005) 'Solidarity and Citizenship Rights in the Charter of Fundamental Rights of the European Union', in de Burca, G. (ed.), *EU Law and the Welfare State: In Search of Solidarity*, Oxford: Oxford University Press.

Ogus, A. (1994) *Regulation*, Oxford: Oxford University Press.

Oliver, P. and Jarvis, M. (2002) *Free Movement of Goods in the European Community* (4th edn), London: Sweet & Maxwell.

Oliver, P. and Roth, W. H. (2004) 'The Internal Market and the Four Freedoms', 41 *Common Market Law Review* 407.

Peers, S. (2000) *EU Justice and Home Affairs Law*, Harlow: Longman.

Peers, S. (2001) 'W.T.O. Dispute Settlement and Community Law', 26 *European Law Review* 605.

Peers, S. (2002) 'Free Movement of Capital: Learning Lessons or Slipping on Spilt Milk?', in Barnard, C. and Scott, J. (eds.), *The Law of the Single European Market: Unpacking the Premises*, Oxford: Hart Publishing.

Peers, S. (2005) 'Transforming Decision-making in EC Immigration and Asylum Law', 30 *European Law Review* 285.

Peers, S. and Ward, A. (eds.) (2004) *The EU Charter of Fundamental Rights: Politics, Law and Policy*, Oxford: Hart Publishing.

Pescatore, P. (1987) 'Some Critical Remarks on the Single European Act', 24 *Common Market Law Reviews* 9.

Peterson, J. and Bomberg, E. (1999) *Decision Making in the European Union*, Basingstoke: Palgrave Macmillan.

Pollack, M.A. and Hafner-Burton, E. (2000) 'Mainstreaming Gender in the European Union', 7 *Journal of European Public Policy* 432.

de la Porte, C. (2002) 'Is the Open Method of Coordination Appropriate for Organising Activities at European Level in Sensitive Policy Areas?', 8 *European Law Journal* 38.

Rhodes, M. (2002) 'Globalization, EMU and Welfare State Futures', in Heywood, P., Jones, E. and Rhodes, M. (eds.), *Developments in West European Politics 2*, Basingstoke: Palgrave Macmillan.

Rhodes, M., Heywood, P. and Wright, V. (eds.) (1997) *Developments in West European Politics*, Basingstoke: Palgrave Macmillan.

Riley, A. (2003a) 'EC Antitrust Modernisation: The Commission Does Very Nicely – Thank You!. Part One', 24 *European Competition Law Review* 604.

Riley, A. (2003b) 'EC Antitrust Modernisation: The Commission Does Very Nicely – Thank You!. Part Two', 24 *European Competition Law Review* 657.

Rogers, N. (2002) 'Minimum Standards for Reception', 4 *European Journal of Migration and Law* 215.

Rosamond, B. (2005) 'The Uniting of Europe and the Foundations of EU Studies: Revisiting the Neofunctionalism of Ernst B. Haas', 12 *Journal of European Public Policy* 237.

Roth, W. H. (2003) 'From *Centros* to *Ueberseering*: Free Movement of Companies, Private International Law, and Community Law', 52 *International and Comparative Law Quarterly* 177.

Ryan, B. (2003) 'The Charter and Collective Labour Law', in Hervey, T. and Kenner, J. (eds.), *Economic and Social Rights under the EU Charter of Fundamental Rights: A Legal Perspective*, Oxford: Hart Publishing.

de Rynck, S. and McAleavey, P. (2001) 'The Cohesion Deficit in Structural Fund Policy', 8 *Journal of European Public Policy* 541.

de Sadeleer, N. (2003) 'Procedures for Derogations from the Principle of Approximation of Laws under Article 95 EC', 40 *Common Market Law Review* 889.

de Sadeleer, N. (2006) 'The Precautionary Principle in European Community Health and Environmental Law', 12 *European Law Journal* 139.

de Sadeleer, N. (ed.) (2007) *Implementing the Precautionary Principle: Approaches from the Nordic Countries, EU and USA*, London: Earthscan.

Sapir, A. *et al* (2004) *An Agenda for a Growing Europe. The Sapir Report*, Oxford: Oxford University Press.

Sargeant, M. (2002) 'Temporary Workers Wait for Increased Protection', *Business Law Review* 205.

Scharpf, F. (2002) 'The European Social Model: Coping with the Challenges of Diversity', 40 *Journal of Common Market Studies* 645–70.

Schmidt, M. (1999) 'Representivity – A Claim Not Satisfied: The Social Partners' Role in the EC Law Making Procedure for Social Policy', 15 *International Journal of Comparative Labour Law and Industrial Relations* 259.

Scott, J. (1995) *Development Dilemmas in the European Community: Rethinking Regional Development Policy*, Buckingham: Oxford University Press.

Scott, J. (1998a) *EC Environmental Law*, Harlow: Longman.

Scott, J. (1998b) 'Law, Legitimacy and EU Governance: Prospects for "Partnership" ', 36 *Journal of Common Market Studies* 175.

Scott, J. (2000) 'Flexibility, "Proceduralization" and Environmental Governance in the EU', in de Burca, G. and Scott, J. (eds.), *Constitutional Change in the EU: From Uniformity to Flexibility?* Oxford: Hart Publishing.

Scott, J. and Trubek, D. (2002) 'Mind the Gap: Law and New Approaches to Governance in the EU', 8 *European Law Journal* 1.

Selamyr, Z.C. (2001) *The Law of the European Central Bank*, Oxford: Hart Publishing.

Shanks, M. (1977) *The European Social Policy Today and Tomorrow*, Oxford: Pergamon.

Shaw, J. (1994) 'Twin-Track Social Europe – The Inside Track', in O'Keeffe, D. and Twomey, P. (eds.), *Legal Issues of the Amsterdam Treaty*, Oxford: Hart Publishing.

Shaw, J. (ed.) (2000) *Social Law and Policy in an Evolving European Union*, Oxford: Hart Publishing.

Shaw, J. (2003) 'Enhancing Cooperation after Nice: Will the Treaty do the Trick?', in Andenas, M. and Usher, J. (eds.), *The Treaty of Nice and the EU Constitution*, Oxford: Hart Publishing.

Shaw, J. (2004) 'Legal and Political Sources of the European Constitution', 55 *Northern Ireland Legal Quarterly* 214.

Shaw, J. (2005) 'Europe's Constitutional Future', *Public Law* 132.

Shaw, J. and More, G. (ed.) (1995) *New Legal Dynamics of European Union*, Oxford: Clarendon.

Simma, B., Aschenbrenner, J.B. and Schulte, C. (1999) 'Human Rights Considerations in Development Co-operation Activities of the EC', in Alston, P. (ed.), *The EU and Human Rights*, Oxford: Oxford University Press.

Sindbjerg Martinsen, D. (2005) 'Social Security Regulation in the EU: The De-Territorialization of Welfare?', in de Burca, G. (ed.), *EU Law and the Welfare State: In Search of Solidarity*, Oxford: Oxford University Press.

Slater, D. (2003) 'Would Chocolate by Any Other Name Taste as Sweet?: A Brief History of the Naming of Generic Foodstuffs in the EC with Regard to the Recent Chocolate Cases (Case C-12/00, *Commission* v. *Spain* and Case C-14/00, *Commission* v. *Italy*)', 4(6) *German Law Journal*.

Slot, P.J. (1996) 'Harmonisation of Law', 5 *European Law Review* 378.

Slot, P. (2003) 'Applying the Competition Rules in the Healthcare Sector', 24 *European Competition Law Review* 580.

Slot, P.J. (2004) 'A View from the Mountain: 40 Years of Developments in Competition Law', 41 *Common Market Law Review* 443.

Slot, P. J. and De la Rochère, J. (2003) 'Case Note, Open Skies cases', 40 *Common Market Law Review* 697.

Smismans, S. (2003) 'Towards a New Community Strategy on Health and Safety at Work? Caught in the Institutional Web of Soft Procedures' , 19 *International Journal of Comparative Labour Law and Industrial Relations* 55.

Smismans, S. (2007) 'The European Social Dialogue between Constitutional and Labour Law', 32 *European Law Review*, forthcoming.

Smith, F. (2000) 'Renegotiating Lomé: the Impact of the World Trade Organisation on the European Community's Development Policy after the Bananas Conflict', 25 *European Law Review* 247.

Snell, J. and Andenas, M. (2000a) 'How Far? The Internal Market and Restrictions on the Free Movement of Goods and Services, Part I', 2 *International and Comparative Corporate Law Journal* 239.

Snell, J. and Andenas, M. (2000b) 'How Far? The Internal Market and Restrictions on the Free Movement of Goods and Services, Part II', 2 *International and Comparative Corporate Law Journal* 361.

Snyder, F. (1985) *Law of the Common Agricultural Policy*, London: Sweet & Maxwell.

Snyder, F. (1999) 'EMU Revisited: Are we Making a Constitution? What Constitution are we Making?', in Craig, P. and de Búrca, G. (eds.), *The Evolution of EU Law*, Oxford: Oxford University Press.

Spaventa, Z.E. (2004) 'From *Gebhard* to *Carpenter*: Towards a (Non)-Economic European Constitution', 41 *Common Market Law Review* 743.

Stöger, K. (2006) 'The Freedom of Establishment and the Market Access of Hospital Operators' , *European Business Law Review* 1545.

Stratigaki, M. (2005) 'Gender Mainstreaming vs Positive Action. An Ongoing Conflict in EU Gender Equality Policy', 12 *European Journal of Women's Studies* 165.

Streeck, W. (1995) 'From Market Making to State Building? Reflections on the Political Economy of European Social Policy', in Leibfried, S. and Pierson, P. (eds.), *European Social Policy: Between Fragmentation and Integration*, Washington DC: Brookings Institute.

Sunstein, C. (2003) 'Beyond the Precautionary Principle', 151 *University of Pennsylvania Law Review* 1003.

Sutcliffe, J. (2000) 'The 1999 Reform of the Structural Fund Regulations: Multi-level Governance or Renationalization?', 7 *Journal of European Public Policy* 290.

Swann, D. (2000) *The Economics of Europe: From Common Market to European Union*, London: Penguin.

Szyszczak, E. (2003) 'Social Policy After Nice', in Andenas, M. and Wincott, D. (eds.), *Accountability and Legitimacy in the European Union*, Oxford: Oxford University Press.

Temple Lang, J. (2004) 'National Measures Restricting Competition, and National Authorities under Article 10 EC', 29 *European Law Review* 397.

Thompson, G. (ed.) (2001) *Governing the European Economy: A Framework for Analysis*, London: Sage.

Tridimas, P. and Nebbia, P. (ed.) (2004) *European Union Law for the Twenty-First Century: Rethinking the New Legal Order*, Oxford: Hart Publishing.

Tsoukalis, L. (1997) *The New European Economy Revisited*, Oxford: Oxford University Press.

Tsoukalis, L. (2005) *What Kind of Europe?*, Oxford: Oxford University Press.

Tsoukalis, L. and Rhodes, M. (1997) 'Economic Integration and the Nation-State', in Rhodes, M. *et al* (eds.), *Developments in West European Politics*, London: Palgrave Macmillan.

Usher, J. (1996) 'Consequences of the Customs Union', in Emiliou, N. and O'Keeffe, D. (eds.), *The European Union and World Trade Law*, London: Wiley.

Usher, J. (2000) *The Law of Money and Financial Services in the European Union*, Oxford: Oxford University Press.

Usher, J. (2002) *EC Agricultural Law* (2nd edn), Oxford: Oxford University Press.

Usher, J. (2006) 'Monetary Movements and the Internal Market', in Nic Shuibhne, N. (ed.), *Regulating the Internal Market*, Cheltenham: Edward Elgar.

Venit, J. (2003) 'Brave New World: The Modernization and Centralization of Enforcement under Articles 81 and 82 of the EC Treaty', 40 *Common Market Law Review* 545.

Verschuuren, J. (2005) 'Shellfish for Fishermen or for Birds? Article 6 Habitats Directive and the Precautionary Principle', 17 *Journal of Environmental Law* 265.

Vickers, J. (2004) 'Merger Policy in Europe: Retrospect and Prospect', 25 *European Competition Law Review* 455.

Vickers, J. (2005) 'Abuse of Market Power', 115 *The Economic Journal* F244.

Vignes, D. (1990) 'The Harmonisation of National Legislation and the EEC', 15 *European Law Review* 358.

Villiers, C. (2006) 'The Directive on Employee Involvement in the European Company: Its Role in European Corporate Governance and Industrial Relations', 22 *International Journal of Comparative Labour Law and Industrial Relations* 183.

Vos, K. (2005) 'Americanisation of the EU social model?', 21 *International Journal of Comparative Labour Law and Industrial Relations* 355.

Waddington, L. (2005) 'Implementing the Disability Provisions of the Framework Employment Directive: Room for National Discretion', in Lawson, A. and Gooding, C. (eds.), *Disability Rights in Europe: From Theory to Practice*, Oxford: Hart Publishing.

Waddington, L. and Bell, M. (2001) 'More Equal than Others: Distinguishing European Union Equality Directives', 38 *Common Market Law Review* 587.

Walker, N. (2004) 'In Search of the Area of Freedom, Security and Justice: A Constitutional Odyssey', in Walker, N. (ed.), *Europe's Area of Freedom, Security and Justice*, Oxford: Oxford University Press.

Wallace, H. (2005) 'An Institutional Autonomy and Five Policy Modes', in Wallace, H., Wallace, W. and Pollack, M. (eds.), *Policy-Making in the European Union* (5th edn), Oxford: Oxford University Press.

Wallace, H., Wallace, W. and Pollack, M. (eds.) (2005) *Policy-Making in the European Union* (5th edn), Oxford: Oxford University Press.

Wallace, W. (2005) 'Post Sovereign Governance', in Wallace, H., Wallace, M. and Pollack, M. (eds.), *Policy-Making in the European Union* (5th edn), Oxford: Oxford University Press.

Wasmeier, M. and Thwaites, N. (2006) 'The Development of *ne bis in idem* into a Transnational Fundamental Right in EU Law: Comments on Recent Developments', 31 *European Law Review* 565.

Weatherill, S. (1994) 'Beyond Preemption? Shared Competence and Constitutional Change in the European Community', in O'Keeffe, D. and Twomey, P. (eds.), *Legal Issues of the Maastricht Treaty*, London: Wiley Chancery Law.

Weatherill, S. (1996) 'After *Keck*: Some Thoughts on How to Clarify the Clarification', 33 *Common Market Law Review* 885.

Weatherill, S. (1997) 'Law and the Economic Objectives of the Community', in Micklitz, H.W. and Weatherill, S. (eds.), *European Economic Law*, Aldershot: Ashgate.

Weatherill, S. (1999) 'Consumer Policy', in Craig, P. and de Burca, G. (eds.), *The Evolution of EU Law*, Oxford: Oxford University Press.

Weatherill, S. (2002) 'Pre-emption, Harmonisation and the Distribution of Competence to Regulate the Internal Market', in Barnard, C. and Scott, J. (eds.), *The Law of the Single European Market: Unpacking the Premises*, Oxford: Hart Publishing.

Weatherill, S. (2004) 'Why Harmonise?', in Tridimas, P. and Nebbia, P. (eds.), *European Union Law for the Twenty-First Century: Rethinking the New Legal Order, Volume 2*, Oxford: Hart Publishing.

Weatherill, S. (2005) *EU Consumer Law and Policy*, Cheltenham: Elgar European Law.

Weatherill, S. (2006) 'Supply of, and Demand for Internal Market Regulation: Strategies, Preferences and Interpretation', in Nic Shuibhne, N. (ed.), *Regulating the Internal Market*, Cheltenham: Edward Elgar.

Weatherill, S. and Beaumont, P. (1999) *EU Law*, Harmondsworth: Penguin.

Weatherill, S. and McGee, A. (1990) 'The Evolution of the Single Market – Harmonisation or Liberalisation?', 53 *Modern Law Review* 578–96.

Weiler, J. (1999a) '*Fin-de-Siècle Europe: Do the New Clothes have an Emperor?*', Cambridge: Cambridge University Press.

Weiler, J. (1999b) 'The Constitution of the Common Market Place: The Free Movement of Goods', in Craig, P. and de Búrca, G. (eds.), *The Evolution of EU Law*, Oxford: Oxford University Press.

Weiss, T. (2000) 'Governance, Good Governance and Global Governance: Conceptual and Actual Challenges', 21 *Third World Quarterly* 795.

Whish, R. (2003) *Competition Law* (5th edn), London: Butterworths.

Wilks, S. (2005) 'Competition Policy', in Wallace, H., Wallace, W. and Pollack, M. (eds.), *Policy-Making in the European Union* (5th edn), Oxford: Oxford University Press.

Williams, R. (1994) 'The European Commission and the Enforcement of Environment Law: An Invidious Position', *Yearbook of European Law* 351.

Willimsky, S. (1997) 'The Concept(s) of Competition', 1 *European Competition Law Review* 54.

Wils, W. (1994) 'Subsidiarity and EC Environmental Policy: Taking People's Concerns Seriously', 6 *Journal of Environmental Law* 85.

Wils, W. (2004) 'The Combination of the Investigative and Prosecutorial Function and the Adjudicative Function in EC Antitrust Enforcement: A Legal and Economic Analysis', 27 *World Competition* 201.

Wishlade, F. (1998) 'Competition Policy or Cohesion Policy by the Back Door? The Commission Guidelines on National Regional Aid', 19 *European Competition Law Review* 343.

De Witte, B. (2004) 'Future Paths of Flexibility: Enhanced Cooperation, Partial Agreements and Pioneer Groups', in De Zwaan, J. *et al* (eds.), *The European Union: An Ongoing Process of Integration*, The Hague: TMC Asser Instituut.

Woods, D., Sinclair, A. and Ashton, D. (eds.) (2004) 'Private Enforcement of Community Competition Law: Modernisation and the Road Ahead', *2004 Competition Policy Newsletter*, No. 2, Summer, 31.

Woolcock, S. (2005) 'Trade Policy: From Uruguay to Doha and Beyond', in Wallace, H., Wallace, W. and Pollack, M. (eds.), *Policy-Making in the European Union* (5th edn), Oxford: Oxford University Press.

Woolfson, C. and Sommers, J. (2006) 'Labour Mobility in Construction: European Implications of the *Laval un Partneri* Dispute with Swedish Labour', 12 *European Journal of Industrial Relations* 49.

Wouters, J. (2000) 'European Company Law: *Quo Vadis?*', 37 *Common Market Law Review* 257.

Wymeersch, E. (2003) 'The Transfer of a Company's Seat in European Community Law', *40 Common Market Law Review* 661.

Young, A. (2005) 'The Single Market', in Wallace, H., Wallace, W. and Pollack, M. (eds.), *Policy-Making in the European Union* (5th edn), Oxford: Oxford University Press.

Zappala, L. (2006) 'Abuse of Fixed-Term Employment Contracts and Sanctions in the Recent ECJ's Jurisprudence', 35 *Industrial Law Journal* 439.

Zeitlin, J. (2005) 'Social Europe and Experimentalist Governance: Towards a New Constitutional Compromise?', in de Burca, G. (ed.), *EU Law and the Welfare State: In Search of Solidarity*, Oxford: Oxford University Press.

Zilioli, C. and Selmayr, M. (2001) *The Law of the European Central Bank*, Oxford: Hart Publishing.

De Zwaan, C. *et al* (eds.) (2004) *The European Union: An Ongoing Process of Integration*, The Hague: TMC Asser Instituut.

# Index